THE COMPLETE BOOK OF DOGS

THE COMPLETE BOOK OF DOGS

M. E. Ensminger

SOUTH BRUNSWICK AND NEW YORK: A. S. BARNES AND COMPANY
LONDON: THOMAS YOSELOFF LTD

© 1977 by A. S. Barnes and Co., Inc.

A. S. Barnes and Co., Inc.
Cranbury, New Jersey 08512

Thomas Yoseloff Ltd
Magdalen House
136–148 Tooley Street
London SE1 2TT, England

Library of Congress Cataloging in Publication Data

Ensminger, M. E.
    The complete book of dogs.

    Includes index.
    SUMMARY: Data on dogs including their selection, breeding, feeding, health, housing, training, grooming, showing, various uses, and general care and management. Lists dog books and magazines, humane organizations, and colleges of veterinary medicine.
    1. Dogs. [1. Dogs] I. Title.
SF426.E57   636.7   74-13
ISBN 0-498-01457-6

PRINTED IN THE UNITED STATES OF AMERICA

To

Duke
Sandy
Blackie
Candy
Bonnie
Tiger
Butch
Happy
 and
King Kong

They brought to their master loyalty,
the will to defend his person and property,
and unswerving devotion;
there was in them a fidelity
which in its steadfastness
far surpassed that of my fellowmen

Contents

Preface		9
Introduction		11
1	The Dog and His Wild Ancestors	15
2	Breeds; Kennel Clubs; Selecting and Buying	24
3	Breeding	133
4	Feeding	183
5	Kennels (Houses) and Equipment	262
6	Training	292
7	Grooming	315
8	Diseases, Parasites, and First Aid	326
9	Business Aspects of Kennels	393
10	Traveling With Your Dog	413
11	People Need Pets	439
12	Dog Shows; Showing	454
13	Dogs as Hunters	474
14	Field Trials	490
15	Coursing and Racing	504
16	Dog Guides for the Blind	513
17	Police Work	526
18	Dogs as Soldiers	533
19	Dogs in Harness; Sled Dogs	542
20	Farm Dogs; Sheep Dog Trials	549
21	Glossary of Terms	556
Appendix		
I	Identifying Your Dog	575
II	Breeding and Health Chart	577
III	Dog License	578
IV	Dog Laws	578
V	Humane Organizations	579
VI	Dog Books	586
VII	Dog Magazines	590
VIII	Colleges of Veterinary Medicine	585
IX	Metric System	591
Index		593

Preface

The unique thing about dogs, not found in most other types of ownership, is the human values derived from them. Dogs are a people's affair, and a way of life for many. There are, in the United States, 32.6 million family-owned dogs, owned by 23.8 million families—representing about 38 percent of the nation's households. That's an average of 1.4 dogs per dog-owning household.[1] They're used for sport, work, protection, and companionship around the house. Thus, it is my fond hope that this book will enhance the human values derived from dogs, by improving the well-being of these pets and insuring greater enjoyment to dog owners everywhere. To this end, as I wrote section by section, and chapter by chapter, I asked myself this simple question: "Is it helpful?"

Also, it is noteworthy that dogs in the United States provide $4¼ billion per year business; ranging all the way from North Atlantic fishermen to 5th Avenue poodle groomers.

As a dog owner and fancier, I also recognize that other dog owners and caretakers, veterinarians, specialists, dog-food manufacturers, pet-shop owners, and others, need an authoritative, up-to-date, in-depth, scientific yet practical book, where, under one cover, they can get information about the whole gamut of dog science— their selection, breeding, feeding, health, housing, training, grooming, showing, various uses, and general care and management. *The Complete Book of Dogs* is designed to fill this need. As one of my reviewers put it, "You don't pay for *The Complete Book of Dogs,* you buy knowledge."

Since the first domestication of the dog, he has taken his place at man's side—as a hunting companion, guardian, general ally, and/or pampered pet. In flood and in fire, in war and in famine, dogs have been faithful to their masters unto death. But in exchange for their fidelity, for giving up their dens and their freedom, man entered into an unwritten covenant with dogs—agreeing to their care. Indeed, people need dogs and dogs need people. Both of them desire to love and to be loved. Of each to the other, it may be said, "They also serve." I trust that *The Complete Book of Dogs* will help them—master and dog —to serve each other better.

Grateful appreciation is expressed to my wife, Audrey Helen, and to my son, John Jacob, for reviewing and editing the entire manuscript. Also, I wish to express my sincere appreciation for the authoritative review accorded certain chapters, due acknowledgment of which is given at the beginning of the chapters that they reviewed.

Clovis, California
June, 1977

M. E. ENSMINGER

---

[1] Estimates by the Pet Food Institute.

Introduction

"OUR 'SANDY' IS GONE"[2]

Out of consideration, the sad news had been withheld from Mrs. Ensminger and our twelve-year-old son, John. Johnny and Sandy had grown up together; they had been pals for ten years. When I arrived at my office, a telephone call awaited me; the word—Sandy was dead. After I collected myself, I proceeded with the difficult and unpleasant task of informing the rest of the family, personally. All of us wept bitterly.

It wasn't as if Sandy had lived to a ripe old age and died of natural causes; he had been run over by a car. We had always feared this sort of thing because Sandy—gentleman that he was—never realized that anything would ever harm him; he trusted people and machines implicitly. But at least there was the consolation that it wasn't a hit-and-run affair. The lady had not left him at the side of the road; instead, she wrapped the body in a blanket, placed it in her car, and delivered it to our home. She was kind and apologetic. Instead of bitterness, I felt sorry for her. But I choked up and couldn't speak. I managed, or hope I did, a faint "thank you—I understand."

Then I gently gathered Sandy's cold body in my arms and walked to our garden. Under a beautiful tree, which will ever be his living monument, we buried Sandy. A friend offered to help, but the assignment was much too sentimental to entrust to others; it was a family affair. In the quiet of the evening, by the light of the moon, we dug a grave of adequate size and depth. John made sure that Sandy would be comfortable therein—that he was in a restfullike, sleeping position. As I closed the grave, Mrs. Ensminger and John walked slowly to the house, arms around each other and weeping. The job was completed; unashamedly, I removed my hat, bowed my head, and said a little prayer:

Oh Lord, I hope that I may be as good a man as Sandy was a dog; he was quiet, patient, considerate, loyal, and a gentleman in the canine world. And, Lord, if there be a dog heaven, may it have a garden with carrots in it, for Sandy loved to dig and eat them. Also, may Sandy be watched over by Angels that love animals. Amen.

Fig. 1 Johnny, Sandy, and Blackie

---
[2] The following tribute to "Sandy" appeared in the author's syndicated column.

"MY NEXT REINCARNATION"[3]

He was one of the most unforgettable characters I've ever known. In love, he could outdo Mark Anthony; in climbing, he could put *Jack and the Beanstalk* to shame; and in pirating, he could make Long John Silver look like a rank amateur.

His love affairs were frequent and ardent—but all quite proper for him. To be near the one being wooed, he would forego sleep and food for days at a time; once he was gone so long that the local police listed him as a "missing person." As an escape artist, he used a high fence for his ladder. He borrowed carrots (he didn't steal them; he just wasn't particular about whose garden they came from); he dug them himself, and then dined on them in a spot to his liking.

When old age crept upon him and infirmity struck, he met it with the dignity and courage befitting his breeding and station in life. He lived in a specially built, insulated house, surrounded by his own private patio and garden of violets; he relished eggnogs, provided they were spoon-fed; and he loved to be held. He didn't want to die; and understandably so, for he was in heaven already. But the end finally came to Blackie, our dog, as it must come to each of us.

If there be such a thing as reincarnation—Oh! Lord—I hope that I may return to earth as Blackie. And, Lord, if this should come to pass, please restrain me lest I should bite a few selected people.

---
[3] The following tribute to "Blackie" appeared in the author's syndicated column.

THE COMPLETE BOOK OF DOGS

1
The Dog and His Wild Ancestors

Chapter 1
From Whence the Dog Came? 17
    From the Wolf and the Jackal 17
    Evolution of the Dog (Table 1) 18
    What the Prehistoric Records Tell Us 19
Position of the Dog in the Zoological Scheme 21
Dog as Man's First Helpmate 21
    Watchdogs 21
    Food 21
    Draft 21
    Hunting 21
    Guarding and Herding 22
    Companionship 22
Some Wild Dogs of Today 22
    Pariah Dogs 22
    Dingo 22
    Galapagos Island Dogs 23
    Dogs of the American Indian 23

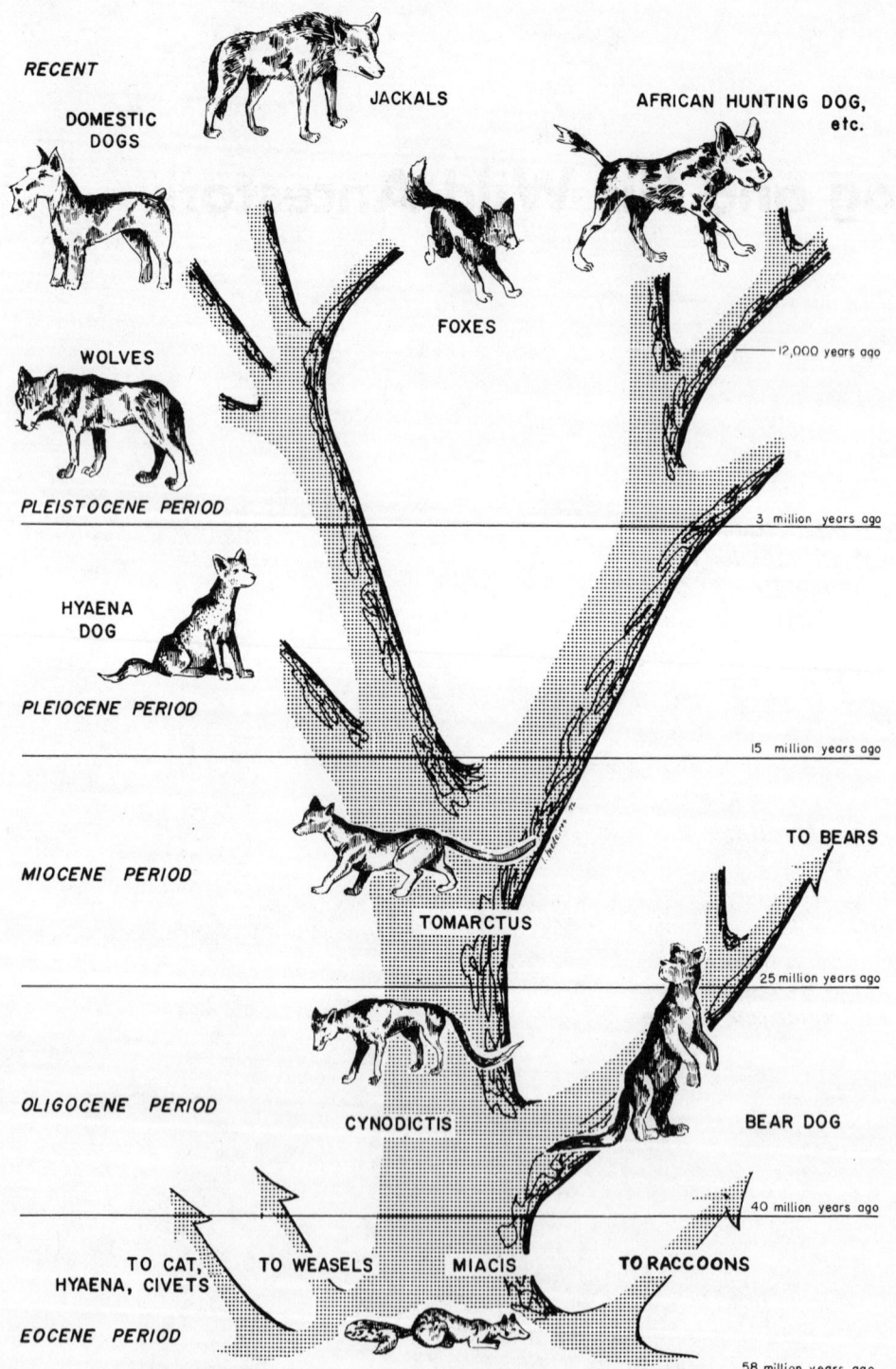

Fig. 2. Dog family tree. (Drawing by J. L. Medeiros)

THE DOG AND HIS WILD ANCESTORS

The domestication of animals marked the first step toward the civilization of the most primitive tribes of men—the transformation from the savage to the civilized way of life. Savage man hunted animals as a source of food and raiment. He lived on what roots, berries, and seeds he could find, and on such insects, animals, and fish as he could catch. In addition, he was only too likely to include his fellow man in his hunting and eating.

The dog appears to have been the very first animal domesticated by man. It took place in the Old Stone Age, 12,000 years ago, based on evidence found in a cave in Iraq. Prehistoric tribes used the dog to assist in hunting and to provide protection by night. Perhaps even more important, the presence of the dog furnished animal companionship, thus filling a deep-rooted need which has always existed in human beings.

FROM WHENCE THE DOG CAME?

Table 1 and Figure 2 tell the story of the evolution of the dog as deciphered from fossil remains.

Figure 2 reveals that *Miacis* began a line of evolution characterized by ever-increasing leg length: *Miacis*→*Cynodicitis*→*Tomarctus*→wolves→dogs. Increased leg length was accompanied by greater running speed and the development of the unique ability to run down prey mile after mile and seize it. This led to important social developments, involving group hunting. Competition, in turn, stimulated the growth of intelligence.

Incredible as it may seem, all the diverse types and breeds of domestic dogs—from the St. Bernard to the Chihuahua, from the Greyhound to the Bulldog—stem from little, tree-climbing *Miacis*, some 40 million years ago.

The author subscribes to the theory that the closest wild relatives of the dog are the wolves and the jackals (with wolves being the main progenitor), which are found in all parts of the world; but he also feels that wild (feral) dogs, such as the Dingo and the Pariah, in widely separated areas throughout the world, had a part in forming a number of breeds of domesticated dogs.

Further evidence of the close kinship of wolves and dogs is found in the fact that their teeth are identical, and they interbreed with no difficulty, given the opportunity. The Eskimos are supposed to have taken advantage of this situation to improve the stamina of their sled dogs, by staking out their bitches when in season, away from their encampments, in order to attract the attention of male wolves.

Domestication probably took place in the following ways: (1) through wolves being attracted to human camps by surplus meat wasted in times of plenty; (2) through wolf cubs being taken as pets by children of the tribe; and (3) through semitame wolves (pets that retreated to the wild as they grew up) joining in the hunt with men. Also, the author theorizes that the jackal was tamed in much the same manner. And furthermore, it is reasonable to assume that domesticated wolves and jackals interbred, as they will even today in captivity. Subsequently, through selective breeding, man created all the various sizes, shapes, and colors of dogs. This is possible because biological material, such as the dog, is flexible in the hands of man. As a result, man has fashioned many sizes, shapes, and colors of other domestic animals—of cattle, sheep, swine, horses, and poultry. So, why not dogs, also?

FROM THE WOLF AND THE JACKAL

From studies of caves, refuse heaps—known as *kitchen middens*—and lake dwellings, it is known that Europeans of the New Stone Age possessed a wolflike breed of dog; and a similar breed has been traced through the successive ages of bronze and iron.

Quite frequently the natives' races of dogs can be shown to resemble closely the native wolf or jackal. For example, the dogs kept by the American Indian differed little from the coyote, while the Eskimo dogs are more closely related to the Arctic wolf.

Fig. 3. Wolf, main progenitor of the dog (Drawing by R. F. Johnson)

TABLE 1
EVOLUTION OF THE DOG AS DECIPHERED FROM FOSSIL RECORDS

Epochs	Approximate Duration in Years	Approximate Number of Years Since Beginning	General Characteristics	The Dog
Recent	12,000+	12,000	Post Glacial Age Rise of Modern Man, *Homo sapiens* Development of complex cultures and civilizations Domestication of animals	*Canis familiaris*—the dog (of some 12,000 years ago). First animal domesticated by man. This was during the Paleolithic Period (Old Stone Age), before the end of the Pleistocene Ice Age, some 10,000 to 15,000 years ago. There are many theories about how domestication took place, among them: (1) that wolves were attracted to human camps by surplus meat wasted in times of plenty; (2) that wolf cubs were taken as pets by children of the tribe; and (3) that semitame wolves joined in the hunt with men. Perhaps the jackal was tamed in like manner. Following domestication, it is reasonable to assume that wolves and jackals interbred (even today, dogs, wolves, and jackals interbreed with no difficulty, given the opportunity). Out of this, the various types and breeds of dogs evolved
Pleistocene (Gr. *pleistos*, most + *kainos*, recent)	2,000,000+	3,000,000	Ice Age: Four major advances Evolution of primitive man, Neanderthal, Heidelberg, Peking, Java, etc Mammoth, mastodon, great sloth, saber-toothed tiger, etc 90–100% modern species Rise of Alps and Himalayas	
Pliocene (Gr. *pleion*, more + *kainos*)	12,000,000	15,000,000	Mammals increase in size 50–90% modern species	*Tomarctus* (of some 20 million years ago). All present-day dogs trace to *Tomarctus*, which lived about 20 million years ago. This creature was a plains dweller, a predator preying on game animals, and very doglike. The wolves, jackals, foxes, and the true wild dogs of today are distant, but not very different, descendants of *Tomarctus*.
Miocene (Gr. *mecion*, less + *kainos*)	10,000,000	25,000,000	The Golden Age of mammals Luxuriant grasses; culmination of plains-dwelling mammals 20–40% modern species	
Oligocene (Gr. *oligos*, little + *kainos*)	15,000,000	40,000,000	Modern mammals, predominate over primitive ones 10–15% modern species	*Cynodictis* (of 30 million years ago). Fast running ground dwellers, rather than tree climbers. At this stage, the family tree of doglike animals split into two groups: (1) the heavyweights, which became more massive and lumbering with the passing of time, and which gave us the "bear dogs" (*Daphaenus*); and (2) *Cynodictis*. In comparison with *Miacis*, *Cynodictis* was bigger (but it was no larger than a mink; and it still had a long body and short limbs), the claws on the toes were less fully retractile, and in the forelimbs some of the bones of the wrist had been fused. *Cynodictis* was adapted to running, rather than climbing. From *Cynodictis* all the true running dogs evolved, although the family tree branched again at this point into (1) the African hunting dogs (*Lycaon*) and its relatives, and (2) the true dogs. Even though these two branches look alike, their separate descent can be traced back some 30 million years. Subsequently, the true dogs branched again, with one branch giving rise to hyaena dogs, which were bone-eating scavengers.

(Continued)

Epochs	Approximate Duration in Years	Approximate Number of Years Since Beginning	General Characteristics	The Dog
Eocene (Gr. *eos*, dawn + *kainos*)	18,000,000	58,000,000	Archaic mammals, the advent of the horse 1–5% modern species	*Miacis* (of 40 million years ago). A small forest-living tree-climbing creature about the size of a ferret, with a long sinuous body and heavy tail, and short but very flexible legs. All paws with five toes, which were retractable. Teeth that shear against each other like scissor blades, equipping it to slice meat (like domestic dogs do). Intelligent and smarter than the animals on which it preyed.

The most outstanding trait of the dog is his loyalty to and affection for the people with whom he lives. These same characteristics are developed to almost the same degree in tamed wolves and jackals, thereby giving further credence to the theory that dogs descended from wolves and jackals.

One of the peculiarities of the dogs, which distinguished them from their wild relatives, is the habit of barking. Wolf and jackal cubs brought up with a litter of puppies learn to bark quite as well as their foster brothers. This is another proof of their similar ancestry.

Wolves, like dogs, are social animals; they run in packs made up of family groups. Within the pack, much cooperation is shown during the hunt. One animal will cut out a member of a herd of deer, or elk, or other game, then other members of the pack will take turns in running it down. Also, it's noteworthy that both the wolf and the dog frequently turn around several times before lying down, and dig up the earth with their forefeet and throw it back with their hind feet.

Other strong evidence that the wolf and the dog are very closely related is provided by (1) their interbreeding with no difficulty, given the opportunity (and their progeny are fertile), and (2) their identical teeth.

Although the jackal will interbreed with both dogs and wolves, they do not show as many doglike habits as the wolf. Jackals are smaller than wolves—only about half the height, and weighing about 40 pounds at maturity. They differ from both dogs and wolves in the structure of their teeth, and in being much more odoriferous.

Foxes have no part in the ancestry of the dog. There are many anatomical differences between the two, the gestation period of the fox is much shorter than that of the dog, and they never cross.

Fig. 4. Jackal, close wild relative of the dog. (Drawing by R. F. Johnson)

WHAT THE PREHISTORIC RECORDS TELL US

From the oldest records supplied by the Chaldean and Egyptian monuments, it is known that several distinct varieties of dogs had been developed 4,000 to 5,000 years ago. Slender dogs of the greyhound type, and a short-legged breed of the terrier type were depicted in Egypt; and the Assyrians of about 600 B.C. had mastifflike hounds.

Also, the early Greeks and Romans had dogs, which they often mentioned in their literature. Both made a distinction between those that hunted by scent and those that hunted by sight, just as we divide hounds of the hunting breeds today. The Roman canine classifications were similar to

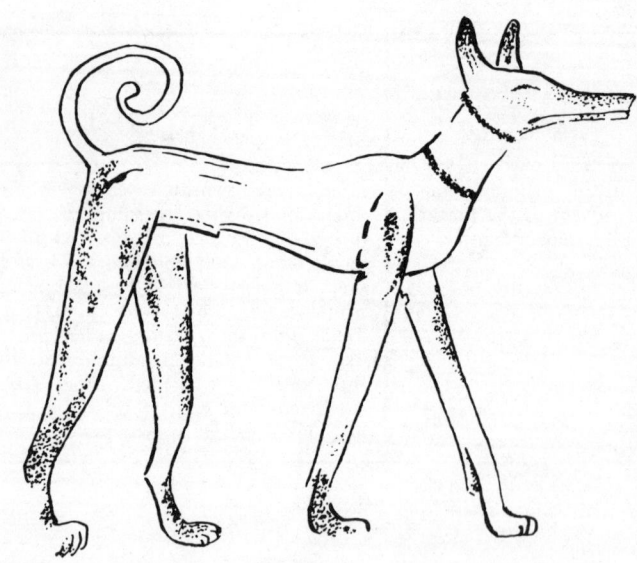

Fig. 5. Egyptian Greyhound with slender head, upright ears, and curled tail, from Beni Hassan, Twelfth Dynasty. (Drawing by J. L. Medeiros)

our present groups; they also had house dogs and sheep dogs.

Upon turning to the much earlier remains of the men of the Stone Age, their deposits give us some definite information. The kitchen middens left by prehistoric man along the coast of the Baltic Sea are composed of the shells of oysters and snails that were eaten by our savage ancestors. In these same mounds, marking the site of this primitive human habitation, we find crude, rough, stone implements, but no traces of the remains of dogs; and, of course, no traces of any other domestic animals. Later, when these early men learned to shape and polish their stone axes and spearheads—which marked the transition from the Old Stone Age to the New Stone Age—the first remains of dogs began to appear in their kitchen middens. These dogs were more like jackals than wolves. It is also noteworthy that they spread all over Europe, and that they appear to have persisted as a well-marked type for thousands of years. At any rate, it has been determined that the Lake Dwellers (about 6,000 years B.C.), when the stone tools had been replaced with bronze and iron was beginning to be used, kept dogs that were still very much like those of the first half-wild dogs that howled by night on the kitchen middens of the shellfish eaters.

But a larger kind of dog is also known from the skulls and other bones found in the refuse deposits of the men of the New Stone Age; and this dog is as clearly derived from the wolf as the other one is from the jackal. The German Shepherd Dog and many hunting dogs seem to be descended from this larger form.

From the above, it seems reasonable to deduct that the crossing of these two types of dogs—the one descending from jackals, the other descending from wolves—gave to man the gene mixture from which he has since molded a bewildering number of breeds of dogs, now totaling more than 400. No domestic animal has evolved with as many breeds as the dog. Likewise, differences in size, body form, coat, ears, tails, and intelligence are unparalleled. The wolflike German Shepherd Dog, the elegant Greyhound, the "sausage dog"—the Dachshund—the smart and lively Poodle, and the stately Great Dane, all evolved out of the ancient mixture of jackal and wolf, under the influence of man. It seems rather clear that many of the breeds, especially the toy dogs, could not have developed without the protection and assistance of civilization. In fact, many of the breeds of dogs today could not exist under natural conditions. It is equally clear that, through selection, man has been able to evolve certain breeds that are adept for certain uses, for example, hunting dogs, sheepherding dogs, and police dogs.

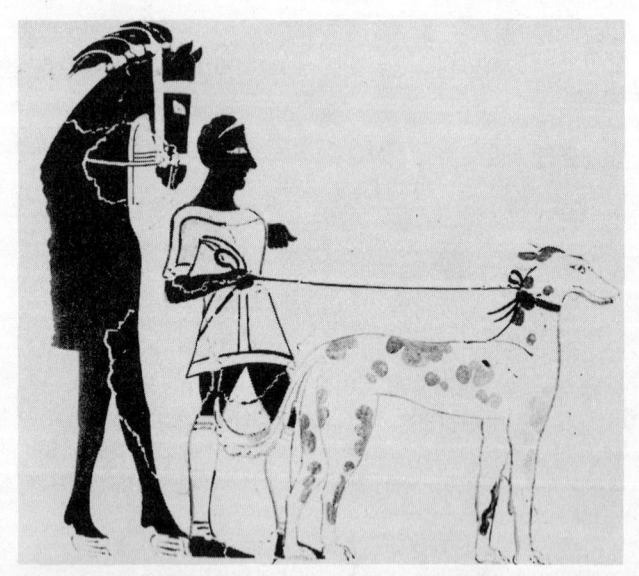

Fig. 6. Minoan painting: Huntsman holding a hound in leash. Detail of a boar hunt, found at Tiryns, a prehistoric fortress, and later a small Greek city. (Courtesy The Bettmann Archive, Inc., New York, N.Y.)

POSITION OF THE DOG IN THE ZOOLOGICAL SCHEME

The following outline shows the basic position of the domesticated dog in the zoological scheme:

Kingdom *Animalia*: Animals collectively; the animal kingdom.

Phylum *Chordata*: One of approximately twenty-one phyla of the animal kingdom, in which there is either a backbone (in the vertebrates) or the rudiment of a backbone, the chorda.

Class *Mammalia*: Mammals are warm-blooded animals that produce their young alive and suckle them for a variable period on a secretion from the mammary glands.

Order *Carnivora*: Animals possessing teeth adapted for flesh eating, a simple stomach and short intestine, feet with four or more usually clawed toes, a well-developed brain, clavicle (called collarbone in man) wanting or vestigial, and zonary deciduate placenta.

Family *Canidae*: There are two branches of *Canidae*: (1) domestic dogs, wolves, jackals, and foxes; and (2) African hunting dogs, Indian wild dogs or *dholes*, and South American bush dogs. All are carnivores, feeding mainly on the flesh of animals, which they run down, rather than stalk or ambush. Except for the fox, they are social animals, working together in family groups, or sometimes larger packs. Foxes live in pairs or solitarily except during the breeding and cub-rearing seasons.

Genus *Canis*: The Genus *Canis* includes four species: (1) *C. familiaris*—dogs, including domesticated dogs, Dingoes, Pariahs, and other wild dogs; (2) *C. lupus*—wolves; (3) *C. aureus*—jackals; and (4) *C. decussatus*—foxes.

Species (Zoological name): *Canis familiaris*. The domestic dog.

DOG AS MAN'S FIRST HELPMATE

Without the dog, man might never have made it. In the early days, they were far more than good friends and companions—they were helpmates.

WATCHDOGS

The first help of dogs to primitive man, when they were still only partially domesticated, was the warning (bark) they made at the approach of savage animals or enemy tribes. This trait is preserved in many breeds of dogs today, which are maintained primarily as watchdogs.

FOOD

Skulls found in the kitchen middens give unmistakable evidence that, in times of need at least, dogs were eaten by savage man. This use of dogs for food persisted until modern times in parts of the world, including in the South Sea islands and among the American Indians. But all this has changed; only rarely is the dog eaten now, even by primitive tribes.

DRAFT

The use of dogs in the Far North as draft animals to pull sleds appears to have been one of their earliest services to mankind. The large, wolflike Eskimo dogs are extraordinarily efficient in this respect, requiring only a few frozen fish for a day's journey and pulling loads of 100 pounds per dog for 30 miles or more in a day. Also, dogs were used as draft animals in the early development of Europe. They were once used for pulling carts loaded with woven goods in Belgium, and for pulling milk carts in Holland. In this country, the Plains Indians often used their dogs, as well as their horses, in moving camp, by making a miniature travois for the dog of the same general type as the larger one used for the horse. Today, the dog is seldom used as a draft animal.

HUNTING

The numerous breeds of dogs used exclusively for hunting today, and the special adaptation of some breeds for certain kinds of game, give evidence that the use of the dog for hunting must have been one of his earliest contributions. Several distinct breeds or types of dogs are shown in early Egyptian sculptures, among them the greyhound type, a hunting dog, is most prominent. It is also noteworthy that hunting dogs soon diverged into two types: those hunting by sight (sight hounds), like the Greyhound, and those in which the sense of smell became of primary importance (scent hounds), like the Bloodhound and Foxhound.

GUARDING AND HERDING

Dogs are natural protectors for those whom they love and for whose care they are entrusted. Thus, since their first domestication they have been used for guarding both man and beast. They have protected man from great beasts of prey when he is satisfying his need for deep sleep; and they have watched over herds and flocks by night, just as they and the shepherds were doing when they first saw the star over Bethlehem. Also, from time immemorial, dogs have been used as drovers in taking cattle and sheep to market.

COMPANIONSHIP

By nature, man needs animal companionship. The affectionate nature and high level of intelligence of dogs fills this inner need. This has led to the development of a great variety of dogs, particularly the toy breeds, that have no other purpose than as pets or "lap dogs." Actually, many of the breeds of dogs have little use along the lines for which they were initially developed —they are simply kept as house dogs and companions.

SOME WILD DOGS OF TODAY

In practically every country where civilized man has explored, he has found some wild dogs, as well as some domesticated and semidomesticated dogs, among the inhabitants. It's easy to understand how wild dogs came about. If left to fend for themselves, some domestic dogs of today would revert to the wild, just as the dogs left on Robinson Crusoe's island did.

Wild dogs and domesticated dogs are quite similar in their habits. For example, both are exceedingly jealous, yet they seem to forget their differences and animosities when hunting in packs. But, in comparison with domesticated dogs, wild dogs possess fewer and have more somber colors.

Wild dogs, like domestic dogs, are able to adapt themselves to the conditions of their habitat; for example, feeding on the land.

Only a few of these wild dogs will be discussed in the sections that follow.

PARIAH DOGS

These are sometimes referred to as the ownerless or street dogs of the Orient. Pariah dogs are found everywhere in North Africa, southern Asia, and southeastern Europe. They are of medium size, thick or short coated, and usually yellow or reddish in color, but in some areas they are also black and white or all black. They interbreed readily with domestic dogs.

These are genuinely wild dogs so far as any care on the part of man is concerned. Yet, they are dependent on the presence of man for their food supply, for they live upon the dead animals found in the fields or on the roadside, and they even enter the towns to eat the street refuse, sharing the role of scavenger with swine. In his travels, the author has observed that the Pariah dogs enjoy a surprising degree of consideration among the Mohammedans, who look upon dogs as unclean.

These Pariah dogs look very much like jackals. Moreover, their scavenging habits are strikingly similar to those of wild jackals, which are camp followers to the larger beasts of prey like the lion and the tiger, instead of to man. It is noteworthy, too, that these Pariahs evidently cross with wild jackals; for in India they resemble most closely the Indian red jackal, in Egypt they are similar to the Nubian jackal, and in South Africa there are similar half-wild dogs like the black-backed jackal.

Where the Pariah dog came from is still a puzzle. One school of thought is that, when the ancient civilizations of the Middle East declined and vanished, the domesticated dogs of the region reverted to the wild. This would account for the diversity of types that are found. Another theory is that the Pariah are descended from some primitive dog, somewhat like the Dingo in appearance, and that they represent a transition stage between truly wild dogs and domestic dogs.

Pariah dogs can be tamed and trained successfully. Puppies reared by humans behave like domesticated dogs.

DINGO

This wild dog of Australia is the most distinct of all the feral races of dogs. It has been closely associated with man for thousands of years. The Dingo was domesticated in the Middle Stone Age, then migrated to Australia with the aborigines, where it reverted to the wild. It is by nature suspicious, alert, and very intelligent; hence, man must wage a relentless war against it in order to keep it from destroying sheep, which are its main food. The Dingo is independent of man because it can easily lead a self-reliant life in the midst of the inferior *marsupial* animals, or pouched types, which throng the plains and forests of Australia.

The Dingo is strikingly like the Pariah dogs of India, especially in the reddish color of its fur. The breed stands about 24 inches at the shoulder. Dingoes are generally nocturnal in their habits, doing their hunting at night. They usually travel in small groups, generally as a family, although packs of as many as 100 have been seen. They interbreed with the domestic dog. Although they do not bark in the wild, when caught as young and tamed, they learn to do so.

GALAPAGOS ISLAND DOGS

A most interesting race of feral dogs (dogs that have reverted to the wild state), exists on the large island of Albemarle, in the Galapagos Islands. These dogs, which apparently escaped from the small settlement at the south end of the island, have acquired a considerable amount of uniformity of appearance. They live like wolves—hunting the native birds, digging up the eggs of the giant land turtles, searching for the eggs laid on the beaches by the sea turtles, and hunting down feral goats and cattle. Despite the fact that they are as shy and difficult to approach as any wild creature, their young are completely tamed when captured and brought up in association with man.

DOGS OF THE AMERICAN INDIAN

The North American Indians had dogs when the white man arrived. They were closely related to the coyote in appearance, size, and habits. There appear to be at least three native wolves in the Americas from which the dogs of the American Indians descended. In Florida, the Seminole dog seems to have been black like the local wolf; in northern South America and the West Indies, the very handsome crab-eating dog is still found as the domestic dog of the Indians; and in South America, the Azara's dog, a foxlike creature, appears to be either the direct ancestor of the dog of the Pampas Indians or to have crossed with it so much that the relationship with any other dog is obscured.

2
Breeds; Kennel Clubs; Selecting and Buying

Chapter 2

Classification of Dogs	25
Relative Popularity of Breeds of Dogs	28
Why So Many Breeds of Dogs?	28
Anatomy and Parts of a Dog	31
How to Measure a Dog	35
Breeds of Dogs and Their Characteristics	35
Kennel Clubs	114
American Kennel Club	114
Registration	115
Registration Procedure	116
United Kennel Club, Inc.	116
Breeds of Coonhounds and Their Characteristics	121
Canadian Kennel Club	128
Kennel Club of England	128
Bermuda Kennel Club, Inc.	129
Selecting and Buying the Dog	129
Summary	132

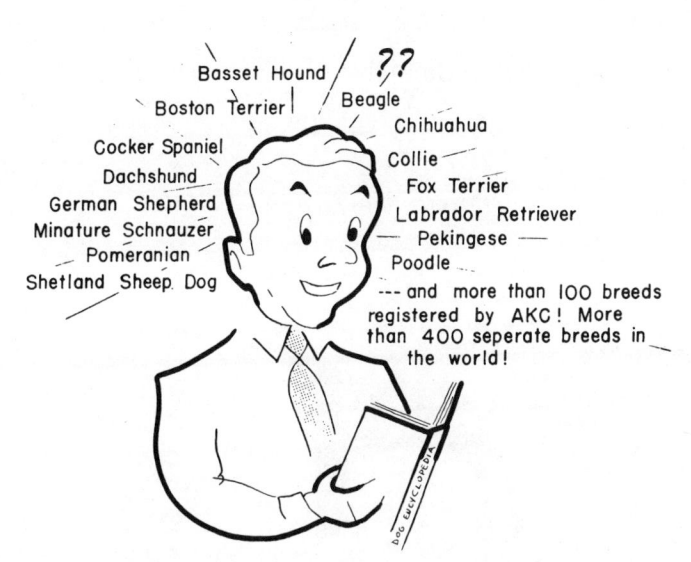

Fig. 7. What kind and breed of dog? (Drawing by R. F. Johnson)

BREEDS; KENNEL CLUBS; SELECTING AND BUYING

All the breeds of dogs were created by man, having come from the process of crossing, selectively breeding, and resolutely propagating specifically favored physical and mental peculiarities. Over a long period, forms were created that continue to breed true. The greatest difficulty is in preventing the breeds from retrogressing towards the original forms from whence they came.

Today, with the science of genetics applied to dog breeding, many breeds are changing rapidly—and new breeds are evolving. These changes will continue; a reminder of the biological flexibility, both physical and mental, that continues to be an important part of the makeup of our dogs of today.

CLASSIFICATION OF DOGS

Breeds of dogs may be and are classified on several different bases, including (1) their external features, (2) by tracing their lineage to five or six prehistoric forms of the domestic dog, and (3) the chief use to which they are put. Each system of classification has its special merits and its advocates.

As dogs increased in importance and numbers in the second half of the nineteenth century, the need to fix a system of grouping the various breeds became urgent. But each country went its separate way, with the result that there is little uniformity of the classifications adopted. Thus, France divides her dog breeds into eight groups, Germany into four, Spain into five, Sweden into eight, England into six, and the United States, Canada, and Bermuda into six. The Federation Cynologique Internationale (F.C.I.), a federation whose members represent several countries—mostly European, with headquarters in Thuin, Belgium—has eleven groups.

The Canadian Kennel Club and the Bermuda Kennel Club classifications of the various breeds generally parallel those of the American Kennel Club.

The American Kennel Club classification follows:

GROUP I: SPORTING BREEDS

Fig. 8.

The sporting breeds serve as hunters' assistants in finding and fetching game birds. This group includes the spaniels—the small, flushing breeds; the pointers—whose sensitive noses point toward a single bird or covey; and the retrievers—the strong, expert swimmers, specialists at recovering water fowl on land or water.

The sporting breeds are:

Pointer
Pointer, German Shorthaired
Pointer, German Wirehaired
Retriever, Chesapeake Bay
Retriever, Curly-Coated
Retriever, Flat-Coated
Retriever, Golden
Retriever, Labrador
Setter, English
Setter, Gordon
Setter, Irish
Spaniel, American Water

Spaniel, Brittany
Spaniel, Clumber
Spaniel, Cocker
Spaniel, English Cocker
Spaniel, English Springer
Spaniel, Field
Spaniel, Irish Water
Spaniel, Sussex
Spaniel, Welsh Springer
Vizsla
Weimaraner
Wirehaired Pointing Griffon

Saluki
Scottish Deerhound
Whippet

GROUP III: WORKING DOGS

Fig. 10.

GROUP II: HOUNDS

Fig. 9.

There are two types of hounds: (1) the sight hounds—long-legged, slender-bodied, keen-visioned hounds, which follow their quarry by sight and capture it by using great speed; and (2) the scent hounds—medium-sized to small hounds, which track their quarry by scent and wear it down by their superior endurance.

The hound breeds are:

Afghan Hound
Basenji
Basset Hound
Beagle
Black-and-Tan Coonhound
Bloodhound
Borzoi
Dachshund
Foxhound, American
Foxhound, English
Greyhound
Harrier
Irish Wolfhound
Norwegian Elkhound
Otter Hound
Rhodesian Ridgeback

The ancestors of the working breeds protected flocks from man and beast, drove cattle and sheep to market, pulled sleds across vast, snow-swept lands, and served as guards on large estates. Through the years, many of the assignments so expertly handled by the working breeds passed into oblivion. But new and important uses evolved. Today, they are working as watchdogs, as guides for the blind, as police dogs, and as soldiers.

The working dog breeds are:

Alaskan Malamute
Belgian Malinois
Belgian Sheepdog
Belgian Tervuren
Bernese Mountain Dog
Bouvier des Flandres
Boxer
Briard
Bullmastiff
Collie
Doberman Pinscher
German Shepherd Dog
Giant Schnauzer
Great Dane
Great Pyrenees
Komondor
Kuvasz
Mastiff
Newfoundland
Old English Sheepdog
Puli
Rottweiler

26

St. Bernard
Samoyed
Shetland Sheepdog
Siberian Husky
Standard Schnauzer
Welsh Corgi, Cardigan
Welsh Corgi, Pembroke

GROUP IV: TERRIERS

Fig. 11.

"Terrier" comes from the Latin word for earth, "terra," because these dogs were developed to follow, serpent like, their hunted quarry into earthen dens. They are small, bold, and alert. They have been assistants to farmers and gamekeepers, as well as to huntsmen. Today, they serve primarily as pets.

The terrier breeds are:

Airedale Terrier
American Staffordshire Terrier
Australian Terrier
Bedlington Terrier
Border Terrier
Bull Terrier
Cairn Terrier
Dandie Dinmont Terrier
Fox Terrier
Irish Terrier
Kerry Blue Terrier
Lakeland Terrier
Manchester Terrier
Miniature Schnauzer
Norwich Terrier
Scottish Terrier
Sealyham Terrier
Skye Terrier
Welsh Terrier
West Highland White Terrier

GROUP V: TOYS

Fig. 12.

Dogs of the toy breeds are, as the name implies, very small. Some are exact miniatures of other breeds, whereas others stemmed from older types prized by royalty of ancient times. They were created for the purpose of pleasure and companionship; and they are noted for their pluckiness and longevity.

The toy breeds are:

Affenpinscher
Brussels Griffon
Chihuahua
English Toy Spaniel
Italian Greyhound
Japanese Spaniel
Maltese
Manchester Terrier (Toy)
Miniature Pinscher
Papillon
Pekingese
Pomeranian
Poodle (Toy)
Pug
Shih Tzu
Silky Terrier
Yorkshire Terrier

GROUP VI: NONSPORTING DOGS

Fig. 13.

The nonsporting group includes various breeds which do not fit into any other category. They have various backgrounds and widely varied characteristics. Some have survived the vicissitudes of time as companion dogs, long after the disappearance of their original specialized work, whereas others have always been valued chiefly as pets.

The nonsporting dog breeds are:

    Boston Terrier
    Bulldog
    Chow Chow
    Dalmatian
    French Bulldog
    Keeshond
    Lhasa Apso
    Poodle
    Schipperke

RELATIVE POPULARITY OF BREEDS OF DOGS

Fig. 14. German Shepherd watchdogs and guards on patrol, within a fenced area surrounding a home.

Table 2 shows the 1970 and 1971 registrations in the American Kennel Club of the various breeds of dogs, with listings by rank. As shown, in 1971 a total of 1,129,200 dogs were registered, representing 116 different breeds. It is noteworthy, however, that two breeds—Poodles and German Shepherd Dogs accounted for nearly one-third of the total registrations. A comparison of 1970 and 1971 registrations by breeds shows a trend for the breeds that are noted as watchdogs and guards to increase, perhaps reflecting the desire of people for protection during these troubled times.

WHY SO MANY BREEDS OF DOGS?

In no other class of animals have so many breeds evolved as in dogs. It is estimated that there are more than 400 distinct dog breeds in the world. By contrast, there are only thirty-six breeds of cats, wild and domestic. Of course, the basic explanation of "why so many breeds?" is the genetic variation that exists in the domestic dog, *Canis familiaris*, and the ability of man to develop a breed by selective breeding. Yet, there must have been motivating forces in order to cause so many new breeds to evolve. These forces were:

1. The diverse needs and uses for which dogs have been produced. For example, shepherd people the world over developed herding dogs—dogs with herding aptitudes and weather-resistant coats; and terriers were developed because of the need for a small but bold animal that would go into the burrows or dens of foxes or other vermin.

2. The fact that many people of wealth and high station have bred dogs. For example, the Egyptians, the most advanced civilization of their day, developed the greyhound type; whereas, by 400 B.C., the Greeks had developed trailing breeds or hounds.

3. Geographical areas were often separated and isolated, with the result that there was a certain amount of inbreeding and fixing of type. Out of this, it was very easy for distinct breeds to evolve in different geographical areas.

4. As primitive men roamed the world for whatever cause—Ice Ages, population pressures, famines, wars, and other causes—they usually took their dogs with them, because they could trail on their own power. As a result, these dogs likely mated with other primitive and different dogs.

5. Dogs are more flexible in the hands of man than other animals—horses or cattle, for example—because of their multiple rate of reproduction, early maturity, and short time interval between generations.

6. Dog shows have had a tremendous impact on fixing new breeds. In the early days of dog shows, in the latter half of the last century, cynologists (those who specialize in the care and training of dogs) had to decide which kinds of dogs should be considered to constitute separate breeds, then they had to draw up the standards for each breed. The world's first dog show was held in England in 1859. American dog shows were started about 1870.

TABLE 2
1970 AND 1971 REGISTRATION OF DOGS BY BREEDS IN THE AMERICAN KENNEL CLUB, WITH THE RANK OF EACH BREED[1]

Breed	Rank	1970 Registrations	Rank	1971 Registrations
Poodles	1	265,879	1	256,491
German Shepherd Dogs	2	109,198	2	111,355
Beagles	4	61,007	3	61,247
Dachshunds	3	61,042	4	60,954
Miniature Schnauzers	5	41,647	5	45,305
St. Bernards	7	27,297	6	35,320
Irish Setters	11	23,357	7	33,516
Labrador Retrievers	10	25,667	8	30,170
Collies	9	26,979	9	28,772
Pekingese	8	27,190	10	27,717
Chihuahuas	6	28,833	11	26,878
Cocker Spaniels	12	21,811	12	24,846
Doberman Pinschers	14	18,636	13	23,413
Basset Hounds	13	20,046	14	20,848
Shetland Sheepdogs	15	16,423	15	18,478
Pomeranians	16	16,158	16	17,079
Great Danes	19	13,180	17	16,349
Yorkshire Terriers	17	13,484	18	15,975
Brittany Spaniels	18	13,400	19	15,662
German Shorthaired Pointers	21	12,724	20	14,468
Golden Retrievers	23	11,437	21	13,589
Boston Terriers	20	12,814	22	13,188
Boxers	22	11,483	23	12,617
Scottish Terriers	25	10,248	24	10,765
Old English Sheepdogs	31	6,785	25	10,511
Siberian Huskies	28	7,891	26	10,471
English Springer Spaniels	27	8,945	27	10,076
Fox Terriers	24	10,670	28	9,988
Pugs	26	10,022	29	9,917
Lhasa Apsos	38	6,014	30	9,671
Afghan Hounds	35	6,127	31	8,049
Dalmatians	29	6,961	32	7,883
Cairn Terriers	32	6,698	33	7,738
Samoyeds	34	6,129	34	7,694
Weimaraners	30	6,898	35	7,615
Norwegian Elkhounds	37	6,080	36	7,517
Airedale Terriers	33	6,325	37	6,976
West Highland White Terriers	39	5,801	38	6,754
Bulldogs	36	6,122	39	6,493
Alaskan Malamutes	40	4,373	40	5,621
Maltese	41	4,197	41	4,819
Shih Tzu	42	3,396	42	4,334
Keeshonden	44	3,045	43	3,829
Basenjis	43	3,258	44	3,288
Silky Terriers	45	2,894	45	3,132
Welsh Corgis (Pembroke)	46	2,446	46	2,354
Chow Chows	48	1,813	47	2,352
Vizslas	47	1,973	48	2,242
Chesapeake Bay Retrievers	49	1,611	49	1,928
Newfoundlands	50	1,557	50	1,763
English Setters	54	1,275	51	1,502
Welsh Terriers	51	1,368	52	1,491

[1] Figures provided by The American Kennel Club, 51 Madison Avenue, New York, N. Y. 10010

(Continued)

TABLE 2 (CONTINUED)
1970 AND 1971 REGISTRATION OF DOGS BY BREEDS IN THE AMERICAN KENNEL CLUB, WITH THE RANK OF EACH BREED

Breed	Rank	1970 Registrations	Rank	1971 Registrations
Borzois	57	1,138	53	1,445
Schipperkes	52	1,345	54	1,408
Great Pyrenees	58	1,131	55	1,402
Australian Terriers	55	1,210	56	1,313
Miniature Pinschers	53	1,297	57	1,294
Kerry Blue Terriers	56	1,163	58	1,194
Standard Schnuazers	59	1,116	59	1,174
Bloodhounds	62	839	60	1,041
Irish Wolfhounds	66	769	61	992
Gordon Setters	65	795	62	937
Whippets	61	928	63	923
Manchester Terriers	60	967	64	888
Pulik	64	811	65	870
Italian Greyhounds	67	699	66	685
Bedlington Terriers	63	813	67	660
English Cocker Spaniels	69	558	68	653
Rhodesian Ridgebacks	68	590	69	630
Bull Terriers	76	398	70	544
German Wirehaired Pointers	73	420	71	542
Irish Terriers	70	529	71	542
Bullmastiffs	72	427	73	535
Rottweilers	71	428	74	508
Pointers	77	396	75	465
Belgian Sheepdogs	79	346	76	427
Skye Terriers	75	405	77	419
Japanese Spaniels	87	285	78	396
American Water Spaniels	81	324	79	387
Salukis	73	420	80	381
Papillons	84	308	81	369
Giant Schnauzers	80	328	82	367
Bouviers Des Flandres	78	348	82	367
Norwich Terriers	89	269	84	365
Welsh Corgis (Cardigan)	85	294	85	360
American Staffordshire Terriers	86	293	86	340
Mastiffs	87	285	87	325
Belgian Tervuren	90	253	88	319
Dandie Dinmont Terriers	83	316	89	273
Sealyham Terriers	82	322	90	247
Black-&-Tan Coonhounds	92	208	91	216
Lakeland Terriers	93	185	92	214
Greyhounds	94	156	92	214
Brussels Griffons	91	230	94	205
Briards	95	144	95	153
Bernese Mountain Dogs	98	103	96	152
Wirehaired Pointing Griffons	96	112	97	131
French Bulldogs	97	107	98	110
Scottish Deerhounds	101	87	99	106
Kuvaszok	99	102	100	94
Affenpinschers	100	95	101	82
Komondorok	106	54	102	73

(Continued)

TABLE 2 (CONTINUED)
1970 AND 1971 REGISTRATION OF DOGS BY BREEDS IN THE AMERICAN KENNEL CLUB,
WITH THE RANK OF EACH BREED

Breed	Rank	1970 Registrations	Rank	1971 Registrations
Foxhounds (American)	105	57	103	65
Flat-Coated Retrievers	103	69	104	63
Irish Water Spaniels	102	80	105	60
Border Terriers	108	39	106	59
English Toy Spaniels	109	37	107	43
Otter Hounds	110	27	108	31
Foxhounds (English)	115	2	109	30
Welsh Springer Spaniels	112	16	110	24
Harriers	111	19	111	23
Curly-Coated Retrievers	104	59	112	19
Clumber Spaniels	107	42	113	13
Field Spaniels	115	2	114	12
Belgian Malinois	114	3	115	6
Sussex Spaniels	113	4	116	5
		1,056,225		1,129,200

In summary, it may be said that all of the existing breeds of dogs are examples of man-made development or evolution. The American Kennel Club recognizes 116 different breeds. In addition, some of the breeds are split into varieties, based on length of coat. Still other varieties that do not have *Stud Book* status can be shown in miscellaneous classes.

ANATOMY AND PARTS OF A DOG

In discussing dogs, especially the breeds, it is necessary to introduce many technical terms, each of which has a precise meaning and significance. Thus, it is important to have a working knowledge of the anatomy and parts of the dog. Nothing so quickly sets an expert apart from a novice as thorough knowledge of the language commonly used in describing the anatomy and parts. In order that there may be no uncertainty about the parts to which these terms refer, a series of drawings of the dog's anatomy and parts, along with captions, is herewith presented in Figs. 15 to 20.

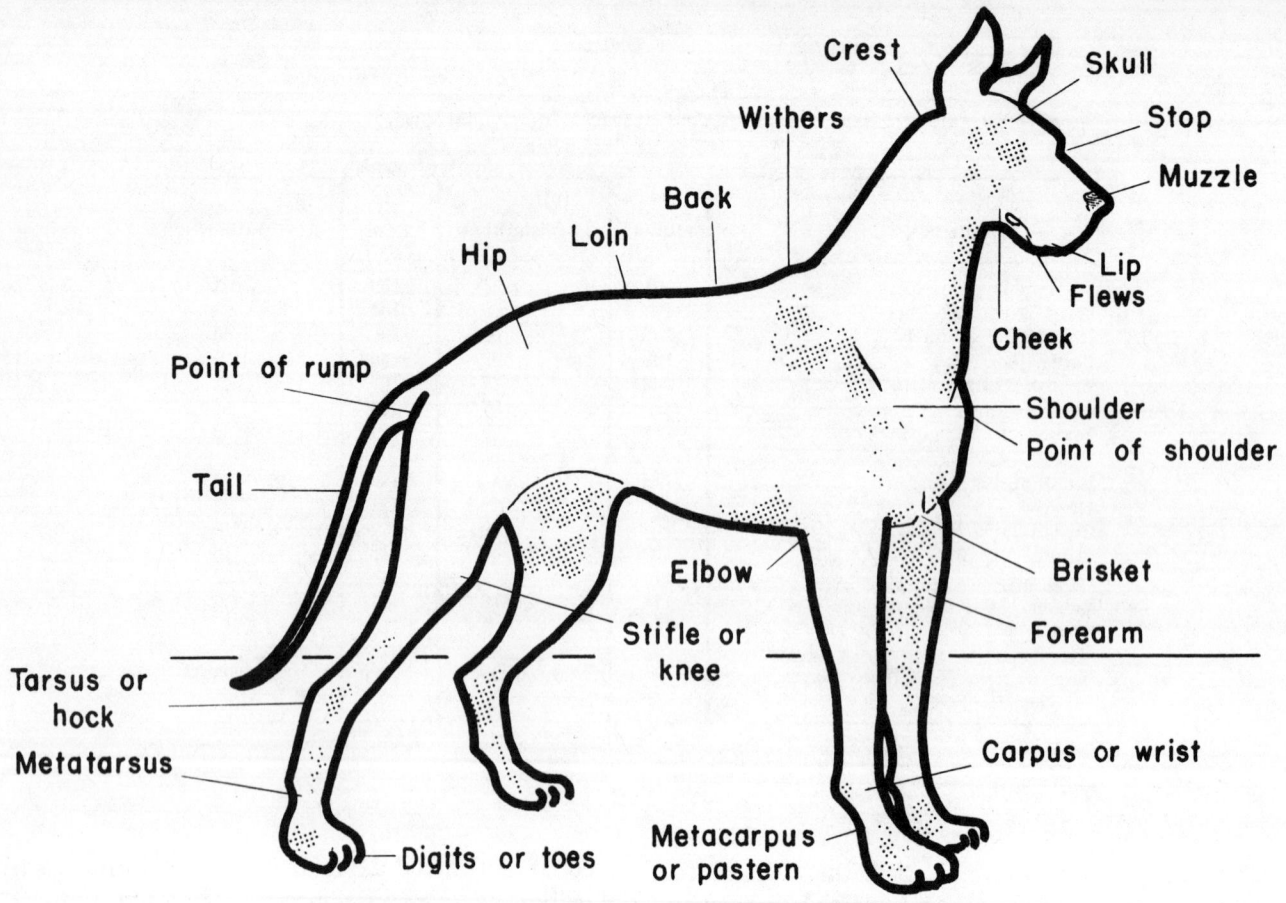

Fig. 15. Parts of a dog. (Drawing by R. F. Johnson)

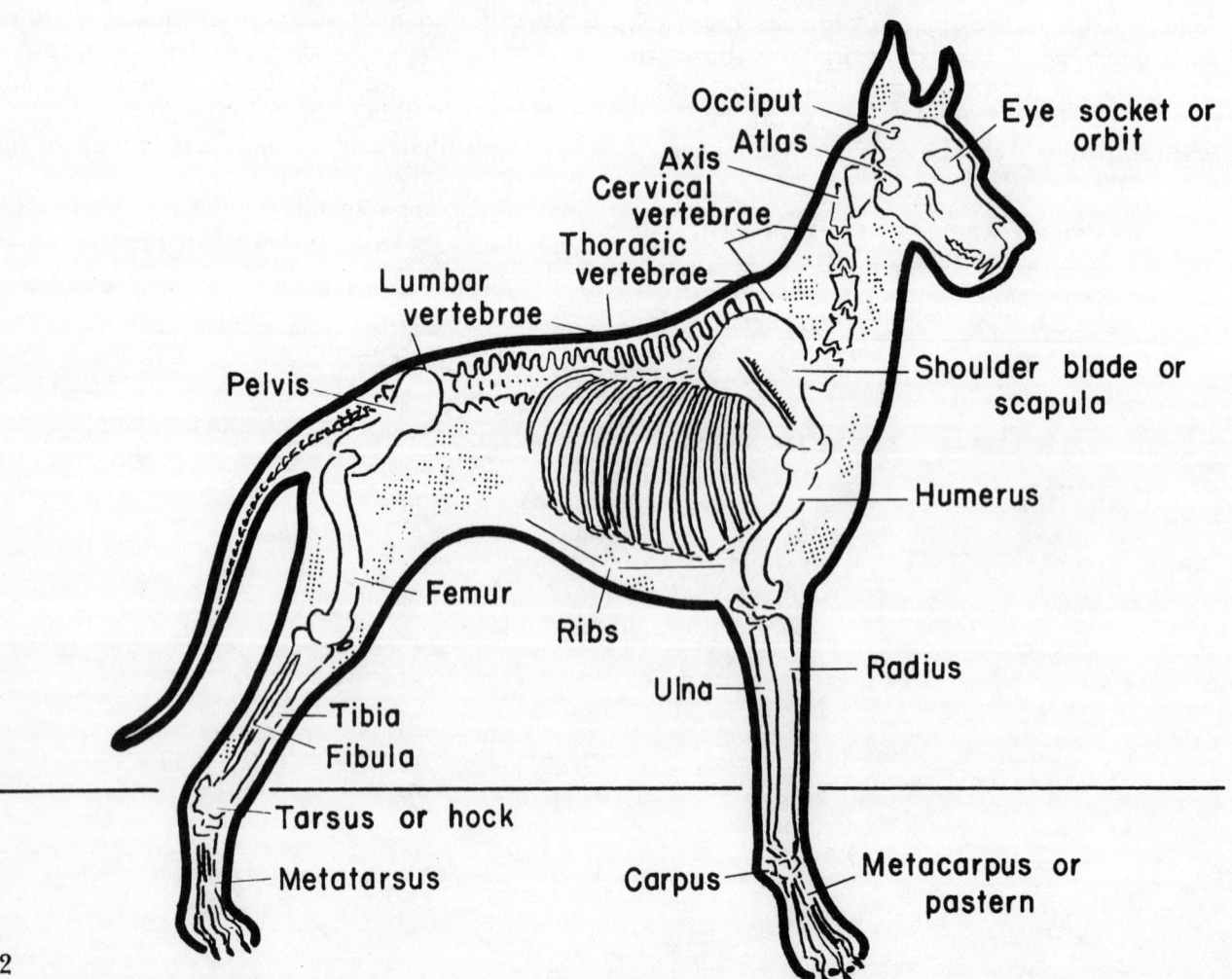

Fig. 16. Skeleton of the dog. (Drawing by R. F. Johnson)

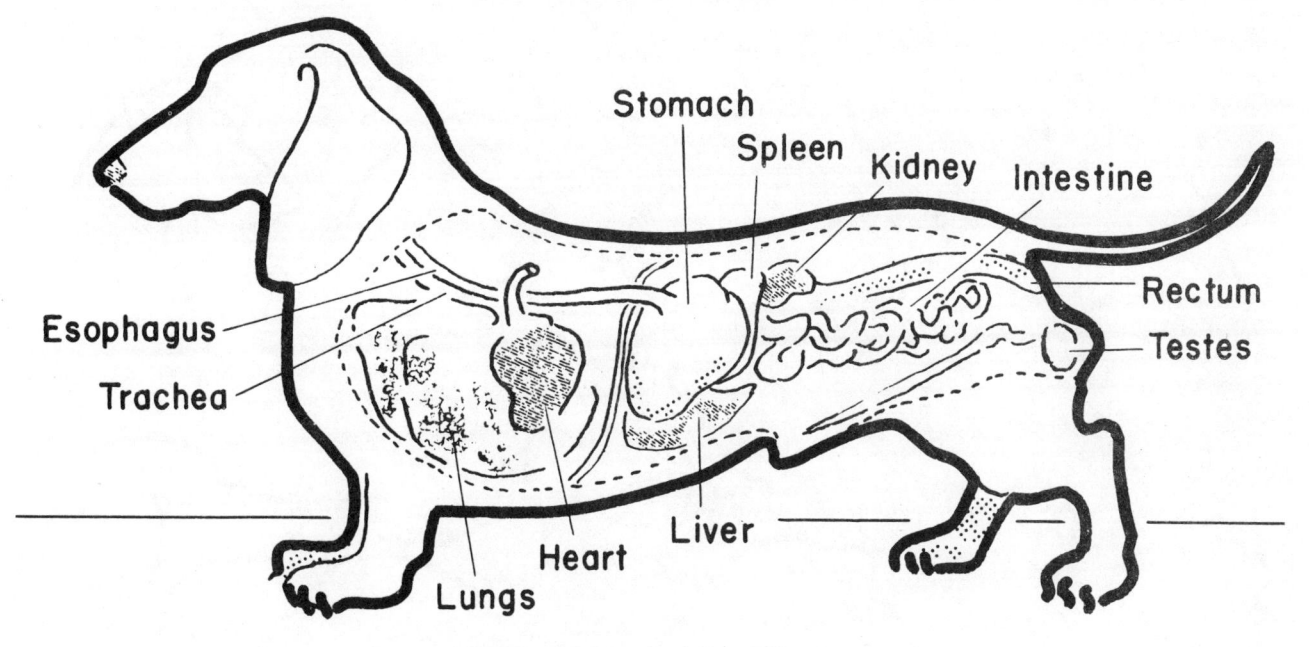

Fig. 17. Internal organs of the dog. (Drawing by R. F. Johnson)

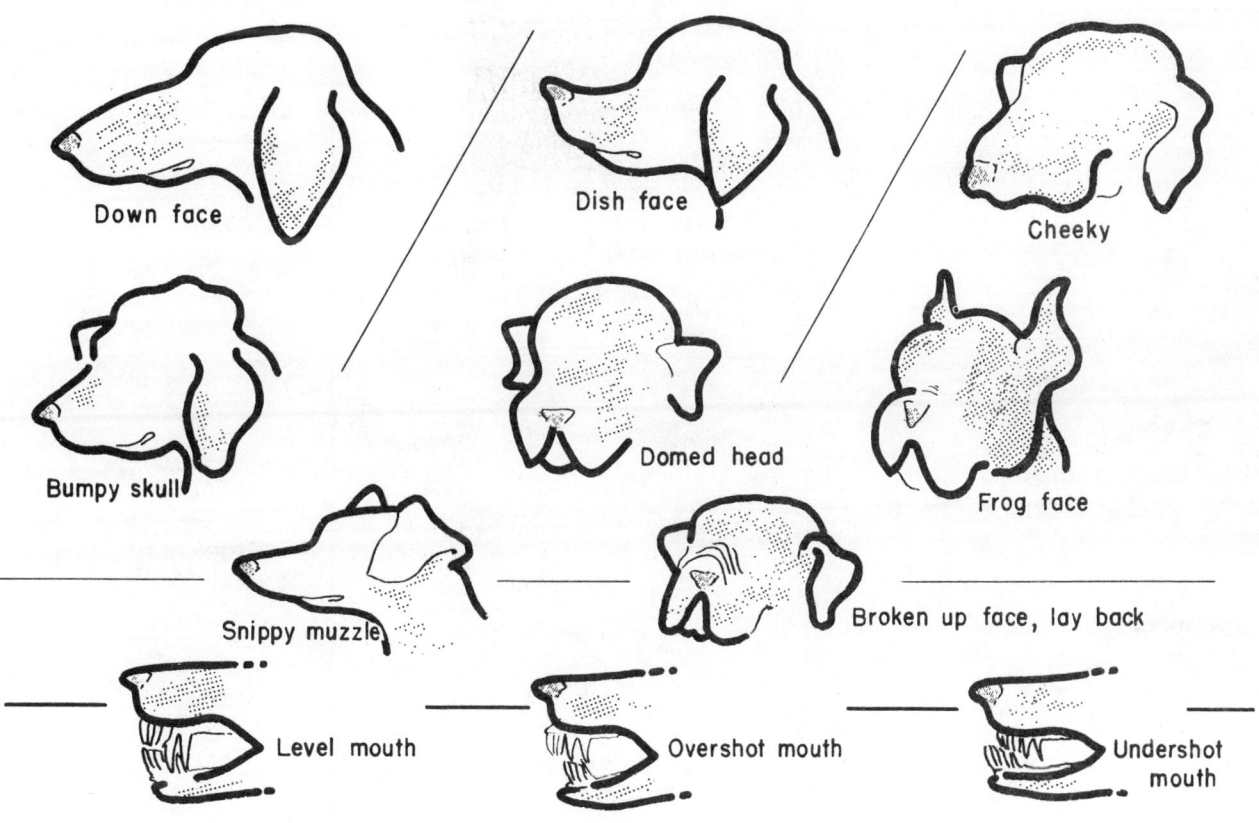

Fig. 18. Head and mouth shapes. (Drawing by R. F. Johnson)

33

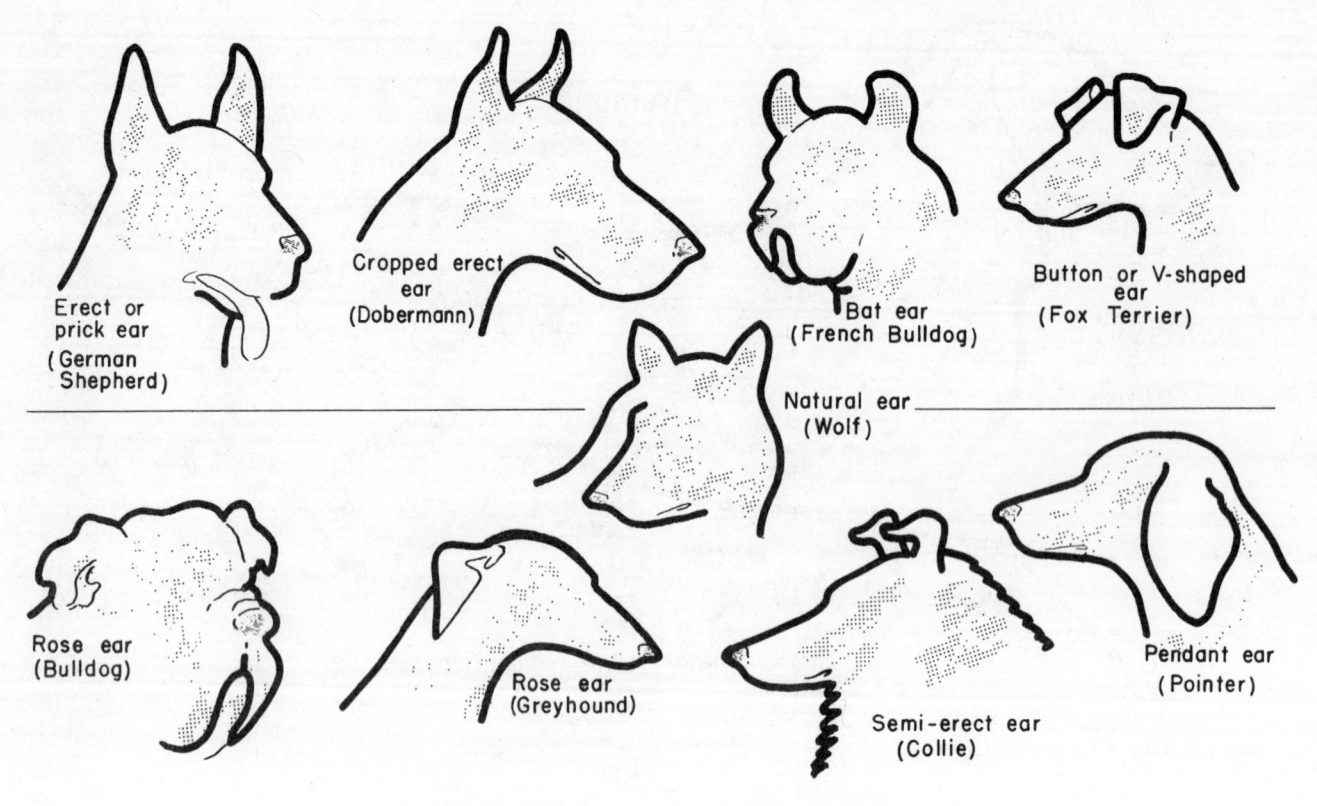

Fig. 19. Ear shapes. (Drawing by R. F. Johnson)

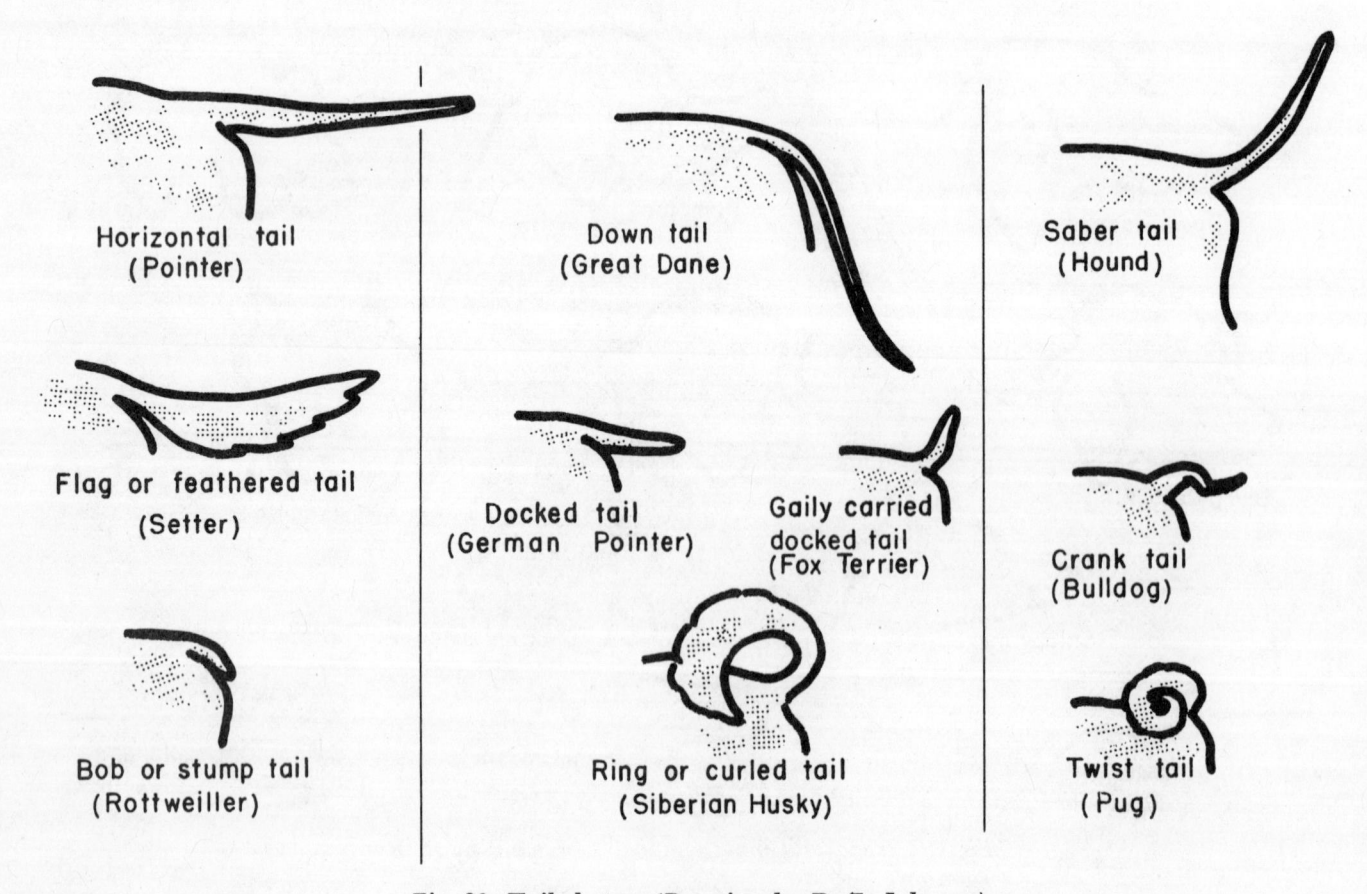

Fig. 20. Tail shapes. (Drawing by R. F. Johnson)

HOW TO MEASURE A DOG

The normal measurements pertinent to a dog are his (1) height to top of shoulder; (2) height at croup; (3) length of body; (4) girth of chest; (5) length of head; (6) length of muzzle; and (7) length of skull. These are illustrated in Fig. 21.

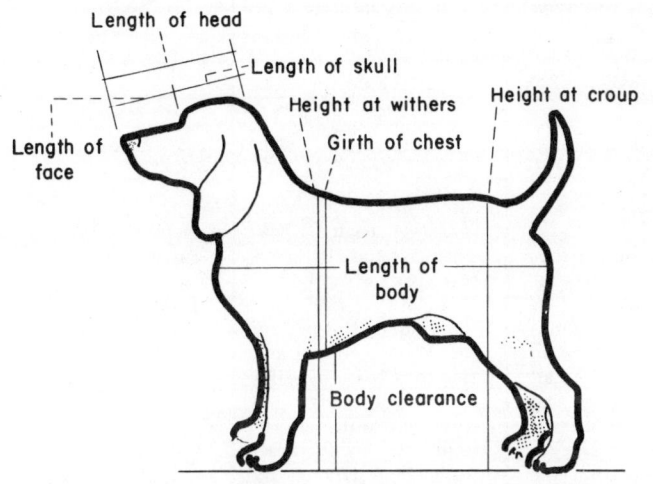

Fig. 21. How to measure a dog. (Drawing by R. F. Johnson)

The height of a dog is measured by standing him squarely on a level area and measuring the vertical distance from the highest point of his withers (or top of shoulders) to the ground. There is some disagreement among dog authorities as to the height range used in describing different size dogs. The author suggests the following:

Miniatures or toys—under 10 inches at the withers
Small dogs—11 to 16 inches
Medium-size dogs—17 to 24 inches
Large dogs—over 24 inches.

BREEDS OF DOGS AND THEIR CHARACTERISTICS

A breed of dogs may be defined as a group of dogs having a common origin and possessing certain well-fixed, distinctive, uniformly transmitted characteristics that are not common to other dogs.

It is estimated that 25 to 30 percent of all dogs in the United States are purebreds, or members of a breed.

There is scarcely a breed of dogs that does not possess one or more distinctive breed characteristics in which it excels all others. By choosing a particular breed, people can get the size, the shape, the color, and the type of coat that they prefer in a dog. The discriminating can also get the kind of temperament desired, for there are temperamental differences between breeds. They can choose among (1) the one-man dog that is aloof with strangers, (2) the bold, aggressive dog, (3) the affectionate, sentimental fellow, and (4) the character that has an independent, impudent attitude to life and authority. Certainly if any strong breed preference exists, it should be an important factor, although it is recognized that certain breeds are better suited to certain uses and conditions than others.

Table 3 lists the 116 breeds of dogs registered in the American Kennel Club and gives their characteristics. Attention is directed to the fact that all breeds are listed alphabetically in order to facilitate finding a particular breed by the person not familiar with the classification according to the six groups used by the American Kennel Club. However, immediately under the listing of the name of the breed, the AKC classification is given.

Because of space limitations, Table 3 does not contain all of the detailed standards of the 116 breeds listed. Rather, it is a condensation of what the author considers pertinent relative to each of the breeds. In the preparation of this table, the author drew heavily from the breed standards published by the American Kennel Club.

The breed standards of each breed are set up by the "parent club" of the breed; that is, the AKC looks to it to evolve with the breed standards for its particular breed, and to make such subsequent revisions in them as it deems necessary—with such changes subject to the final approval of the AKC. The first club of each breed elected to AKC membership is recognized as the parent club.

Colored pictures of some of the leading breeds of dogs, Figs. 140 to 181,[2] follow page 128.

---

[2] Figs. 140 to 181 courtesy of Carnation Company (makers of Friskies), Los Angeles, Calif., and Frye & Smith, San Diego, Calif.

TABLE 3 BREEDS OF DOGS

Breed	Place of Origin; Present Popularity	Color; Coat	General Appearance	Size
Affenpinscher —*toy* *Fig. 22.*	Germany In 1936, the breed was admitted to the American Kennel Club's *Stud Book* and to dog show classification	*Color:* Black, black with tan markings; red, gray, and other colors *Coat:* Varies on body parts from short and dense to long, and shaggy. It is long, loose, shaggy, stiff, and wiry on the legs and around the eyes, nose and chin	A small, shaggy-haired, upstanding toy dog with apple head, upright ears, and short, docked tail Sometimes called the "monkey dog" because of its large dark eyes, whiskers, and bushy eyebrows	*Height:* Not over 10½ in. *Weight:* About 7 lb
Afghan Hound —*hound* *Fig. 23.*	It originated on the Sinai peninsula, but takes its name from nearby Afghanistan, where it was once used to hunt gazelles. Sinai is where Jehovah delivered to Moses the tablets of the Ten Commandments. Thus, the history of the Afghan Hound can be traced back to the period 3000 to 4000 B. C. The breed was first introduced to the U.S. about 1926. But it did not become popular until recently. Today, it is the rage in America, India, Iran (Persia) and Arabia	*Color:* All colors are permissible *Coat:* The hindquarters, flanks, ribs, forequarters, and legs should be well covered with thick, silky hair, very fine in texture; the ears and all four feet should be well feathered; from in front of the shoulders and extending back from the shoulders along the topline, the hair is short and close — giving a smooth back	A large, slender dog with profusely coated, pendent ears and characteristic coat on the body The unique features of the Afghan Hound are: (1) the coat of silky hair, (2) the high tail carriage, and (3) the high and wide apart hipbones. The latter structure gives him a motion like that of a monkey and adapts him to travel in rough, hilly country	*Height:* Dogs: 27 in. Bitches: 25 in. *Weight:* Dogs: 60 lb. Bitches: 50 lb.
Airedale Terrier —*terrier* *Fig. 24.*	England, where it was originally used for hunting otter and other small game. The name "Airedale" was taken from a show by that name in Yorkshire, England, where this breed was first exhibited extensively. Today, it's the favorite terrier in Germany The Airedale reached its height in popularity in the U.S. in the period from 1905 to 1920	*Color:* Head and ears tan, with dark markings on each side of the skull; ears slightly darker in shade than the rest of the head; body black or dark grizzle; legs up to the thighs and elbows tan. A small white mark on the chest is not objectionable *Coat:* Hard, dense, and wiry; lying straight and close	A medium-sized, upstanding, rough-coated dog with small V-shaped and folded ears	*Height:* Approximately 23 in. *Weight:* Variable, but an average of 50 lb.

[3] The author wishes to express grateful appreciation to the following for providing the breed drawings that appear in the Missouri; Carnation Company (makers of Friskies), Los Angeles, California; and artist J. L. Medeiros, Clovis, California, who

AND THEIR CHARACTERISTICS[3]

Head	Body	Tail	Character: Use	Faults or Disqualifications
Round, with well-domed forehead *Ears:* Rather small, set high, pointed and erect, usually clipped to a point	As long as high Back straight; chest reasonably deep; shoulders sloping; belly only slightly tucked up	Set high and carried high Short	Generally quiet and devoted, but can be vehemently excited. When attacked, it is fearless toward any aggressor *Use:* Pet and companion	*Faults:* Very light colors and white markings
Long, narrow, and clean, with slightly arched skull, level forehead, and slight stop *Ears:* Long, set approximately on level with outer corners of eyes, the leather of the ear reaching nearly to the end of the dog's nose, and covered with long, silky hair	Back of moderate length with slight depression behind the shoulders; strong, slightly arched loins; prominent hipbones; deep chest; tucked up flanks	Fairly long, carried low, usually with a ring at the end; sparsely feathered	Aloof and dignified, seldom barks, and reserved with strangers *Use:* As a show and companion dog	*Faults:* Overshot or undershot jaw; absence of topknot; and lack of short-haired saddle in mature dogs. White markings, especially on the head, are undesirable
Elongated; the skull and muzzle of equal length. Skull wedge shaped, long and flat, not too wide between the ears and narrowing somewhat toward the eyes *Ears:* V-shaped, with carriage to the side of the head; rather small	Short, strong, and level body. Loins muscular and of good width; ribs well sprung; hindquarters strong and muscular	Set well up on the back; of good strength and substance; fair length; carried gaily but not curled over the back	An intelligent, reliable, and powerful guard; very tractable and quick at learning; very responsive to owner *Use:* For hunting game (including big game in Africa, India, and Canada); as police dogs; as guards and family pets	*Faults:* Yellow eyes; hound ears; white feet; soft coat; much oversized or undersized; undershot or overshot jaw; poor movement

(Continued)

left column of this table: Ralston Purina Company (makers of Purina dog food products), Checkerboard Square, St. Louis, made several drawings especially for this book.

TABLE 3 (CONTINUED) BREEDS OF

Breed	Place of Origin; Present Popularity	Color; Coat	General Appearance	Size
Alaskan Malamute —*working dog* *Fig. 25.*	Alaska: named after the native human tribe of Alaska called the Mahlemuts (now spelled Malamutes), who used them to pull sleds Between the two World Wars, the Alaskan Malamute Club was founded and recognized by the American Kennel Club. Although the Alaskan Malamute is still quite rare in the U. S., it is increasing in numbers	*Color:* Wolf gray, black, or white; with white markings *Coat:* A thick, coarse, guard coat; and a dense undercoat 1 to 2 in. in depth, oily and woolly	A compact, rather large, long-coated dog, with erect ears and bushy tail curled over the back. The Alaskan Malamute is the "draft horse" of the dog world	*Height:* Dogs: 25 in. Bitches: 23 in. *Weight* Dogs: 85 lb. Bitches: 75 lb
American Foxhound —*hound* *Fig. 26.*	United States, from English Foxhound foundation The American Foxhound is America's oldest sporting dog. His ancestors were among the first settlers	*Color:* Any color *Coat:* Close, hard, hound coat of medium length	A medium-sized, short-coated hound with long pendent ears and saber-shaped tail, of various colors	*Height:* Dogs: 22–25 in. Bitches: 21–24 in. *Weight:* Average weight 60 lb
American Staffordshire Terrier (formerly Staffordshire Terrier) —*terrier* *Fig. 27.*	England The breed was named after Staffordshire, England, where it was developed for dogfighting. They are a cross between the Bulldog and the Old English Terrier. They were brought to America in 1870. The breed was recognized by the American Kennel Club in 1935	*Color:* Any color *Coat:* Short, close, stiff, and glossy	A medium-sized, rather upstanding, sturdily built, short-haired terrier of any color. Flashy looking	*Height:* Dogs: 18–19 in. Bitches: 17–18 in. *Weight:* Dogs: 40–50 lb Bitches: 35–45 lb

DOGS AND THEIR CHARACTERISTICS

Head	Body	Tail	Character; Use	Faults or Disqualifications
Broad between the ears and moderately domed, narrowing between the eyes, with slightly curved cheeks *Ears:* Medium size; triangular; slightly rounded at the tips and set wide apart. When the dog is working, the ears may be folded against the skull	Back gently sloping to hips; loins well muscled; croup slightly sloping; chest full and deep; belly line only slightly drawn up; hindquarters broad and powerful with plenty of muscle	Well furred and feathered; carried curled over the back	An affectionate, friendly dog. A staunch and hardy sled dog *Use:* Sled dog racing; Antarctic expeditions; and servicing cold, remote areas when they're weathered in	*Faults:* High set ears; any unsoundness in the legs or feet; a long loin and weak back
Fairly long, slightly domed at occiput, with a broad, full cranium *Ears:* Set on moderately low; long, reaching to, or nearly to, the tip of the nose; fine in texture; fairly broad; and setting close to the head	Back moderately long, muscular, and strong; loins broad and slightly arched; chest deep; ribs well sprung	Set moderately high; carried gaily, in a slight curve; with a small brush	The American Foxhound is very versatile. He can be trained to trail any species of ground game; and he possesses endurance, speed, a good cry, the agility to negotiate any kind of terrain, intelligence, determination, and a homing instinct *Uses:* 1. Field trials 2. Hunting foxes with guns 3. "Trial" hounds or drag hounds, which are raced or hunted on a drag, with only speed counting 4. Hounds to hunt in large numbers (perhaps 15 to 20) in a pack—the type used by hunt clubs	*Disqualifications:* Overshot or undershot jaw
Medium length; broad skull; very pronounced cheek muscles; distinct stop *Ears:* Ears set high. Either cropped or uncropped, the latter preferred. Uncropped ears should be short and held half-rose or prick	Moderately short bodied. Loins slightly arched; chest deep and broad; shoulders strong, muscular, and sloping; ribs well sprung	Short in comparison to size; tapering to a fine point; low set; not curled or held over back; not docked	Keenly alive to his surroundings; courageous; an intelligent and tractable companion, and an enthusiastic sportsman *Use:* As a guard dog and as a companion	*Faults:* Dudley nose; light or pink eyes; undershot or overshot mouth; tail too long or badly carried (Continued)

39

TABLE 3 (CONTINUED) BREEDS OF

Breed	Place of Origin; Present Popularity	Color; Coat	General Appearance	Size
American Water Spaniel —*sporting dog* Fig. 28.	U. S., principally in the Midwest, for use in hunting in swamps and river areas. Recognized as a breed by the AKC in 1940. Despite its U. S. origin and virtues, the breed has always been limited in numbers. Lack of popularity is attributed to not being a pretty dog, and the breed being in the hands of practical hunting men, rather than those who show	*Color:* Solid liver or dark chocolate; a little white on toes or chest permissible *Coat:* Closely curled or marcel effect, with sufficient density to give protection against weather, water, or punishing cover; but not coarse	A medium-sized, long-coated, curly-haired dog, with long ears and long, saber-shaped tail	Medium size *Height:* 15–18 in. *Weight:* Dogs: 28–45 lb Bitches: 25–40 lb
Australian Terrier —*terrier* Fig. 29.	Australia, dating from 1885 The Australian Terrier was introduced into the U. S. during the first quarter of the present century and admitted for registry by the American Kennel Club in 1960 (the 114th breed to be admitted to the AKC)	*Color:* Blue black or silver black, with rich tan markings on head and legs; sandy color; or clear red *Coat:* Outercoat harsh, straight, and about 2½ in. long; undercoat short and soft; topknot of finer texture and lighter color than body coat	A small, low-set, rough-coated terrier with soft topknot and prick or drop ears	*Height:* About 10 in. *Weight:* 12–14 lb
Basenji (the "barkless dog") —*hound* Fig. 30.	Central Africa, where it served as a companion to the Egyptian pharaohs; and was highly prized for its intelligence, speed, hunting power, and silence In 1937, the first pair of Basenjis was brought to America. In 1943, the American Kennel Club accepted the breed for registration. A bright future for the breed seems assured	*Color:* Chestnut red (the deeper the better), pure black, or black and tan; all with white feet, chest and tail tip *Coat:* Short and silky	A small, long-limbed, short-haired dog with conical skull, broad forehead deeply furrowed with wrinkles, erect ears, a ring tail, and no bark	*Height:* Dogs: 17 in. Bitches: 16 in. *Weight:* Dogs: 24 lb Bitches: 22 lb

DOGS AND THEIR CHARACTERISTICS

Head	Body	Tail	Character; Use	Faults or Disqualifications
Moderate in length; skull rather broad and full; stop moderately defined *Ears:* Lobular, long and wide, not set too high on head, but slightly above eyeline. Leather extending to end of nose and well covered with curls	Strong but not too compact. Symmetrical. Back and loins strong; loins slightly arched; chest deep but not wide, with well-sprung ribs; shoulders well laid in and muscular; hindquarters well muscled	Strong at root, tapering to fine point, about long enough to reach the hock Carriage straight or curving slightly upward, nearly level with the back	Agreeable and obedient. His enthusiasm and thoroughness are an inspiration to huntsmen, and his desire to please makes him easily taught *Use:* Gundog and retriever. He springs game, rather than points; he swims like a seal Also, an efficient watchdog	*Faults:* Very flat skull, narrow across the top, or long, slender, or snipy muzzle; cow hocks; rat or shaved tail; coat too straight, soft, fine, or tightly kinked *Disqualifications:* Yellow eyes
Long, flat skulled, full between the eyes, with a moderate stop *Ears:* Set high and well apart; small and pricked; the leather either pointed or slightly rounded and free from long hairs	Low set; slightly longer than high. Back straight; chest medium wide and deep; ribs well sprung; hindquarters strong and well muscled	Set on high and carried erect, but not too gay; docked leaving two-fifths	An affectionate and intelligent dog, with the aggressiveness of the natural ratter and hedge hunter *Use:* As a hunter in the Australian bushland. Also, used for guarding the mines and herding sheep. Used as a house pet in the U. S.	*Faults:* Light colored and protruding eyes
Wedge shaped, with narrow skull, tapering to the nose. Wrinkles on the forehead are characteristic *Ears:* Small, pointed and erect, of fine texture, and set well forward on top of head	Short body. Level back; well-sprung ribs; deep brisket; broad, deep chest, ending in a definite waist	Set on top and curled tightly over to either side	The Basenji is known as the "barkless dog." It should not bark, but it is not mute. The Basenji's sound of happiness, which is pleasant to hear, is somewhere between a chortle and a yodel He's very fastidious; he cleans himself all over in the manner of a cat. As a result, he is free of doggy odors *Use:* In Central Africa, the Basenji is used for hunting—for pointing, retrieving, driving game into nets, and hunting wounded quarry. Also, the breed is used to hunt and destroy rats In the U. S., the Basenji is primarily a family pet	*Faults:* Overshot or undershot jaw; cream, shaded, or off colors

(Continued)

TABLE 3 (CONTINUED) BREEDS OF

Breed	Place of Origin; Present Popularity	Color; Coat	General Appearance	Size
Basset Hound —*hound* *Fig. 31.*	France, where it was used for slow trailing of game The Basset Hound has never been very popular in the U. S., perhaps due to his grotesque appearance. However, it is the favorite hound in Italy	*Color:* Any recognized hound color; and the distribution of color and markings are unimportant *Coat:* Hard, smooth, and short	A short-legged, heavy-boned hound. Capacious but narrow and long skull; very long, pendulous ears; and gaily carried tail. The Le Couteulx strain, with the downcast look and sad expression, is most popular in the U. S.	*Height:* 11–15 in. *Weight:* 40–60 lb
Beagle —*hound* *Fig. 32.*	The origin of the Beagle is clouded in obscurity, although the earliest known varieties were British The Beagle is the favorite hound in both the U. S. and Canada	*Color:* Any hound color. The most popular color is a mixture of white, black, and tan *Coat:* Close, hard, hound coat of medium length	A small, short-coated hound with strong head, long ears, and gaily carried tail—a foxhound in miniature	*Height:* Under 15 in. *Weight:* 25–30 lb
Bedlington Terrier —*terrier* *Fig. 33.*	England Named after the English coal mining region of Bedlington, where it was used as a ratter and for hunting badger For many years, the Bedlington Terrier never became popular in the U. S., primarily because of the laborious trimming necessary to prepare them for show purposes	*Color:* Blue, sandy, liver, blue and tan, sandy and tan, liver and tan *Coat:* Thick and linty, tending to curl	A medium-sized terrier with hanging ears, moderately long tail, and curly coat. Looks like a baby lamb	*Height:* Dogs: 16½ in. Bitches: 15½ in. *Weight:* 17 to 23 lb

Head	Body	Tail	Character; Use	Faults or Disqualifications
Large, with long, narrow skull. Hind skull very capacious, narrowing toward the eyes and covered with loose skin, which forms wrinkles or folds on the face and cheeks. Prominent occiput. Powerful muzzle *Ears:* Extremely long and low set. When drawn forward, they will fold over the end of the nose. Velvety. Hang in loose folds with the ends curving slightly inward. Set far back on the head at the base of the skull	The back should be long and level, the loins and croup strong and muscular, the chest deep and roomy, the shoulders sloping, and the thighs muscular	Long and strong; carried with terminal half curved upward; undocked	The build of the Basset Hound equips it admirably to follow a trail over and through difficult terrain. It possesses a mild temperament and great devotion. He's a one-man dog *Use:* Slow hunting of foxes, rabbits, pheasants, coon, opossum, and squirrels, over and through difficult terrain. As a companion	*Faults:* Overshot or undershot jaw; and cow hocks or bowed legs *Disqualifications:* More than 15 in. high; knuckled-over front legs; distinctly long coat
The skull should be fairly long, slightly domed at occiput, with a broad full cranium *Ears:* Set on moderately low; long, reaching to, or almost to, the end of the nose; fine in texture; fairly broad; setting close to the head, with the forward edge slightly turned in toward the cheek	Back and loins compact, straight, and muscular; croup slightly drooping; shoulders slightly sloping and well muscled; ribs fairly well sprung; flanks and belly not tucked up	Set moderately high; carried gaily, but not turned forward over the back; rather short; with a moderate amount of hair underneath	A small, keen hound with an excellent nose and voice *Use:* As a gundog, he is a specialist on the cottontail rabbit, but he is effective on squirrels and pheasants. Also, popular as a house dog	*Faults:* A long tail; teapot curve to tail, or inclined forward from the root; rat tail with absence of brush *Disqualifications:* Measuring more than 15 in.
Pear-shaped head; skull narrow, rounded, and deep, without stop; an unbroken line from the crown to the end of the nose *Ears:* Medium size, set on low, triangular with rounded tips and hanging flat; covered with soft fine hair	Muscular but markedly flexible. Back roached; loins arched; croup indexed forward; chest deep and fairly broad; shoulders sloping and well laid in; belly tucked up; hindquarters muscular	Set low, thick at the root, of moderate length, and tapering to the tip; carried in a graceful curve, never over the back	Lovable, devoted, obedient, intelligent, and easily managed. Needs careful grooming *Use:* Today, the Bedlington Terrier is primarily used as a pet	

(Continued)

TABLE 3 (CONTINUED) BREEDS OF

Breed	Place of Origin; Present Popularity	Color; Coat	General Appearance	Size
Belgian Malinois —*working dog* Fig. 34.	Belgium, in the grazing country about Malinois; hence, its name In 1948, some Belgian Malinois were imported to the U.S. from Belgium. These dogs, along with the Belgian Tervuren, were registered and shown as Belgian Sheepdogs up to July 1, 1959, at which time the AKC established them as three separate breeds— Belgian Malinois, Belgian Tervuren, and Belgian Sheepdog Today, Malinois are relatively rare in the U.S.; they have not caught the American fancy	*Color:* Rich fawn to mahogany, with black overlay. Black mask and ears *Coat:* Comparatively short, straight, with dense undercoat. Very short hair on the head, ears, and lower legs	A medium-sized, well-balanced, square dog, elegant in appearance, with a very proud carriage of the head and neck	*Height:* Dogs: 24–26 in. Bitches: 22–24 in. *Weight:* Average 60 lb
Belgian Sheepdog (Groenendael) —*working dog* Fig. 35.	Belgium Prior to 1891, the Belgian Sheepdog was the genuine shepherd's dog throughout the greater part of Europe	*Color:* Black; either solid or with white limited to the forechest, between pads of feet, on tips of toes, and on chin and muzzle *Coat:* The guard hairs of the coat must be long, straight, and dense. The undercoat should be very dense	A black, well-balanced, square dog, elegant in appearance, with an exceedingly proud carriage of the head and neck	*Height:* Dogs: 24–26 in. Bitches: 22–24 in. *Weight:* Average 60 lb
Belgian Tervuren —*working dog* Fig. 36.	Belgium; formerly a variety of Belgian Sheepdog, named after the town of origin	*Color:* Rich fawn to russet mahogany with black overlay. The coat is characteristically double pigmented, wherein the tip of each fawn hair is blackened *Coat:* Guard hairs long, straight, and dense. Undercoat very dense	A well-balanced, square dog, elegant in appearance and proud in carriage of head and neck	*Height:* Dogs: 24–26 in. Bitches: 22–24 in. *Weight:* Average 55 lb

Head	Body	Tail	Character; Use	Faults or Disqualifications
Clean-cut and strong; top flattened; stop moderate *Ears:* Triangular, stiff, erect, and in proportion to head size. Base of ear should not come below the center of the eye	Withers are slightly higher than the back; back straight; loins relatively short, broad and strong; croup medium long and sloping gradually; chest deep; shoulders long, sloping, and flat; hindquarters broad and heavily muscled	Strong at the base; bone to reach hock; at rest it is held low, with the tip bent back level with the hock	The dog is strong, agile, well muscled, alert, and full of life *Use:* An outstanding sheepdog. Also, used for show and guard work	*Faults:* Washed-out fawn color on the body; ears hanging like a hound's; tail cropped or stumpy; dogs under 22½ or over 27½ in. in height; bitches under 20½ or over 25½ in. in height
Clean-cut and strong; top flattened rather than rounded; stop moderate *Ears:* Triangular, stiff, erect, and in proportion to the head size. Base of ear should not come below the center of the eye	Withers slightly higher than the back; back straight; loins short, broad, and strong; croup medium long and sloping gradually	Strong at the root; bone to reach hock; at rest, the dog holds the tail low, the tip bent back level with the hock	Intelligence, courage, alertness, and devotion to master. Inherent aptitude as guardian of flocks and protectiveness of the person and property of his master *Use:* Initially a sheep dog. In Europe, Belgian Sheepdogs are sometimes used as police dogs. During World War I, thousands of these dogs were used as messengers	*Faults:* Any deviation from the specifications is considered a fault, with the seriousness of each fault determined by the extent of the deviation, and the extent to which such deviation affects the working ability of the dog *Disqualifications:* Viciousness; any color other than black, or black with white marks; ears hanging like a hound's; tail cropped or stumpy; dogs under 22½ in. or over 27½ in. high; bitches under 20½ in. or over 25½ in. high
Well chiseled; top of skull flattened rather than rounded; stop moderate *Ears:* Triangular, well cupped, stiff, erect, not too large, and set high	Topline straight; loins short, broad, and strong; croup medium long and sloping gradually; shoulders long, sloping, and well laid in; hindquarters powerful and well muscled	Strong at the base; last vertebra to reach the hock; at rest, the dog holds the tail low, the tip bent back level with the hock	Intelligence, alertness, and devotion to master *Use:* Guardian of flocks. Protector of property and master	*Faults:* Washed-out color or color so black that it resembles the Belgian Sheepdog *Disqualifications:* Ears hanging like a hound's; tail cropped or stumpy; white anywhere except on the chest, tips of the toes, or on the chin or muzzle; undershot teeth; dogs under 22½ in. or over 27½ in. high; bitches under 20½ in. or over 25½ in. high

(Continued)

TABLE 3 (CONTINUED) BREEDS OF

Breed	Place of Origin; Present Popularity	Color; Coat	General Appearance	Size
Bernese Mountain Dog —*working dog* Fig. 37.	Switzerland, where they once pulled weaver's wagons. Today, their life in harness is a thing of the past; they're used as house pets all over Switzerland A few of these Bernese Mountain Dogs were imported to the U.S., beginning in 1930. In 1937, they were admitted to the American Kennel Club. But they are rare	*Color:* Jet black; with russet brown or deep tan markings on all four legs; a spot just above the forelegs on each side of the white markings on the chest and spots over eyes—spots may never be missing *Coat:* Soft and silky with bright, natural sheen; long and slightly wavy but may never curl	Above medium-size and sturdily built dog, with a long coat, small drop ears, and a long bushy tail. They resemble Collies	*Height:* Dogs: 23–27½ in. Bitches: 21–26 in. *Weight:* Average 65 lb
Black-and-Tan Coonhound —*hound* Fig. 38.	U.S., descended from hounds of eleventh century England. The Black-and-Tan Coonhound was admitted for registry in the American Kennel Club in 1945. It is growing in popularity	*Color:* Black, with rich tan markings above eyes, on sides of muzzle, chest, legs and breeching, and black pencil markings on toes *Coat:* Short but dense	Above medium-sized hound with very long, folded ears and long saber-shaped tail	*Height:* Dogs: 25–27 in. Bitches: 23–25 in. *Weight:* Average 60 lb
Bloodhound —*hound* Fig. 39.	England. It appears that the name "Bloodhound" was given these dogs because they were so adept at following the trails of wounded criminals Today, the use of Bloodhounds in the U.S. is largely restricted to tracking down missing persons and criminals, but modern transportation facilities have made this usage pretty obsolete. So, numbers are limited	*Color:* Black and tan, red and tan, and tawny. The darker colors are sometimes interspersed with lighter or badger-colored hair, and sometimes flecked with white *Coat:* Short, hard, smooth, and dense	A large, massively built, short-coated hound with characteristic head, very long ears, wrinkled face, and long tail	*Height:* Dogs: 25–27 in. Bitches: 23–25 in. *Weight:* Dogs: 90 lb Bitches: 80 lb

DOGS AND THEIR CHARACTERISTICS

Head	Body	Tail	Character; Use	Faults or Disqualifications
Skull flat, with defined stop and strong muzzle. *Ears:* V-shaped, set on high, not too pointed at tips, and rather short. When in repose, hanging close to head; when alert, brought slightly forward and raised at bases	Back straight; loins strong; chest broad and deep; shoulders sloping; hindquarters powerful	Tail of fair thickness and good length; well covered with hair, but not to form a flag; when in repose, carried low, and may swirl upward but should not curl	Hardy and faithful. Once he has centered his attention upon a person, he does not make friends with strangers. *Use:* Originally, they were used as a draft dog. Today, in Switzerland, and elsewhere, they are family pets	*Faults:* Too massive in head; light or staring eyes; too heavy or long ears; too narrow or snipy muzzle; undershot or overshot mouth; pendulous dewlap; body too long; splay or bare feet; curled tail; white legs.
The head should be chiseled, with medium stop midway between occiput bone and nose. The skin should be free of folds. *Ears:* Low set and well back. They should hang in graceful folds. In length, they should extend well beyond the tip of the nose	Powerful shoulders; deep chest; well-sprung ribs; and a powerful back, with a visible slope from the withers to the rump	Strong, with base slightly below level of back line, carried free, and when in action at about a right angle to the back	A powerful, agile, alert hound. The Black-and-Tan Coonhound works entirely by scent, "barking up" or giving voice the moment his quarry is treed. *Use:* Hunting raccoon and opossum. Also, the Black-and-Tan Coonhound is used for hunting deer, mountain lion, bear, and other big game	*Faults:* Dewclaws; white on chest or other parts of body. *Disqualifications:* White, if it exceeds 1½ in. in diameter
Narrow with skull tapering from temples to end of nose and appearing to be flattened at the sides. Forehead narrow; occiput pronounced. Entire head covered with abundant loose skin, which forms loose folds and pendulous ridges. *Ears:* Thin and soft; extremely long; set very low; fall in graceful folds, with the lower parts curling inward and backward	Back and loins straight and muscular; croup falling away slightly; shoulders muscular and well laid in; chest broad and deep, with well-sprung ribs; flank strong and belly not tucked up	Set on level with back; carried gaily, but not curled over back; covered with harsh hair on under side	An outstanding tracking and trailing hound. The Bloodhound is without a peer when it comes to following a scent. He's so accurate that he is the only dog whose evidence is accepted in a court of law. Unlike the police-trained dog, the Bloodhound does not attack the man he is trailing. Despite his formidable appearance, deep, roaring bay, and fantastic trailing ability, the Bloodhound is one of the most gentle of all dogs	

(Continued)

TABLE 3 (CONTINUED) BREEDS OF

Breed	Place of Origin; Present Popularity	Color; Coat	General Appearance	Size
Border Terrier —terrier Fig. 40.	On either side of the Cheviot Hills—the Border country between England and Scotland, where they were used to bolt foxes from their holes. When hunting, the Border farmers and shepherds rode horseback. Hence, the Border Terrier had to be fast enough to keep up with a horse, yet small enough to follow the fox to earth. Few Border Terriers are found in the U.S.	*Color:* Red, grizzle and tan, blue and tan, or wheaten. A small amount of white on the chest is acceptable. *Coat:* A short and dense undercoat covered with a very wiry and closely lying top coat	A small, rather short-legged, rough-coated terrier with small drop ears and upward curved tail of medium length	*Height:* Average of 12 in. *Weight:* Dogs: 13–15½ lb Bitches: 11½–14 lb
Borzoi (formerly called Russian Wolfhound) —hound Fig. 41.	The U.S.S.R., where it has been used since the seventeenth century for hunting wolves and coursing hare and other game. The first Borzoi were brought to America in 1889. In 1935, U.S. breeders changed the name from Russian Wolfhound to Borzoi. Only limited numbers are found in the U.S.	*Color:* Pure white, or white with fawn, tan, gray or brindle markings. Also, solid-colored specimens of the colors listed occasionally appear. *Coat:* Long, silky (not woolly); either flat, wavy, or rather curly. On the head, ears, and front of legs, it should be short and smooth; on the neck the frill should be profuse and rather curly. The feather on the hindquarters and tail should be long and profuse	A big, handsome, long-coated dog with long, lean head, small folded ears and long, feathered tail	*Height:* Dogs: 28–31 in. Bitches: 26–29 in. *Weight:* Dogs: 75–105 lb Bitches: 60–85 lb
Boston Terrier —nonsporting dog Fig. 42.	United States; developed in the Boston area about 1875. It's the result of a cross between the English Bulldog and the white English Terrier. The American Kennel Club admitted the breed for registry in 1893. At one time, the Boston Terrier was the most popular show dog in America; they still rank high	*Color:* Brindle or black, with white markings. *Coat:* Short, smooth, bright, and fine in texture	A smooth-coated, short-headed, short-bodied but upstanding dog; a short tail; brindle or black color and evenly marked with white	*Height:* 16 in. *Weight:* Not exceeding 25 lb

48

DOGS AND THEIR CHARACTERISTICS

Head	Body	Tail	Character; Use	Faults or Disqualifications
Otterlike head; moderately broad and flat skull; plenty of width between the eyes and ears; a slight curve at the stop *Ears:* Small, V-shaped, dropping forward close to the cheeks	Back long, straight and fairly narrow; chest not too deep; ribs deep and carried well back; thighs strong	Not set on too high; moderately short; thick at the base, then tapering; carried gaily when at the alert, but not over the back	A keen, lively dog, capable of following a mounted horseman *Use:* In their native land, they were used to hunt fox, badger, and otter In the U. S. as a pet	
Long, narrow, and clean; pointed at the end; skull long and narrow *Ears:* Small and fine in quality, lying back when in repose, and raised when at attention	Back fairly short, rising in a graceful arch over the loins; chest deep; belly well tucked up	Long; set on low; carried low in a graceful curve	An elegant, graceful, aristocratic dog, possessing courage and combining muscular power with speed *Use:* In Eastern U.S., the breed is used principally as a show dog and pet. In the West, it is used by ranchers to hunt coyotes. Also, they have been used in both the theater and movies	
Square with flat skull; free from wrinkles; stop well defined; muzzle short, square, wide, and deep *Ears:* Carried erect; either cropped to conform to the shape of the head, or natural bat	Short but not chunky. Back short; loins short and muscular; rump curving slightly to root of tail; chest wide; shoulders sloping; ribs deep and well sprung; flank very slightly cut up	Set on low; short and tapering to a fine point; straight or screw; not carried over the back	Intelligent, affectionate, faithful, and not noisy. He is not a fighter, but is able to take care of himself. The Boston Terrier's kind and gentle disposition has won the designation, "American Gentleman" *Use:* As a companion and pet	*Faults:* Eyes light color or walleye; protruding teeth; protruding lower jaw; a long or gaily carried tail, or a tail that is extremely gnarled or curled against the body *Disqualifications:* Solid black, black and tan, liver, or mouse colors; a flesh colored nose; docked tail or any artificial means used to deceive the judge

(Continued)

49

TABLE 3 (CONTINUED) BREEDS OF

Breed	Place of Origin; Present Popularity	Color; Coat	General Appearance	Size
Bouvier des Flandres —*working dog* Fig. 43.	In Southwest Flanders Developed by farmers, butchers, and cattle merchants for use in their work. The word "bouvier" means cow herd or ox driver Today, the breed is popular in France, Holland and Belgium The Bouvier des Flandres first began to appear in the U.S. in the 1930s. It has steadily gained in popularity	*Color:* Fawn to black; pepper and salt, gray and brindle. A white star on the chest is allowed *Coat:* Rough and shaggy. The topcoat is harsh and wiry, and the undercoat is fine and soft	A large, coarse-haired prick-eared dog with conspicuous beard and short, docked tail	*Height:* Dogs: 23½–27½ in. Bitches: 22¾ in. minimum *Weight:* Average 70 lb
Boxer —*working dog* Fig. 44.	Germany In spite of his German ancestry, the name "Boxer" is English. It stems from his manner of fighting. Invariably, a Boxer begins a fight with his front paws, much like a man boxing In 1904, the first Boxer was registered. But it was not until the 1930s that the public began to take an interest in the breed. Today, Boxers rank among the 20 most popular U.S. breeds The Boxer is one of the most popular breeds in Germany, France, Australia, Great Britain, Holland, India, and Sweden, as well as the U.S.	*Color:* Fawn of various shades, or brindle. White markings must be limited to one-third of the ground color *Coat:* Short, shiny, lying smooth and tight to the body	A medium-sized, smooth-coated, powerful dog, with short, square body, distinctive head, small ears, and docked tail	*Height:* Dogs: 22½–25 in. Bitches: 21–23½ in. *Weight:* Dogs: 66 lb Bitches: 62 lb
Briard —*working dog* Fig. 45.	France, where they evolved primarily as sheep dogs In 1922, the first Briard was registered by the American Kennel Club Although not numerous, one feature most favorable to the Briard is that it requires a minimum of attention—no clipping, no bathing, and only a minimum of combing	*Color:* Dark colors preferred. But all solid colors except white are accepted *Coat:* Long, slightly wavy, stiff and strong	A powerful, upstanding, long-bodied dog with a long or shaggy coat, usually cropped erect ears, and a long tail	*Height:* Dogs: 23–27 in. Bitches: 22–25½ in. *Weight:* Average 70 lb

Head	Body	Tail	Character; Use	Faults or Disqualifications
Moderately long, with broad, flat skull; fairly wide between the ears; sloping slightly toward the muzzle *Ears:* Set high, cropped to a triangular shape; erect; rough coated	Back short and straight; loins short and slightly arched; rump broad and square; brisket deep; ribs deep and well sprung	Set high, carried high, and docked to about 4 in.	Rugged, powerfully built, alert, intelligent, and adept at driving cattle *Use:* As a working dog for driving cattle; as an ambulance and messenger dog in World War I; as a utility, service, and police dog	*Faults:* Light colored eyes, and staring or wild expression; brown, pink, or spotted nose; narrow muzzle; soft, silky, or woolly topcoat; chocolate brown with white spots
Slightly domed, neither wedge shaped nor flat and not too broad; occiput not too pronounced; stop well defined; forehead showing indication of central furrow. The Boxer is normally undershot *Ears:* Set at highest points of the sides of the skull; cut rather long without too broad a shell; carried erect	Square. Back short, straight, broad, well muscled; withers clearly defined; chest deep; ribs well sprung; loins short and strong; shoulders long, sloping, and not too heavily muscled; middle slightly tucked up; hindquarters strong; thighs broad and curved	Attached high; docked and carried erect	An alert, vigorous, and powerful guard and protector *Use:* A family dog; show purposes	*Faults:* Head not typical; bulldoggy appearance; light bone; lack of balance; lack of noble bearing *Disqualifications:* Boxers with white or black ground color, or entirely white or black, or any color other than fawn or brindle (white markings, when present, must not exceed one-third of the ground color)
Large and rather long; stop well marked and about equal distance from top of head and tip of nose; forehead very slightly rounded *Ears:* Placed high; alert; may be cropped or left natural	Back and loins straight; croup falling away slightly; chest deep and broad; shoulders and thighs well muscled	Well feathered; forming a crook at the the end; carried low. Uncut	Briards seldom bark unless it is necessary to give warning. They are well suited as stock dogs, companions, and guardians *Use:* In France, they are used to guard the small farms, to herd sheep and cattle, and to care for property and animals. In the U.S., Briards are primarily family dogs — companions and guardians	*Faults:* Rump either too straight or too sloping; white spot on breast (a large white spot is very bad); tail too short or carried over back *Disqualifications:* Too small in size; absence of dewclaws; short hair on the head, face, or feet; cut tail; curly hair; white hair on the feet; spotted colors of the coat

(Continued)

TABLE 3 (CONTINUED) BREEDS OF

Breed	Place of Origin; Present Popularity	Color; Coat	General Appearance	Size
Brittany Spaniel —*sporting dog* *Fig. 46.*	France Although a relative newcomer to the U.S. (since 1931), the breed has made great strides in popularity with Eastern and Midwestern gunners The Brittany Spaniel is the favorite gundog in Belgium, and is very popular in France and Italy	*Color:* Dark orange and white, or liver and white. Some ticking is desirable *Coat:* Dense, flat, or wavy; never curly	A compact, closely knit dog of medium size. It's unusual in that it is a pointing spaniel	Medium size *Height:* 17½–20½ in. *Weight:* 30–40 lb
Brussels Griffon —*toy* *Fig. 47.*	Belgium The term *griffon* means thick haired. Importations to the U.S. began about 1900	The Brussels Griffon may be either rough coated or smooth coated *Rough Coated:* *Coat:* Wiry and dense *Color:* (1) Reddish brown, with a little black on the whiskers and chin allowable; (2) black and reddish brown mixed; (3) black with uniform reddish brown markings; or (4) solid black *Smooth Coated:* *Coat:* The smooth coated variety is just what the designation implies—they are smooth coated *Color:* Same as for rough coated except that solid black is not allowed	An active, thick-set, short-bodied toy dog with docked tail. Distinctive	*Height:* 8 in. *Weight:* 8–12 lb
Bulldog —*nonsporting dog* *Fig. 48.*	British Isles The Bulldog is the symbol of British courage and tenacity the world over. The name "Bull" was given to the breed because their early use was in connection with the then popular English sport of "bullbaiting," in which a dog would seize a bull by the nose or ear and hold on at all costs. In 1835, bullbaiting became illegal in England, but the name Bulldog lived on	*Color:* The colors, listed in order of preference, are: (1) red brindle, (2) all other brindles, (3) solid white, (4) solid red, fawn, or fallow, (5) piebald, and (6) inferior qualities of all the foregoing *Coat:* Straight, short, flat, close, of fine texture, smooth, and glossy	A low-set, compact, powerfully built, smooth-coated dog with a very large square head, and a short tail that may be either straight or screwed	*Height:* 15 in. *Weight:* Dogs: 50 lb Bitches: 40 lb

DOGS AND THEIR CHARACTERISTICS

Head	Body	Tail	Character; Use	Faults or Disqualifications
Medium length, rounded. *Ears:* Set high, above the level of the eyes. Short and leafy, rather than pendulous, reaching about half the length of the muzzle. Should lie flat and close to the head, with the tip rounded very slightly	Compact. Length equal to height at the withers. Loins short and strong; croup falling away slightly; chest deep; shoulders well laid in and muscular; hindquarters well muscled	The breed is often naturally tailless. But if not, it should be docked to 4 in.	Courage, endurance, and perseverance, together with an excellent nose, characterize the breed. *Use:* Gundog and retriever. The Brittany is unique in that it is the only spaniel that points its game. Also, a fine family pet	*Disqualifications:* Measuring under 17½ in. or over 20½ in. Black in the coat, or a black nose. Tail more than 4 in. in length
Skull large and round, with a domed forehead; stop very prominent. *Ears:* Small, set high, may be shown cropped or natural. If natural, they are carried semierect	Back short and straight; chest broad and deep; ribs well sprung	Set and held high; docked to about a third	Intelligent, alert, with almost a human expression; easy to train. *Use:* Companion and pet	*Disqualifications:* Dudley or butterfly nose; white spot or blaze anywhere on coat; hanging tongue; jaw overshot; solid black coat in the smooth type
Large and square; skull flat between the ears; forehead flat and broad; cheeks broad and rounded; a deep furrow running from stop to occiput; stop broad and very deep; muzzle broad, square, and turned upward; jaws broad, massive, and square. *Ears:* Set high on the head; wide apart; small and thin; rose ear most desirable	Short and stocky. Back short, broad over the shoulders and narrowing over the loins; croup curved downward; chest broad and deep with well-sprung ribs; shoulders sloping and well muscled; hindquarters strong and muscular	Set on low; thick at the root; either straight or screwed	A good natured, quiet, child-loving companion that is ready to defend its master with unflinching tenacity when necessary. *Use:* As a companion	*Disqualifications:* Dudley or flesh colored nose

(Continued)

53

TABLE 3 (CONTINUED) BREEDS OF

Breed	Place of Origin; Present Popularity	Color; Coat	General Appearance	Size
Bullmastiff —*working dog* Fig. 49.	England; developed about 1860 from a cross between the Bulldog and Mastiff In 1933, the American Kennel Club granted recognition to the Bullmastiff. Since that time, the breed has made numerous friends in this country. It gained particular fame among Hollywood celebrities	*Color:* Red, fawn, or brindle. May have small white spot on chest *Coat:* Short and dense	A large, short-coated dog with a broad, square head, short muzzle, small drop ears and long, down-carried tail	*Height:* Dogs: 25–27 in. Bitches: 24–26 in. *Weight:* Dogs: 110–130 lb Bitches: 100–120 lb
Bull Terrier —*terrier* Fig. 50.	England, where it was developed as a fighting dog, or "gladiator," by the sporting gentry of England	*Color:* There are two varieties: 1. White 2. Colored; which may be any color other than white, or any color with white markings. Brindle is the preferred color. The "Colored" was declared a separate variety of Bull Terrier in 1936 *Coat:* Short, flat, harsh to the touch, with a fine gloss	A strongly-built, muscular, symmetrical, short-coated dog with a rather long head, pointed, erect ears, and low-carried tail	*Height:* About 20 in. *Weight:* Dogs: 50 lb Bitches: 45 lb
Cairn Terrier —*terrier* Fig. 51.	Scotland, on the misty Isle of Skye. Named after the rocky piles into which it burrowed after game — badgers, foxes, and other vermin. Also, they were used for otter hunting The first Cairn Terriers were brought to the U. S. in 1913. On the following year, the breed was recognized by the American Kennel Club. It has made steady growth in numbers and popularity	*Color:* Any color except white. Dark ears, muzzle, and tail tip are desirable *Coat:* Hard and weather resistant. Must be double coated; with a profuse coarse outercoat, and a short, soft, furry undercoat	A small, rough-coated, low-set, prick-eared terrier, with moderately long, up-curved tail	*Height:* Dogs: 10 in. Bitches: 9½ in. *Weight:* Dogs: 14 lb Bitches: 13 lb

Head	Body	Tail	Character; Use	Faults or Disqualifications
Broad and square, with moderately defined central furrow; flat forehead; broad, powerful cheek muscles; muzzle straight, deep, and broad; mouth may be slightly undershot *Ears:* V-shaped; carried close to cheeks; set on wide and high, giving a square appearance to the skull	Compact Chest wide and deep; ribs well sprung; forequarters muscular but not loaded; back short; loins wide, muscular, and slightly arched; hindquarters broad and muscular	Set on high, strong at the root. It may be straight or curved, but never carried hound fashion	Good natured, affectionate, quiet, strong, and agile *Use:* As a guard, protector, and house companion	*Faults:* Cow hocks and splay feet
Long, strong, and deep clear to the end of the muzzle; skull flat; cheeks well developed *Ears:* Small, thin, placed close together; capable of being held stiffly erect	Deep, fairly narrow, and fairly long. Back and loins strong; ribs deep and carried well back; underline fairly straight; hindquarters muscular and racy	Moderately short, thick at the base, then tapering; carried gaily when at the alert, but not over the back	Alert, fearless, and keen; completely trustworthy. Pound for pound, he is the strongest of all terriers *Use:* Very versatile. Among his recent, or current uses are: herding sheep, hunting, as an actor on the stage and screen, in war work, and in obedience work. Also, as a children's pet	*Disqualifications:* 1. *White*, with blue eyes 2. *Colored (which is a separate variety),* with blue eyes or predominantly white color
Broad skull; decided stop; well covered with hair on the forehead *Ears:* Small, pointed, carried erectly, set well apart, free from long hairs	Medium length. Back moderately long, and straight; loins straight and muscular; chest deep with well-sprung ribs; shoulders sloping; hindquarters strongly muscled	Set on at back level; carried gaily but must not curve over the back; well furnished with hair but not feathery	Active and hardy; game and always eager to go hunting *Use:* As a rugged hunting dog in his native land; as a companion in the U.S.	*Faults:* Overshot or undershot mouth; yellow or ringed eyes; white on chest, feet, or other parts of the body *Disqualifications:* Flesh colored nose

(Continued)

TABLE 3 (CONTINUED) BREEDS OF

Breed	Place of Origin; Present Popularity	Color; Coat	General Appearance	Size
Chesapeake Bay Retriever —*sporting dog* *Fig. 52.*	U.S., in the Chesapeake Bay region of Maryland, from which it derives its name. Descended from two Newfoundland puppies from England that were shipwrecked near Maryland. Recognized as a breed by the American Kennel Club in 1933 The Chesapeake trails the Labrador and Golden Retrievers in popularity	*Color:* Any shade of brown, from dark brown to faded tan *Coat:* Thick and short, not over 1½ in. long, with a dense, fine, woolly undercoat. A Chesapeake's coat should resist water in the same manner that a duck's feathers do	A rough and ready character, but not beautiful. A medium-sized, thick-coated, compactly-built dog, with small pendent ears and a medium-length tail	*Height:* Dogs: 23–26 in. Bitches: 21–24 in. *Weight:* Dogs: 65–75 lb Bitches: 55–65 lb
Chihuahua —*toy* *Fig. 53.*	Mexico, in the state of Chihuahua, from which the breed takes its name. The Chihuahua's ancestors trace back as far as the ninth century in Mexico. Legend has it that the progenitors of the modern Chihuahua served in a dual role for the ancient Techichi and Aztec tribes of Mexico— (1) as a popular pet, and (2) as an object of worship Chihuahuas were first registered by the American Kennel Club in 1903 The Chihuahua has been bred to its greatest perfection in the U.S., where it is very popular. It ranks among the top twelve breeds in registrations	*Color:* Any color; solid, marked, or splashed. Mexico favors the jet black with tan markings, and the black-and-white spotted. The U.S. prefers the solid colors There are two varieties; smooth coated, and long coated 1. *Smooth Coat:* Smooth, soft, close, and glossy. The smooth coated are the most numerous in the U.S. 2. *Long Coat:* The long-coated Chihuahuas are judged by the same standards as the smooth-coated variety except that the coat is longer, preferably with an undercoat	A graceful, alert, swift-moving, shorthaired, little dog, with a saucy expression	The world's smallest breed of dog *Height:* 5 in. *Weight:* From 1 to 6 lb, with 2 to 4 lb being preferable

Head	Body	Tail	Character; Use	Faults or Disqualifications
Broad and round, with medium stop *Ears:* Rounded but not too broad; hang close to the head	Medium length. Back short and strong; loins well muscled and slightly arched; chest deep and broad; shoulders sloping and well laid in; flanks well drawn up; upper thighs powerful	Medium length, with moderate feathering	A tough, unsophisticated dog, with a no nonsense attitude toward his work, rather than a lovable pet *Use:* Duck hunting; retrieving downed waterfowl	*Disqualifications:* Black or liver colored. White on any part of body except breast, belly, or spots on feet. Feathering on legs or tail over 1¾ in. long. Dewclaws on hind legs. Overshot or undershot jaw
Well-rounded, apple dome skull, with or without molera. Cheeks and jaw lean *Ears:* Large; held erect when alert, but flaring out at about a forty-five degree angle in repose	Slightly long. Back level; ribs rounded, but not barrel shaped; hindquarters muscular	Moderately long, carried sickle—either up or out, or in a loop over the back	The Chihuahua is clannish, recognizing and claiming his own kind; and, generally, not liking dogs of other breeds *Use:* House pets	*Disqualifications:* Cropped tail; broken down or cropped ears. Additionally, long-coated Chihuahuas are disqualified if they have too thin a coat that approaches bareness

(Continued)

TABLE 3 (CONTINUED) BREEDS OF

Breed	Place of Origin; Present Popularity	Color; Coat	General Appearance	Size
Chow Chow —*nonsporting dog* *Fig. 54.*	China, where it has been known for over 2,000 years and was used as a hunter. Without doubt, the most lavish kennel of all time was maintained by a Tang emperor of the seventh century A.D., which involved 2,500 pairs (5,000 breeding animals) and a staff of 10,000 huntsmen. The Chow is still one of the most popular breeds in China, especially in the Canton area The first Chow was exhibited in the U.S. in 1890. Today, the breed is firmly established in this country	*Color:* Any clear color, solid throughout, with lighter shading on ruff The Chow is the only breed in the world possessing a blue black tongue *Coat:* Outercoat abundant, dense, straight, and sticking outward. Undercoat soft and woolly	A medium-sized, powerfully built dog with profuse coat, a lionlike mane, blunt muzzle, deepset eyes, prick ears, and curled tail	*Height:* Minimum of 18 in. *Weight:* Average 60 lb
Clumber Spaniel —*sporting dog* *Fig. 55.*	England, where the breed was first shown in 1859 The Clumber Spaniel has been registered in the U.S. since 1883. But it has never been numerous in this country	*Color:* Lemon and white, and orange and white *Coat:* Silky and straight, not too long, extremely dense; feather long and abundant	A long, low, heavy-looking dog, with a thoughtful expression indicative of great intelligence. The heaviest of the British sporting spaniels	*Height:* 17–18 in. *Weight:* Dogs: 55–65 lb Bitches: 35–50 lb
Cocker Spaniel —*sporting dog* *Fig. 56.*	England; first registered in 1900. The name of the breed is derived from their early use in hunting woodcock Probably the most popular dog in the world today Has long been among America's favorites	*Color:* Black, red, shades of cream or buff and liver, as well as particolors of black and white, black and tan; and tricolors of black, tan, and white. A few liver and whites *Coat:* Dense, flat or wavy (never curly). The hair on the head should be short and fine.	A small, long-coated dog with very long ears and docked tail	*Height:* Dogs: under 15½ in. Bitches: under 14½ in. *Weight:* 22 to 28 lb

DOGS AND THEIR CHARACTERISTICS

Head	Body	Tail	Character; Use	Faults or Disqualifications
Large and massive, with broad flat skull; well filled under the eyes; moderate stop; proudly carried *Ears:* Small, slightly rounded at tips, stiffly carried	Short and compact. Back short, straight, and strong; loins broad, deep, and powerful; ribs well sprung; let down well in the flank	Set high; carried closely to back, following line of spine at start	Reserved, aloof, dignified, and not prone to nervous barking. Alert, intelligent, and fearless *Use:* As a pet and guard dog. In China, the Chow is also used as a hunting dog	*Disqualifications:* Nose spotted or color other than black, except in blue Chows, which may have solid blue or slate noses; tongue red, pink, or obviously spotted with red or pink; drop ear or ears
Large and massive; round above eyes; flat on top; a marked stop *Ears:* Long and broad at the top, turned slightly over on the front edge; close to the head; set on low and feathered only on the front edge	Long, low, and well ribbed up. Deep, wide chest; long, broad, and level back, with a very slight arch over the loins; strong hindquarters	Set on low and carried in line with back	A dignified, rather slow worker, but a sure finder and a splendid retriever when trained. The Clumber is perhaps the most easily trained of any of the spaniel family *Use:* Shooting dog	
Somewhat heavy and long; rounded crown; stop clearly defined *Ears:* Lobular; set on a line no higher than the lower part of the eye; leather extending to nostrils; covered with long, silky, straight or wavy hair	Short, compact, and firmly knit together, giving the impression of strength and sturdiness	Docked	The temperament is free and merry *Use:* Originally a hunting dog. They love hunting and take to the water readily. Today, they are used as a pet and show dog	*Disqualifications:* (1) Blacks, with white markings other than on chest or throat; (2) solid colors other than black, with white markings except on chest and throat; (3) parti-colors, with 90% or more of primary color, or secondary color or colors limited solely to one location; (4) black and tans, with tan markings in excess of 10%, total absence of tan markings at any of the specified locations, white markings except on chest and throat Dogs over 15½ in. Bitches over 14½ in.

(Continued)

59

TABLE 3 (CONTINUED) BREEDS OF

Breed	Place of Origin; Present Popularity	Color; Coat	General Appearance	Size
Collie —*working dog* *Fig. 57.*	Scotland, in the Highlands. It is not uncommon today to hear the Collie referred to as the "Scotch Collie." The smooth-coated Collie was originally a cattle-driving dog Today, the rough-coated Collie is popular in Great Britain, Belgium, Holland, America, Denmark, Germany, and New Zealand Collie popularity started in the U.S. about 1880; the breed was first registered in the American Kennel Club *Stud Book* in 1885. It has been among or close to the first ten breeds in the U.S. for nearly a century	*Color:* Sable and white, tricolor (predominantly black, carrying white markings, and with tan shadings on and about the head and legs), blue merle, or white; with or without white markings *Coat:* There are two varieties of Collies: rough coated, and smooth coated. The rough coated is the more popular of the two varieties On the *rough-coated* variety, the coat should be well fitted and properly textured; abundant except on the head and legs; the outercoat should be straight and harsh; and the undercoat should be soft, furry, and close together On the *smooth-coated* variety, the coat is hard, dense, and smooth	A medium-sized dog with narrow, aristocratic-looking head and high-set, tipped ears	*Height:* Dogs: 24–26 in. Bitches: 22–24 in *Weight:* Dogs: 60–75 lb Bitches: 50–65 lb
Curly-Coated Retriever —*sporting dog* *Fig. 58.*	England; descended from an early type of English water spaniel. The Curly-Coated Retriever Club was formed in England in 1896 The breed has never been popular except in New Zealand, where it is used for both wildfowling and quail shooting The Curly-Coated Retriever was first seen in America in 1907. It is rare today	*Color:* Black or liver *Coat:* A mass of crisp curls all over	A strong, smart, upstanding dog, showing activity, endurance, and intelligence	*Height:* 24 in. *Weight:* 70 to 80 lb

Head	Body	Tail	Character; Use	Faults or Disqualifications
Small in proportion to the size of the dog; long and noble; flat skull; moderately broad between the ears, with slight stop. Muzzle rather long and tapering gradually toward the nose *Ears:* Of medium size. When in repose, they are folded lengthwise and thrown back into the frill. When alerted, they are drawn well up and carried nearly erect, with about one-fourth of the ear tipping or breaking forward	Rectangular; somewhat long in proportion to the height. Chest deep; shoulders sloping; ribs well rounded; back strong and level; loins powerful and slightly arched; croup sloping and rounded; thighs powerful	Moderately long, the bone reaching to the hock joint or below When the dog is quiet, the tail is carried low, with an upward twist or swirl. When in motion or excited, it is carried gaily, but not over the back	Distinctive features, calm, peaceful, affectionate, home loving, and easily trained *Use:* As a show dog and companion. An excellent dog for children	*Faults:* Overshot or undershot jaw; prick or low ears; undersize or oversize
Long and well proportioned, not too flat *Ears:* Small, set on low, lying close to the head, and covered with short curls	Rather short, muscular and well ribbed up, squarely built	Moderately short, carried fairly straight, tapering toward the point, covered with curls	The breed possesses an eagerness for the water and a stamina in cold water. Most Americans consider them a bit slow *Use:* Retrieving downed waterfowl. Also, most of them are good landworkers	*Faults:* A saddle back or patch of uncurled hair behind the shoulder should be penalized. Also, a prominent white patch on the breast is undesirable

(Continued)

TABLE 3 (CONTINUED) BREEDS OF

Breed	Place of Origin; Present Popularity	Color; Coat	General Appearance	Size
Dachshund —*hound* *Fig. 59.*	Germany, where the breed got its name from its early use in badger hunting; "dachs" meaning badger and "hund" meaning dog in German. Importations of Dachshunds to the U.S. antedate the earliest American shows and stud books. Eleven animals were registered in the AKC *Stud Book* in 1885. By 1913–14, it was among the 10 most numerous breeds in the Westminster Kennel Club shows. But during and immediately following World War I, the breed declined in popularity. Today, the Dachshund ranks among the 20 most popular breeds in the U.S. Also, the Dachshund is a favorite breed in Australia, Great Britain, Denmark, Holland, and India	*Color:* Solid red (tan) of various shades, black with tan points, and chocolate and tan. Animals of the first two colors should have black noses and nails, and a narrow black line edging lips and eyelids. Chocolate with tan permits brown nose *Coat:* Three coat types— 1. smooth or shorthaired; 2. wirehaired; 3. longhaired. The shorthaired coat type predominates in the U.S.	A short-legged, long-bodied dog of graceful build, bold head carriage, pendent ears of medium length, and long, upward curved tail. He is sometimes referred to as "the sausage dog."	*Height:* Average 9–10 in. *Weight:* Dogs: up to 25 lb Bitches: up to 23 lb *Miniature Dachshunds:* Under 10 lb. They are bred in all three coats
Dalmatian —*nonsporting dog* *Fig. 60.*	The origin of the Dalmatian is clouded in obscurity. But it is known that the breed takes its name from the Adriatic province of Dalmatia, where it was used as a guard dog As a watch dog, the Dalmatian is without a peer. In the days of coaches, he was a mark of prestige as he trotted along (1) under the rear axle, (2) under the front axle, or (3) under the pole between the wheelers and leaders	*Color:* The ground color should be pure white. The spots may either be black or liver (but not both on the same dog) *Coat:* Short, hard, dense, fine, sleek, and glossy	Graceful, medium-sized, short-coated, black or liver-spotted dog with pendent ears and a long tail. His markings are distinct and different from any other breed In the Dalmatian dog, as in man, uric acid is excreted as the end product of purine metabolism, rather than allantoin (see Table 8 of this book)	*Height:* 19 to 23 in. *Weight:* Dogs: 55 lb Bitches: 50 lb
Dandie Dinmont Terrier —*terrier* *Fig. 61.*	In the Border country between England and Scotland, where they were first recorded as a distinct breed about 1700 and noted for preeminence in hunting otter and badger. Named after the character, Dandie Dinmont, in Sir Walter Scott's *Guy Mannering,* published in 1814	*Color:* Pepper or mustard, usually with some white on the chest *Coat:* About 2 in. long. From the skull to the root of the tail, there should be a mixture of hard and soft hair	A long-bodied, short-legged terrier with a long tail, pendulous ears, and a topknot of soft hair	*Height:* 8–11 in. *Weight:* 18–24 lb

Head	Body	Tail	Character; Use	Faults or Disqualifications
Long, uniformly tapered, clean-cut *Ears:* Broad, long, rounded, set on high and well back	Long and fully muscled. Back long, broad and muscular; withers high and long; loins only slightly arched; croup straight, long, broad, round, and well muscled; chest rounding and not too deep; breastbone prominent; belly moderately drawn up	Long, strong at the root and tapering; carried horizontally with a slight upward curve	A versatile sporting dog and an intelligent, alert, and affectionate house dog and companion *Use:* In the U.S., he is a house pet and companion. The Dachshund is especially clean, with practically no doggy odor	*Serious Faults:* Overshot and undershot jaws; knuckling over; very loose shoulders *Secondary faults:* Cow hocks; walleyes, except for dapple dogs; a bad coat *Minor faults:* Absence of, too profuse, or too light tan markings in the case of two-colored dogs
Fair length and flat; broad between the ears; moderate stop; skin without wrinkles *Ears:* Set high, of moderate size, rather wide at the base, gradually tapering to a rounded point	Back strong and straight; loins powerful and muscular, lightly arched; chest deep but not too broad; shoulders moderately sloping, well muscled; ribs moderately sprung, but not barrel shaped; hindquarters muscular	Strong at the root and tapering toward the end; long enough to reach the hock joint; carried with a slight curve upward, but never curled	The instinct of coaching is born in the Dalmatian; he takes to a horse like a duck takes to water. Also, he is aristocratic, a gentleman, and rather quiet—he barks only when there's a purpose *Use:* A handsome show dog, a delightful companion, and a picturesque and characteristic mascot on horse establishments	*Major faults:* Butterfly or flesh colored nose; cow hocks; flat feet; lack of pigment in the eye rims; trichiasis (abnormal position or direction of the eyelashes); shyness *Faults:* Ring or low-set tail; undersize or oversize *Disqualifications:* Any color markings other than black or liver Patches; tricolor; over 24 in. at the withers; undershot or overshot bite
Strongly made and large; skull broad between the ears, narrowing toward the eyes; forehead well domed; topknot soft and silky *Ears:* Pendulous, set well back, wide apart, low on the skull, and hanging close to the cheeks	Long, strong and flexible. Arching over the loins; chest full and deep, with well-sprung ribs; shoulders muscular; thighs well developed	Rather short; thick at the root and tapering off to a point; covered with wiry hair; carried in a scimitar-shaped curve	An ardent hunter, and an attractive family companion. More serene than most terriers *Use:* Both as an outdoor dog and as a house or apartment dog.	

(Continued)

TABLE 3 (CONTINUED) BREEDS OF

Breed	Place of Origin; Present Popularity	Color; Coat	General Appearance	Size
Doberman Pinscher —*working dog* *Fig. 62.*	Germany, around 1890. The breed is named after a Mr. Ludwig Doberman, of Apolda, Germany, who set out to develop a breed that would attack man, beast, or even the devil himself Importations of Dobermans to the U.S. have been sporadic Official war dog of U.S. Marines in World War II, with a distinguished record	*Color:* Black, red, blue, and fawn; with markings of rust above each eye, and on the muzzle, throat, forechest, all legs and feet, and below the tail *Coat:* Smooth haired, short, hard, thick, and close lying	A streamlined, smooth-coated dog with erect, cropped ears and docked tail	Medium size *Height:* Dogs: 26–28 in. Bitches: 24–26 in. *Weight:* Dogs: 67–75 lb Bitches: 57–65 lb
English Cocker Spaniel —*sporting dog* *Fig. 63.*	England The breed derives its name from the early use of these small spaniels to hunt woodcock The English Cocker Spaniel Club of America was formed in 1935. In 1940, the Canadian Kennel Club recognized the English Cocker Spaniel as a breed, as did the American Kennel Club in 1947	*Color:* Various. In self colors, a white-shirt frill is undesirable *Coat:* The head coat should be short and fine. The body coat should be flat or slightly wavy and silky in texture, and should be of medium length and have enough under-coating to give protection	A small, lively, long-coated dog with very long ears and docked tail	*Height:* Dogs: 16–17 in. Bitches: 15–16 in. *Weight:* Dogs: 28–34 lb Bitches: 26–32 lb
English Foxhound —*hound* *Fig. 64.*	England, where the stud books of the Masters of Foxhounds Association date back prior to 1800. But the foxhound existed in England long before that time The English Foxhound was first imported to the U. S. in 1738. Today, it is the best known of all pack hounds	*Color:* Any hound color. Hound colors are black, tan, and white; or any combination of these three *Coat:* Short, dense, hard, and glossy	A medium-sized, well-proportioned hound with pendent ears, gaily carried tail, and a smooth coat; of various hound colors. The English Foxhound is stouter in appearance than his American cousin	*Height:* Average 23 in. *Weight:* Average 70 lb

64

Head	Body	Tail	Character; Use	Faults or Disqualifications
Long and clean; skull wedge shaped and flat on front and sides; stop slight; muzzle wedgelike and strong *Ears:* Trimmed and carried erect (in those states where ear-trimming is prohibited, or where dogs with cropped ears cannot be shown, the foregoing requirement is waived). The upper attachment of the ear, when erect, should be on a level with the top of the skull	Back short, firm and muscular; loins well muscled and slightly arched; croup slightly rounded and not too short; forechest prominent; shoulders long, sloping, muscular, and well laid in; ribs well sprung and deep; thighs broad and powerful	Docked at approximately second joint	Alertness, agility, muscular power, and temperamental fire *Use:* Guard and home watchdog; police dog; war dog; guide dogs for the blind	*Faults:* Coarseness; fine, greyhound build; undersized or oversized; head out of balance to body; slit or glassy eyes *Disqualifications:* Jaw overshot more than 3/16 in. or undershot more than 1/8 in.; four or more missing teeth
The skull and forehead should be well developed with no suggestion of coarseness, and should be arched and slightly flattened on top *Ears:* Lobular; set low and close to the head; leather fine and extending at least to the nose, well covered with long, silky, straight or slightly wavy hair	Close coupled, compact and firmly knit, giving the impression of great strength without heaviness	Set on to conform with the topline of the back. Merry in action — a "wiggle tail"	His love and faithfulness to his master and household, and his alertness and courage are characteristic. He is noted for his intelligence and merry disposition *Use:* A hunting dog; a house companion	*Faults:* In the breed description and standards adopted by the American Kennel Club, a large list of faults is given, a few of which follow: white feet in any specimen of self color; insufficient coat, or coat too soft, curly, or wavy
Strong but not heavy, sufficiently long and broad in skull; muzzle powerful and blunt *Ears:* Set on low and lying close to the cheeks. Most English Foxhounds are "rounded," which means that about 1½ in. is taken off the end of the ears	Back straight and muscular, without any depression behind the withers; chest broad and deep; shoulders long, sloping, and well covered; and thighs muscular	Strong at the root and carried gaily, but never curled over the back	A combination of grace and strength *Use:* In packs for hunting as followed in the traditional English fashion of riding to hounds	*Disqualifications:* Overshot or undershot jaw

(Continued)

TABLE 3 (CONTINUED) BREEDS OF

Breed	Place of Origin; Present Popularity	Color; Coat	General Appearance	Size
English Setter —*sporting dog* Fig. 65.	England, where it has been used on game birds for more than 400 years. The first show for the breed was held in England in 1859. The English Setter has been firmly entrenched in the affections of the American gunner since 1874, before the Pointer arrived. It has been said, "Once a Setter man, always a Setter man"	*Color:* Black, white, and tan; black and white; blue belton (belton means two colors on one hair); lemon and white; lemon belton; orange and white; orange belton; liver and white; liver belton; and solid white. *Markings:* Dogs with heavy patches of color on the body, but flecked all over preferred. *Coat:* Flat and of good length, without curl	A large, long-coated dog, white with colored markings, moderately long ears, and well-feathered tail	*Height:* Dogs: 25 in. Bitches: 24 in. *Weight:* 50 to 70 lb
English Springer Spaniel —*sporting dog* Fig. 66.	England. The breed descends from what were originally known as Land Spaniels (to distinguish them from Water Spaniels). The name "Springer" comes from the purpose for which the breed was used in the Middle Ages–for springing game from cover. In 1902, the Kennel Club of England recognized the English Springer Spaniel as a distinct breed. English Springer Spaniels were popular in America up to the time of the Civil War. Thereafter, with the opening up of the Great Plains, they gave way to longer-legged, wider-ranging Pointers and Setters	*Color:* Liver or black with white markings; liver and white (or black and white), with tan markings; blue or liver roan; or predominantly white with tan, black, or liver markings. *Coat:* The body coat is flat or wavy, of medium length, and sufficiently dense to be waterproof, weatherproof, and thornproof. On the head, front of forelegs, and below the hocks on front of hind legs, the hair is short. Hair should be of fine texture	A medium-sized sporting dog with moderately long ears, docked tail, and coat of any recognized spaniel color	*Height:* Dogs: 20 in. Bitches: 19 in. *Weight:* 45–55 lb

Head	Body	Tail	Character; Use	Faults or Disqualifications
Long and lean, with a well-defined stop *Ears:* Carried close to the head, well back and set low, of moderate length, slightly rounded at the ends, and covered with silky hair	Back short and straight; loins slightly arched, broad, strong and muscular; croup falling away slightly; chest deep and rounded; shoulders sloping; hindquarters powerful	Straight and taper to a fine point, with only sufficient length to reach the hocks, or less. The tail should not curl sideways or above the level of the back	Mild, sweet disposition, along with beauty, intelligence, and aristocratic appearance. The English Setter thrives on attention and affection *Use:* Gundog, companion for children, and show dog The setter crouches or "sets" on finding game, then creeps toward the birds with its body close to the ground	
The head is impressive without being heavy. Its beauty lies in a combination of strength and refinement *Ears:* Set on a level with the line of the eye; on the side of the skull and not too far back. The flaps should be long and fairly wide and hang close to the cheeks with no tendency to stand up or out. The leather should be thin and long enough to touch the tip of the nose	Well coupled, strong, compact. Back broad and strong; loins muscular and slightly arched; chest deep and well developed; shoulders sloping; ribs deep and extending well back; hindquarters muscular	Somewhat low, following the natural line of the croup; carriage should be nearly horizontal; should not be docked too short	An active, lively, and keen gundog, and an agreeable house companion. The typical Springer is friendly, eager to please, quick to learn, and willing to obey *Use:* Gundog The Springer is a flushing dog; hence, for pheasant hunting they are generally considered more satisfactory than Pointers or Setters, because of the tendency of pheasants to scurry off. A good retriever. Also, they are widely used as house companions	*Faults:* In the breed description and standards adopted by the American Kennel Club, a large list of faults and penalties is given, a few of which follow: Lacking breed type; excessive timidity or viciousness; oversize, undersize, cloddy, leggy, and/or overweight; rough, curly coat; off colors such as lemon, red, or orange; under or overshot jaw; short, round ears, or ears not properly set; tail carried upright; cow hocks

(Continued)

TABLE 3 (CONTINUED) BREEDS OF

Breed	Place of Origin; Present Popularity	Color; Coat	General Appearance	Size
English Toy Spaniel —*toy* *Fig. 67.*	England The breed was well known in the U. S. throughout the nineteenth century	*Color:* There are two varieties, the colors of which are: 1. *King Charles and Ruby*—These are solid colored dogs. a. The *King Charles* is black and tan (considered a solid color). The body is black, rich and glossy), and there are deep mahogany tan markings over the eyes and on the muzzle, chest, and legs. White hairs on the chest are faulted; a white patch on the chest or white elsewhere disqualifies b. The *Ruby* is a rich chestnut red and whole colored. White hair on the chest is faulted; a white patch on the chest or elsewhere disqualifies 2. *Blenhein and Prince Charles*—These are broken colored dogs a. The *Blenhein* is red and white. The ears and cheeks should be red, with a blaze of white extending from the nose up the forehead and ending between the ears. On top of the forehead, there should be a spot of red the size of a dime b. The *Prince Charles* is a tricolored dog; white, black and tan. The ground color is pearly white; the tan appears as spots over the eyes, on the muzzle, chest, and legs; the ears and vent should be lined with tan *Coat:* Long, silky, soft, and wavy, but not curly. Profuse mane, extending well down in front of the chest. Feather well displayed on ears and feet	A small, compact, "cobby" dog, with long hair and a feathered tail	*Height:* Average 10 in. *Weight:* 9–12 lb

Head	Body	Tail	Character; Use	Faults or Disqualifications
Well domed, preferably semiglobular, with a well-marked stop *Ears:* Set low on the head, long, hanging flat to the cheeks, and heavily feathered	Compact and "cobby," with a broad back and a wide chest	Not carried above the level of the back; feathered, forming a marked flag	An affectionate, intelligent, little dog that captivated royalty, aristocrats, and wealthy for at least three centuries	*Disqualifications:* In King Charles and Ruby, a white patch on the chest, or white on any other body part, constitutes a disqualification

(Continued)

TABLE 3 (CONTINUED) BREEDS OF

Breed	Place of Origin; Present Popularity	Color; Coat	General Appearance	Size
Field Spaniel —*sporting dog* Fig. 68.	England At one period, an English breed fancier almost drove the breed to extinction, by selecting and breeding for such heavy bone and length of body that Field Spaniels were almost grotesque The Field Spaniel is the least known of the sporting spaniels, but it has been in America since the 1880s	*Color:* Black, liver, golden liver, mahogany red, or roan; or any one of these colors with tan over the eyes and on the cheeks, feet, and pasterns *Coat:* Dense, flat or slightly wavy; silky and glossy	A medium-sized dog, long coated, with moderately long ears and feathered tail. It's a larger dog than the Cocker Spaniel	*Height:* 18 in. *Weight:* 35–50 lb
Flat-Coated Retriever —*sporting dog* Fig. 69.	England, where it was once favored by British gamekeepers It was brought to America in 1870 Very rare now	*Color:* Black or liver *Coat:* Dense, fine quality and texture, and flat	A medium-sized, sturdily made, long-haired dog, with small pendent ears and a long tail	*Height:* 23 in. *Weight:* 60–70 lb
Fox Terrier —*terrier* Fig. 70.	England An ancient sporting breed, which derived its name because it was used for driving the fox from its hole The American Fox Terrier Club was founded, and adopted a standard, in 1885	*Color:* White should predominate; brindle, red or liver markings are objectionable *Coat:* There are two varieties: 1. smooth haired 2. wirehaired The smooth haired Fox terrier is the most popular in the U. S.	A small, upstanding dog with V-shaped drop ears and docked tail, and either smooth coated or wire coated	*Height:* Dogs: maximum of 15½ in. Bitches: maximum of 12 in. *Weight:* Dogs: 18 lb Bitches: 16 lb
French Bulldog —*nonsporting dog* Fig. 71.	France The first major U. S. French Bulldog show was held in the ballroom of the Waldorf-Astoria in New York City in 1898	*Color:* All brindle, fawn, white, brindle and white, and any color except those which constitute disqualification *Coat:* Moderately fine, brilliant, short, and smooth	A small, smooth-coated, low-set dog with broad, squarish head, short muzzle, bat ears, and a short tail. The two distinctive features of the French Bulldog are: the bat ears, and flat skull and curved forehead	*Height:* Average 12 in. *Weight:* Not over 28 lb. The most popular size is between 19 and 22 lb

DOGS AND THEIR CHARACTERISTICS

Head	Body	Tail	Character; Use	Faults or Disqualifications
The head should be very characteristic of the breed, with well-developed skull and prominent occiput *Ears:* Moderately long and wide, set on low, and hanging in graceful folds with the lower parts curling inwards and backwards	Moderate length; somewhat barrel shaped, with well-sprung ribs; back and loins short and broad; chest deep but not too wide; hindquarters strong and muscular	Strong at the root, carried in line with the back or slightly below, and nicely fringed with wavy feather	Level headed, intelligent, easily trained, and possessed with great perseverance *Use:* Gundog; companion	
Long and nicely molded *Ears:* Small and well set on, held close to the side of the head	The back should be short, square, and well ribbed up; chest deep and fairly broad; belly not drawn up; shoulder and thigh well muscled	The tail should be short, straight, well set on, and carried gaily but not much above the level of the back	A bright, active dog, with an intelligent expression *Use:* As a water dog, and for upland shooting	
Wedge shaped; skull flat, moderately narrow, gradually decreasing in width to the eyes; stop slight *Ears:* V-shaped, small, moderate thickness, drooping forward close to the cheeks	Back short, straight, and firm; loins strong and slightly arched; croup slightly curved; chest deep and oval; shoulders long and sloping; ribs moderately rounded; belly slightly drawn up; thighs strong and muscular	Set on rather high and carried gaily, but not over the back or curled	Strong and gay, with a brave, wise way in the field or at home *Use:* Primarily as a family dog in the U. S. In England, it is used as a sporting dog, also	*Disqualifications:* Nose white, cherry, or spotted to a considerable extent with either of these colors; ears prick, tulip, or rose; mouth undershot or overshot
Large and square; skull flat between the ears; forehead slightly rounded; stop well defined; muzzle broad, deep, and well laid back *Ears:* Bat ears—they're broad at the bases, elongated, with round tops; set high on the head; carried erect	Short and well rounded. Back strong and short, broad at the shoulders, narrowing at the loins, and slightly roached; chest broad, deep and full; well ribbed, with the belly tucked up	Either straight or screwed (but not curly), short, hung low, thick root, and fine tip; carried low in repose	A charming, intelligent, obedient, alert dog. As a rule, they bark very little *Use:* Principally as companions and pets. But they are also good watchdogs	*Disqualifications:* Ears other than bat ears; colors of black and white, black and tan, liver, mouse, or solid black; eyes of different color; other than black nose except in the case of light-colored dogs; harelip; any mutilation; over 28 lb in weight

(Continued)

TABLE 3 (CONTINUED) BREEDS OF

Breed	Place of Origin; Present Popularity	Color; Coat	General Appearance	Size
German Shepherd Dog —*working dog* Fig. 72.	Germany, where the parent club of the breed was founded in 1899. A worldwide favorite and among the first three in American dogs. Their heroism in World War I, rocketed them to popularity in the U. S.	*Color:* Jet black to light gray. May be black and tan, brindle, iron gray, or gray with sable markings. White is not desired. *Coat:* Dense, double, and usually flat	Above average size, long bodied, well muscled, with erect ears and long tail. A "natural" dog, unchanged by the show ring	*Height:* Dogs: 24–26 in. Bitches: 22–24 in. *Weight:* 75 to 85 lb or more
German Shorthaired Pointer —*sporting dog* Fig. 73.	Germany, where it was developed for hunting game birds and trailing large game. The German *Stud Book* established this breed in the 1870s. The breed has been in America since 1922. It is increasing in popularity	*Color:* Solid liver, liver-and-white spotted, liver-and-white spotted and ticked, liver-and-white ticked, liver roan. *Coat:* Short and thick and feels tough and hard to the hand	An aristocratic, well-balanced, symmetrical animal with conformation indicating power, endurance and agility, and a look of intelligence and animation	*Height:* Dogs: 23–25 in. Bitches: 21–23 in. *Weight:* Dogs: 55–70 lb Bitches: 45–60 lb
German Wirehaired Pointer (Deutsche Drahthaar) —*sporting dog* Fig. 74.	Germany, where it was developed as a gundog. Recognized as a breed in 1870. Brought to America in 1920. Has achieved considerable popularity in the Midwest. Accepted for registration in AKC and granted separate show classification in 1959	*Color:* Liver; or liver and white (liver-and-white spotted, liver roan, or liver-and-white spotted with ticking and roaning). *Coat:* Outercoat is straight, harsh, wiry, and rather flat lying, from 1½ to 2 in. in length. Undercoat is dense in winter and thin in summer	Pointer in type, sturdy, lively, and an intelligent, determined expression	*Height:* Dogs: 24–26 in. Bitches: Over 22 in. *Weight:* Average 55 lb
Giant Schnauzer —*working dog* Fig. 75.	Germany, where they were developed as a cattle-driving dog. Later, the Germans used them to guard breweries and for police work. A few of the Giant Schnauzers were brought to America prior to World War I. After the war, more were brought over. But their appearance in the U. S. coincided with the time when the German Shepherd was reaching its peak of popularity. Hence, they had little chance to make headway. Someday, they may	*Color:* Solid black or pepper and salt. *Coat:* Hard, wiry, coarse, and dense	A large, strong, rough-haired dog with the characteristic Schnauzer head and beard. The Giant Schnauzer has the build of a terrier, but the strength and agility of the finest working dogs	*Height:* Dogs: 25½–27½ in. Bitches: 23½–25½ in. *Weight:* Average 75 lb

DOGS AND THEIR CHARACTERISTICS

Head	Body	Tail	Character; Use	Faults or Disqualifications
Clean-cut, moderately broad between the ears, powerful muzzle *Ears:* Pointed, erect, and turned to front	Longer than tall. Back straight and strong; loins moderately arched; hips broad and strong; croup long and falling away slightly; chest deep but not too broad; shoulders long, sloping, and well muscled; ribs flat rather than barrel shaped	Bushy, reaching to hocks, and slightly curved at tip	A bit distant, but loyal. Very intelligent *Use:* Watchdog, leader of the blind, police work, and armed service	*Disqualifications* Cropped or hanging ears; undershot jaw; docked tail; white dogs; dogs with noses not predominantly black
Clean-cut and in proportion to the body. Skull slightly rounded on top *Ears:* Broad and set fairly high; lie flat and never hang away from the head	Withers high; back short and straight; loins muscular; hips broad; croup long and slanting; chest deep and moderately long, with well-sprung ribs; shoulders slanting; belly long and drawn up	Set high. Must be docked, leaving approximately 2/5 of length	Exceedingly kind and mild disposition *Use:* Pointing game and/or retrieving from land and water	*Faults:* Flesh colored nose; any color other than liver and white (gray white)
The head and muzzle are moderately long *Ears:* Rounded but not too broad; hang close to the sides of the head	Sturdy build. Longer than it is high. Withers high; back short and straight; loins muscular; croup long and slanting; chest deep and moderately broad with well-sprung ribs; shoulders slanting; belly long and drawn up; thighs muscular	Docked, approximately 2/5 of original length	Friendly, but not overly friendly *Use:* An all-purpose gundog; one that will point birds and will retrieve from land and water	*Faults:* A short, smooth coat; a soft, woolly coat; or an excessively long coat is to be severely penalized. Any black in the coat, or spotted or flesh colored noses should be penalized
Strong and elongated; skull tapering to the nose; stop well defined by prominent eyebrows; muzzle straight, practically parallel with the top line of the skull; length of muzzle to that of the skull in the proportion of 4:5; the whole being shaped like a moderately blunt wedge, and wearing a hard bristly beard *Ears:* Small and V-shaped; set well on the head and either dropping forward closely to the cheek, or cropped, with ears evenly cut	Back straight, short, not too broad, and muscular; deep chest, oval ribbed; shoulders sloping, flat but muscular; belly slightly drawn up; thighs strong and well muscled	Set on high, docked short (cut down to 2 or 3 joints), and carried erect	An outstanding and gentle worker with cattle; a versatile utility dog; intelligent, hardy, and eager to learn *Use:* As a utility dog and guard	*Faults:* Any deviation from the standard, with the degree of the deviation determining the penalty. Shyness. Viciousness *Disqualifications:* Overshot or undershot jaw

(Continued)

TABLE 3 (CONTINUED) BREEDS OF

Breed	Place of Origin; Present Popularity	Color; Coat	General Appearance	Size
Golden Retriever —*sporting dog* Fig. 76.	England. In 1913, the British Kennel Club recognized them as a separate breed. The Golden Retriever has been known in America since 1932. It appears to be destined to increase in numbers	*Color:* Lustrous golden of various shades. *Coat:* Dense and water repellent, with good undercoat. Lies flat against the body and may be straight or wavy	A beautiful, medium-sized golden-colored, long-coated dog with small pendent ears and a long tail	*Height:* Dogs: 23–24 in. Bitches: 21–22½ in. *Weight:* Dogs: 65–75 lb Bitches: 60–70 lb
Gordon Setter —*sporting dog* Fig. 77.	Scotland, dating back to at least 1620. Named after the Duke of Gordon. The British Gordon Setter Club was formed in 1927. The Gordon Setter was first introduced to America in 1874. Due to the scarcity of game in some places, and the fact that the Gordon Setter is not a fast dog, the breed has declined in importance in the U.S.	*Color:* Black with tan markings, either of rich chestnut or mahogany color. *Coat:* Soft and shiny; straight or slightly waved, but not curly; with long hair on ears, under stomach, on chest, on back of legs, and on the tail	A large, powerful, black and tan, long-coated dog with pendent ears	*Height:* Dogs: 24–27 in. Bitches: 23–26 in. *Weight:* Dogs: 55–80 lb Bitches: 45–70 lb
Great Dane —*working dog* Fig. 78.	Germany; over 400 years ago as a boar hunter. A Great Dane Club was founded in Germany in 1891, in England in 1885, and in the U. S. in 1889. The German standards for the breed are accepted in all countries. Throughout the world, the Great Dane has developed steadily in popularity and numbers. It is the most popular and numerous of the big breeds of dogs	*Brindle,* in which the ground color may vary from pale gold to any shade of orange, with black stripes. *Fawn,* from the palest buff to the deepest orange, preferably with a black mask and black nails. *Blue,* which should be a steel blue. Blues may have light eyes and white markings on the chest and feet. *Black,* which should be glossy. *Harlequin,* in which the ground should be white with irregularly shaped patches of black or blue distributed over the body. *Coat:* Short, thick, smooth, and glossy	A big, powerful, well-built dog with a rectangular head, small ears, and a long tail. The Great Dane is the Apollo of dogs. He's "statuesque."	*Height:* Dogs: over 30 in. Bitches: over 28 in. *Weight:* Over 120 lb

Head	Body	Tail	Character; Use	Faults or Disqualifications
Broad skull. Good stop *Ears:* Rather short, hanging flat against the head, with rounded tips slightly below jaw	Well balanced; short coupled; back straight; loins powerful; croup falling away slightly; chest deep and fairly broad, with well-sprung ribs; fore and rear quarters well developed	Well set on; length extends to hock; carried with merry action, with some upward curve	Gentle, sensitive, intelligent, and willing *Use:* Primarily a hunting dog. His particular forte is retrieving from water, but he is equally useful on upland birds. In recent years, some Golden Retrievers have been used as guide dogs for the blind. Also, a popular companion and pet	Deviation in height of more than 1 in. from standard either way Undershot or overshot jaw Abnormal position or direction of the eyelashes (Trichiasis)
Deep, rather than broad; nicely rounded skull; clearly defined stop *Ears:* Set low on the head, about in line with the eye; fairly large and thin; well folded and carried close to the head	Back muscular; loins slightly arched; chest deep and not too wide; shoulders long and sloping; hindquarters long, flat, and well muscled	Short, should not reach below the hocks, carried horizontally, thick at the root and finishing in a point. Feather, which starts near the root, should be slightly waved or straight	Beauty, brains, bird sense, and devoted loyalty. A one-man dog *Use:* Primarily as a bird dog	*Disqualifications:* Predominantly tan, red, or buff dogs which do not have the typical pattern of markings of a Gordon Setter
Of good length, with narrow skull; well proportioned; stop well marked; bridge of nose broad; square appearing from all angles. Muzzle square, and well lipped, with distinct lip furrow *Ears:* Set high, not too far apart, medium size, moderate thickness, drooping forward close to the cheek. Cropped ears well pointed and carried erect	Withers slightly raised; back straight and powerful; loins slightly arched and strong; croup sloping slightly to the set of the tail; chest deep and fairly broad; shoulders long and sloping; ribs well sprung; belly well drawn up; thighs broad and muscular	Thick at the root, tapering to end; moderate length, reaching to hocks; carried straight and hanging downward in repose, and never raised above the level of the back even when the dog is excited	Proud, reserved, and suspicious with strangers, but friendly, affectionate, and obedient with friends. An alert and fearless guard *Use:* House dog and companion	*Faults:* Undershot teeth *Disqualifications:* Under minimum height; white Danes without any black marks (albinos); off colors; docked tails; split noses

(Continued)

TABLE 3 (CONTINUED) BREEDS OF

Breed	Place of Origin; Present Popularity	Color; Coat	General Appearance	Size
Great Pyrenees —working dog Fig. 79.	In the isolated Pyrenees Mountains, on both the Spanish and French sides, where it was used to guard flocks The first pair of Great Pyrenees was brought to this country in 1824; and a few scattered importations followed. But the American Kennel Club did not recognize the breed until 1933	*Color:* White, or white with markings of badger, gray, or varying shades of tan *Coat:* A long, thick outercoat, which is straight or slightly undulating; and a fine, white undercoat	A massive, long-coated, white dog with pendent ears and a long bushy tail. He has been called, "an animated snowdrift of the Pyrenees Mountains"	*Height:* Dogs: 27–32 in. Bitches: 25–29 in. *Weight:* Dogs: 100–125 lb Bitches: 90–115 lb
Greyhound —hound Fig. 80.	The origin of the Greyhound is clouded in obscurity. No one knows how old he is, where he originated, or how he acquired his name. It seems fairly certain, however, that his fame was first written in the hot sands of Egypt, where he coursed gazelle. From there he can be traced to almost every country, on every continent on the globe The first successful dog tracks were established in England, but it is now a growing sport in the U. S.	*Color:* Any color *Coat:* Short, smooth, and firm	A large, graceful, smooth-coated dog with ears folded to the rear and a long, down-carried tail. He's the canine symbol of speed	*Height:* Average 26 in. *Weight:* Dogs: 65–70 lb Bitches: 60–65 lb
Harrier —hound Fig. 81.	The origin of the Harrier is unknown, but it is known that the first English pack was established in 1260. The name comes from their early use in pursuit of hare, which was a popular sport in early-day England The Harrier has been known in America since Colonial days	*Color:* Black, tan, or white, or any combination of these *Coat:* Short, dense, hard, and smooth	A medium-sized, short-coated pack hound with pendent ears and a long tail. The Harrier is very similar in type to the English Foxhound, although smaller	*Height:* 19–21 in. *Weight:* 45 lb

Head	Body	Tail	Character; Use	Faults or Disqualifications
Large and wedge shaped, with rounded crown and no apparent stop *Ears:* V-shaped, but rounded at the tips; medium size; set parallel with the eyes; carried low and close to the head except when raised at attention	Back and loins short coupled, straight, and broad; rump sloping slightly; chest deep; shoulders sloping and well laid in; ribs flat sided; haunches fairly prominent	Long enough to hang below the hocks; well plumed; carried low in repose, but carried high over the back when alert—making the wheel (a circle like a wheel)	Gentle and docile with those he knows; faithful and devoted to his master even to the point of self-sacrifice; and courageous in the protection of the flock placed in his care and of the ones he loves *Use:* Protector of the shepherd and his flock. As a watchdog and companion. Also, suitable for sled work and for pack and guide work on ski trips	
Long and narrow, fairly wide between the ears, scarcely perceptible stop, and good length of muzzle, which should be powerful without coarseness *Ears:* Small and fine, thrown back and folded, except when excited, when they are semipricked	Back broad and very muscular; loins slightly arched and higher than the withers; croup broad and drooping to the set of the tail in an unbroken line; chest deep and broad; and belly well tucked up	Long, fine, and tapering with a slight upward curve	The Greyhound is a sight hunter. He is constructed to run in huge leaps, driving his hind legs ahead of his front ones It is the popular English racing dog, whose skill and speed are seen at their best when he is pursuing a hare The Greyhound is gentle and well behaved in the house, but comparatively few are kept as companions	
Medium size with bold forehead *Ears:* Set low and hanging close to the cheeks	Back straight and muscular; loins broad and arched; croup level; chest large; shoulders sloping and well laid in	Set high, long, and gracefully curved	A strong, agile pack hound for hare hunting, with a good nose *Use:* Hunting, especially rabbits	

(Continued)

TABLE 3 (CONTINUED) BREEDS OF

Breed	Place of Origin; Present Popularity	Color; Coat	General Appearance	Size
Irish Setter —*sporting dog* Fig. 82.	Ireland Special classes were provided for the breed in the Dublin Show in 1874. The Ulster Irish Setter Club was organized in 1876 The Irish Setter was brought to America in the 1870s	*Color:* Mahogany or rich chestnut red. His ancestors in Ireland were often spotted *Coat:* Short and fine on head, forelegs, and tips of ears; of moderate length and flat on all other body parts; forming feathering behind the limbs, under the belly, and on the tail	A large, long-coated, elegant dog, solid red in color, with pendent ears, and handsome tail	There is no disqualification as to size; overall balance is considered more important than size *Height:* Dogs: 27 in. Bitches: 25 in. *Weight:* Dogs: 70 lb Bitches: 60 lb
Irish Terrier —*terrier* Fig. 83.	Ireland, where they were developed for their working qualities and hunting ability	*Color:* Whole colored; of either bright red, red wheaten, or golden red. A small patch of white on the chest is permissible *Coat:* Topcoat should be harsh and wiry, with a broken appearance. Undercoat should be soft and fine	An upstanding, rough-coated, red terrier, with small, drop ears, and docked tail The body is longer than that of the other terriers	*Height:* 18 in. *Weight:* Dogs: 27 lb Bitches: 25 lb
Irish Water Spaniel —*sporting dog* Fig. 84.	Ireland It's Erin's most ancient breed. The first special class for Irish Water Spaniels was provided in 1859 In 1878, the breed was first registered in the U.S. in the National American Kennel Club, which later became the American Kennel Club. From about 1880 to 1925, it was the leading retriever breed in the U.S. In the 1930s, registrations of Irish Water Spaniels in the U.S. dropped as the popularity of the newer imports of other retrieving breeds increased	*Color:* Solid liver *Coat:* The neck, back, and flanks should be covered with dense, tight ringlets, free from woolliness. The hair should be longer on the belly and shorter on the throat. The forelegs should be well covered with curls or ringlets down to the feet. A topknot is characteristic	A medium-sized, curly-coated dog, with topknot, long, ringlet-covered ears, and a characteristic rattail. It's the tallest and most distinctive of the spaniels	*Height:* Dogs: 22–24 in. Bitches: 22–23 in. *Weight:* Dogs: 55–65 lb Bitches: 45–58 lb

Head	Body	Tail	Character; Use	Faults or Disqualifications
Long and lean, its length at least double the width between the ears. Oval skull *Ears:* Set well back and low, not above level of eye; leather thin, hanging in a neat fold close to the head and nearly long enough to reach the nose	Well proportioned; sufficiently long to permit a straight and free stride. Back moderate length and well muscled; loins slightly arched; croup long, muscular, and slightly sloping; chest deep but rather narrow; shoulders well laid in; ribs well sprung and belly slightly drawn up; hindquarters strong and well muscled	Strong at root, tapering to fine point, about long enough to reach the hock, carried straight or curved slightly upward	Beautiful, keen, hardy, and fast bird dog with an excellent nose; a good retriever and watchdog; very affectionate, and long lived. He is typically Irish, with a devil-may-care attitude that makes him very likeable. A one-man dog *Use:* Bird dog. An ideal companion in the home	
Long, with flat skull; rather narrow between the ears and narrowing still more toward the eyes; very slight stop *Ears:* Small, V-shaped, moderate thickness, set well on top of the head, and covered with short dark hair	Moderately long. Back strong and straight; loins strong, muscular, and slightly arched; hindquarters strong and muscular; ribs fairly sprung, deep rather than round	Set on high; docked to ¾ its natural length; carried gaily but not over back; covered with rough hair	Of good temper, affectionate, and loyal; a courageous guard; and brave against vermin *Use:* Daredevil and courageous messengers in war. As pets and protectors	*Faults:* Light or yellow eye; a "dead" ear (ears that do not respond or prick up), houndlike in appearance; single, curly, or kinky coat *Disqualifications:* Nose of any color other than black; undershot or overshot mouth; cropped ears; any color other than red, golden red, or red wheaten
Rather large, with well-domed skull and prominent occiput *Ears:* Long and lobular, set low, with leathers reaching to about the end of the nose when extended forward	Medium length and somewhat barrel shaped. Back and loins short and broad; chest deep but not too wide; hindquarters long, strong, and well muscled	Set low enough to give a rounded appearance to the hind quarters and carried nearly level with the back	An energetic gundog; a strong swimmer and indefatigable in the water. Loyal to those he knows, but forbidding to strangers *Use:* For retrieving waterfowl and upland game	*Faults:* White on the chest is objectionable

(Continued)

TABLE 3 (CONTINUED) BREEDS OF

Breed	Place of Origin; Present Popularity	Color; Coat	General Appearance	Size
Irish Wolfhound —*hound* Fig. 85.	The origin of the Irish Wolfhound has been traced back to 391 A.D. in Ireland, where he was originally a wolf and elk hunter. Abroad, this big dog is still used in various hunts—for wild boar, larger animals, and even lions in Kenya. The Irish Wolfhound was brought to America in the 1800s. In this country, he is occasionally used in running down and killing coyotes and wolves. But, for the most part, he finds his way into a private home, where he is quiet mannered and dignified	*Color:* Gray, brindle, red, black, pure white, and fawn. *Coat:* Rough and hard on body, legs, and head; especially wiry and long over eyes and on the under jaw	A huge, rough-coated hound, with proudly carried long, narrow head, piercing eyes, shaggy brows, small folded ears, and low-carried tail. The Irish Wolfhound, which is the tallest of all breeds of dogs, is built along Greyhound lines	*Height, minimum:* Dogs: 32 in. Bitches: 30 in. *Weight, minimum:* Dogs: 120 lb Bitches: 105 lb
Italian Greyhound —*toy* Fig. 86.	Italy, where dogs similar to the present Italian Greyhound are known to have existed for more than 2,000 years. In the U.S., the breed enjoyed reasonable popularity between 1875 and 1900	*Color:* Any color and markings acceptable, except tan markings. *Coat:* Hair thin and glossy like satin	A small, very refined, long-legged, smooth-coated dog with small rose ears, and a long, fine tail. It's a miniature Greyhound	*Height:* 9–10 in. *Two Weights:* 1. 8 lb and under 2. Over 8 lb
Japanese Spaniel —*toy* Fig. 87.	China, centuries ago. It is reported that one of the Chinese emperors gave a pair to the emperor of Japan. The present Japanese Spaniel Club of America was founded in 1912	*Color:* Either black and white, or red and white. *Coat:* Profuse, long, straight, rather silky, with a tendency to stand out	A small, long-coated dog with small ears, very short face, and a plumed, curly tail. They must look Oriental—aristocratic in appearance, and stylish in carriage	*Height:* 9 in. *Weight:* Two classes: 1. Under 7 lb 2. Over 7 lb

DOGS AND THEIR CHARACTERISTICS

Head	Body	Tail	Character; Use	Faults or Disqualifications
Long; skull not too broad, with the forehead very slightly raised and very little stop. Muzzle long and moderately pointed. Nose dark *Ears:* Small; carried folded back	Back long; loins arched; croup dropping to the root of the tail; shoulders sloping and muscular; and thighs muscular	Long, slightly curved, of medium thickness and well covered with hair	The Irish Wolfhound possesses a commanding appearance and combines, to a remarkable degree, power and swiftness with keen sight. As the occasion demands, he can be either (1) a ferocious hunter-fighter, overtaking marauders (like the timber wolf), seizing them by the neck and shaking them to death, or (2) a handsome and imposing companion and show dog. Thus, it has been well said of the Irish Wolfhound that he is, "gentle when stroked, fierce when provoked" *Use:* Hunting, house guard, companion, and/or show dog	*Faults:* Large ears, and hanging flat to the face; too curly a tail; lips or nose liver-colored or lacking pigmentation
Skull long, flat, and narrow, with a slight stop *Ears:* Rose shaped, placed well back, soft and delicate	Back curved and drooping over the croup; chest deep and narrow; shoulders long and sloping; ribs slightly arched; belly well tucked up; thighs muscular	Rather long, fine, and with low carriage	A marvelous disposition; and, despite their fragile appearance, they are strong and active, and no more injury prone than other toy breeds *Use:* As a pet	*Faults:* Badly undershot or overshot mouth; very dark eyes; erect or button ears; ring tail, or gay tail *Disqualifications:* Tan markings
Large; broad, rounded skull and very pronounced stop; muzzle short; upper and lower jaws slightly upturned *Ears:* Small, V-shaped, set high and wide apart on head, and feathered	Squarely and compactly built; "cobby"; back short and straight; chest wide and deep	Twisted to either right or left from root and carried over back; profusely covered with long hair	Smart, lively, sensitive, and tough. He rarely forgets either friend or foe *Use:* As a pet	*Disqualifications:* In black and whites, a nose any other color than black

(Continued)

TABLE 3 (CONTINUED) BREEDS OF

Breed	Place of Origin; Present Popularity	Color; Coat	General Appearance	Size
Keeshond —*nonsporting dog* *Fig. 88.*	Holland During the troubled years preceding the French revolution, the Keeshond became the symbol of a political party in Holland. One version has it that it was named after a dog named Kees, owned by Kees de Gyselaer, leader of the political party known as "The Patriots." In any case, the Keeshond was popular as a watch dog and a pet on the canal barges	*Color:* A mixture of gray and black, varying from light to dark *Coat:* Abundantly covered with long, straight, harsh hair, which protrudes out from the body. The hair around the neck and forepart of the shoulders and chest forms a lionlike mane. Also, there is a thick, downy undercoat	A short-coupled, long-haired, fox-headed dog with pointed ears, and a richly plumed tail well carried over the back	*Height:* Dogs: 18 in. Bitches: 17 in. *Weight:* Average 40 lb
Kerry Blue Terrier —*terrier* *Fig. 89.*	Ireland, in County Kerry, from which it takes its name. Originally, it was an all-purpose dog In the U.S., they were first shown at Westminster in 1922; and recognized by the American Kennel Club in 1924	*Color:* Any shade of blue gray or gray blue *Coat:* Soft, dense, and wavy	A medium-sized, upstanding, wavy-coated, blue colored terrier with drop ears and docked tail The most alert of all terriers	*Height:* Dogs: 18–19½ in. Bitches: 17½–19 in. *Weight:* 33–40 lb
Komondor —*working dog* *Fig. 90.*	Hungary, where he has been used as a protector of cattle and sheep for 1,000 years In 1935, the breed began to appear in the U.S. In 1937, the American Kennel Club recognized the breed and adopted a standard In dog shows, his ragamuffin appearance has mitigated against him. In order to make him attractive in bench shows, exhibitors have combed out the mats and dressed up the dog	*Color:* White *Coat:* Long, shaggy, woolly, thick, and unkempt; forming flat mats	A large, shaggy dog with white matted coat, which completely obscures the shape of the head; and with a long tail	*Height:* Dogs: 25½ in. and up Bitches: 23½ in. and up *Weight:* Average 90 lb

Head	Body	Tail	Character; Use	Faults or Disqualifications
A foxlike head; wedge shaped, with a definite stop. Eyes dark, with well-defined "spectacles" (a line connecting each eye to an ear on the same side) *Ears:* Set high on the head, small, triangular in shape, and carried erect	Compact A short, straight back; chest deep and strong; barrel well rounded; belly moderately tucked up	Set high, moderately long, well feathered, tightly curled over the back	The Keeshond has no desire to hunt; he would much rather remain with his master *Use:* As a companion and guard	*Faults:* Absence of "spectacles"; apple head, or absence of stop; overshot or undershot; protruding round eyes or light-colored eyes; ears not carried erect at attention; black markings below the knee; white foot or feet; tail not carried over and lying close to the back; silky, wavy, or curly coat *Very serious faults:* Entirely black or white, or any other solid color; and marked deviations from the gray color
Long; skull flat, with very slight stop, of moderate width between the ears and narrowing very slightly to the eyes *Ears:* V-shaped, small, of moderate thickness, and carried forward close to the cheeks	Moderately long. Back short, strong, and straight; loins short and powerful; chest deep with well-sprung ribs; shoulders flat; deep bodied; hindquarters strong and muscular	Set on high, moderate length, and carried gaily and erect	An affectionate and intelligent companion; very hardy; keen on game. He will fight unto death in combat *Use:* In Ireland and England, the Kerry Blue Terrier is used as an all-around working dog—for hunting small game and birds, for retrieving from land and water, and for herding sheep and cattle. In the U.S., he is primarily a watchdog and companion	*Disqualifications:* Solid black; dewclaws on hind legs
Medium size, round with broad skull and slight stop. Covered with long hair *Ears:* Low set and hang along side of head; medium sized; surface covered with long hair	Withers joining the neck smoothly; back straight, broad, and long; loins broad and muscular; shoulders well laid in; chest broad and deep; ribs slightly rounded; belly slightly tucked up	Long, reaching to the hocks, with tip curved upward; covered with very long hair	As a protector of herds and flocks, and as a household guardian, the Komondor is earnest, courageous, and faithful. He is much devoted to his master and flock (or herd) and will defend them against attack by man or beast. The Komondor is recognized as the king of the world's shepherd dogs *Use:* Guard dogs for country estates and children	*Faults:* Size below limit. Short or too curly coat; straight or silky coat; any missing teeth; looseness or slackness; short or curly tail; light colored eyes; erect ears; dewlaps on neck *Disqualifications:* Blue white eyes; color other than white; undershot or overshot bite; bobtails; flesh colored nose, short, smooth hair on head and legs

(Continued)

TABLE 3 (CONTINUED) BREEDS OF

Breed	Place of Origin; Present Popularity	Color; Coat	General Appearance	Size
Kuvasz *—working dog* Fig. 91.	Hungary; descended from dogs that came from Asia with the Magyars 1,000 years ago. They were the guard dogs of King Matthias, about 1458. The name "Kuvasz" is derived from the Turkish word "Kawasz," meaning a steadfast guardian. The Kuvasz Club of America was formed in 1966	*Color:* White preferred, but ivory white accepted *Coat:* Short and smooth on the head and front of the limbs, but longer on all other body parts; thick, close, and wavy; forming a ruff around the neck	A sturdily-built, white, wavy-coated dog of medium size with droop ears and long, bushy tail	*Height:* Dogs: 28–29½ in. Bitches: 26–27½ in. *Weight:* Dogs: 100–120 lb. Bitches: 75–95 lb
Labrador Retriever *—sporting dog* Fig. 92.	Newfoundland They gradually died out in Newfoundland due to the heavy dog tax The English Kennel Club recognized them as a separate breed in 1903 The Labrador has become one of the most popular gundogs in the U.S. and undisputed king in the retrieving field. Also, the breed is a favorite gundog in Australia, Great Britain, New Zealand, and South Africa	*Color:* Black, yellow, or chocolate *Coat:* Short, very dense, and without wave	A medium-sized, short-coated, black dog with small pendent ears and otter tail. A strong swimmer	*Height:* Dogs: 22½–24½ in. Bitches: 21½–23½ in. *Weight:* 60 lb
Lakeland Terrier *—terrier* Fig. 93.	England, in the Lake district around Cumberland; hence, the name. Originally, they were used for destroying the foxes that preyed on the sheep	*Color:* Blue, black, liver, black and tan, blue and tan, red, red grizzle, grizzle and tan, or wheaten *Coat:* Double coated The outercoat is hard and wiry; the undercoat is soft	A small, upstanding, rough-coated terrier, with small, V-shaped drop ears and usually a docked tail	*Height:* 14–15 in. *Weight:* Average of 17 lb
Lhasa Apso *—nonsporting dog* Fig. 94.	Tibet, in the land of the Dalai Lama; under the shadow of Mt. Everest, the highest peak in the world	*Color:* Golden, sandy, honey, dark grizzle, slate, smoke, parti-color, black, white, or brown. Because this is the Tibetan Liondog, golden or lionlike colors are preferred *Coat:* Hard and straight, of good length and very thick	A small, short-legged, shaggy dog with pendent ears and curled tail	*Height:* Dogs: 10–11 in. Bitches: 9–10 in. *Weight:* Average 15 lb

Head	Body	Tail	Character; Use	Faults or Disqualifications
Skull broad and flat; stop slight; covered with short, smooth hair *Ears:* Rather small, set well back, folded over level with the top of the skull, and lying close to the head. Covered with fine, short hair	Powerful Strong and fairly broad back; chest deep; shoulders sloping and well laid in; belly slightly drawn up; hindquarters well muscled	Set on low; moderate length with the tip curving upward; thickly covered with hair and fringed	A reliable, sensible, and hardy herding dog. A decorative, affectionate, and obedient watch and companion dog *Use:* As a herding dog in its native Hungary In the U.S., used as a watchdog and companion; primarily a one-family dog	*Faults:* Light eyes; yellowish coat color *Disqualifications:* Curled up tail; undershot or overshot bite; overly pronounced stop; matting or wiry coat; dogs smaller than 26 in., bitches smaller than 24 in.
Wide head, (sometimes they're heavy headed) with slight stop *Ears:* Hang moderately close to the head	Square body, with good balance. Wide over the loins and strong and muscular in the hindquarters	The tail is a distinctive feature of the breed. It should be very thick at the base and taper toward the tip. It is covered with a short, thick, dense coat of hair, which gives it the rounded appearance referred to as otter tail	High-spirited and easily trained gundogs; obedient and faithful *Longevity:* The oldest recorded age for a dog is attributed to an English Labrador who lived to the age of 27 years and 3 months *Use:* Retriever of both waterfowl and upland birds. Also, the breed has demonstrated its versatility by working as a guard, stock dog, police dog, children's playmate, and companion	*Faults:* Tail should not curl over back. A pink nose without pigmentation should be penalized
Fairly long, with a flat skull and barely perceptible stop *Ears:* Small; V-shaped; their fold just above the top of the skull, the inner edge close to the cheeks, and the flap pointed down	Square Back straight and short coupled; loins strong; chest deep but rather narrow; shoulders sloping; belly slightly drawn up; hindquarters strong and muscular	Set high; usually docked; carried gaily and upright, with slight curve in the direction of the head	Bold, gay, and friendly, with a self-confident, cock-of-the-walk attitude *Use:* As an earth (hunting) dog in England; and as a house dog in the U.S.	*Faults:* Tail curled over the back; paddling, moving close, or toeing in *Disqualifications:* Overshot or undershot jaw
Narrow; skull conical; stop well defined; with a head fringe falling over the eyes; whiskers and a beard *Ears:* Pendent and well feathered	Longer than high. Straight back; loins strong and straight; croup level; well ribbed up; well-developed quarters and thighs	Carried well over the back in a screw; there may be a kink at the end; well feathered	Keen watchfulness, hardy, and obedient	*Faults:* Low carriage of the tail

(Continued)

TABLE 3 (CONTINUED) BREEDS OF

Breed	Place of Origin; Present Popularity	Color; Coat	General Appearance	Size
Maltese —toy Fig. 95.	Malta, the Mediterranean Isle after which they were named. At the time of the Apostle Paul, Publius, the Roman governor of Malta, had a Maltese dog, named *Issa*, of which he was very fond	*Color:* Pure white *Coat:* Single; that is, without undercoat. It hangs long, flat, and silky over the sides, almost to the ground	A toy dog covered from head to foot with a mantle of long, silky, white hair	*Height:* 5 in. *Weight:* Under 7 lb with 4–6 lb preferred
Manchester Terrier —terrier Fig. 96. Fig. 97.	England, in the Manchester district; hence, the name. Originally, they were used for rat killing and rabbit coursing, two poor-men's sports	*Color:* Jet black and rich mahogany, which should form clear color divisions and not blend *Coat:* Smooth, short, thick, dense, close, and glossy; not soft	A small, short-haired terrier, with V-shaped, drop ears and a tail of medium length. The Manchester Terrier has a sleek, breedy look about him; he's known as the "gentleman's terrier"	There are two sizes; the standard variety, and the toy variety. The only difference between the two varieties is in their size and their ears *Weight:* 1. Standard variety, 12–22 lb. 2. Toy variety, under 12 lb
Mastiff —working dog Fig. 98.	England, where it has been bred for over 2,000 years as a watchdog. Also, the Mastiff was used for dogfighting and bull and bearbaiting in England up to 1835, at which time the sport was made illegal In 1941, the American Kennel Club recognized the Mastiff	*Color:* Apricot, silver fawn, or dark fawn brindle; in all cases with dark muzzle, ears, and nose *Coat:* Outercoat moderately coarse. Undercoat should be dense, short, and close lying	A large, massive, smooth-coated dog, with broad, square head, blunt muzzle, small drop ears, and down-carried tail	*Height:* Dogs: minimum of 30 in. Bitches: minimum of 27½ in. *Weight:* Average 185 lb
Miniature Pinscher —toy Fig. 99.	Germany It's the favorite breed of Denmark, Holland, and Italy In 1929, the Miniature Pinscher Club of America was organized	*Color:* 1. Solid red or stag red 2. Lustrous black with sharply defined tan, rust red markings on cheeks, lips, lower jaw, throat, twin spots above eyes and chest, lower half of forelegs, inside of hind legs and vent region, and lower portion of hocks and feet 3. Solid brown or chocolate with rust or yellow markings *Coat:* Smooth, hard, short, straight, lustrous, closely adhering to the body	A well-balanced, sturdy, compact, short-coupled, smooth-coated toy dog with cropped, erect ears, and a docked tail. A small version of the Doberman Pinscher	*Height:* 11–11½ in. *Weight:* 8 lb

Head	Body	Tail	Character; Use	Faults or Disqualifications
Medium length; skull slightly rounded on top; stop moderate *Ears:* Drop; low set; heavily feathered with long hair that hangs close to the head	Compact Topline level; loins strong; chest fairly deep; shoulders sloping; ribs well sprung	A long-haired plume carried gracefully over the back, with tip lying to the side over the quarter	Without fear, yet gentle mannered; lively, playful, and vigorous *Use:* As a household pet	*Faults:* Kinkiness, curliness, or woolly coat; cow hocks, or hind legs toeing in or out
Long and narrow; wedge shaped; flat, narrow, level skull *Ears:* 1. Standard variety: erect or button, small and thin. If cropped, they should be to a point and carried erect 2. Toy variety: pointed tips; naturally erect carriage	Moderately short. Back slightly arched over the strong loins; slightly sloping rump; chest deep and narrow; ribs well sprung	Moderately short; thick at the base and tapering to a point; not carried higher than the back	Lively, attractive, and intelligent, with a sensible alert temperament *Use:* Pet and house dog	*Faults:* Toy variety: blunt-tipped or "bell" ears *Disqualifications:* White in any part of the coat, forming a patch or coat measuring as much as ½ in. in its longest dimension Weight of standard variety over 22 lb Ears of toy variety cropped or cut
Skull broad and flat, with not too decided a stop; forehead well wrinkled; muzzle short, rather square, and covered with short, fine hair *Ears:* Small, V-shaped, rounded at the tips, set high and wide apart, and lying close to cheeks	Back muscular, powerful, and straight; loins broad, well muscled, and slightly arched; chest broad and deep; shoulders slightly sloping, muscular, and well laid in; ribs well sprung; belly slightly drawn up; upper thighs broad and muscular	Set on moderately high, broad at the root and tapering to the end, reaching to the hocks and carried low	A combination of grandeur and good nature, courage and docility *Use:* Guard; family dog	
Long; skull round, without pronounced stop *Ears:* Well set; upstanding (when cropped, pointed and carried erect in balance with the head)	Height and length about equal. Back strong; loins slightly arched; chest deep and oval; shoulders sloping; hindquarters straight when viewed from behind	Set high, held erect, docked ½ to 1 in.	Lively, alert, and bold; presents a neat appearance; possesses an affectionate disposition, particularly towards its master. The Miniature Pinscher has a distinct Hackney gait *Use:* As a house dog	*Faults:* Overshot or undershot jaws; ears poorly placed, low set, or hanging; tail set too low, too thin, drooping, hanging, or poorly docked; coat too long, or curly; any color other than listed *Disqualifications:* A dog of either sex measuring under 10 or over 12½ in.; thumb marks or any area of white on feet or forechest exceeding ½ in. in its longest dimension

(Continued)

TABLE 3 (CONTINUED) BREEDS OF

Breed	Place of Origin; Present Popularity	Color; Coat	General Appearance	Size
Miniature Schnauzer —*terrier* Fig. 100.	Germany, where they were developed as a guard and destroyer of vermin, especially rats. The German word for muzzle is *schnauze*, hence, Schnauzer means the breed with a beard on the muzzle Miniature Schnauzers have been bred in the U.S. since 1925. The American Miniature Schnauzer Club was formed in 1933	*Color:* Salt and pepper, black and silver, or solid black *Coat:* Double A hard, wiry outercoat, and a close undercoat	A small Schnauzer of square build, with wiry coat, small ears, docked tail, a pronounced mustache, and a beard The Miniature Schnauzer resembles his larger cousin, the Standard Schnauzer; he's just a smaller edition	*Height:* 12–14 in. *Weight:* Average 15 lb
Newfoundland —*working dog* Fig. 101.	Newfoundland, where it gained fame for saving lives in shipwrecks off Newfoundland The breed began a resurgence in America about 1935, and it has made slow and steady progress ever since	*Color:* Black A slight tinge of bronze or a splash of white on chest and toes is not objectionable *Other than black:* Any color other than black, but the preferred colors are bronze, or white and black (*Landseer*) with black head marked with narrow blaze, evenly marked saddle, and black rump extending to the tail *Coat:* Flat, dense, coarse, and oily	A large, powerful, long-coated dog with massive head, small drop ears, and long, bushy tail	*Height:* Dogs: 28 in. Bitches: 26 in. *Weight:* Dogs: 150 lb Bitches: 120 lb
Norwegian Elkhound —*hound* Fig. 102.	Norway, where, since 4000 to 5000 B.C., he has been comrade to the Vikings, guardian of lonely farms, keeper of flocks, and defender from wolves and bear. He was especially proficient in hunting elk, from which he gets his name The breed is neither old nor numerous in the U.S.	*Color:* Gray with black tips to the hairs. The color is somewhat lighter on the chest, stomach, legs, underside of tail, and around the anus. Yellowish or fawn markings are undesirable *Coat:* Topcoat rather long, straight, and harsh; undercoat soft	A medium-sized, thick-coated dog with prick ears and a tail that is curled and carried over the back.	*Height:* Dogs: 20½ in. Bitches: 19¼ in. *Weight:* Average 50 lb

DOGS AND THEIR CHARACTERISTICS

Head	Body	Tail	Character; Use	Faults or Disqualifications
Strong and elongated; wedge shaped; moderately wide between the ears, with flat forehead; a slight stop *Ears:* When cropped, they are pointed and stand erect When uncropped, the ears are small and V-shaped, folding close to the skull	Short, deep, and rectangular. Topline strong and sloping slightly from the withers to the base of the tail; chest moderately deep and broad, with well-sprung ribs; shoulders sloping and well muscled; belly well drawn up; thighs powerfully muscled	Set high, carried erect, docked	A robust, active dog of terrier type, fond of children, and a good ratter *Use:* As a family pet and guard, especially suited for town life and small quarters	*Faults:* Toyishness, raciness, or coarseness in type; undershot or overshot jaw; light and/or large and prominent eyes *Disqualifications:* Dogs or bitches under 12 in. or over 14 in.; solid white color or white patches on the body
Broad and massive, with slightly domed skull and well-developed occiput; no decided stop *Ears:* Small, set well back, lie close to the head, covered with short hair, and no fringe	Back straight, broad, and powerful; loins and croup well muscled, broad and rounded laterally; chest broad and deep; shoulders sloping and well muscled; ribs well sprung; belly a bit drawn up; thighs broad and well muscled	Strong at the base; medium length, carried low with a slight curl at the end; very thick and bushy	A natural guard and lovable companion; obedient, tractable, and intelligent; and an inherent love of water. A strong swimmer *Use:* As a guard, companion, and friend	*Faults:* Low over the loin; cow hocks; splayed or turned-out feet; tail with a kink or turned over back *Disqualifications:* Markings other than white on a solid colored dog
Broad between the ears; skull only slightly domed *Ears:* Set high, firm, and erect; higher than they are wide at the base; pointed; very mobile	Powerful, compact. Broad, deep, chest; well-sprung ribs; straight back; well-developed loins; and stomach drawn up very little	Set high; short; thickly and closely haired, but without brush; tightly curled, not carried too much to one side	A game, fearless hunter and a devoted companion *Use:* In Norway, the Norwegian Elkhound was, and still is, used for hunting elk; and as a gundog and retriever for upland game birds, notably the blackcock. In the U. S., he is used primarily as a companion or farm dog	*Disqualifications:* Pronounced variation from gray color

(Continued)

TABLE 3 (CONTINUED) BREEDS OF

Breed	Place of Origin; Present Popularity	Color; Coat	General Appearance	Size
Norwich Terrier —*terrier* Fig. 103.	England. The foundation animals of the Norwich Terrier were first introduced into England in 1880. Soon thereafter, they became the fad with undergraduates of Cambridge University. In 1936, the breed was recognized by the American Kennel Club	*Color:* All shades of red (including red wheaten), black and tan, and grizzle. White markings on the chest are allowable, but not desirable. *Coat:* Hard, wiry, straight, and close lying. Also, there's a definite undercoat	A small, rough-coated, moderately short-bodied terrier, with ears that may either be erect or dropped	*Height:* 10 in. *Weight:* 11–12 lb
Old English Sheepdog —*working dog* Fig. 104.	England, about 150 years ago; developed for the purpose of driving sheep and cattle to market. It is not known when Old English Sheepdogs were first introduced into the U.S., but classes were provided for them in the Westminster Show, in New York, in 1903. In both the U.S. and Canada, the breed has remained neither a rare dog nor a common one. Perhaps the main reason for the failure of the breed to gain great popularity in the U.S. is its heavy, dense coat, which is somewhat difficult to care for if the dog is not to look like a ragamuffin. Also, some dog owners object to the "hair blindness"	*Color:* Any shade of gray, grizzle, blue, or blue merled, with or without white markings; or in reverse. *Coat:* Profuse, but not excessive; of hard texture; shaggy, and neither straight nor curled	A medium-sized, long-coated, bobtailed dog with pendent ears and gray or blue color. A rolling, bearlike gait	*Height:* Dogs: 32 in. and above. Bitches: 28 in or above. *Weight:* Average 95 lb
Otter Hound —*hound* Fig. 105.	Although the Otter Hound is an old breed, its origin is shrouded in mystery. Both England and France contributed to the early development of the breed. Its ancestors were used for hunting otter in England as early as A.D. 1199. Otter Hounds were first brought to the U.S. about 1900. Registrations were made in 1907. The breed has not attained wide popularity in this country	*Color:* Any color or combination of colors is acceptable. The nose should be darkly pigmented, black, or liver, depending on the color of the hound. *Coat:* Thick, dense, hard, and waterproof	A large, shaggy-coated hound with long, fringed, pendent ears and a long, thick tail. The Otter Hound looks very much like a Bloodhound wearing the wrong coat	*Height:* Dogs: 24–27 in. Bitches: 22–26 in. *Weight:* Dogs: 75–115 lb Bitches: 65–100 lb

DOGS AND THEIR CHARACTERISTICS

Head	Body	Tail	Character; Use	Faults or Disqualifications
"Foxy" appearance Skull wide, slightly rounded, with good width between the ears *Ears:* Prick or drop If prick, they should be small, pointed, erect, and set well apart. If drop, they should be neat, small, with break just above the skull line	Moderately short, compact, and deep, with level topline and well-sprung ribs	Medium, docked; carriage not too gay	Game, very active, a loveable disposition, and hardy. They enjoy accompanying a mounted horseman. Despite their short legs, they have no trouble keeping up *Use:* Primarily as a house dog. Also, they make good rabbit dogs	*Faults:* Over or undershot jaw; silky or curly coat *Disqualifications:* Cropped ears
Capacious; skull squarely formed, with well-defined stop; well covered with hair which falls over the eyes *Ears:* Medium sized, carried flat to side of head, and coated moderately	Short and compact Straight back and powerful, slightly arched loins; croup strong and curved; chest broad and deep; shoulders sloping; ribs well sprung; thighs rounded and muscular	Preferably none When not born tailless, puppies should be docked at first joint when 3 to 4 days old; and it should never be longer than 1½ to 2 in. in length at maturity	A quiet, reliable, faithful, obedient, and friendly dog. Not prone to roam or fight *Use:* As a house dog Also, it can be trained as a retriever, and it makes a good sled dog	*Faults:* Long, narrow head; light colored eyes; slabsidedness; any shade of brown or fawn
Large, with a rather broad skull and high forehead *Ears:* Long, thin, and pendulous; fringed with hair	Back and loins strong, broad and straight; chest deep; and quarters powerful	Strong; covered thickly with hair; carried well up, but not curled over the back	Especially adept at hunting otter Fast and untiring in the water, where he is aided by his webbed toes and strong tail. It has great scenting powers, along with tenacity *Use:* Hunting otter But otters are seldom hunted in the U.S. Hence, those that have been imported were brought over primarily because of their novelty	*Faults:* Undershot or overshot jaw; outercoat that is soft, woolly, textured or longer than 6 in.; lack of undercoat

(Continued)

TABLE 3 (CONTINUED) BREEDS OF

Breed	Place of Origin Present Popularity	Color; Coat	General Appearance	Size
Papillon —*toy* Fig. 106.	The origin of the breed is clouded in obscurity. Some authorities class it as a Belgian breed. However, Spain, France, and England all had a hand in the development of the Papillon When carried erect, the ears of a Papillon resemble butterfly wings; hence, the name Papillon, which means butterfly Although they were exhibited for many years in the U.S., it was not until 1935 that Papillons were represented in the American Kennel Club by their own breed club, the Papillon Club of America	*Color:* White with colored markings which may be of any color except liver. Head markings should be symmetrical, and the white blaze on the face should be clearly defined. Head markings and blaze are preferable, but not essential *Coat:* Abundant, long, fine, silky, flowing, straight, flat on back and sides of body. No undercoat	A small, long-haired toy dog distinguished from other breeds by its beautiful butterflylike ears	*Height:* 8–11 in. *Weight:* 4 to 7 lb
Pekingese —*toy* Fig. 107.	China, where it was the *Sacred Lion Dog* of Chinese emperors for 2,000 years. The exact date of its origin is unknown, but record of its existence can be traced to the Tang Dynasty of the eighth century. The oldest strains were kept pure, and the theft of one of these sacred dogs was a criminal offense, punishable by death. It is also noteworthy that the Pekingese played an important role in Chinese Buddhist art The Pekingese Club of America became a member of the American Kennel Club in 1909. The breed is very popular in America. Also, it is the favorite toy breed in Australia, Germany, South Africa, Sweden, and Great Britain	*Color:* All colors allowable Red, fawn, black, black and tan, sable, brindle, white; with or without white markings, or parti-color. In solid colors, a black muzzle is desirable *Coat:* Long, straight and flat, rather coarse; feather long and profuse on thighs, legs, tail, and toes; mane profuse, extending beyond the shoulder blades, forming ruff or frill around the neck	A long-bodied, short-legged little dog with profuse coat, medium-sized ears and long, well-plumed tail. Looks like a lion because of its massive front, heavy mane, and tapering hindquarters; hence, sometimes referred to as "the little lion dog of Peking"	*Height:* Average 6 in. *Weight:* Maximum of 14 lb

DOGS AND THEIR CHARACTERISTICS

Head	Body	Tail	Character; Use	Faults or Disqualifications
Small, skull of medium width and slightly rounded between the ears; stop well defined *Ears:* Large with rounded tips and set on the sides and toward the back of the head; may be either erect or drop type 1. *Erect type* — carried obliquely and move like the spread wings of a butterfly. When alert, each ear forms an angle of approximately 45 degrees to the head 2. *Drop type* — similar to erect type, but ears are carried drooping and must be completely down	Back rather long and straight; loins only slightly arched; chest fairly deep; shoulders sloping and well laid in; ribs not too round; belly slightly drawn up; hindquarters well developed	Set high, long, carried well arched over the body, with the plume hanging to either side of the body	Friendly, lively, and hardy *Use:* As a house dog	*Faults:* Overshot or undershot mouth; ears small, pointed, set too high, one ear up, or ears partly down; tail low set or not arched over back; height over 11 in. (over 12 in. disqualifies) *Disqualifications:* Over 12 in. high; liver color, coat of solid color, all white, or one with no white, white patches on ears or around eyes; pink, spotted, or liver colored nose
Skull massive, broad, wide and flat between the ears (not domeshaped); wide between the eyes; eyes large, dark, and prominent; stop deep; muzzle wrinkled, very short, and broad *Ears:* Heart shaped, not set too high, leather never long enough to come below the muzzle, not carried erect, but rather drooping, with long feather	Heavy in front, broad chest, falling away behind the shoulders, to give a lionlike shape. Back level; not too long a body; hindquarters comparatively light	Set high; lying well over the back to either side; long, profuse, straight feather	Lively, intelligent, independent, loyal, and regal. Not afraid of the devil himself; they have never been known to turn tail and run *Use:* House dog and pet	*Faults:* Protruding tongue; badly blemished eye; overshot; wry mouth *Disqualifications:* Over 14 lb; dudley nose

(Continued)

TABLE 3 (CONTINUED) BREEDS OF

Breed	Place of Origin; Present Popularity	Color; Coat	General Appearance	Size
Pointer —*sporting dog* Fig. 108.	England, from Spanish Pointers taken to England about 1650. Pointers have been popular in America since 1876	*Color:* Liver, lemon, black, orange; either solid colored or in combination with white. *Coat:* Short, flat	A large, refined, symmetrically built, short-haired dog, with pendent ears and lashing tail	Balance and symmetry are more important than size, for the Pointer is an athlete. *Height:* Dogs: 25–28 in. Bitches: 23–26 in. *Weight:* Dogs: 55–75 lb Bitches: 45–65 lb
Pomeranian —*toy* Fig. 109.	Descended from the sled dogs of Iceland and Lapland. However, the name traces to the Duchy of Pomerania, a territory of Germany, where the breed was probably reduced in size. Pomeranians were first exhibited in the U.S. in 1892, although the first importation of the breed came in in 1899. Today, the Pomeranian ranks among the nation's twenty most popular breeds, based on registrations	*Color:* Any solid color; any solid color with lighter or darker shadings of the same color; any solid color with sable or black shadings; parti-color; sable; and black and tan. *Coat:* Two coats. The undercoat should be soft and fluffy. The outercoat should be long, straight, and glistening. In judging the breed, the coat is the most important single factor	A compact, short-coupled dog with long hair, a fox-shaped head, and a profusely-haired tail which is turned over the back and carried flat. A miniature copy of the Baltic sled dog	*Height:* 7 in. *Weight:* 3 to 7 lb, with the ideal 4 to 5 lb
Poodle —*nonsporting dog* Fig. 110. Fig. 111.	Most likely of German origin, where it was developed as a water retriever. However, the Poodle is the national dog of France. Also, it is a favorite breed in the U.S., Canada, Denmark, and Sweden; and the favorite non-sporting breed in Germany, Austria, and Italy. The Poodle is the most popular dog in the U.S.	*Color:* In blues, grays, silvers, browns, cafe-au-laits, apricots, and creams, the coats may show varying shades of the same color. *Coat:* Very profuse, dense, and of harsh texture. There are two types of coats, the curly and the corded. The show clips are: "puppy" clip, "continental" clip, and "English saddle" clip. Poodles under one year of age may be shown with the "puppy" clip; whereas dogs one year old or over must be shown with either the "continental" clip or the "English saddle" clip	A lively, attractive dog which is usually clipped and docked. Fashion decrees that Poodles be clipped	Three sizes: 1. *Standard*— over 15 in. 2. *Miniature*— 10–15 in. 3. *Toy*— 10 in. or under Average 7 lb The words *standard, miniature,* and *toy* are used to denote size only; the rest of the standards are the same

Head	Body	Tail	Character; Use	Faults or Disqualifications
Long head, with square jaws A pronounced stop midway between nostrils and occiput *Ears:* Set on at eye level; when hanging naturally, they should be close to the head, with little or no folding, and should extend just below the lower jaw; should be somewhat pointed at the tip—never round	A strong, muscular back, with a slight raise; a slightly tucked up appearance	Heavy at the root and tapering to a point. Carried straight, preferably level with the back	Full of energy; even temperament; speed; endurance; ability to concentrate on his job *Use:* A gundog They will work satisfactorily for someone other than their own master	*Faults:* Lack of true pointer type; hound or terrier characteristics; timid or unruly; long hair or curl; soft silky coat; weak or washed-out colors; light nose on a dark colored dog; faulty gait
Foxy in outline, or wedge shaped; skull slightly flat and large in proportion to muzzle; slight stop; hair on head and face smooth and short coated *Ears:* Small, carried perfectly erect, and covered with short, soft hair	Compact Back short and level; chest fairly deep and not too broad; shoulders well laid in; well ribbed up, and barrel well rounded	The tail is characteristic of the breed. It should be set high, turned over the back and carried flat, and profusely covered with long, spreading hair	Diminutive size, docile temper, and a vivacious spirit *Use:* House dog and pet	
Moderately rounded, with a definite stop; muzzle long, straight and fine, with slight chiseling under the eyes *Ears:* Set low and hanging close to the head; leather long, wide, and heavily feathered	Back short, strong, and slightly hollowed; loins short, broad, and muscular; chest deep and moderately wide; ribs well sprung	Set high; docked to sufficient length to insure a balanced outline; carried high	The Poodle is one of the most intelligent of the canine race. In fact, there is something more human than canine about most Poodles; and this quality makes them unique among dogs, and enchanting as companions *Use:* As a companion	*Major faults:* Eyes round, protruding, large, or very light; jaws undershot or overshot, or wry mouth; cow hocks; feet flat or spread; tail set low, curled, or carried over the back; shyness or sharpness *Disqualifications:* Parti-colored; clips other than those listed under coat; not within the height range listed under size

(Continued)

TABLE 3 (CONTINUED) BREEDS OF

Breed	Place of Origin; Present Popularity	Color; Coat	General Appearance	Size
Pug —*toy* Fig. 112.	Probably a native of China Taken to Holland, then developed in Britain Today, the Pug ranks among the twenty most popular breeds in America	*Color:* Silver, apricot fawn, or black *Coat:* Fine, soft, short, and glossy; neither hard nor woolly	A small, short-haired dog with rounded head, short, compressed muzzle, small button or rose ears, and curled tail. They look somewhat like a Bulldog in miniature	*Height:* Not over 12 in. *Weight:* 14 to 18 lb
Puli —*working dog* Fig. 113.	Hungary, where the Puli has been the helper and companion of Hungarian shepherds for 1,000 years In the 1930s, the Puli began to appear in America. The American Kennel Club approved a standard for the breed in 1936	*Color:* Solid colors of black, rusty black, various shades of gray, or white *Coat:* Long and matted in cords; completely covering the head, muzzle, and eyes	A squarely built, medium-sized dog with a shaggy coat, pendent ears, and fairly long, often curled tail	*Height:* Dogs: 17–19 in. Bitches: 16–18 in. *Weight:* Average 30 lb
Rhodesian Ridgeback —*hound* Fig. 114.	They were developed in South Africa. However, they were taken to Rhodesia in 1877, from which country they were named In 1950, the Rhodesian Ridgeback Club of America was formed; and, in 1959, the breed was admitted to the American Kennel Club *Stud Book.* Although a newcomer to the U.S., the Ridgeback has won many admirers	*Color:* Light wheaten to red wheaten *Coat:* Short, dense, sleek, and glossy; but neither woolly nor silky	A large, powerful, active, short-haired hound with moderately long, pendent ears and long tail, whose most distinctive characteristic is the ridge of wrong-way hair on the back	*Height:* Dogs: 25–27 in. Bitches: 24–26 in. *Weight:* Dogs: 75 lb Bitches: 65 lb
Rottweiler —*working dog* Fig. 115.	Germany, in and around the town of Rottweil from which they take their name The Rottweiler was developed from the cattle dogs that helped drive the Roman invader's livestock over the Alps They were first brought to the U.S. in limited numbers in the early 1930s. The breed was recognized by the American Kennel Club in 1935	*Color:* Black, with tan or mahogany brown markings on cheeks, muzzle, chest, legs, and over both eyes *Coat:* Short, coarse, and flat Undercoat required on neck and thighs, but should not show through outercoat	Above average size; strong; short-coated, black and tan; small drop ears; and short, docked tail The Rottweiler somewhat resembles the Doberman Pinscher, although it is heavier, slower, and less volatile than the Doberman	*Height:* Dogs: 23¾–27 in. Bitches: 21¾–25¾ in. *Weight:* Average 85 lb

DOGS AND THEIR CHARACTERISTICS

Head	Body	Tail	Character; Use	Faults or Disqualifications
Large, massive, round—not apple headed, with well-marked stop and well-wrinkled forehead *Ears:* There are two kinds— 1. rose 2. button The latter is preferred	Short and cobby Back short, broad, straight, and strong; loins short, broad, and well muscled; chest wide and deep with well-sprung ribs; shoulders well laid; thighs strong	Curled tightly over the hip The double curl is perfection	A very intelligent, faithful, affectionate, obedient, easy-to-keep pet and companion *Use:* A house dog The Pug requires less care than the other members of the toy group	
Medium size; skull short, narrow, and slightly domed; completely covered with long hair *Ears:* Hanging, medium sized, V-shaped, covered with long hair	Square Back medium length, straight, and level; loins broad; rump sloping moderately; chest deep and fairly broad; ribs well sprung; middle well tucked up	Bushy Either carried low with end curled up or curled over the back. Occasionally born bobtail	Vigorous, alert, very active; affectionate and devoted *Use:* In its native land, the Puli is a herder and drover; in other countries it is a pet and house dog	*Faults:* Overshot or undershot; short or sparse coat, lack of undercoat; white markings; flesh color on nose, flews, or eyelids
Fair length, with a flat skull and rather broad between the ears; free from wrinkles; the stop fairly well defined *Ears:* Set high; medium size; rather wide at the base, and tapering to a rounded point; carried close to the head	Back powerful; loins strong, muscular, and slightly arched; chest not too wide, but very deep; ribs moderately well sprung, but not rounded	Strong at the root and tapering to a point; carried with a slight curve upward	This big hound has a fine tracking nose combined with a volatile temperament *Use:* In its native land, it is used to hunt big game, especially lions	
Medium length, skull broad between the ears, stop and occiput well pronounced *Ears:* Small, set on high, and wide apart	Somewhat long. Back straight and strong; loins short and strong; croup broad and sloping slightly; chest deep and broad; shoulders long and sloping; belly not drawn up; thighs muscular	Either born with a short stump tail or docked	Bold and loyal. Not suspicious, bad tempered, or noisy *Use:* As a guard and protector	*Faults:* Light or flesh colored nose; overshot or undershot; heavy, long, narrow, or rose ears; too long or too thin tail; white markings

(Continued)

TABLE 3 (CONTINUED) BREEDS OF

Breed	Place of Origin; Present Popularity	Color; Coat	General Appearance	Size
St. Bernard —*working dog* Fig. 116.	The origin of the St. Bernard is debatable, but the first records of the breed can be traced to the Swiss Alps, in 1707. Presumably, the breed takes its name from the noted Monk, Bernard de Menthon. As the rescue dog of the Swiss Alps, they have saved thousands of lives in the 300 years use at St. Bernard Hospice The St. Bernard Club of America was organized in 1888	*Color:* White with red, or red with white; or brindle patches with white markings. White markings are necessary: white blaze, and white on the chest, neck, nose, feet, and tail tip; and black shadings on the face and ears *Coat:* There are two types of coats: (1) short haired, and (2) long haired. Both types are similar, except that the coat of the long haired type is of medium length and plain to slightly wavy. On both types, the tail is bushy	A large, powerful, tall dog, with smooth or long coat, massive head, pendent ears, and long tail	*Height:* Dogs: 27½ in. minimum Bitches: 25½ in. minimum *Weight:* Up to 200 lb
Saluki —*hound* Fig. 117.	The Saluki probably originated in Syria. It is the oldest pure breed in the world, having been a distinct breed and type as long ago as 329 B.C., when Alexander the Great invaded India. The word "Saluki" is Arabic. The Arab referred to his Saluki as *el hor,* meaning "the noble one" The Saluki was officially recognized by the American Kennel Club in 1927. Today, it is a familiar sight in the dog world, and no longer a curiosity. It is becoming more and more popular each year	*Color:* White, cream, fawn, golden, red, grizzle, and tan, tricolor (white, black, and tan) and black and tan *Coat:* Smooth and of a soft, silky texture; slight feather on the legs, feather at the back of the thighs, and sometimes slightly woolly feather on the thigh and shoulder. There is a smooth variety of Saluki, which has no feathering	A medium to large dog with a short coat, blunt, wedge-shaped skull, pendent ears, and a long tail	*Height:* Average 23–28 in. *Weight:* Average 60 lb
Samoyed —*working dog* Fig. 118.	The early development of the Samoyed took place in Iran. But their nomadic masters were forced north to Siberia (the U.S.S.R.) where they have lived for centuries, with the Samoyed serving as their pet, sled dog, and reindeer herder The breed was introduced to America soon after 1900. Several importations were made from 1936 to 1943	*Color:* Pure white, white and biscuit, (beige), cream, or all biscuit *Coat:* Doublecoated The undercoat should be soft, short, thick, and close; and the outercoat should be straight	A medium-sized, long-coated dog, most commonly white in color, with small prick ears and bushy tail which is usually carried over the back	*Height:* Dogs: 21–23½ in. Bitches: 19–21 in. *Weight:* Average 55 lb

DOGS AND THEIR CHARACTERISTICS

Head	Body	Tail	Character; Use	Faults or Disqualifications
Large and massive with somewhat domed skull; cheek muscles well developed and powerful; distinct furrow between eyes; and skin of forehead wrinkled. Stop abrupt and well defined *Ears:* Medium size, set on fairly high; falling close to the cheeks; lobes rounded and triangular	Back broad and straight; croup sloping slightly; chest deep; shoulders sloping, muscular; ribs well rounded and deep; belly only slightly drawn up; thighs well muscled	Well set on, carried low, with the last third of its length curved somewhat upward	Famous as "the good samaritan dog"; an excellent pathfinder in the snow, with an uncanny sense of smell for finding helpless persons. Placid disposition; gentle with children *Use:* As a companion, and for rescue work in the Alps	*Faults:* Overshot bite
Long and narrow; skull moderately wide between the ears, not domed; stop not pronounced *Ears:* Set on high; 5 to 6 in. long; hanging close to the skull and mobile; and covered with long, silky hair	Back long and slightly arched from back of the withers; loins not overloaded with muscle; croup sloping slightly; chest deep and broad; ribs flat; belly drawn up; shoulders sloping and muscular; hindquarters very muscular	Long; set on low and carried naturally in a curve; well feathered on the underside with long, silky hair, but not bushy	The Saluki is a fast dog that hunts largely by sight. He has been called the "Persian Greyhound." The Saluki shows great attachment to his master; he's affectionate, without being demonstrative *Use:* Originally, the Arabs used the Sáluki to bring down gazelle, the fastest of antelopes. They were likely used on jackals, foxes, hares, and wild boars, also In the U.S., the Saluki is esteemed as a show dog and companion	
Wedge shaped; broad and flat across the creaseless forehead *Ears:* Small, triangular, set wide apart, erect with thick cartilage and slightly rounded tips	Back short and broad; loins broad and powerful; croup long and broad; chest broad and deep; withers high and well defined; shoulders sloping; ribs well sprung; flanks deep	Moderately long; profusely covered with long hair; carried forward over the back or side when alert, but sometimes dropped when at rest	Faithful, obedient, and adaptable; beautiful and glamorous *Use:* Guard and watchdog; sled dog; herder	*Faults:* Unsound stifles or cow hocks; oversize or undersize; choppy or stilted gait; overshot or undershot *Disqualifications:* Any other color than pure white, cream, biscuit, or white and biscuit. Blue eyes (Continued)

99

TABLE 3 (CONTINUED) BREEDS OF

Breed	Place of Origin; Present Popularity	Color; Coat	General Appearance	Size
Schipperke —*nonsporting dog* Fig. 119.	Belgium But the name *Schipperke* is Flemish for "little captain" The breed was first imported to America in 1888	*Color:* Solid black *Coat:* Short, dense, and hard Shorter and softer on the head and ears; longer on the neck, chest, and back of the thighs. Also, a dense short undercoat	A small, black, dense-coated, tailless dog, with a well-developed mane and small prick ears	*Height:* 12 in. *Weight:* Under 18 lb
Scottish Deerhound —*hound* Fig. 120.	Scotland, where as early as the sixteenth and seventeenth centuries, he was the hunter of stags and the companion of Highland Chieftains. Because of its suitability to pursue and kill deer, it was named "deerhound" In 1927, the breed was officially recognized by the American Kennel Club. They are limited in numbers	*Color:* Dark blue gray, dark or light gray, brindle, yellow, sandy or red fawn, with black mask and ears *Coat:* Hard and wiry, from 3 to 4 in. long; ragged and rough—not woolly or silky. Slightly fringed behind the legs	A very large, rugged, rough-coated dog with small drop ears and low-carried tail. It resembles a rough-coated Greyhound of larger size and bone	*Height:* Dogs: 30–32 in. Bitches: 28 in. *Weight:* Dogs: 85–110 lb Bitches: 75–95 lb
Scottish Terrier —*terrier* Fig. 121.	Considerable speculation surrounds the early origin and early history of the Scottish Terrier, with England and Scotland vying for the honor. In 1882, the Scottish Terrier Club was organized, with joint officers for England and Scotland. Later, separate clubs were organized in the two countries, but they have always worked harmoniously together The first importation of the Scottish Terrier was brought into the U.S. in 1883. The first Scottish Terrier registered in America was "Dake," a brindle dog whelped in 1884	*Color:* Steel or iron gray, brindled or grizzled, black sandy, or wheaten. White markings are objectionable and can be allowed only on the chest and that to a slight extent *Coat:* Rather short, about 2 in.; outercoat very harsh and wiry; undercoat dense	A small, compact, heavily-built, short-legged terrier, with a strong, bearded head, high-set prick ears, and a gaily carried tail	*Height:* 10 in. *Weight:* Dogs: 19–22 lb Bitches: 18–21 lb

DOGS AND THEIR CHARACTERISTICS

Head	Body	Tail	Character; Use	Faults or Disqualifications
Foxlike Skull wide between the ears, narrowing over the eyes, and tapering to the tip of the nose. Wedge shaped with moderate stop *Ears:* Very erect, small, triangular, placed high, strong enough not to be capable of being lowered except in line with the body	Short, thick set, and cobby. Broad behind the shoulders; back strong, short, and level or slightly sloping to the rump; loins muscular; chest broad and deep, with well-sprung ribs and belly drawn up; hindquarters somewhat lighter than forequarters	Either born tailless or docked to no more than 1 in. in length	A merry and attractive family companion, especially good with children. Also, a good guard and a keen hunter of rabbits and small vermin *Use:* House dog and watchdog	*Faults:* Light eyes; ears too long or too rounded; smooth, short coat with short ruff and culotte; lack of undercoat; curly or silky coat; body coat more than 3 in. long; overshot or undershot; cow hocks *Disqualifications:* Any color other than solid black; drop or semierect ears; badly overshot or undershot
Long; broad at the ears, narrowing slightly to the eyes; and a flat skull *Ears:* Set on high; small; folded toward the rear and carried low, except when the dog is excited when they may be raised semierect; covered with fine glossy hair; black or dark colored	Back and loins well arched; croup sloping to root of tail; chest deep but not broad; shoulders sloping; thighs muscular; hips prominent	Very long and thin, reaching to about 2 in. from the ground. In repose, carried straight down or curved. In excitement, may be curled, but never carried over back	Tremendous courage in the chase; gentle dignity in the home. He has fine powers of scent and is a good tracker; and he is friendly, tractable, easily trained, and devoted and loyal to his master *Use:* In the U.S., the Scottish Deerhound is used as a companion	*Faults:* Straight shoulders; curl or ring tail *Disqualifications:* White blaze on the head, or a white collar
Long, of medium width; skull nearly flat with slight but distinct stop; covered with short hard hair *Ears:* Small, prick, set well up on the skull, rather pointed but not cut	Moderately short and well ribbed up. Strong loins, deep flanks, and very muscular hindquarters	Never cut; about 7 in long; carried with a slight curve but not over the back	Independent nature and philosophical disposition; self-confident; courageous *Use:* As a companion	*Faults:* Soft coat; round or very light eye; overshot or undershot jaw; oversize or undersize; failure to show with head and tail up

(Continued)

101

TABLE 3 (CONTINUED) BREEDS OF

Breed	Place of Origin; Present Popularity	Color; Coat	General Appearance	Size
Sealyham Terrier —terrier Fig. 122.	Wales The breed derives its name from Sealyham, Wales, where it was developed between 1850 and 1891. Originally, it was used for quarrying badger, otter, and fox The Sealyham Terrier was recognized by the American Kennel Club in 1911. Today, it is one of the nation's most popular breeds	*Color:* White, with lemon, tan, or badger markings on head and ears *Coat:* A soft, dense undercoat and a hard, wiry topcoat	A sturdy, powerfully-built, short-legged, white, rough-coated terrier with a rather large head, medium-sized drop ears, and a docked tail carried upright	*Height:* 10½ in. *Weight:* Dogs: 21 lb Bitches: 20 lb
Shetland Sheepdog (Sheltie) —working dog Fig. 123.	Shetland Isles, the land of small breeds It traces to the Border Collie of Scotland, but it is a separate and distinct breed Shetland Sheep dogs were first introduced to America in 1911. Today, the Sheltie is firmly entrenched in America, as a companion and working dog. Range sheep operators have found them well suited to herding duties	*Color:* Black, blue merle, and sable (ranging from golden through mahogany); marked with varying amounts of white and/or tan *Coat:* A double coat. The outercoat should consist of long, straight, harsh hair. The undercoat should be short, furry, and dense	A small, long-coated dog with narrow skull, drop ears, and long, handsome tail. It's a working Collie in miniature	*Height:* 13–16 in. *Weight:* Average 16 lb
Shih Tzu —toy Fig. 124.	Tibet The Delai Lamas gave them to the emperors of China, who used them as pets. The name Shih Tzu means "lion" in Chinese The Shih Tzu was recognized by the American Kennel Club in 1969. The breed is increasing in numbers in the U.S.	*Color:* All colors permissible *Coat:* A luxurious, long, dense topcoat. May be slightly wavy but not curly. Woolly undercoat	A short-legged, rather long dog, with long pendent ears. Moves with its head well up, tail carried gaily over the back, and a distinctly arrogant carriage	*Height:* 9–10½ in. *Weight:* 12–15 lb

DOGS AND THEIR CHARACTERISTICS

Head	Body	Tail	Character; Use	Faults or Disqualifications
Long, broad, powerful; broad between the ears, with slightly domed skull and a moderate stop *Ears:* Folded level with top of head, and with forward edge close to cheek; well rounded at tip; long enough to reach outer corner of eye; thin	Noticeably longer than high; back, loins, and croup straight and broad; chest deep and wide; shoulders sloping; hindquarters powerful	Docked and carried upward	A plucky, courageous, easily-trained dog *Use:* A house companion	*Faults:* Overshot or undershot; white, cherry, or butterfly nose; prick, tulip, rose, or hound ears; thin, spread, or flat feet; capped or cow hocks
Long with flat skull; narrowing toward the eyes, and with slight stop *Ears:* Small and flexible, placed high, carried three-fourths erect, with tips breaking forward. In repose, the ears fold lengthwise and are thrown back into the frill	Moderately long. Straight back and powerful loins; chest deep with well-sprung ribs; shoulders well laid in; thighs muscular	Set on low; long; abundant hair; carried low with an upward curve at the tip	They obey willingly and naturally, and they guard property and places well, with watch-dog warning *Use:* Sheep dog; pet and house dog	*Faults:* Coat short, flat, wavy, curly, soft, or silky; too-angled head; overshot or undershot *Disqualifications:* Heights above or below the desired range, i.e. 13–16 in. Brindle color
Broad and round; wide between the eyes; stop definite; muzzle square and short; covered with long hair *Ears:* Large; long leathers; carried drooping; set slightly below the crown of the skull; so heavily coated that they appear to blend with the hair of the neck	Strong, longer than high Back and loins straight; chest broad and deep; shoulders well laid in; fore and hind legs short, heavy boned, and muscular	Set on high; heavily plumed; curved well over the back; carried gaily	Active and alert; attractive in temperament and character *Use:* Indoor guards; family pets	*Faults:* Narrow head, lack of definite stop, snipiness, pink on nose or eye rims, small or light eyes; legginess; sparse coat

(Continued)

103

TABLE 3 (CONTINUED) BREEDS OF

Breed	Place of Origin; Present Popularity	Color; Coat	General Appearance	Size
Siberian Husky (Siberian Chuchi) —*working dog* Fig. 125.	Siberia (U.S.S.R.), where they have been kept pure for untold centuries, and where the natives used them as beasts of burden, as guards for their possessions, and as companions for their children The name "Husky" was given to the Eskimos by the early North American explorers; hence, the name of their dogs, Siberian Huskies The first Siberian Huskies were imported to Alaska in 1909 for sled dog racing purposes. Next to the Samoyed, he is the most popular of the Arctic sled dogs in America	*Color:* All colors from black to pure white; and all markings *Coat:* Double The undercoat is dense, soft, and downy. The outcoat is usually medium length, thick, smooth textured, and soft	A medium-sized dog, moderately compact and powerfully built, with erect ears, a well-furred body, and brush tail curved over the back	*Height:* Dogs: 21–23½ in. Bitches: 20–22 in. *Weight:* Dogs: 45–60 lb Bitches: 35–50 lb
Silky Terrier —*toy* Fig. 126.	Australia, where it has long been a house dog The Silky Terrier was admitted for registry in the American Kennel Club *Stud Book* in 1959	*Color:* Blue and tan *Coat:* Fine, glossy, and silky; flat, 5 to 6 in. long on mature dogs; forming a topknot on the head. The hair is parted on the head and down over the back to the root of the tail	A lightly-built, low-set, long, silky-haired toy dog with the pronounced terrier spirit	*Height:* 9–10 in. *Weight:* 8–10 lb
Skye Terrier —*terrier* Fig. 127.	Scotland, on the misty Isle of Skye, from which it takes its name In the U.S., the Skye has been surpassed in popularity by many of the modern breeds of terriers, primarily because the coat requires much attention. But it retains great popularity in Scotland and England	*Color:* Black, blue, dark or light gray, silver, platinum, fawn, or cream. Black points of ears, muzzle, and tip of tail desirable *Coat:* Double. Undercoat short, close, soft, and woolly. Outercoat 5½ in. long, hard, straight, and flat	A profusely coated, long-bodied, short-legged terrier, with prick or drop ears, feathered head, and long, feathered tail	*Height:* 10 in. *Weight:* Average 25 lb

Head	Body	Tail	Character; Use	Faults or Disqualifications
Of medium size, in proportion to the body; skull rather broad between the ears and slightly domed, narrowing toward the eyes *Ears:* Medium size, set high, carried erect, moderately rounded at the tips, and well furred on the inner side	Moderately compact Chest deep and moderately wide; ribs well sprung; shoulders sloping and powerful; back of medium length, level, and strong; loins slightly raised	A well-furred brush carried over the back in a sickle curve when the dog runs or stands at attention, and trailing out behind when working or in repose	A willing and hardy sled dog, and a trustworthy house dog. The Siberian Husky is a very clean dog, free from dog odors *Use:* As a sled dog, or house dog The Siberian Husky is considered to be the toughest draft dog that lives, pound for pound	*Faults:* Ears not strongly erect; cow hocks; long, rough, or shaggy coat, texture too harsh or too silky *Disqualifications:* Height over 23½ in. in dogs; over 22 in. in bitches
Strong, wedge shaped, and moderately long; skull slightly longer than muzzle, flat, and not too wide between the ears; stop shallow *Ears:* Set high, small, V-shaped, and pricked	Low set and moderately long. Top line strong, rounding over the loins, brisket medium wide, and deep	Set high; carried erect or semi-erect, but not too gay; docked; well coated but devoid of plume	Keenly alert, quick, friendly, and responsive *Use:* A house dog and pet	*Faults:* Shyness or excessive nervousness; toeing in or out; light eyes; markedly overshot or undershot
Long and powerful; skull broad across the forehead and tapering gradually to a strong muzzle; slight stop *Ears:* Either prick or drop; symmetrical and gracefully carried	Very long and low Backline level; chest deep; ribs well sprung, but sides appear flat due to straight falling and profuse coat	Long and well feathered; normally carried low	Fearless, goodtempered, loyal, and canny; friendly and gay with those he knows and reserved and cautious with strangers *Use:* Show dog and/or companion	

(Continued)

TABLE 3 (CONTINUED) BREEDS OF

Breed	Place of Origin; Present Popularity	Color; Coat	General Appearance	Size
Standard Schnauzer —*working dog* *Fig. 128.*	Germany, where the breed has been popular since the fifteenth century; used as a ratter, farm guard, and cattle dog The Standard Schnauzer has been in America since 1905. The Schnauzer Club of America was founded in 1925	*Color:* Pepper and salt or pure black *Coat:* Tight, hard, wiry, and thick. The undercoat is soft and close; the outercoat is neither short nor close lying	A medium-sized dog of square build, with rough coat, small ears, docked tail, arched eyebrows, bristly mustache, and a beard	Midway between large breeds and toys *Height:* Dogs: 18½–19½ in. Bitches: 17½–18½ in. *Weight:* 35 lb
Sussex Spaniel —*sporting dog* *Fig. 129.*	Sussex, England Specimens of the breed competed in Britain as early as 1862. It has been in America since the 1880s. But the breed has never been popular, perhaps due to their lack of speed desired by our sportsmen	*Color:* Rich golden liver *Coat:* Abundant, flat or slightly waved, with no tendency to curl, moderately well feathered on legs and tail, but clean below the hocks	A low-set, rather massive golden liver colored dog with large ears and docked tail	*Height:* 15–16 in. *Weight:* 35–45 lb
Vizsla —*sporting dog* *Fig. 130.*	Hungary, where the breed is known as the Hungarian Pointer. In the Hungarian language, the word "vizsla" means "alert or responsive" In 1960, the Vizsla was admitted to the *Field Dog Stud Book,* and joined the breeds registered in the American Kennel Club *Stud Book.* Because of being a newcomer, the breed is still relatively rare in the U.S. But they are giving a good account of themselves in the shooting field, in field trials, and in dog shows; hence, they are growing more popular day by day	*Color:* Solid Rusty gold or rather dark sandy yellow in different shades, with darker shades preferred *Coat:* Short, smooth, dense, and close lying, without woolly undercoat	A medium-sized, lightly-built, short-haired dog with long ears and docked tail. They are Pointer in type	*Height:* Dogs: 22–24 in. Bitches: 21–23 in. *Weight:* Average about 65 lb

Head	Body	Tail	Character; Use	Faults or Disqualifications
Strong, elongated, and wedge shaped; size in proportion to body *Ears:* Set high, cropped to a point, and carried erect. When uncropped, they are small, V-shaped, button ears, carried high and close to the head. In Germany, the ears must be cropped. In America, both cropped and natural ears are permitted, so as to comply with different state laws	Square Back strong and straight; loins well developed; chest moderately deep and broad; shoulders sloping and well laid in; ribs well sprung; belly well drawn up; thighs powerfully muscled	Set high; carried erect; docked to not less than 1 in. nor more than 2 in.	Affectionate, adaptable, stable, good natured, intelligent, and responsive. A reliable guard and natural enemy to vermin. Makes a tractable companion *Use:* As a house dog and guard, and as a ratter	*Faults:* Overshot or undershot mouth; squirrel tail; soft, smooth, curly, wavy, shaggy, or too long or too short coat; shy or highly nervous dogs *Disqualifications:* Vicious dogs Dogs under 18 in. or over 20 in. in height; bitches under 17 in. or over 19 in.
Moderately long, with broad skull, definite central furrow, and a decided stop; occiput full *Ears:* Thick, fairly large and lobe shaped; set moderately low; carried close to the head and covered with soft, wavy hair	Low, long, and level. Back and loins long and muscular; ribs deep	Set low, not carried above the level of the back, thickly covered with moderately long feather, and docked from 5 to 7 in.	A reliable gundog, easily managed, inclined to give tongue on scent. Nice tail action, indicative of a cheerful and tractable disposition *Use:* Upland shooting Skilled in working dense cover	
Refined and clean; skull slightly domed, rather shorter than the muzzle, with moderate stop *Ears:* Set on low, proportionately long, with rounded tips; lying close to the cheeks	Square appearing Short back, high withers, and slightly rounded over the loins	Set just below the level of the back; thick at the root and tapering to a point; one-third docked off	An excellent nose; careful ranging and tracking ability; and a reliable retriever *Use:* As a hunting dog, with the combined ability to find and point game and to serve as a retriever. Also, he is a tractable and an affectionate companion in the home	*Faults:* Dark brown and pale yellow are undesirable. Hare feet are objectionable *Disqualifications:* Deviation of more than 2 in. in height above or below the standard

(Continued)

107

TABLE 3 (CONTINUED) BREEDS OF

Breed	Place of Origin; Present Popularity	Color; Coat	General Appearance	Size
Weimaraner —*sporting dog* *Fig. 131.*	Germany, in the German Court of Weimar in the 1800s Originally, the Weimaraner was used as a big game dog. But with the demise of big game hunting in Germany, the breed was trained as a bird dog. The first pair of Weimaraners was brought to the U.S. in 1929. The "Gray Ghost," as the breed has been dubbed in this country, is still very limited in numbers. Moreover, its owners would have it remain that way, because the Weimaraner Club of America, which is perhaps the nation's most exclusive dog club, confines ownership to those who meet certain qualifications	*Color:* Solid color, in shades of mouse gray to silver gray, usually blending to lighter shades on the head and ears. A small white mark on the chest is permitted *Coat:* Short, smooth, and sleek	A large, gray dog with moderately long ears and docked tail The Weimaraner is a striking dog in appearance	Large size *Height:* Dogs: 25–27 in. Bitches: 23–25 in. *Weight:* Dogs: 65–85 lb Bitches: 55–75 lb
Welsh Corgi (Cardigan) —*working dog* *Fig. 132.*	Wales, in the high country now known as Cardiganshire, from which it takes its name, and where it has been known for 3,000 years The Welsh Corgi is relatively rare in the U.S. There are two distinct breeds of Welsh Corgi, the Cardigan and the Pembroke. The latter is the most popular	*Color:* Red, sable, red brindle, black, tricolor, blue merle; usually with white markings *Coat:* Medium length but dense; slightly harsh texture	Low slung and long, sturdily built, heavy boned, deep chest, with low tail and foxlike brush	*Height:* Approximately 12 in. *Weight:* About 20 lb
Welsh Corgi (Pembroke) —*working dog* *Fig. 133.*	Wales, from Pembrokeshire, in South Wales They're an ancient breed, descended from the dogs of Flemish weavers The breed first began to appear in America about 1930	*Color:* Red, sable, fawn, black, and tan; may have white markings *Coat:* Medium length and dense; not wiry	A low-slung, short-legged dog with erect ears and a short or bobtail The Pembroke has longer legs and is shorter bodied than the Cardigan	*Height:* 10–12 in. *Weight:* Dogs: 20–24 lb Bitches: 18–22 lb

DOGS AND THEIR CHARACTERISTICS

Head	Body	Tail	Character; Use	Faults or Disqualifications
Moderate size; perceptible occiput; slight stop; and slight median line extending back over the forehead *Ears:* Medium size, flat or slightly curled, set rather high, lightly covered with hair	A moderately long, but strong back; broad and slightly arched loins; slightly sloping croup; deep chest; well-sprung ribs; moderately tucked-up flank	Docked, to measure about 6 in. at maturity. Carried in a manner expressing confidence and sound temperament	Friendly, fearless, alert, and obedient *Use:* Initially, for big game hunting Presently, the Weimaraner is used as a bird dog, in upland shooting, and as a water retriever. Also Weimaraners are used as family pets and watchdogs	*Minor* faults: Tail too short or too long Pink nose *Major faults:* Badly overshot or undershot jaw Snipy muzzle Short ears *Serious faults:* White, other than a spot on the chest Eyes other than gray, blue gray, or light amber Nondocked tail *Disqualifications:* Deviation in height of more than one inch either way from the standard. A distinctly long coat. A distinctly blue or black coat
Foxlike in shape and expression; rather broad between the eyes; flat skull *Ears:* Large and prominent in proportion to size of dog, slightly rounded at the tips, and carried erect	Rather long Back and loins straight and powerful; chest deep and moderately broad; shoulders well set and muscular; ribs well sprung; thighs strong and muscular	Foxlike, moderately long; carried low when standing or moving slowly, streaming out when running fast, and lifted when tracking or excited	A handsome, sturdy, powerful, intelligent dog; capable of both speed and endurance *Use:* As a cattle dog (he's a heeler) and family dog by the Welsh farmers. As a house dog in the U.S.	*Faults:* Flop ears; a rattail or whip tail; predominately white *Disqualifications:* Pure white; a distinctly long coat
Foxy in shape and appearance; skull fairly wide and flat between the ears; moderate amount of stop *Ears:* Pricked, medium sized, and slightly pointed	Medium length Straight back; chest broad and deep; ribs well sprung; hindquarters strong	Short, preferably natural; otherwise docked at birth	Agreeable; affectionate, without forcing its attention on anyone; intelligent; alert; and an ever-vigilant guard *Use:* In Wales, the Pembroke is used to drive cattle and round up Welsh ponies; he's a heeler, which means that he nips at the heels As a small house dog	

(Continued)

109

TABLE 3 (CONTINUED) BREEDS OF

Breed	Place of Origin; Present Popularity	Color; Coat	General Appearance	Size
Welsh Springer Spaniel —*sporting dog* *Fig. 134.*	Wales, where it has been popular since the sixteenth century. Likely the first of the spaniel breeds to be used in front of the sportsman's gun Large numbers exported from England to America, India, Australia, and Thailand (Siam). Wide distribution due to breed's ability to withstand extremes of heat and cold. In the U.S., the Welsh Springer Spaniel hasn't been as popular as his cousin, the English Springer, perhaps because the Welshman is more independent and not so easily trained	*Color:* Dark rich red and white *Coat:* Straight or flat, and thick, of silky texture	A medium-sized, symmetrical, long-coated dog with feathered tail	*Height:* 15–16 in. *Weight:* 35–45 lb
Welsh Terrier —*terrier* *Fig. 135.*	Wales, where he is a sporting dog; used for hunting otter, fox, and badger Welsh Terriers were first brought to the U.S. in 1888. The nation's first show classification for the breed was offered at Westminster in 1901	*Color:* Black and tan, or black grizzle and tan *Coat:* Wiry, hard, very close, and abundant	A small, upstanding, rough-coated, black-and-tan terrier with drop ears and docked tail	*Height:* Dogs: 15 in. Bitches: 14 in. *Weight:* 20 lb
West Highland White Terrier —*terrier* *Fig. 136.*	Scotland Originated by the Duke of Argyll The West Highland White Terrier Club of America was admitted to membership in the American Kennel Club in 1909	*Color:* White, with a black nose *Coat:* Doublecoated Outercoat of hard hair, about 2 in. long and free from curl Undercoat should be short, soft, and close, resembling fur. Requires little or no trimming for showing	A white, rough-haired, short-legged terrier with a foxlike head and an undocked tail	*Height:* Dogs: 11 in. Bitches: 10 in. *Weight:* Average 16 lb

Head	Body	Tail	Character; Use	Faults or Disqualifications
Moderate length, slightly domed, clearly defined stop *Ears:* Set moderately low and hanging close to the cheeks, comparatively small for a spaniel and narrowing toward the tip, covered with nice setterlike feathering	Not long Strong and muscular back; deep brisket; well-sprung ribs; well balanced	Set on low, never carried above the level of the back, lightly feathered, and with lively action	A reliable, hard-working spaniel *Use:* As a gundog, a companion, and guard. He can be happy living in town as well as in the country	*Faults:* A short chubby head is objectionable
More masculine appearing than the Fox Terrier Skull flat and rather wide between the ears; stop not too well defined *Ears:* V-shaped, small, not too thin, set on fairly high, carried forward and close to the cheek	Back short; loins strong; chest moderately wide; shoulders long, sloping, and well laid in; ribs well sprung; hindquarters strong with muscular thighs	Set on high; docked; not carried too gaily	Gay, affectionate, hardy, and game. By nature quiet and not quarrelsome. Not as excitable as the Fox Terrier *Use:* House companion. The Welsh is especially devoted to children	*Disqualifications:* Nose white, cherry, or spotted; ears prick, tulip, or rose; undershot or overshot jaw; black below hocks or white to an appreciable extent
Skull rather wide and slightly domed; stop defined; eyebrows heavy; head thickly coated with hair *Ears:* Small, carried erect, set wide apart, and terminating in a sharp point. Never cropped	Compact Back short and well ribbed up; loins strong; chest moderately wide; shoulders long, sloping, and well laid in; hindquarters strong with muscular thighs	Set on moderately high, but not carried too gaily. Never docked	Bold, independent, affectionate, lively, and hardy *Use:* As a house dog Also, as a hunter	*Faults:* Any coat color other than white and any nose color other than black; coat with any silkiness or tendency to curl; much over or under height limits; too long or too narrow skull; overshot or undershot teeth; missing teeth; round-pointed drop, broad, large, or mule ears; too small, too full, or light colored eyes; cow hocks; tail carried at half-mast or over back; extreme timidity or pugnacity

(Continued)

TABLE 3 (CONTINUED) BREEDS OF

Breed	Place of Origin; Present Popularity	Color; Coat	General Appearance	Size
Whippet —*hound* Fig. 137.	England, where the Whippet was recognized as a breed by the English Kennel Club in 1891. With the inception of straight racing in England, the Whippet was dubbed "the poor man's race horse"	*Color:* Immaterial *Coat:* Close, smooth, and firm	A medium-sized, slender, but robust, dog with rose ears and a low-carried tail—a Greyhound in miniature	*Height:* Dogs: 19–22 in. Bitches: 18–21 in. *Weight:* Variable, 10–28 lb
Wirehaired Pointing Griffon —*sporting dog* Fig. 138.	Holland, where it was developed by a Dutch sportsman as a hunting dog and retriever. But the major portion of its development took place in France. Hence, some authorities regard it as a French breed. This breed has never been numerous or popular in America, although it has been here since 1900	*Color:* Steel gray with chestnut splashes; gray white with chestnut splashes; chestnut; dirty white mixed with chestnut; never black *Coat:* Hard, dry, and stiff; never curly; downy undercoat	An unkempt appearance due to the long, harsh coat; pendent ears	*Height:* Dogs: 21½–23½ in. Bitches: 19½–21½ in. *Weight:* 55 lb
Yorkshire Terrier —*toy* Fig. 139.	England The breed was developed in Yorkshire and Lancashire. It's the favorite toy breed in Great Britain The Yorkshire Terrier was first introduced into the U.S. in 1880	*Color:* Dark steel blue from the occiput to the root of the tail; a rich, golden tan on the head, and a bright tan on the chest Puppies are born black *Coat:* Glossy, fine, silky, long, and straight. The hair requires a great deal of attention	A long, silky-haired, steel-blue toy terrier with docked tail	*Height:* 8–9 in. *Weight:* Not over 7 lb

Head	Body	Tail	Character; Use	Faults or Disqualifications
Long and lean, flat and broad between the eyes; muzzle long and powerful without being coarse; nose black *Ears:* Small and fine; thrown back and folded, but semipricked when at attention	Rectangular. Back broad and rather long; loins and croup slightly arched; chest deep and roomy; shoulders sloping and muscular; hindquarters strong and broad, with muscular thighs	Long and tapering; carried low with slight curve at the end	Friendly and affectionate, but retiring; clean nature. An enthusiastic race dog of great speed. He is capable of speeds up to 35 miles per hour. An attractive house dog and companion *Use:* Primarily a race dog Also, rabbit coursing, and as a show dog	*Faults:* Gay ears; thin, flat, open foot; steep croup *Disqualifications:* Undershot mouth; overshot ¼ in or more; blue or china colored eyes; eyes of different colors; ½ in. above or below stated heights
Long, with a harsh coat, forming a mustache and eyebrows. Square muzzle *Ears:* Medium size, flat or sometimes slightly curled, set rather high	Short backed; well-developed loins	Carried straight Generally cut to one-third its length	Intelligent air; rather slow *Use:* Hunting dog	
Small and rather flat on top; skull not too prominent or round; hair on the head long and deep golden tan in color *Ears:* Small, V-shaped, carried erect, and not set too wide apart	Compact Level back and good loins	Docked to a medium length and carried slightly higher than the level of the back	Affectionate, lively, and bold, with the spirit of a terrier *Use:* A pet	

Figs. 140–181 (color pictures of some of the leading breeds) follow page 128.

KENNEL CLUBS

There are several kennel clubs, national and international in scope, in different countries of the world. Space limitations will permit covering only a few of them in this book.

Kennel clubs consist of specialty clubs, rather than individuals. They are banded together for the purposes of: (1) establishing standards for the breed, (2) recording the lineage of their animals, (3) protecting the purity of the breeds, (4) encouraging further improvement of the breed, and (5) promoting interest in dogs in general.

There are several registry clubs or associations in the United States. The American Kennel Club (AKC), which is the largest organized body of American dogdom, in 1971 registered 1,129,200 dogs, comprised of 116 different breeds. The United Kennel Club (UKC) registers most of the foxhounds and coonhounds in this country. The *American Field Publishing Company* registers by far the largest number of pointers and setters; and it also registers other sporting dogs.

AMERICAN KENNEL CLUB

The address:

American Kennel Club
51 Madison Avenue
New York, New York 10010

The American Kennel Club came into being on September 17, 1884, eleven years after the Kennel Club of England was founded. It is a nonprofit organization devoted to the advancement of purebred dogs. Its membership is made up of more than 380 autonomous dog clubs (not individuals) throughout the United States. Each club's voting privileges may be exercised by a representative known as a *delegate*. The delegates are the legislative body of the AKC—they make the rules and elect the directors from among their numbers. The management of the club's affairs is in the hands of the Board of Directors, whose responsibility it is to make regulations and policies in conformity with the rules. Funds for the operation of the AKC are derived from (1) registration of dogs, (2) membership dues, and (3) issuance of licenses for shows and trials that are held by nonmember clubs.

The stated objectives of the American Kennel Club are: to adopt and enforce rules and regulations governing dog shows, obedience trials, and field trials; to publish an official *Stud Book* and an official *Kennel Gazette;* and to advance in every way possible the development and interest in purebred dogs. More specifically, here are a few of the programs of the AKC:

1. *Stud Book*—The registration of dogs is the Club's biggest and most important business. It should be pointed out, however, that the AKC does not have a monopoly on dog registrations in the United States, for there are other registry organizations. The AKC symbol on a certificate has won wide acceptance and respect, as evidenced by the fact that thousands of breeders over the country feature this symbol in their advertising. Furthermore, it is noteworthy that the AKC has registered more than 15 million dogs since its inception.

The *Stud Book* contains the ancestry record of every dog that has been registered in the AKC since the breed was recognized.

Before a new breed is accepted in the *Stud Book,* it must be proved that it breeds true to type, that it has the sponsorship of a well-established club in this country, and that there are sufficient dogs in the hands of many owners to justify setting up a record system for it.

2. *The Stud Book Register*—This is a monthly publication of the AKC, in which is listed the sire and dam of each dog that has sired or whelped a litter, if not previously published.

3. *Purebred Dogs—American Kennel Gazette* —This is a monthly publication. It contains reading matter of general interest on dogs, news of the various breed clubs, a list of forthcoming events that have been approved to be held under AKC rules, identification of those dogs that have finished their championships, the awards of all dog shows, obedience trials, and field trials, as well as a "Secretary's Page," which contains action taken by the Club's Board of Directors.

4. *The Complete Dog Book*—This book contains the standards of each of the breeds eligible to be shown at dog shows held under the AKC rules, along with other valuable information about dogs.

5. *Library*—The AKC maintains, at its New York headquarters, a reference library consisting of 9,750 volumes, all devoted to the dog. It is one of the most complete collections of its kind in the world. The public is invited to use the facilities of the library, which are open for reference purposes Monday through Friday, from 10:00 a.m. to 4:00 p.m.

6. *Information Service*—The AKC maintains an information service designed to assist breeders, dog owners, and potential dog owners, and to handle inquiries concerning any of the 116 breeds that are registerable in the AKC *Stud Book*.

7. *License Department*—This division licenses dog shows, obedience trials, and judges. Club policy forbids the scheduling of two major events of the same type on the same day if they are less than 200 miles apart. Following approval of a date, the applying club must also secure approval of its list of judges and of its premium list.

The licenses of several thousand judges is a major responsibility of this department. The Club maintains a list of qualified judges, but, for the most part, judges are licensed for only one show at a time.

Nearly all dog shows and obedience trials in the United States are cleared through the AKC. However, the Club does not fill the same role in field trials, as many of the trials for pointing dogs are not run under the Club's rules. The same applies to coonhounds, Foxhounds, and certain other field trials. However, Beagle trials, Retriever trials, and Spaniel trials are almost exclusively under the auspices of the AKC.

Immediately after the conclusion of any AKC show or trial, the superintendent or secretary is required to file a complete report with the American Kennel Club. These become a part of the Club's permanent record. The AKC then checks the eligibility of each dog exhibited, and, finally, each placement of each dog is recorded on the dog's own card in the Club file.

8. *Grievances*—Any dog owner or exhibitor who fails to abide by the AKC rules, and who prejudices people against purebred dogs by his activities, may be disciplined by the Board of Directors of the AKC, which is empowered to suspend all club privileges, or to fine if there is no question of fact involved.

If it becomes necessary to settle a question of fact, such a case is referred to a trial board. The latter consists of three men appointed by the board, with nine such trial boards strategically located throughout the United States. These trial boards operate very much like a court of law. Every accused person is given an opportunity to defend himself. Also, any person or any club is privileged to file charges with the AKC against either another person or another club.

9. *Rules and Regulations*—Up-to-date copies of AKC rules and regulations may be secured by writing to the American Kennel Club. Usually, separate booklets are available for rules applying to registration and field trials, regulations and standards for obedience trials, and rules applying to registration and dog shows.

10. *Member clubs*—The AKC will also make available, on request, the listings of member clubs together with the names and addresses of their respective delegates and secretaries.

11. *Buyers and Sellers Department*—This department is for the purpose of bringing together buyers and sellers. Any breeder whose dogs are registered with the AKC may list his available stock with this department. The services are free. The AKC also provides assistance to anyone wishing to contact breeders of specific breeds of dogs.

REGISTRATION

A purebred dog may be defined as a member of a breed, the animals of which possess a common ancestry and distinctive characteristics; and he is either registered or eligible for registry in the Stud Book. Every purebred dog has a pedigree, but he may or may not have a registration certificate. A Pedigree Form is a family tree, showing the dog's ancestry; whereas a Registration Certificate is a certification of registration in the *Stud Book*. Registration in the AKC is primarily restricted to dogs whose sires and dams were registered or eligible for registration in the Club. However, reciprocal agreements with other stud books, particularly those abroad, make it possible to register some dogs that do not meet the general requirements.

When you buy a dog that is represented as being eligible for registration with the American Kennel Club, you are entitled to receive an AKC application form, properly filled out by the seller, which, when completed by you and submitted to the AKC with the proper fee, will enable you to effect the registration of the dog. Before an individual dog can be registered, however, the litter, of which it is a member, must be enrolled in the AKC by the breeder.

Under AKC rules, any person who sells dogs that he represents as eligible for registration in the AKC must maintain records to give full identifying information with every dog he delivers, even though AKC papers may not be available yet. *Therefore, no buyer should accept a promise of later identification.*

The rules and regulations of the AKC stipulate that whenever someone sells or delivers a dog that he claims may be registered with the AKC, he must identify the dog either (1) by putting into the hands of the buyer a properly completed AKC registration application, or (2) by giving the buyer a bill of sale or a written statement, signed by the seller, giving the dog's full breeding information as follows:

Breed, sex, and color of the dog
Date of birth of the dog
Registered names of the dog's sire and dam
Name of the breeder

Persons who purchase dogs that are represented as being eligible for registration with the AKC, and who encounter problems in acquiring the necessary registration application forms, should write to the American Kennel Club at the address given at the beginning of this section, giving all of the information they received at the time of purchase. Then, the AKC will attempt to assist in the matter.

Registration Procedure

Step by step, and form by form (Forms presented as Figs. 182 through 187 provided through the courtesy of the American Kennel Club), the procedure for registering a dog in the American Kennel Club is as follows:

Step 1—Figs. 182 and 183, Litter Registration Application. This form, which is for the purpose of enrolling the entire litter, must be filled out and submitted to the AKC by the breeder; and this must be done before an individual dog can be registered.

Step 2—Figs. 184 and 185, Application for Registration of Dog of This Registered Litter. This form must be filled out by the seller; then completed by the new owner and submitted to the AKC along with the $3.00 registration fee.

Step 3—Figs. 186 and 187, Registration Certificate, which you will receive from the AKC after the application is processed. Note that the reverse side (Fig. 187) of this form is used to record transfer of the dog; and that the fee for the first transfer is $2.00.

UNITED KENNEL CLUB, INC.

The address:

United Kennel Club, Inc.
321 West Cedar Street
Kalamazoo, Michigan 49009

Between 1875 and 1900, there was no widely recognized U.S. standard of perfection for the various dog breeds. There were few breed clubs, and both breed clubs and breeders went their own independent ways. Some individual breeders kept their own pedigree records. A few dog registration organizations came into being. Many of the so-called registrations were poorly kept and unreliable. But the United Kennel Club, Inc., founded by Mr. Chauncy Zachariah Bennet in 1898, proved an exception. This registry went on to become what is today the second oldest and second largest registration office of purebred dogs in the United States.

Some pertinent facts about the United Kennel Club, Inc. follow:

1. *First breed registered by the UKC*—The American (Pit) Bull Terrier was the first breed registered by the UKC. The registration of other breeds followed—Black-and-Tan Coonhound, Redbone Coonhound, and English Coonhound.

2. *Bloodlines Journal*—This publication, which was started a number of years ago, is published every two months and mailed to all breeders and fanciers doing business with the UKC.

3. *Purple Ribbon pedigree*—This is a merit or special advanced registration system, which is highly coveted as the top caliber pedigree record achievable under UKC registration. To earn a Purple Ribbon pedigree, an unbroken pedigree chain must be recorded with the UKC for six or seven generations of breeding. This system and seal is trademarked and registered with the U.S. Department of Commerce.

4. *Promotion of field trials and other activities*—The UKC helped promote English Beagle Field Trials in America, and licensed field trials for coonhounds.

In time, UKC also licensed (for all breeds) bench shows and inaugurated its own system of benching and awards, with provision for ribbons and trophies.

5. *More licensed shows; night hunts*—Next, in period of time, the UKC licensed shows for six breeds of coonhounds, and added UKC-licensed Night Hunts. Today, the UKC lists something like 1,200 recognized hunting clubs in the United States and Canada that are holding these events. Also, UKC Water Races have been inaugurated.

The UKC-licensed Night Hunts have probably been the fastest growing dog event in the United States, attracting wide interest from old and young alike. This event calls for trying out the hounds in the woods under actual hunting conditions, with a judge who scores the dogs according to their hunting ability—all overseen by

FEE $5.00
Fee Subject To Change Without Notice
DO NOT SEND CASH

LITTER REGISTRATION APPLICATION

To register a litter born in the U.S.A. out of an AKC registered female and sired by an AKC registered male of the same breed.

Mail with fee to: **THE AMERICAN KENNEL CLUB, 51 MADISON AVE., NEW YORK, N. Y. 10010**

PLEASE READ REVERSE SIDE BEFORE COMPLETING APPLICATION

PRINT IN CAPITAL LETTERS ONLY — USE INK

DO NOT WRITE IN THIS SPACE

BREED ________ Place of Birth of Litter: **CITY** ________ **STATE** ________

Number of living dogs in this litter on the date this application is submitted to the **AKC**· MALES | FEMALES

Date of birth of Litter: (Use Numbers) MONTH | DAY | YEAR

AKC Champion Title (if any) — REGISTERED NAME OF SIRE — AKC Obedience Title (if any) — AKC NUMBER OF SIRE

AKC Champion Title (if any) — REGISTERED NAME OF DAM — AKC Obedience Title (if any) — AKC NUMBER OF DAM

SEC. A. OWNER OF SIRE ON DATE OF MATING COMPLETES THIS SECTION.

Name of Owner of **SIRE** — FIRST NAME & INITIAL — LAST NAME

I **CERTIFY** that the above-named Dam was mated to the above-named Sire and that the Sire was owned or co-owned by me on the date of mating.

Place of mating (check one) ☐ **U.S.A.** ☐ **FOREIGN** (print country ________).

SIGNATURE of Owner or Co-Owner of Sire ________

Date of Mating: MONTH | DAY | YEAR

SEC. B. OWNER (OR IF LEASED, LESSEE) OF DAM ON DATE OF BIRTH OF LITTER COMPLETES THIS SECTION.

Note: If ownership of Dam changed while Dam was in whelp, SEC. C below must also be completed.

Name & Address of Owner (or if Leased, Lessee) of **DAM** — FIRST NAME & INITIAL — LAST NAME

STREET ADDRESS

CITY — STATE — ZIP

Co-Owner (If Any) of **DAM** — FIRST NAME & INITIAL — LAST NAME

I apply to register this litter and **CERTIFY** that I was the Owner, Co-owner, or Lessee of the above-named Dam on the date of birth of the Litter, and that this Dam was not mated to any other dog during her season. I further **CERTIFY** that all of the representations on this application are true. I agree to comply with AKC rules and regulations. I have read the "Notice" and instructions on the reverse side of the application.

SIGNATURE of Owner, Co-Owner, or Lessee of Dam ________

SEC. C. DO NOT COMPLETE UNLESS OWNERSHIP OF DAM CHANGED OR LEASE TERMINATED WHILE DAM WAS IN WHELP.

Note: Before completing, carefully read instructions on reverse side.

Owner (or if Leased, Lessee) of DAM on Date of Mating — FIRST NAME & INITIAL — LAST NAME

Co-Owner of the DAM on Date of Mating — FIRST NAME & INITIAL — LAST NAME

I CERTIFY that I was the Owner, Co-owner, or Lessee of the above-named Dam on the date the Dam was mated to the above-named Sire. **I CERTIFY** that the Dam, while in my possession, was not mated to any other dog during her season.

FOR OFFICE USE ONLY

SIGNATURE of Owner, Co-Owner, or Lessee of Dam ________

Fig. 182. Litter Registration Application, Front Side. (See Fig. 183 for reverse side of form.)

FOR OFFICE USE ONLY

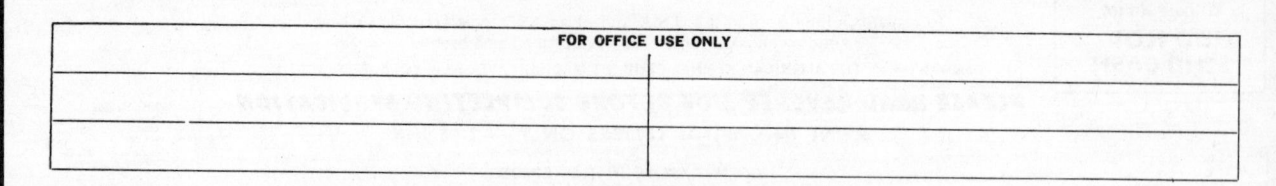

IMPORTANT NOTICE
The American Kennel Club reserves the right to correct or cancel for cause the registration of this litter. Any misrepresentation on this application is a cause for cancellation and may result in loss of all AKC privileges.

- Single copies of AKC "Registration Rules" and "Regulations for Record Keeping and Identification of Dogs" are available on request without charge.
- If this application is accepted, AKC will send the litter owner one application for the individual registration of each dog in the litter.
- When completed and submitted, this application becomes the property of The American Kennel Club.

The Following Instructions and Sample Application Will Guide You in Completing Your Application

1. Sire and Dam must have been AKC registered **and** recorded in the ownership of the persons who were the actual owners on the dates of mating and whelping, **before** this application is submitted to the AKC. If registration or transfer applications for Sire or Dam accompany this application, **all** applications will be returned.

2. To ensure proper registration of this litter, print in capital letters and stay within the boxes. Skip a box where a space would normally appear.

3. SIGNATURES: Wherever an owner's signature is required **and** dog is co-owned, only one signature is necessary. *Signatures of persons other than owners or lessees will be accepted only if power of attorney or other official authorization has been filed with AKC.* Power of Attorney cards are obtainable on request.

4. LEASE OF DAM: If Dam was leased at time of mating or birth of litter, a "Report of Lease of Bitch" card (obtainable from AKC) **must** be filed with AKC.

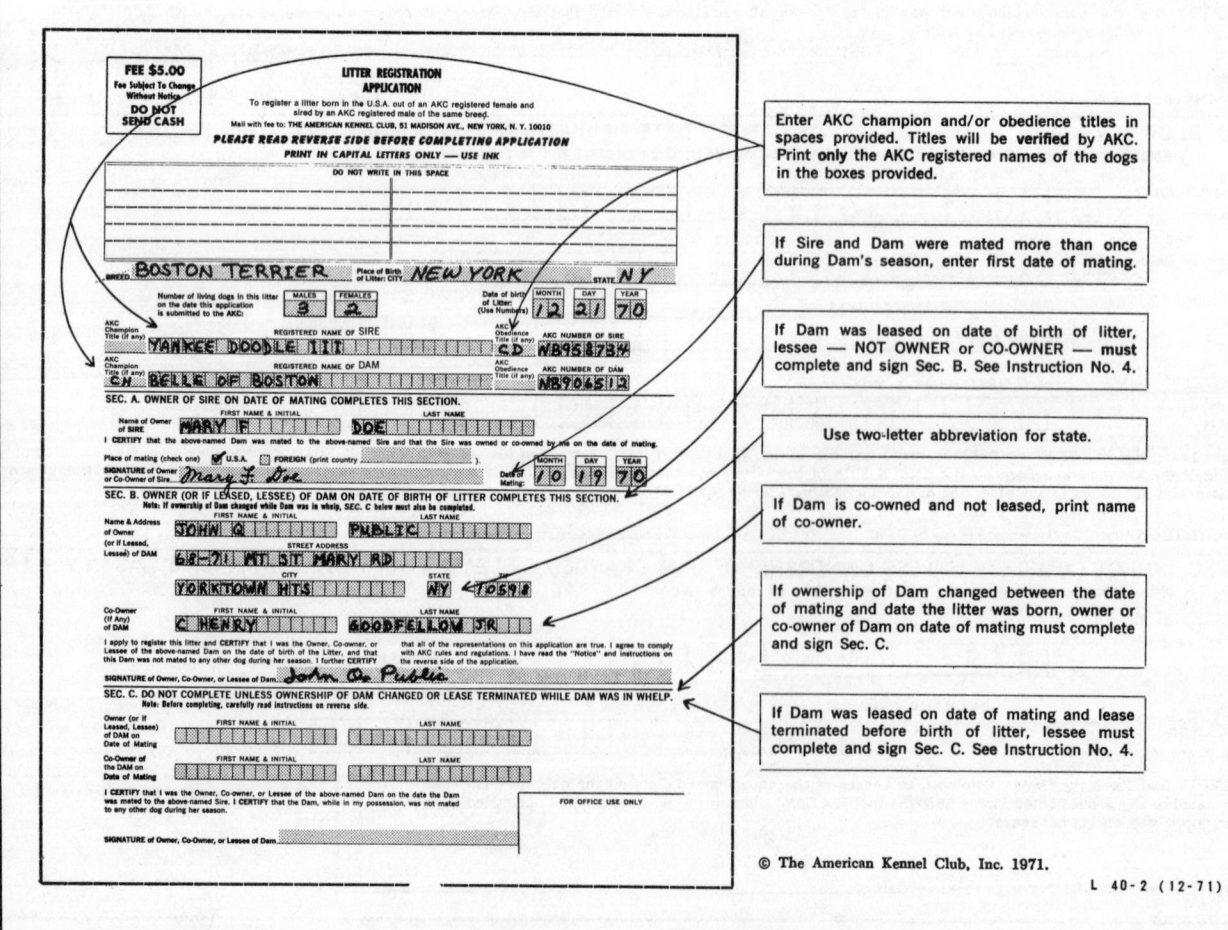

Fig. 183. Litter Registration Application, Reverse Side. (See Fig. 182 for front side of form.)

The person who owns this dog and applies to register it as owner has the right to name it.

Do NOT use a number as a part of a name. The American Kennel Club reserves the right to assign a number suffix, if necessary.

NAME OF DOG—PLEASE **PRINT** — (LIMIT NAME TO 25 LETTERS)

1st CHOICE

2nd CHOICE

DO **NOT** WRITE IN THIS SPACE

KN____NAME____OK____

FILE NO.____

FEE____

REC'D____

ISSUED____

I hereby give permission to use my AKC registered Kennel Name IN NAMING THIS DOG____

SIGNATURE OF OWNER OF KENNEL NAME

BREED

SEX

LITTER NUMBER

WHELPED

COLOR____

SIRE

DAM

BREEDER

LITTER OWNER

MUST BE COMPLETED BY OWNER OF LITTER

SPECIMEN COPY

ISSUED

APPLICATION

FOR REGISTRATION OF DOG OF THIS REGISTERED LITTER.

PLEASE READ BOTH SIDES OF THIS FORM

THE AMERICAN KENNEL CLUB RESERVES THE RIGHT TO CORRECT OR REVOKE FOR CAUSE ANY REGISTRATION CERTIFICATE ISSUED.

THE USE OF THIS APPLICATION TO REGISTER A DOG FROM A LITTER OTHER THAN THE LITTER NUMBERED ABOVE OR ANY OTHER MISUSE OF THIS FORM WILL RESULT IN THE INVALIDATION OF THIS APPLICATION.

IF THIS FORM IS NOT USED TO REGISTER A DOG OF THIS LITTER, PLEASE RETURN IT TO THE A.K.C. WITH EXPLANATION.

Fig. 184. Application for Registration of Dog of This Registered Litter, Front Side. (See Fig. 185 for reverse side of this form.)

INSTRUCTIONS: PLEASE TYPE — OR USE **PEN. NO PENCIL.** Erasures or Corrections may cause return of application for an explanation.

SEC. A MUST BE COMPLETED IN FULL and SIGNED BY OWNER OF LITTER (AND CO-OWNER, IF ANY) SHOWN ON REVERSE SIDE.

ONE box MUST BE checked

☐ I (we) still own this dog, and I (we) apply to The American Kennel Club to register it and have ownership recorded in my (our) name(s).

☐ I (we) certify that this dog was transferred DIRECTLY TO THE FOLLOWING PERSON(S) ON____ mo. day year

MUST be filled in by owner(s) of Litter.

PRINT NAME(S) OF PERSON(S) TO WHOM DOG WAS DIRECTLY TRANSFERRED____

ADDRESS____

Signature____ OWNER OF LITTER AT BIRTH

Signature____ CO-OWNER (IF ANY) OF LITTER AT BIRTH

SEC. B TO BE COMPLETED and SIGNED BY THE PERSON(S) NAMED IN SEC. A ABOVE, PROVIDED the person(s) owns the dog at the time this application is submitted to the A.K.C. If the person(s) named in SEC. A has transferred the dog to some other person(s), DO NOT COMPLETE SEC. B. Instead - obtain a Supplemental Transfer Statement form from the A.K.C. Instructions for its completion and use are on the form.

I apply to The American Kennel Club to have Registration Certificate for this dog issued in my/our name(s), and certify that I/we acquired it DIRECTLY from the person(s) who Signed Sec. A above, and that I/we still own this dog. I agree to abide by American Kennel Club rules and regulations.

New Owner's Signature____

PRINT Address____ City, State____

New Co-Owners Signature____

PRINT Address____ City, State____

→ ***REGISTRATION FEE MUST ACCOMPANY APPLICATION.*** MAKE CHECKS, MONEY ORDERS PAYABLE TO THE AMERICAN KENNEL CLUB. **DO NOT SEND STAMPS OR CASH.**

FEE: $3.00—plus $1.00 for each additional transfer of dog represented by Supplemental Transfer Statement. FEES SUBJECT TO CHANGE WITHOUT NOTICE

When completed and submitted, this Application becomes the property of The American Kennel Club

Mail to: THE AMERICAN KENNEL CLUB, 51 Madison Avenue, New York, N. Y. 10010

Fig. 185. Application for Registration of Dog of This Registered Litter, Reverse Side. (See Fig. 184 for front side of this form.)

AMERICAN KENNEL CLUB

No.

NAME

BREED

SEX

COLOR

DATE OF BIRTH

SIRE

DAM

BREEDER

OWNER

CERTIFICATE ISSUED

SPECIMEN COPY

AMERICAN KENNEL CLUB · A·K·C · INCORPORATED

IF A DATE APPEARS AFTER THE NAME AND NUMBER OF THE SIRE AND DAM, IT INDICATES THE ISSUE OF THE STUD BOOK REGISTER IN WHICH THE SIRE OR DAM IS PUBLISHED.

THIS CERTIFICATE ISSUED WITH THE RIGHT TO CORRECT OR REVOKE BY THE AMERICAN KENNEL CLUB.

See Transfer Instructions on Back of Certificate

REGISTRATION CERTIFICATE

Fig. 186. Registration Certificate, Front Side. (See Fig. 187 for reverse side of this form.)

TO RECORD TRANSFER OF THIS DOG

SEC. A MUST BE **COMPLETED** AND **SIGNED** PERSONALLY BY FORMER OWNER (AND CO-OWNER, IF ANY) NAMED ON FACE OF CERTIFICATE.

INVALID IF SIGNED IN BLANK

I transferred this dog on (month)________(day)________(year)________DIRECTLY to:

PRINT NAME

PRINT ADDRESS

SIGNED________ PRESENT RECORDED OWNER   SIGNED________ PRESENT RECORDED CO-OWNER (IF ANY)

SEC. B MUST BE **COMPLETED** AND **SIGNED** PERSONALLY BY NEW OWNER (AND NEW CO-OWNER, IF ANY) NAMED IN SEC. A ABOVE, provided he still owns the dog and wants NEW REGISTRATION certificate issued in his name. If the dog has again been transferred, DO NOT USE THIS SEC. B, but write AMERICAN KENNEL CLUB for transfer application forms.

I apply to American Kennel Club to have registration certificate for this dog issued in my/our name(s) and certify that I/we acquired it directly from the owner(s) who signed Sec. A above, and that I/we still own the dog. I agree to abide by all the rules and regulations of AMERICAN KENNEL CLUB.

New owner's personal signature________   New co-owner's personal signature________

Print { Address________ City, State________   Print { Address________ City, State________

INCLUDE ZIP CODE   INCLUDE ZIP CODE

SEND THIS CERTIFICATE WITH CORRECT FEE TO

AMERICAN KENNEL CLUB

51 MADISON AVENUE, NEW YORK, NEW YORK 10010

FEE:—$2.00 FEES ARE SUBJECT TO CHANGE WITHOUT NOTICE.

WHEN COMPLETED AND SUBMITTED, THIS APPLICATION BECOMES THE PROPERTY OF AMERICAN KENNEL CLUB.

WARNING

Every transfer must be recorded. The complete chain of transfers must be shown. American Kennel Club may cancel the registration of this dog and its descendents if this application contains any error or misrepresentation.

Copyright 1961, AMERICAN KENNEL CLUB

Fig. 187. Registration Certificate, Reverse Side. (See Fig. 186 for front side of this form.)

a Master of Hounds from a local hunting club sponsoring the event under the club name. In a typical event, the six breeds of coonhounds compete. Regular UKC-licensed shows have the second largest following; and these are followed next in order by the UKC Water Races, then, the UKC Field Trials.

6. *Breeds recognized and presently registered by UKC*—The following list shows the breeds recognized and presently registered by UKC. Those followed by an asterisk are the breeds originally recognized by UKC, for which the organization served as original registrar:

    American (Pit) Bull Terrier*
    American Eskimo*
    American Toy Terrier*
    Airedale Terrier
    American Water Spaniel*
    Alaskan Malamute
    Arctic Husky*
    Basset Hound
    Beagle
    Bloodhound
    Boston Terrier
    Boxer
    Miniature Boxer*
    Chihuahua
    Chow Chow
    Collie
    Collie, Columbian*
    Collie, Smooth
    Dachshund, Smooth
    Dachshund, Longhaired
    Dalmatian
    English Shepherd*
    Fox Terrier, Smooth
    Fox Terrier, Wire
    Toy Fox Terrier*
    German Shepherd Dog
    Great Dane
    Greyhound
    Pekingese
    Pomeranian
    Poodle
    St. Bernard
    Scottish Terrier
    Spaniel, Cocker
    Whippet

COONHOUND BREEDS

    American Black-&-Tan Coonhound*
    Bluetick Coonhound*
    English Coonhound*
    Plott Hound*
    Redbone Coonhound*
    Walker (Treeing) Coonhound*
    American Black-and-Tan Fox & Coonhound*

BREEDS OF COONHOUNDS AND THEIR CHARACTERISTICS

The United Kennel Club has established coonhound breed standards for two purposes:

1. To act as a guide for judges at bench shows.
2. To furnish suggestions for breeders in their aims toward improving the breed.

Table 4 is a pertinent summary of coonhound breed standards based on literature and pictures provided by the United Kennel Club.

TABLE 4 BREEDS OF COONHOUNDS

Breed	Place of Origin; Present Popularity	Color; Coat	General Appearance	Size
American Black-and-Tan Coonhound *Fig. 188.*	U. S.	*Color:* Predominately deep rich black, with tan trim covering not more than 10–15% of body; small pumpkin seed over eyes; a little white on breast is not a fault *Coat:* Smooth haired, fine, glossy, but thick enough for protection	Power, agility, alertness	*Height:* Dogs: 23–26 in. Bitches: 22–25 in. *Weight:* Dogs: 50–75 lb Bitches: 40–65 lb
Bluetick Coonhound *Fig. 189.*	Descended from several strains of English Foxhounds	*Color:* Preferred color is a dark blue, thickly mottled body, spotted by various shaped black spots on back, ears, and sides. Preference running to more blue than black on body *Coat:* Medium coarse and lying close to the body; smooth and glossy; neither rough nor short	Speedy; well muscled; of racy type, not clumsy. Rather large in size	*Height:* Dogs: 22–27 in. Bitches: 20–25 in. *Weight:* Dogs: 55–80 lb Bitches: 45–65 lb

Head	Body	Tail	Character; Use	Faults or Disqualifications
Carried well up, slightly domed, and broad between ears *Ears:* Set medium low, devoid of erectile power, and should reach to end of nose when drawn out	Chest deep and moderately wide; shoulders muscular and sloping; back short and slightly arched, well muscled and strong; muscular at loins	Heavy; strong; tapering; rather long; without brush; carried free, well up, saberlike	Active, fast, bright, kind, confident, courageous, with great trailing and treeing instinct and ability	Teeth overshot or undershot White on tip of tail
Skull very slightly domed and broad between ears. Stop prominent *Ears:* Well attached slightly below top of skull; thin, and taper to point; should reach well towards end of nose	Slightly higher at shoulders than hips. Chest deep but not excessively wide; shoulders well laid in, sloping, and muscular; ribs well sprung with good depth; back moderately long and muscular; loins well muscled and slightly arched	Attached slightly below back line, well rooted, tapering, moderate length, carried high with a forward curve as a half moon	A pleading hound expression; active, ambitious, and speedy on trail	Off colors Overshot or undershot

(Continued)

TABLE 4 (CONTINUED) BREEDS OF

Breed	Place of Origin; Present Popularity	Color; Coat	General Appearance	Size
English Coonhound	Unknown	*Color:* Any good hound color, coming in ticks, the tricolor, and black saddle *Coat:* Hair is hard, medium length, or good hound type for protection	Strong and racy	*Height:* Dogs: 22–25 in. Bitches: 21–24 in.
Plott Hound	In the Great Smoky Mountains of Tennessee and North Carolina Named after Jonathan Plott, who came from Germany in 1750 and settled in North Carolina In 1946, the UKC recognized the Plott Hound as a breed	*Color:* Brindle or brindle with black saddle. Some white *Coat:* Smooth haired, fine, glossy	Strong and attractive	*Height:* Dogs: 22–25 in. Bitches: 21–24 in. *Weight:* Dogs: 50–65 lb Bitches: 40–55 lb

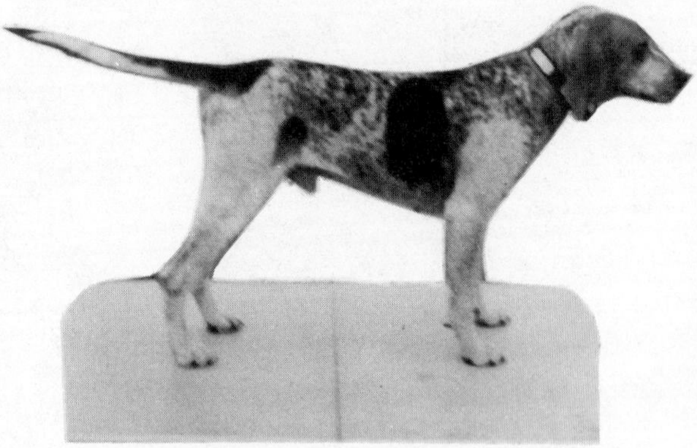

Fig. 190.

Fig. 191.

COONHOUNDS AND THEIR CHARACTERISTICS

Head	Body	Tail	Character; Use	Faults or Disqualifications
Skull very slightly domed, wide *Ears:* Hung a little low; fine textured; reach nearly to end of nose if drawn out	Deep, broad chest; strong, slightly-arched back; shoulders and thighs well muscled	Set high; medium length; just a little brush; carried gaily	For coon hunting	
Carried well up; dome moderately flat; moderate width between and above eyes	Chest deep with adequate lung space; back slightly arched, well muscled, and strong; muscular loins and quarters	Moderately heavy; strong at root and tapering; rather long without brush; carried free, well up, saberlike	Active, fast, bright, kind, confident, courageous, vicious fighter on game, tremendous treeing instinct, takes readily to water, alert, quick to learn, has great endurance *Use:* To hunt bears and wild boars, and as a tree dog	(Continued)

TABLE 4 (CONTINUED) BREEDS OF

Breed	Place of Origin; Present Popularity	Color; Coat	General Appearance	Size
Redbone Coonhound *Fig. 192.*	In Georgia, from foundation stock owned by George F. L. Birdsong	*Color:* Solid red preferred Small amount of white on brisket or feet not objectionable *Coat:* Smooth and hard, medium to short in length, sufficient for protection		*Height:* Dogs: 22–26 in. Bitches: 21–25 in.
Walker (Treeing) Coonhound *Fig. 193.*	Developed from certain strains of Walker Foxhounds. Great credit for developing the Walker Foxhounds goes to George Washington Maupin and John W. Walker, of Kentucky	*Color:* White predominating, with black-and-tan spots. Any other color combination may be penalized at the discretion of the judge, but not barred *Coat:* Smooth haired, glossy, fine, yet dense enough for protection	In appearance, they cannot be distinguished from the Walker Foxhound	*Height:* Dogs: 22–27 in. Bitches: 20–25 in. *Weight:* Dogs: 50–75 lb Bitches: 40–65 lb

Head	Body	Tail	Character; Use	Faults or Disqualifications
Skull moderately broad, well proportioned with body; muzzle never dished or upturned *Ears:* Set moderately low, fine in texture, and reaching near end of nose when stretched out	Chest deep and broad; ribs well sprung; back strong and slightly arched; thighs and shoulders clean and muscular	Medium length, slight brush	Specialists in coon hunting. But they are also proficient in trailing and treeing bear, cougar, and wildcat	Overshot or undershot jaw
Carried well up; occiput prominent; wide between eyes; flat rather than dome shaped *Ears:* Set medium low; of medium length; should hang gracefully, with inside part tipping toward muzzle; not too pointed	Chest moderately wide and deep; shoulders muscular and sloping; back short, gracefully arched, muscular, and strong; hips round, smooth, wide and muscular	Strong at root, tapering, moderately long, without flag, carried free, well up, saberlike	Energetic, bright, intelligent, active, quick, fearless, pleasant, kind, graceful, ambitious, speedy with super-abundance of sense, endurance, trailing, hunting and treeing instinct, and ability Specialists in coon hunting, but can be trained to trail any species of ground-furred game	

CANADIAN KENNEL CLUB

The address:

Canadian Kennel Club, Inc.
2 Eva Road
Etobicoke, Ontario, Canada

The Canadian Kennel Club was formed in 1888, four years after the American Kennel Club was established. At the outset, a reciprocity agreement was drawn up, whereby provision was made for Canadian dogs to compete at shows held under the auspices of the American Kennel Club rules without compelling such dogs to register in the AKC *Stud Book,* provided they were already registered in the Canadian Kennel Club *Stud Book.* Further, it was agreed that each Club would uphold all the qualifications made by the other. In 1926, this reciprocity agreement was further expanded and solidified so as to place the two Clubs on a more satisfactory basis. Thus, there has been a long and pleasant relationship between the Canadian Kennel Club and the American Kennel Club. However, not all Canadian breed standards correspond to those adopted by the American Kennel Club. Some differences exist between the rules under which dog shows, field trials, obedience trials, etc., are held; but the line of demarcation between them is not very great. In general, whatever has been accepted in one country has been duplicated in the other.

Other pertinent points about the CKC follow:

1. *Official magazine or organ*—The first organ established by the CKC was known as the *Canadian Kennel Gazette.* In time, it was sold to Winnipeg interests. On May 2, 1917, the magazine was repurchased by the CKC; and in June, 1917, the first issue of the *Kennel and Bench* went forth. In March, 1940, the name of the official organ was changed to *Dogs in Canada.*

2. *Incorporation under the* Live Stock Pedigree Act—In 1915, the CKC filed application for incorporation under the Live Stock Pedigree Act of Canada, which was subsequently accepted. Since that time, the CKC has risen to an honored place among the most prominent livestock associations of Canada.

3. *Statistics*—The CKC has some 9,700 members and registers approximately 50,000 dogs each year. In 1971, there were 298 championship shows (all breed and specialty), 185 licensed obedience trials, 132 licensed field trials, and 6 tracking tests, held under the CKC rules. In 1971, the total dogs entered in championship events held under CKC rules exceeded 96,000.

KENNEL CLUB OF ENGLAND

The address:

Kennel Club
1 Clarges Street
Piccadilly, London
WIY 8AB, England

The Kennel Club of England is simply known as the *Kennel Club* in that country.

The Kennel Club was formed in 1873, with the Prince of Wales, who was later to become King Edward, as Patron of the Club. Its foundation marked the beginning of the modern cult of the dog, not only in Britain but throughout the world. It was the first authority set up to govern and direct the conditions under which dog shows should be held and conducted, and to establish the standards by which the dogs entered should be judged. Also, it became the pattern for similar bodies that subsequently formed in other countries as interest in breeding and exhibiting purebred dogs gradually spread to every civilized region of the world. A few noteworthy points about the Kennel Club follow:

1. *A Stud Book published*—In 1874, the Kennel Club of England published the first dog *Stud Book,* which contained the pedigrees of 4,027 dogs which had won prizes at shows in the previous fourteen years (1859–1873).

2. *Cropping dogs' ears prohibited*—In 1895, the Kennel Club prohibited the cropping of dogs' ears.

3. *Two main groups, with each of these divided into three subgroups*—In England, all breeds are classed as "sporting breeds" or "nonsporting breeds." However, there are three subdivisions under each. These are:

Sporting Breeds	*Nonsporting Breeds*
Hound group	Utility group
Gundog group	Working group
Terrier group	Toy group

The German Shepherd Dog (known as Alsatian in England) is the most popular breed, with 16,834 registrations in 1970, followed by the Labrador Retriever with 14,827 registrations that same year.

4. *Statistics*—Some noteworthy statistics about the Kennel Club are: In 1970, it registered a total of 175,074 dogs, of which 77,772 were sporting breed dogs, and 97,302 were nonsporting breed dogs; and 2,371 shows were held throughout England.

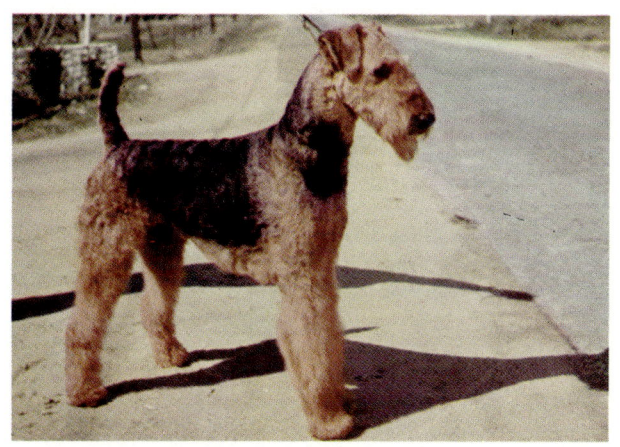

Fig. 140. Airdale Terrier.

Fig. 141. Afghan Hound.

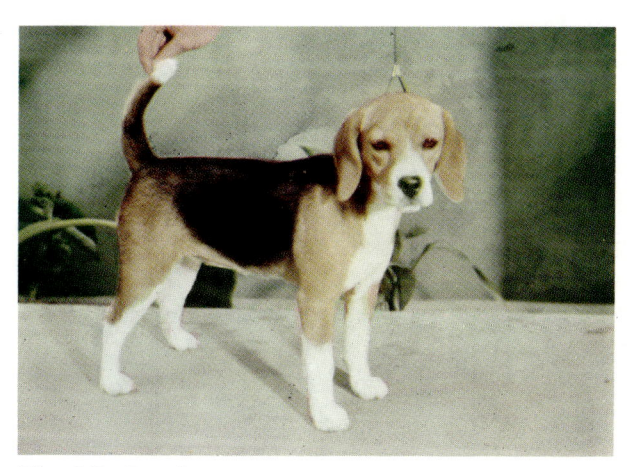

Fig. 142. Beagle.

Fig. 143. Bedlington Terrier.

Fig. 144. Boston Terrier.

Fig. 145. Boxer.

Fig. 146. Bulldog.

Fig. 147. Bull Terrier.

Fig. 148. Cairn Terrier.

Fig. 149. Chow Chow.

Fig. 150. Cocker Spaniel.

Fig. 151. Collie.

Fig. 152. Dachshund.

Fig. 153. Dalmatian.

Fig. 154. Doberman Pinscher.

Fig. 155. English Setter.

Fig. 156. English Springer Spaniel.

Fig. 157. Fox Terrier.

Fig. 158. German Shepherd Dog.

Fig. 159. Golden Retriever.

Fig. 160. Gordon Setter.

Fig. 161. Great Dane.

Fig. 162. Greyhound.

Fig. 163. Irish Setter.

Fig. 164. Irish Terrier.

Fig. 165. Irish Wolfhound.

Fig. 166. Kerry Blue Terrier.

Fig. 167. Labrador Retriever.

Fig. 168. Miniature Pinscher.

Fig. 169. Old English Sheepdog.

Fig. 170. Pekingese.

Fig. 171. Pointer.

Fig. 172. Pomeranian.

Fig. 173. Poodle.

Fig. 174. Pug.

Fig. 175. St. Bernard.

Fig. 176. Scottish Terrier.

Fig. 177. Sealyham Terrier.

Fig. 178. Standard Schnauzer.

Fig. 179. Weimaraner.

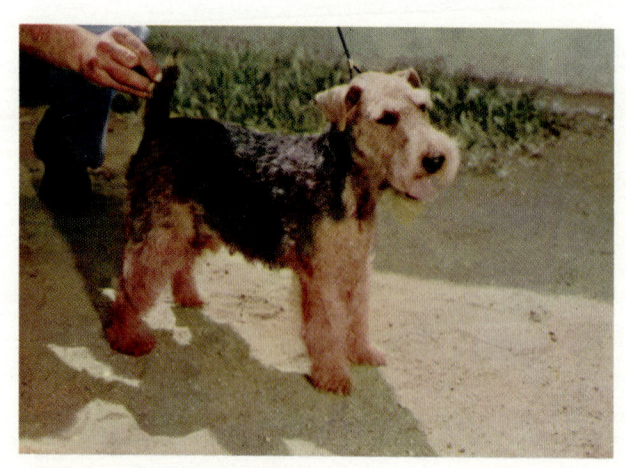

Fig. 180. Welsh Terrier.

Fig. 181. Yorkshire Terrier.

BERMUDA KENNEL CLUB, INC.

The address:

Bermuda Kennel Club, Inc.
P. O. Box 1455
Hamilton, Bermuda

The Bermuda Kennel Club, Inc., was founded in 1955. The Club held its first show the following year. Until 1967, its shows were conducted under the rules of the Canadian Kennel Club. In 1967, the Bermuda Kennel Club, Inc., adopted its own show rules; and, in 1968, it set up its own registration system.

The Club conducts an International Show each autumn, usually in November. Within a one-week period, four all-breed shows and five obedience trials are held. The shows are held in Bermuda's beautiful Botanical Gardens, with entries from the U.S., Canada, and England. The Bermuda show affords dog owners and enthusiasts an opportunity to participate in a wonderful show in a pleasant environment.

SELECTING AND BUYING THE DOG

The dog lover can make a choice between the large and the small, the powerful and the elegant, the vivacious and the placid, the long and the short coated; between a great array of colors, head and ear shapes, and tails; between specialists for different uses; and between animals adapted to hot or cold climates. In short, there is a breed for every need and a dog for each person.

The following points should be considered when selecting and buying the dog:

1. *What's your reason for owning a dog?*—First and foremost, you should determine the primary reason for owning a dog. The house dog or pet may be quite small. The person desiring a watchdog should select one of the breeds that is quick to give warning—is noisy, powerful, or vicious enough to frighten away intruders. The person who likes to hunt should choose one of the breeds adapted for that purpose, rather than a Pekingese, for example. A farmer should think of a Collie or a sheep dog.

2. *What size dog?*—You should consider your home as well as your yard. If space is limited, perhaps you should select one of the smaller breeds. Also, you should consider the cost involved in feeding a big dog, in comparison with a small one.

Most big dogs need considerable room. On the other hand, the Great Dane and the St. Bernard, two of the largest breeds, often get along very well in small quarters. They're so big that they do not romp about as much as some of the smaller dogs.

Most of the intermediate-sized dogs, like the German Shepherds, Boxers, Doberman Pinschers, and others, are built for heavy work. They have a vast store of energy and need much exercise while growing. Once grown, however, they fit into small homes quite well.

The toys and terriers are great house dogs. They are the right size for almost any home. Yet, they are limited from the standpoint of use. For example, no one would like to have a Chihuahua as a hunting dog.

3. *What's your temperament?*—If you are quiet

Fig. 194. Bermuda International Dog Show winner, Kay Hill's Dealer's Choice, a Doberman Pinscher owned by Mrs. J. Bruce Morey of St. Charles, Illinois. Looking on are (left to right): the breed judge, Mr. Stanley Dangerfield, Camberley, Surrey, England; the handler (name unknown); and the Governor of Bermuda, the Right Honorable Lord Martonmere, who presented the trophy. (Courtesy Bermuda News Bureau)

and easygoing, you might not appreciate the cheery liveliness of a Terrier. If you are the rugged, outdoor variety, you would likely prefer a more rugged dog than a Poodle. Also, you should consider your own disposition. If you are a relaxed person, then perhaps you should select one of the less active breeds. On the other hand, if you are the "eager beaver" type that relaxes through exercise, then you should consider a lively sporting breed. Elderly people usually prefer a quiet, philosophical, complacent dog—one that will be content with a sedate walk or a quiet game in the park. Usually the toys and smaller breeds best meet the latter needs.

4. *What's the personality and health of the dog?*—Like people, some dogs are shy. Remember that a dog that's shy with his litter mates (the little fellow who's over in the corner) will be shy with you, also. Remember, too, that a normal, healthy dog is aggressive and wants to make friends with you and the whole world. If he's without bad personality traits and in good health, he'll be bright eyed, alert, full of bounce and vigor, and agressively interested in you and others.

Unless you are sure that the newly acquired pet is healthy, and came from a healthy environment, it is an excellent idea to let your veterinarian examine him before you take him home, preferably before you buy him.

5. *Are there children?*—Children want a rather rugged, spirited dog—one that will romp and play with them. Their dog should be able to take a lot of roughhousing and mauling, and should not require a lot of trimming or expert attention. They generally prefer a dog that ranges in size from a Terrier to a Springer Spaniel.

6. *What sex shall you choose?*—Your choice of a female (bitch) or a dog (male) may be governed by many factors.

Females have the following advantages over males:
a. Cleaner in the house
b. More apt to stay home
c. More devoted and affectionate as a companion
d. Better disposition; more gentle
e. Mentally quicker
f. More graceful
g. Likely to be cheaper to buy.

However, in comparison with males, females have the following disadvantages:
a. Special precautions needed during period of estrus (heat)
b. Lack of the rugged strength of the male
c. Higher license fee in most localities
d. Less aggressive.

Of course, the only time the bitch is attracted to the dog (male) is during the heat period. She can be bred only at this time. Likewise, the only time the dog is particularly interested in the bitch is during her period of heat which, normally, occurs twice a year.

Actually, the female has much in her favor; the only thing against her is the mating season which may be expected to occur about every twenty-six weeks (twice a year), with these periods lasting about twenty-two days each, during which time she can be bred on about twelve days. Thus, twice a year, and for three weeks each time, she must be confined or otherwise protected during these heat periods, provided mating is not desired.

On the other hand, the male is constantly "in season," so to speak. This is the reason that he roams if given the opportunity.

Of course, the danger of mating can be eliminated by spaying a female. Spaying is not a dangerous type of surgery, and they usually recover fairly rapidly. But there are some disadvantages. Spayed females have a tendency toward obesity, with the result that their diet has to be more limited and their exercise stepped up. Further, they are apt to be more lethargic and less on the alert as watchdog. Spaying also eliminates the possibility of raising puppies anytime in the future, should that time ever come.

Today, there are sprays that can be used on females that make them less attractive to males; and there are birth control pills for both males and females. Yet, none of these methods is entirely satisfactory.

7. *Long hair vs short hair*—This point should be carefully considered. Long-haired dogs require more brushing and grooming to keep them attractive and to control shedding, which is a problem indoors. Although short-haired dogs shed, they are easier to bathe, brush, and groom. Wirehaired dogs are less apt to shed, but their coats must be plucked out at intervals in order to keep them trim. Persons who are allergic to dogs usually encounter more difficulty when they're around long-haired dogs than with short-haired or wirehaired dogs.

8. *Indoors or outdoors?*—Generally long-coated dogs can stand cold weather better than short-haired ones. Hence, where the dog is to sleep outside, it's usually best either to (a) select a long-haired dog, or (b) provide warm, comfortable quarters.

9. *Best age to buy*—Generally speaking, puppies make an adjustment and can be moved more easily than older dogs. This means that they are usually acquired anywhere from one month of age to past weaning, at 4 to 5 months of age. Older puppies (4 to 5 months of age) have a firmer hold on life, are more easily house broken, and are past the dangers of early puppyhood. Moreover, you can earn a puppy's love and affection when he is 6 months of age just as easily and quickly as you can at one month of age— and with less inconvenience to you or whoever bears the brunt of those first few weeks of his new environment.

Of course, there are those who insist on the pleasure of bringing up a "wee little pup." This is fine, provided they are prepared to accept with it the not-so-adorable mischief and lack of training that goes with it. You, and you alone, must judge at what age will be best for you to secure the puppy.

10. *Pedigreed or just plain dog*—Purebreds have the advantage over dogs of nondescript breeding in that it is possible more nearly to predict their physical and mental make up at maturity; a purebred will likely resemble its parents. This built-in predictability causes police forces, those training dogs for the blind, and the Armed Services to select purebreds. Also, if used for breeding purposes, purebreds will transmit their desirable qualities to their offspring, for like produce like. Moreover, to many people, fine breeding in a pedigree imparts pride of ownership. But every puppy—whether purebred or not —is blessed with the ability to capture your heart and satisfy your desires for canine companionship. A long, wet tongue lapping at your hands and face, and needle-sharp teeth that for some reason never really hurt you, know no pedigree. In short, the puppy of unknown ancestry will make you just as true a pal and will think just as much of you as the "blueblood."

11. *Where to buy; what price to pay*—You can buy a dog from a kennel operator or breeder, dealer, pet shop, or private owner; or you can adopt it from the Humane Society shelter or dog pound.

The good kennel owner or breeder has built up a reputation for careful selection of breeding stock, clean quarters, and integrity in his business methods. Generally dogs purchased from a reputable kennel are healthy, free from parasites, and vaccinated. Also, most of them will agree to sell on a trial basis, allowing up to two weeks time to see how the dog and new owner make out. True enough, such a kennel may ask a higher price for puppies than other sources, but the buyer receives higher quality in return. Also, the services available from the kennel after you buy a puppy may be more important from your viewpoint than the saving of a few dollars and going without pedigree papers.

Reliable pet shops are also a popular source. Often high quality puppies are offered for sale in classified columns of local newspapers.

There is a wide range in prices. Generally speaking, purebreds cost more than dogs of nondescript breeding. Furthermore, the offspring of champions sell at higher than normal prices. For example, the son or daughter of a champion bitch and a champion dog might bring $1,000 or more, whereas the puppy of an unknown ancestry may be available for $10 to $20. But, like buying a suit of clothes or a hamburger, you usually get what you pay for.

12. *Buy a healthy dog*—Make certain that the dog is in good health. Do not accept a dog whose

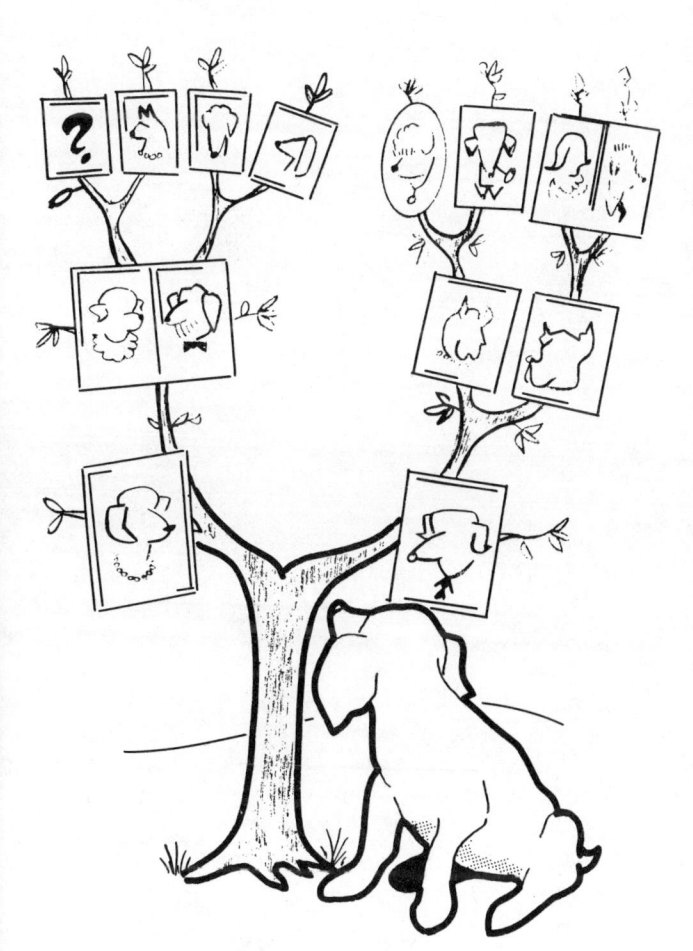

Fig. 195. The Family tree. (Drawing by R. F. Johnson)

eyes or nose are running. Check his teeth and gums; the teeth should be clean and white, and the gums should be pink. Examine his ears—make sure that they are free from signs of infection or inflammation. Feel his body—it should be firm and solid, and not soft and flabby. Stand him up—see that he has correct stance and straight legs, and that he doesn't favor a limb.

13. *Get experienced help if you need it*—If the person who is selecting and buying a dog has had little experience with animals, especially with dogs, it's generally best to get the counsel and advice of someone who knows dogs; either an experienced dog owner or a veterinarian. Have such a person accompany you when you select and buy; the fee involved will be a good investment.

SUMMARY

The dog lover may make a choice between breeds; between the large and the small, the quiet and the vivacious, the long coated and the short coated, and between a great array of colors. Also, he can select from among those breeds best adapted to the intended use. For coursing fleet-footed game in the open, the hunter may select from among the breeds with long legs, pointed heads, slender bodies, and long tails. For hunting in cover, he will want one of the breeds with a short body, shaggy coat, and a good bark. For protection or guard duty, a powerful, muscular breed should be selected. For a house dog and pet, one of the smaller breeds is usually best. For cold climates, a thick-coated dog is needed, while a short, thin coat is best adapted for hot climates. Indeed, the almost bewildering diversity of traits and breeds, makes it possible for the dog lover to select a dog adapted to every need and each person.

3
Breeding

Chapter 3

PART I. SOME PRINCIPLES OF DOG GENETICS

Mendel's Contribution to Genetics	*137*
Some Fundamentals of Heredity in Dogs	*138*
The Gene as the Unit of Heredity	*138*
Mutations	*144*
Simple Gene Inheritance (Qualitative Traits)	*144*
Dominant and Recessive Factors	*145*
Incomplete or Partial Dominance	*147*
Multiple Gene Inheritance (Quantitative Traits)	*147*
Genetics of Coat Color	*148*
Litter Size; Identical Twins	*151*
Sex Determination	*152*
Lethals and Abnormalities of Development	*153*
The Relative Importance of Sire and Dam	*155*
Prepotency	*155*
Nicking	*156*
Family Names	*156*
Heredity and Environment	*156*
Systems of Breeding	*157*
Purebreeding	*157*
Inbreeding	*157*
Close breeding	*158*
Linebreeding	*159*
Outcrossing	*159*
Grading Up	*160*
Crossbreeding	*160*
Selection in Dog Breeding	*160*
Bases of Selection	*160*
Selection Based on Type and Individuality	*161*
Selection Based on Pedigree	*161*

(Continued)

    Selection Based on Show-Ring Winnings   *161*
    Selection Based on Performance Testing   *162*
        Performance Testing Not New   *162*
  Selection for Several Characters   *163*

PART II. SOME PHYSIOLOGICAL ASPECTS OF REPRODUCTION IN DOGS

The Reproductive Organs of the Male   *163*
The Reproductive Organs of the Female   *165*
Normal Breeding Habits of Dogs   *166*
  Age of Puberty   *166*
  Age to Breed   *167*
  Signs of Heat   *167*
  Heat (Estrus) Period   *167*
  Time of Ovulation   *168*
  Fertilization   *168*
  Gestation Period   *168*
Conditioning the Bitch for Breeding   *168*
The Stud Dog   *169*
  Care and Management of the Stud Dog   *169*
  Age and Service of the Stud   *170*
  The Stud Fee   *170*
  Selecting the Stud Dog   *170*
Mating (The Act of Copulation)   *171*
Artificial Insemination   *171*
  Advantages of Artificial Insemination   *172*
  Limitations of Artificial Insemination   *172*
  Frozen Dog Semen   *173*
  Some Practical Considerations of Artificial Insemination   *173*
    Ways in Which to Make Artificial Insemination of Dogs More Successful   *174*
Sterility and Infertility   *174*
  Pregnancy Determination   *174*
  False Pregnancy   *175*
Care of the Pregnant Female   *175*
Whelping Time   *176*
  Signs of and Preparation for Whelping   *176*
  The Whelping Box   *176*
  Whelping (Delivery)   *177*
    Abnormal Conditions: Rendering Assistance   *178*
    The Afterbirth   *178*
    Cleaning Up   *178*
  Handling Newborn Puppies   *178*
    Colostrum   *179*
    The First Week   *179*
    Supplemental Feeding   *179*
  The Nursing Period   *180*
  Raising Orphan Puppies   *181*
  Weaning   *181*
  Register the Litter   *182*

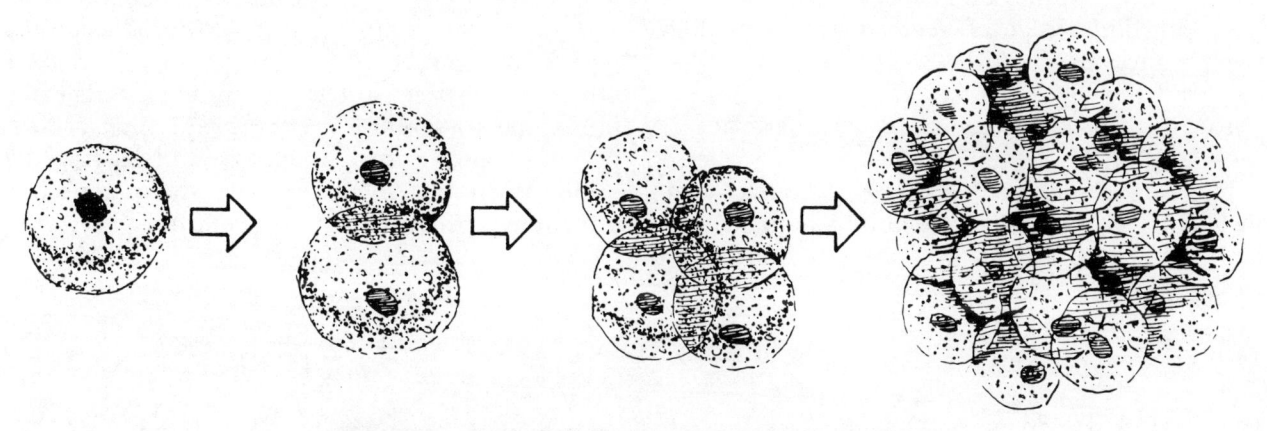

Fig. 196. When an egg cell is fertilized, it begins to divide; first in two, then in four, and finally into a cluster that looks something like a mulberry. (Drawing by J. L. Medeiros)

BREEDING[1]

All life begins with life. Each living thing must come from another living thing of the same kind. In all nature, there is never an exception. Thus, the life of each puppy begins with the mating of a male and a female. This process of creating a new life is called *reproduction*. Today, dog breeding is a science, the successful pursuance of which requires great study and careful planning. Thus, all those who breed dogs, whether as a business or as a hobby, should have a working knowledge of genetics and physiology of reproduction.

PART I. SOME PRINCIPLES OF DOG GENETICS

The height and speed of the Greyhound—coupled with his generally lithe build—is in marked contrast to the massiveness of the Bulldog and the size of the Chihuahua. Yet, there is good and substantial evidence that all three breeds descended from a common ancestry. Because of the diversity of genes carried by the original parent stock, it has been possible, through selection and the application of genetic principles, to evolve with three distinct breeds—the Greyhound for running at great speed, the Bulldog for guard duty, and the Chihuahua for a lap dog and pet. Also, through selection and planned matings, the parent stock of dogs has been altered to produce some breeds that are specialists at sight hunting and others at scent hunting; to produce some breeds that excel in water retrieving whereas others are better suited to finding land game birds; and to produce certain breeds that are superior for police duty, war duty, and leading the blind. Wittingly or unwittingly, and planned or unplanned, this transition—from the wolf, the

Fig. 197. All life begins with life. (Puppies. Courtesy Smithsonian Institution, Washington, D.C.)

---

[1] The author acknowledges with thanks the authoritative review accorded this chapter by: Mr. Herbert N. Holmes, Gunsmoke Kennels, 1541 East Lake Shore Drive, Springfield, Illinois 62705.

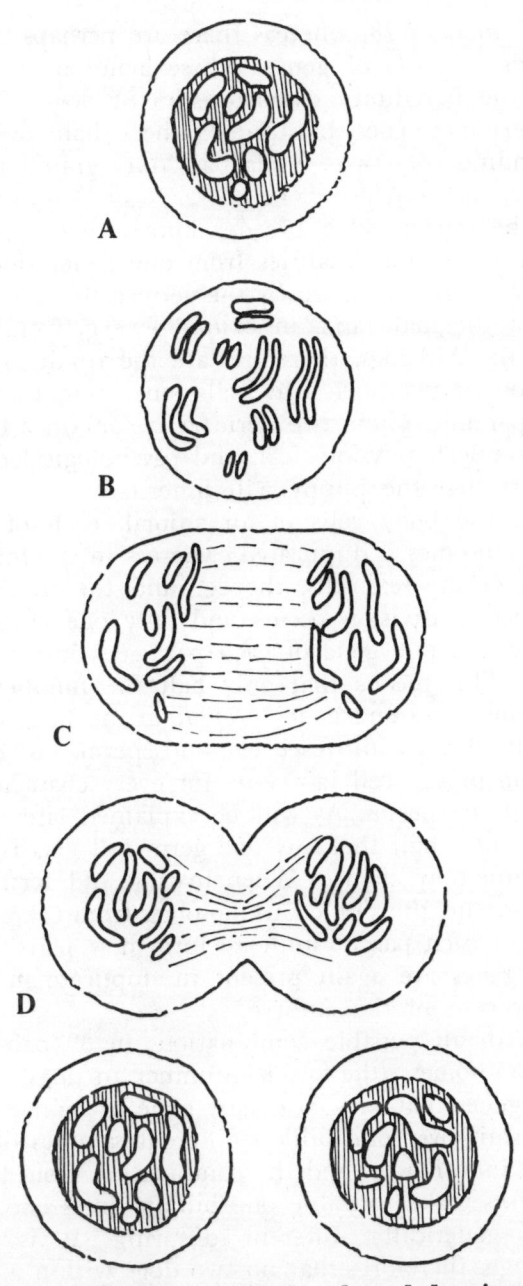

Fig. 198. A highly simplified, enlarged drawing of a single dog cell with chromosomes in nucleus. Actual cell would have 78 chromosomes in nucleus and nucleus would be much smaller in proportion to rest of cell.

B. Chromosomes begin to split lengthwise.

C. Split chromosomes move to opposite ends.

D. Two new cells begin to develop.

E. Two new cells are formed.

(Drawing by J. L. Medeiros)

jackal, and various wild dogs—has come about through the application of the principles of genetics.

MENDEL'S CONTRIBUTION TO GENETICS

Modern genetics was really founded by Gregor Johann Mendel, a cigar-smoking Austrian monk, who conducted breeding experiments with garden peas from 1857 to 1865, during the time of the U.S. Civil War. In his monastery at Brunn (now Brno, in Czechoslovakia), Mendel applied a powerful curiosity and a clear mind to reveal some of the basic principles of hereditary transmission. In 1866, he published in the proceedings of a local scientific society a report covering eight years of his studies, but for thirty-four years his findings went unheralded and ignored. Finally, in 1900, sixteen years after Mendel's death, three European biologists independently duplicated his

Fig. 199. Gregor Johann Mendel (1822–1884) a cigar-smoking Austrian monk, whose breeding experiments with garden peas founded modern genetics. (Courtesy The Bettmann Archive)

findings, and this led to the dusting off of the original paper published by the monk thirty-four years earlier.

The essence of Mendelism is that inheritance is by particles or units called *genes,* that these genes are present in pairs—one member of each pair having come from each parent—and that each gene maintains its identity generation after generation. Thus, Mendel's work with peas laid the basis for two of the general laws of inheritance: (1) the law of segregation, and (2) the independent assortment of genes. Later genetic principles have been added; yet all the phenomena of inheritance, based upon the reactions of genes, are generally known under the collective term, *Mendelism.*

Thus, modern genetics is really unique in that it was founded by an amateur who was not trained in science and who did his work merely as a hobby. During the years since the rediscovery of Mendel's principles (in 1900), many additional genetic principles have been added, but the fundamentals as set forth by Mendel have been proved correct in every detail. It can be said, therefore, that inheritance in both plants and animals follows the biological laws discovered by Mendel.

SOME FUNDAMENTALS OF HEREDITY IN DOGS

Space limitations will not permit covering all of the diverse field of genetics and animal breeding. Rather the author will present a condensation of the pertinent facts in regard to the field and summarize their applications to dog breeding.

THE GENE AS THE UNIT OF HEREDITY

Genes determine all the hereditary characteristics of dogs, from body size to the color of the hair. They are truly the fundamental unit of genetics.

The bodies of all dogs are made up of millions or even billions of tiny cells, microscopic in size. Each cell contains a nucleus in which there are a number of pairs of bundles, called *chromosomes.* In turn, the chromosomes carry pairs of minute particles, called *genes,* which are the basic hereditary material. The nucleus of each body cell of dogs contains 39 pairs of chromosomes, or a total of 78, whereas there are perhaps thousands of pairs of genes. These genes determine all the hereditary characteristics of dogs. Thus, inheritance goes by units rather than by the blending of two fluids, as our grandfathers thought.

The modern dog breeder knows that the job of transmitting qualities from one generation to the next is performed by the germ cells—a *sperm* from the male and an *ovum,* or *egg,* from the female. All dogs, therefore, are the result of the union of two such tiny cells, one from each of its parents. These two germ cells contain all the anatomical, physiological, and psychological characters that the puppy will inherit.

In the body cells of an animal, each of the chromosomes is duplicated; whereas in the formation of the sex cells, the egg and the sperm, a reduction division occurs and only one chromosome and one gene of each pair goes into a sex cell. This means that only half the number of chromosomes and genes present in the body cells of the dog go into each egg and sperm, but each sperm or egg cell has genes for every characteristic of its species. As will be explained later, the particular half that any one germ cell gets is determined by chance. When mating and fertilization occur, the single chromosomes from the germ cell of each parent unite to form new pairs, and the genes are again present in duplicate in the body cells of the embryo.

With all possible combinations in 39 pairs of chromosomes (the species number in dogs) and the genes that they bear, any male or female can transmit over one billion different samples of its own inheritance; and the combination from both parents makes possible one billion times one billion genetically different offspring. It is not strange, therefore, that no two dogs within a given breed (except identical twins from a single egg split after fertilization) are exactly alike. We can marvel that the members of a given breed bear as much resemblance to each other as they do.

Even between such closely related individuals as full sisters, it is possible that there will be quite wide differences in size, growth rate, temperament, conformation, and in almost every conceivable character. Admitting that many of these differences may be due to undetected differences in environment, it is still true that in such animals much of the variation is due to hereditary differences. A male, for example, will sometimes transmit to one offspring much better inheritance

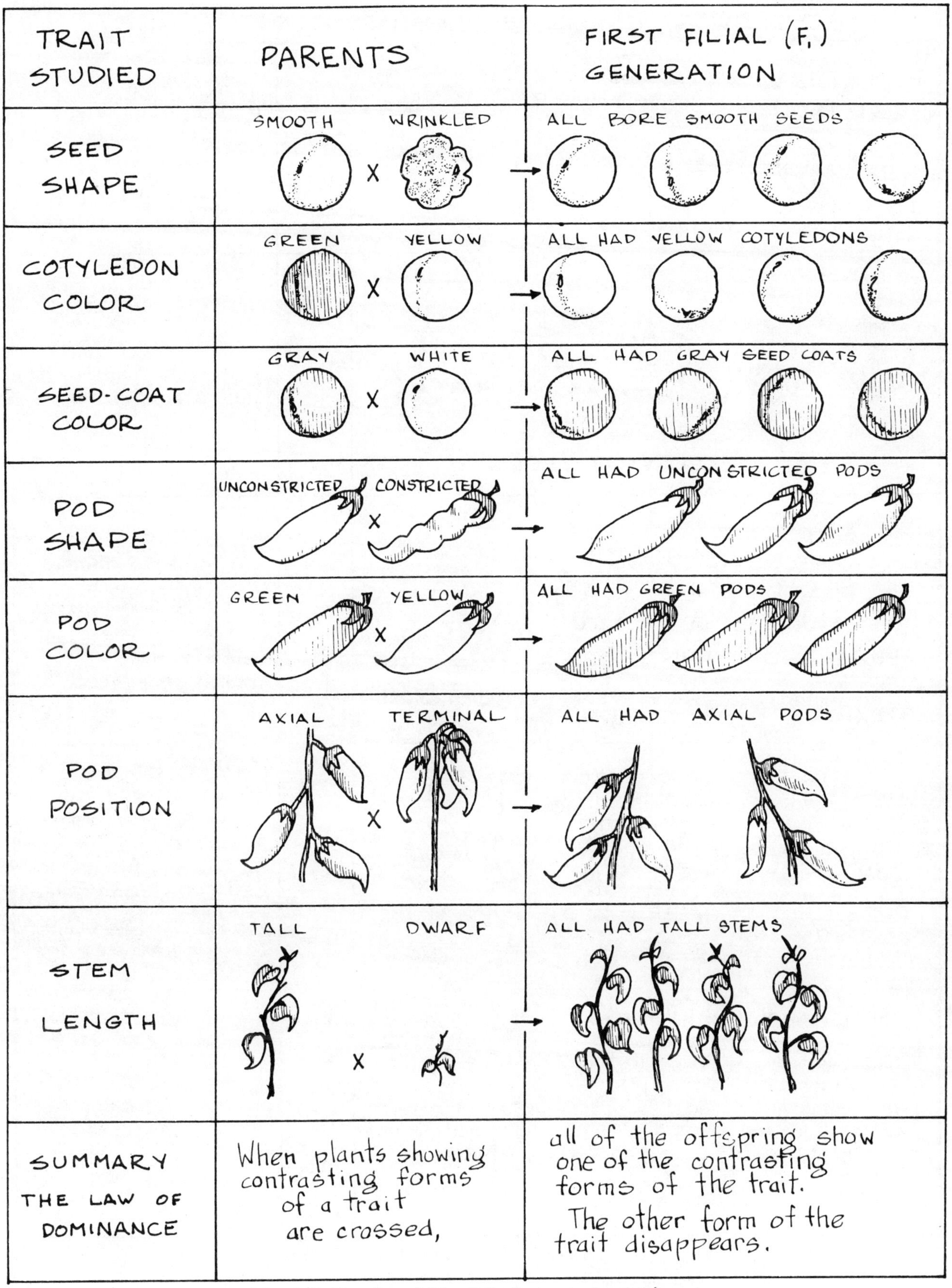

TRAIT STUDIED	PARENTS	FIRST FILIAL (F₁) GENERATION
SEED SHAPE	SMOOTH × WRINKLED	ALL BORE SMOOTH SEEDS
COTYLEDON COLOR	GREEN × YELLOW	ALL HAD YELLOW COTYLEDONS
SEED-COAT COLOR	GRAY × WHITE	ALL HAD GRAY SEED COATS
POD SHAPE	UNCONSTRICTED × CONSTRICTED	ALL HAD UNCONSTRICTED PODS
POD COLOR	GREEN × YELLOW	ALL HAD GREEN PODS
POD POSITION	AXIAL × TERMINAL	ALL HAD AXIAL PODS
STEM LENGTH	TALL × DWARF	ALL HAD TALL STEMS
SUMMARY — THE LAW OF DOMINANCE	When plants showing contrasting forms of a trait are crossed,	all of the offspring show one of the contrasting forms of the trait. The other form of the trait disappears.

Fig. 200. Results of Mendel's first set of experiments. (Drawing by J. L. Medeiros)

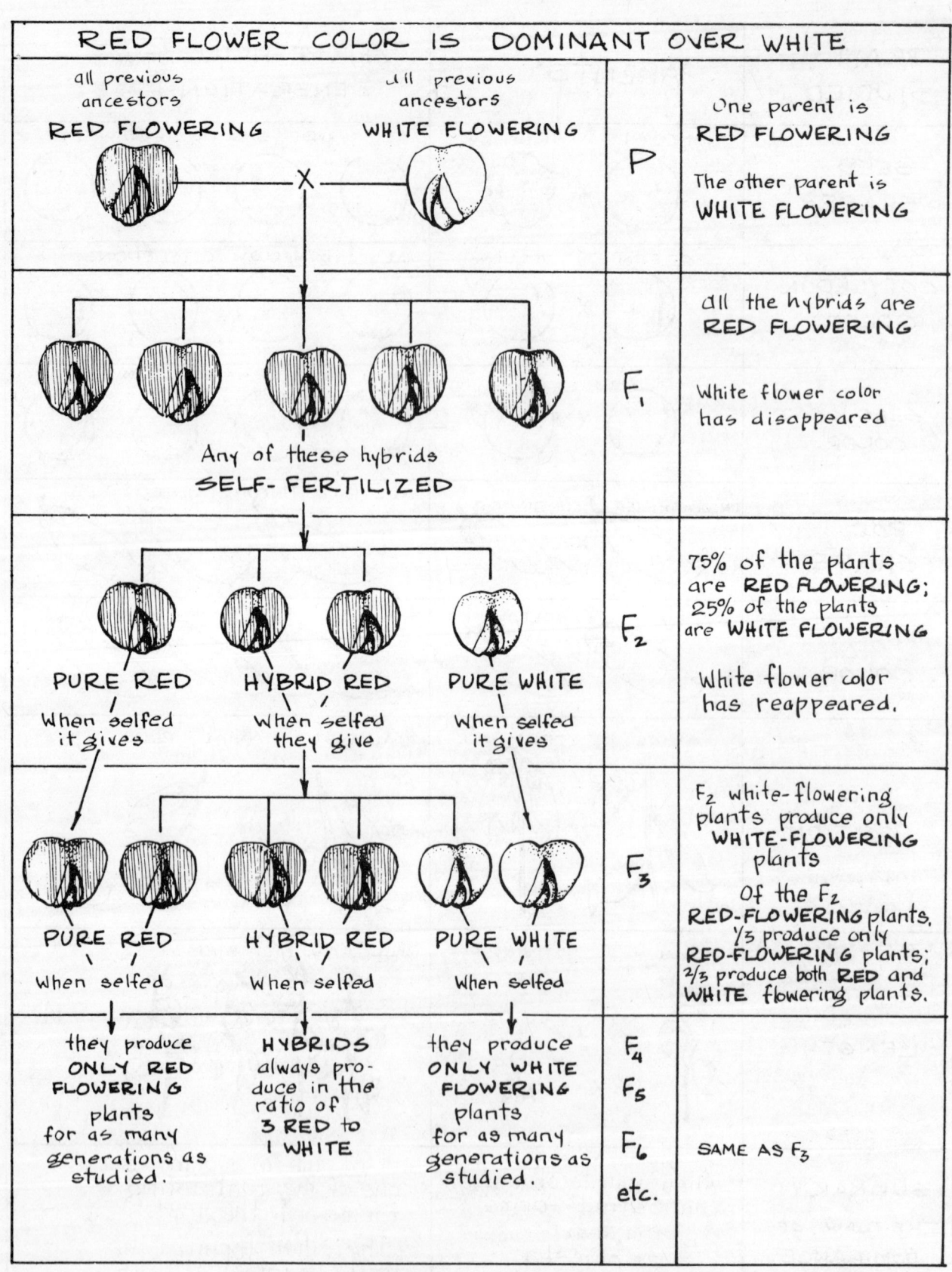

Fig. 201. Inheritance of flower color in Mendel's experiment. (Drawing by J. L. Medeiros)

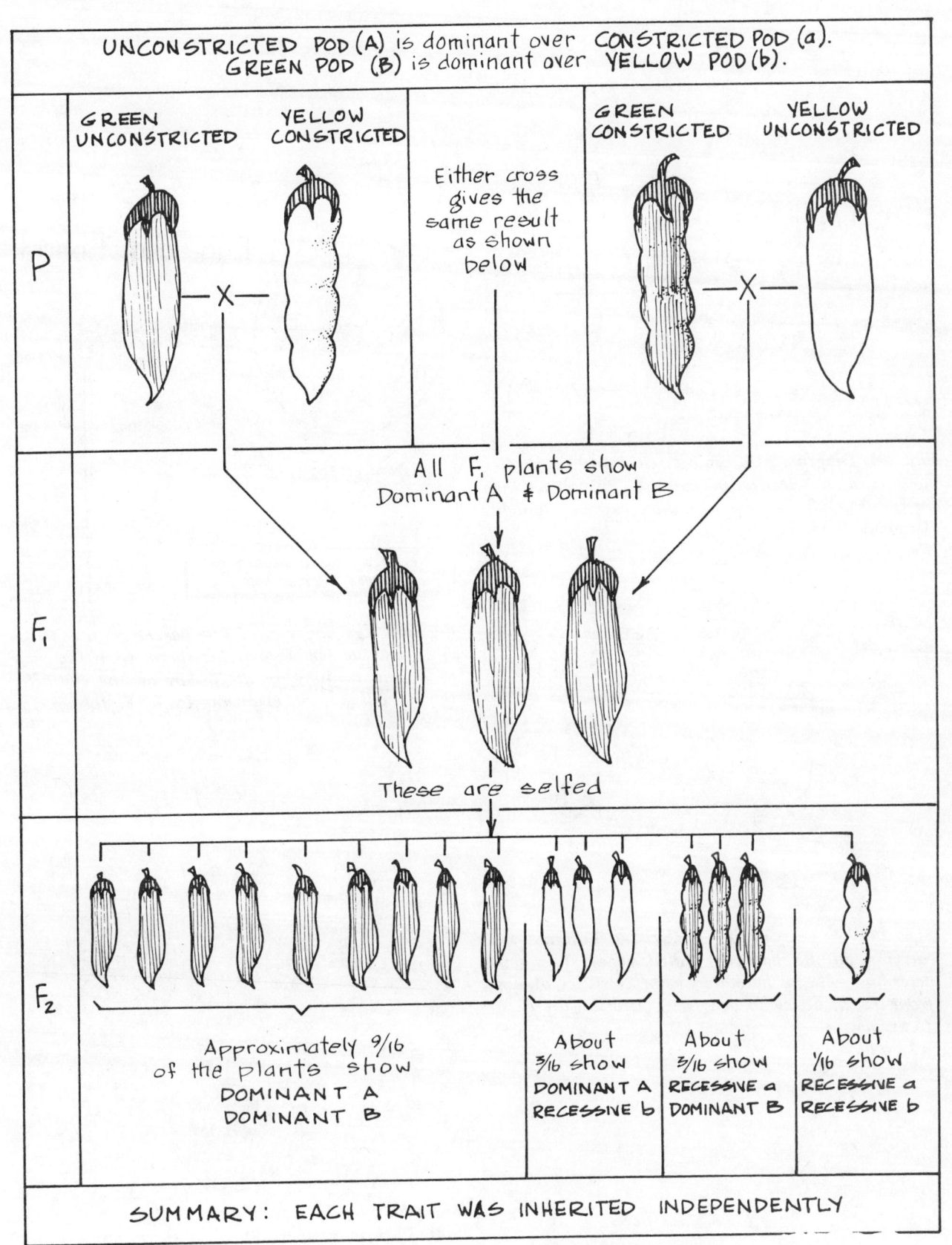

Fig. 202. The inheritance of two traits simultaneously as demonstrated by Mendel's experiment. (Drawing by J. L. Medeiros)

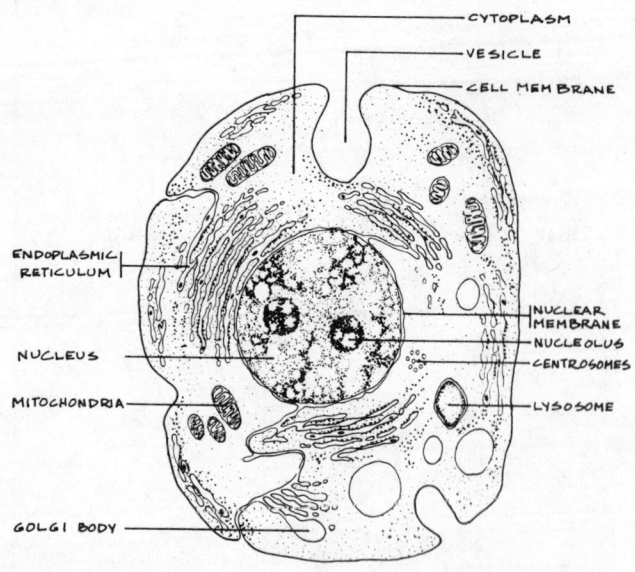

Fig. 203. Diagram of a typical cell, based on studies made with the electron microscope. This shows that the cell is much more complex than was once thought. (Drawing by J. L. Medeiros)

Schematic Drawing of a Pair of Chromosomes

Note: The shaded discs represent pairs of genes. The various characteristics which the respective gene pairs govern is indicated. A large disc in a pair denotes a dominant.

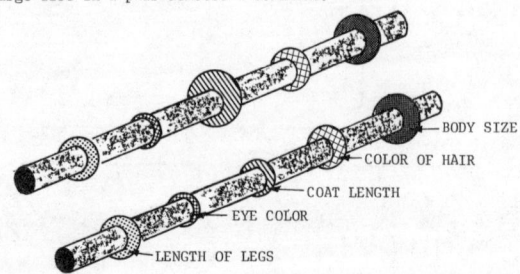

Fig. 204. A pair of bundles, called chromosomes, carrying minute particles, called genes. The genes determine all the hereditary characteristics of dogs, from length of leg to body size. (Drawing by R. F. Johnson)

Egg and Sperm

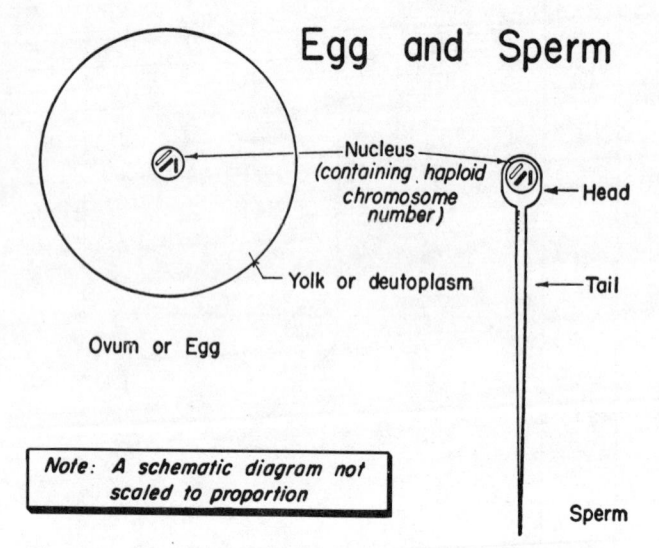

Note: A schematic diagram not scaled to proportion

Fig. 205. Egg and sperm. The parent germ cells, the egg from the female and the sperm from the male, unite and transmit to the puppy all the characters that it will inherit. (Drawing by R. F. Johnson)

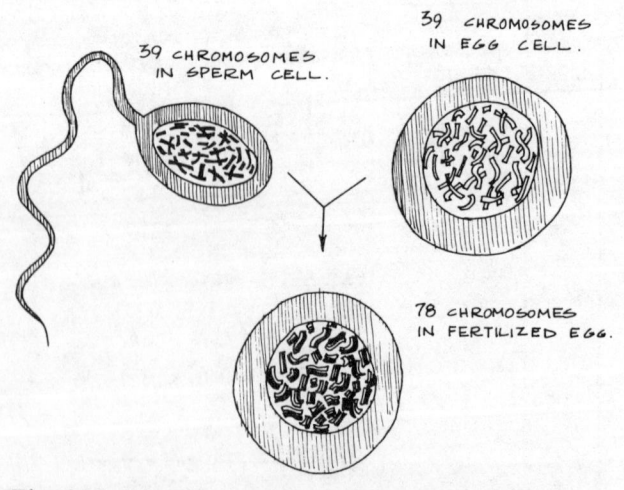

Fig. 206. The dog sperm and the dog egg each contains 39 chromosomes. When the sperm and egg join, the single fertilized egg cell that results has 78 chromosomes, arranged in pairs. These chromosomes, in turn, carry thousands of genes that determine what each living dog will be like. (Drawing by J. L. Medeiros)

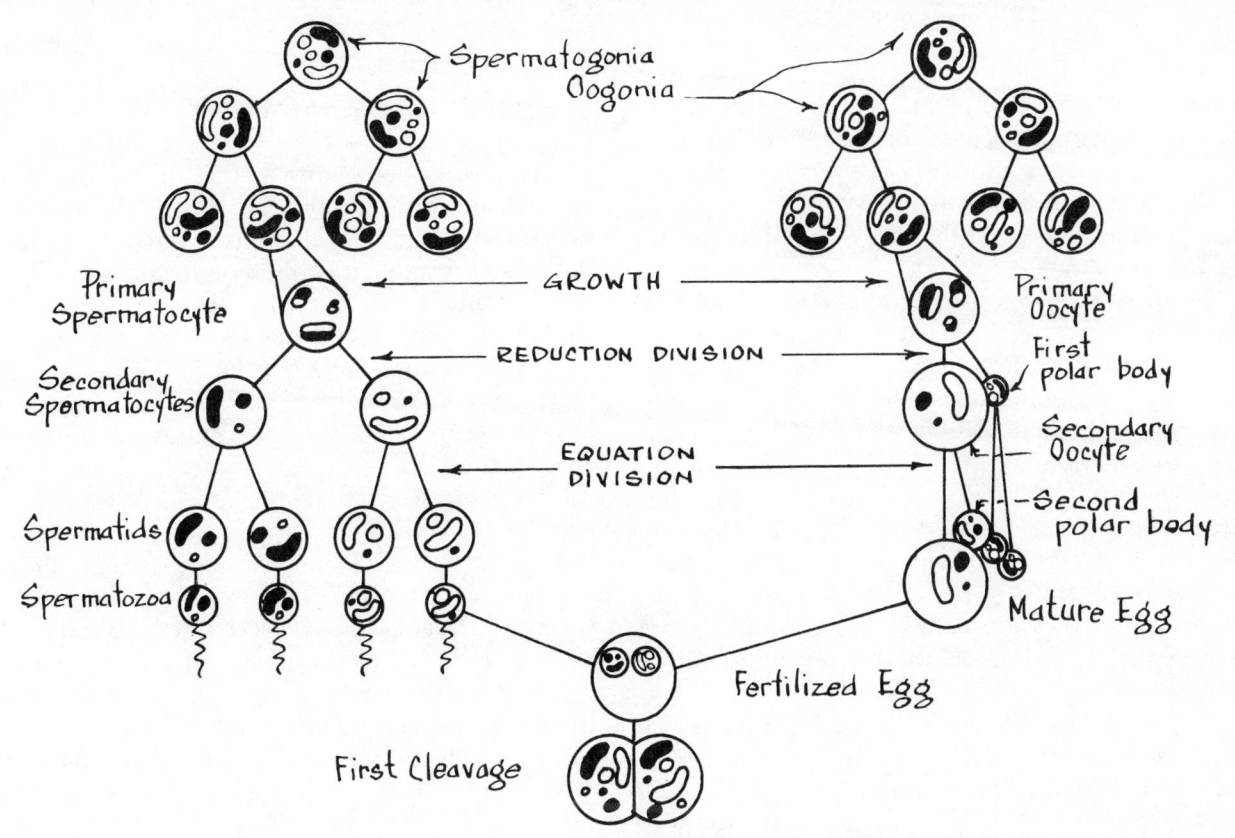

Fig. 207. Maturation, or meiosis, of germ cells in animals. The process begins with the third row of cells; maternal chromosomes white, paternal black. All chromosomes in the fertilized egg received from the mature egg are thereafter maternal, and those received from the spermatozoon are thereafter paternal, regardless of what they were in the mature germ cells. (Drawing by J. L. Medeiros)

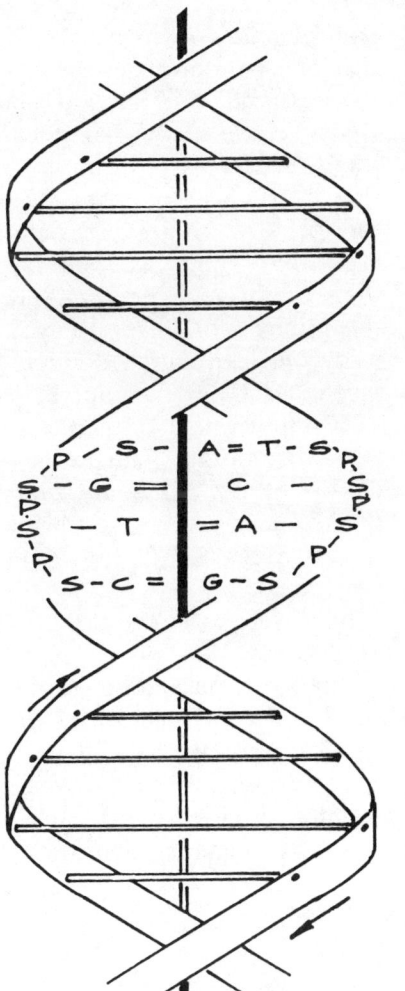

Fig. 208. Diagrammatic representation of the Watson-Crick DNA structure. P, phosphate; S, sugar; A, adenine; T, thymine; G, guanine; and C, cytonsine. The horizontal parallel lines symbolize hydrogen bonding between complimentary bases. (Drawing by J. L. Medeiros)

than he does to most of his get, simply as the result of chance differences in the genes that go to different sperm at the time of the reduction division. Such difference in inheritance of offspring has been called both the hope and the despair of the dog breeder.

If an animal receives similar determiners or genes from each parent, it will produce a uniform set of offspring; because any half of its inheritance is just like any other half. For example, regardless of what combination of chromosomes go into a particular germ cell, it will be just like any other egg or sperm from the same individual. Such animals are referred to as being *homozygous*. Few, if any, of our dogs are in this hereditary state at the present time. Instead of being homozygous, they are *heterozygous*. This explains why there may be such wide variation within the offspring of any given male and female.

Variation between the offspring of animals that are not pure or homozygous, to use the technical term, is not to be marveled at, but is rather to be expected. No one would expect to draw exactly 35 sound apples and 15 rotten ones every time he took a random sample of 50 from a barrel containing 70 sound ones and 30 rotten ones, although on the average—if enough samples were drawn—he would expect to get about that proportion of each. Individual drawings would, of course, vary rather widely. Exactly the same situation applies to the relative numbers of "good" and "bad" genes that may be present in different germ cells from the same dog. Because of this situation, the mating of a Greyhound bitch with a fine track record to a Greyhound dog that on the average transmits relatively good performance will not always produce a puppy of a merit equal to that of its parents. The puppy could be markedly poorer than the parents or, happily, it could in some cases be better than either parent.

Selection and close breeding are the tools through which dog breeders can obtain males and females whose chromosomes and genes contain similar hereditary determiners—dogs that are genetically more homozygous.

MUTATIONS

Gene changes are technically known as *mutations. A mutation may be defined as a sudden variation which is later passed on through inheritance and that results from changes in a gene or genes*. Mutations are not only rare, but they are prevailingly harmful. For example, albino mutations in dogs (white animals with pink eyes) are not as well equipped to survive as their parents. The observed differences between animals are usually due to different combinations of genes being present rather than to mutations. Each gene probably changes only about once in each 100,000 to 1,000,000 animals produced. This wide range in frequency indicates what is generally recognized—some genes mutate more often and more easily than others.

The short legs of the Pembroke Welsh Corgi are the result of a mutation. Being a mutation, it bred true; and being considered desirable, it was perpetuated.

Gene changes can be accelerated by exposure to X rays, radium, mustard gas, and ultraviolet light. Such changes may eventually be observed in the offspring of both people and animals of Japan who were exposed to the intense radiation of the atom bombs unleashed in World War II.

SIMPLE GENE INHERITANCE (QUALITATIVE TRAITS)

In the simplest type of inheritance, only one pair of genes is involved. Thus, Mendel found that one pair of genes was responsible for height in peas, and that tall was dominant over dwarf. Likewise, we know that one pair of genes is responsible for eye color in Pointers, and that brown eyes are dominant over pearl eyes. If both the pairs of genes are determiners for brown eyes, the puppy will be brown eyed; if both the pairs of genes are determiners for pearl eyes, the puppy will be pearl eyed. If we cross a homozygous brown-eyed Pointer (EE) with a homozygous pearl eyed Pointer (ee), the first cross (F_1) puppies will be *monohybrids* (Ee); and all first cross animals will be brown eyed. However, if two of these monohybrids (Ee) are crossed, the second cross (F_2) offspring will be in the ratio of three (75%) brown eyed to one (25%) pearl eyed.

But were we to make further crosses, we would find that not all these F_2 brown eyed Pointers are pure for eye color. Actually, in the F_2 puppies, 25% of them are pure brown eyed, 50% of them are hybrids for that trait, and 25% of them are pure pearl eyed. The 50% hybrids are not species hybrids, like the mule. Rather, they are genetic hybrids (or heterozygotes), which involve a single pair of genes, one of which is dominant and the other recessive. This phenomenon is explained and understood by assuming that one parent has the genes for the dominant brown eyed characteristic and the other parent the genes for the recessive pearl eyed characteristic at similar loci in paired homologous chromosomes; that one pair of each of these genes is present in the monohybrid; but that these genes separate or segregate out when the monohybrid produces germ cells (sperms and eggs) with the half (*haploid*) number of chromosomes.

In addition to eye color, other examples of single gene inheritance—involving one pair of genes only—in dogs include coat color and coat length.

It should be borne in mind that the eye colors and percentages given in the F_2 cross referred to above occur at random and that eye color will appear in the offspring in the proportions indicated only when relatively large numbers are concerned. The possible gene combinations, therefore, are governed by the laws of chance, operating in much the same manner as the results obtained from flipping coins. For example, if a penny is flipped often enough, the number of heads and tails will come out about even. However, with the laws of chance in operation, it is possible that out of any four tosses one might get all heads, all tails, or even three to one. For this reason, dog breeders should not make the mistake of trying to apply Mendel's law to a single litter of puppies, then assume that it doesn't hold when the proportions don't come out according to expectations.

DOMINANT AND RECESSIVE FACTORS

Some genes have the ability to prevent or mask the expression of others, with the result that the genetic makeup of such animals cannot be recognized with perfect accuracy. This ability to cover up or mask the presence of one member of a set of genes is called *dominance*. The gene which masks the one is the *dominant gene;* the one which is masked is the *recessive gene*.

In Pointers, the brown-eyed character is dominant to the pearl-eyed character. Thus, if a pure brown-eyed male is mated to pearl-eyed females (or the sexes may be reversed), the resulting progeny are not midway between the two parents but are all brown eyed. It must be remembered, however, that not all brown-eyed Pointers are pure for the brown-eyed character, many of them carry a factor for pearl eyes in the hidden or recessive condition. In genetic terminology, animals that are pure for a certain character—for example, the brown-eyed character—are termed *homozygous,* whereas those that have one dominant and one recessive factor are termed *heterozygous*.

A simple breeding test can be used in order to determine whether a brown-eyed Pointer male is homozygous or heterozygous, but it is impossible to determine such purity or impurity merely through inspection. The breeding test consists of mating the brown-eyed sire with a number of pearl-eyed females. If the male is pure or homozygous for the brown-eyed character, all of the puppies will be brown eyed; if he is impure or heterozygous, only half of the resulting offspring will, on the average, be brown eyed and half will have pearl eyes. Dog breeders may test their stud dogs in this manner.

It is clear, therefore, that a dominant character will cover up a recessive. Hence an animal's breeding performance cannot be recognized by its *phenotype* (how it looks), a fact which is of great significance in practical breeding.

As can be readily understood, dominance often makes the task of identifying and discarding all animals carrying an undesirable recessive factor a difficult one. Recessive genes can be passed on from generation to generation, appearing only when two animals, both of which carry a recessive factor, happen to mate. Even then, only one out of four offspring produced will, on the average, be homozygous for the recessive factor and show it.

In German Shepherd Dogs, white color (with dark eyes) is an example of such an undesirable recessive factor. Although jet black to tan have been the accepted colors of the breed since its founding in Germany in 1899, white has persisted through the years as a recessive. For this reason, a white puppy occasionally and unexpectedly shows up in a purebred German Shepherd litter. This appearance of a white puppy in the German Shepherd breed does not signify any impurity of breeding, but merely the outcropping of a long-hidden recessive gene. When a white puppy does appear, however, one can be very certain that both the sire and the dam contributed equally to the condition and that each of them carried the recessive gene for white color. This fact should be given consideration in the culling program.

As the factor for white is recessive, the white animals are pure for color. The mating of two white animals, therefore, will always produce

Figs. 209–210. A white German Shepherd puppy, due to a recessive.

white puppies. Hence, when dark-eyed, white German Shepherd Dogs are mated, all the offspring will be dark eyed and white—never any other color.

If such an undesirable recessive appears in purebreds, the action should be drastic. A reputable breeder of purebreds has an obligation not only to himself but to his customers. Purebred animals must be purged of undesirable genes and lethals (see section on "Lethals and Abnormalities of Development" in this chapter). This can be done by:

1. Eliminating those sires and dams that are known to have transmitted the undesirable recessive character.

2. Eliminating both the abnormal and normal offspring produced by these sires and dams (approximately half of the normal animals will carry the undesirable character in the recessive condition).

3. By, in some instances, breeding a prospective stud dog to a number of females known to carry the factor for the undesirable recessive, thereby making sure that the new sire is free from the recessive.

Such action is expensive, and it calls for considerable courage. Yet it is the only way in which purebred dogs can be freed from such undesirable genes.

Table 5 contains a list of those characters of dogs that are generally recognized as dominant or recessive. Unfortunately, few dog genetic studies have been made under controlled experimental conditions; hence, much of the information that is presently accepted, including the dominant-recessive list that follows, is based on observations, and, therefore, subject to the errors and misinterpretations that usually characterize such data.

TABLE 5
DOMINANT AND RECESSIVE CHARACTERS OF DOGS

	Dominant	Recessive
Color Inheritance:	All colors	Albino (pink eyes) white
	All colors	Dark-eyed white
	Black-and-brindle	Black-and-tan
	Black-and-tan	Liver-and-tan
	Brindle	Tan
	Merling	Black-and-tan
	Red	Cream
	Sable	Black-and-tan
	Sable	Merling
	Ticking	Nonticking
Coat:	Coarse hair	Fine hair
	Short hair	Long hair
	Sparse coat	Dense coat
	Straight hair	Curly hair
	Wire coat	Smooth coat
Eye color:	Brown eye	Pearl eye
	Brown eye	Yellow eye
Others:	Dewclaws (the fifth toe, located on the inside of the legs and close to the ground)	No dewclaws
	Short ears	Long ears
	Straight tail	Curly tail
	Short legs	Long legs

INCOMPLETE OR PARTIAL DOMINANCE

The results of crossing brown-eyed with pearl-eyed Pointers are clear-cut because the brown-eyed character is completely dominant over its *allele*–pearl eyed (see Glossary for definition of allele). But, there are varying degrees of dominance—from complete dominance to an entire lack of dominance. In the vast majority of cases, however, dominance is neither complete nor absent, but incomplete or partial. Also, the fact that one trait in an organism is completely dominant over its allele does not mean that every trait in that organism will illustrate complete dominance. For example, in man, dark hair color is completely dominant over light hair color, and dark eye color is completely dominant over light eye color. But skin color shows incomplete dominance, with the result that a negro-white marriage gives rise to mulatto children.

MULTIPLE GENE INHERITANCE (QUANTITATIVE TRAITS)

Relatively few of the utility traits in dogs which we value highly are one-gene traits, or simple-gene inherited traits like the eye color of Pointers described in the section "Simple Gene Inheritance (Qualitative Traits)." Rather, such characters as racing ability (speed and endurance) in Greyhounds, bird-hunting ability in Pointers, trailing ability in Bloodhounds, guard duty in German Shepherd Dogs, and livestock savvy in Collies are due to many genes; thus, they are called *multiple-factor characters* or *multiple-gene characters*. Because such characters show all manner of gradations—from high to low ability, for example—they are sometimes referred to as *quantitative traits*.

In quantitative inheritance, the extremes (ei-

147

ther good or bad) tend to swing back to the average. Thus, the offspring of a winning Greyhound male and a winning Greyhound female are not apt to be as good as either parent. Likewise, and happily so, the progeny of two very mediocre parents will likely be superior to either parent.

Estimates of the number of pairs of genes affecting each important characteristic vary greatly, but the majority of geneticists agree that, for most such characters, ten or more pairs of genes are involved. Growth rate in dogs, therefore, is affected by: (1) the animal's appetite; (2) food consumption; (3) food utilization—that is, the proportion of the food eaten that is absorbed into the bloodstream; (4) food assimilation—the use to which the nutrients are put after absorption; and (5) food conversion—whether used for muscle, fat, or bone formation. This should indicate clearly enough that such a characteristic as growth rate is controlled by many genes and that it is difficult to determine the mode of inheritance of such characters.

GENETICS OF COAT COLOR[2]

The genetics of coat color in dogs has received considerable attention. Although a number of conclusions relative to the inheritance of coat color have been reached by research workers, many of them are tentative, and several of them are in disagreement. The most complete work on the subject is by Dr. Clarence C. Little, the noted American geneticist, working at the Jackson Laboratory, Bar Harbor, Maine. Dr. Little makes the following pertinent points relative to coat color in dogs:

1. Color in living tissues is caused by granules of pigment called *melanin,* of which there are two basic varieties, dark (black and brown) and light (yellow). The shade is determined by the size of these granules and the density in which they are packed together.

2. The wild type of coat color is called *agouti,* a hair pattern which is banded with light and dark shades alternately; the tip of the hair is dark, the base light. Puppies with the agouti type of coloring are born black, because only the black tips of the hairs come through the skin at birth. The characteristic banding of the hair develops later.

3. At least ten different gene pairs are concerned with coat color in dogs. They are situated on corresponding loci of homologous pairs of chromosomes. Some are multiple alleles, others dominant-recessive gene pairs. Every dog must carry a pair of each of these ten, but no dog can carry more than one pair from each series. In some cases, however, there is a "choice" as to which of several allelic genes shall compose the pair. At four of the ten pairs of loci concerned with coat color, there are series of alleles, and any two members of a series can be present. The remaining six loci are concerned with single gene pairs only.

Dr. Little has arranged his series in the order in which genes mask each other, each gene being masked by the gene above it in the series—that is, in the order of *epistasis*. He calls his series of multiple alleles A, C, E, and S; and his single gene pairs B, D, G, M, P, and T, the capitals indicating the dominant. The gene summaries given in Table 6 are taken from Dr. Little's book (see footnote No. 2).

---

[2] This section is based on the classical work of Dr. Clarence C. Little, Sc.D., as reported in *The Inheritance of Coat Color in Dogs,* Cornell University Press, Ithaca, New York, 1957. Also, the author gratefully acknowledges the authoritative review accorded this section by Dr. John L. Fuller, who, for ten years, was associated with Dr. Little at the Jackson Laboratory; now Professor, State University of New York, Binghamton, New York.

TABLE 6

IMPORTANT GENES IN CONTROL OF COAT COLOR IN DOGS

Series or Pair	Gene	Effect	Comments
Series A	A	All its alleles control the relative distribution of dark and light pigment	
	A^s	Permits distribution of dark color over the whole body	Epistatic to a^y, a^t
	a^y	Restricts the area of dark pigment, and may produce tan or sable	Epistatic to a^t
	a^t	Produces bicolors, black-and-tan, liver-and-tan	
	a^w	A possible allele which would produce the wild agouti type of color	
Series C	C	Gives full pigmentation in its most usual form, dense black, brown, or red	Epistatic to c^{ch}, c^a
	c^{ch}	Reduces red and yellow more than it does black, to give the chinchilla type of coloring. Has no visible influence in solid black dogs, but its effects may be shown in liver coloring	Epistatic to c^a
	c^a	Complete albinism, absence of all pigment and very rare in dogs	
	c^e	For extreme dilution, to account for extremely pale pigmentation with reduced eye pigment	
Series E	E	Allows the formation of black or brown pigment over the whole body	Epistatic to e^{br}, e
	e^{br}	Brindle In the presence of a^y or a^t, this gives the bands of dark pigment on a lighter ground, which constitute brindle markings. e^{br} is epistatic to e, but incompletely hypostatic to E	Epistatic to e
	e	Red yellow pigmentation, from deep mahogany to lemon. No black pigment is found in the hair	Radically restricts effect of A
	e^m	A superextension of dark pigment, to form a mask, typically in fawn breeds, i.e., Pug. If present, is epistatic to E	

A complicated relationship exists between the E and the A series

Series or Pair	Gene	Effect	Comments
Series S		This series deals with the pattern of white and color distribution, and contains at least four alleles	
	S	Solid color, with no white except for very small markings—toes or chest	

(Continued)

TABLE 6 (CONTINUED)

Series or Pair	Gene	Effect	Comments
	s^i	The so-called "Irish spotting." One or more of several areas may be white, for example, muzzle, forehead, feet, tail tip, belly, throat, neck	
	sp	Piebald spotting	
	sw	Extreme piebald spotting	

The six single gene pairs concerned in coat color follow:

Series or Pair	Gene	Effect	Comments
The B pair	B	Gives black	
	b	Gives brown—liver	
The D pair		Controls density of pigmentation	
	D	Dense pigment	
	d	Maltese or blue dilution, i.e., blue Great Danes, Chows, etc.	
The G pair		For graying or paling from birth to old age	
	G	Paling or becoming progressively grayer in puppies born black, i.e., Kerry Blue Terrier	
	g	Absence of paling	
The M pair		For merling	
	M	Produces irregular patches of color, black or liver, against a lighter background, and usually increases the amount of white in the coat	
	MM	The double dominant, is semilethal. In some breeds it causes deformities, deafness, blindness, sterility, and completely white coat color	
	Mm	Normal merle, c.f. Collies	
	mm	Nonmerle	
The P pair		Unusual genes, causing reduction in dark pigment only when in the double recessive pp, without reduction in red or yellow. It produces pale blue, "lilac," liver; dogs with pp become pale yellowish fawn, "champagne," "silver" and so on	
The T pair		The gene for "ticking" applied generally to spotting, though in Dalmatians it has a different connotation to the breeder	
	TT	Spotting, ticking	
	tt	No spotting, clear white areas	

TABLE 7
GENES FOR COAT COLOR IN CERTAIN BREEDS OF DOGS

Breed and Color	Genes
Basenji (red)	a^y B C D E g m P s^i t
Beagle (tricolor-clear-white areas)	a^t B C D E g m P s^p t
Beagle (tricolor-ticked-white areas)	a^t B C D E g m P s^p T
Dachshund (black, tan points)	a^t B C D E g m P S t
Dachshund (liver, tan points)	a^t b C D E g m P S t
Dalmatian (black spots)	A^s B C D E g m P s^w T
Great Dane (blue)	A^s B C d E g m P S t
Great Dane (merle)	A^s B C D E g M P S t
Irish Terrier (red)	a^y B C D E g m P S t
Irish Water Spaniel (liver)	A^s b C D E g m P S t
Kerry Blue Terrier (blue)	A^s B C D E G m P S t
Labrador Retriever (black)	A^s B c^{ch} D E g m P S t
Newfoundland (black)	A^s B C D E g m P S t
Norwegian Elkhound	a^w B c^{ch} D E g m P S t
Pekingese (pink-eyed dilute)	A^s B C D E g m p S t
Poodle (blue; born blue)	A^s B C d E g m P S t
Poodle (gray; born black)	A^s B C D E G m P S t
Poodle (light silver; born gray)	A^s B C d E G m P S t
Scottish Terrier (black)	A^s B C D e^{br} g m P S t
Scottish Terrier (brindle)	a^y B C D e^{br} g m P S t
Weimaraner	A^s b C d E g m P S t

According to present thinking, the gene complex of every dog's coat color consists of ten pairs of genes. Six of these are caused by single gene pairs in the dominant-recessive relationship. In the case of the first four series of Table 6 (Series A, C, E, and S), there are a number of allelic genes from which the pairs may be made up, and only one pair of each character can exist in any one dog. Table 7 shows how these patterns work out for several breeds of dogs.

LITTER SIZE; IDENTICAL TWINS

There are wide species differences with respect to multiple birth; the dog and the hog being the most prolific and the cow and the horse the least.

Litter size is inherited; thus, larger litters are produced in some breeds and in some families more than in others. But factors other than heredity also play a part in determining litter size. For example, obese females produce smaller litters than females in proper breeding condition, because they shed fewer eggs and implantation may be impaired.

Some opinions to the contrary, the stud dog has little effect on litter size, provided he is fertile, because far more sperm are ejaculated than are needed.

Most litters number 6 to 7, with the larger dogs having more—Foxhounds, Mastiffs, and St. Bernards may have 20 or more—and the toy breeds having fewer—often twins and triplets.

Litter brothers or sisters (always of the same sex) that develop from the same ovum and spermatazoon are known as *identical twins,* as distinguished from *fraternal twins.*

Fraternal twins are produced from two separate ova that were fertilized by different sperm. Identical twins result when a single fertilized egg divides, very early in its embryology, into two separate individuals.

In humans, nearly half of the like-sexed twins are identical, whereas in cattle only 5 to 12 percent of such births are identical. The frequency of identical twins in dogs is unknown. Such twins are always of the same sex, a pair of males or a pair of females, and alike genetically—their chromosomes and genes are alike; they are 100 percent related. When the bodies of identical twins are not entirely separated, they are known as *Siamese twins.*

Genetically, fraternal twins are no more alike

than full brothers and sisters born at different times; they are only 50 percent related. They usually resemble each other more, however, because they were subjected to the same intrauterine environment before birth and generally they are reared under much the same environment. Also, fraternal twins may be of different sexes.

SEX DETERMINATION

On the average, and when considering a large population, approximately equal numbers of males and females are born in all common species of animals. To be sure, many notable exceptions can be found. This is why the field of sex control is a fertile one for fraudulent operators.

The accepted theory of sex determination is that sex is determined by the chromosomal makeup of the individual. One particular pair of the chromosomes is called the *sex chromosomes*. In dogs, the female has a pair of similar chromosomes (usually called X chromosomes), whereas the male has a pair of unlike sex chromosomes (usually called X and Y chromosomes).

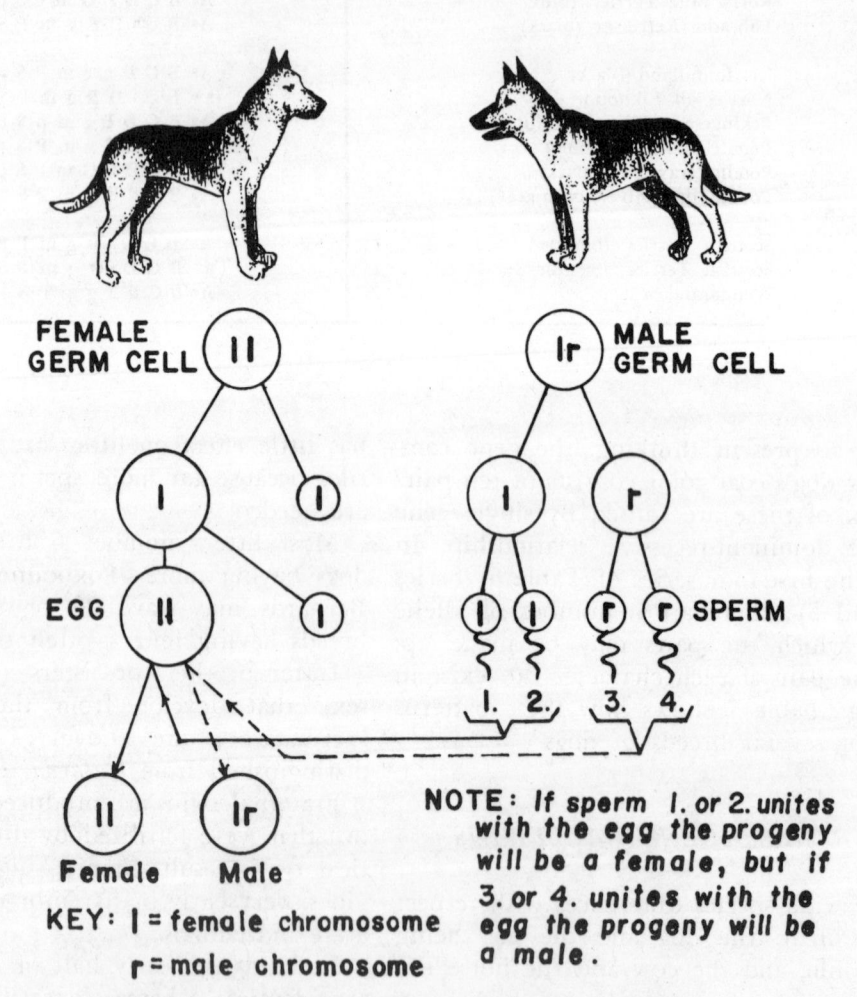

Fig. 211. Diagrammatic illustration of the mechanism of sex determination in dogs, showing how sex is determined by the chromosomal makeup of the individual. The female has a pair of like sex chromosomes, whereas the male has a pair of unlike chromosomes. Thus, if an egg and sperm of like sex chromosomal makeup unite, the offspring will be a female; whereas if an egg and sperm of unlike sex chromosomal makeup unite, the offspring will be a male. (Drawing by J. L. Medeiros)

The pairs of sex chromosomes separate out when the germ cells are formed. Thus, each of the ova or eggs produced by the bitch contains the X chromosome. The sperm of the male, on the other hand, are of two types, one half containing the X chromosome and the other half the Y chromosome. Since, on the average, the eggs and sperm unite at random, it can be understood that half of the progeny will contain the chromosomal makeup XX (females),[3] with the other half XY (males).[3]

LETHALS AND ABNORMALITIES OF DEVELOPMENT

Lethals may be defined as congenital abnormalities which result in the death of an animal, either at birth or later in life. Other defects occur that are not sufficiently severe to cause death but which do impair the usefulness of the affected animals. Many such abnormal dogs are born each year. Unfortunately, the purebred breeder, whose chief business is that of selling breeding stock, is likely to keep quiet about the appearance of any defective animals because of the justifiable fear that it may hurt his sales.

The embryological development—the development of the young from the time that the egg and the sperm unite until the animal is born—is very complicated. Thus, the oddity probably is that so many of the offspring develop normally rather than that a few develop abnormally.

Many such abnormalities (commonly known as *monstrosities* or *freaks*) are hereditary, being caused by certain "bad" genes. Moreover, the bulk of such lethals are recessive and may, therefore, remain hidden for many generations. The prevention of such genetic abnormalities requires that the germ plasm be purged of the "bad" genes. This means that, where recessive lethals are involved, the dog breeder must be aware of the fact that both parents carry the gene. For the total removal of the lethals, test matings and rigid selection must be practiced. The best test mating to use for a given sire consists of mating him to some of his own daughters.

In addition to hereditary abnormalities, there are certain abnormalities that may be due to nutritional deficiencies, or to "accidents of development"—the latter including those which appear to occur sporadically and for which there is no well-defined reason. When only a few defective individuals occur within a particular kennel, it is often impossible to determine whether their occurrence is due to: (1) defective heredity, (2) defective nutrition, or (3) merely to accidents of development. If the same abnormality occurs in any appreciable number of animals, however, it is probably either hereditary or nutritional. In any event, the diagnosis of the condition is not always a simple matter.

The following conditions would tend to indicate a hereditary defect:

1. If the defect had previously been reported as hereditary in the same breed of dogs

2. If it occurred more frequently within certain families or when there had been inbreeding

3. If it occurred in more than one season and when different rations had been fed.

The following conditions might be accepted as indications that the abnormality was due to a nutritional deficiency:

1. If it had previously been reliably reported to be due to a nutritional deficiency

2. If it appeared to be restricted to a certain area

3. If it occurred when the ration of the mother was known to be deficient

4. If it disappeared when an improved ration was fed.

If there is suspicion that the ration is defective, it should be improved, not only from the

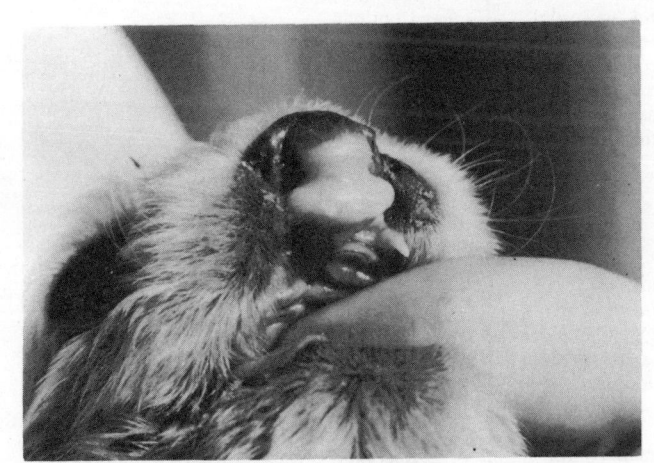

Fig. 212. Harelip and cleft palate. (Courtesy Dr. J. H. Reed, D.V.M., Ph.D., Ontario Veterinary College, University of Guelph, Guelph, Ontario, Canada)

---

[3] The scientists' symbols for the male and female, respectively, are: ♂ (the sacred shield and spear of Mars, the Roman god of war) and ♀ (the looking glass of Venus, the Roman goddess of love and beauty).

TABLE 8

SOME HEREDITY LETHALS AND ABNORMALITIES IN DOGS

Kind of Abnormality	Description of Abnormality	Probable Mode of Inheritance
Lethals:		
Canine hemophilia	Blood lacks the ability to clot. Even at teething, a pup may bleed to death	Recessive, sex linked (always males)
Cleft palate (and harelip)	Puppies cannot nurse	Probably recessive
Nonlethals:		
Cataract	An opacity of the lens of the eye	Dominant
Cryptorchidism	One or both testicles retained in the body	Recessive
Dalmatian urine	Low ability to break down uric acid in the body and form allantoin	Recessive
Deafness	Cannot hear. Afflicted dogs show a characteristic alertness and generally stay away from other dogs. Can be detected at early age by making a squeaking noise with your lips; deaf puppies will not prick up their ears. Appears to be more prevalent in white dogs	Recessive
Double nose	Born with a double nose	Incomplete dominant
Glaucoma	Internal pressure and eventual swelling of the eyeball, sometimes producing a complete displacement of the lens. The cornea, the outside transparent part of the eye, sometimes becomes opaque	Dominant
Hairlessness	Born without hair	Dominant. Lethal in the homozygotes
Hernia, umbilical (navel)	Weakness at umbilicus; a lump forms due to the intestines protruding	Probably recessive
Hydrocephalas	Excess fluid in portions of the brain	Recessive
Missing teeth	Not having the normal compliment of teeth	Recessive
Overshot jaw	The lower jaw is shorter than the upper	Recessive
Undershot jaw	The lower jaw is longer than the upper	Mode of inheritance complicated

standpoint of preventing such deformities, but from the standpoint of good and efficient management.

If there is good and sufficient evidence that the abnormal condition is hereditary, the steps to be followed in purging the dogs of the undesirable gene are identical to those for ridding them of any other undesirable recessive factor. An inbreeding program, of course, is the most effective way in which to expose hereditary lethals in order that purging may follow.

Some of the lethals and other abnormalities that have been reported in dogs are summarized in Table 8; and the probable mode of inheritance of each one, based on presently available information, is given. It is emphasized, however, that this summary should not be regarded as absolute and final. Research in this area has been scanty. Nevertheless, based on various reports, the data presented in Table 8 represents the author's best judgment at the time of writing this book.

THE RELATIVE IMPORTANCE OF SIRE AND DAM

As a sire can have so many more offspring during a given season or a lifetime than a dam, he is from a hereditary standpoint a more important individual than any one female so far as the whole breeding program is concerned, although both the sire and the dam are of equal importance so far as concerns any one litter of puppies. Because of their wider use, therefore, stud dogs are usually culled more rigidly than bitches, and the breeder can well afford to pay more for an outstanding stud than for an equally outstanding bitch.

Experienced dog breeders have long felt that daughters often more closely resemble their sires, whereas the sons resemble their dams. Some sires and dams, therefore, enjoy a reputation based almost exclusively on the merit of their sons, whereas others owe their prestige to their daughters. Although this situation is likely to be exaggerated, any such phenomenon that may exist is due to sex-linked inheritance, which may be explained as follows: The genes that determine sex are carried on one of the chromosomes. The other genes that are located on the same chromosome will be linked or associated with sex and will be transmitted to the next generation in combination with sex. Thus, because of sex linkage, there are more color-blind men than color-blind women. In poultry breeding, the sex-linked factor is used in a practical way for the purpose of distinguishing the pullets from the cockerels early in life, through the process known as "sexing" the chicks. When a black cock is crossed with barred hens, all the cocks come barred and all the hens come black. It should be emphasized, however, that under most conditions, it appears that the influence of the sire and dam on any one litter of offspring is about equal. Most dog breeders, therefore, will do well to seek excellence in both sexes of breeding animals.

PREPOTENCY

Prepotency refers to the ability of the animal, either male or female, to stamp its own characteristics on its offspring. The offspring of a prepotent stud dog, for example, resemble both their sire and each other more closely than usual. The only conclusive and final test of prepotency consists of the inspection of the get.

From a genetic standpoint, there are two requisites that an animal must possess in order to be prepotent: dominance and homozygosity. Every offspring that receives a dominant gene or genes will show the effect of that gene or genes in the particular character or characters which result therefrom. Moreover, a perfectly homozygous animal would transmit the same kind of genes to all of its offspring. Although entirely homozygous dogs probably never exist, it is realized that a system of inbreeding is the only way to produce dogs that are as nearly homozygous as possible.

It should be emphasized that it is impossible to determine just how important prepotency may be in dog breeding, although many sires of the past have enjoyed a reputation of being extremely prepotent. Perhaps these animals were prepotent, but there is also the possibility that their reputation for producing outstanding animals may have rested upon the fact that they were mated to some of the best bitches of the breed.

In summary, it may be said that if a given sire or dam possesses a great number of genes that are completely dominant for desirable type and performance and if the animal is relatively homozygous, the offspring will closely resemble the parents, they will resemble each other, and they will be uniform. Fortunate, indeed, is the breeder who possesses such dogs.

NICKING

If the offspring of certain matings are especially outstanding and in general better than their parents, dog breeders are prone to say that the animals *nicked well*. For example, a bitch may produce outstanding puppies to the service of a certain stud dog, but when mated to another male of apparent equal merit as a sire, the offspring may be disappointing. Or sometimes the mating of a rather average male to an equally average female will result in the production of a most outstanding individual both from the standpoint of type and performance.

So-called successful nicking is due, genetically speaking, to the fact that the right combination of genes for good characters are contributed by each parent, although each of the parents within itself may be lacking in certain genes necessary for excellence. In other words, the animals *nicked well* because their respective combinations of good genes were such as to complement each other.

Because of the very nature of successful nicks, outstanding dogs arising therefrom must be carefully scrutinized from a breeding standpoint, because, with their heterozygous origin, it is quite unlikely that they will breed true.

FAMILY NAMES

Family names are traced through either the males or the females.

Unfortunately, the value of family names is generally grossly exaggerated. Obviously, if the foundation male or female, as the case may be, is very many generations removed, the genetic superiority of this head of a family is halved so many times by subsequent matings that there is little reason to think that one family is superior to another. The situation is often further distorted by breeders placing a premium on family names of which there are few members, little realizing that, in at least some cases, there may be unfortunate reasons for the scarcity in numbers.

Such family names have about as much significance as human family names. Who would be so foolish as to think that the Joneses as a group are alike, but different from the Smiths? Perhaps, if the truth were known, there have been many individuals with each of these family names who have been of no particular credit to the clan, and the same applies to all dog family names.

On the other hand, certain linebred families—linebred to a foundation sire or dam so that the family is kept highly related to it—do have genetic significance. Moreover, if the programs involved have been accompanied by rigid culling, many good individuals may have evolved, and the family name may be in good repute.

HEREDITY AND ENVIRONMENT

A purebred dog, penned in an attractive kennel and with plenty of food before him, is undeniably the result of two forces—heredity and environment (with the latter including training). If turned out on the street to fend for himself, an identical twin to the placid kennel dog would present an entirely different appearance. By the same token, optimum environment could never make a champion out of a mongrel with scrub ancestry, but it might well be added that "condition, training, and grooming will cover up a multitude of sins."

These are extreme examples, but they do emphasize the fact that any particular animal is the product of heredity and environment. Stated differently, heredity may be thought of as the foundation, and environment as the structure. Heredity has already made its contribution at the time of fertilization, but environment works ceaselessly away until death.

Admittedly, after looking over a dog, a breeder cannot with certainty know whether it is genetically a high or a low producer; and there can be no denying the fact that environment—including feeding, management, and disease—plays a tremendous part in determining the extent to which hereditary differences that are present will be expressed in dogs.

Experimental work has long shown conclusively enough that the vigor and size of animals at birth are dependent upon the environment of the embryo from the minute the ova or egg is fertilized by the sperm, and now we have evidence to indicate that newborn animals are affected by the environment of the egg and sperm long before fertilization has been accomplished. In other words, perhaps due to storage of factors, the kind and quality of the ration fed to young, growing females may later affect the quality of their progeny. Generally speaking, then, environment may inhibit the full expression of potentialities from a time preceding fertilization until physiological maturity has been attained.

It is generally agreed, therefore, that maximum development of characters of importance—speed, hunting ability, guard duty, etc.—cannot be achieved unless there are optimum conditions of nutrition and management.

SYSTEMS OF BREEDING

The many diverse types and breeds of dogs in existence today originated from the wolf, the jackal, and the wild dogs common to certain areas of the world. These ancestors possessed the pool of genes, which, through controlled matings and selection, proved flexible in the hands of man. Out of this evolved breeds of dogs of many different appearances and uses. In appearance, they differ in size, color, coat length and density, ears, and tails. In adaptation, they differ markedly in their usefulness for racing; for pursuing game by sight or scent, on water or land, on the prairie or in dense cover; for working stock; for guard dogs; for leading the blind; and for pets. Few of these diverse uses and breeds occurred by happenstance. Rather, the vast majority of them were the result of carefully conceived systems of breeding; some involving one mating, others many. It should be just so today whenever dogs are bred; whether it be by a one-dog owner or in a large kennel.

At the outset it should be stated that there is no one best system of breeding or secret of success for any and all conditions. Each breeding program is an individual case, requiring careful study. The choice of the system of breeding should be determined primarily by the size and quality of the breeder's dogs, his finances, his skill, and the ultimate goal ahead.

PUREBREEDING

A purebred animal may be defined as a member of a breed, the animals of which possess a common ancestry and distinctive characteristics, which is either registered or eligible for registry in the Stud Book *of that breed.*

It must be emphasized that purebreeding and homozygosity may bear very different connotations. The term *purebred* refers to animals whose entire lineage, regardless of the number of generations removed, traces back to the foundation animals accepted by the breed or to any animals that have been subsequently approved for infusion. On the other hand, homozygosity refers to the likeness of the genes.

Yet there is some interrelationship between purebreds and homozygosity. Because most breeds had a relatively small number of foundation animals, the unavoidable inbreeding and linebreeding during the formative stage resulted in a certain amount of homozygosity. Moreover, through the normal sequence of events, it is estimated that purebreds become more homozygous by from 0.25 to 0.5 percent per animal generation.

It should be emphasized that the word *purebred* does not necessarily guarantee superior type or high performance. That is to say, the word *purebred* is not, within itself, magic, nor is it sacred. Many a person has found to his sorrow that there are such things as purebred mongrels. Yet, on the average, purebred dogs are much superior to nonpurebreds.

The breeding of purebred dogs offers unlimited challenges and opportunities. It has been well said that honor, fame, and fortune are all within the realm of possible realization of the purebred breeder; but it should also be added that only a few achieve this high calling. Although we have had many constructive dog breeders and great progress has been made, it must be remembered that only a few achieve sufficient success to classify as master breeders.

INBREEDING

Most scientists divide inbreeding into various categories, according to the closeness of the relationship of the animals mated and the purpose of the mating. There is considerable disagreement, however, as to both the terms used and their intended meanings. For the purposes of this book and the discussion which follows, the following definitions will be used:

Inbreeding is the mating of animals more closely related than the average of the population from which they came.

Close breeding is the mating of closely related animals: sire to daughter, son to dam, and brother to sister.

Linebreeding is the mating of animals more distantly related than in closebreeding and in which the matings are usually directed toward keeping the offspring closely related to some highly admired ancestor; such as half-brother to half-sister, female to grandsire, and cousin to cousin.

CLOSE BREEDING

In close breeding there are a minimum number of different ancestors. In the repeated mating of a brother with his full sister, for example, there are only two grandparents instead of four, only two great-grandparents instead of eight, and only two different ancestors in each generation farther back—instead of the theoretically possible 16, 32, 64, 128, etc. The most intensive form of inbreeding is self-fertilization. It occurs in some plants, such as wheat and garden peas, and in some lower animals; but dogs and other domestic animals are not self-fertilized. Close breeding is rarely practiced by present-day dog breeders, though it was common in the foundation animals of most of the breeds.

The reasons for practicing close breeding are:

1. It increases the degree of homozygosity within dogs, making the resulting offspring pure or homozygous in a larger proportion of their gene pairs than in the case of linebred or outcross dogs. In so doing, the less desirable recessive genes are brought to light so that they can be more readily culled. For example, breeders of Boxers can, and do, use close breeding as a means through which to expose those animals that are carriers of the undesirable recessive white color known to exist in the breed. Thus, close breeding, together with rigid culling, affords the surest and quickest method of fixing and perpetuating a desirable character or group of characters and of weeding out the undesirable ones.

2. If carried on for a period of time, it tends to create lines or strains of dogs that are uniform in type and other characteristics.

3. It keeps the highest relationship to a desirable ancestor.

4. Because of the greater homozygosity, it makes for greater prepotency. That is, selected close bred dogs are more homozygous for desirable genes (genes which are often dominant) and they, therefore, transmit these genes with greater uniformity.

5. Through the production of inbred lines or families by close breeding and the subsequent crossing of these lines, it affords a modern approach to breed improvement. Moreover, the best of the closebred animals are likely to give superior results in outcrosses.

6. Where a breeder is in the unique position of having dogs so superior that to go on the outside for seed stock would merely be a step backward, it offers the only sound alternative for maintaining existing quality or making further improvement.

The precautions in close breeding may be summarized as follows:

1. As close breeding greatly enhances the chances that recessives will appear during the early generations in obtaining homozygosity, it is almost certain to increase the proportion of worthless breeding stock produced—that with such so-called degenerate characteristics as reduction in size, fertility, and general vigor. Lethals and other genetic abnormalities often appear with increased frequency in close bred dogs.

2. Because of the rigid culling necessary in order to avoid the "fixing" of undesirable characters, especially in the first generations of a close breeding program, it is almost imperative that this system of breeding be confined to a relatively large breeder and to instances when the owner has sufficient finances to stand the rigid culling that must accompany such a program.

3. It requires skill in making planned matings and rigid selection, thus being most successful when applied by master breeders.

4. It is not adapted for use by the breeder with average or below average dogs because the very fact that his animals are average means that a very good share of undesirable genes are present. Close breeding would merely make the animals more homozygous for undesirable genes and, therefore, worse.

Judging from outward manifestations alone, it might appear that close breeding is predominantly harmful in its effects—often leading to the production of defective dogs lacking in vitality. But this is by no means the whole story. Although close breeding often leads to the production of dogs of low value, the resulting superior animals can confidently be expected to be homozygous for a greater than average number of good genes and thus more valuable for breeding purposes. Figuratively speaking, therefore, close breeding may be referred to as trial by fire, and the breeder who practices it can expect to obtain many animals that fail to measure up and have to be culled. On the other hand, if close breeding is properly handled, he can also expect to secure animals of exceptional merit.

Although close breeding is practiced less after the formative period of different breeds of dogs, it has real merit when its principles and limitations are fully understood. Perhaps it had best be confined to use by the skilled master breeder who is in a sufficiently sound financial position to endure rigid and intelligent culling and delayed returns and who has both large numbers and above average quality.

LINEBREEDING

From a biological standpoint, close breeding and linebreeding are the same thing, differing merely in intensity. In general, close breeding has been frowned upon by dog breeders, but linebreeding (the less intensive form) has been looked upon with favor in many quarters. In a linebreeding program, the degree of relationship is not closer than half-brother and half-sister or matings more distantly related; cousin matings, grandparent to grand offspring, etc.

Linebreeding is usually practiced in order to conserve and perpetuate the good traits of a certain outstanding dog or bitch. Because such descendents are of similar lineage, they have the same general type of germ plasm and therefore exhibit a high degree of uniformity in type and performance.

In a more limited way, a linebreeding program has the same advantages and disadvantages as a close breeding program. However, it offers fewer possibilities both for good and harm than close breeding. It is a more conservative and safer type of program, offering less probability to either "hit the jackpot" or "sink the ship." It is a middle-of-the-road program that the vast majority of small dog breeders can safely follow to their advantage. Through it, reasonable progress can be made without taking any great risk. A degree of homozygosity of certain desirable genes can be secured without running too great a risk of intensifying undesirable ones.

Usually a linebreeding program is best accomplished through breeding to an outstanding dog rather than to an outstanding bitch because of the greater number of offspring of the former. If a breeder found himself in possession of a great stud dog, proved to be so by a large number of his get, a linebreeding program might be initiated in the following way:
Select two of the best sons of the noted stud dog and mate them to their half-sisters, balancing all possible defects in the subsequent matings. The next generation matings might well consist of breeding the daughters of one of the males to the son of the other, etc. If, in such a program, it seems wise to secure some outside "blood" (genes) to correct a common defect or defects, this may be done through selecting one or more outstanding, proved bitches from the outside—animals whose get are strong where the dogs in the breeding program are deficient—and then mating this female (females) to one of the linebred stud dogs with the hope of producing a son that may be used.

The dog owner with limited numbers can often follow a linebreeding program by breeding his bitch or bitches to a stud dog owned by a large breeder who follows such a program—thus, in effect, following the linebreeding program of the larger breeder.

Naturally, a linebreeding program may be achieved in other ways. Regardless of the actual matings used, the main objective in such a system of breeding is that of rendering the animals homozygous—in desired type and performance—to some great and highly regarded ancestor, while at the same time weeding out homozygous undesirable characteristics. The success of the program, therefore, is dependent upon having desirable genes with which to start and an intelligent intensification of these good genes.

It should be emphasized that some dog owners should almost never close breed or linebreed. This includes all those whose dogs are of average quality.

With purebred dogs of only average quality, more rapid progress can usually be made by introducing superior outcross sires. Moreover, if the animals are of only average quality, they must have a preponderance of "bad" genes that would only be intensified through a close breeding or linebreeding program.

OUTCROSSING

Outcrossing is the mating of animals that are members of the same breed but which show no relationship close up in the pedigree (for at least the first four or six generations).

Most of our purebred dogs of all breeds are the result of outcrossing. It is a relatively safe system of breeding, for it is unlikely that two such unrelated animals will carry the same undesirable genes and pass them on to their offspring.

Perhaps it might well be added that the majority of purebred breeders with average or below average dogs had best follow an outcrossing program, because, in such dogs, the problem is that of retaining a heterozygous type of germ plasm with the hope that genes for undesirable characters will be counteracted by genes for desirable characters. With such average or below average dogs, an inbreeding program would merely make the animals homozygous for the less desirable characters, the presence of which already makes for their mediocrity. In general, continued outcrossing offers neither the hope for improvement nor the hazard of retrogression of linebreeding or close breeding programs.

Judicious and occasional outcrossing may well be an integral part of linebreeding or close breeding programs. As closely inbred animals become increasingly homozygous with germ plasm for good characters, they may likewise become homozygous for certain undesirable characters even though their general overall type and performance remains well above the breed average. Such defects may best be remedied by introducing an outcross through an animal or animals known to be especially strong in the character or characters needing strengthening. This having been accomplished, the wise breeder will return to the original close breeding or linebreeding program, realizing full well the limitations of an outcrossing program.

GRADING UP

Grading up is that system of breeding in which purebred sires of a given breed are mated to grade females.

Generally speaking, grading up has little to offer the dog breeder. Nevertheless, it is a recognized system of breeding; and, too, many of our breeds of dogs evolved through it. Also, it is sometimes followed when a bitch is bred accidentally, or when a dog owner has an outstanding bitch of unknown ancestry from which he desires to raise a litter of pups.

Naturally, the greatest single step toward improved quality and performance occurs in the first cross. The first generation of such a cross results in offspring carrying 50% of the hereditary material of the purebred parent (or 50% of the "blood" of the purebred parent, as many breeders speak of it). The next generation gives offspring carrying 75% of the "blood" of the purebred breed, and in subsequent generations the proportion of inheritance remaining from the original scrub females is halved with each cross. Later crosses usually increase quality and performance still more, though in less marked degree.

After the third or fourth cross, the offspring compare very favorably with purebred stock in conformation, and only exceptionally good sires can bring about further improvement. This is especially so if the males used in grading up successive generations are derived from the same strain within a breed.

CROSSBREEDING

Crossbreeding is the mating of animals of different breeds.

The proved value of crossbreeding in the creation of new breeds of dogs especially adapted to certain uses is generally recognized. Many of our breeds of dogs evolved in this manner. However, purebreeding will continue to control the destiny of further improvement in each breed of dogs, and furnish the desired homozygosity and uniformity which many breeders insist is a part of the art of breeding better dogs.

SELECTION IN DOG BREEDING

In simple terms, selection in dog breeding is an attempt to secure or retain the best of those animals in the current generation as parents of the next generation. Obviously, the skill with which selections are made is all-important in determining the future of the dogs in any given kennel or breed. It becomes perfectly clear, therefore, that the destiny of improvement is dependent upon selecting for breeding purposes those animals that are genetically superior.

The desirability of any individual animal is determined by the following two factors:

1. Type or individuality based upon how well the dog measures up to the breed standard;

2. Performance or use for which it is intended. Whenever possible this should be measured objectively. For example, racing dogs should be tested on the track and hunting dogs should be tested in field trials.

BASES OF SELECTION

Whether establishing a new breeding program or improving an old one, there are four bases of selection: (1) selection based on type and individuality, (2) selection based on pedigree, (3) selection based on show-ring winnings, and (4)

Fig. 213. The Boston Terrier, with short, round head and deformed tail end of vertebral column, crossed with long-headed, long-tailed Dachshund with short, bent legs. The first generation hybrids have long heads, long bodies and tails, and short, bent legs. The second generation hybrids exhibit various combinations of short heads and short legs and long heads and long legs. (Drawing by J. L. Medeiros)

selection based on performance or use. At the outset, it should be said that each method of selection has its own particular place. Certainly the progressive dog breeder will make judicious use of all of them.

SELECTION BASED ON TYPE AND INDIVIDUALITY

This implies selecting those animals that most closely approach an ideal or standard of perfection—the breed standards—and culling out those that fall short of these standards. The vast majority of dogs are selected on this basis.

SELECTION BASED ON PEDIGREE

In pedigree selection, the individuality and performance of the ancestors are relied upon for an estimate of the probable transmitting ability. Pedigree selection is of special importance when performance data is not available or when the animals are so young that their individual merit cannot be ascertained with any degree of certainty. Also, when selection is being made between dogs of comparable individual merit, the pedigree may well be the determining factor. In making use of pedigree selections, however, it must be remembered that ancestors close up in the pedigree are much more important than those many generations removed.

SELECTION BASED ON SHOW-RING WINNINGS

The show-ring has long been a major force in shaping the breeds of dogs.

As now conducted, our dog shows have both advantages and disadvantages from the standpoint of breed improvement.

Among the *advantages* are the following:

1. The show-ring is the best medium yet discovered for molding breed type. For this reason, it behooves the kennel clubs and the purebred breeders alike to accept their rightful responsibility in seeing that the animals that win top honors are those that most nearly meet the breed standards.

2. It serves as one of the very best advertising or promotional mediums for both the breed and the breeder.

3. It brings breeders together for exchange of ideas and experiences.

4. It provides an incentive to breed better dogs, for only by comparing animals in the show-ring can the breeder ascertain whether or not he is keeping up with his competitors.

Some of the *disadvantages* of the show-ring are as follows:

1. The desire to win often causes exhibitors to resort to artificial means, including surgical means, in order to correct defects. Such man-made corrections are not hereditary, and their effects are often not too durable—as is belatedly discovered by some innocent purchaser.

2. Heavy fitting, in order to win, sometimes results in temporary or permanent sterility.

3. Valuable animals are frequently kept out of use or from reproduction in order to enhance their likelihood of winning in the show-ring.

Thus, in making selections from among show animals, one should do so with a full understanding of both the virtues and the limitations inherent therein.

Selection based on show-ring winnings implies the selection of animals that have placed well in one or more dog shows. Perhaps the principal value of selection based on show-ring winnings lies in the fact that shows focus the attention of the amateur to those types and strains of animals that at the moment are meeting with the approval of the better breeders and judges.

SELECTION BASED ON PERFORMANCE TESTING

Selection of breeding stock on the basis of performance records is a requisite in modern dog improvement. It should be emphasized that this involves the taking of accurate records rather than just casual observations. Moreover, in order to be most effective, selection must be based on characteristics of utility value (rather than breed fancy points), and an objective measure or "yardstick" must be placed upon each of the characteristics that is to be measured. Finally, those breeding animals that fail to meet the high standards set forth must be culled out promptly and unflinchingly.

As most characters of utility value—for example, speed in racing dogs and hunting ability in hunting dogs, and body type—are due to many genes; a method of measuring and selecting for these characters must be used. Performance on the track works well for Greyhounds and Whippets, and field trials are the answer for hunting dogs, coon hounds, and the like.

In performance testing programs, it must be realized that training and feeding play a major role in producing outstanding animals, making it difficult to separate out environmental from hereditary influences. For greatest effectiveness and progress, therefore, the conditions under which the tests are made should be standardized as much as possible.

Despite all the difficulties enumerated, and the admitted fact that much more research work is needed in the testing of dogs in field trials or on the race track, there is ample evidence to indicate that selection on the basis of performance is imperative in those breeds having an important utility value if breed improvement is to take place at the maximum rate. To select intelligently on the basis of a testing program, the breeder must have adequate records and use them.

Performance Testing Not New

Performance testing is not new. It was advocated by the Roman, Varro, 2,000 years ago, and it was effectively used by Robert Bakewell, the English patriarch, in the eighteenth century in his practice of bull and ram letting (leasing).

The breeders of race horses have always followed a program of mating animals of proved performance on the track. It is interesting to note that the first breed register, which appeared in 1791, recorded the pedigrees of all the Thoroughbred horses winning important races. In a similar way, the Standardbred horse, which is an American creation, takes its name from the fact that, in its early history, animals were required to trot a mile in 2 minutes and 30 seconds or pace a mile in 2 minutes and 25 seconds before they could be considered as eligible for registry. The chief aim, therefore, of the early-day breeders of race horses was to record the pedigrees of outstanding performers rather than all members of the breed.

Milk production has long been used as a criterion for selecting dairy cattle, and with the invention of the Babcock test in 1890, butterfat content also became a measuring device. Testing in dairy cattle is now the most widely known record of performance used in the United States.

The invention of the trap nest shortly before 1900 made it possible to keep individual egg-production records on hens.

These performance tests have exerted a powerful influence in developing high genetic merit in those classes of animals to which they have been applied.

SELECTION FOR SEVERAL CHARACTERS

Sometimes dog breeders have been burdened by attempting to select for too many characters. For example, Greyhound breeders may select for speed, beauty, temperament, size, color, etc. It must be remembered, however, that selection for two or more characteristics automatically cuts down the effectiveness of selection for any one of them. Thus, the breeder who selects with equal intensity for type and speed is likely to be left in the position of the dog that chased two rabbits and caught neither. A realization of this fact, together with the fact that in many cases such things as type and beauty are correlated only slightly, if at all, with performance is undoubtedly behind the current emphasis on performance testing with all classes of animals.

PART II. SOME PHYSIOLOGICAL ASPECTS OF REPRODUCTION IN DOGS

Anyone planning to breed a dog should first have an understanding of reproductive physiology and the application of scientific practices therein.

THE REPRODUCTIVE ORGANS OF THE MALE

The male's functions in reproduction are: (1) to produce the male reproductive cells, the *sperm* or *spermatozoa,* and (2) to introduce sperm into the female reproductive tract at the proper time. In order that these functions may be fulfilled, those who breed dogs should have an understanding of the anatomy of the reproductive system of the male and of the functions of each of its parts. Fig. 214 is a schematic drawing of the reproductive organs of the male. A description of each part follows:

1. *Scrotum*—The scrotum, a diverticulum of the abdomen, encloses the testicles. It is situated about half way between the inguinal region and the anus. The skin covering it is pigmented and is covered sparsely with fine hairs.

The chief function of the scrotum is thermoregulatory—to maintain the testicles at temperatures several degrees lower than that of the body proper.

Cryptorchids are males one or both of whose testicles have not descended to the scrotum. Monorchids are males one of whose testicles has failed to descend to the scrotum. Undescended testicles are usually sterile because of the high temperature in the abdomen.

2. *Testicles*—The testicles are relatively small and round-oval shaped. Their primary function is to produce sperm, each about 1/2500 inch in diameter. The testicles communicate through the inguinal canal with the pelvic cavity, where accessory organs and glands are located.

3. *Epididymis*—The efferent ducts of each testis unite into one duct, thus forming the epididymis. This greatly coiled tube consists of three parts:

a. *The head*—This includes several tubules that are grouped into lobules.

b. *The body*—The part of the epididymis that passes down along the sides of the testis.

c. *The tail*—The part located at the bottom of the testis.

The epididymis has four functions: (a) as a passage way for sperm from the seminiferous tubules, (b) the storage of sperm, (c) the secretion of a fluid that probably nourishes the sperm, and (d) the maturation or "ripening" of the sperm.

4. *Vas deferens (Ductus deferens)*—This slender tube, which is lined with ciliated cells, leads from the tail of the epididymis to the pelvic part of the urethra in the penis. Its primary function is to move sperm into the urethra at the time of ejaculation.

The vas deferens—together with longitudinal strands of smooth muscle, blood vessels, and nerves; all encased in a fibrous sheath—make up the spermatic cord (there are two of them), which passes up through an opening in the abdominal wall, the inguinal canal, into the pelvic cavity. The spermatic cords suspend the testicles.

The cutting or closing off of the ductus deferens, known as *vasectomy,* is the most usual operation performed to produce sterility, where sterility without castration is desired.

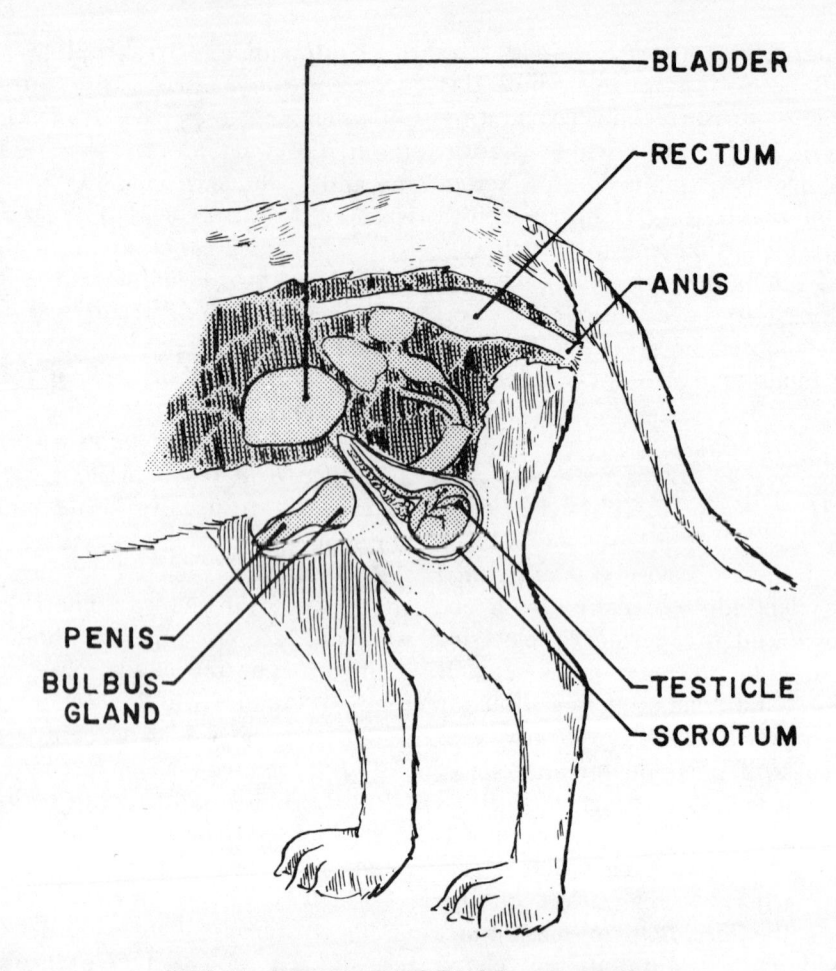

MALE REPRODUCTIVE ORGANS

Fig. 214. Male reproductive organs. (Drawing by J. L. Medeiros)

5. *Prostate gland*—This gland is located at the neck of the bladder. It completely surrounds the prostatic portion of the urethra, to which it is closely adhered. The prostate empties into the urethra through many small openings in the urethral wall on either side of the urethral crest. During the act of mating, the prostate secretes a copious alkaline fluid which is conveyed to the urethra, taking the sperm with it. Hypertrophy of the prostate gland is common in older dogs.

6. *Urethra*—This is a long tube that extends from the bladder to the glans penis. The vas deferens and seminal vesicle open to the urethra close to its point of origin. The urethra serves for the passage of both urine and semen.

7. *Penis*—This is the male organ of copulation. It is long and pointed. At mating, it transmits the semen from the male's epididymis, where the semen is stored, into the female's vagina. The penis consists of a *root* attached to the *ischium*, a *body*, and relatively large *glans* with a *bulb* at its caudal end. The cranial portion of the body, and most of the glans, has a bone (the *os penis*) passing through it. This os penis has a deep ventral groove through which the urethra passes. At the time of copulation, the glans on the penis swells after passing the sphincter muscle of the vagina, thereby "tying" or "locking" the two animals together.

The reproductive organs of the dog are designed to produce semen and to convey it to the bitch at the time of mating. The semen consists of two parts: (1) the sperm, which are produced by the testes, and (2) the liquid portion, or semen plasma, which is secreted by the seminiferous tubules, the epididymis, the vas deferens, and the prostate. Actually, the sperm make up only a small portion of the ejaculate. On the average, at the time of each service, a dog ejaculates 10 milliliters; and the average ejaculate contains 1¼ billion normal, live sperm.

THE REPRODUCTIVE ORGANS OF THE FEMALE

The bitch's functions in reproduction are: (1) to produce the female reproductive cells, the *eggs* or *ova,* (2) to develop the new individual, the *embryo,* in the uterus, (3) to expel the fully developed young at the time of birth or *parturition,* and (4) to produce milk for the nourishment of the young. Actually, the part played by the female in the generative process is much more complicated than that of the male. It is imperative, therefore, that those who breed dogs have an understanding of the anatomy of the reproductive organs of the bitch and the functions of each part. Fig. 215 shows the reproductive organs of the bitch; and a description of each part follows:

1. *Ovaries*—The paired ovaries are small, elongated-oval in outline, and flattened. They average less than an inch long. Each ovary is commonly situated a short distance behind, or in contact with, the posterior pole of the corresponding kidney.

The ovaries have three functions: (a) to produce the female reproductive cells, the *eggs* or *ova,* (b) to secrete the female sex hormone, *estrogen,* and (c) to form the *corpora lutea.* The ovaries may alternate somewhat irregularly in the performance of these functions.

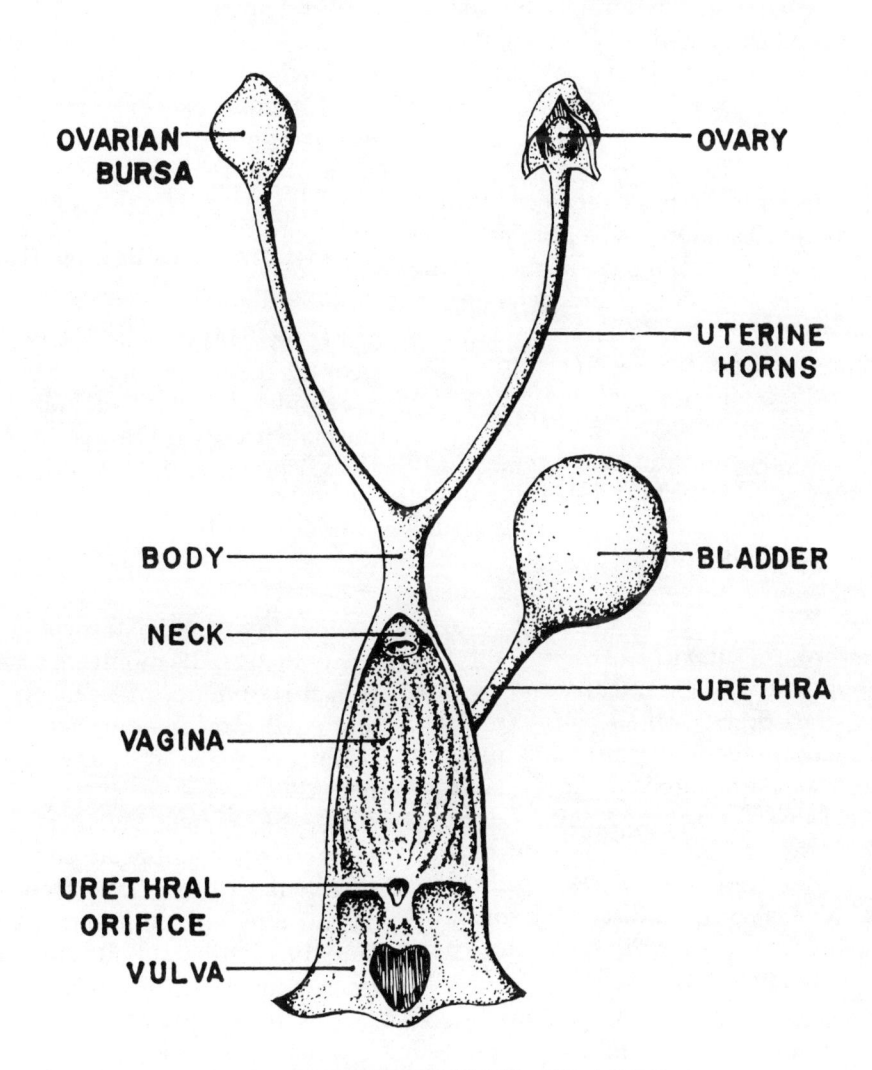

FEMALE REPRODUCTIVE ORGANS

Fig. 215. Female reproductive organs. (Drawing by J. L. Medeiros)

The ovaries differ from the testes in that eggs are produced in very limited numbers and at intervals, during or shortly after heat. Each miniature egg is contained in a sac, called *Graafian follicle,* a large number of which are scattered throughout the ovary. Generally, the follicles remain in an unchanged state until the advent of puberty, at which time some of them begin to enlarge through an increase in the follicular liquid within. Toward the end of heat, the follicles rupture and discharge the eggs, the process known as *ovulation.* As soon as the eggs are released, the corpora lutea make their appearance. The corpora lutea secrete a hormone called *progesterone,* which (a) acts on the uterus so that it implants and nourishes the embryo, (b) prevents other eggs from maturing and puts an end to the heat period—so that the bitch is no longer willing to mate, (c) maintains the animal in a pregnant condition, and (d) assists the female hormone in the development of the mammary glands. If the eggs are not fertilized, however, the corpora lutea atrophy and allow new follicles to ripen.

The egg-containing follicles also secrete into the blood the female sex hormone, *estrogen.* Estrogen is necessary for the development of the female reproductive system, for the mating behavior or *heat* of the female, for the development of the mammary glands, and for the development of the secondary sex characteristics, or femininity, in the bitch.

From the standpoint of the dog breeder, the ripening of the first Graafian follicle in a dog generally coincides with puberty, and this marks the beginning of reproduction.

2. *Fallopian tubes (or oviducts)*—These small, cilia-lined tubes or ducts lead from the ovaries to the "horns" of the uterus. They are about 2 to 3 inches long in the bitch and the end of each tube nearest the ovary, called *infundibulum,* flares out like a funnel. They are not attached to the ovaries but lie so close to them that they seldom fail to catch the released eggs.

At ovulation, the eggs pass into the infundibulum where, within a few minutes, the ciliary movement within the tube, assisted by the muscular movements of the tube itself, carries them down into the oviduct.

3. *Uterus*—The uterus is the muscular sac, connecting the fallopian tubes and the vagina, in which the fertilized eggs attach themselves and develop until expelled from the body of the bitch at the time of parturition. The uterus consists of a very short body and extremely long "horns" in which embryos develop. In a medium-sized bitch, the body is about an inch long and the horns 5 to 6 inches. The horns of the uterus present dilations, the *ampullae,* which contain the fetuses, and are separated by constrictions.

4. *Vagina*—The vagina, which is relatively long, admits the penis of the male at the time of copulation and receives the semen. At the time of birth, it expands and serves as the final passageway for the fetus.

5. *Vulva (or urogenital sinus)*—The vulva, which lies some distance below the anus, is the external opening of the genital tract. It is relatively small during anestrus. But, during heat, the vulva becomes engorged, enlarged, and, as the proper time for mating approaches, changes in texture from a hard, rigid organ to one that is soft and spongy. The vestibule is that part of the female genital canal that extends from the vulva to the urethral opening. It is nearly vertical in direction except during the copulatory act, when it may assume an almost horizontal position.

NORMAL BREEDING HABITS OF DOGS

Because of the close association of dogs and people, it is reasonable to expect that we have a considerable store of knowledge relative to the normal breeding habits of dogs—perhaps more than we have for any other class of animals.

AGE OF PUBERTY

Dogs, whether male or bitch, reach sexual maturity at 6 to 12 months of age. This rather wide range is due to differences in breeds, families, and environment—especially nutrition. In general, males do not reach puberty quite so early as females.

In the female, reaching sexual maturity is marked by coming in heat. Even though it is intended to breed the bitch, it is not well to do so during the first heat period, when she is only 6 to 10 months old. Rather, it is best to wait for her second heat, which means that the bitch may be 14 to 16 months old before she is mated.

Usually, one becomes aware of the male's sexual maturity (puberty) when he rubs his genitals against the furniture or against your ankle or hand. He may also rub against children in the same way. This is a perfectly natural reaction. If, and when, it happens, simply be firm and tell the dog to stop. Even though the male reaches sexual maturity at 8 to 9 months of age, usually it is not well to use him in service until he is at least one year old. In fact, according to the American Kennel Club rules, a litter cannot be registered if sired by a male under 7 months of age (likewise, they give an upper limit of 12 years of age).

AGE TO BREED

Bitches are usually bred at 14 to 16 months of age, at the time of their second heat period in life. It is to be emphasized, however, that the age to breed depends primarily upon development, rather than age itself. Proper development is essential in order that animals may be able to withstand the strain of lactation, the demands of which are much more rigorous than gestation.

Males are usually not used in service until they are 12 months of age; and the number of services should be limited until they are two years of age, because they are still making rapid growth as yearlings.

SIGNS OF HEAT

The signs of a bitch's heat period are a swollen vulva, an erratic appetite, which may either increase or decrease, general restlessness, and frequent urination. She may even ignore her house training during this period. This phase, which usually lasts 4 or 5 days, is followed by a bloody discharge from the vulva. Some females bleed a great deal, whereas others bleed very little; either type of bleeding may be normal for the particular bitch. Following the bleeding stage, which may last from 4 to 7 days, the unmistakable sign of heat in the female is the acceptance of the male.

HEAT (ESTRUS) PERIOD

After the bitch reaches sexual maturity, heat periods occur twice per year—about every 6 months.

Because of the nuisance of having a lot of male dogs around, many local ordinances require that females in season be confined indoors.

The entire heat cycle, which usually lasts from 18 to 21 days, is divided naturally into the following 4 stages:

1. *Preparatory stage* (lasts 4 to 5 days)—This stage generally lasts from 4 to 5 days. Signs of this stage are: a swollen vulva, either increased or poor appetite, restlessness, perhaps increased urination, and breaking of house-training rules. During this period, the bitch appears to attract dogs, or at least those dogs that approach her are not repelled.

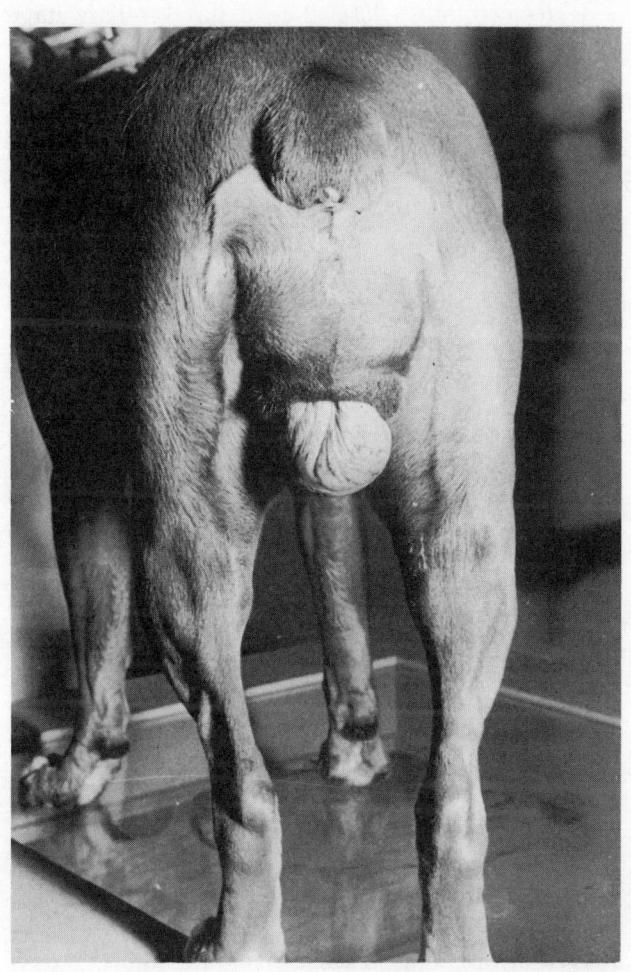

Fig. 216. Prolapse of the vagina. This may occur during estrus. (Courtesy Dr. J. H. Reed, D.V.M., Ph.D., Ontario Veterinary College, University of Guelph, Guelph, Ontario, Canada)

2. *Bleeding stage* (lasts 4 to 7 days)—This stage usually lasts from 4 to 7 days. It is generally marked by bleeding, which may vary from heavy to light. Also, during the first part of this period the vagina is exceedingly tender. The bitch continues to urinate frequently. During

this stage, males will be interested in the bitch, but she will not allow them to mate.

3. *Receptive stage* (lasts 3 to 5 days)—This stage usually lasts 3 to 5 days, although it may last as long as 2 weeks in exceptional cases. During this stage, the bitch is receptive to males. Also, the discharge usually tapers off just prior to the beginning of this stage. During the receptive stage, the bitch will usually continue to accept the male for several days. Hence, it is important to make sure that only the selected sire can get to her at this time.

4. *Reject stage* (lasts 2 to 3 days)—This stage lasts from 2 to 3 days. It follows the receptive stage, about 14 days from the beginning of heat signs. This stage is characterized by the bitch suddenly rejecting males, sometimes viciously. Her season is over, and no impregnation is physically possible during this period. Nevertheless, the males will continue to be around and seek her out.

TIME OF OVULATION

Ovulation takes place during the third stage referred to above—the receptive stage. It is recommended that a bitch be bred on the first or second day of the receptive stage (generally, this is about the twelfth to fourteenth day after the onset of heat), at which time ovulation is taking place. If the male dog is not being overworked at the time, a second service a day later (some prefer 2 days later) would be desirable. Ovulation ends at the close of the receptive stage.

FERTILIZATION

Fertilization refers to the union of the sperm and ovum.

Ovulation takes place during the 3 to 5 days receptive stage, which occurs some 12 to 14 days following the onset of the heat period. When mating occurs at this time, sperm (or male germ cells) are deposited in the female reproductive tract. They ascend the female reproductive tract, and, under favorable conditions, they meet the eggs, and only one sperm fertilizes only one egg in the upper part of the oviduct near the ovary.

A series of delicate time relationships must be met, however, or the eggs will not be fertilized. The sperm cells live only 24 to 48 hours in the reproductive tract of the female, and it probably requires 4 to 6 hours for them to ascend the female reproductive tract. Moreover, the eggs are viable for an even shorter period of time; probably for not more than 24 hours after ovulation. For conception, therefore, breeding must take place at the right time. Also, it is good protection to allow more than one service during the receptive stage—the period of ovulation.

As bitches usually stay in the receptive stage for 3 to 5 days, it is reasonable to assume that the highest conception rate—the best chances of fertilization—may be obtained by mating at least twice during the receptive stage, with the services spaced a day or two apart.

GESTATION PERIOD

The gestation period or period of pregnancy is approximately nine weeks, or 63 days. But, as happens in all species, birth may be early or late, so it is well to expect puppies anytime between the fifty-eighth and sixty-fifth day of gestation.

CONDITIONING THE BITCH FOR BREEDING

Proper conditioning of the bitch prior to breeding is very important. This includes not being overweight or underweight; not showing deficiencies in the diet; freedom from internal and external parasites; and immunity against certain diseases.

A bitch that is in hard, vigorous physical condition, on the lean side but gaining in weight, is most likely to have a healthy litter. If the bitch is undernourished, the puppies may be born weak, and the dam's milk supply may be poor or nonexistent. Also, a poor start in life may show up later in bone deficiencies or lack of disease resistance. Overweight bitches are less likely to conceive, and they may have difficulty at whelping time. Also, too high a condition (too fat) can result in small litters.

Prior to breeding, it is recommended that a few specimens of the droppings of the female be taken to your veterinarian for him to determine whether or not she is infested by any type of worms. If worms are present, the bitch should be wormed under the supervision of your veterinarian prior to breeding her. It is possible to worm females up to two to three weeks after breeding, but it is much preferable to get it over with prior to mating.

The owner should make certain that the bitch is free from all lice, ticks, or fleas before sending her to the stud dog owner for breeding. If this precaution is not taken, the stud dog owner will likely isolate the bitch upon arrival and treat her before breeding, simply because he does not want to infest his stud dog or his kennel.

Prior to breeding the female, it is also good practice to make sure that she is immunized against distemper, hepatitis, and leptospirosis. If this immunity is present, temporary resistance to these diseases is passed on to the puppies; otherwise, the puppies may die before they have a chance to be protected by their own inoculations. Your veterinarian will advise you on this point. He will probably suggest giving the bitch a booster shot for added protection prior to breeding her.

THE STUD DOG

The selection of the stud dog is most important. If possible, he should be more outstanding than the female to which he is to be mated.

It is never wise to utilize for stud the family pet or the neighbor's pet just because such a dog is available at little or no cost. If the bitch is worth breeding, she is worth shipping clear across the continent, if necessary, to obtain for her a mate that will enable her to realize her possibilities.

The following three criteria may be used to evaluate the merits of a stud dog:

1. *His individual excellence*—As an individual, the stud dog should be bold and aggressive (not vicious) and structurally typical of his breed, without any freakish exaggerations of type. He must be sound, a free and true mover, possess quality, and be a gentleman of his breed. Accidentally acquired scars or injuries may be disregarded.

2. *His pedigree*—A pedigree is particularly valuable where a young, untried stud dog is involved. Superior relatives, close up in the pedigree, impart confidence that the dog will breed true to type.

3. *His progeny*—Where an older stud dog has been used in service, an evaluation can best be made of him on the basis of his progeny. In evaluating the progeny, one must also give consideration to the type of bitches to which the stud dog was mated. Sometimes a stud dog with a great show or field trial record attracts the top bitches of the entire country on the strength of his winning record. Because of the outstanding females to which he is bred, he is bound to produce some creditable progeny. So, it is necessary to take into consideration the opportunities the dog has had in relation to the progeny produced; that is, what quality bitches were mated to him.

In the choice of a stud dog, no attention whatsoever need be paid to claims that he sires big litters. Unless the sire is deficient in sperm, the number of puppies in the litter depends entirely upon the bitch. At one service, a dog deposits enough spermatozoa to produce a million puppies, if there were so many ova to be fertilized and space for them to develop. In any event, the major purpose of selecting a stud dog is to obtain good puppies, not large numbers of them.

CARE AND MANAGEMENT OF THE STUD DOG

Although certain general recommendations can be made, it should be recognized that each stud dog should be studied as an individual, and his care, feeding, exercise, and handling should be varied accordingly.

The immediate reason that a stud dog should be properly fed, exercised, and groomed is the maintenance of his strength and virility. A second, and most important, reason is that a stud dog is on exhibition at all times. Hence, when clients with bitches to be bred appear without notice to examine a dog that stands at public stud, the dog should be presented to them in the best possible condition—clean, hard, in the most becoming state of flesh, and with a gleaming, lively coat. These qualities depend largely upon the care and management accorded the stud dog.

The amount and quality of the food should be varied according to the frequency of services. Where a dog is serving two or more bitches per week over a long period of time, he should be fed at least two meals each day; and his diet should include a specially prepared dog food, or he should be given meat, milk, eggs, cottage cheese, liver, and other foods of animal origin, properly reinforced with vitamins and minerals. Also, he will need a larger quantity of food than is normally given in the maintenance diet.

An interval of an hour or two should intervene between a dog's meal and his employment for breeding. He may be fed following breeding, but it should be a light meal only.

It has always been assumed that forced exercise is of importance in improving semen quality. However, recent studies with dairy bulls cast considerable doubt on the relationship of exercise to fertility. Nevertheless, exercise is good for the health of the dog, and should be accorded.

Proper grooming of the stud dog is necessary, not only to make him more attractive in appearance, but to assist the exercise accorded in maintaining the best of health and condition.

AGE AND SERVICE OF THE STUD

It should be remembered that the number and kind of puppies that a stud dog sires in a given season or year is more important than the total number of services. The number of services will vary with the age, development, temperament, health, and breeding condition of the dog, and the distribution of the services. Therefore, no definite best number of services can be recommended for any and all conditions, and yet the practices followed by good kennels are not far different. All are agreed that excessive service of the dog may reduce his fertility.

Some of the great stud dogs whose progeny became famous, and who were in great demand as studs, have been used daily. Others have been used every other day. Generally speaking, the author recommends that services not be more frequent than every other day.

Dogs should not be used in service until they are at least 1 year of age. Even then, they should be well developed and limited to 1 service per week; and not more than 12 to 15 services in total until they are 2 years of age.

Dogs often remain virile and valuable breeders until 12 years of age, especially if they have been properly handled. However, it is usually best to limit the number of services on a valuable old dog in order to preserve his usefulness and extend his longevity as long as possible.

THE STUD FEE

Well ahead of breeding, the owner of the bitch and the owner of the stud dog should agree on the price. Also, breeding contracts should always be in writing; and the higher the stud fee, the more important it is that good business methods prevail. "Gentlemen's agreements" are not good enough. From a legal standpoint, a breeding contract is binding to the parties whose signatures are affixed thereto. Thus, it is important that the contract be carefully read and fully understood before signing.

If desired, it is usually possible to arrange for the service of a stud dog in the immediate locality, either on the basis of one of the puppies, a very low fee (maybe $10), or no charge at all. Sometimes, the owner of a male takes a fancy to a bitch that he has seen and offers to breed her as a means of proving his stud dog, at little or no charge.

With a valuable bitch, it is recommended that a valuable stud dog be secured. Usually such dogs are available in kennels and handled by professionals. The stud fee for such dogs may range up to $200, or more, depending on the caliber and reputation of the stud dog, the current popularity of the breed, and the demand for it in your locality. A common rule of thumb in setting stud fees is that the value of each puppy, if well reared, should at the time of weaning approximate the stud fee of its sire. For this reason, when a good bitch is involved, sometimes the owner of a good stud dog will arrange to take his pick of one or more of the puppies in lieu of a cash stud fee. This may appear to be a rather practical arrangement, but it does have disadvantages. What if the owner of the stud dog picks that very same puppy that you wanted for yourself? This sort of thing happens. If this method of payment is used, one should be certain to specify at what age the stud-fee puppy is to be taken. Naturally, prolonging the time of selection adds to your food and care costs. In most instances where the stud dog is handled by a professional, if the mating does not produce puppies, it is understood that you have a return privilege—that is, you may take the bitch back for a second service at no added cost. But, as previously emphasized, regardless of the arrangements—whether it's for a puppy, a certain fee, or with or without repeat service—you should always get a breeding agreement in writing. It will avoid any misunderstanding and possible hard feeling at a later date.

SELECTING THE STUD DOG

Careful study should be given to the selection of the stud dog. It is easy to choose the nearest male in the neighborhood; however, you will be better satisfied with the quality and value of the pups if you choose a stud of proper bloodlines, size, conformation, and disposition.

The experienced dog breeder will be able to make his own selection of the stud. Those with less experience may do well to seek the counsel and advice of a kennel owner; they're reputable, and they know the breeding of the dogs involved. Also, the American Kennel Club (51 Madison Avenue, New York, New York) will supply you with information about breeders in your area.

Once you have decided on the stud dog to which you would like to breed your bitch, you should contact the owner of the stud dog as far in advance as possible. Remember that a professional kennel, or stud owner, makes and maintains his reputation on the basis of the quality of the dogs that he breeds. Thus, he will likely want to approve your bitch before he allows his stud to mate her. Most stud owners require a copy of the bitch's registration papers (which certify that she is purebred), a photograph of the bitch, and a certification of health from a veterinarian. Some even want an X ray, since certain large breeds are subject to hip problems (hip dysplasia—poorly formed joints), and should not be bred. If he feels that your bitch is below standard, he will not accept her. In this case, you should not be offended. To you, your dog is still the best female in the world—she's your dog. So, you may proceed to make arrangements to have her bred elsewhere, provided you still want to raise a litter of puppies.

MATING (THE ACT OF COPULATION)

Obviously, great care must be exercised in determining when the dog and the bitch should be put together. Because the length of time between the beginning of estrus and the time of ovulation varies in different bitches, no hard and fast rule can be established, although the twelfth to fourteenth day is in most cases the correct time. The wise breeder will keep a daily record of the changes in the bitch's condition and arrange to put the bitch and dog together when the discharge has become almost clear and the external parts are soft and spongy. Of course, if the bitch is to be shipped to a distant point for breeding, such shipment should be sufficiently far in advance of the receptive stage.

The mating area itself is usually the home ground of the male. Moving him might upset him and make the mating more difficult than necessary. Also, the dog may be bashful and require assistance at the first service; and, if the female is not ready to be bred, she may inflict injury upon the male provided no one is present. Thus, it is usually recommended that both the owner of the bitch and the owner of the stud dog be present at the time of service.

A quiet place should be selected for the mating, to insure privacy. Kennels usually have a special breeding room or shed. Private individuals may use a garage, a cellar, or some other empty room.

If there is great difference in the size of the two animals being mated, you can ease the male's difficulty by providing a platform for whichever animal is smaller. If the female is considerably larger, a pit may be used for her. Also, you may wish to muzzle the bitch if she creates problems and becomes hysterical.

If the bitch refuses the advances of the dog, it is preferable to separate the two, wait a day, then again permit the dog to approach the bitch. If everything goes right, they will begin to mate. Male dogs have the glans on the penis that swells after passing the sphincter muscle of the vagina and "tie" the animals together. The tie may last for a period of a few minutes, a half hour, or occasionally up to an hour or more, but it will end naturally when the locking glands have deflated the needed amount. Once the dogs are locked like this you must take precautions that the bitch or dog does not try to break away. Either or both might be injured. The long tie or lock between the dogs is nature's device to make propagation certain because the bitch is receptive for such a short period of time each year.

Once the lock or tie is broken, the event is over. The owner of the male should take away his dog, while you should remove the bitch, unmuzzle her (if you have provided a muzzle), and offer her water.

Ordinarily, if the bitch accepts the dog, fertilization of the ovum will take place. Usually one good service will suffice. However, if you wish to make sure that your bitch is pregnant, a second mating 24 hours later (some prefer 48 hours later) should be made. Of course, if the bitch rejects the male entirely the second time, it means that she has passed her period of receptivity.

ARTIFICIAL INSEMINATION

By definition, *artificial insemination is the deposition of spermatozoa in the female genitalia by artificial rather than by natural means.*

The first scientific research in artificial insemination of domestic animals was conducted with dogs by the Italian physiologist, Lazarro Spallanzani, in 1780. The Italian scientist is reported to have artificially impregnated a bitch at the time, and, after 62 days, she whelped 3 puppies, 2 males and 1 female. Subsequently, sporadic and successful attempts were made to inseminate bitches artificially. Only in recent years, however, has artificial insemination been practiced in order to effect certain matters that otherwise would be impossible with dogs. Even today, the use of this procedure is not nearly so prevalent in the breeding of dogs as it is in the breeding of cattle and some of the other animal species.

To date, the American Kennel Club has not encouraged the practice of artificial insemination, although it will cooperate with the breeder if he wishes to employ the method or if he finds it necessary to do so. When a natural mating cannot be consummated, application for registration of a litter born as a result of A.I. will be considered by the American Kennel Club provided there is compliance with certain stipulations. The AKC requires that the litter application form be accompanied by an affidavit by the owner of the sire certifying that he witnessed the extraction of the semen and its insemination by a licensed veterinarian, identified by him; and an affidavit from the veterinarian that he made the extraction and the insemination, and that this was done in the presence of the sire's owner.

ADVANTAGES OF ARTIFICIAL INSEMINATION

Some of the advantages of artificial insemination of dogs are:

1. *It extends geographical distances*—By using air transportation for shipping semen, it is possible to effect a mating between a stud and a bitch that are located many miles apart.

2. *It makes it possible to overcome certain physical handicaps to mating*—Artificial insemination is of value (a) in mating animals of greatly different sizes—for example, a heavy, mature dog and a bitch that is just coming in heat for the first time, (b) in using crippled males that are unable to perform natural service, (c) in making possible the use of a dog that has premature erection, thereby preventing entry of the penis into the vagina, and (d) in making possible the use of dogs that are impotent because of lack of sexual drive.

3. *It makes it possible to overcome certain psychological handicaps*—Artificial insemination becomes necessary if the bitch has developed a neurosis as a result of being trained as a watchdog, or if she has become thoroughly upset due to transportation.

4. *It makes it possible to cope with certain cases of vaginitis*—Bitches with vaginitis frequently fail to conceive following a natural service, but many of them will conceive when impregnated artificially.

5. *Other possible advantages of artificial insemination*—With other classes of livestock, where artificial insemination has been used more extensively, breeders have come to think of several added advantages, which, to date, have not occurred to dog breeders. With greater use, the author predicts that dog breeders will come to recognize the same advantages to A.I. Among these are the following:

   a. It increases the use of outstanding sires
   b. It reduces the likelihood of costly delays through using sterile sires
   c. It helps control disease
   d. It makes it possible to prove more sires
   e. It creates large families of dogs.

LIMITATIONS OF ARTIFICIAL INSEMINATION

Like many other wonderful techniques, artificial insemination is not without its limitations. A full understanding of such limitations, however, will merely accentuate and extend its usefulness. Some of the limitations of artificial insemination of dogs are:

1. *Survival time for semen is short*—To date, it has been thought that the survival time of normal semen is about 21 hours. It appears, however, that this limitation exists primarily because so little A.I. has been used among dogs, with the result that only limited studies have been made. It is noteworthy, for example, that recently it was found that the survival time of dog semen can be extended to as much as 173 hours through the addition of such extenders as pasteurized milk or egg-yolk citrate.

2. *Other possible limitations of artificial insemination*—Based on other classes of domestic animals in which artificial insemination has been used more extensively, it can be concluded that the following limitations will apply to the A.I. of dogs, also:

   a. It must conform to physiological principles

b. It requires skilled technicians

c. It may accentuate the damage of a poor male

d. It may restrict the stud dog market

e. It may increase the spread of disease if not done with proper care

f. It may be subject to certain abuses.

FROZEN DOG SEMEN

A research program was started at the University of Oregon Medical School in 1968 to investigate the feasibility of freezing and the long-term storage of canine semen. As a result of this study, the Oregon researchers reported (*The Veterinary Record*, Jan. 6, 1973) that canine semen which had been stored in liquid nitrogen showed good motility upon thawing, and that the future prospects for the preservation of canine semen would seem to be comparable with those presently attained in the cattle industry.

SOME PRACTICAL CONSIDERATIONS OF ARTIFICIAL INSEMINATION

Artificial insemination has practical application in dairy cattle and beef cattle, but, as yet, it has only limited application with other classes of animals, including dogs. Someday it may.

Some practical considerations relative to artificial insemination in dogs follow:

1. *Meeting the requirements of the American Kennel Club*—The AKC must be furnished with a properly completed official litter application form, along with the two affidavits; one affidavit from the owner of the sire certifying that he witnessed the extraction of the semen and its insemination by a licensed veterinarian, with the veterinarian identified by him, and a second affidavit from the veterinarian to the effect that he made the extraction and the insemination and that this was done in the presence of the sire's owner. Both affidavits must identify the sire and dam by the AKC name and number and must state the time and place of the mating.

2. *Semen volume and characteristics*—Table 9 shows the semen volume and sperm concentration of dogs, along with similar information relative to other common animals.

Among the noteworthy characteristics of dog semen are the following:

a. There is no appreciable alteration in semen quality when collections are made as frequently as every other day for short intervals. Further, it is reported that when a stud dog ejaculates daily for short periods, a 24-hour rest will usually provide sufficient time for complete restoration of sperm reserves.

b. The survival time of sperm in the reproductive tract of the bitch is greater than previously supposed. One group of investigators found motile sperm in the uterus as long as 11 days after copulation.

c. Individual movements of the spermatozoa are intense in fresh samples, and mass movements are sometimes seen, also.

3. *Semen collection*—As a first step in collecting semen, a bitch should be presented to the stud. Then, just as soon as he shows interest, the collecting can proceed. Either of the following methods may be used in collecting semen:

a. Collecting semen directly into a syringe by simple digital pressure posterior to the bulb of the penis.

b. Collecting semen with an artificial vagina.

4. *Semen quality*—Dog semen should be examined for quality before inseminating. The following criteria may be used to evaluate quality:

a. Motility (70 to 90% of the sperm should be actively motile)

b. Morphological studies (the total irregular forms should not exceed 20%)

TABLE 9

SEMEN VOLUME AND SPERM CONCENTRATION OF ANIMALS

Class of Animal	Av. Volume of Semen per Ejaculate	Av. Concentration of Sperm	Total Sperm Ejaculate
	(ml)	(millions/ml)	(millions)
Dog	10	125	1,250
Bull	8	1,200	9,600
Ram	1	3,000	3,000
Boar	215	250	53,750
Stallion	125	120	15,000

c. Sperm count (a semen sample should contain a minimum of 100,000 spermatozoa per cubic millimeter)

d. Volume (males weighing approximately 25 pounds should ejaculate about 500 million sperm per collection).

5. *Insemination procedure*—The only equipment needed for inseminating the bitch is a sterile tube; an ordinary 1-ml glass pipette may be used for this purpose, or one may procure plastic insemination tubes, which are sterile-wrapped.

In preparation for the inseminating, the bitch is usually placed on a table of convenient height and held by an attendant. The genitalia are next cleansed with a mild soap and warm water, then thoroughly dried. Then the inseminating tube is inserted and the semen is injected directly into the uterus. The average insemination requires about 200 million sperm.

WAYS IN WHICH TO MAKE A.I. OF DOGS MORE SUCCESSFUL

Based on present knowledge, gained through research and practical observation, along with work with other classes of livestock, it may be concluded that dog owners can make artificial insemination more successful through the following:

1. By keeping record of heat periods and noting irregularities and peculiarities;

2. By watching carefully for heat signs, especially the onset;

3. By having the semen arrive at the time it is needed, without having to store or hold it any longer than possible;

4. By avoiding breeding diseased females or females discharging cloudy mucus. The latter condition indicates an infection somewhere in the reproductive tract;

5. By having the veterinarian examine females that have failed to conceive or that show other reproductive abnormalities.

STERILITY AND INFERTILITY

Sterility is a condition of infertility. Whatever the cause, there are no cure-alls for the condition. Rather, each individual case requires careful diagnosis and specific treatment for what is wrong. Also, it should be recognized that there are two types of sterility—temporary and permanent—although no sharp line of demarcation can be drawn between them.

1. *Temporary sterility*—Some common causes of temporary sterility are:

a. Overfeeding and lack of exercise, accompanied by extremely high condition

b. Underfeeding and extremely thin, run-down condition

c. Nutritional deficiencies

d. Infections of various kinds

e. Some types of physiological imbalances characterized by such things as cystic ovaries or failure to ovulate at the proper time

f. Failure to mate during the receptive stage, after the congestion has left the vulva

g. Failure to keep the male and female tied together sufficiently long during the act of copulation

h. Mating of animals (dog and bitch) of different sizes, with the result that copulation was not successful.

Temporary sterility can be reduced by removing the cause and correcting the difficulty, whatever it may be.

2. *Permanent sterility*—Naturally, permanent sterility is much more serious to the dog breeder. Perhaps the most common causes of permanent sterility are:

a. Some obstruction in the bitch—a closure of the female genital organs

b. Prostate disease in the dog

c. Old age, which is usually accompanied by irregular breeding and eventual total sterility

d. Infections in the reproductive tract, usually in the cervix, uterus, or fallopian tubes

e. Some types of physiological imbalances characterized by such things as cystic ovaries or failure to ovulate at the proper time.

Sometimes a veterinarian is able to correct certain types of permanent sterility. Accordingly, it may be worthwhile to obtain professional advice in an effort to bring about conception.

PREGNANCY DETERMINATION

For practical reasons, it is often very worthwhile to be able to determine whether a bitch is pregnant before she shows it by the distention of the abdomen. Also, one needs to be on the alert relative to phantom (false) pregnancies, so common in bitches, when the abdomen enlarges and the mammary glands increase in size.

Almost anyone with experience can determine 5 or 6 weeks after breeding whether or not a bitch is going to whelp, especially if she is going to have a large litter. But not everyone can tell at the third week, and only a few are able to tell, until whelping time, when a bitch is carrying just 1 or 2 puppies.

Pregnancy can be diagnosed by palpation. By gentle examination of the bitch's abdomen, trained fingers can feel the lumps that will later be puppies. A very skilled person can accurately diagnose pregnancy as early as 22 days after fertilization; and most anyone with experience can do so from the twenty-fourth to the thirty-fifth day after fertilization. Unless the person is very experienced, it is best to let the veterinarian do the palpating.

By the end of the 6th week, or the beginning of the 7th, there should be a perceptible enlargement of the abdomen.

By the 7th week, an X ray of the bitch will show the fetal skeletons and you can determine, once and for all, if the pregnancy is real or false; also, you can determine the number of puppies.

FALSE PREGNANCY

An unspayed bitch may suffer from false pregnancy. Such bitches show all the symptoms of real pregnancy—expanded belly, swollen and sensitive breasts, making a nest for her litter, and even general nervousness as the make-believe whelping time approaches. Only she is not pregnant. If the condition reoccurs, you have a problem dog. Hormone injections by the veterinarian may help; if not, the dog will have to be spayed.

CARE OF THE PREGNANT FEMALE

The duration of pregnancy of the bitch is usually estimated at 63 days, or roughly 9 weeks. However, you should be ready for the puppies to arrive anytime after the 60th day and on through the 65th day. Puppies may arrive early or late, just as other births do.

The following points are pertinent to the care of the pregnant female:

1. *Halting pregnancy*—In case you have encountered an accident—that unplanned parenthood has occurred—you can halt the pregnancy by a series of hormone injections, given by your veterinarian. These are usually most effective if given within 2 to 5 days after mating. The longer you wait, of course, the less chance you have of success.

2. *Worming and vaccinating*—As indicated under the section, "Conditioning the Bitch for Breeding," it is best that treatments for internal and external parasites and vaccinations be administered prior to breeding. If this was overlooked, or if the bitch gets pregnant by accident, it can be handled during the early stages of pregnancy —during the first two to three weeks. So, have her stool examined for worms, then if treatment is indicated, proceed to give it. Also, if you fail to give the usual inoculations against distemper, hepatitis, and leptospirosis, these can be given in the early stages of pregnancy, although it is strongly recommended that this be done prior to breeding. This is important because immune bitches pass along their immunity to the newborn pups.

3. *Exercising*—Pregnant females should be exercised moderately in the normal manner. Walking and running are better for the pregnant bitch than sedentary existence, but she should not be permitted to jump, hunt, fight, or otherwise exert during the latter half of her gestation period. Violent activity may cause her to abort her puppies.

4. *Feeding*—When the bitch shows evidence of being in whelp, usually by the sixth week, the amount of food should be increased, and the frequency of feedings should be increased to 3 times per day. Remember that the pregnant female may be eating for 10 to 12 puppies in addition to herself. This calls for more food, for an increase in the protein content of the diet, and for fortification with minerals and vitamins. During this stage, it is also well to make sure that the bitch receives ample quantities of calcium and phosphorus; that is, more than her normal, non-pregnant requirements. Otherwise, she may suffer from eclampsia either during pregnancy or lactation, because nature ordained that the puppies draw on her supply of minerals whether she can spare them or not. Should this condition develop, get in touch with your veterinarian immediately.

But do not overdo the liberal feeding during the pregnancy period. Excess weight is detrimental. A very fat dog, like a very fat person, has a harder time delivering. As a rule of thumb, a 10-pound gain during pregnancy for a 30-pound dog may be considered excessive. When such an overweight condition occurs, you should cut down on the bitch's food while making sure that she is getting sufficient protein, vitamins, and minerals.

5. *Constipation*—Proper food and adequate exercise will usually regulate the bowel movement. If constipation occurs during pregnancy, it

should be treated immediately, because constipation means an accumulation of waste material and its toxins. But you should avoid violent purgatives as they may cause a miscarriage. A small dosage of milk of magnesia (a teaspoonful or tablet for each 10 pounds of body weight) or a lubricant like mineral oil mixed with the food will usually take care of the situation. Infant suppositories inserted in the rectum of the bitch are especially recommended for they usually work without creating any stomach or intestinal upset. Check with your veterinarian to see what he recommends, especially if the constipation persists for 2 or 3 days.

6. *Coddling*—A bitch that is pregnant for the first time is apt to be somewhat nervous and anxious. Thus, it is quite alright for you to show your concern and affection; speak to her gently, do not make any great demands upon her, let her feel your presence, and assure her of your concern through your tone and manner. But don't hover over her day and night; too much coddling can spoil her, with the result that she may expect such treatment long after she has whelped.

WHELPING TIME

By the end of the 6th week, or the beginning of the 7th, there should be unmistakable signs of approaching parturition—a perceptible enlargement of the abdomen, and the breasts may be enlarged, full of milk, and about ready for the nursing puppies.

At about 8 weeks, with one more week to go, you should do some preliminary work in preparation for the new arrivals. All long hair around the bitch's nipples should be clipped, as well as the hair around her vulva and rectum; that is, if it is necessary. The cleared area around the nipples and teats will make it easier for the pups to nurse, and the cleared space around the hindquarters will allow for more sanitary delivery. If the bitch is unusually hairy, it may be best to call upon the veterinarian to do the clipping. At this time, it is also well to examine the breasts. If they seem especially sensitive to the touch, or if the bitch seems to be worrying about them with her teeth and tongue, wash them gently with warm water and a mild soap, then apply some mineral or baby oil to soften them.

Toward the end of the 8th week, the whelping box should be ready and the bitch should have an opportunity to get accustomed to it several days before her puppies are due to arrive. Place her regular mattress or blanket in the whelping box so that she will feel at home in it, and so that she will be content to have her puppies there. Otherwise she is apt to have them in the corner of the room, or most any other place.

SIGNS OF AND PREPARATION FOR WHELPING

A few hours, or perhaps a day or two, before whelping, the bitch will likely begin arranging the bedding of the box to suit herself; tearing blankets or cushions, and nosing the parts into the corners. At this time, it is best to substitute rubber matting or burlap sacking, securely tacked to the floor of the box. This will provide traction for the puppies so that they can reach the dam's breast.

Be prepared several days in advance, as the normal gestation period is from 58 to 65 days, and 61 is as common as 63. The bitch will generally show some signs of uneasiness and discomfort before the puppies arrive. However, a sure way to predict the time of whelping is to take the dam's temperature with a rectal thermometer, twice daily beginning with the fifty-ninth day. It will drop from a normal of 101°-102°F. to 99° or 100°F., then finally it will fall below 99°F. about 12 hours before whelping.

THE WHELPING BOX

A whelping box should be provided for the birth of the puppies and for use during the nursing period. If such a box is not available, it can be easily constructed. It is enclosed on 3 sides and has an entrance cut on the 4th side. The entrance side should have a barrier, or sill, from 4 to 6 inches high, which makes it easy for the mother to step into it but impossible for the puppies to get out. The box should be large enough so that the bitch can stretch out at full length on her side and have room to spare at both head and tail. A good rule of thumb is to figure on a box 1½ to 2 times the length of the bitch.

The box may be left open on top during warm weather. However, it is always well to have a cover or hinged lid in order to prevent drafts. Should the puppies be born during cold weather, some artificial heat may be advisable, also. You

Fig. 217. Whelping room, with whelping box in near-right corner. (Courtesy Mrs. Charles R. Anderson, Cedwood Puli Kennels, Bristol, Conn.)

will want to keep the room temperature at least 75°F. for the newborn puppies. It is very important to prevent them from chilling during the first few days of life. Puppies whimper when they are too cold, thereby giving you a warning signal.

The whelping box should also be equipped with a railing, which projects out from the walls 3 to 4 inches from the floor. This will prevent a bitch from crushing or suffocating a pup that may get between her and the sides of the box.

The whelping box should be located in a quiet place, away from the usual family traffic pattern. It should be so situated that the mother can be alone with her babies. Immediately before the puppies arrive, the bitch's regular mattress or regular blanket should be removed and replaced with several layers of newspaper laid flat.

WHELPING (DELIVERY)

In normal presentation, the head comes first with the paws alongside the head. A breech birth, with the buttocks presented first, is not uncommon. Each puppy will arrive completely enclosed in a somewhat transparent membrane or sac. Although the sacs are rather tough, sometimes they are ruptured during delivery. As each puppy emerges from the vagina, a bulge will be seen first and then the whitish appearing membrane sac. Immediately you will see the puppy, then the umbilical cord, to which is attached the placenta or afterbirth. At this point, the bitch's instinct usually takes over; she'll tear the sac from around the puppy, nip the umbilical cord with her teeth, and eat the afterbirth. This is perfectly normal procedure, and as nature intended. She will clean the puppy's nostrils of mucus with her tongue and lick the puppy dry. You should not be alarmed if the mother seems to rough up her new baby; she is just getting its breathing started and its circulation going normally.

If the mother fails to take on the duties just enumerated, and there is danger of the newly arrived puppies suffocating, you may have to become midwife. Help her break the sac and encourage her to lick the puppy dry. You may even rub the puppy vigorously with a rough towel, thereby replacing the action of her tongue.

If the newborn puppy does not start to breathe fairly soon, you should assist. Swing it gently by the back legs and tap it lightly on the back until it gasps for breath.

If the mother does not bite the cord in two, or if she leaves it too long, you should sever it with dull scissors and then swab the end with iodine. Occasionally, a bitch will bite the cord off too close to the body, with the result that infection may get in, bleeding will be excessive, or there may be possible hernias. In this case, you should take over and sever the cord with the dull scissors.

If the weather is cold and uncomfortable, and if the mother is not handling the puppies well, it may be wise to remove all of them except one, placing them in a box or basket covered with a woolen cloth; then returning them once whelping is finished.

It is best that the midwife be somebody with whom the bitch is on intimate terms and in whom she has confidence. Usually, the mother will appear grateful for gentle assistance through this ordeal.

If presentation has been normal, the puppies should arrive at intervals of 10 to 30 minutes, or not over an hour apart. If the interval is more than an hour, you should take the bitch out, using a leash if necessary to make her leave the puppies. A bit of exercise and a chance to relieve herself, plus a drink of water, may help matters. If the bitch is straining without getting anywhere, and whelping does not seem to be progressing normally, it is time to call your veterinarian. An experienced veterinarian can usually be depended upon to withdraw with obstetrical forceps an abnormally presented puppy. As a last resort, he may do a Caesarian section. Sometimes, he will administer a hormone to stimulate contraction of the uterus. After a protracted or difficult whelping, especially if the placenta is retained, the veterinarian may inject antibiotics into the uterus to prevent infection.

Once the bitch appears to be through whelping take her out to relieve herself, then spread fresh papers in the whelping box. The bitch will normally have a slight drainage for several weeks following whelping, so keep her off of rugs. Such drainage is nothing to worry about, and it will gradually cease. On the other hand, fresh blood could mean serious internal injury; in this case you should consult your veterinarian.

ABNORMAL CONDITIONS: RENDERING ASSISTANCE

If the bitch has been in labor for more than an hour, or if there has been more than a 2-hour interval between presentations, you should call a veterinarian. Long labor, therefore, is the first danger signal. Additional signs of trouble are: the bitch whining and yelping more than normal during whelping; vomiting; symptoms of shock—chills, trembling or shivering; or a state of collapse. Kind and gentle words may reassure and calm the bitch at this time, but only the veterinarian can give the medical help that is obviously needed. So, you should get in touch with him as soon as you recognize these trouble signs.

THE AFTERBIRTH

Be sure to count the afterbirths to make certain that all of them have been expelled. A retained afterbirth usually spells serious difficulties for the new mother. The dark red discharge following whelping usually indicates that all afterbirths have been expelled, whereas a bright red discharge could indicate danger of hemorrhage. If a discharge is any other color, particularly greenish, it may indicate that one of the afterbirths has been retained and is decomposing, and that an infection has set in. If any of these conditions exist, you should consult your veterinarian immediately. Above all, do not attempt to treat the female yourself.

Remember, it is important to make sure that the number of placentas equals the number of puppies.

CLEANING UP

After the entire litter has arrived, you should clean up the whelping box by putting in a new supply of newspaper, so that the puppies will have a clean nest. Continue to replace the papers as they become soiled by the puppies. Let the new mother out so that she can relieve herself, even though she may be reluctant to leave the whelping box and her babies. She will not be gone long because she will be uneasy about the puppies and unwilling to leave them for more than a few minutes at a time.

Fig. 218. A good start in life. Puli puppies and mother. (Courtesy Mrs. Charles R. Anderson, Cedwood Puli Kennels, Bristol, Conn.)

HANDLING NEWBORN PUPPIES

The mother and her newborn puppies should be left in peace and quiet. Here are some don'ts:

1. Don't allow small children to run into the room.
2. Don't allow adults to enter the room unless they are involved in caring for the mother and litter.
3. Don't bring the sire of the pups into the room. The bitch will not recognize him as the father, and after her excitement from whelping, she may attack him viciously.

Puppies are born with their eyes closed, and they will not open their eyes until about the 9th day following birth. They should not be exposed to bright sunlight when their eyes are opening and for about 10 days thereafter.

You need not worry about puppies learning to eat. Instinctively, they will crawl by themselves to the source of food, even though they are blind, and they have no trouble in doing what comes naturally to them at this stage of their life—nursing.

Puppies should be left alone as much as possible—to sleep and grow. Excessive handling at this stage is detrimental and may introduce infection or cause injury.

COLOSTRUM

The first secretion of the mammary glands following parturition is known as *colostrum*. Colostrum is nature's product, designed to give the young puppies a good start in life. It is higher than normal milk in dry matter, protein, vitamins, and minerals. Also, it is high in globulin, and most important, it contains antibodies that give newborn puppies protection against certain diseases. It is somewhat laxative, also. Without this first milk, the puppy is protected against distemper for only about a week, whereas he is generally immune to distemper until his first inoculation at 4 to 6 weeks of age provided he has received colostrum. Thus, if you plan to formula-feed from the beginning, the formula should not be used exclusively until after the puppies have obtained the colostrum in the first 24 hours. If, for some reason or other, the bitch fails to give colostrum, you should immediately check with your veterinarian about an early distemper injection.

THE FIRST WEEK

During the first week, puppies sleep much of the time, as do babies of other species, and they should not be awakened or played with. They will grow more and be more playful as they mature.

During the first week, it is important that the following rules and procedures be observed:

1. *No visitors*—During the first 3 days of life, no visitors should be permitted in the nursery. Thereafter, one visitor may be permitted at a time, but you should make sure that the guest is very careful about the new arrivals. Some females become very upset over strangers and the handling of their puppies, with the result that they are apt to hurt their own puppies or even the visitor.

2. *Postnatal watch*—Most puppy mortalities occur at birth or within the first week. So, it is important that the caretaker see that each of the puppies is getting his fair share of food and growing normally. If one or more of the puppies seems weak and is being crowded out, it may be necessary to give him an assist to a nursing station.

3. *Dock the tails*—In the breeds that require docking, this should be done on the third day, by your veterinarian. Dewclaws should be removed at the same time. The puppies will hardly notice these things being done at this time.

SUPPLEMENTAL FEEDING

It is most important that the puppies receive plenty of milk. If they do not, they will whine almost constantly and be uneasy. If this happens, a bitch-replacer milk, of which several brands are on the market, can be used; or a commercial baby formula works very well. A home-mixed formula can be prepared as follows: mix 1 can of evaporated milk, 1¼ can of water, an egg yolk, and 2 teaspoons of cream. If hand-feeding is supplementary to the bitch's milk, half of the litter may be kept away from her at one time, then fed once each 3 to 4 hour period. By alternating the shifts, all of the puppies may be left with the dam overnight.

Formula feeds should be well mixed, with commercial formulas mixed according to directions and stored in the refrigerator until needed, then such quantities as needed for one feeding warmed just prior to feeding. All utensils should be kept absolutely clean and sanitary at all times.

A lamb or baby nipple may be used for the larger breeds, but an eyedropper or doll-size nipple is necessary for puppies of the smaller breeds. Do not enlarge the nipple hole too much, as the puppies will not nurse if the milk flows too freely, just as they get discouraged and give up if the nipple is clogged by overheating or undermixing the formula. If you use an eyedropper, drip the milk very slowly into the puppy's mouth, so as to prevent it going down the windpipe and producing mechanical pneumonia. Experienced breeders sometimes prefer to use a tube or "gavage" feeding. This consists of a narrow plastic tube, like those used for premature babies. One end of the tube is inserted through the mouth into the puppy's stomach, the other end is attached to a syringe containing the formula. Then, the formula is slowly released through the tube and into the stomach. Very small or weak puppies without strong sucking reflexes may do best when fed in this manner. It is important, however, that the feeder know how to use this method. Before trying it for the first time, the inexperienced person should rely upon the veterinarian showing him how to do it.

The amount of formula required will vary according to the amount of milk that the puppies are getting from their mother. A puppy of a medium-sized breed may take about a half-ounce per feeding at first, gradually increasing to two ounces per feeding at the age of two weeks. By that time, the eyes are open and puppies may be gradually shifted to drink or eat from a saucer.

THE NURSING PERIOD

Proper care during the nursing period will make for a good start in life. In earlier sections, the care and management during the first few days following whelping was covered. This section covers from about the first week of age to weaning. The "to do" list for this period follows:

1. *Check the mother's vaginal discharge*—The vaginal discharge is a sloughing off of the lining of the uterus to which the placentas were once attached. It has to be eliminated, so such a discharge is perfectly normal. However, if it persists longer than 5 days, or if it seems particularly heavy, you should check with your veterinarian.

2. *Watch for infected breasts*—The caretaker should be on the alert for infected breasts, which can appear anytime from immediately following whelping to weaning. This condition can prove serious to both the dam and the puppies if it goes unnoticed and unrectified. An infected breast is easy to detect; it is inflamed, very tender to the touch, and it does not secrete milk. Infected breasts may lead to the early death of any puppies sucking them, because of failure to get required nourishment and of possibly contracting the infection. Thus, if an infected breast is observed, you should immediately call the veterinarian.

3. *Keep weekly weight records of puppies*—Many kennels keep a weekly weight record of the puppies. They have a special notebook in which the birth weight and identifying characteristics of each puppy are recorded at the time of birth. Then, weekly weight records are subsequently recorded therein. With such a record, it is very easy to see how the puppies are doing. Those who raise just one litter of puppies for the fun of it will find it interesting to follow this same procedure. During the first 3 to 4 weeks of life, the puppies should at least quadruple their birth weight.

4. *Change bedding daily*—Throughout the nursing period, the bedding should be changed daily.

5. *Give small and weak puppies a special assist*—The caretaker should check frequently to make sure that all puppies are receiving an equal supply of food. Large puppies are apt to push the smaller ones out of the way and thus get most of the milk. If this happens, it is well to give the smaller puppies a chance to feed before the larger ones are permitted to nurse. In case of a large litter where there are more puppies than feeding stations, all of the puppies may be given an equal opportunity for nourishment by dividing them into two groups, then feeding them alternately.

6. *Give puppies supplemental milk if necessary*—With proper feeding, most bitches will give sufficient milk for the litter. Like some cows, however, some bitches are just poor milkers. Sometimes, health reasons make for a poor milk supply. In any event, if the dam is not giving sufficient milk for the puppies, supplemental feeding of milk should be resorted to. Instructions relative to this have been given in an earlier section.

7. *Feed the bitch a balanced and liberal diet*—The lactating requirements are far more rigorous than the gestating requirements. Hence, it is exceedingly important that the diet of the bitch be well balanced at this time; that it be high in protein, adequate in energy, and that it be well fortified with minerals, vitamins, and unidentified factors. Also, after giving birth to the litter, increased consumption of food is necessary in order to enable sufficient quantities of milk to be produced. At the height of lactation, about the 4th week, the female will consume about twice the normal quantity of food.

With a large litter, it may be well to supplement the bitch's diet with horse meat or raw hamburger; adding 1 part of these products to 3 parts of her normal ration.

8. *Blunt the puppies' nails*—After about the second week, the puppies' nails grow long and sharp. When pawing at the breast, they sometimes lacerate it. To prevent this sort of thing happening, the puppies' nails should be blunted with scissors from time to time.

9. *Worm the puppies if necessary*—Every precaution should be taken to prevent the puppies from becoming infested with parasites, particularly roundworms. If the bitch harbors such parasites, she should be wormed before she is bred;

and her teats and rearquarters should be washed thoroughly with mild soap and water just before she whelps, in order to remove adhering roundworm eggs. Also, the whelping quarters should be clean and sanitary at all times. Despite all these precautions, puppies are apt to have roundworms. Thus, treatment may be in order.

10. *Remove the protective door sill*—When the puppies are about 3 weeks old, they will begin to wander about. Let them do so. Remove the protective door sill or board previously placed across the doorway of their whelping box. Instinctively, young puppies refuse to soil their own sleeping quarters if given an opportunity to relieve themselves elsewhere.

11. *Provide separate rations for puppies*—Puppies are great imitators. As they observe their mother eating her ration, they will become curious and try it for themselves. This stage occurs when the puppies are about 3 to 3½ weeks of age. When this happens, the puppies should be given their own ration, separate and apart from their mother. If the same food is used for the puppies that is used for their mother, it is well to add some milk to it for the youngsters.

By the time puppies reach weaning age, at 5 to 8 weeks, they should be consuming enough food to avoid any setback.

Self-feeding is recommended for puppies; that is, keeping feed before them at all times. This applies from the time feeding is initiated at 3 to 3½ weeks of age up to 16 to 20 weeks of age. Thereafter, one feeding a day may suffice, or, if the puppies do not overeat and get too heavy, self-feeding can be continued.

12. *Crop the ears at 6 to 8 weeks of age*—If you intend to crop (clip short) the puppies' ears—the procedure usually decreed for reasons of style and show with Great Danes, Boxers, and Dobermans—it is best that it be done early, at about 6 to 8 weeks of age. At this stage, there is almost no pain. Thus, if you plan to show your dog, or if you wish it to conform to standards set by show winners, this procedure should be carried out.

RAISING ORPHAN PUPPIES
(Also, see chapter 4, section on "Orphaned and Rejected Puppies")

Occasionally, a bitch dies during or immediately after parturition, leaving a litter of orphaned puppies to be raised. At other times, a bitch may fail to give sufficient milk. In such cases, the puppies may be (1) shifted to another bitch, known as a foster mother or nurse bitch, or (2) placed on a milk replacer, or synthetic milk, which is mixed and fed according to the manufacturer's directions.

If at all possible, however, it is very important that orphan puppies receive colostrum. If this is not possible, you should confer with your veterinarian as to the procedure to follow.

For the first few days, the orphans should be fed with a bottle and rubber nipple, an eyedropper, or a tube (see section on Supplemental Feeding). All receptacles must be kept sanitary (clean and scald each time they are used) and feeding must be at regular intervals.

Milk replacers should be warmed to 100° to 105°F. prior to feeding.

WEANING

Weaning is made easy by prior preparation. Even nature gives an assist in this regard. Instinctively, the dam lets her young know that she is tired of nursing them and that it is time to eat on their own. At about 4 weeks of age, she will start her young on solid food. First she eats some of the food, then she regurgitates it (vomits it up) semidigested for the puppies, in much the same way as the mother bird feeds her young. This is nature's way of giving the puppies what they need. Of course, you will give nature an assist by starting puppies on food when they are about 3½ weeks of age.

Puppies should be weaned at about 6 weeks of age. It is recommended that the mother be taken from the whelping box and that the puppies be left in the quarters to which they have become accustomed. Even at its best, weaning creates a stress on both the bitch and young. Nevertheless, the separation of the mother and young should be complete and final, with no opportunity for them to see each other until the weaning is final.

At weaning time, the same schedule and the same type of food should be accorded the puppies as was being followed prior to weaning; only they will need more food.

During the nursing period, the bitch has been receiving about 3 times the normal amount of food as that required during the gestating stage. Thus, at the time of weaning, her food allowance needs to be sharply reduced. She should not be fed on the day that weaning takes place. Then, on the 2nd day, she may be given 1/5 of her normal ration; on the 3rd day, 2/5 of her normal ration; and so on until, on the 5th day following weaning, she is receiving what she consumed before whelping. Cutting down on the ration of the female at weaning time reduces the quantity of milk that she produces and helps restore the milk-producing organs to normal.

It is not necessary to milk the bitch out following weaning. If you cut down on the ration, nature will take care of the rest. The back pressure built up in the udder automatically stops milk production. If the udder seems congested and hot, it may be desirable to rub an oil preparation (such as camphorated oil or a mixture of lard and spirits of camphor) on it. But do not milk it out.

REGISTER THE LITTER

If the litter is purebred—that is, out of a registered stud and a registered bitch of the same breed—you should register the litter with the American Kennel Club or other registry. Remember, puppies that are registered, or eligible for registry, are always more readily sold at a higher price. Remember, too, that only purebred dogs are eligible to be shown in AKC approved shows, and that registration papers are proof of lineage. So, prior to arrival of the litter of puppies you should have litter registration forms on hand. Then all you have to do is fill it out in keeping with the instructions, listing the number of puppies and their sexes, etc. After you have been notified that the litter has been registered with the American Kennel Club, you will simply give an individual litter registration application, which will be sent to you by the AKC, along with a copy of the puppy's pedigree, to the new owner. Then, he may register the puppy with the American Kennel Club. Further instructions relative to registration are given in chapter 2, "Breeds; Kennel Clubs; Selecting and Buying."

4
Feeding

Chapter 4
Functions of Food   *187*
   Maintenance   *187*
   Growth   *187*
   Show Conditioning   *187*
   Reproduction and Lactation   *188*
   Work (Hunting, Racing, Etc.)   *188*
Nutrients   *188*
   Balanced Ration   *189*
   Nutritive Needs of Dogs   *189*
      Protein   *189*
         Quality of Protein   *189*
         Quantity of Protein   *198*
         Protein Toxicity   *201*
      Energy   *201*
         Carbohydrates   *201*
         Fats   *202*
            Rancidity of Fat   *203*
         Quantity of Energy   *203*
         Calorie System of Measuring Energy   *203*
      Minerals   *204*
         Calcium and Phosphorus   *204*
         Dog Mineral Chart   *206*
      Vitamins   *205*
         Dog Vitamin Chart   *212*
         Unidentified Factors   *219*
      Water   *220*
Food for Dogs   *220*
   Home Formula   *220*
   Commercial (Manufactured) Dog Foods   *221*
      How to Select Commercial Foods   *221*
      Types of Dog Foods   *221*
         Canned Dog Food (Complete, 75% Moisture)   *221*
            Canned Meat (Straight Pack, 75% Moisture)   *222*

(Continued)

Dry Dog Foods (10% Moisture)	*222*
Semimoist Dog Foods (25% Moisture)	*222*
Supplements	*222*
Palatability (Taste, Aroma)	*224*
Fads, Foibles, and Trade Secrets	*224*
Formulating Diets; Some Suggested Formulations	*224*
Special Feeding	*226*
Feeding the Pregnant Female	*226*
Feeding the Lactating Female	*226*
Feeding Puppies	*227*
Weaning	*228*
Orphaned and Rejected Puppies	*228*
Feeding Breeding Stock	*230*
Feeding Working Dogs	*230*
Feeding Older Dogs	*230*
Feeding Obese Dogs	*231*
Feeding Sick Dogs	*231*
Feeding Rules	*232*
Amount to Feed	*232*
When to Feed	*233*
Self-Feeding	*233*
Some Don'ts of Feeding	*233*
Nutritional Diseases and Ailments	*234*
Composition of Dog Food Ingredients	*235*

Fig. 219. Feeding! Hot Smoke and her litter of puppies. (Courtesy H. N. Holmes, Gunsmoke Kennels, Springfield, Ill.)

FEEDING[1]

Feeding America's dogs is big and important business; it's big business to the companies engaged in manufacturing and marketing dog food, and it's important business to every dog owner.

At last count, some 3,000 pet food manufacturers were selling their products under 15,000 different labels, to be eaten by about 32.6 million dogs and 22 million cats.[2] Gross sales of pet foods now total more than $1.352 billion annually.[2] Approximately $1 out of every $100 spent for groceries goes for pet food. Dollar-wise, the pet industry is 2½ times bigger than baby food.

But more growth lies ahead! And the race is on as pet food manufacturers go after it. The quarry: the approximately 50 percent of U.S. dogs that are still fed on table scraps or home-mixed preparations, all or in part; a pet food market that's been expanding at the phenomenal rate of 10 percent, or more, per year; and a dog population explosion of 2 to 3 percent per year.

Dog nutrition and feeding has changed more than the feeding of any other class of animal. Nowadays, fewer and fewer dogs are fed on table scraps alone; and no self-respecting master would admit to his dog being the neighborhood scavenger, ransacking garbage cans and living off the land. Instead, old Rover and his kind are devouring gourmet dinners of beef burgundy, kidney stew, ribs of lamb and veal, fricassees, burgers, river herring feasts, and chunks of meat. And that's not all! They come in onion or garlic flavors, as gravies, sauces, and the like; and there's a choice of dry, semimoist, or canned form. Most of them are so exotic that it's difficult to recognize what's in them. All of them possess human qualities of taste, aroma, and eye appeal; the idea being that your dog shares *your* senses of taste, smell, and sight. (He doesn't; he's an animal, with tastes and needs different from yours.)

The typically American dog is better fed than his master, for the following reasons:

1. He is protected by his primitive tastes and the never ending application of modern science and technology to the manufacture of dog foods. Man, on the other hand, loses the inherited ability to select the foods that are best for him. Very early in life, he's conditioned to eating an excess of refined foods, such as sugar.

2. Each man is his own nutritionist, since he pretty much selects his food at home or at a restaurant. By contrast, those owners who feed commercial dog foods rely on the manufacturer, back of whom is a staff of nutritionists and a research laboratory.

3. More is known about the nutritional requirements of the dog than is known about the nutritional requirements of man.

Also, foods for discriminating pets are inspected for wholesomeness and sanitation. Many producers of canned dog foods are subject to federal inspection because they also process meat and meat products for human consumption.

But challenges in dog feeding still remain! Futuristic dog feeding calls for more owners who know what their pets need, who will not be misled by a few well-chosen words or folktales of overenthusiastic advertising, and who will not be swayed by a product that merely looks good, smells good, and tastes good.

Futuristic dog feeding calls for owners who recognize that no amount of expertise in dog care, and no amount of love and affection, can overcome deficiencies in nutrition.

It calls for owners who recognize that, unless the dog is fed properly, his maximum potential in body form, style, attractiveness, endurance, reproduction, use, and longevity cannot be achieved.

It calls for dog owners who recognize that all dogs cannot be fed the same; that the nutritive requirements of dogs differ according to age, size, use, individuality, physiological state (pregnant, lactating, etc.), and temperature.

It calls for owners who recognize that, although the dog is a carnivorous animal, he cannot live on meat alone.

It calls for dog owners who know about the 43 or more nutrients required by dogs.

It calls for owners who, no matter how well-meaning their intent, do not create imbalances by adding their own pet ingredients to a complete, nutritionally balanced food.

It calls for knowledgable and discriminating dog owners who recognize that, although most dog foods are well balanced and wholesome, others are deficient in nutrient value.

Furthermore, futuristic dog feeding calls for owners (1) who, although recognizing that a

---

[1] The author acknowledges with thanks the authoritative review accorded this chapter by: Mr. Herbert N. Holmes, Gunsmoke Kennels, 1541 East Lake Shore Drive, Springfield, Illinois 62705.
[2] Pet Food Institute figures.

dog must eat his food if it is to do him any good, are aware that obvious liking for a particular product does not necessarily assure its nutritional qualities; (2) who are aware that onion and garlic flavors, among others, practically guarantee enthusiastic consumption even if the food is nutritionally poor; (3) who are aware that advertising claims for "flavor" are actually selling the master by appealing to his taste for garlic, sauces, and the like; and (4) who are aware that such expensive goodies as beef burgundy, kidney stew, and ribs of lamb and veal are aimed at the master, who believes that his pet cannot survive on ordinary foods. It calls for dog owners who recognize that results are more important than cost per can, package, or bag.

Futuristic dog feeding calls for progressive owners who have the tomorrow mind, instead of the yesterday mind; for owners who accept and follow scientific feeding, rather than age-old fads, foibles, and trade secrets.

FUNCTIONS OF FOOD

The food consumed by dogs is used for a number of functions, with the exact usage varying according to age, size, use, individuality, physiological state, and temperature. With all dogs, a certain part of the food is used for bodily functions, aside from any useful production. This is known as the *maintenance requirement*. In addition, young, growing dogs need nutrients suitable for building muscle tissue and bone; breeding females require food for the development of their fetuses, and, following parturition, for the production of milk; whereas working dogs (such as hunting and racing dogs) use food to supply energy for productive work. Each of these needs will be discussed separately.

MAINTENANCE

A dog differs from an engine in that the latter has no fuel requirement when idle; whereas a dog requires fuel every second of the day, whether he is idle or not.

The maintenance requirement may be defined as a ration that is adequate to prevent any loss, or gain, of tissue in the body when there is no production. Although these requirements are relatively simple, they are essential for life itself. A mature dog must have heat to maintain body temperature, sufficient energy to cover the internal work of the body and the minimum movement of the animal, and a small amount of protein, vitamins, and minerals for the repair of body tissues.

No matter how quietly a dog may be lying in his quarters, he still requires a certain amount of fuel, and the least amount on which he can exist is called his *basal maintenance requirement*. A dog requires about nine percent more fuel when standing than when lying, and still more for any movement he may make. Even under the best of conditions, about one-half of all the food consumed by dogs is used in meeting the maintenance requirements.

GROWTH

Growth may be defined as the increase in size of the muscles, bones, internal organs, and other parts of the body. Naturally, the growth requirements become increasingly acute when dogs are forced into some use at an early age, such as showing, hunting, or racing.

Growth has been referred to as the foundation of dog production. Breeding females may have their productive ability seriously impaired if they have been raised improperly. Hunting dogs cannot perform the maximum amount of work, and racing dogs do not possess the desired speed and endurance, if their growth has been stunted or if their skeletons have been injured by inadequate rations during the growth period.

SHOW CONDITIONING

Show conditioning may be defined as the production of a hard, trim finish, along with a beautiful hair coat.

Conditioning of mature dogs for show is usually obtained by increasing the allowance of high energy foods—the carbohydrates and fats—along with insuring plenty of exercise. For older dogs, very little additional protein, minerals, and vitamins are required for maintenance. In conditioning young, growing dogs for show, however, it is essential that, in addition to supplying more carbohydrates and fats, more protein, minerals, and vitamins be added; with all nutrients kept in proper balance.

REPRODUCTION AND LACTATION

There are many causes of reproductive failure in dogs, but most scientists are agreed that inadequate nutrition is a major one.

It is known that the diet exerts a powerful effect on sperm production and semen quality. Too fat a condition in the stud dog can even lead to temporary or permanent sterility. There is abundant evidence that greater fertility of dogs exists under conditions where a well-balanced ration and plenty of exercise are provided.

Most of the growth of the fetus occurs during the last half of pregnancy, thus making the reproductive requirements most critical during this period. The diet of the pregnant female should supply sufficient amounts of protein, minerals, and vitamins. In the case of young, growing, pregnant females, additional protein, minerals, and vitamins, above the ordinary requirements, must be provided; otherwise, the fetus will not develop properly or milk will be produced at the expense of the tissues of the dam.

The nutritive requirements for moderate to heavy milk production are much more rigorous than the pregnancy requirements. Thus, there is special need for a rather liberal protein, mineral, and vitamin allowance during lactation.

WORK (HUNTING, RACING, ETC)

Work, such as hunting, racing, police work, leading the blind, war work, etc., requires high energy foods.

For mature work dogs, not in reproduction, work is performed primarily at the expense of the carbohydrates and fats of the diet. Theoretically, protein is not drawn upon so long as the other nutrients are present in adequate amounts. From a practical standpoint, however, it is usually desirable that protein supply 20 to 25 percent of the calories, to insure that the dog can make efficient use of the remainder of the nutrients in the ration. For work dogs, the mineral and vitamin requirements are practically the same as for comparably idle animals.

NUTRIENTS

Nutrients are the chemical substances found in food materials that can be used, and are necessary, for the maintenance, production, and health of dogs. The chief classes of nutrient substances are proteins, carbohydrates, fats, minerals, vitamins, and water. These nutrients are needed by the dog in definite amounts, with the quantities varying according to the age, size, use, and individuality of the dog. A deficiency in a nutrient can be, and often is, a limiting factor in growth, reproduction, performance (work), or health. This is clearly illustrated by the "egg story" in Fig. 220, which the author told to hundreds of students and dog owners during his 25 years as a university professor.

HOW MANY EGGS WILL BE PRODUCED?

If the following nutrients are required for egg production, with each nutrient identified by No. only (for example, No. 1 might be an essential amino acid, No. 2 might be vitamin A, etc., etc.):	*If* to produce 12 (one doz.) eggs, the total units of each nutrient required are:	*If* the units of each nutrient present in the ration are:	Comments
No. 1	12	9	The ration lacks 3 units of having enough of this nutrient for 12 eggs
No. 2	20	30	A surplus, ⅓ more of the nutrient than needed
No. 3	12	13	Barely over
No. 4	11	11	Even with the board

Fig. 220. An "egg story." Nutrient number 1 will be the limiting factor; only 9 eggs can be produced.

Note that the question posed at the top of Fig. 220 is, "How many eggs will be produced?" Note, too, that the "If" heading each of the first three columns sets forth certain facts on which the question is predicated. Of course, nutrient number 1 is the limiting factor—there is only enough of it for nine eggs; hence, only nine eggs will be produced. In the dog, the same principle applies to growth, reproduction, lactation, speed, and endurance. A shortage of just one required nutrient can limit every conceivable type of performance.

BALANCED RATION

To supply all the needs—for maintenance, growth, show conditioning, reproduction, lactation, and work—the different classes of dogs must receive sufficient food to furnish the necessary quantity of protein, energy (carbohydrates and fats), minerals, vitamins, and water. A ration that meets all these needs is said to be balanced. More specifically, by definition, *a balanced ration is one that provides a dog the proper proportions and amounts of all the required nutrients for a period of 24 hours.* However, by common usage, the word *ration* implies the feeds fed to an animal or animals without limitation to the time in which they are consumed.

NUTRITIVE NEEDS OF DOGS

The nutritive requirements of dogs have been published by the National Research Council. These, with adaptations by the author, are herewith presented in Tables 10, 11, 12, 13, and 14. The nutritive requirements given in these tables may not represent the minimum requirements for each nutrient, but they will provide for adequate nutrition. However, dog food manufacturers and dog owners will find it desirable, in some cases, to increase the level of certain nutrients to compensate for variations in ingredient composition, environment, and possible losses of nutrients during storage and processing. Also, it is generally recognized that individual dogs differ in their nutritive requirements, and that stress conditions, including subclinical disease level, influence the quantity of nutrients needed in the diet of the dog.

Table 15 summarizes the pertinent known facts relative to the nutritive needs of dogs.

PROTEIN

Proteins are complex organic compounds made up chiefly of amino acids, which are present in characteristic proportions for each specific protein. This nutrient always contains carbon, hydrogen, oxygen, and nitrogen, and in addition it usually contains sulphur and frequently phosphorus. Proteins are essential in all plant and animal life as components of the active protoplasm of each living cell.

In plants, the protein is largely concentrated in the actively growing portions, especially the leaves and seeds. Plants also have the ability to synthesize their own proteins from such relatively simple soil and air compounds as carbon dioxide, water, nitrates, and sulfates. Thus, plants, together with some bacteria, which are able to synthesize these products, are the original sources of all proteins.

About fifty percent of the dog's body is protein. It is the primary constituent of structural and protective tissues—such as bones, ligaments, hair, skin, and the soft tissues that include the organs and muscles. Also, protein is combined with carbohydrates, fats, and minerals in the body to form enzymes, hormones, various body fluids, and antibodies. They enter into practically every phase of the dog's bodily activity. Except for the bacterial action in the rumen of cows, sheep, and the like, animals lack the ability of plants to synthesize proteins from simple materials. They must depend upon plants or other animals as a source of dietary protein; they must have amino acids or more complete protein compounds in the ration. Of course, the latter situation applies to dogs.

Dogs of all ages and kinds require adequate amounts of protein of suitable quality—for maintenance, growth, fitting, reproduction, and work. Of course, the protein requirements for growth and reproduction are the greatest and most critical.

Quality of Protein

Merely providing an adequate level, or quantity, of protein in the diet will not suffice, because quality of protein is an essential determinant in meeting the needs of the animal. Thus, the quality, or value, of a protein depends on its amino acid content. Since proteins vary widely in content and relative proportions of amino acids, it follows that they vary widely in quality. For these reasons, an understanding of amino

TABLE 10

NUTRIENT REQUIREMENTS OF DOGS[3]

(Amounts per lb or kg of body weight per day)

Nutrient		Adult Maintenance		Growing Puppies	
		(per lb)	(per kg)	(per lb)	(per kg)
Protein	(g)	2.18	4.8	4.36	9.6
Fat	(g)	0.5	1.1	1.0	2.2
Linoleic Acid	(g)	0.1	0.22	0.2	0.44
Minerals:					
Calcium	(mg)	110	242	220	484
Phosphorus	(mg)	90	198	180	396
Potassium	(mg)	60	132	120	264
Sodium Chloride	(mg)	110	242	220	484
Magnesium	(mg)	4.0	8.8	8.0	17.6
Iron	(mg)	0.6	1.32	1.2	2.64
Copper	(mg)	0.07	0.16	0.15	0.32
Manganese	(mg)	0.05	0.11	0.1	0.22
Zinc	(mg)	0.5	1.1	1.0	2.2
Iodine	(mg)	0.015	0.034	0.031	0.068
Selenium	(mcg)	1.1	2.42	2.2	4.84
Vitamins:					
Vitamin A	(IU)	50	110	100	220
Vitamin D	(IU)	5	11	10	22
Vitamin E	(IU)	0.5	1.1	0.1	2.2
Thiamin	(mcg)	10	22	20	44
Riboflavin	(mcg)	21.8	48	43.6	96
Pantothenic Acid	(mcg)	100	220	200	440
Niacin	(mcg)	113.6	250	227.3	500
Pyridoxine	(mcg)	10	22	20	44
Folic Acid	(mcg)	1.8	4.0	3.6	8.0
Biotin	(mcg)	1.0	2.2	2.0	4.4
Vitamin B_{12}	(mcg)	0.23	0.5	0.45	1.0
Choline	(mg)	11.8	26	23.6	52

[3] From No. 8, *Nutrient Requirements of Dogs*, Revised 1974, National Academy of Sciences, NRC, p. 36, Table 2, with U.S. customary added by the author.

These data may be related to those in Table 11 by assuming 0.35 ounces of dry matter consumption per pound (or to Table 12 by assuming 22 g of dry matter consumption per kilogram) of body weight by adult dogs for maintenance and double this consumption by growing puppies. Adult dogs which are working or lactating will consume 2–3 times the food consumed by the adult dog for maintenance, and thus daily nutrient intakes per pound, or per kilogram, body weight will equal or exceed those levels ingested by growing puppies.

TABLE 11
NUTRIENT REQUIREMENTS (AND SELECTED RECOMMENDED ALLOWANCES) OF DOGS [4]
(percentage or amount per lb of food)

		Type of Diet			
		Dry Basis	Dry Type	Semimoist	Canned or Wet
Moisture level	(%)	0	10	25	75
Dry Matter Basis	(%)	100	90	75	25
Nutrient		**Requirement**			
Protein	(%)	22	20	16.5	5.5
Fat	(%)	5.0	4.5	3.75	1.25
Linoleic Acid	(%)	1.0	0.9	0.75	0.25
Minerals:					
Calcium	(%)	1.1	1.0	0.8	0.3
Phosphorus	(%)	0.9	0.8	0.7	0.22
Potassium	(%)	0.6	0.5	0.45	0.2
Sodium Chloride	(%)	1.1	1.0	0.8	0.3
Magnesium	(%)	0.040	0.036	0.03	0.01
Iron	(mg)	27.3	24.5	20.5	6.8
Copper	(mg)	3.3	3.0	2.5	.82
Manganese	(mg)	2.3	2.0	1.73	.55
Zinc[5]	(mg)	22.73	20.45	17.3	5.45
Iodine	(mg)	0.7	0.63	.53	0.18
Selenium[5]	(mg)	0.05	0.045	0.04	0.014
Vitamins:					
Vitamin A	(IU)	2273[6]	2045	1705	568
Vitamin D	(IU)	227.3[7]	204.5	170.5	56.8
Vitamin E	(IU)	22.73[8]	20.45	17.05	5.68
Thiamin	(mg)	0.45	0.41	0.34	0.114
Riboflavin	(mg)	1.0	0.91	0.73	0.23
Pantothenic Acid	(mg)	4.5	4.1	3.4	1.14
Niacin	(mg)	5.18	4.7	3.9	1.3
Pyridoxine	(mg)	0.45	0.41	0.34	0.114
Folic Acid	(mg)	0.08	0.07	0.06	0.02
Biotin[5]	(mg)	0.05	0.04	0.034	0.01
Vitamin B$_{12}$[5]	(mg)	0.01	0.009	0.008	0.003
Choline	(mg)	545	500	409	136

[4] From No. 8 *Nutrient Requirements of Dogs*, Revised 1974, National Academy of Sciences, NRC, p. 35, Table 1, with U.S. customary added by the author.

Based on diets with ME concentrations in the range of 99–113 kcal/oz of dry matter. If energy density exceeds this range, it may be necessary to increase nutrient concentrations proportionately. Recommended nutrient levels selected to meet the requirements of the most demanding life cycle segments, i.e., rapid growth and lactation.

[5] Recommended allowance based on research with other species.

[6] This amount of vitamin A activity corresponds to 0.68 mg of all-*trans* retinol per pound of dry diet (One IU of vitamin A activity equals 0.03 µg of all-*trans* retinol).

[7] This amount of vitamin D activity corresponds to 5.68 µg of cholecalciferol per pound of dry diet (One IU of vitamin D activity equals 0.025 µg of cholecalciferol).

[8] This amount of vitamin E activity corresponds to 22.7 mg of *dl-a*-tocopheryl acetate per pound of dry diet (One IU of vitamin E activity equals 1 mg of *dl-a*-tocopheryl acetate).

TABLE 12

NUTRIENT REQUIREMENTS (AND SELECTED RECOMMENDED ALLOWANCES) OF DOGS [9]

(percentage or amount per kg of food)

		Type of Diet			
		Dry Basis	Dry Type	Semimoist	Canned or Wet
Moisture level	(%)	0	10	25	75
Dry Matter Basis	(%)	100	90	75	25
Nutrient		Requirement			
Protein	(%)	22	20	16.5	5.5
Fat	(%)	5.0	4.5	3.75	1.25
Linoleic acid	(%)	1.0	0.9	0.75	0.25
Minerals:					
Calcium	(%)	1.1	1.0	0.8	0.3
Phosphorus	(%)	0.9	0.8	0.7	0.22
Potassium	(%)	0.6	0.5	0.45	0.2
Sodium Chloride	(%)	1.1	1.0	0.8	0.3
Magnesium	(%)	0.040	0.036	0.030	0.010
Iron	(mg)	60	54	45	15
Copper	(mg)	7.3	6.5	5.5	1.8
Manganese	(mg)	5.0	4.5	3.8	1.2
Zinc[10]	(mg)	50	45	38	12
Iodine	(mg)	1.54	1.39	1.16	0.39
Selenium[10]	(mg)	0.11	0.10	0.08	0.03
Vitamins:					
Vitamin A	(IU)	5000[11]	4500	3750	1250
Vitamin D	(IU)	500[12]	450	375	125
Vitamin E	(IU)	50[13]	45	37.5	12.5
Thiamin	(mg)	1.00	0.90	0.75	0.25
Riboflavin	(mg)	2.2	2.0	1.6	0.5
Pantothenic Acid	(mg)	10.0	9.0	7.5	2.5
Niacin	(mg)	11.4	10.3	8.6	2.8
Pyridoxine	(mg)	1.0	0.9	0.75	0.25
Folic Acid	(mg)	0.18	0.16	0.14	0.04
Biotin[10]	(mg)	0.10	0.09	0.075	0.025
Vitamin B$_{12}$[10]	(mg)	0.022	0.020	0.017	0.006
Choline	(mg)	1200	1100	900	300

[9] From No. 8, *Nutrient Requirements of Dogs*, Revised 1974, National Academy of Sciences, NRC, p. 35, Table 1.
Based on diets with ME concentrations in the range of 3.5–4.0 kcal/g of dry matter. If energy density exceeds this range, it may be necessary to increase nutrient concentrations proportionately. Recommended nutrient levels selected to meet the requirements of the most demanding life cycle segments, i.e., rapid growth and lactation.

[10] Recommended allowance based on research with other species.

[11] This amount of vitamin A activity corresponds to 1.5 mg of all-*trans* retinol per kilogram of dry diet (one IU of vitamin A activity equals 0.3 µg of all-*trans* retinol).

[12] This amount of vitamin D activity corresponds to 12.5 µg of cholecalciferol per kilogram of dry diet (One IU of vitamin D activity equals 0.025 µg of cholecalciferol).

[13] This amount of vitamin E activity corresponds to 50 mg of *dl-a*-tocopheryl acetate per kilogram of dry diet (One IU of vitamin E activity equals 1 mg of *dl-a*-tocopheryl acetate).

TABLE 13

ESTIMATED DAILY FOOD REQUIREMENTS FOR MAINTENANCE OF DOGS OF VARIOUS WEIGHTS [14]

(U. S. Customary weights)

Weight of Dog		ME Required (kcal/day)	Dry Type[15]		Semimoist[16]		Canned or Wet			
							High fat, Meat[17]		Low fat, Low meat[18]	
(lb)	(kg)		(oz/lb body wt)	(oz/dog)	(oz/lb body wt)	(oz/dog)	(oz/lb body wt)	(oz/dog)	(oz/lb body wt)	(oz/dog)
5	2.3	247	0.53	2.65	0.61	3.05	1.33	6.65	1.91	9.55
10	4.5	408	0.43	4.3	0.51	5.1	1.12	11.2	1.62	16.2
15	6.8	556	0.40	6.00	0.46	6.9	1.01	15.15	1.46	21.9
20	9.1	692	0.37	7.4	0.43	8.6	0.93	18.6	1.35	27.0
30	13.6	935	0.34	10.2	0.38	11.4	0.85	25.5	1.22	36.6
50	22.7	1373	0.29	14.5	0.34	17.0	0.75	37.5	1.07	53.5
70	31.8	1768	0.27	18.9	0.32	22.4	0.69	48.3	0.99	69.3
110	49.8	2475	0.24	26.4	0.29	31.9	0.61	67.1	0.88	96.8

[14] Adapted by the author from No. 8, *Nutrient Requirements of Dogs*, Revised 1974, National Academy of Sciences, NRC, p. 37, Table 4. Approximate requirements for growth may be estimated by multiplying maintenance requirements by 2. If ME values of a particular food vary from those used in these calculations, the estimated food requirement in the table will vary accordingly. Dogs of different breeds, temperament, and physical condition utilize foods with differing degrees of effectiveness. Therefore, these requirements will vary with individual dogs in different environments and stress conditions. Working or lactating adult dogs may require 2–3 times more food than is required for maintenance.

[15] Assumed for purposes of calculation that this diet contained 90% dry matter, 24% crude protein, 10% fat, 46% starch and sugar and 10% fiber and ash. The apparent digestibility of crude protein was assumed to be 80%, fat 92%, starch and sugar 85%. Gross energy (GE) values used for protein, fat, and starch and sugar were 124.7 [160.2–35.44 (urinary losses)], 266.5 and 117.6 kcal/oz respectively. To calculate ME concentration, the above values were used as follows:

	Apparent Digestibility Coefficient	Nutrient/Diet	GE (kcal/oz)	ME (kcal)
Crude protein	0.80	0.24	124.7	23.9
Fat	0.92	0.10	266.5	24.52
Starch and sugar	0.85	0.46	117.6	46.0
				94.42

Thus, the estimated ME concentration was 94.4 kcal/oz.

[16] Assumed for purposes of calculation that this diet contained 75% dry matter, 20% crude protein, 8% crude fat, 34% starch and sugar, 8% fiber and ash and 5% propylene glycol. The same apparent digestibility and ross energy values were used as in footnote 15, with the addition of an ME value of 133.2 kcal/oz for propylene glycol (Weil, C.S., et al., 1971. Results of feeding propylene glycol in the diet to dogs for two years. Food Cosmet. Toxicol. 9:479). The estimated ME concentration was 79.4 kcal/oz.

[17] Assumed for purposes of calculation that this diet contained 25% dry matter, 9.2% crude protein, 11.0% fat, 1.2% starch and sugar and 3.6% fiber and ash. The apparent digestibility of crude protein was assumed to be 75%, fat 92%, and starch and sugar 85%. Gross energy values were as in footnote 15. The estimated ME concentration was 36.9 kcal/oz.

[18] Assumed for purposes of calculation that this diet was comparable in composition to dry-type dog food with water added and canned. Dry matter 25%. The estimated ME concentration was 25.5 kcal/oz.

TABLE 14
ESTIMATED DAILY FOOD REQUIREMENTS FOR MAINTENANCE OF DOGS OF VARIOUS WEIGHTS [19]

Weight of Dog		ME Required (kcal/day)	Dry Type[20]		Semimoist[21]		Canned or Wet			
							High Fat, Meat[22]		Low Fat, Low Meat[23]	
kg	lb		g/kg body wt	kg/dog	g/kg body wt	kg/dog	g/kg body wt	kg/dog	g/kg body wt	kg/dog
2.3	5	247	33	0.07	38	0.09	83	0.19	119	0.27
4.5	10	408	27	0.12	32	0.14	70	0.31	101	0.45
6.8	15	556	25	0.17	29	0.20	63	0.43	91	0.62
9.1	20	692	23	0.21	27	0.24	58	0.53	84	0.77
13.6	30	935	21	0.28	24	0.33	53	0.72	76	1.04
22.7	50	1,373	18	0.42	21	0.49	47	1.06	67	1.53
31.8	70	1,768	17	0.54	20	0.62	43	1.36	62	1.96
49.8	110	2,475	15	0.75	18	0.87	38	1.90	55	2.75

[19] From No. 8, *Nutrient Requirements of Dogs*, Revised 1974, National Academy of Sciences, NRC, p. 37, Table 4.
[20] Assumed for purposes of calculation that this diet contained 90% dry matter, 24% crude protein, 10% fat, 46% starch and sugar and 10% fiber and ash. The apparent digestibility of crude protein was assumed to be 80%, fat 92%, starch and sugar 85%. Gross energy (GE) values used for protein, fat, and starch and sugar were 4.4 [5.65–1.25 (urinary losses)], 9.4 and 4.15 kcal/g, respectively. To calculate ME concentration, the above values were used as follows:

	Nutrient/Diet	Apparent Digestibility Coefficient	GE (kcal/g)	ME (kcal)
Crude protein	0.24	0.80	4.4	0.84
Fat	0.10	0.92	9.4	0.86
Starch and sugar	0.46	0.85	4.15	1.62
				3.32

Thus, the estimated ME concentration was 3.3 kcal/g.
[21] Assumed for purposes of calculation that this diet contained 75% dry matter, 20% crude protein, 8% crude fat, 34% starch and sugar, 8% fiber and ash and 5% propylene glycol. The same apparent digestibility and gross energy values were used as in footnote 20, with the addition of an ME value of 4.7 kcal/g for propylene glycol (Weil, C. S., et al., 1971. Results of feeding propylene glycol in the diet to dogs for two years. Food Cosmet. Toxicol. 9:479). The estimated ME concentration was 2.8 kcal/g.
[22] Assumed for purposes of calculation that this diet contained 25% dry matter, 9.2% crude protein, 11.0% fat, 1.2% starch and sugar and 3.6% fiber and ash. The apparent digestibility of crude protein was assumed to be 75%, fat 92%, and starch and sugar 85%. Gross energy values were as in footnote 20. The estimated ME concentration was 1.3 kcal/g.
[23] Assumed for purposes of calculation that this diet was comparable in composition to dry-type dog food with water added and canned. Dry matter 25%. The estimated ME concentration was 0.9 kcal/g.

TABLE 15

NUTRITIVE NEEDS OF DOGS

Nutrient	Function of Nutrient	Some Deficiency Symptoms	Sources	Comments
Protein—for growth and repair	Maintenance and building of muscle tissue and bone, including growth of hair; development of fetus; milk production; growth of puppies About 50% of the dog's body is protein, with the majority being contained in structural tissues	Depressed appetite, poor growth, loss of weight, rough and dull hair coat, reduced milk production, irregular estrus, and lowered reproduction.	Meat, fish, eggs, and soybeans are the most commonly used proteins Plant proteins are well utilized by dogs, provided they contain the proper amino acids in the right proportions. For example, soybean protein supplemented with methionine is an excellent protein for dogs	A 23% protein diet, in which the fat does not exceed 5% of the dry matter, will supply 20 to 25% of the calories, and meet the needs of growing puppies and lactating bitches
Energy — for maintenance work, reproduction, and conditioning	Essential for the normal life processes of the dog, including body maintenance, reproduction, and lactation. Because energy is necessary for life itself, it is the most important nutrient	*Puppies:* Slow and stunted growth. A deficiency of fat in the ration of young puppies will result in— 1. Dry, harsh hair and dry, flaky skin 2. Increased susceptibility to infection. The effectiveness of dietary fat in preventing and curing fat deficiency is directly related to its linoleic acid content *Mature dog:* Loss of weight, poor condition, and excessive fatigue *Breeding animals:* Poor reproduction; failure of some bitches to show heat, more services per conception, and light weight puppies	Carbohydrates, fats, and excess protein of food. About 94% of the energy from fat and 86% of the energy of most rations is available for use by dogs Dogs can meet their energy needs from plant or vegetable sources provided their supply of essential amino acids is adequate	Carbohydrates usually supply the most inexpensive source of energy and form a large part of most dog foods Fat provides (1) a concentrated source of energy (9.3 calories/gram vs. 4.1 calories/gram for carbohydrates and protein), (2) fatty acids needed by the body as a physiological requirement, and (3) a carrier of vitamins A, D, E, and K

(Continued)

TABLE 15 (CONTINUED)

Nutrient	Function of Nutrient	Some Deficiency Symptoms	Sources	Comments
Minerals—for that all important 2 to 5% of the dog's weight, chiefly the skeleton, and for normal physiological processes Dogs require calcium, phosphorus, iron, copper, potassium, magnesium, sodium, chlorine, iodine, manganese, cobalt, and zinc	Minerals (1) furnish the structural material for the growth of bones and teeth, (2) are found in various tissues, (3) maintain the acid-base balance in the body, and (4) regulate many of the vital processes Also, see Table 20, Dog Mineral Chart	Unsoundnesses and nutritional deficiency diseases Also, see Tables 20 and 25	Mineral supplements and food ingredients	Excess minerals are expensive; and imbalances may actually be injurious. Hence, it is recommended that proper kinds and amounts of be incorporated in the ration
Vitamins—for growth, development, health, and reproduction There are two groups of vitamins, based on their solubility: 1. Fat soluble vitamins—A, D, E, and K 2. Water soluble vitamins—thiamin (B_1), riboflavin (B_2), niacin, pyridoxine (B_6), pantothenic acid, biotin, folic acid, choline, B_{12}—all members of the B-complex; and ascorbic acid (vitamin C)	Vitamins are necessary for growth, reproduction, performance and health The vitamins are sometimes called the spark plugs or ignition system of the animal Also, see Table 21, Dog Vitamin Chart	Single, uncomplicated vitamin deficiencies are the exception rather than the rule Also, see Tables 21 and 25	Synthetic products Vitamin rich foods	Although deficiency symptoms are the most striking result of vitamin deficiencies, mild deficiencies affect performance and health more than severe deficiencies, because they go unrectified Do not shower the dog with mistaken kindness through using "shotgun"-type vitamin preparations. Instead, the quantity of each vitamin should be based on available scientific knowledge

> Animal proteins are complete in the ten essential amino acids, in adequate amounts to support the body needs.

> Vegetable proteins are incomplete or insufficient in the ten essential amino acids (not always the three shown in diagram) thus unable to support body needs.

The Ten Essential Amino Acids:

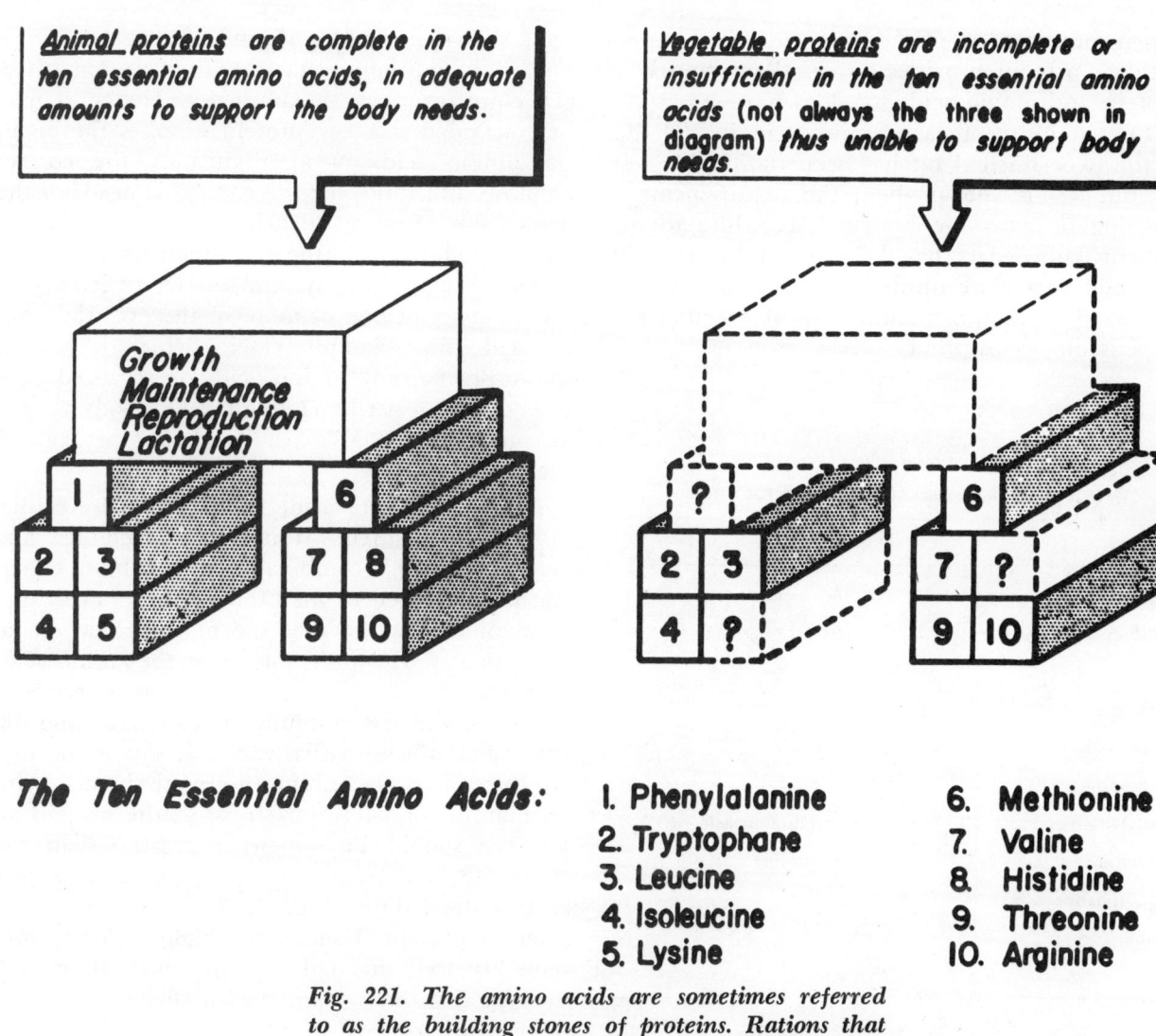

1. Phenylalanine
2. Tryptophane
3. Leucine
4. Isoleucine
5. Lysine
6. Methionine
7. Valine
8. Histidine
9. Threonine
10. Arginine

Fig. 221. The amino acids are sometimes referred to as the building stones of proteins. Rations that furnish an insufficient amount of the essential building stones (amino acids) are said to have proteins of poor quality. In general, proteins of animal origin are of better quality than proteins of plant origin. (Drawing by R. F. Johnson)

acids is requisite to understanding proteins.

Proteins are very complex compounds with each molecule made up of hundreds of thousands of amino acids combined with each other. The amino acids, of which some twenty-three are known, are sometimes referred to as the *building stones of proteins*. Certain of these amino acids can be made by the dog's body to satisfy its needs. Others cannot be formed fast enough to supply the body's needs and, therefore, are known as *essential* (or *indispensable*) amino acids. These must be supplied in the food. Moreover, they must be provided simultaneously in the correct proportions since they are not stored as such for any significant period of time. Thus, rations that furnish an insufficient amount of any of the essential amino acids are said to have proteins of poor quality, whereas those that provide the proper proportions of the various necessary amino acids are said to supply proteins of good quality, or to be complete. Eggs, meat, milk, soybeans, peanuts, and yeast provide good quality protein for dogs. But even these vary. For example, meat from muscle and glandular organs ranks high, whereas skins, tendons, and gullets contribute less to protein quality. Plant proteins can be well utilized by dogs. However, the relative value of different sources depends on their amino acid patterns.

When properly supplemented with methionine, soybean protein provides an excellent source of protein and amino acids for dogs.

The necessity of each amino acid in the diet of the experimental rat has been thoroughly tested, but less is known about the requirements of the dog or even the human. According to our present knowledge, based largely on work with rats, and to a more limited extent with dogs, the following division of amino acids as essential and dispensable seems proper.

TABLE 16
ESSENTIAL AND DISPENSABLE AMINO ACIDS FOR THE DOG

Essential	Dispensable
Arginine	Alanine
Histidine	Aspartic acid
Isoleucine	Citrulline
Leucine	Cystine
Lysine	Glutamic acid
Methionine	Glycine
Phenylalanine	Hydroxyglutamic acid
Threonine	Hydroxyproline
Tryptophane	Proline
Valine	Serine
	Tyrosine

Some authorities do not consider arginine essential. But the author has included it in the above grouping because it may be essential under some conditions.

Fortunately, the amino-acid content of proteins from different sources varies. Thus, the deficiencies of one protein may be improved by combining it with another, and the mixture of the two proteins often will have a higher feeding value than either one alone. It is for this reason that a considerable variety of ingredients in the ration of the dog is usually recommended.

Tables 17 and 18 show the variation in the minimum quantity of various proteins needed to maintain the tissue proteins of an adult dog. Of course, the minimum of each dietary protein will vary somewhat according to the source. For example, not all fish meals will have as high nutritive value as the sample shown in Tables 17 and 18, and some samples of beef may have a higher nutritive value than the one given. Of all the proteins shown in Tables 17 and 18, egg protein is needed in minimum amounts to maintain nitrogen equilibrium in the adult dog. Hence, it may be concluded that egg protein supplies the essential amino acids in approximately the correct amounts and ratios for the metabolic needs of the dog's body. Larger quantities of other proteins are needed to meet the requirements for maintenance because they have a relative deficiency in the quantity of one or more of the essential amino acids. For example, casein, which is low in sulphur-containing amino acids, is required at a level of 0.73 g per lb (1.60 g per kg) body weight as compared to 0.57 g per lb (1.25 g per kg) of egg protein.

Normal diets are made up of a mixture of dietary protein sources—from meat, vegetables, and cereal—to give a combination that almost equals egg protein. Hence, one protein may tend to supplement another so that the mixture may be of high quality. However, the closer the amino acids of a protein come to the amounts and proportions shown in the last columns of Tables 17 and 18, the higher the nutritive value. It should be noted that these are minimum requirements, with no margins of safety for stress, so the protein allowance should be somewhat greater than the values given therein.

Also, digestibility is an important factor in considering protein. Usually the higher quality proteins are well digested and absorbed. In mixed, dry-type dog foods supplying an adequate amount of protein, from 70 to 80 percent of the protein may be expected to be digested and absorbed. Moderate heat treatment, if materials are processed, does not significantly reduce the value of the protein. But excessive heat treatment may cause partial destruction of certain of the amino acids, especially lysine.

Table 19 lists the protein, calorie, and total sulfur amino acid content of a number of ingredients commonly used in dog foods. Sulfur amino acid contents of ingredients are sometimes used to calculate protein score, a value that serves as an indicator of protein quality.

Quantity of Protein

We have already noted that the required level of protein in the diet is influenced by the amino acid content, or the quality. Required protein levels are also influenced by calories—by the protein-calorie ratio, and the total calorie intake.

TABLE 17

COMMON SOURCES OF PROTEIN, GRAMS OF PROTEIN REQUIRED FROM EACH SOURCE TO MAINTAIN NITROGEN EQUILIBRIUM IN AN ADULT DOG, AND MILLIGRAMS OF AMINO ACID SUPPLIED BY EACH OF THESE AMOUNTS OF PROTEIN [24]

Protein Required Per Lb Body Weight Per Day In Grams

	Egg White	Fish Meal	Beef Lean Muscle	Casein	Casein and 3% Methionine	Peanut Flour	Wheat Gluten	Wheat Gluten and Lysine	Minimum Values
grams	0.57	0.62	0.73	0.73	0.57	0.10	1.41	0.71	0.57

Milligrams Of Amino Acid Supplied By Above Amounts Of Protein

Arginine	34	43	47	20	22	113	52	26	21.8
Histidine	10	11	23	23	17	23	28	14	10
Isoleucine	36	32	38	50	36	42	63	32	32
Leucine	50	48	57	78	57	72	102	51	47.8
Lysine	40	55	53	62	46	35	31	—	30.9
Phenylalanine	33	23	29	42	31	50	71	36	22.8
Tyrosine	19	16	22	40	29	29	40	19	15.9
Phenylalanine and Tyrosine	53	39	51	82	60	79	110	55	39
Methionine	23	18	20	25	27	9	23	12	9.1
Cystine	17	9	10	3	3	15	33	17	15
Methionine and Cystine	40	27	30	28	30	24	56	29	24
Threonine	28	28	32	35	25	29	40	20	20
Tryptophan	7	7	7	7	6	8	10	6	5.9
Valine	42	32	38	57	42	47	61	28	30

[24] From No. 8, *Nutrient Requirements of Dogs*, Revised 1972, National Academy of Sciences, NRC, p. 28, Table 5, with U. S. customary added by the author. (It is assumed that only one source of protein will be used in any one day in experiments studying nitrogen equilibrium.)

TABLE 18

COMMON SOURCES OF PROTEIN, GRAMS OF PROTEIN REQUIRED FROM EACH SOURCE TO MAINTAIN NITROGEN EQUILIBRIUM IN AN ADULT DOG, AND MILLIGRAMS OF AMINO ACID SUPPLIED BY EACH OF THESE AMOUNTS OF PROTEIN [25]

	Egg White	Fish Meal	Beef Lean Muscle	Casein	Casein and 3% Methionine	Peanut Flour	Wheat Gluten	Wheat Gluten and Lysine	Minimum Values
Protein Required Per Kg Body Weight Per Day In Grams									
grams	1.25	1.36	1.60	1.60	1.25	2.24	3.10	1.56	1.25
Milligrams of Amino Acids Supplied By Above Amounts of Protein									
Arginine	74.8	94.6	103.4	66.0	48.4	248.6	114.4	57.2	48
Histidine	22.0	24.2	50.6	50.6	37.4	50.6	61.6	30.8	22
Isoleucine	79.2	70.4	83.6	110.0	79.2	92.4	138.6	70.4	70
Leucine	110.0	105.6	125.4	171.6	125.4	158.4	224.4	112.2	105
Lysine	88.0	121.0	116.6	136.4	101.2	77.0	68.2	——	68
Phenylalanine	72.6	50.6	63.8	92.4	68.2	110.0	156.2	79.2	50
Tyrosine	41.8	35.2	48.4	88.0	63.8	63.8	88.0	41.8	35
Phenylalanine and tyrosine	114.4	85.8	112.2	180.4	132.0	173.8	242.0	121.0	86
Methionine	50.6	39.6	44.0	55.0	59.4	19.8	50.6	26.4	20
Cystine	37.4	19.8	22.0	6.6	6.6	33.0	72.6	37.4	33
Methionine and cystine	88.0	59.4	66.0	61.6	66.0	52.8	123.2	63.8	53
Threonine	61.6	61.6	70.4	77.0	55.0	63.8	88.0	44.0	44
Tryptophan	15.4	15.4	15.4	15.4	13.2	17.6	22.0	13.2	13
Valine	92.4	70.4	83.6	125.4	92.4	103.4	134.2	66.0	66

[25] From No. 8, *Nutrient Requirements of Dogs*, Revised 1972, National Academy of Sciences, NRC, p. 28, Table 5. (It is assumed that only one source of protein will be used in any one day in experiments studying nitrogen equilibrium.)

200

TABLE 19

PROTEIN, CALORIES, AND SULFUR AMINO ACIDS IN SOME COMMON FOOD PRODUCTS [26]

Product[27]	Dry Matter (%)	On a Dry Basis Protein (g per 100 g of food)	Kilo-calories (per g)	Total Sulfur Amino Acids in Each Gram of Protein (mg)
Barley, grain, (4)	89.0	13.0	3.3	34
Carrot, roots, fresh, (4)	12.9	6.6	3.5	—
Corn, grits, cracked fine screened, (4)	88.2	9.0	3.8	32
Cattle, meat, lean, (5)	37.5	75.0	4.4	43
Oats, cereal by-product, mx 4% fiber, (4)	91.2	12.0	3.9	32
Pea, seeds, (5)	89.5	13.0	3.6	33
Potato, tubers, fresh, (4)	23.1	8.5	3.7	26
Rice, groats, polished, (4)	88.5	8.0	3.8	32
Cattle, milk, skimmed dehy, mx 8% moisture, (5)	94.3	36.0	3.6	37
Soybean, flour, solv-extd fine sift, mx 3% fiber, (5)	92.3	50.0	3.4	37
Wheat, grain, (4)	88.9	20.0	3.8	38
Chicken, eggs wo shells, raw, (5)	26.3	47.0	6.0	63
Reference protein[28]	—	100.0	4.0	42

[26] From No. 8, *Nutritional Requirements of Dogs*, Revised 1972, National Academy of Sciences, NRC, p. 29, Table 6.

[27] NRC names. The (4) following the name of a product indicates energy feeds, whereas (5) indicates protein supplements. See section on "Composition of Dog Food Ingredients" for further explanation.

[28] A highly digestible protein to which other proteins are compared.

The National Research Council recommendation is that proteins should contribute a minimum of 12% of the energy (calorie) value of the diet of the adult dog. Remember that this is the lower level. Remember, too, that: (1) some proteins are of relatively low biological value; (2) both the protein and calorie needs increase during growth, pregnancy, and lactation; (3) there are individual differences—some dogs require more protein and energy than others; (4) protein intake must be increased beyond these minimal levels if provision is to be made for maintaining the protein reserves; and (5) during periods of stress (hunting, racing, etc.), protein intake should be increased above maintenance levels. Also, protein requirements increase with rate of growth; during the latter part of pregnancy, and with litter size; and in keeping with the amount of milk given during lactation. Hence, a margin of safety is important.

Based on a 100% dry diet containing 3.5 to 4 kcal ME per gram and protein equivalent in quality to casein, experiments indicate that the following percentages of protein in the diet will meet the needs of dogs: for growth, 20%; for reproduction and lactation, 22%; and for old age, 17.8%. Diets that contain higher levels of fat require more protein to maintain a proper protein:calorie ratio—sometimes as much as 30%.

Protein Toxicity

There appears to be a general belief, based on professional experiences, that prolonged intake of high-protein diets can be harmful to dogs. Any adverse effects of this nature can be avoided by adherence to the guidelines on dietary protein levels recommended in this book, including the accompanying tables of nutrient requirements.

Excess protein can be extremely harmful to dogs that have had some disease that has resulted in kidney or liver damage and to older dogs that have impaired circulation. Such dogs tend to accumulate excess nitrogen in the blood when a high protein diet, e.g., too much meat, is fed.

ENERGY

Dietary energy (calories) is derived from fats, carbohydrates, and excess protein. Both fats and carbohydrates are economical sources of energy. Fats contribute 2.25 times more energy per pound on oxidation than carbohydrates and proteins. A smaller quantity of fat is required, therefore, to serve the same function.

Carbohydrates

The carbohydrates are organic compounds composed of carbon, hydrogen, and oxygen. This group includes the sugars, starch, cellulose, gums, and related substances. They are formed in the plant by photosynthesis as follows: $6CO_2 + 6H_2O$ + energy from sun = $C_6H_{12}O_6$ (glucose) + $6O_2$. On the average, the carbohydrates comprise about three-fourths of all the dry matter in plants, the chief source of animal feed. They form the woody framework of plants as well as the chief reserve food stored in seeds, roots, and tubers.

When consumed by dogs, carbohydrates are used as a source of heat and energy, and any excess of them is stored in the body as fat.

From the standpoint of supplying the normal energy needs of dogs, the carbohydrates are by far the most important, more of them being consumed than any other compound. The fats are next in importance for energy purposes. Up to 65% of a complete food may be carbohydrates (dry basis) while still allowing for sufficient protein, fat, and mineral.

Carbohydrates are usually more abundant and cheaper than fats. Also, they may be more easily stored in warm weather and for longer periods of time.

Carbohydrates are well utilized by normal dogs provided they are properly prepared. Some starches—like those from oats, corn, and potatoes—are poorly utilized and will produce diarrhea, unless first subjected to heat treatment—by baking, cooking, toasting, or other means. Studies show that dogs may utilize diets containing 81% cooked cereal.

Some sugars are effectively used and tolerated by normal dogs, whereas others, like milk sugar (lactose), may be poorly utilized by some dogs. Older dogs, in particular, do not synthesize adequate quantities of the enzyme, lactose, which is required for the digestion of milk sugar. Thus, when the lactose level is low and milk sugar is high, the milk sugar tends to ferment in the digestive tract and produce diarrhea. This is why some dogs, particularly older dogs and puppies, scour when given too much cow's milk, which is high in lactose.

For dogs with certain liver and kidney ailments, a well-balanced diet with ample carbohydrates prevents excessive work of denaturing proteins and is valuable in this respect.

Fats

Lipids (fat and fat-like substances), like carbohydrates, contain the three elements; carbon, hydrogen, and oxygen. As dog food, fats function much like carbohydrates in that they serve as a source of heat and energy and for the formation of fat. Because of the larger proportion of carbon and hydrogen, however, fats liberate more heat than carbohydrates when digested, furnishing approximately 2.25 times as much heat or energy per pound on oxidation as do the carbohydrates. A smaller quantity of fat is required, therefore, to furnish the same amount of calories.

From a chemical standpoint, a molecule of fat consists of a combination of three molecules of certain fatty acids, with one molecule of glycerol. Most fats contain many different kinds of fatty acids. As a result, they differ in their melting points and other properties, depending on the particular fatty acids that they contain. Thus, because of the high content of unsaturated acids (such as oleic and linoleic) and acids of low molecular weight, corn fat is a liquid at ordinary temperatures; whereas, because of the high content of stearic and palmitic acids, beef fat is solid at ordinary temperatures. The source of dietary fat influences and helps determine the type of fat deposited in the dog's body; hence, the resulting body firmness is determined thereby.

Fat is included in the dog's diet to provide (1) a concentrated source of energy, (2) needed fatty acids, (3) palatability, and (4) a carrier for the fat soluble vitamins A, D, E, and K.

The fat and fatty acid composition of some common dog food ingredients are shown in Table 31. The linoleic acid content is given in this table because the effectiveness of dietary fat in preventing and curing a fatty-acid deficiency is related thereto.

It is recommended that a dog food contain at least 5% fat on a dry basis, including 1% of the diet as lineoleic acid. Since not all fats are rich in lineoleic acid (Table 31), supplemental fats must be chosen judiciously when the total fat of the ration is only 5%. Although these levels (5% total fat on a dry basis, of which 1% is linoleic acid) appear to be sufficient for normal physiological functions, higher fat levels may be desirable in practical dog foods to enhance acceptability and to improve hair coat and sheen.

Most dogs can tolerate high levels of fat, up to 40% in the diet. However, excess fat will reduce the food intake and retard the growth of puppies. Also, with high fat diets, the intake of calories must be adjusted in relation to all nutrients for proper nutritional balance.

Some dogs may have had certain diseases that have affected their dietary fat utilization. For example, dogs with pancreatic damage do not have the ability to utilize fats efficiently. The pancreas secretes pancreatic lipase, an enzyme which aids in the digestion of fats. When this enzyme is deficient, fat may pass through the digestive tract in varied quantities without being efficiently utilized by the dog. Such dogs often develop dermatitis, dandruff, a dull hair coat, itching, and other indications of a dry skin.

Pancreatic deficiency in the dog can be compensated for in either of two ways: (1) by adding pancreatic enzyme to the diet so that the fat can be digested, or (2) by adding larger quantities of short-chain fats, such as corn oil, to the diet. Corn oil is absorbed through the digestive tract with a minimum of pancreatic activity. This is why veterinarians usually recommend additional corn oil for dogs that have pancreatic problems. It is noteworthy that this is also the reasoning behind the addition of extra quantities of corn oil to the diet of show dogs in order to produce a more glossy hair coat.

Most fatty acids associated with cereals are highly unsaturated; hence, some cereal grains are a good source of fatty acids.

Rancidity of Fat

Because of their unsaturation, fats often become rancid through oxidation or hydrolysis, resulting in disagreeable flavors and odors. Rancid fat is undesirable for dogs, primarily because of its well-known destructive effect on fat-soluble vitamins. Use of an antioxidant is, therefore, recommended as a means of retarding rancidity. Also, the development of rancidity may be retarded through proper cold storage.

Quantity of Energy

At the outset, it must be recognized that not all the energy in a ration is available to dogs. Some of it is present in the cell walls of the ingredients, and some of it will pass through the dog's body undigested. On the average, however, 94% of the energy from fat and 86% of the energy from most rations is available for use by the dog.

Secondly, the quantity of energy needed is affected by (1) individuality, (2) condition, (3) size, (4) age, (5) gestation and lactation, (6) kind, amount, and severity of work, (7) weather, and (8) the food. Each of these factors exerts an influence on food allowance; hence, they are discussed later in this section under the heading "Amount to Feed."

Calorie System of Measuring Energy

Energy is used in many forms—as light, electricity, atomic force, work, or heat—and it is measured by several units such as candle power, kilowatts, foot pounds, joules, and calories. In animals, energy is expended as work and/or heat or stored as products. It would appear, therefore, that it should be measured in units suitable for these purposes. Thus, a *heat unit* is an excellent way in which to measure the potential energy of feeds, the energy of animal products, and the heat that results from body processes. The heat unit used by animal nutritionists is the *calorie*.

A calorie (or *cal*, always written with a small c) is the amount of heat required to raise the temperature of one gram of water one degree Centigrade. To measure this heat, an instrument known as the *bomb calorimeter* is used, in which the feed (or other substance) tested is placed and burned with the aid of oxygen (see Fig. 222).

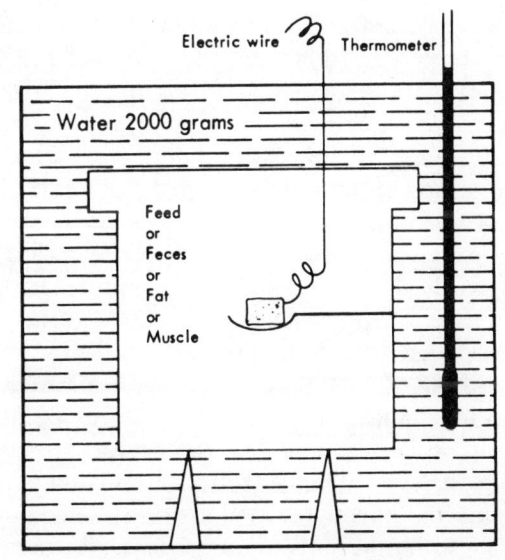

Fig. 222. Diagrammatic sketch of a bomb calorimeter used for the determination of the gross energy value (caloric content) of various materials.

It is noteworthy that the determination of the heat of combustion with a bomb calorimeter is neither difficult nor time-consuming. Briefly stated, the procedure is as follows: An electric wire is attached to the material being tested, so that it can be ignited by remote control; 2,000 grams of water are poured around the bomb; 25 to 30 atmospheres of oxygen are added to the bomb; the material is ignited; the heat given off from the burned material warms the water; and a thermometer registers the change in temperature of the water. For example, if one gram of material is burned and the temperature of the water is raised one degree Centigrade, 2,000 cal are given off. Hence, the material contains 2,000 cal per g, or 907,200 cal per pound.

MINERALS

When we think of minerals, we instinctively think of bones, or skeleton and teeth. But in addition to furnishing structural material for the growth of bones and teeth, minerals are found in various tissues. They maintain the acid-base balance within the body and regulate many of the vital life processes.

At Washington State University, the author and one of his associates, Dr. W. W. Heinemann, clearly demonstrated the importance of minerals in animal nutrition in a study with rabbits, involving one mineral only—phosphorus.[23] Rabbits were used because, with their early breeding and short generation interval, the results could be obtained in six years. Dogs would have taken much longer. However, there is reason to believe that the results apply to dogs and all other classes of animals, including man—in growth, reproduction, and soundness. In this experiment, generation after generation of rabbits were fed on alfalfa hay, with one group receiving hay produced on low phosphorus soils and the other group eating alfalfa grown on high phosphorus soils. The rabbits in the low-phosphorus soil-alfalfa group (1) were retarded in growth—with 9.8% lower weaning weights, (2) required 12% more matings per conception, and (3) had 47% lower breaking strength of bones than the rabbits on the high-phosphorus soil-alfalfa group. Remember that these adverse effects resulted from a deficiency of just one mineral only—phosphorus. Remember, too, that the dog requires at least 12 minerals; hence, the chances of encountering a deficiency are greatly multiplied.

The minerals that have been shown to be essential for dogs are calcium, phosphorus, iron, copper, potassium, magnesium, sodium, chlorine, iodine, manganese, zinc and selenium. Certain other minerals may be necessary under some conditions. Pertinent information relative to dog minerals is summarized in Table 20. (See pp. 206–211.)

Since approximately 70% of the mineral content of the dog's body consists of calcium and phosphorus, these two major minerals will be discussed further.

---
[29] Heinemann, W. W., *et al., Wash. Agri. Expt. Sta., Tech Bul. 24,* June, 1957.

Fig. 223. Rabbit with bowed legs and enlarged joints resulting from eating alfalfa produced on low phosphorus soils. There is reason to believe that the same thing happens to dogs. (Courtesy Washington State University)

Calcium and Phosphorus

Calcium and phosphorus comprise about ¾ of the ash of the skeleton and from ⅓ to ½ of the minerals of milk. Dogs are more likely to suffer from a lack of either or both of these minerals than from any other minerals. About 99% of the calcium and over 80% of the phosphorus are found in the bones and teeth. But both minerals have additional functions concerned with the blood and muscles.

In considering the calcium and phosphorus requirements of the dog, it is important to realize that the proper utilization of these minerals by the body is dependent upon three factors: (1) an adequate supply of calcium and phosphorus in an available form, (2) a suitable ratio between them (1.2–1.4 calcium: 1 phosphorus), and (3) sufficient vitamin D to make possible the assimilation and utilization of the calcium and phosphorus.

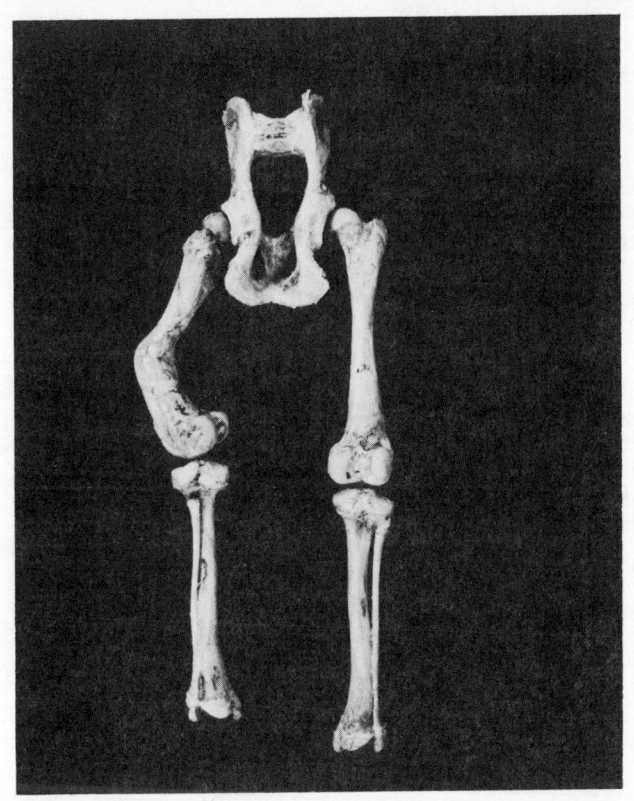

Figs. 224–225. Calcium made the difference! Two puppy pelvises.

Upper picture shows pelvis of a puppy that received an inadequate level of calcium in the diet. Note bowed bone, narrow pelvic opening, and hairline fractures.

Lower picture shows good pelvis and sound bones of a puppy that received an adequate level of calcium, and a balanced Ca : P ratio, in the diet. (Courtesy Ralston Purina Company, St. Louis, Mo.)

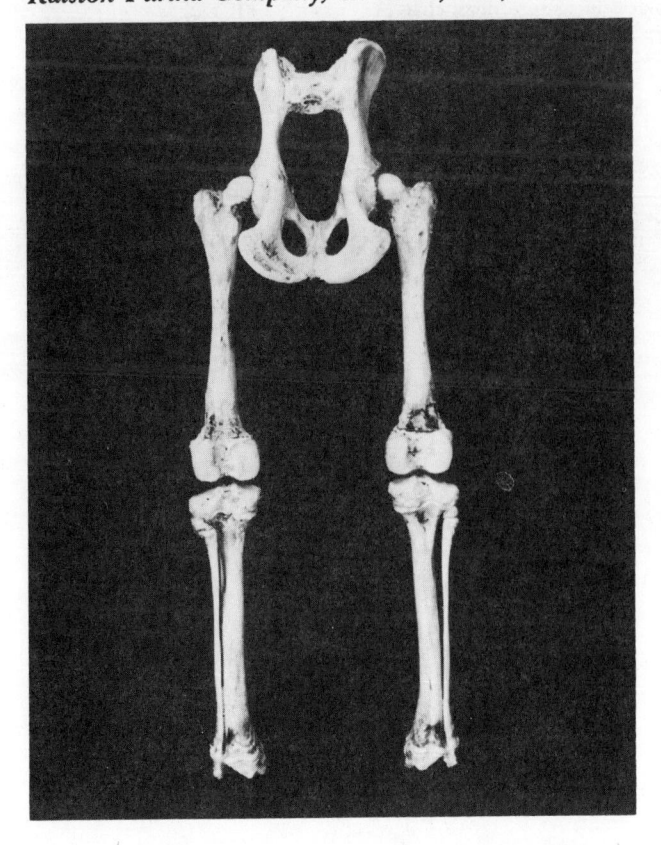

If plenty of vitamin D is present, the ratio of calcium to phosphorus becomes less important. Also, less vitamin D is needed when there is a desirable calcium-phosphorus ratio.

Some foods are very poorly balanced from the standpoint of calcium and phosphorus. For example, lean meat contains approximately 0.01 percent calcium and 0.18 percent phosphorus. This is a ratio of 1 part calcium to 18 parts phosphorus, whereas a ratio of 1.2–1.4 parts of calcium to 1 part of phosphorus is considered to be near optimum. Thus, when lean meat is fed by the dog owner, it needs to be supplemented with a good commercial dry feed that can contribute to the needed calcium. Otherwise, there will be a serious imbalance of calcium and phosphorus.

Dogs in periods of growth, gestation, and lactation require liberal amounts of calcium and phosphorus in their diets. This point, and other pertinent facts, is presented in Table 20.

VITAMINS

Until early in the twentieth century, if a ration contained proteins, fats, carbohydrates, and minerals—together with a certain amount of fiber—it was considered to be a complete diet. True enough, the disease known as *beriberi* (having been known to the Chinese as early as 2600 B.C.) made its appearance in the rice-eating districts of the Orient when milling machinery was introduced from the West; and scurvy was long known to occur among sailors fed on salt meat and biscuits. However, for centuries these diseases were thought to be due to toxic substances in the digestive tract caused by pathogenic organisms rather than food deficiencies, and more time elapsed before the discovery of vitamins. Of course, there was no medical profession until 1835, the earlier treatments having been based on superstition rather than science.

Largely through the trial-and-error method, it was discovered that specific foods were helpful in the treatment of certain of these maladies. In 1747, Lind, a British naval surgeon, showed that the juice of citrus fruits was a cure for scurvy. Lunin, as early as 1881, had come to the conclusion that certain foods, such as milk, contain, beside the principal ingredients, small quantities of unknown substances essential to life. Eijkman, working in Java in 1897, had satisfied himself that the disease beriberi was due to the continued consumption of a diet of *polished rice*. We are told also that, at a very early date, the

TABLE 20

Mineral	Function of Mineral	Deficiency Symptoms	Unit	Nutritional Per lb or kg Body Wt/Day Adult Maintenance (lb)	Adult Maintenance (kg)	Growing Puppies (lb)	Growing Puppies (kg)
Calcium	Essential for the development and maintenance of good strong bones and teeth; maintains the contractability, rhythm, and tonicity of the heart muscles; antagonizes the action of the sodium and potassium on the heart; is required for normal coagulation of the blood; is necessary for proper nerve irritability; and appears to be essential for selective cellular permeability	Rickets, bowed legs and other bone malformations in puppies; osteomalacia in adults; hyperirritability of muscles and nerves; reduced lactation Rickets is more commonly observed in the heavy breeds of dogs than in the small breeds	mg	110.0	242.0	220.0	484.0
Phosphorus	Essential for sound bones and teeth, and for the assimilation of carbohydrate and fats. A vital ingredient of the proteins in all body cells. Necessary for enzyme activation. Acts as a buffer in blood and tissue. Occupies a key position in biologic oxidation and reactions requiring energy	Poor growth, poor calcification of bone, and rickets in young dogs Osteomalacia in mature dogs, characterized by frequent lameness and fractures	mg	90.0	198.0	180.0	396.0
Potassium	Essential for proper enzyme, muscle, and nerve functions, and appetite Protects the dog against endotoxin or gram-negative bacteria	Poor growth, restlessness, and paralysis of the neck and foreparts of the body	mg	60.0	132.0	120.0	264.0

DOG MINERAL CHART [30]

Requirements					Practical Sources of the Mineral	Comments
	In % or Amt./lb or kg of Food					
Unit	Dry Basis	Dry Type	Semi-Moist	Canned or Wet		
%	1.1	1.0	0.8	0.3	Oyster shell (flour) Limestone (ground) Tricalcium phosphate	A calcium to phosphorus ratio of 1.2–1.4:1 is considered best for maximum utilization of these two minerals, and also of vitamin D. A large excess of either Ca or P promotes the conversion of the other into insoluble tricalcium phosphate Growing dogs and pregnant or lactating bitches require liberal amounts of calcium. Calcium reserves are deposited in the spongy formations of the bones for mobilization against some future need such as pregnancy, lactation, or periods of deficient intake On the average, only 50% availability of Ca should be assumed. Diets high in phytates and low in vitamin D adversely influence calcium absorption Calcium that is not utilized is excreted mainly in the feces
%	.9	.8	.7	.22	Monosodium phosphate Dicalcium phosphate Steamed bone meal	The phosphorus requirements increase slightly when the calcium is increased High levels of dietary fat increase the phosphorus requirement by about 20% On the average, only 50% availability of P should be assumed
%	.6	.5	.45	.2	Soybean oil meal Dried skim milk Animal liver meal	Feeding low potassium diets to pregnant bitches will not affect litter size or birth weight of puppies

[30] The nutritional requirements of this table were taken from No. 8, *Nutrient Requirements of Dogs*, Revised 1974, National Academy of Sciences, NRC. (see Tables 10, 11, and 12 in this chapter)

(Continued)

TABLE 20 (CONTINUED)

Mineral	Function of Mineral	Deficiency Symptoms	Unit	Adult Maintenance (lb)	Adult Maintenance (kg)	Growing Puppies (lb)	Growing Puppies (kg)
Salt (Sodium chloride)	Sodium chloride helps maintain osmotic pressure in body cells, upon which depends the transfer of nutrients to the cells, the removal of waste materials, and the maintenance of water balance among the tissues. Also, sodium is important in making bile, which aids in the digestion of fats and carbohydrates; and chlorine is required for the formation of hydrochloric acid in the gastric juice so vital to protein digestion. It is noteworthy that when salt is omitted, sodium expresses its deficiency first	Reduced appetite, fatigue, exhaustion, lower protein efficiency	mg	110.0	242.0	220.0	484.0
Magnesium	Helps maintain good skeletal growth, deposition of the minerals in the right place, and maintenance of body secretions	Keyed up, high strung and jumpy. Anorexia, slower weight gain, and muscular weakness with pronounced relaxation of muscles and tendons of legs. Altered carbohydrate metabolism in young puppies	mg	4.0	8.8	8.0	17.6
Iron	Iron is a part of the hemoglobin molecule, essential for oxygen transport	Anemia; fatigue; sometimes diarrhea. A deficiency of iron is associated with coat color changes in some dogs. Dogs on low iron-low protein diets are severely affected by hookworm infestations	mg	0.6	1.32	1.2	2.64

Nutritional Per lb or kg Body Wt/Day

DOG MINERAL CHART

| Requirements ||||| Practical Sources of the Mineral | Comments |
Unit	Dry Basis	Dry Type	Semi-Moist	Canned or Wet		
%	1.1	1.0	.8	.3	Salt (sodium chloride)	There is little likelihood of a deficiency of sodium chloride when natural foodstuffs are fed Fresh meat contains very little salt Higher levels of salt will increase water intake
%	0.04	0.036	0.03	0.01	Meat and bone meal Soybean meal	Magnesium is closely associated with calcium and phosphorus in the body, in both distribution and metabolism
mg/lb mg/kg	27.3 60	24.5 54	20.5 45	6.8 15	Ferric ammonium citrate Ferrous sulphate Liver and heart Soybeans	Iron of inorganic salts, liver, heart, muscle, and soybeans is readily available (50% or more utilized), while that of oysters, alfalfa, spinach, blood, wheat, oats, and yeast are less efficient (25% utilized) Milk is very low in iron. This fact must be kept in mind when feeding puppies About 2/3 of the total iron in the body is present in the blood. Storage deposits of iron are found in the bone marrow, liver, and spleen Iron deficiency anemia responds to administration orally, intramuscularly, or intraperitoneally Iron toxicity occurs in dogs. It is characterized by anorexia, weight loss, and a decrease in serum albumin concentrations

(Continued)

TABLE 20 (CONTINUED)

Nutritional

Mineral	Function of Mineral	Deficiency Symptoms	Unit	Adult Maintenance (lb)	Adult Maintenance (kg)	Growing Puppies (lb)	Growing Puppies (kg)
Copper	Copper, along with iron and vitamin B_{12}, is necessary for hemoglobin formation, although it forms no part of the hemoglobin molecule (or red blood cells). Copper is essential in enzyme systems, hair development and pigmentation, bone development, reproduction, and lactation	Anemia, rough-and-dull coat	mg	0.07	0.16	0.15	0.32
Manganese	Occurs in tissues of dogs and plays a role in catalyzing certain metabolic reactions	Improper bone formation, retarded growth, and lowered reproduction	mg	0.05	0.11	0.1	0.22
Zinc	A component of enzymes, such as insulin; and necessary for normal bone, muscle, skin, and hair growth	Depressed growth; emaciation; skin disorder	mg	0.5	1.1	1.0	2.2
Iodine	Iodine is needed by the thyroid gland in making thyroxin (an iodine-containing hormone that controls the rate of body metabolism or heat production)	Goiter	mg	0.015	0.034	0.031	0.068
Selenium	Not completely known. Thought to be involved in Vitamin E absorption and retention	Dystrophy of skeletal and cardiac muscles	mcg	1.1	2.42	2.2	4.84
Other minerals: Chromium Cobalt Fluorine Molybdenum Nickel Silicon Tin Vanadium	Little is known of the absolute requirements of these trace minerals. Hence, dietary requirements of the dog for these elements have not been established						

210

DOG MINERAL CHART

Requirements

Unit	In % or Amt./lb or kg of Food								Practical Sources of the Mineral	Comments
	Dry Basis		Dry Type		Semi-Moist		Canned or Wet				
	(lb)	(kg)	(lb)	(kg)	(lb)	(kg)	(lb)	(kg)		
mg	3.3	7.3	3.0	6.5	2.5	5.5	0.82	1.8	Trace mineralized salt Animal liver meal Fish meal	Without copper in the diet, iron is absorbed but hemoglobin is not formed efficiently The liver appears to be the principal storage organ for copper in the body
mg	2.3	5.0	2.0	4.5	1.73	3.8	0.55	1.2	Manganese sulfate or oxide	
mg	2.73	50.0	20.45	45.0	17.3	38.0	5.45	12.0	Zinc oxide Zinc carbonate Fish meal Liver	Where zinc in the diet is low, the addition of zinc makes for a more attractive hair-coat
mg	0.7	1.54	0.63	1.39	0.53	1.16	0.18	0.39	Inclusion of 1% stabilized iodized salt (.007% iodine) in the dog's diet Trace mineralized salt supplying 4.5 mg of iodine per kg of diet	Iodine deficiencies are worldwide. In the U.S., the northwestern states, the Pacific Coast, and the Great Lakes regions are classed as goiter areas High amounts of iodine are toxic and must be avoided
mg	0.05	0.11	0.045	0.10	0.04	0.08	0.014	0.03	Sodium selenite	Dry-type diets should supply a minimum of 0.1 mg/kg selenium

(Continued)

TABLE 21

Vitamin	Function of Vitamin	Deficiency Symptoms	Unit	Adult Maintenance (lb)	Adult Maintenance (kg)	Growing Puppies (lb)	Growing Puppies (kg)
A	Essential for (1) normal maintenance and functioning of the epithelial tissues, particularly of the eye and the respiratory, digestive, reproductive, nerve, and urinary systems; (2) the production of visual pigments in the eye, which are necessary for vision in dim light; and (3) growth of bony structures	Loss of appetite; poor growth in puppies; skin lesions—dryness, scaling, and scratching; weak and infected eyes; respiratory infections; changes in the blood picture, primarily a lag in the neutrophile index; degeneration of certain nerves; reproductive failure Poor vision at night	I.U.	50.0	110.0	100.0	220.0
D	Vitamin D is associated with calcium absorption, transportation, and deposition Vitamin D, phosphorus, and calcium all play a role in the prevention of rickets, and their effectiveness depends upon proper amounts of each	Rickets In rickets, bones are not calcified and bend or "bow" readily, teeth are irregular and slow to erupt, and blood levels of Ca and P are altered	I.U.	5.0	11.0	10.0	22.0
E (alpha tocopherol)	Necessary for reproduction Protection of vitamin A and carotene from oxidation. Hence, it "stretches" the supply of vitamin A As an antioxidant in food	Poor reproduction and lactation; young born dead or weak, and those living suffer from muscular dystrophy	I.U.	0.5	1.1	0.1	2.2

Nutritional Per lb or kg Body Wt/Day

DOG VITAMIN CHART [31]

Requirements								Practical Sources of the Vitamin	Comments
	Amount/lb or kg of Food								
Unit	Dry Basis		Dry Type		Semimoist		Canned or Wet		
	(lb)	(kg)	(lb)	(kg)	(lb)	(kg)	(lb)	(kg)		
I.U.	2,273	5,000	2,045	4,500	1,705	3,750	568	1,250	Stabilized vitamin A Liver Milk fat Carrots Dehydrated alfalfa meal	Large doses of vitamin A will relieve certain types of experimentally produced hypertension Dogs can convert most of the carotene in pigments found in carrots, peaches, green plants, etc., to vitamin A within their bodies High levels of vitamin A may result in a more lustrous coat Excessive amounts of vitamin A in puppies produces loss of appetite, adverse skeletal changes, weight loss, hyperesthesia, and exophthalmos
I.U.	227.3	500	204.5	450	170.5	375	56.8	125	Vitamin D_2 from animal sources and/or vitamin D_3 from irradiated plant sterols, both of which are utilized by the dog Cod liver oil There is some evidence of the absence of 7-dehydrocholesterol, or pro-vitamin D, in the skin of dogs. Hence, dogs may have to rely solely upon dietary sources, and sunshine may be ineffective in producing vitamin D	Of all the known vitamins, vitamin D has the most limited distribution in common animal feeds Deficiencies of vitamin D are most common in rapidly growing puppies; and heavy-boned breeds are more susceptible than smaller breeds Overly high doses of vitamin D will produce adverse effects: calcification of the soft tissues, excess mineralization of the bones, deformation of the teeth, excessive thirst, and prostration. But intakes producing these effects are far above normal feeding levels
I.U.	22.73	50.0	20.45	45.0	17.05	37.5	5.68	12.5	Alpha-tocopherol (highest vitamin E activity) supplement Wheat germ oil Liver Cereal grains	Fats in the process of becoming rancid destroy the vitamin E in the ration and in the dog's body

[31] The nutritional requirements of this table were taken from No. 8, *Nutritional Requirements of Dogs*, Revised 1974, National Academy of Sciences, NRC (see Tables 10, 11, and 12 of this chapter).

(Continued)

TABLE 21 (CONTINUED)

Vitamin	Function of Vitamin	Deficiency Symptoms	Unit	Nutritional Per lb or kg Body Wt/Day Adult Maintenance (lb)	(kg)	Growing Puppies (lb)	(kg)
B_{12}	Necessary for growth Red blood formation. It is essential to prevent and cure anemia, and to facilitate the development of lots of erythroyctes capable of carrying ample oxygen from the lungs to the muscle Increased food utilization	Poor growth and anemia	mcg	0.23	0.5	0.45	1.0
Folic Acid	Enters into certain enzyme systems that are concerned with nucleic acid metabolism Essential for the formation of blood cells	Anemia Decrease in hemoglobin concentration and hematocrit values	mcg	1.8	4.0	3.6	8.0
Thiamin (B_1)	Carbohydrate metabolism of all living cells Promotes growth, appetite, and digestion	Loss of appetite, constipation, weakness and sometimes drowsiness, loss of weight, paralysis, convulsions, decreased ability to respond to conditioned reflexes, and impaired gastric secretion Poor growth of young and decreased fertility	mcg	10.1	22.0	20.0	44.0
Riboflavin (B_2)	Primarily in protein metabolism Essential for normal growth and maintaining a healthy condition of the skin	Acute deficiency causes collapse in dogs accompanied by fall in temperature, a variable heart rate, and low respiratory rate Chronic deficiency causes loss of weight, weakness, and, frequently, diarrhea; and watery eyes and bloodshot eyeballs sometimes. With prolonged deficiency, there may be fatty livers and corneal opacities	mcg	21.8	48.0	43.6	96.0

DOG VITAMIN CHART

Requirements									Practical Sources of the Vitamin	Comments
	\multicolumn{8}{c}{Amount/lb or kg of Food}		
Unit	Dry Basis		Dry Type		Semimoist		Canned or Wet			
	(lb)	(kg)	(lb)	(kg)	(lb)	(kg)	(lb)	(kg)		
mg	0.01	0.022	.009	0.020	.008	.017	.003	.006	Fish meal Meat scraps Animal liver meal Dried skim milk Commercial B_{12} concentrate	Normally, either the diet contains sufficient B_{12}, especially those with significant amounts of animal proteins, or there is sufficient intestinal synthesis to prevent deficiencies Some sled dog owners inject their dogs with B_{12} prior to a race to increase the level of red blood cells. The increase in cells requires several days B_{12} injections are frequently given to dogs infested with hookworms, as a means of helping in blood replenishment
mg	.082	.18	.077	.16	0.06	.14	0.02	.04	Yeast Soybean meal Alfalfa meal Liver Wheat	Practical rations appear to provide adequately for this vitamin without supplementation
mg	0.45	1.00	0.41	0.90	0.34	0.75	0.114	0.25	Pork Cereal grains Oil seed meals Milk products Brewer's yeast Synthetic thiamine	High-fat diets require less thiamine than those high in carbohydrates, such as potatoes and bread Hunting and racing dogs, and dogs kept in cold areas, probably need more thiamine than other dogs
mg	1.0	2.2	0.91	2.0	0.73	1.6	0.23	.5	Riboflavin (synthetic) Liver Milk products Kidney Heart Soyflour Eggs	A deficiency of riboflavin in the diets of dogs under practical conditions is not known to occur

(Continued)

TABLE 21 (CONTINUED)

Vitamin	Function of Vitamin	Deficiency Symptoms	Unit	Nutritional Per lb or kg Body Wt/Day Adult Maintenance (lb) / (kg)	Growing Puppies (lb) / (kg)
Pyridoxine (B$_6$)	Functions in the metabolism of protein. Also, necessary for nerves, proper heart function, blood regeneration, and prevention of anemia	Anemia, failure of the heart to function properly, degeneration of nerves, and convulsions Loss of appetite, poor growth, and diarrhea Blood not regenerated normally	mcg	10.0 / 22	20.0 / 44.0
Pantothenic Acid	Part of coenzyme A, a necessary factor for intermediary metabolism Maintenance of hair and skin	Erratic appetites, intestinal disorders, poor growth, and depigmentation or discoloration of hair In severe cases, hemorrhage, convulsions, collapse, and coma; also, liver damage may be extensive	mcg	100.0 / 220.0	200.0 / 440.0
Niacin (nicotinic acid)	As a constituent of coenzymes I and II. These coenzymes are essential in biologic oxidation, especially in the oxidation of carbohydrates	Blacktongue, which is similar to pellagra in man; characterized by sensitivity of the mucous membranes in the mouth, and by a sore purplish black tongue if the niacin deficient diet is continued. Emaciation follows, then death, unless niacin is supplied Also, a deficiency of niacin will cause dermatitis, loss of appetite, ulcers, and alternating diarrhea and constipation	mcg	113.6 / 250.	227.3 / 500.
Choline	In fat transportation within the body and in many biochemical reactions	Deposits of fat in and around the liver On a choline-deficient diet, the growth of puppies stops within a week	mg	11.8 / 26.0	23.6 / 52.0

DOG VITAMIN CHART

Requirements									Practical Sources of the Vitamin	Comments
	Amount/lb or kg of Food									
Unit	Dry Basis		Dry Type		Semimoist		Canned or Wet			
	(lb)	(kg)	(lb)	(kg)	(lb)	(kg)	(lb)	(kg)		
mg	.45	1.0	.41	.9	.34	.75	.114	.25	Yeast Liver Cereal grains Meat Egg yolk Fish Legumes Milk	The anemia caused by pyridoxine deficiency cannot be cured by supplementation with iron and copper B_6 functions in the metabolism of protein. Hence, rations high in protein require extra B_6 for complete protection
mg	4.5	10.0	4.1	9.0	3.4	7.5	1.14	2.5	Pure calcium pantothenate Organ meats Eggs Certain vegetables Cereals Fish solubles	An unknown quantity of this vitamin is synthesized by intestinal bacteria, then absorbed
mg	5.18	11.4	4.7	10.3	3.9	8.6	1.3	2.8	Synthetic niacin Meat Yeast Cereals	Under natural conditions, blacktongue occurs only in areas where corn forms a major part of the diet of both man and the dog, such as used to occur in the deep South High quality proteins supply tryptophan from which niacin may be synthesized in the intestinal tract Requirements are highest when the diet is high in corn. The niacin in corn is relatively unavailable
mg	545.4	1,200	500.	1,100	409.	900	36.3	300	Synthetic vitamin Liver Eggs Soybean oil Yeast	Choline is inexpensive. Hence, there is no excuse for a deficiency ever occurring Many factors determine the need for choline; among them: protein, cystine, methionine, fat, and vitamin B_{12}

(Continued)

TABLE 21 (CONTINUED)

Vitamin	Function of Vitamin	Deficiency Symptoms	Nutritional Per lb or kg Body Wt/Day Unit	Adult Maintenance (lb)	(kg)	Growing Puppies (lb)	(kg)
Vitamin K	Necessary for the production of prothrombin at its site of formation, the liver	Lowered prothrombin level in the blood, the clotting power is impaired, and a hemorrhagic tendency develops					
Vitamin C (ascorbic acid)	To form and maintain intercellular material. Vitamin C is necessary to form the normal epithelial cement substance of the vascular tissues, especially capillaries	Scurvy in dogs under special circumstances, especially in certain disease conditions					
Biotin	As an essential component of a coenzyme concerned in carbon dioxide fixation. Biotin enters into several reactions of intermediary metabolism	A progressive paralysis; dermatitis. Hard pad (podakeratosis). Pulmonary edema, delayed opening of eyelids, and possible blindness	mcg	1.0	2.2	2.0	4.4

Chinese used a concoction rich in vitamin A as a remedy for night blindness. Also, codliver oil was used in treating or preventing rickets long before anything was known about the cause of the disease.

The significance of these observations relative to diet, however, was not fully appreciated until scientists found it desirable in many types of investigations to use the biological approach, with purified diets to supplement chemical analyses in measuring the value of feeds. These rations were made up of relatively pure nutrients—proteins, carbohydrates, fats, and minerals—from which the unidentified substances were largely excluded. With these purified rations, all investigators shared a common experience; the animals limited to such diets not only failed to thrive, but they even failed to survive if the investigations were continued for any length of time. At first, many investigators explained such failures on the basis of unpalatability and monotony of the rations. Finally, it was realized that these purified rations were lacking in certain substances, minute in amount and the identity of which was unknown to science. These substances were essential for the maintenance of health and life itself and the efficient utilization of the main ingredients of the food. With these findings, a new era of science was ushered in. The modern approach to nutrition was born.

Funk, a Polish scientist working in London, first referred to these nutrients as "vitamines" in 1912. Presumably, the name vitamines alluded to the fact that they were essential to life, and they were assumed to be chemically of the nature of amines (the chemical asumption was later proved incorrect, with the result that the *e* was dropped—thus, the word *vitamin*).

The actual existence of vitamins, therefore, has been known only since 1912, and only within the last few years has it been possible to see or touch most of them in a pure form. Previously, they were merely mysterious invisible "little things" known only by their effects. In fact, most of the present fundamental knowledge relative to the vitamin content of both human foods and animal

DOG VITAMIN CHART

Requirements									Practical Sources of the Vitamin	Comments
Unit	\multicolumn{8}{c}{Amount/lb or kg of Food}		
	Dry Basis		Dry Type		Semimoist		Canned or Wet			
	(lb)	(kg)	(lb)	(kg)	(lb)	(kg)	(lb)	(kg)		
									Menadione, a synthetic product	Vitamin K is normally synthesized in sufficient quantities in the intestinal tract of dogs. However, when some drugs are included in the diet or specific stress occurs, sufficient vitamin K may not be produced to meet the requirements. Hence, vitamin K is usually added to most commercial dog foods; it's cheap insurance
									Synthetic vitamin C	It is estimated that one dog in each thousand may need added vitamin C in his diet
mg	0.05	0.10	0.04	0.09	0.034	0.075	0.01	0.025	Yeast Liver Molasses Milk	Biotin is widely distributed in foods and is synthesized in the intestinal tract. However, deficiencies do occur once in a while. For example, excessive quantities of raw egg white will produce a biotin deficiency in dogs. The protein "avidin" in raw egg white binds biotin produced by intestinal bacteria

feeds was obtained through measuring their potency, in promoting growth, or in curing certain disease conditions in animals—a most difficult and tedious method. For the most part, small laboratory animals were used, especially rats, guinea pigs, pigeons, chicks, and dogs.

The absence of one or more vitamins in the dog's ration may lead to a failure in growth or reproduction, or to characteristic disorders known as *deficiency diseases*. In severe cases, death itself may follow. Although the occasional deficiency symptoms are the most striking result of vitamin deficiencies, it must be emphasized that, in practice, mild deficiencies probably cause higher total losses than do severe deficiencies. It is relatively uncommon for a ration, or diet, to contain so little of a vitamin that obvious symptoms of a deficiency occur. When one such case does appear, it is reasonable to suppose that there must be several cases that are too mild to produce characteristic symptoms but which are sufficiently severe to lower the state of health.

There are two groups of vitamins based on their solubility:
1. *Fat soluble vitamins*—A, D, E, and K;
2. *Water soluble vitamins*—thiamine (B_1), riboflavin (B_2), niacin, pyridoxine (B_6), pantothenic acid, biotin, folic acid, choline, B_{12}—all members of the B complex; and ascorbic acid (vitamin C).

The fat-soluble vitamins can be stored in the liver and other parts of the body, while only very limited amounts of the water-soluble vitamins are stored. For this reason, it is important that the water-soluble vitamins be fed regularly in the ration in adequate amounts.

Pertinent information relative to dog vitamins is summarized in Table 21. (See pp. 214–221.)

Unidentified Factors

In addition to the vitamins listed in Table 21, certain unidentified or unknown factors appear to be important in dog nutrition. They are referred to as "unidentified" or "unknown," factors, because they have not yet been isolated or synthesized in the laboratory. Nevertheless, rich sources of these factors and their effects have been well established, especially in poultry and swine. A diet that supplies the specific levels of all the known nutrients but which does not supply the unidentified factors is inadequate for best performance, particularly during the critical periods —gestation, lactation, growth, and when under extreme stress. There is evidence that these unidentified factors exist in dried whey, marine and packinghouse by-products, distillers' solubles, antibiotic fermentation residues, alfalfa meal, fish solubles, and green forage. Most of the unidentified factor sources are added to the diet at a level of one to three percent.

WATER

Water is one of the most vital of all nutrients. In fact, dogs can survive for a longer period without food than they can without water. Yet comparatively little discussion will be devoted to this nutrient simply because, under ordinary conditions, it can be readily provided in abundance and at little cost.

Water is one of the largest single constituents of the dog's body. The percentage of water varies with condition and age, but it averages about sixty percent. The younger the animal, the more water it contains. Also, the fatter the animal, the lower the water content. Thus, as a dog matures, it requires proportionately less water on a weight basis, because it consumes less feed per unit of weight and the water content of the body is being replaced by fat.

Water is the essential medium in which chemical reactions of the body take place. It performs the following important functions:

1. It participates in the regulation of body temperature
2. It is involved in the transportation of nutrients
3. It facilitates excretion
4. It serves as the medium in which buffering agents regulate pH and osmotic relationships of body fluids.

Surplus water is excreted from the body, principally through the urine, feces, respiration, tongue, and perspiration. In the lactating female, considerable water is eliminated in the milk. Excessive water loss caused by diarrhea, vomiting, damaged skin, hyperventilation, and excessive urination associated with diabetes, may lead to dehydration. Also, fluid loss may be caused by high sodium chloride, magnesium, potassium, and other excessive intakes.

In general the needs for water can best be met by allowing the dog free access to plenty of clean, fresh water at all times. The quality of water offered to dogs should be equal to that consumed by people. Also, the temperature of water is important. In the winter, the chill should be removed, and it should be kept from freezing; in the summer, it should be cooled to 60° to 70° F.

Dogs will adjust their water content in keeping with the amount that they receive in the food. For example, when they are switched from canned dog food to dry-type food, they drink more, thereby making up for the water formerly received in the canned food, which has about 7.5 times more water than dry-type food.

FOOD FOR DOGS

The essential nutrients—proteins, fats, carbohydrates, minerals, and vitamins—can be supplied to the dog in either of two ways; by home formulation, or by commercial dog foods. Under most conditions, a commercially prepared dog food supplied by a reputable dealer may be the most economical and the least irksome. Nevertheless, dog foods can be formulated, prepared, mixed, and cooked in the home or kennel, provided the person doing so has sufficient knowledge, training, and time, and either enjoys doing it or can hire the labor involved in preparing a nutritious diet expertly and correctly. It is generally recognized, however, that the increasing use of manufactured dog foods has brought better health and longer life to dogs, since most commercial foods are carefully balanced from the standpoint of the forty-three, or more, nutrients required by a dog.

HOME FORMULA

Home formula implies that the food is formulated, prepared, mixed, and cooked in the home or kennel. It may consist of anything from table scraps to breakfast cereals mixed with ground round steak, vegetables, liver, and vitamin supplements. Most of these home formulas are much more expensive than the best brands of commercially prepared dog foods, and more important, they take longer to prepare and are not generally so well balanced. To do a good job of formulating a home dog food requires knowledge, training, and time, and generally involves more expense than using a commercially prepared food.

COMMERCIAL (MANUFACTURED) DOG FOODS

The commercial dog food manufacturer has the distinct advantages of: (1) purchase of ingredients in quantity lots, making possible price advantages; (2) economical and controlled preparation; (3) the hiring of scientifically trained personnel for use in formulating the ration; and (4) having research laboratories, with the result that the foods that they prepare are products of research. Because of these several advantages, commercial dog foods are finding a place of increasing importance in feeding America's dogs.

HOW TO SELECT COMMERCIAL FOODS

There is a difference in commercial dog foods! That is, there is a difference from the standpoint of what a dog owner can purchase with his dog food dollars. The smart operator will know how to determine what constitutes the best in commercial foods for his specific needs. He will not rely solely on how the dog food looks and smells or on the salesman. The most important factors to consider or look for in buying a commercial dog food are:

1. *The reputation of the manufacturer*—This should be determined by (a) checking on who is back of it, (b) conferring with other dog owners who have used the particular product, and (c) checking on whether or not the commercial food under consideration has consistently met its guarantees. The latter can be determined by reading the bulletins or reports published by the respective state departments in charge of enforcing feed laws.

2. *The specific needs*—Food needs vary according to (a) age, size, and individuality of the animal, and (b) whether the animal is fed primarily for maintenance, growth, show conditioning, reproduction, lactation, or work (hunting, running, etc.). The wise operator will buy different formula feeds for different needs.

3. *The feed label or tag*—The state laws require that mixed feeds carry a tag or label that guarantees the ingredients and the chemical makeup of the feed. Ingredients must be listed in descending order of their predominance by weight.

4. *Flexible formulas*—Feeds with flexible formulas are usually the best buy. This is because the price of feed ingredients in different source foods varies considerably from time to time. Thus, a good dog food manufacturer will shift his formulas as prices change in order to give the dog owner the most for his money. This is as it should be, for (a) there is no one best ration, and (b) if substitutions are made wisely, the price of the feed can be kept down and the dog owner will continue to get equally good results.

TYPES OF DOG FOODS

From the standpoint of preparation, dog foods can be divided into three general types: (1) wet or canned food (sales of $446 million in 1971), (2) dry dog food (sales of $337 million in 1971), (3) semimoist dog food (sales of $149 million in 1971).[32]

Many folks are under the erroneous impression that all dry dog foods are cereals and that all canned dog foods are meat. Nothing could be further from the truth. Both types of products contain meat, but in the dry type most of the water has been removed. Additionally, there is an intermediate type of product—with more moisture than dry dog foods, but less moisture than canned dog foods—which we commonly refer to as *semimoist dog food*. Each of these products, along with certain types of preparation peculiar to some of them, will be discussed briefly.

Canned Dog Food (Complete, 75% Moisture)

Canned dog food (complete) has been around for a very long time. These products are a blend of meat or meat by-products with the addition of cereals, various other ingredients, vitamins, minerals, and fats. These foods are prepared by blending, cooking, canning, and sterilizing the ingredients. They contain about 75% moisture and 25% food solids. Most of them contain about 10% protein, 4% fat, 8% carbohydrates, and up to 75% water. The better canned foods contain approximately 650 to 700 calories per pound.

---
[32] Pet Food Institute figures.

In canned (complete) dog food, usually about 50% of the protein comes from meat products, with the remainder from such products as eggs, fish, dried milk, corn germ, wheat germ, yeast, soybeans, cereal grains, and perhaps some connective tissue and bone.

Canned Meat (Straight Pack, 75% Moisture)

Canned meats vary greatly in content and quality, depending on the brand. They may consist of meat from horses or other animals, or fish or poultry, or they may be made from ground by-products of the meat packing industry, such as udders, lungs, lips, spleen, blood and bone, as well as smooth muscle from the gastro-intestinal tract of animals.

Meat alone is not considered a complete diet for a dog; it's low in calcium, relatively high in phosphorus, and the quality of the protein varies according to the source. Straight meat packs are usually expensive, but very palatable. They are used primarily for mixing with complete dog food in order to add palatability. Usually they run 500 to 800 calories per pound, depending on the fat content.

Dry Dog Foods (10% Moisture)

As indicated by the designated type, these products are relatively dry—only containing about 10% moisture.

Complete dry dog foods are generally made by mixing cooked cereal products with other dry products—meat meal, cheese, soybean and fish meals, dry milk solids, dried by-products of vegetables or fruit processing, and dried bakery by-products; with mineral and vitamin supplements added. Most dry dog foods contain about 23% protein, 7% fat, 24% carbohydrates (often expressed as nitrogen-free extract or NFE on the label), and 10% water. The average caloric value is on the order of 1,650 to 2,000 kilocalories per pound.

The dry foods come in several forms; some of them are bulky and designed to keep dogs from overeating, some are fed dry, others with water mixed in, and still others may be fed either way. Some common forms of dry dog foods are:

1. *Meal in flakes*—This is simply a dry dog food rolled out in flake form.
2. *Homogenized expanded meal (complete)*—This consists of expanding the product as a means of increasing palatability. Such products come in either chunk or nugget form.
3. *Biscuits and knibbles*—These are baked products that are prepared in much the same manner as cookies or crackers. Generally speaking, it is not intended that these products be used as complete dog foods. Rather, they are used as snacks or treats, and as supplements to fresh meat or meat products. Most of them are high in carbohydrates, and their energy value runs about 1,500 calories per pound.

Semimoist Dog Foods (25% Moisture)

These new, and very convenient, semimoist dog foods are intermediate in moisture between dry dog foods and canned dog foods. They generally contain the same basic nutrients found in dry dog foods, with the addition of moisture, often in the form of broths or fatty materials. They are easy to store—not requiring refrigeration—and they are relished by most dogs.

Five ounces of semimoist food (25% moisture) are nutritionally equivalent to about sixteen ounces of a canned food (75% moisture).

SUPPLEMENTS

Generally speaking, the author favors the use of a complete dog food, because each bite is a balanced diet. Where complete dog foods are used, however, it is important that there be a different type of dog food for a specific need. For example, working dogs require more energy than mature, idle dogs. Where special foods for special uses are not available, a supplement may be used. Also, owners sometimes use supplements as a treat, or with the intent of improving the nutrition. The latter is hazardous, however, unless the dog owner is a nutrition expert and has full knowledge of both the ration being fed, the supplement being used, and the nutritive requirements of the dog.

Among the supplements commonly used are the following:

1. *Mineral and/or vitamin supplements*—The dog does need minerals and vitamins. But these should be provided only in the amounts, and in the relationship to each other, as recommended in Tables 10, 11, 12, 20 and 21, with reasonable margins of safety added. Moreover, the mineral and vitamin requirements given in these tables are based on the total food consumed by the dog, rather than any additives of supplementation. Thus, any supplementation of minerals and vitamins should be done solely on the basis of correcting any deficiencies of these nutrients or addi-

Fig. 226. Chow time. These puppies, eager for their dinner, are 10 weeks old. (Courtesy The Seeing Eye, Inc., Morristown, N.J.)

tives that may exist in the total ration. The real hazard, of course, is that by using supplements of vitamins and minerals an imbalance may be created, which is likely to do more harm than good.

2. *Eggs*—If eggs are added to the diet, they should always be cooked. Raw eggs contain the enzyme *avidin*, which ties up the vitamin *biotin*. Thus, if raw eggs are fed continuously over a period of time, a biotin deficiency will occur, the symptoms of which are: dermatitis, loss of hair, and poor growth.

3. *Charcoal*—Sometimes, dog owners add charcoal to the diet. The reasons given for the practice are: to correct diarrhea, to absorb gases, and to add needed minerals. The truth of the matter is that charcoal consists chiefly of carbon in elemental form and supplies but little mineral matter. Animal experiments also show that feeding charcoal decreases feed efficiency, results in the charcoal absorbing the vitamins and holding them so that they are not available, and lessens only very mild forms of diarrhea. Thus, the feeding of charcoal is not recommended.

4. *Special supplements for pups*—Prior to weaning, many owners insist on feeding puppies various mixtures of milk, baby cereal, vitamins, eggs, and meat. Such mixtures are expensive and time consuming. Moreover, they are quite unnecessary. A good commercial dog food that has been properly moistened with water or milk, and fed according to the manufacturer's directions, will be palatable and nutritious for puppies.

PALATABILITY (TASTE, AROMA)

Like people, dogs have taste and aroma preferences—some foods are more appetizing to them than others. For this reason, the additions of milk, meat, broth, or other materials, are made to improve palatability. But they do not necessarily provide greater nutritional value than properly balanced dry diets.

Certainly, palatability is important, for dogs must eat their food if it is to do them any good. But many dogs are finicky simply because they are spoiled. For the latter, stepping up the exercise and halving the ration will usually effect a miraculous cure.

It is probable that well-liked foods are digested somewhat better than those that are equally nutritious, but less palatable. This is explained on a physiological basis.

Palatability is particularly important when feeding dogs that are being worked hard, as in hunting or racing. Unless the ration is consumed, such dogs will not obtain sufficient nutrients to permit maximum performance.

Familiarity and habit are important factors concerned with the palatability of dog foods. For example, dogs have to learn to eat carrots, and very frequently they will back away from foods with new and unfamiliar odors. For this reason, any change in food should be made gradually.

Occasionally, the failure of dogs to eat a normal amount of food is due to a serious nutritional deficiency. For example, if dogs are fed a ration made up of palatable ingredients, but deficient in one or more required vitamins or minerals, they may eat normal amounts for a time. Then when the body reserves of the lacking nutrient(s) are exhausted, they will usually consume much less food, due to an impairment of their health and consequent lack of appetite. If the deficiency is not continued so long that the dogs are injured permanently, they will usually recover their appetites if some ingredient is added that supplies the nutritive lack and makes the ration complete.

So long as the dog food manufacturer does not use taste and aroma as a means of making poor quality feed ingredients more appetizing, there is no harm from having a highly palatable feed for dogs. However, more than likely, the exotic tastes and flavors do the owner more good than the dog, for they give him the grand feeling of showering the maximum amount of love and affection on his pet.

FADS, FOIBLES, AND TRADE SECRETS

By definition a *fad is a matter of no importance or an important matter imperfectly understood, taken up and urged with more zeal than sense.* Only horse owners approach dog owners in their store of fads, foibles, and trade secrets. Also, dog owners are great imitators. They will single out some dog that has made a fine record—in showing, hunting, or racing—and, in one way or another, find out what he's getting. Then they will get some of the "same stuff" and use it from then till doomsday. Among the most common fads, foibles, and trade secrets of dog owners are the following:

1. *The common belief that dogs are carnivorous animals and should have nothing but meat*—After all, the argument goes, in the wild state dogs ate flesh, and nothing else. Of course, the fact is that wild animals devour all of their kill—the innards, bones, marrow, and blood—while meats prepared for dogs in cans consist mainly of drained muscle and fat. Furthermore, the wild ancestors of dogs supplemented their diets with everything from berries and edible grasses to mud. A dog would actually have to eat several times his own weight in lean hamburger everyday to obtain the calcium that he needs, and some nutrients would simply be unobtainable from such a diet.

2. *The belief that dogs cannot utilize starch*—Perhaps the most common fad among dog owners is to attempt to feed diets without starch. The fact remains that dogs utilize all starches, including potatoes, just as well as their masters, provided they are properly prepared—by heating.

3. *The belief that dog bones make for sound teeth*—Many dog owners believe that dogs cannot have sound teeth if they are fed soft diets. However, both experiments and experiences show that puppies fed soft diets, with nothing to gnaw on, usually have perfect teeth.

FORMULATING DIETS; SOME SUGGESTED FORMULATIONS[33]

This book gives the nutrient requirements of dogs on a 100% dry-matter (moisture-free) basis and on 90%, 75%, and 25% dry-matter bases (Ta-

---

[33] Both narrative and Table 22 of this section were taken from No. 8, *Nutrient Requirements of Dogs,* Revised 1972, National Academy of Sciences, NRC.

bles 11 and 12). Data on the composition of feeds (Tables 29 and 30) are expressed on a dry basis.

Diets or feed mixtures can readily be calculated on a dry basis. When this is done, nutrient requirements can be compared directly with the percentages of nutrients in the dry diet without additional calculation. The diet can then be converted to an as-fed basis by taking the following steps:

1. Percent of ingredients in the dry diet ÷ by percent dry matter of ingredient x 100 = parts of ingredient in the diet as fed
2. Parts of ingredient in the diet as fed are totaled
3. Parts of ingredient ÷ by total parts x 100 = percent of the ingredient in the diet as fed

An example of calculating a diet on a dry basis and correcting to an as-fed basis is given in Table 22. The diet was formulated to contain 3,785 kcal per kg of metabolizable energy and 15% of protein on a dry basis.

The calculations for the next to the last column (Parts) in Table 22 were as follows:

$$\frac{81.0}{86.0} \times 100 = 94.2$$

$$\frac{13.3}{9.6} \times 100 = 138.5$$

$$\frac{5.7}{89.0} \times 100 = 6.4$$

The calculations for the last column (In Diet) in Table 22 were as follows:

$$\frac{94.2}{239.1} \times 100 = 39.4\% \text{ of corn as fed}$$

$$\frac{138.5}{239.1} \times 100 = 57.9\% \text{ of skimmed milk as fed}$$

$$\frac{6.4}{239.1} \times 100 = 2.7\% \text{ of solvent-extracted soybean meal}$$

Formulas for two meal-type diets are given in Table 23. These diets have been used successfully, but there is no asurance that all dogs will accept them readily. Other combinations of ingredients may serve as well as, or better than, those suggested in the table.

Palatability is an important factor in formulating diets. Dogs like well-formulated dry products, and these products can be satisfactory as the sole diet.

Although additions of milk, meat, broths, or other materials may improve palatability, they do not necessarily increase the nutritional value of properly balanced dry diets.

A dry, semimoist, or canned diet can provide all the nutrients required by dogs if the diet is properly formulated and processed. The water content of a product must be considered in calculating dietary intake.

TABLE 22
EXAMPLE OF CALCULATING A DIET ON A DRY BASIS AND CORRECTING TO AN AS-FED BASIS [34]

Ingredient	Composition of Foods			Amount in Diet (dry basis)			Amount in Diet (as-fed basis)	
	Dry Matter (as-fed basis)	ME (dry basis)	Protein (dry basis)	In Diet	ME	Protein	Parts	In Diet
	(%)	(kcal/kg)	(%)	(%)	(kcal/kg)	(%)		(%)
Corn, grain, (4) [35]	86.0	3,808	10.2	81.0	3,084	8.3	94.2	39.4
Cattle, milk, skimmed, (5) [36]	9.6	3,910	28.5	13.3	520	3.8	138.5	57.9
Soybean, seeds, solv-extd grnd, mx 7% fiber, (5) [36]	89.0	3,174	51.5	5.7	181	2.9	6.4	2.7
Total				100.0	3,785	15.0	239.1	100.0

[34] From No. 8, *Nutrient Requirements of Dogs*, Revised 1972, National Academy of Sciences, NRC, p. 49, Table 14.
[35] The (4) is the NRC designation of energy feeds.
[36] The (5) is the NRC designation of protein supplements.

TABLE 23

MEAL-TYPE DIETS FOR DOGS (DRY MATTER 90%) [37]

Ingredient [38]	Diet 1	Diet 2
	(%)	(%)
Animal, carcass residue w bone, dry rendered dehy grnd, mx 9% indigestible material mn 4.4% phosphorus, (5)	8.00	15.00
Fish, whole or cuttings, cooked mech-extd dehy grnd, salt declared above 3% mx 7%, (5)	5.00	3.00
Soybean, seed, solv-extd grnd, mx 7% fiber, (5)	12.00	—
Soybean, flour, solv-extd fine sift, mx 3% fiber, (5)	—	19.00
Wheat, germ, grnd, mn 25% protein mn 7% fat, (5)	8.00	5.00
Cattle, milk, skimmed dehy, mx 8% moisture, (5)	4.00	2.50
Grains, cereal, (4)	51.23	—
Corn, grain, flaked, (4)	—	26.75
Wheat, bran, dry milled, (4)	4.00	—
Wheat, grain, flaked, (4)	—	26.70
Animal, fat, hydrolyzed, feed gr mn 85% fatty acids mx 6% unsaponifiable matter mx 1% insoluble matter, (4)	2.00	—
Animal, bone, steamed dehy grnd, (6)	2.00	—
Yeast, brewers saccharomyces, dehy grnd, (7)	2.00	0.50
Grains, fermentation solubles, dehy, (5)	1.00	—
Salt, iodized	0.50	0.25
Vitamin A and D mix[39]	0.25	0.50
Riboflavin supplement[40]	—	0.80
Ferric oxide, red, Fe_2O_3, commercial, (4)	0.02	—

[37] From No. 8, *Nutrient Requirements of Dogs,* Revised 1974, National Academy of Sciences, NRC, p. 59, Table 11. While these rations have been used satisfactorily with some dogs, there is no assurance that all dogs will accept them readily. The numbers in parentheses following each product are NRC designations as follows: (4) indicates energy feeds; (5) indicates protein supplements; (6) indicates minerals; and (7) indicates vitamins.
[38] NRC names. See section under "Composition of Dog Food Ingredients" of this book.
[39] 2,250 IU of A, 400 IU of D per g.
[40] Supplies 500 mg/kg of riboflavin.

SPECIAL FEEDING

Throughout most of this chapter, the accent is on the average dog. This is as it should be, for there are more average dogs than any other kind —that's the reason they're "average." But this section is different! It is devoted to special feeding required for certain phases or uses of dogs. Also, it is the author's intent to point up the fact that the nutritive requirements of dogs, like other classes of animals, differ according to age, weight, use or demands, growth, stage of gestation or lactation, and environment.

FEEDING THE PREGNANT FEMALE

The nutrients fed the pregnant female must first take care of the usual maintenance needs. If the female is not fully mature, nutrients are required for maternal growth as well as for growth of the fetus. Quality and quantity of proteins, minerals, and vitamins become particularly important in the rations of young pregnant bitches, for their requirements are much greater and more exacting than those of the mature dog.

Although an overweight condition is undesirable, it is necessary that body reserves be stored for subsequent use during lactation. With a large litter of puppies and a bitch that is a heavy milker, the demands for milk production will be greater than can be supplied by the ration fed at the time of lactation. Thus, during gestation, bitches are generally fed an average of 20 percent more food than during the maintenance period. Moreover, it is a good plan to increase the food allowance of the pregnant bitch between the fourth and sixth weeks of pregnancy, at which time her energy requirements increase. In addition to eating for herself, she must consume food for 4 or 5, or possibly for 10 or 12, puppies. Actually, this increase during the latter half of gestation accounts for the majority of the overall 20 percent increase in food allowance during pregnancy.

FEEDING THE LACTATING FEMALE

Lactation imposes special demands on the bitch because of the large amounts of proteins and minerals secreted in the milk. Hence, the nutritive requirements of lactation are more rigorous than those during gestation. They are very similar to those of the milk cow, except they are more exacting relative to quality of proteins and the B vitamins because of the absence of rumen synthesis in the dog.

After giving birth to the litter, the food allowance should be increased so that more milk will be produced. When the maximum quantity of milk is being produced (about the fourth week), the female should be consuming two to three times the normal maintenance quantity of food. In addition to receiving more energy, the lactating female should be given a ration rich in protein, minerals, and vitamins. The lactating diet should include meat and liver, some fat and cereal, milk, eggs, and cottage cheese.

With a normal number of pups in the litter, generally a good commercial dog food will be adequate for a lactating bitch. However, if the litter is large, with ten or more pups, it may be well to supplement the diet for maximum milk production, using one part of horse meat or raw hamburger to three parts of dry ration.

Since the lactating female is being fed for milk production, it is helpful to compare the composition of bitch's milk with milk of other species. This is given in Table 24. It is particularly noteworthy that, in comparison with cow's milk, bitch's milk is higher in total solids, protein, and fat, but lower in lactose. In addition to the information presented in Table 24, the following facts relative to the chemical composition of bitch's milk are pertinent: calcium, 0.28 percent; phosphorus, 0.24 percent; and calcium to phosphorus ratio, 1.2:1. This would indicate that feeding bitches is more critical than feeding milk cows; and this is doubly so when it is recognized that the dog is a monogastric animal, whereas the cow is a ruminant.

FEEDING PUPPIES

The growth of a puppy is determined primarily by heredity and food. No dog will grow beyond the dictates of his genes, no matter how well or what he is fed; but withholding food can stunt growth.

The first secretion of the mammary gland following parturition is known as *colostrum*. This is nature's product, designed to give the young a good start in life; and it is vitally important that puppies get it. It is higher than normal milk in dry matter, protein, vitamins, and minerals. Additionally, and most important, it contains antibodies that give newborn animals protection against certain diseases.

While the puppies are nursing, they should be watched carefully to make sure that all of them get a chance to nurse. As they grow, some of the ration fed to the mother should be made available to them, also. By the time they are ready to wean at six weeks, they should be consuming sufficient food that no setback occurs.

Puppies have much higher food requirements than adult dogs. In some breeds, they increase their birth weight by as much as sixty times during the first year, with the most rapid growth increase occurring between the first and the sixth months. Hence, they need to be fed much and often. Although the amount of food will vary with the breed, activity, rate of growth, and other individual factors, a doubling or tripling of the maintenance food allowance, on a per pound of body weight basis, is usually advisable.

Authorities differ on the subject of number of feedings per day for puppies. Some recommend feeding puppies six times daily, others three times daily, and still others recommend self-feeding. After attaining maturity, dogs are generally fed once or twice daily. Actually, successes can be cited in support of various frequencies of feeding. Perhaps the most important thing is that one system or program be selected, then followed. There are, of course, some exceptions that should

TABLE 24

THE CHEMICAL COMPOSITION OF BITCHES' MILK IN COMPARISON WITH OTHER SPECIES [41]

Animal	Water	Total Solids	Fat	Protein	Lactose	Ash
< - % - >
Dog	79.6	20.4	8.3	7.5	3.7	0.90
Cow	86.2	13.8	4.4	3.8	4.9	0.7
Goat	87.1	12.9	4.1	3.7	4.2	0.8
Human	88.0	12.0	3.8	1.2	7.0	0.21
Horse	90.1	9.9	1.0	2.6	6.9	0.35
Pig	82.8	17.2	5.1	7.1	3.7	1.1
Sheep	82.0	18.0	6.4	5.6	4.7	0.91

[41] *Story of Milk Production*, published by Chas. Pfizer & Co., Inc., Vol. 3, No. 2, 1959, Table 2, p. 16; with the composition of the dog's milk provided by author.

be made in whatever frequency system is selected. For example, puppies that are kept in unheated kennels during the cold, winter months need more food and more frequent feeding than those kept in warm kennels.

In general, satisfactory results may be secured from feeding puppies complete dog foods manufactured by reputable companies; and they may be either (1) dry, (2) semimoist, or (3) wet mixtures. With puppies of the larger breeds, however, it is sometimes desirable to supplement normal dog foods with liver and fat, thereby providing more energy.

WEANING

Weaning of puppies is more a matter of preparation than of absolute separation from the mother. The simplicity with which it is accomplished depends very largely upon the thoroughness of the preparation. Most pups start eating the same solid food as their mother at about 3 weeks of age, and by the time they are 5 to 6 weeks old the mother has usually started to wean them. Pups are generally weaned at 6 weeks of age.

At weaning time, the food allowance of the female should be decreased, as this helps to reduce the quantity of milk produced and to restore the milk-producing organs to normal. To facilitate weaning, it is recommended that the female not be fed on the day weaning takes place. On the second day, limit her feed to one-fifth the normal allowance, then over the next week gradually increase her food until she is on a normal maintenance ration (not a lactating ration).

ORPHANED AND REJECTED PUPPIES

About 30% of all puppies born fail to reach weaning age. There are two primary reasons for these high death losses: (1) chilling, and (2) orphaned and rejected puppies. Without doubt, the vast majority of such losses could be alleviated were more dog owners informed of satisfactory hand-raising regimens.

Puppies are generally orphaned because of their mother (1) dying, (2) not having any milk, (3) not giving sufficient milk, or (4) rejecting or refusing to nurse them. Whatever the cause, owners can have a greater degree of success in raising such orphaned or rejected puppies provided they have certain basic information, then apply it. The following points are pertinent to raising orphaned and rejected puppies:

1. *Substitutes for bitch's milk*—The most satisfactory food substitute for an orphaned or rejected puppy is the one that most nearly approaches that of its dam's milk. As noted in Table 24, bitch's milk is richer than cow's milk; it is higher in protein, fat, calcium, phosphorus, total solids, and calories. Most significantly, it is lower in lactose. The latter point is important because a high concentration of lactose tends to produce diarrhea in puppies.

The raising of an orphaned puppy will be simplified if it has first received colostrum. This is so because scientists have not yet discovered how to duplicate colostrum.

Where necessity demands, one of the following products may be substituted for the bitch's milk:

a. *Milk replacers*—Several reputable commercial companies produce and sell milk replacers. When used according to manufacturer's directions, these products are very satisfactory. In addition to correcting the iron and copper deficiencies of normal milk, these replacers are usually fortified with vitamins, other minerals, and antibiotics.

b. *Goat's milk*—The milk of goats is very satisfactory as a substitute for bitch's milk. It stores well and does not require mixing or measuring.

c. *Evaporated milk*—If diluted to 20% solids (5 parts of evaporated milk plus 1 part of boiled water), evaporated milk is nearer the composition of bitch's milk than is fresh cow's milk.

2. *Suitable environment*—Puppies have a very poor temperature regulatory mechanism; hence, they must be kept very warm. The ideal temperatures for newborn puppies follow:

Age	Degrees Fahrenheit
Birth to the 5th day	85–90°
2nd week	80°
4th through 6th week	75°
After the 6th week	70°

Also, it is recommended that orphaned puppies be kept in separate compartments. Unless this is done for the first two or three weeks of life, they will suckle, or otherwise disturb, each other.

Torn newspaper may be used as bedding. But better footing can be provided by cotton quilted bed pads or other washable cloth. Disposable paper diapers work very well, also. Whatever the bedding, it should be changed at frequent intervals, and the feces should be examined for signs of trouble.

3. *Feeding schedule and management*—Where a commercial milk replacer is used, usually the caretaker had best follow the mixing and feeding directions given by the manufacturer on the container.

Generally speaking, the calorie content and the nutritive quality of the formula used dictate the feeding schedule. The author favors a minimum of 6-times-a-day feeding for the first 2 weeks of life, then gradually increasing the volume of milk replacer fed at each feeding and lengthening the interval between feedings. After about 2 weeks, feed only 4 times daily.

4. *Feeding Equipment*—The following equipment is needed for hand-feeding:

A measuring cup
Mixing bowl
Spoon
Baby nursing bottles and nipples
Eyedropper

Blind (without holes) lamb nipples work particularly well for all but the smallest toy breeds. By punching holes in the nipple with a needle, the flow of milk can be regulated as desired. It is important that the hole not be too large, for a puppy will not nurse unless the flow of milk is proper. An eyedropper can be used for feeding newborn puppies of the small breeds.

Before feeding, the formula should be warmed to about 100°F., or near body temperature.

Fig. 227. Stainless steel dishes in a kennel should be cleaned daily to protect the health and well-being of dogs. (Courtesy The Seeing Eye, Inc., Morristown, N.J.)

It is important that all receptacles be kept absolutely clean and sanitary.

FEEDING BREEDING STOCK

The feeding of pregnant and lactating females has already been covered, so repetition at this point is unnecessary.

It is recognized that poor nutrition, even before sexual maturity, can result in reproductive trouble at a later date, for both the stud dog and the bitch. It is important, therefore, that prospective breeding animals be well fed early in life.

A well-balanced diet is essential to assure the highest fertility of the stud dog as well as of the female. The program throughout the entire year should be such as to keep the stud dog in a vigorous, thrifty condition at all times. Also, when in heavy service, the stud dog should receive additional proteins of high quality, and his ration should be well fortified with minerals and vitamins—all in the proper ratios.

Either obesity or a thin, run-down condition should be avoided in both breeding males and females. Either condition can result in infertility, which may be permanent or temporary. Where obesity exists, the best advice is to reduce the ration and increase the exercise.

FEEDING WORKING DOGS

Working dogs—dogs used in hunting, racing, police work, war work, leading the blind, etc.—are canine athletes. Hence, they should be fed accordingly.

Many working dogs are started in training early in life. In the case of dogs used in racing and hunting, and in certain other working dogs, they are moved from one location to another under all sorts of conditions. They are trained over a long period of time (some of them the year around), used innumerable times each year, used irregularly, and forced to work when they are fatigued.

Often they are not fed balanced rations. Sometimes they are given concoctions of questionable value—if not downright harmful. By contrast, human athletes—college football teams and participants in the Olympics, for example—are usually required to eat at a special training table, supervised by nutrition experts. They are fed the best diet that science can formulate and technology can prepare. It is high in protein, rich in readily available energy, and fortified and balanced in vitamins and minerals. As a result, human athletes generally compete year after year until overtaken by age.

Indeed, working dogs, which are usually highly stressed, need special rations just as human athletes do—and for the same reasons; and the younger the age, the more acute the need. This calls for rations high in protein, rich in readily available energy, fortified with vitamins, minerals, and unidentified factors—and with all nutrients in proper balance. Also, increased thiamine should be provided because thiamine needs increase with the amount of carbohydrate metabolized; riboflavin should be increased because more of this vitamin is needed as the calorie output is increased; and added vitamin E may be needed because of the relationship between vitamin E and muscular function.

A Greyhound in a race, or a Retriever in the water, is asked to develop a large amount of power in a very short period of time. The oxidations that occur under these conditions are at a high pitch, with the result that readily available energy and more vitamins are required.

The increased nutritional requirements of the working dog may be met in any of the following ways, or in combinations of two or more of them:

1. By increasing the intake of the complete and balanced commercial dog food that is being fed.
2. By the addition of raw hamburger or meat to the ration that is being fed, as a means of increasing appetite and the caloric intake. Horsemeat or hamburger are normally good sources of both high-quality, palatable protein and fat. Usually, 1 part of meat is added to 3 parts of dry ration.
3. By adding fat, which is the most concentrated source of energy. A small amount of added fat will sometimes increase both feed intake and palatability. Although most commercial dog foods have ample fat, if it is necessary to add some fat, it is recommended that lard, bacon grease, or corn oil be used.

FEEDING OLDER DOGS

The food requirements of older dogs, like those of elderly people, differ from those of their juniors. Older dogs spend much more time sleeping and are less active. The general level of physical activity is decreased to a point that moderate exercise must be enforced. Also in aging, a gradual, but constant, reduction of tissues takes place. The numbers of individual cells of a specific tissue are reduced, and the cells become progressively smaller. Total enzymatic activity of these tissues is reduced and metabolism is slowed. Even cardiac output and renal function are lower than in puppies.

To meet the above transition that occurs in senile dogs, a marked reduction in caloric intake is necessary. Less carbohydrate and fat should be fed; only sufficient fat should be fed to meet the dog's requirement for essential fatty acids. Unless there is kidney damage (chronic nephritis), older dogs should be fed increased quantities of protein, and the protein should be of high biological value. Also, older dogs may need more vitamins, and more calcium appears to be necessary, with particular attention given to the calcium:phosphorus ratio. Usually more iron is necessary. Thus, special foods for older dogs may be indicated, and elderly pets should be placed under the supervision of a veterinarian.

FEEDING OBESE DOGS

Obesity frequently occurs in small house dogs and in older dogs of all sizes. It results from ingesting more calories than are expended in daily living, usually accentuated by lack of exercise. Obesity (1) has a significant deleterious effect on the response of dogs to distemper infection, (2) may result in sterility in breeding animals, and (3) may shorten the life of the dog; all compelling reasons why the condition should be rectified.

Where a serious overweight problem exists, it is best that the regime and the diet be prescribed by the veterinarian. The weight of the patient must be charted at frequent intervals so that progress can be followed, and the prescribed diet must not be deviated from.

The reducing diet should be low in fat, moderate in carbohydrate, high in protein, and well-fortified with vitamins and minerals. Ground horsemeat, cooked heart from which the fat has been removed, cottage cheese, and boiled eggs are all good sources of protein which are comparatively low in fat. Commercial low-calorie dog foods are available. Usually these contain approx-

Fig. 228. Scales give a big assist in preventing overfeeding and obesity. (Drawing by R. F. Johnson)

imately 300 calories per pound of food, whereas normal commercial canned dog food contain about 500 calories per pound. Since a 20-pound adult dog requires approximately 600 to 700 calories per day for maintenance, by feeding somewhat less than two cans of the low-calorie (300 calories per pound) dog food per day, the animal should, theoretically, receive fewer calories than his maintenance requirement; and should lose weight. But there are individual animal differences, so only through experimentation can one satisfactorily reduce an animal.

When on a reducing diet, it is recommended that the dog be fed twice daily, thereby minimizing the hunger problems.

FEEDING SICK DOGS

The proper feeding of sick dogs is extremely important. Most infectious diseases reduce the amount of food consumed and alter the nutritional status considered most suitable to combating infectious diseases; conditions that can best be overcome by special diets. Also, nutritional deficiencies can reduce the capacity of the dog to resist the consequences of infection, whereas good nutrition can bolster the resistance to infection.

The feeding of sick dogs is dictated by the condition of the patient and the cause of the illness. Thus, a veterinarian should first diagnose the sickness, following which he should prescribe treatment and diet. Fortunately, the feeding of sick dogs has been simplified by the availability of several prescription dog food formulations available through veterinarians.

FEEDING RULES

Observance of the following general rules will help to avoid some of the common difficulties encountered in feeding dogs:

1. Dogs should be fed as individuals, for each one is different, just as people are different.
2. Know the weight and age of each dog.
3. Never feed moldy, spoiled, or rotten food.
4. Keep the feed and water containers clean.

Fig. 229. Know the weight and age of each dog. This can be accomplished by weighing yourself on an ordinary bathroom scale; then weighing a second time with your dog in your arms; then subtracting the first weight from the second. (Courtesy The Seeing Eye, Inc., Morristown, N.J.)

5. Make certain that the dog's teeth are sound.
6. See that the dog gets adequate exercise. It improves appetite, digestion, and overall well-being.
7. Dogs that are obese should be let down in condition gradually. This should be accomplished by decreasing the food allowance and increasing the exercise.

AMOUNT TO FEED

The following food allowances will keep most mature dogs in proper condition:

1. *Dry dog food*—Feed 1/2 ounce per pound body weight per day. Thus, a 32-pound dog would get one pound (16 oz) of food per day.
2. *Canned dog food*—Feed 1-3/4 ounces of canned food per pound of body weight per day. More canned dog food than of dry food must be fed because the canned product contains approximately 75 percent water.
3. *Semimoist dog food*—Feed 6/10 ounce of semimoist dog food per pound of body weight per day.

Of course, the main qualities desired in dogs are trimness, spirit, and endurance. To this end, the caretaker must alter the above feeding guides as necessary, bearing in mind that the amount to feed is affected by the following:

1. *Individuality*—Dogs vary in their metabolism—in their keeping qualities. Thus, the nutritional requirements of two litter-mate sisters may be quite different; one may need an extra helping to maintain condition, whereas the other may have to be restricted to avoid obesity.
2. *Condition*—Dogs that are thin need to be fed more liberally than those that are obese. The desired condition in all dogs may best be described as "strong, firm, and hard."
3. *Size*—The food allowance per pound body weight decreases with increased weight; hence, on a per pound basis, larger dogs require fewer calories than smaller dogs.
4. *Age*—Growing puppies require two to three times as much food per pound of body weight as mature dogs of the same breed require. Adjustment in their allowance should be made as they mature so as to permit steady growth without excess fatness.
5. *Gestation and lactation*—As pregnancy advances and gestating females increase in body weight, they will eat more total pounds per day. However, on a per pound body weight basis their

allowance will change very little from the guidelines given above.

Lactating females must be fed more liberally, to meet the rigorous demands of producing milk. During the height of milk production, about a month after whelping, the lactating bitch will need three to four times the allowance given above.

6. *Kind, amount and severity of work*—When hunting, especially when retrieving in cold water, or when running in a dog race, a dog may expend up to 100 times more energy than when at rest.

7. *Weather*—During cold, winter weather, dogs in unheated quarters require 25 to 50 percent more food than during ideal October weather. In a study on the effect of temperature, it was found that Huskies required 1.8 times more calories in the winter (at $-22°$ C, or $-8°$ F) than in the summer (at $+17°$ C, or $+62°$ F).

8. *The food*—There's a difference in dog foods—a difference in moisture content; in kind, proportion, and quality of ingredients; and in balance of nutrients. All these factors affect food allowance.

Again it is emphasized that the recommended allowances given at the outset of this section are intended as guides only, and that the eye of the caretaker and a pair of scales should make the final determination for each dog as an individual—more for some, less for others.

WHEN TO FEED

The common practice is to feed one meal a day. Because people eat 3 meals a day, sometimes a dog owner thinks it cruel to feed his dog only once a day. However, this is normally adequate for mature dogs. Of course, dogs that are working hard, lactating females, and young puppies should be fed more frequently. Twice a day feeding is recommended for working dogs; and lactating females with large litters should be fed 3 to 5 times daily. Puppies should either have food free-choice or receive several meals daily. When hand-fed at intervals, they are usually started on a 6-times-a-day feeding schedule, which is gradually lessened (see section entitled "Feeding Puppies").

Most people feed their dogs in the evening, just ahead of their own dinner. This helps to keep the dog from begging if he is kept in the house. On the other hand, many kennels and many people having housebreaking troubles feed in the morning. Still others feed at noon. Morning feeding is often inconvenient to people who are rushing off to work or to school. So, when you feed should be determined by your own convenience.

Dogs learn to anticipate their food. Accordingly, they should be fed with regularity, as determined by a timepiece. During warm weather, they will eat better if the feeding hours are early and late, in the cool of the day.

SELF-FEEDING

Self-feeding is the practice of allowing free access to food in unlimited quantities. Self-feeding with animals is not new; it has been practiced with chickens, hogs, cattle, and sheep for many years. It should be pointed out, however, that there are two primary differences between meat-producing animals and dogs:

1. Chickens, hogs, cattle, and sheep are usually self-fed when forced production is desired.
2. With breeding animals, usually some feed "governor" is used in order to limit consumption of self-fed animals—for example, a high level of salt or fat, or considerable roughage may be included in the ration of breeding cows that are self-fed.

In recent years, some of the major dog food manufacturers have developed complete rations, which they consider satisfactory for self-feeding most dogs. Among the claims made by manufacturers for self-feeding dogs are the following:

1. Each individual dog regulates his food intake to the amount needed by him.
2. Dogs eat less at a time and more frequently, which makes for more effective use of the nutrients.
3. The level of nutrients in the blood is maintained at a more constant and uniform level.
4. Dogs are more contented, quieter, and less bored.
5. It makes for greater convenience and saving in labor.

The main hazard to self-feeding is that some dogs may eat too much and become too fat.

SOME DON'T'S OF FEEDING

There are both "do's" and "don't's" of feeding dogs. This section pertains to the latter.

Fig. 230. Dogs love bones; and they should have them. But don't give them fowl, fish, or chop bones. (Drawing by R. F. Johnson)

1. *Don't feed tidbits at the table*—Feeding tidbits, or treats, at the table makes beggars and nuisances out of dogs. The "cuteness" is not appreciated by friends, and it may wear thin with you.

2. *Don't give dogs fowl bones, fish bones, or chop bones*—Dogs like to chew on bones, and they should have them. But don't give them fowl bones; they splinter and they may puncture the throat or digestive tract. Fish bones are apt to get caught in the throat. Too many chop bones may cause impaction in the intestines and bring about serious illness or death. So, when bones are given to the dog, use large, fresh bones—the kind that he can gnaw away on without consuming.

3. *Don't feed baby foods or raw eggs*—Leave human baby foods for babies. Don't feed raw eggs because they contain the enzyme, avidin, which destroys the vitamin biotin.

4. *Don't create imbalances*—Don't create imbalances by making needless additions to a complete, well-balanced dog food. It is cruel and unkind to add nutrients that make for an imbalance in the diet of a dog.

5. *Don't experiment with feeding a sick dog*—Where a sick dog is involved, seek the advice of your veterinarian. He will first diagnose the ailment, then he will prescribe the proper diet.

NUTRITIONAL DISEASES AND AILMENTS

Nutritional deficiencies may be brought about either by (1) too little food, (2) rations that are too low in one or more nutrients, or (3) an imbalance of nutrients produced by an excess or deficiency of one nutrient, which changes the requirements of the others.

Nutritional diseases and ailments with dogs came hand in hand with their increased confinement, many dogs being confined to homes or kennels most of their lives. Under these conditions, they are not permitted to forage for themselves; rather, they are dependent upon what food the caretaker gives them. If the diet is not complete, or if there are imbalances, these are apt to be reflected in nutritional diseases and ailments, with the severity of the problem dependent upon the extent of the deficiency or imbalance.

Although the cause, prevention, and treatment of most nutritional diseases and ailments are known, they continue to plague many dogs simply because the available knowledge is not put into practice. Moreover, those nutritional diseases that are not of sufficient proportions to produce clear-cut deficiency symptoms go unnoticed and unrectified. Table 25 contains a summary of the important nutritional diseases and ailments of dogs. Of course, it should be recognized that if

Fig. 231. Dog with blacktongue (top), due to a deficiency of niacin. Same dog (bottom) after receiving meat, a good source of niacin.

Figs. 232–233. Rickets. Vitamin D made the difference! Upper picture shows Bluetick Coonhound pup with rickets (note bowed legs), due to a deficiency of vitamin D. Lower picture shows same puppy after receiving a diet adequate in vitamin D. (Courtesy Ralston Purina Company, St. Louis, Mo.)

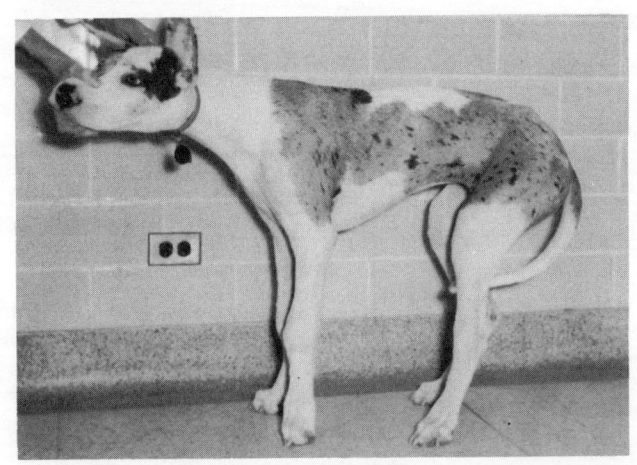

Fig. 234. Scurvy, or Avitaminosis C. Note the enlargement of the limbs. (Courtesy Dr. J. H. Reed, D.V.M., Ph.D., Ontario Veterinary College, University of Guelph, Guelph, Ontario, Canada)

any one of these conditions is seen, the diet is probably deficient in more than one nutrient.

COMPOSITION OF DOG FOOD INGREDIENTS[42]

Tables 29 and 30 give the composition of feeds commonly used in dog diets. The sections which follow, including Tables 26, 27, and 28, will help interpret and explain Tables 29 and 30.

NRC NOMENCLATURE

In Tables 29 and 30, names of the feeds are based on a scheme proposed by Harris et al (1968). The names, called *NRC (National Research Council) names*, are designed to give a qualitative description of each product, where such information is available and pertinent. A complete NRC name consists of as many as eight components separated by commas and written in linear form. The components are as follows:

- Origin (or parent material)
- Species, variety, or kind
- Part eaten

---

[42] The narrative of this section was taken from No. 8, *Nutrient Requirements of Dogs*, Revised 1974, National Academy of Sciences, NRC.

235

TABLE 25

Disease	Cause	Symptoms (and age or group most affected)	Distribution and Losses Caused
Anemia, nutritional	Commonly an iron deficiency, but it may be caused by a deficiency of copper, cobalt, pyridoxine, or folic acid Hookworm infestation and sucking lice may also produce anemia, because of loss of blood	Loss of appetite, progressive emaciation, and death Most prevalent in suckling young	Worldwide Losses consist of slow and inefficient gains, and deaths
Blacktongue	Deficiency of the vitamin niacin	Sensitivity of the mucous membranes in the mouth, and a sore, purplish black tongue if the niacin deficiency continues; also, dermatitis, loss of appetite, ulcers, and alternating diarrhea and constipation; and emaciation follows, then death	Occurs in areas where corn forms a major part of the diet, such as was formerly the case in the deep South
Enclampsia	Inadequate amounts of calcium	Excitability, stiffness, staggering, and convulsions; affected dogs are unable to stand; the muscles become rigid; respiration is rapid; the temperature rises; and the patient emits cries of pain; it is a disease of females in lactation or late pregnancy	Most common in females nursing large litters, especially where there has been insufficient calcium and/or vitamin D
Goiter (Iodine Deficiency)	A failure of the body to obtain sufficient iodine from which the thyroid gland can form thyroxin (an iodine-containing compound)	Goiter (big neck) is the most characteristic symptom Also, puppies may be born hairless and weak	Northwestern U.S. and the Great Lakes region
Night blindness	Vitamin A deficiency	Night blindness, the first symptoms of vitamin A deficiency, is characterized by faulty vision, especially noticeable when the afflicted dog is forced to move about in twilight in strange surroundings	Worldwide

NUTRITIONAL DISEASES AND AILMENTS

Treatment	Control and Eradication	Prevention	Remarks
Provide dietary sources of the nutrient or nutrients the deficiency of which is known to cause the condition	When nutritional anemia is encountered, it can usually be brought under control by supplying dietary sources of the deficient nutrient or nutrients	Supply dietary sources of iron, copper, cobalt, pyridoxine, and folic acid Supplement milk with other foods at an early age	Anemia is a condition in which the blood is either deficient in quality or quantity (a deficient quality refers to a deficiency in hemoglobin and/or red cells) Most commercial dog foods are properly fortified with the nutrients the deficiency of one or more of which may cause anemia
Add niacin to the diet, at following levels per pound body weight/day: adult maintenance, 114 mcg; growing puppies, 228 mcg	Add niacin to the diet, and lessen the corn in the food	Avoid a high corn diet Include in the complete diet the following levels of niacin per pound body weight/day: adult maintenance, 114 mcg; growing puppies, 228 mcg	Good commercial dog foods usually supply adequate amounts of niacin
Administer calcium salts; remove nursing puppies, at least temporarily; sedatives may be necessary	Add the correct amount of calcium to the diet	Include recommended levels of calcium and vitamin D in the diet	Meat alone is low in calcium. Such a diet may cause enclampsia unless it is properly supplemented
Once the iodine deficiency symptoms appear in dogs, no treatment is very effective	At the first signs of iodine deficiency, 1% iodized salt (containing .007% iodine) should be included in the diet, with the hope of preventing more goiter, rather than curing existing cases	In iodine deficient areas, include in the diet 1% iodized salt, containing .007% iodine	The enlarged thyroid gland (goiter) is nature's way of attempting to make sufficient thyroxine under conditions where a deficiency exists
Treatment consists in adding the proper quantity of vitamin A to the diet; until the night blindness disappears, double the quantities of vitamin A recommended in the column headed "prevention"	(See Prevention and Treatment)	Include vitamin A in the diet at the following level per pound body weight/day: adult dog, 50 I.U., growing puppy, 100 I.U.	Dogs can convert most of the carotene found in carrots, peaches, green plants, etc., to vitamin A

(Continued)

TABLE 25 (CONTINUED)

Disease	Cause	Symptoms (and age or group most affected)	Distribution and Losses Caused
Osteomalacia	Lack of vitamin D. Inadequate intake of calcium and phosphorus, and/or incorrect ratio of calcium to phosphorus	Osteomalacia, which is a disease of adult dogs, is characterized by frequent lameness and fractures	Southwestern U.S. is classed as a phosphorus-deficient area, whereas calcium-deficient areas have been reported in parts of Florida, Louisiana, Nebraska, Virginia, and West Virginia
Rickets	Lack of either calcium, phosphorus, or vitamin D, or an incorrect ratio of the two minerals	Rickets is a disease of puppies; in rickets, the bones are not calcified and bend or "bow" readily, teeth are irregular and slow to erupt, and blood levels of Ca and P are altered	Worldwide. It is seldom fatal
Scurvy	Deficiency of vitamin C	Dog shows severe pain after being in one position for an extended period of time; for example, after sleeping; when scurvy is severe, the gums may be bleeding and swollen, and there may be extensive hemorrhages under the skin	About one dog in each thousand is affected

- Process(es) and treatment(s) to which product has been subjected
- Stage of maturity
- Cutting or crop
- Grade or quality designations
- Classification

Feeds of the same origin (and the same species, variety, or kind, if one of these is stated) are grouped into eight classes, each of which is designated by a number in parentheses. The numbers and the classes they designate are as follows:

(1) Dry forages or dry roughages
(2) Pasture, range plants, and feeds fed green
(3) Silages
(4) Energy feeds
(5) Protein supplements
(6) Minerals
(7) Vitamins
(8) Additives

Feeds that in the dry state contain on the average more than 18% of crude fiber are classified as *forages or roughages*. Feeds that contain 20% or more of protein are classified as *protein supplements*. Products that contain less than 20% of protein are classified as *energy feeds*. (These guidelines are approximate, and there is some overlapping.)

Abbreviations have been devised for some of the terms in the NRC feed names (Table 26).

The following list shows how three feeds are described:

NUTRITIONAL DISEASES AND AILMENTS

Treatment	Control and Eradication	Prevention	Remarks
Select natural foods that contain sufficient quantities of calcium and phosphorus; include in the diet adequate calcium, phosphorus, and vitamin D; and keep the calcium phosphorus ratio at about 1.2–1.4:1	(See Treatment)	Feed balanced rations	Calcium deficiencies are fairly common in dogs because meats, which are their chief food, are low in this mineral
If the disease has not advanced too far, treatment may be successful by supplying adequate amounts of vitamin D, calcium, and phosphorus, and/or adjusting the ratio of calcium to phosphorus	(See Prevention)	Provide (1) sufficient calcium, phosphorus, and vitamin D, and (2) a correct ratio of the two minerals—a calcium:phosphorus ratio of 1.2–1.4:1	Rickets is characterized by a failure of growing bone to ossify, or harden properly In adult animals this disease is called *osteomalacia* (bone softening)
Add vitamin C to the diet	50 mg of ascorbic acid/dog/day	Include vitamin C in the diet	Many commercial dog foods contain vitamin C, as insurance against scurvy

Components of Name	Feed No. 1	Feed No. 2	Feed No. 3
Origin (or parent material)	Alfalfa	Animal	Cattle
Species, variety, or kind	—	—	—
Part eaten	aerial part	carcass residue	milk
Process(es) and treatment(s) to which product has been subjected	dehy grnd	dry rendered, dehy grnd	skim dehy
Stage of maturity	early bloom	—	—
Cutting or crop	cut 1	—	—
Grade or quality designations	mn 17% protein	mx 4.4% phosphorus	mx 8% moisture
Classification	(1) (dry forages)	(5) (protein supplements)	(5) (protein supplements)

239

Thus, the NRC names of the three feeds are written as follows:

No. 1: Alfalfa, aerial part, dehy grnd, early bloom, cut 1, mn 17% protein, (1)

No. 2: Animal, carcass residue, dry rendered, dehy grnd, mx 4.4% phosphorus, (5)

No. 3: Cattle, milk, skim dehy, mx 8% moisture, (5)

The analytical data are expressed in the metric system (with the exception of the bushel weights of the cereal grains) and are shown on a dry basis. See Table 27 for weight-unit conversion factors and Table 28 for weight equivalents.

LOCATING NAMES IN THE TABLES

To locate in Tables 29 and 30 the NRC name of a feed, one must know the name of the parent material (i.e., the origin of the feed) and usually the variety or kind of parent material. The first word of each NRC name is the name of the parent material. For a feed derived from a plant, the origin term is the name of the plant (e.g., alfalfa, barley, oats), not the word *plant*.

Names having the same origin term are arranged in an order that depends on whether the names include references to species, variety, or kind. Names lacking such references are arranged under the origin term as follows:

First: numerically, by classes

Second (within a class): alphabetically, by parts eaten, process(es), stage of maturity (in the order in which stages occur), cutting, and grade

Names that include references to species, variety, or kind are arranged under the origin term as follows:

First: alphabetically, by species, variety, or kind

Second (within species, variety, or kind): numerically, by classes

Third (within a class): alphabetically, by parts eaten, process(es), stage of maturity (in the order in which the stages occur), cutting, and grade

Many feeds have names that were given to them by the Association of American Feed Control Officials (AAFCO), the Canada Feed Act (CFA), or the Canada Grain Act (CGA). In addition, some feeds have regional or local names. The reader will find these names in their alphabetical place, where they are cross-referenced to the NRC names; he will also find them under the NRC names.

A 6-digit reference number is listed after the NRC name and other names. The first digit is the class of the feed. The number may be used as the "numerical name" of a feed when performing linear programming with electronic computers.

The common name of the parent material is followed by the scientific name. (Example: Alfalfa *Medicago sativa*)

CAROTENE CONVERSION

International standards for vitamin A activity as related to vitamin A and beta-carotene are as follows:

1 IU of vitamin A = 1 USP unit
    = vitamin A activity of 0.300 ug of crystalline vitamin A alcohol, which corresponds to 0.344 ug of vitamin A acetate or 0.550 ug of vitamin A palmitate

Beta-carotene is the standard for provitamin A.

1 IU of vitamin A = 0.6 ug of beta-carotene

1 mg of beta-carotene = 1667 IU of vitamin A

International standards for vitamin A are based on the utilization of vitamin A and beta-carotene by the rat. Since dogs do not convert carotene to vitamin A in the same ratio as rats, it is suggested that the values in Tables 29 and 30 (when used in connection with Tables 10, 11, and 12) be converted as follows:

Converting mg of beta-carotene to IU of vitamin A	1 mg = 833 IU
IU of vitamin A activity (%)[43]	50.0
Factor for converting carotene to vitamin A	2.0

---
[43] Calculated from carotene.

TABLE 26

ABBREVIATIONS FOR TERMS USED IN TABLES 29 AND 30 [44]

AAFCO	Association of American Feed Control Officials	mech	mechanical
Can	Canadian	mech-extd	mechanically extracted, expeller-extracted, hydraulic-extracted, or old process
CE	Canadian Eastern		
CGA	Canada Grain Act	µg	microgram
CFA	Canada Feeds Act	mg	milligram
cp	chemically pure	mm	millimeter
cw	Canadian Western	mn	minimum
dehy	dehydrated	mx	maximum
extd	extracted	NRC	National Research Council
extn	extraction	ppm	parts per million
extn unspec	extraction unspecified	s-c	suncured
g	gram(s)	solv-extd	solvent-extracted
grnd	ground	spp	species
ICU	International Chick Unit	US	United States
IU	International Units	USP	United States Pharmacopeia
kcal	kilocalories	w	with
kg	kilogram(s)	wo	without
lb	pound(s)	wt	weight

[44] From No. 8, *Nutrient Requirements of Dogs*, Revised 1974, National Academy of Sciences, NRC, p. 58, Table 8.

TABLE 27

WEIGHT-UNIT CONVERSION FACTORS [45]

Units Given	Units Wanted	For Conversion Multiply by
lb	g	453.6
lb	kg	0.4536
oz	g	28.35
kg	lb	2.2046
kg	mg	1,000,000.
kg	g	1,000.
g	mg	1,000.
g	µg	1,000,000.
mg	µg	1,000.
mg/g	mg/lb	453.6
mg/kg	mg/lb	0.4536
µg/kg	µg/lb	0.4536
Mcal	kcal	1,000.
kcal/kg	kcal/lb	0.4536
kcal/lb	kcal/kg	2.2046
ppm	µg/g	1.
ppm	mg/kg	1.
ppm	mg/lb	0.4536
mg/kg	%	0.0001
ppm	%	0.0001
mg/g	%	0.1
g/kg	%	0.1

[45] From No. 8, *Nutrient Requirements of Dogs*, Revised 1974, National Academy of Sciences, NRC, p. 58, Table 9.

TABLE 28

WEIGHT EQUIVALENTS [46]

1 lb = 453.6 g = 0.4536 kg = 16 oz
1 oz = 28.35 g
1 kg = 1,000 g = 2.2046 lb
1 g = 1,000 mg
1 mg = 1,000 µg = 0.001 g
1 µg = 0.001 mg = 0.000001 g
1 µg per g or 1 mg per kg is the same as ppm

[46] From No. 8, *Nutrient Requirements of Dogs*, Revised 1974, National Academy of Sciences, NRC, p. 58, Table 10.

TABLE 29

COMPOSITION OF SOME COMMON DOG FOOD INGREDIENTS, EXCLUDING AMINO ACIDS

Line Number	SCIENTIFIC NAME / National Research Council Name (NRC) / American Feed Control Name (AAFCO) / Canada Feed Act Name (CFA) / Other Names	International Reference Number	Dry Matter (%)	ME (kcal/g)	Protein (%)	Ether Extract (%)	Crude Fiber (%)	Nitrogen-Free Extract (%)	Calcium (%)	Copper (mg/kg)	Iodine (mg/kg)	Iron (%)	Magnesium (%)	Manganese (mg/kg)
1	ALFALFA. *Medicago sativa*													
2	-aerial part, dehy grnd, mn 15% protein, (1)	1-00-022	93.1	2.34	16.3	2.5	28.4	43.8	1.32	11.2	.129	.033	.31	31.1
3	-aerial part, dehy grnd, mn 17% protein, (1)	1-00-023	93.0	2.43	19.2	3.2	26.1	41.8	1.43	10.6	.161	.049	.31	31.2
4	-aerial part, dehy grnd, mn 20% protein, (1)	1-00-024	93.1	2.57	22.1	3.9	21.7	41.2	1.63	11.4	.150	.043	.38	36.5
5	ANIMAL. Scientific name not used													
6	-blood, dehy grnd, (5)	5-00-380	91.0	3.36	87.8	1.8	1.1	3.1	.31	10.9	—	.413	.24	5.8
7	Blood meal (AAFCO)													
8	Blood meal (CFA)													
9	-blood, spray dehy, (5)	5-00-381	91.0	3.35	90.3	1.1	1.1	2.2	.49	8.9	—	.330	.04	7.0
10	Blood flour													
11	-carcass residue, dry rendered dehy													
12	grnd, mx 4.4% phosphorus, (5)	5-00-385	93.5	3.02	57.1	10.6	2.6	2.8	8.49	10.4	—	.047	.29	10.2
13	Meat meal (AAFCO)													
14	Meat scrap													
15	-carcass residue w blood, dry or wet													
16	rendered dehy grnd, mx 4.4%													
17	phosphorus, (5)	5-00-386	92.0	3.07	65.0	8.8	2.2	.7	6.46	42.1	—	—	.17	20.8
18	Meat meal tankage													
19	Digester tankage													
20	-carcass residue w bone, dry rendered dehy													
21	grnd, mn 4.4% phosphorus, (5)	5-00-388	94.0	2.87	53.8	10.1	2.3	2.8	11.24	1.6	—	.053	1.20	13.1
22	Meat and bone meal (AAFCO)													
23	Meat and bone scrap													
24	-liver, dehy grnd, (5)	5-00-389	92.6	4.08	71.8	16.3	1.4	4.0	.54	96.4	—	.068	—	9.5
25	Animal liver meal (AAFCO)													
26	Animal liver meal (CFA)													
27	Liver meal													
28	-bone, steamed dehy grnd, (6)	6-00-400	95.0	—	12.7	3.4	2.1	—	30.51	17.2	—	.088	.67	32.0
29	Bone meal, steamed (AAFCO)													
30	-bone phosphate, precipitated dehy,													
31	mn 17% phosphorus, (6)	6-00-406	99.0	—	.4	.3	—	—	28.03	—	—	—	—	—
32	Bone phosphate (AAFCO)													
33	ANIMAL—POULTRY.													
34	-fat, heat rendered, mn 90% fatty acids													
35	mx 2.5% unsaponifiable matter													
36	mx 1% insoluble matter, (4)	4-00-409	99.5	8.65	—	99.5	—	—	—	—	—	—	—	—
37	Animal fat (AAFCO)													
38	BARLEY. *Hordeum vulgare*													
39	-grain, (4)	4-00-530	89.0	3.34	13.0	2.1	5.6	76.6	.09	8.5	—	.005	.13	18.3
40	-grain, Pacific coast, (4)	4-07-939	89.0	3.32	10.9	2.5	7.0	77.0	.07	—	—	—	—	18.0
41	-malt sprouts w hulls, dehy, mn 24%													
42	protein, (5)	5-00-545	93.0	2.83	28.2	1.5	15.1	48.3	.24	—	—	—	.19	34.1
43	Malt sprouts (AAFCO)													
44	BEET, SUGAR. *Beta saccharifera*													
45	-molasses, mn 48% invert sugar mn 79.5													
46	degrees brix, (4)	4-00-668	77.0	3.17	8.7	.3	—	80.4	.21	22.9	—	.013	.30	6.0
47	Beet molasses (AAFCO)													
48	Molasses (CFA)													
49	-pulp, dehy, (4)	4-00-669	91.0	2.69	10.0	.7	20.9	64.5	.74	13.7	—	.033	.30	38.5
50	Dried beet pulp (AAFCO)													
51	Dried beet pulp (CFA)													
52	BLOOD—see ANIMAL													
53	BONE—see ANIMAL													
54	BREAD.													
55	-dehy, (4)	4-07-944	95.0	3.49	11.6	1.1	.5	84.8	.03	—	—	—	—	—
56	BREWERS—see GRAINS													
57	BUTTERMILK—see CATTLE													
58	CALCIUM PHOSPHATE, DIBASIC													
59	-commercial, (6)	6-01-080	96.0	—	—	—	—	—	23.12	—	—	—	—	—
60	Dicalcium phosphate (AAFCO)													
61	CALCIUM—also see LIMESTONE													
62	Calcium Carbonate, $CaCO_3$													
63	-commercial mn 38%													
64	calcium, (6)	6-01-069	96.6	—	—	—	—	—	39.34	—	—	—	.05	—
65	CASEIN—see CATTLE													
66	CATTLE. *Bos* spp													
67	-whey, dehy, mn 65% lactose, (4)	4-01-182	94.0	3.21	14.7	.9	.0	74.1	.93	45.9	—	.017	.14	.49
68	Dried whey (AAFCO)													
69	Whey, dried													
70	-whey low lactose, dehy, mn													
71	lactose, declared, (4)	4-01-186	91.0	3.04	17.3	1.4	.2	65.4	1.70	—	—	—	—	—
72	Dried whey-product (AAFCO)													
73	-buttermilk, condensed, mn 27% total													
74	solids w mn 0.055% fat mx 0.14% ash													
75	per 1% solids, (5)	5-01-159	29.0	3.54	36.7	8.6	—	42.6	1.52	—	—	—	.66	—
76	Condensed buttermilk (AAFCO)													
77	Buttermilk, concentrated													
78	Buttermilk, condensed													
79	Buttermilk, evaporated													
80	-buttermilk, dehy, feed gr mx 8% moisture													
81	mx 13% ash mn 5% fat, (5)	5-01-160	93.0	3.46	34.4	6.2	.0	48.6	1.44	—	—	—	.41	3.8
82	Dried buttermilk, feed grade (AAFCO)													
83	Buttermilk, dried													
84	-casein, milk acid precipitated dehy,													
85	mn 80% protein, (5)	5-01-162	90.0	3.42	90.9	.6	.0	4.8	.68	—	—	—	—	4.9

(1) dry forages and roughages; (2) pasture, range plants, and forages fed green; (3) silages:

(From No. 8, *Nutrient Requirements of Dogs*, Revised 1974, National Academy of Sciences, NRC, pp. 40–51, Table 6.)

TABLE 29 (CONTINUED)
COMPOSITION OF SOME COMMON DOG FOOD INGREDIENTS, EXCLUDING AMINO ACIDS

Dry Basis

Line Number	Potassium (%)	Sodium (%)	Zinc (mg/kg)	Biotin (mg/kg)	Choline (mg/kg)	Folic acid (mg/kg)	Niacin (mg/kg)	Pantothenic acid (mg/kg)	Provitamin A (Carotene) (mg/kg)	Pyridoxine (mg/kg)	Riboflavin (mg/kg)	Thiamin (mg/kg)	Vitamin B$_{12}$ (µg/kg)	Vitamin E (mg/kg)	Vitamin K (mg/kg)
1															
2	2.50	.08	21.5	–	1665.	1.65	45.0	22.4	109.5	6.98	11.4	3.2	–	105.3	10.63
3	2.67	.10	17.2	.35	1632.	2.26	49.2	32.2	108.8	6.77	13.2	3.5	–	137.6	9.35
4	2.71	.92	19.3	–	1738.	2.87	58.7	35.2	232.4	–	16.6	4.2	–	–	–
5															
6	.99	.35	–	–	832.	–	34.6	1.2	–	–	1.6	–	–.	.0	–
7															
8															
9	.45	.36	–	–	306.	–	31.4	5.8	–	–	4.6	.4	–	–	–
10															
11															
12	.59	1.80	–	.10	2091.	.05	60.8	5.1	–	3.21	5.7	.2	54.7	1.1	–
13															
14															
15															
16															
17	.61	1.82	–	–	2358.	1.63	42.6	2.6	–	–	2.6	–	–	–	–
18															
19															
20															
21	1.55	.78	104.2	.15	2329.	.05	50.8	3.9	–	2.65	4.7	1.2	47.6	1.1	–
22															
23															
24	–	–	–	.02	–	6.00	220.0	48.8	–	–	50.0	.2	541.6	–	–
25															
26															
27															
28	–	.48	446.9	–	–	–	4.4	2.5	–	–	.9	.4	–	–	–
29															
30															
31	–	–	–	–	–	–	–	–	–	–	–	–	–	–	–
32															
33															
34															
35															
36	–	–	–	–	–	–	–	–	–	–	–	–	–	–	–
37															
38															
39	.63	.02	17.2	.22	1157.	.56	64.5	7.3	–	3.26	2.2	5.7	–	6.8	–
40	.56	.02	16.8	.17	1053.	.56	49.6	8.2	–	3.26	4.8	4.5	–	40.4	–
41															
42	.22	–	–	–	1703.	.22	46.6	9.2	–	–	1.6	.8	–	–	–
43															
44															
45															
46	6.19	1.52	–	–	–	–	54.8	6.0	–	–	3.1	–	–	–	–
47															
48															
49	.23	–	.8	–	911.	–	17.9	1.6	–	–	.8	.4	–	–	–
50															
51															
52															
53															
54															
55	–	–	–	–	–	–	–	–	–	–	–	–	–	–	–
56															
57															
58															
59	–	–	–	–	–	–	–	–	–	–	–	–	–	–	–
60															
61															
62															
63															
64															
65															
66															
67	1.28	.51	–	.42	21.	.96	11.9	50.7	–	2.66	31.8	3.9	.03	–	–
68	–	–	–	–	–	–	–	–	–	–	–	–	–	–	–
69															
70															
71	–	–	–	–	1944.	–	65.8	75.8	–	–	61.0	–	–	–	–
72															
73															
74															
75	.79	1.07	–	–	–	–	–	–	–	–	49.3	–	–	–	–
76															
77															
78															
79															
80															
81	.76	1.02	–	.32	1944.	.43	9.2	32.4	–	2.58	33.3	3.8	.02	6.8	–
82															
83															
84															
85	–	–	–	–	232.	.44	1.4	2.9	–	.44	1.7	.4	–	–	–

(4) energy feeds; (5) protein supplements; (6) minerals; (7) vitamins; (8) additives.

TABLE 29 (CONTINUED)
COMPOSITION OF SOME COMMON DOG FOOD INGREDIENTS, EXCLUDING AMINO ACIDS

Line Number	SCIENTIFIC NAME / National Research Council Name (NRC) / American Feed Control Name (AAFCO) / Canada Feed Act Name (CFA) / Other Names	International Reference Number	Dry Matter (%)	ME (kcal/g)	Protein (%)	Ether Extract (%)	Crude Fiber (%)	Nitrogen Free Extract (%)	Calcium (%)	Copper (mg/kg)	Iodine (mg/kg)	Iron (%)	Magnesium (%)	Manganese (mg/kg)	Phosphorus (%)
86	Casein (AAFCO)														
87	Casein, dried														
88	-lips, raw, (5)	5-07-940	30.0	—	60.0	23.3	—	—	—	—	—	—	—	—	
89	-liver, raw, (5)	5-01-166	27.2	3.99	73.6	12.5	.0	9.1	.04	—	—	—	—	—	
90	Beef liver														
91	-lungs, raw, (5)	5-07-941	20.0	—	80.0	15.0	—	—	—	—	—	—	—	—	
92	-milk, dehy, feed gr mx 8% moisture mn 26% fat, (5)	5-01-167	93.7	4.76	26.9	28.2	.2	38.9	.95		—	.018	—	.4	
93															
94	Dried whole milk (AAFCO)														
95	Milk, whole, dried														
96	-milk, skimmed dehy, mx 8% moisture, (5)	5-01-175	94.0	3.28	35.6	1.0	.2	55.1	1.34	12.2		.005	.12	2.3	
97	Dried skimmed milk, feed grade (AAFCO)														
98	Milk, skimmed, dried														
99	-spleen, raw, (5)	5-07-942	25.0	3.92	72.0	16.0	—	—	—	—		—	—	—	
100	Cattle, melts, raw														
101	-udders, raw, (5)	5-07-943	25.0	5.74	48.0	48.0	—	—	—	—		—	—	—	
102	CHICKEN. *Gallus domesticus*														
103	-broilers, whole, raw, (5)	5-07-945	24.3	4.27	76.5	20.2	—	—	—	—	—	—	—	—	
104	-cull hens, whole, raw, (5)	5-07-950	57.9	3.95	27.6	35.2	.9	—	—	—	—	—	—	—	
105	-day-old chicks, whole, raw, (5)	5-07-946	24.4	4.04	57.0	23.5	3.6	—	—	—	—	—	—	—	
106	-eggs w shells, raw, (5)	5-01-213	34.1	4.01	37.5	31.1	.0	.0	4.40	—	—	—	—	—	
107	-feet, raw, (5)	5-07-947	47.0	3.15	53.2	23.4	—	—	—	—	—	—	—	—	
108	-gizzards, raw, (5)	5-07-948	25.0	5.14	80.4	10.5	.0	2.8	—	—	—	—	—	—	
109	-heads, raw, (5)	5-07-949	33.0	3.47	57.6	18.2	—	—	—	—	—	—	—	—	
110	-offal w feet, raw, (5)	5-07-951	31.0	4.64	42.3	41.6	—	—	2.64	—	—	—	—	—	
111	-offal wo feet, raw, (5)	5-07-952	27.0	5.09	43.7	42.2	.7	—	1.00	—	—	—	—	—	
112	CITRUS. *Citrus* spp														
113	-pulp wo fines, shredded dehy, (4)	4-01-237	90.0	3.04	7.3	5.1	14.4	66.5	2.18	6.3	—	.018	.18	7.6	
114	Dried citrus pulp (AAFCO)														
115	Citrus pulp, dried														
116	COCONUT. *Cocos nucifera*														
117	-meats, mech-extd grnd, (5)	5-01-572	93.0	3.17	21.9	7.1	12.9	50.7	.23	20.1	—	.211	.28	59.6	
118	Coconut meal, mechanical extracted (AAFCO)														
119	Copra meal, expeller (AAFCO)														
120	Coconut meal, hydraulic														
121	Copra meal, hydraulic														
122	-meats, solv-extd grnd, (5)	5-01-573	92.0	2.83	22.9	2.0	16.1	52.5	.18					59.8	
123	Coconut meal, solvent extracted (AAFCO)														
124	Solvent extracted copra meal (AAFCO)														
125	CORN. *Zea mays*														
126	-grain, flaked, (4)	4-02-859	97.0	3.20	8.0	.3	.4	82.0	.01	—	—	—	—	—	
127	Flaked corn (AAFCO)														
128	Corn grain, flaked														
129	-grits byproduct, mn 5% fat, (4)	4-02-887	90.6	3.60	11.8	7.2	5.5	72.7	.06	16.1	—	.007	.26	16.1	
130	Hominy feed (AAFCO)														
131	Hominy feed (CFA)														
132	-distillers grains w solubles, dehy, mn 75% original solids, (5)	5-02-843	91.0	3.48	29.7	8.8	9.3	47.5	.38	54.9	.05	.022	.38	33.0	
133															
134	Corn distillers dried grains with solubles (AAFCO)														
135															
136	-distillers solubles, dehy, (5)	5-02-844	95.5	3.57	29.8	9.4	4.2	48.4	.31	57.6	.05	.021	.62	62.8	
137	Corn distillers dried solubles (AAFCO)														
138	-germ wo solubles, wet milled solv-extd dehy grnd, (5)	5-02-898	93.0	3.07	19.4	2.2	12.9	62.2	.11	—	—	—	—	17.2	
139															
140	Corn germ meal, solvent extracted, (wet milled) (AAFCO)														
141															
142	-gluten, wet milled dehy, (5)	5-02-900	91.0	3.40	47.1	2.5	4.4	43.4	.18	31.0	—	.044	.05	8.0	
143	Corn gluten meal (AAFCO)														
144	Corn gluten meal (CFA)														
145	CORN, DENT YELLOW. *Zea mays indentata*														
146	-grain, (4)	4-02-935	86.0	3.62	10.2	4.4	2.3	81.8	.03	4.0	—	.003	.17	4.8	
147	-grain, grnd cooked, (4)	4-07-953	88.0	3.60	10.5	4.5	2.4	80.6	.02	—	—	—	—	—	
148	CORN, FLINT. *Zea mays indurata*														
149	-grain, (4)	4-02-948	89.0	3.64	11.1	4.8	2.2	80.3	—	13.0	—	.003	—	7.9	
150	CORN, WHITE. *Zea mays*														
151	-grits by-prod, mn 5% fat, (4)	4-02-990	89.9	3.53	12.0	6.3	5.2	72.7	.06	—	—	—	—	—	
152	White hominy feed (AAFCO)														
153	White hominy feed (CFA)														
154	Hominy, white corn, feed														
155	Corn, white, hominy feed														
156	COTTON. *Gossypium* spp														
157	-seed w some hulls, mech-extd grnd, mn 41% protein mx 14% fiber mn 2% fat, (5)	5-01-617	94.0	3.08	43.6	4.6	12.8	32.4	.17	20.7	—	.032	.60	22.9	
158															
159	Cottonseed meal, 41% protein														
160	-seed w some hulls, pre-press solv-extd grnd, 41% protein, (5)	5-07-872	92.5	2.88	43.6	1.5	12.7	34.5	.17	20.7	—	.032	.60	22.9	
161															
162	Cottonseed meal, pre-press solvent extracted, 41% protein														
163															
164	-seed w some hulls, solv-extd grnd, mn 41% protein mx 14% fiber mn 0.5% fat, (5)	5-01-621	91.5	2.94	44.8	2.2	13.1	33.1	.17	21.3	—	.033	.61	23.5	
165															
166	Cottonseed meal, solvent extracted, 41% protein														
167															
168	-seed wo hulls, pre-press solv-extd grnd, mn 50% protein, (5)	5-07-874	92.5	3.03	54.0	1.3	9.2	28.8	.17	19.4	—	.012	.50	24.6	
169															
170	Cottonseed meal, pre-press solvent extracted, 50% protein														
171															

(1) dry forages and roughages; (2) pasture, range plants, and forages fed green; (3) silages;

TABLE 29 (CONTINUED)
COMPOSITION OF SOME COMMON DOG FOOD INGREDIENTS, EXCLUDING AMINO ACIDS

Dry Basis

Line Number	Potassium (%)	Sodium (%)	Zinc (mg/kg)	Biotin (mg/kg)	Choline (mg/kg)	Folic acid (mg/kg)	Niacin (mg/kg)	Pantothenic acid (mg/kg)	Provitamin A (Carotene) (mg/kg)	Pyridoxine (mg/kg)	Riboflavin (mg/kg)	Thiamin (mg/kg)	Vitamin B₁₂ (µg/kg)	Vitamin E (mg/kg)	Vitamin K (mg/kg)
86															
87															
88	—	—	—	—	—	—	—	—	—	—	—	—	—	—	—
89	—	—	—	—	—	—	—	—	—	—	—	—	—	—	—
90															
91															
92															
93	1.08	.38	—	.39	—	—	9.0	24.2	7.5	4.94	20.9	3.9	—	—	—
94															
95															
96	1.78	.53	42.6	3.5	1517.	.66	12.2	35.8	—	4.22	21.4	3.7	44.57	9.8	—
97															
98															
99	—	—	—	—	—	—	—	—	—	—	—	—	—	—	—
100															
101	—	—	—	—	—	—	—	—	—	—	—	—	—	—	—
102															
103	—	—	—	—	—	—	—	—	—	—	—	—	—	—	—
104	—	—	—	—	—	—	—	—	—	—	—	—	—	—	—
105	—	—	—	—	—	—	—	—	—	—	—	—	—	—	—
106	—	—	—	—	—	—	—	—	—	—	—	—	—	—	—
107	—	—	—	—	—	—	—	—	—	—	—	—	—	—	—
108	—	—	—	—	—	—	—	—	—	—	—	—	—	—	—
109	—	—	—	—	—	—	—	—	—	—	—	—	—	—	—
110	—	—	—	—	—	—	—	—	—	—	—	—	—	—	—
111	—	—	—	—	—	—	—	—	—	—	—	—	—	—	—
112															
113	.69	—	16.1	—	939.	—	24.0	14.4	—	—	2.7	1.7	—	—	—
114															
115															
116															
117	1.20	.04	—	—	989.	1.40	26.8	7.1	—	—	3.3	.8	—	—	—
118															
119															
120															
121															
122	—	.04	—	—	1196.	.33	26.0	7.2	—	4.78	14.3	1.0	—	—	—
123															
124															
125															
126	—		—	—	—	—	21.6	—	—	—	1.3	4.2	—	—	—
127															
128															
129	.74	.44	—	.14	1104.	.31	56.4	8.3	10.1	12.14	2.2	8.7	—	—	—
130															
131															
132															
133	1.10	.05	87.9	.33	3700.	1.10	84.6	12.1	4.0	7.10	9.9	3.8	1.60	43.4	—
134															
135															
136	2.20	.16	104.7	.52	6100.	1.80	125.6	23.0	.8	13.60	23.0	7.3	7.00	59.1	—
137															
138															
139	.22	—	—	3.22	1935.	.22	37.7	4.4	—	—	4.4	1.1	—	93.5	—
140															
141															
142	.03	.11	—	.16	363.	.22	54.8	11.3	—	8.79	1.6	.2	—	46.2	—
143															
144															
145															
146	.38	.01	12.1	.07	624.	.22	26.6	5.8	4.8	8.37	1.3	4.6	—	25.6	—
147	—	—	—	—	—	—	—	—	—	—	—	—	—	—	—
148															
149	—	—	—	—	—	—	17.8	—	—	—	—	—	—	—	—
150															
151	—	—	—	—	—	—	61.5	7.5	—	—	2.4	14.6	—	—	—
152															
153															
154															
155															
156															
157															
158	1.49	.04	—	—	2957.	2.45	42.0	14.9	—	5.64	5.3	6.9	—	42.6	—
159															
160															
161	1.49	.04	—	—	3042.	2.45	42.0	14.9	—	—	5.3	6.9	—	—	—
162															
163															
164															
165	1.53	.04	—	.11	3126.	2.51	43.2	15.3	—	6.99	5.5	7.1	—	16.4	—
166															
167															
168															
169	1.36	.05	79.2	.11	3568.	1.19	55.1	16.2	—	7.57	6.2	—	—	16.2	—
170															
171															

(4) energy feeds; (5) protein supplements; (6) minerals; (7) vitamins; (8) additives.

TABLE 29 (CONTINUED)
COMPOSITION OF SOME COMMON DOG FOOD INGREDIENTS, EXCLUDING AMINO ACIDS

Line Number	SCIENTIFIC NAME / National Research Council Name (NRC) / American Feed Control Name (AAFCO) / Canada Feed Act Name (CFA) / Other Names	International Reference Number	Dry Matter (%)	ME (kcal/g)	Protein (%)	Ether Extract (%)	Crude Fiber (%)	Nitrogen-Free Extract (%)	Calcium (%)	Copper (mg/kg)	Iodine (mg/kg)	Iron (%)	Magnesium (%)	Manganese (mg/kg)	Phosphorus (%)
172	CRAB. *Callinectes sapidus, Cancer* spp														
173	*Paralithodes canschatica*														
174	-processed residue, dehy grnd, mn 25%														
175	protein salt declared above 3%														
176	mx 7%, (5)	5-01-663	93.0	1.62	33.4	1.9	11.8	9.1	16.47	35.3	—	.473	.95	143.9	1.71
177	Crab meal (AAFCO)														
178	DISTILLERS—see CORN														
179	FAT—see ANIMAL														
180	FISH.														
181	-livers, extn unspecified dehy grnd,														
182	salt declared above 4%, (5)	5-01-968	93.0	4.17	71.5	16.8	1.1	5.8	.54	95.8	—	.075	—	9.5	1.34
183	Fish liver meal (CFA)														
184	-soluble, condensed, mn 30% protein, (5)	5-01-969	51.0	3.41	61.6	12.7	2.0	4.1	1.20	94.5	—	.059	.04	23.3	1.37
185	Condensed fish solubles (AAFCO)														
186	-stickwater soluble, cooked dehy, mn														
187	60% protein, (5)	5-01-971	92.0	3.30	68.3	8.3	1.1	5.1	—	—	—	—	—	—	—
188	Dried fish solubles (AAFCO)														
189	Fish solubles, dried														
190	FISH, ALEWIFE. *Pomolobus pseudoharengus*														
191	-whole, raw, (5)	5-07-964	26.0	4.30	75.0	19.2	—	—	—	—	—	—	—	—	—
192	-whole or cuttings, cooked mech-extd														
193	dehy grnd, (5)	5-09-830	91.0	2.07	62.6	—	—	—	—	—	—	—	—	—	—
194	Fish meal, alewife														
195	FISH, ANCHOVY. *Engraulis* spp														
196	-whole or cuttings, cooked mech-extd														
197	dehy grnd, (5)	5-01-985	93.0	2.84	70.9	5.8	1.1	—	4.84	—	—	—	—	23.6	3.06
198	Fish meal, anchovy														
199	FISH, CARP. *Cyprinus carpio*														
200	-whole, raw, (5)	5-01-986	22.0	3.86	84.1	10.4	—	—	—	—	—	—	—	—	—
201	-whole or cuttings, cooked dehy grnd, (5)	5-09-831	90.8	2.46	74.4	—	.8	—	—	—	—	—	—	—	—
202	Fish meal, carp														
203	FISH, CATFISH. *Ictalurus* spp														
204	-whole, raw, (5)	5-07-965	17.5	3.52	94.3	2.3	—	—	—	—	—	—	—	—	—
205	-whole or cuttings, cooked mech-extd dehy														
206	grnd, (5)	5-09-835	93.9	1.82	55.3	—	—	—	7.77	27.7	—	—	—	—	—
207	Fish meal, catfish														
208	-whole or cuttings, cooked mech-extd														
209	press cake, (5)	5-09-834	47.1	1.73	52.4	—	—	—	—	—	—	.040	.18	40.4	4.04
210	-whole or cuttings, cooked pasteurized, (5)	5-09-833	39.9	2.45	69.7	—	—	—	—	7.5	—	.050	1.25	15.0	2.43
211	-whole or cuttings, raw, (5)	5-09-832	42.2	2.27	64.5	—	—	—	5.57	7.1	—	.009	.12	10.6	2.55
212	FISH, FLOUNDER. Bothidae (family),														
213	Pleuronectidae (family)														
214	-whole, raw, (5)	5-01-996	17.0	3.36	88.2	2.9	—	—	—	—	—	—	—	—	—
215	FISH, HADDOCK. *Melanogrammus aeglefinus*														
216	-whole, raw, (5)	5-07-966	18.0	3.47	94.4	1.7	—	—	—	—	—	—	—	—	—
217	FISH, HAKE. *Merluccius* spp. *Urophycis* spp														
218	-whole, cooked (5)	5-07-967	30.0	3.65	57.4	18.8	—	—	—	—	—	—	—	—	—
219	-whole, cooked acidified, (5)	5-07-968	25.0	—	—	21.2	1.1	—	—	—	—	—	—	—	—
220	-whole, raw, (5)	5-07-969	19.0	3.65	89.5	5.8	—	—	—	—	—	—	—	—	—
221	FISH, HERRING. *Clupea harengus harengus*,														
222	*Clupea harengus pallasi*														
223	-whole, raw, (5)	5-01-999	26.0	4.26	69.2	21.1	—	—	—	—	—	—	—	—	—
224	-whole or cuttings, cooked mech-extd														
225	dehy grnd, (5)	5-02-000	92.0	3.36	76.7	8.2	1.1	3.4	3.20	—	—	—	—	10.8	2.39
226	Fish meal, herring														
227	FISH, MACKEREL ATLANTIC. *Scomber scombrus*														
228	-whole, raw, (5)	5-07-971	32.0	5.28	57.8	37.5	—	—	—	—	—	—	—	—	—
229	FISH, MACKEREL PACIFIC. *Scomber japonicus*														
230	-whole, raw, (5)	5-07-972	31.0	4.62	71.0	24.5	—	—	—	—	—	—	—	—	—
231	FISH, MENHADEN. *Brevoortia tyrannus*														
232	-whole or cuttings, cooked mech-extd														
233	dehy grnd, (5)	5-02-009	92.0	3.02	66.6	8.4	1.1	2.6	5.97	9.1	—	.061	—	27.9	3.05
234	Fish meal, menhaden														
235	FISH, REDFISH. *Sciaenops ocellata*														
236	-whole, raw, (5)	5-08-113	19.8	3.37	90.9	2.0	.6	—	—	—	—	—	—	—	—
237	Drumfish, whole, raw														
238	Ocean perch, whole, raw														
239	-whole or cuttings, cooked mech-extd dehy grnd, (5)	5-07-973	94.2	2.66	58.4	8.5	1.1	—	4.20	—	—	—	—	—	2.40
240	Fish meal, drum														
241	Fish meal, redfish														
242	FISH, ROCKFISH. *Sebastodes* spp														
243	-whole, raw, (5)	5-07-974	32.0	3.74	50.7	22.6	—	—	—	—	—	—	—	—	—
244	FISH, SALMON. *Oncorhynchus* spp. *Salmo* spp														
245	-whole, raw, (5)	5-02-011	35.0	5.42	62.8	37.1	—	—	—	—	—	—	—	—	—
246	-whole or cuttings, cooked mech-extd														
247	dehy grnd, (5)	5-02-012	93.0	3.20	62.4	10.4	—	6.8	5.85	12.8	—	.020	—	7.9	3.26
248	Fish meal, salmon														
249	FISH, SARDINE. *Clupea* spp, *Sardinops* spp														
250	-whole or cuttings, cooked mech-extd														
251	dehy grnd, (5)	5-02-015	93.0	2.97	70.4	4.6	1.1	7.0	5.27	21.7	—	.032	.11	23.9	2.98
252	FISH, SMELT. *Asmerus* spp														
253	-whole, raw, (5)	5-07-975	21.0	3.76	85.7	8.6	—	—	—	—	—	—	—	—	—
254	FISH, SOLE. Soleidae (family)														
255	-whole, raw, (5)	5-07-976	19.0	3.33	72.3	9.1	—	—	3.32	—	—	—	—	—	2.30
256	FISH, TUNA. *Thunnus thynnus*														
257	-process residue, (5)	5-07-977	44.0	3.69	54.8	21.8	—	—	—	—	—	—	—	—	—

(1) dry forages and roughages; (2) pasture, range plants, and forages fed green; (3) silages;

TABLE 29 (CONTINUED)
COMPOSITION OF SOME COMMON DOG FOOD INGREDIENTS, EXCLUDING AMINO ACIDS

Dry Basis

Line Number	Potassium (%)	Sodium (%)	Zinc (mg/kg)	Biotin (mg/kg)	Choline (mg/kg)	Folic acid (mg/kg)	Niacin (mg/kg)	Pantothenic acid (mg/kg)	Provitamin A (Carotene) (mg/kg)	Pyridoxine (mg/kg)	Riboflavin (mg/kg)	Thiamin (mg/kg)	Vitamin B$_{12}$ (μg/kg)	Vitamin E (mg/kg)	Vitamin K (mg/kg)
172															
173															
174															
175															
176	.48	.91	—	—	2150.	—	47.3	6.1	—	—	6.3	—	—	—	—
177															
178															
179															
180															
181															
182	—	—	—	—	—	—	—	—	—	—	—	—	—	—	—
183															
184	3.43	6.00	75.1	.39	7898.	—	330.8	69.4	—	—	28.4	10.8			
185															
186															
187	—	—	—	—	5677.	—	251.2	48.8	—	—	8.4	—	—	—	—
188															
189															
190															
191	—	—	—	—	—	—	—	—	—	—	—	—	—	—	—
192															
193	—	—	—	—	—	—	—	—	—	—	—	—	—	—	—
194															
195															
196															
197	.54	.86	118.2	.39	3978.	.22	68.8	9.46	—	3.76	7.1	—	.11	3.6	—
198															
199															
200	—	—	—	—	—	—	—	—	—	—	—	—	—	—	—
201	—	—	—	—	—	—	—	—	—	—	—	—	—	—	—
202															
203	—	—	—	—	—	—	—	—	—	—	—	—	—	—	—
204	—	—	—	—	—	—	—	—	—	—	—	—	—	—	—
205															
206	—	—	—	—	—	—	—	—	—	—	—	—	—	—	—
207															
208															
209	.58	.65	121.4	—	—	—	—	—	—	—	—	—	—	—	—
210	.45	.50	90.2	—	—	—	—	—	—	—	—	—	—	—	—
211	.25	.34	67.9	—	—	—	—	—	—	—	—	—	—	—	—
212															
213															
214	—	—	—	—	—	—	—	—	—	—	—	—	—	—	—
215															
216	—	—	—	—	—	—	—	—	—	—	—	—	—	—	—
217															
218	—	—	—	—	—	—	—	—	—	—	—	—	—	—	—
219	—	—	—	—	—	—	—	—	—	—	—	—	—	—	—
220	—	—	—	—	—	—	—	—	—	—	—	—	—	—	—
221															
222															
223	—	—	—	—	—	—	—	—	—	—	—	—	—	—	—
224															
225	.54	.54	—	.46	4352.	2.61	96.6	12.4	—	4.02	9.8	—	237.70	29.3	.00
226															
227															
228															
229															
230	—	—	—	—	—	—	—	—	—	—	—	—	—	—	—
231															
232															
233	.76	.33	163.0	.28	3348.	.22	60.8	9.6	—	—	5.2	.8	.11	9.8	—
234															
235															
236	1.36	.30	—	—	—	—	176.8	—	—	—	2.5	7.6	—	—	—
237															
238															
239	—	—	—	—	1486.	—	28.7	2.6	—	—	3.1	—	—	—	—
240															
241															
242															
243	—	—	—	—	—	—	—	—	—	—	—	—	—	—	—
244															
245	—	—	—	—	—	—	—	—	—	—	—	—	—	—	—
246															
247	—	—	—	—	2772.	—	24.9	6.8	—	—	5.7	.9	—	—	—
248															
249															
250															
251	.35	.19	—	—	3182.	—	66.7	9.9	—	—	6.3	.4	—	—	—
252															
253	—	—	—	—	—	—	—	—	—	—	—	—	—	—	—
254															
255	—	—	—	—	—	—	—	—	—	—	—	—	—	—	—
256															
257	—	—	—	—	—	—	—	—	—	—	—	—	—	—	—

(4) energy feeds; (5) protein supplements; (6) minerals; (7) vitamins; (8) additives.

TABLE 29
COMPOSITION OF SOME COMMON DOG FEEDS, EXCLUDING AMINO ACIDS

Dry Basis

Line Number	SCIENTIFIC NAME / National Research Council Name (NRC) / American Feed Control Name (AAFCO) / Canada Feed Act Name (CFA) / Other Names	International Reference Number	Dry Matter (%)	ME (kcal/g)	Protein (%)	Ether Extract (%)	Crude Fiber (%)	Nitrogen-Free Extract (%)	Calcium (%)	Copper (mg/kg)	Iodine (mg/kg)	Iron (%)	Magnesium (%)	Manganese (mg/kg)	Phosphorus (%)
258	-whole or cuttings, cooked mech-extd														
259	dehy grnd, (5)	5-02-023	87.0	2.82	65.9	7.5	1.1	3.6	6.11	—	—	—	—	—	3.53
260	Fish meal, tuna														
261	FISH, TURBOT. *Psetta maxima*														
262	-whole, raw, (5)	5-07-978	27.0	5.22	53.2	38.7	—	—	1.46	—	—	—	—	—	1.17
263	FISH, WHITE. Gadidae (family), Lophiidae (family),														
264	Rajidae (family)														
265	-whole or cuttings, cooked mech-extd														
266	dehy grnd, mx 4% oil, (5)	5-02-025	92.0	2.90	68.7	4.8	1.1	1.8	8.55	—	—	—	—	15.5	3.92
267	White fish meal (CFA)														
268	Fish, cod, meal														
269	Fish, cusk, meal														
270	Fish, haddock, meal														
271	Fish, hake, meal														
272	Fish, pollock, meal														
273	Fish, monkfish, meal														
274	Fish, skate, meal														
275	FISH, WHITING. *Gadus merlangus*														
276	-whole, raw, (5)	5-07-979	23.0	3.21	69.9	8.7									
277	FLAX. *Linum usitatissimum*														
278	-seed, mech-extd grnd, mx 0.5% acid														
279	insoluble ash, (5)	5-02-045	91.0	3.25	38.8	5.7	9.9	39.4	.48	29.0	—	.019	.64	43.3	9.8
280	Linseed meal, mechanical extracted (AAFCO)														
281	Linseed meal (CFA)														
282	Linseed oil meal, expeller extracted														
283	Linseed oil meal, hydraulic extracted														
284	Linseed meal, old process														
285	-seed screenings, mech-extd grnd, (5)	5-02-054	91.0	3.33	17.4	10.3	13.2	51.7	.41	—	—	—	—	—	.47
286	Flaxseed screenings meal (AAFCO)														
287	-seed, solv-extd grnd, mx 0.5% acid														
288	insoluble ash, (5)	5-02-048	91.0	3.05	38.6	1.9	9.9	43.2	.44	28.2	—	.036	.66	41.3	.91
289	Linseed meal, solvent extracted (AAFCO)														
290	Solvent extracted linseed meal (CFA)														
291	Linseed oil meal, solvent extracted														
292	GRAINS.														
293	-brewers grains, dehy, mx 3% dried														
294	spent hops, (5)	5-02-141	92.0	3.16	28.2	6.7	16.3	45.0	.29	23.2	—	.027	.15	40.9	.54
295	Brewers dried grains (AAFCO)														
296	Brewers dried grains (CFA)														
297	-distillers grains, dehy, (5)	5-02-144	92.5	3.24	29.2	8.2	13.8	42.5	.05	16.2	.05	.014	.08	10.8	.40
298	HOMINY FEED—see CORN														
299	HORSE. *Equus caballus*														
300	-meat, raw, (5)	5-07-980	24.0	4.08	75.0	16.7	—	—	.13	—	—	—	—	—	1.6
301	-meat w bone, raw grnd, (5)	5-07-981	36.0	3.49	51.4	19.4									
302	LARD—see SWINE														
303	LIMESTONE.														
304	-grnd, mn 33% calcium, (6)	6-02-632	100.0	—	—	—	—	—	33.84	—	—	.330	—	275.6	.0
305	Limestone, ground (AAFCO)														
306	LINSEED—see FLAX														
307	LIVER—see ANIMAL														
308	MAIZE—see CORN														
309	MALT—see BARLEY														
310	MEAT—see ANIMAL														
311	MILK—see CATTLE														
312	MILLET. *Setaria* spp														
313	-grain, (4)	4-03-098	90.0	3.31	13.3	4.4	8.9	69.9	.06	24.0	—	.004	.18	32.3	.3
314	MOLASSES—see BEET, SUGAR, see SUGARCANE														
315	OATS. *Avena sativa*														
316	-hulls, (1)	1-03-281	93.0	2.39	6.0	2.2	29.0	56.3	.17	5.5	—	.011	.09	19.9	.2
317	Oat hulls (AAFCO)														
318	Oat hulls (CFA)														
319	-cereal byproduct, mx 4% fiber, (4)	4-03-303	91.0	3.61	17.4	6.4	4.3	69.3	.09	—	—	.042	—	48.4	.5
320	Feeding oat meal (AAFCO)														
321	Oat middlings (CFA)														
322	-grain, (4)	4-03-309	89.0	3.22	13.2	5.1	12.4	65.7	.11	6.6	—	.008	.19	42.9	.3
323	-grain, gr 1 US mn wt 34 lb per bushel														
324	mx 2% foreign material, (4)	4-03-313	91.0	3.21	13.3	5.3	13.2	64.7	.09	—	—	—	—	41.8	.3
325	-grain, gr 2 heavy US mn wt 36 lb per														
326	bushel mx 3% foreign material, (4)	4-03-315	89.5	3.25	13.5	4.5	10.9	67.6	—	—	—	—	—	—	
327	Oats, grain, heavy														
328	-grain, gr 2 US mn wt 32 lb per bushel														
329	mx 3% foreign material, (4)	4-03-316	89.0	3.21	12.7	4.7	12.4	66.9	.07						
330	OATS. *Avena sativa*														
331	-grain, gr 3 US mn wt 30 lb per bushel														
332	mx 4% foreign material, (4)	4-03-317	91.0	3.15	13.3	5.1	14.3	63.6	—						
333	-grain, gr 4 US mn wt 27 lb per bushel														
334	mx 5% foreign material, (4)	4-03-318	91.2	3.01	13.2	4.9	16.6	60.2	—						
335	Oats, grain, light														
336	-groats, (4)	4-03-331	91.0	3.65	18.4	6.4	3.3	69.5	.08	0.4	—	—	.98	31.4	.4
337	Oat groats (AAFCO)														
338	Oat groats (CFA)														
339	Hulled oats (CFA)														
340	-groats, grnd cooked, (4)	4-07-982	91.0	3.65	18.4	6.4	3.3	69.5	.08	—	—	—	—	—	.4
341	OATS, WHITE. *Avena sativa*														
342	-grain, Can 2 CW mn wt 36 lb per bushel														
343	mx 3% foreign material, (4)	4-03-378	86.5	3.25	13.2	5.2	12.0	66.1	—						

(1) dry forages and roughages; (2) pasture, range plants, and forages fed green; (3) silages;

TABLE 29 (CONTINUED)

COMPOSITION OF SOME COMMON DOG FEEDS, EXCLUDING AMINO ACIDS

Dry Basis

Line Number	Potassium (%)	Sodium (%)	Zinc (mg/kg)	Biotin (mg/kg)	Choline (mg/kg)	Folic acid (mg/kg)	Niacin (mg/kg)	Pantothenic acid (mg/kg)	Provitamin A (Carotene) (mg/kg)	Pyridoxine (mg/kg)	Riboflavin (mg/kg)	Thiamin (mg/kg)	Vitamin B$_{12}$ (µg/kg)	Vitamin E (mg/kg)	Vitamin K (mg/kg)
258															
259	–	–	–	–	–	–	–	–	–	–	–	–	–	–	
260															
261				,											
262	–	–	–	–	–	–	–	–	–	–	–	–	–	–	–
263															
264															
265															
266	.54	.65	–	.09	9692.	.22	75.7	9.6	–	3.59	9.8	2.0	.11	9.8	–
267															
268															
269															
270															
271															
272															
273															
274															
275	–	–	–	–	–	–	–	–	–	–	–	–	–	–	–
276															
277															
278															
279	1.36	.12	–	–	2047.	3.19	39.1	19.6	.2	–	3.8	5.6	–	–	–
280															
281															
282															
283															
284	–	–	–	–	–	–	–	–	–	–	–	–	–	–	–
285															
286															
287															
288	1.52	.15	–	–	1346.	–	33.1	–	–	–	3.2	10.4	–	–	–
289															
290															
291															
292															
293															
294	.09	.28	–	–	1725.	.24	47.2	9.3	–	.72	1.6	.8	–	–	–
295															
296															
297	.16	.05	54.1	.22	1100.	1.20	45.4	7.1	8.4	4.30	3.4	2.2	.25	–	–
298															
299															
300	–	–	–	–	–	–	–	–	–	–	–	–	–	–	–
301	–	–	–	–	–	–	–	–	–	–	–	–	–	–	–
302															
303															
304	–	.06	–	–	–	–	–	–	–	–	–	–	–	–	–
305															
306															
307															
308															
309															
310															
311															
312															
313	.48	.04	15.4	–	877.	–	58.4	8.2	–	–	1.8	7.3	–	–	–
314															
315															
316	.63	.04	–	–	473.	–	10.7	3.5	–	–	4.9	–	–	–	–
317															
318															
319	.55	.05	483.5	.24	1319.	.38	30.9	25.4	–	2.42	2.0	7.7	–	26.4	–
320															
321															
322	.42	.07	–	.34	1206.	.45	17.8	14.5	–	1.35	1.8	7.0	–	6.6	–
323															
324	.41	.07	–	.12	1209.	.33	19.8	14.3	–	1.43	1.2	–	–	22.0	–
325															
326	–	–	–	–	–	–	–	–	–	–	–	–	–	–	–
327															
328															
329	–	–	–	–	–	–	–	–	–	–	–	–	–	–	–
330															
331															
332	–	–	–	–	–	–	–	–	–	–	–	–	–	–	–
333															
334	–	–	–	–	–	–	–	–	–	–	–	–	–	–	–
335															
336	.37	–	–	–	–	–	8.9	16.2	–	1.21	1.4	7.5	–	–	–
337															
338															
339															
340	–	–	–	–	–	–	–	–	–	–	–	–	–	–	–
341															
342															
343															–

(4) energy feeds; (5) protein supplements; (6) minerals; (7) vitamins; (8) additives.

TABLE 29 (CONTINUED)
COMPOSITION OF SOME COMMON DOG FEEDS, EXCLUDING AMINO ACIDS

Dry Basis

Line Number	SCIENTIFIC NAME / National Research Council Name (NRC) / American Feed Control Name (AAFCO) / Canada Feed Act Name (CFA) / Other Names	International Reference Number	Dry Matter (%)	ME (kcal/g)	Protein (%)	Ether Extract (%)	Crude Fiber (%)	Nitrogen-Free Extract (%)	Calcium (%)	Copper (mg/kg)	Iodine (mg/kg)	Iron (%)	Magnesium (%)	Manganese (mg/kg)	Phosphorus (%)
344	-grain, Can 2 feed mn wt 28 lb per bushel mx 22% foreign material, (4)	4-03-379	86.5	3.24	12.7	5.1	12.0	66.8	—	—	—	—	—	—	—
345															
346	-grain, Can 3 CW mn wt 34 lb per bushel mx 6% foreign material, (4)	4-03-380	86.5	3.25	12.7	5.3	12.1	66.5	—	—	—	—	—	—	—
347															
348	OYSTERS. *Crassostrea* spp, *Ostrea* spp														
349	-shells, fine grnd, mn 33% calcium, (6)	6-03-481	100.0	—	1.0	—	—	—	38.05	—	—	.290	.30	133.3	.07
350	Oyster shell flour (AAFCO)														
351	PEA. *Pisum* spp														
352	-seed, grnd, (5)	5-03-598	91.0	3.14	24.7	2.1	9.9	59.2	.19	—	—	—	—	—	.55
353	PEANUT. *Arachis hypogaea*														
354	-kernels, mech-extd grnd, mx 7% fiber, (5)	5-03-649	92.0	3.44	49.8	8.2	12.0	27.7	.18	—	—	—	.36	27.7	.62
355	Peanut meal, mechanical extracted (AAFCO)														
356	Peanut meal (CFA)														
357	Peanut oil meal, expeller extracted														
358	-kernels, solv-extd grnd, mx 7% fiber, (5)	5-03-650	92.0	2.92	51.5	1.3	14.1	28.2	.22	—	—	—	.04	31.5	.71
359	Peanut meal, solvent extracted (AAFCO)														
360	Groundnut oil meal, solvent extracted														
361	Peanut oil meal, solvent extracted														
362	PHOSPHATE ROCK														
363	-defluorinated grnd, mx 1 part fluorine per 100 part phosphorus, (6)	6-01-780	99.8	—	—	—	—	—	32.07	—	—	.922	—	—	18.04
364															
365	Phosphate, defluorinated (AAFCO)														
366	Defluorinated phosphate (CFA)														
367	POTATO. *Solenum tuberosum*														
368	-tubers, dehy grnd, (4)	4-07-850	90.3	3.04	6.5	.6	1.6	78.1	.08	—	—	—	—	3.2	.22
369	Potato meal														
370	POULTRY.														
371	-feathers, hydrolyzed dehy grnd, mn 75% of protein digestible, (5)	5-03-795	94.0	3.50	93.0	2.6	.6	.0	.21	—	—	—	—	—	.89
372															
373	Hydrolyzed poultry feathers (AAFCO)														
374	POULTRY FAT—see ANIMAL														
375	RICE. *Oryza sativa*														
376	-bran w germ, dry milled, mx 13% fiber CaCO₃ declared above 3% mn, (4)	4-03-928	91.0	3.53	14.8	16.6	12.1	44.5	.07	14.3	—	.021	1.04	459.1	2.00
377															
378	Rice bran (AAFCO)														
379	-grain w hulls, grnd, (4)	4-03-938	89.0	3.10	8.2	2.1	10.1	74.6	.04	—	—	—	.16	20.2	.29
380	Ground rough rice (AAFCO)														
381	Ground paddy rice (AAFCO)														
382	-groats, grnd, (4)	4-03-935	89.0	3.53	9.6	1.3	1.1	87.2	.04	4.8	—	.004	.06	4.8	.20
383	Ground brown rice (AAFCO)														
384	Rice grain without hulls, ground														
385	-groats, polished, (4)	4-03-942	89.0	3.51	8.2	.4	.4	90.4	.03	3.3	—	.002	.02	12.2	.13
386	Rice, white, polished														
387	-polishings, dehy, (4)	4-03-943	90.0	3.85	13.1	14.7	3.3	60.0	.04	—	—	—	.72	—	1.58
388	Rice polishings (AAFCO)														
389	Rice polish (CFA)														
390	RYE. *Secale cereale*														
391	-grain, (4)	4-04-047	89.0	3.47	13.4	1.8	2.2	80.7	.07	8.8	—	.009	.13	75.2	.38
392	SESAME. *Sesamum indicum*														
393	-seed, mech-extd grnd, (5)	5-04-220	93.0	3.26	51.5	5.5	5.4	27.6	2.18	—	—	—	—	51.6	1.39
394	Sesame oil meal, expeller extracted														
395	SEAWEED. Laminariales (order), Fucales (order)														
396															
397	-entire plant, s-c grnd, (1)	1-04-190	89.4	—	10.7	—	8.6	—	2.05	—	—	—	7.12	—	.20
398	SHRIMP. *Pandalus* spp, *Penaeus* spp														
399	-process residue, dehy grnd, salt declared above 3% mx 7%, (5)	5-04-226	90.0	2.19	52.7	3.2	12.2	1.7	8.17	—	—	.010	.60	33.4	1.77
400															
401	Shrimp meal (AAFCO)														
402	SODIUM PHOSPHATE, MONOBASIC														
403	-technical, (6)	6-04-288	96.7	—	—	—	—	—	—	—	—	—	—	—	22.46
404	Monosodium phosphate (AAFCO)														
405	SODIUM TRIPOLYPHOSPHATE														
406	-commercial, (6)	6-08-076	96.0	—	—	—	—	—	—	—	—	—	—	—	25.98
407	Sodium tripolyphosphate (AAFCO)														
408	SORGHUM, GRAIN VARIETY. *Sorghum vulgare*														
409	-grain, (4)	4-04-383	89.0	3.55	12.5	3.4	2.2	79.9	.45	10.9	—	—	.19	16.3	.35
410	SORGHUM, MILO. *Sorghum vulgare*														
411	-grain, (4)	4-04-444	89.0	3.54	12.4	3.1	2.2	80.4	.45	15.8	—	—	.22	14.5	.33
412	SOYBEAN. *Glycine max*														
413	-oil, (4)	4-07-983	100.0	8.93	—	100.0	—	—	—	—	—	—	—	—	—
414	-seed, mech-extd grnd, mx 7% fiber, (5)	5-04-600	90.0	3.33	48.7	5.2	6.7	33.1	.30	20.0	—	.018	.28	35.9	.70
415	Soybean meal, mechanical extracted (AAFCO)														
416	Soybean meal, expeller extracted														
417	Soybean meal, hydraulic extracted														
418	Soybean oil meal, expeller extracted														
419	Soybean oil meal, hydraulic extracted														
420	-seed, solv-extd grnd, mx 7% fiber, (5)	5-04-604	89.0	3.11	51.5	1.0	6.7	34.3	.36	40.8	—	.013	.30	30.9	.75
421	Soybean meal, solvent extracted (AAFCO)														
422															
423	Soybean meal, solvent extracted														
424	Soybean oil meal, solvent extracted														
425	-seed wo hulls, solv-extd grnd, mx 3% fiber, (5)	5-04-612	89.8	3.24	56.7	.9	3.1	33.1	.29	—	—	—	—	50.7	.69
426															
427	Soybean meal, dehulled, solvent extracted (AAFCO)														
428															

(1) dry forages and roughages; (2) pasture, range plants, and forages fed green; (3) silages;

TABLE 29 (CONTINUED)

COMPOSITION OF SOME COMMON DOG FEEDS, EXCLUDING AMINO ACIDS

Dry Basis

Line Number	Potassium (%)	Sodium (%)	Zinc (mg/kg)	Biotin (mg/kg)	Choline (mg/kg)	Folic acid (mg/kg)	Niacin (mg/kg)	Pantothenic acid (mg/kg)	Provitamin A (Carotene) (mg/kg)	Pyridoxine (mg/kg)	Riboflavin (mg/kg)	Thiamin (mg/kg)	Vitamin B₁₂ (µg/kg)	Vitamin E (mg/kg)	Vitamin K (mg/kg)
344															
345	—	—	—	—	—	—	—	—	—	—	—	+	—	—	—
346															
347	—	—	—	—	—	—	—	—	—	—	—	—	—	—	—
348															
349	.10	.21	—	—	—	—	—	—	—	—	—	—	—	—	—
350															
351																
352	1.13	.04	33.0	.20	713.	.40	18.9	5.1	—	1.10	.9	2.0	—	—	—
353															
354	1.25	—	—	—	1829.	—	183.7	52.4	—	—	5.8	7.9	—	—	—
355															
356															
357															
358	1.30	.08	21.7	.42	2174.	.39	184.9	57.6	—	10.87	12.0	7.9	—	3.3	—
359															
360															
361															
362															
363															
364	.09	3.96	—	—	—	—	—	—	—	—	—	—	—	—	—
365															
366															
367															
368	2.18	—	—	—	—	—	—	—	—	—	—	—	—	—	—
369															
370															
371															
372	—	—	—	—	977.	—	34.2	12.2	—	—	2.4	—	—	—	—
373															
374															
375															
376															
377	1.91	.08	32.9	4.62	1378.	—	333.2	25.8	—	—	2.9	24.6	—	65.9	—
378															
379	.38	.07	16.9	—	899.	.45	34.0	.37	—	—	1.2	3.1	—	15.7	—
380															
381															
382	.13	.04	—	—	—	—	19.2	—	—	—	.3	1.2	—	—	—
383															
384															
385	.15	.03	2.0	—	1019.	.17	15.8	3.7	—	.45	.7	.7	—	4.0	—
386															
387	1.30	.12	—	.67	1452.	—	590.8	64.8	—	—	2.0	21.9	—	100.0	—
388															
389															
390															
391	.51	.02	34.3	.07	—	.67	1.3	7.8	—	—	1.8	4.4	—	16.8	—
392															
393	1.29	.04	107.5	—	1648.	—	32.3	6.9	—	13.44	4.0	3.1	—	—	—
394															
395															
396															
397	—	—	—	—	—	—	—	—	—	—	—	—	—	—	—
398															
399															
400	—	—	—	—	6476.	—	—	—	—	—	4.4	—	—	—	—
401															
402															
403	—	33.4	—	—	—	—	—	—	—	—	—	—	—	—	—
404															
405															
406	—	—	—	—	—	—	—	—	—	—	—	—	—	—	—
407															
408															
409	.38	.04	15.4	2.92	762.	.22	48.4	12.5	—	5.95	1.5	4.6	—	—	—
410															
411	.39	.01	19.1	.20	762.	.27	48.0	12.8	—	4.61	1.3	4.8	—	13.5	—
412															
413	—	—	—	—	—	—	—	—	—	—	—	—	—	—	—
414	1.90	.27	—	.33	2970.	7.33	33.8	—	—	—	—	4.4	—	—	—
415															
416															
417															
418															
419															
420	2.21	.38	30.3	.36	3082.	.79	30.1	16.3	—	8.99	3.7	7.4	—	3.4	—
421															
422															
423															
424															
425															
426	2.25	.01	50.1	.36	3075.	4.01	24.1	16.1	—	8.91	3.5	2.7	—	3.7	—
427															
428															

(4) energy feeds; (5) protein supplements; (6) minerals; (7) vitamins; (8) additives.

TABLE 29 (CONTINUED)
COMPOSITION OF SOME COMMON DOG FEEDS, EXCLUDING AMINO ACIDS

Line Number	SCIENTIFIC NAME / National Research Council Name (NRC) / American Feed Control Name (AAFCO) / Canada Feed Act Name (CFA) / Other Names	International Reference Number	Dry Matter (%)	ME (kcal/g)	Protein (%)	Ether Extract (%)	Crude Fiber (%)	Nitrogen-Free Extract (%)	Calcium (%)	Copper (mg/kg)	Iodine (mg/kg)	Iron (%)	Magnesium (%)	Manganese (mg/kg)	Phosphorus (%)
429	Soybean oil meal, dehulled, solvent														
430	extracted														
431	SUGARCANE. *Saccharum officinarum*														
432	-molasses, dehy, (4)	4-04-695	96.0	3.10	10.7	1.0	5.2	74.8	—	—	—	—	—	—	—
433	Cane molasses, dried														
434	Molasses, cane, dried														
435	-molasses, mn 48% invert sugar mn 79.5														
436	degrees brix, (4)	4-04-696	75.0	3.15	4.3	.1	—	84.8	1.19	79.5	—	.025	.47	56.3	.11
437	Cane molasses (AAFCO)														
438	Molasses, cane														
439	SUNFLOWER. *Helianthus* spp														
440	-seed wo hulls, mech-extd grnd, (5)	5-04-738	93.0	3.19	44.1	8.2	14.0	26.4	.46	—	—	—	—	24.6	1.12
441	Sunflower meal (AAFCO)														
442	Sunflower oil meal, without hulls,														
443	expeller extracted														
444	-seed wo hulls, solv-extd grnd, (5)	5-04-739	93.0	2.97	50.3	3.1	11.8	26.5	.43	—	—	—	—	24.7	1.08
445	Sunflower meal (AAFCO)														
446	Sunflower oil meal, without hulls,														
447	solvent extracted														
448	SWINE. *Sus scrofa*														
449	-lard, (4)	4-04-790	100.0	8.93	.0	100.0									
450	TANKAGE-see ANIMAL														
451	TOMATO. *Lycopersicon esculentum*														
452	-pulp, dehy, (5)	5-05-041	92.0	—	23.6	14.1	31.5		.30	—	—	—	—	—	.62
453	Dried tomato pomace (AAFCO)														
454	TURKEY. *Meleagris gallapavo*														
455	-offal mature birds, raw, (5)	5-07-984	28.0	—	—	43.9	1.4	—	—	—	—	—	—	—	—
456	-offal young birds, raw, (5)	5-07-985	35.0	—	—	42.6	.9	—	—	—	—	—	—	—	—
457	-meat, raw, (5)	5-07-986	26.0	3.58	81.9	8.1	.0								
458	WHEAT. *Triticum* spp														
459	-bran, dry milled, (4)	4-05-190	89.0	3.12	18.0	4.6	11.2	59.3	.16	13.8	—	.019	.62	130.0	1.31
460	Wheat bran (AAFCO)														
461	Bran (CFA)														
462	WHEAT. *Triticum* spp														
463	-flour, coarse bolted, feed gr mx 2%														
464	fiber, (4)	4-05-199	89.0	3.49	17.8	3.3	3.4	73.1	.03	5.2	—	.002	—	50.4	.31
465	Wheat feed flour, mx 1.5% fiber (AAFCO)														
466	Feed flour, mx 2.0% fiber (CFA)														
467	-flour byproduct, coarse sifted, mx 7%														
468	fiber, (4)	4-05-201	90.0	3.42	20.4	4.7	5.6	65.0	.12	10.2	—	.011	.29	116.1	.84
469	Wheat shorts, mx 7% fiber (AAFCO)														
470	Shorts, mx 8% fiber (CFA)														
471	-flour byproduct, fine sifted, mx 4%														
472	fiber, (4)	4-05-203	89.0	3.55	20.2	4.0	2.2	70.8	.09	4.9	—	.007	.33	42.2	.58
473	Wheat red dog, mx 4.0% fiber (AAFCO)														
474	Middlings, mx 4.5% fiber (CFA)														
475	-flour byproduct, mill run, mx 9.5%														
476	fiber, (4)	4-05-206	90.0	3.23	17.0	4.4	8.9	63.9	.10	20.8	—	.010	.57	114.1	1.13
477	Wheat mill run (AAFCO)														
478	-grain, (4)	4-05-211	89.0	3.44	14.3	1.9	3.4	78.6	.06	8.1	—	.006	.18	54.8	.40
479	-grain, Pacific coast, (4)	4-08-142	89.2	3.46	11.1	2.2	3.0	81.6	.14	—	—	—	—	—	.34
480	-grain screenings, (4)	4-05-216	89.0	3.29	16.9	3.4	7.9	68.2	.09	—	—	—	—	32.1	.40
481	-grits, cracked fine screened, (4)	4-07-852	88.0	3.53	12.6	1.2	.3	84.5	—	—	—	—	—	—	—
482	Farina														
483	Wheat endosperm														
484	-germ, grnd, mn 25% protein 7% fat, (5)	5-05-218	90.0	3.86	29.1	12.1	3.3	50.7	.08	9.8	—	.012	—	149.9	1.16
485	Wheat germ meal (AAFCO)														
486	WHEAT, DURUM. *Triticum durum*														
487	-grain, (4)	4-05-224	89.5	3.48	15.0	2.2	2.5	78.3	.17	8.6	—	.004	—	32.1	.45
488	-grain, Can 4 CW mn wt 56 lb per bushel														
489	mx 2.5% foreign material, (4)	4-05-225	86.5	3.47	15.7	1.9	2.6	78.0						—	—
490	WHEAT, HARD RED SPRING. *Triticum aestivum*														
491	-grain, (4)	4-05-258	86.5	3.45	16.1	2.2	3.5	76.3	.06	12.2	—	.006	—	71.9	.46
492	WHEAT, HARD RED WINTER. *Triticum aestivum*														
493	-grain, (4)	4-05-268	89.1	3.44	14.6	1.8	3.0	78.6	.06	5.0	—	—	.11	36.8	.45
494	WHEAT, RED SPRING. *Triticum aestivum*														
495	-grain, Can 4 No mn wt 56 lb per bushel														
496	mx 2.5% foreign material, (4)	4-05-282	86.5	3.47	16.3	2.0	2.8	77.2	—	—	—	—	—	—	—
497	WHEAT, SOFT. *Triticum aestivum*														
498	-grain, (4)	4-05-284	90.0	3.46	12.0	1.9	2.6	81.5	.10	10.8	—	.006	.11	57.0	.33
499	WHEAT, SOFT RED WINTER. *Triticum aestivum*														
500	-grain, (4)	4-05-294	89.1	3.46	12.3	1.8	2.5	81.4	.10	11.0	—	—	.11	42.9	.33
501	WHEY-see CATTLE														
502	YEAST. *Saccharomyces cerevisiae*														
503	-brewers saccharomyces, dehy grnd, mn														
504	40% protein, (7)	7-05-527	93.0	3.23	48.0	1.2	3.2	40.8	.14	35.5	—	.011	.25	6.1	1.54
505	Brewers dried yeast (AAFCO)														
506	-petroleum saccharomyces, dehy grnd, (7)	7-09-836	92.0	—	51.1	—	—	—	.02	—	—	—	—	—	5.8
507	-primary saccharomyces, dehy, mn 40%														
508	protein, (7)	7-05-533	93.0	3.16	51.6	1.1	3.2	35.5	.39	—	—	.030	.39	4.0	1.85
509	Dried yeast (AAFCO)														
510	Primary dried yeast (AAFCO)														
511	YEAST, TORULOPSIS. *Torulopsis utilis*														
512	-dehy, mn 40% protein, (7)	7-05-534	93.0	3.29	51.9	2.7	2.2	34.8	.61	14.4	—	.010	.14	1.81	2.0
513	Torula dried yeast (AAFCO)														

(1) dry forages and roughages; (2) pasture, range plants, and forages fed green; (3) silages;

TABLE 29 (CONTINUED)
COMPOSITION OF SOME COMMON DOG FEEDS, EXCLUDING AMINO ACIDS

Dry Basis

Line Number	Potassium (%)	Sodium (%)	Zinc (mg/kg)	Biotin (mg/kg)	Choline (mg/kg)	Folic acid (mg/kg)	Niacin (mg/kg)	Pantothenic acid (mg/kg)	Provitamin A (Carotene) (mg/kg)	Pyridoxine (mg/kg)	Riboflavin (mg/kg)	Thiamin (mg/kg)	Vitamin B$_{12}$ (µg/kg)	Vitamin E (mg/kg)	Vitamin K (mg/kg)
429															
430															
431															
432	—	—	—	—	—	—	—	—	—	—	—	—	—	—	—
433															
434															
435															
436	3.17	—	—	—	1168.	—	45.7	51.1	—	—	4.4	1.2	—	—	—
437															
438															
439															
440	1.16	—	—	—	—	—	—	—	—	—	—	—	—	—	—
441															
442															
443															
444	1.08	—	—	—	3118.	—	236.6	10.1	—	17.20	3.3	—	—	11.8	—
445															
446															
447															
448											—				—
449															
450															
451															
452	—	—	—	—	—	—	—	—	—	—	6.7	12.9	—	—	—
453															
454															
455	—	—	—	—	—	—	—	—	—	—	—	—	—	—	—
456	—	—	—	—	—	—	—	—	—	—	—	—	—	—	—
457															
458															
459	1.39	.07	—	.54	1110.	2.02	235.1	32.6	—	11.24	3.5	8.9	—	12.1	—
460															
461															
462															
463															
464	—	—	—	—	—	—	47.1	1.0	—	—	—	6.6	—	—	—
465															
466															
467															
468	.94	.08	—	.41	1031.	1.22	105.1	19.6	—	12.22	2.2	17.6	—	33.2	—
469															
470															
471															
472	.67	.74	—	.42	1247.	1.25	59.1	15.3	—	12.47	1.7	21.2	—	64.7	—
473															
474															
475															
476	1.42	.24	—	—	1090.	—	124.4	14.7	—	—	2.7	16.9	—	—	—
477															
478	.58	.10	15.4	.11	933.	.45	63.6	13.6	—	—	1.3	5.5	—	17.4	—
479	—	—	—	—	—	—	66.3	12.9	—	—	1.2	5.5	—	—	—
480	—	—	—	—	—	—	—	—	—	—	—	—	—	—	—
481	—	—	—	—	—	—	—	—	—	—	—	—	—	—	—
482															
483															
484	—	.06	—	.24	3344.	2.22	52.6	12.4	—	14.44	5.7	31.0	—	147.4	—
485															
486															
487	—	—	—	—	—	.44	—	—	—	—	—	7.0	—	—	—
488															
489															
490															
491	.58	.07	16.2	.13	899.	.49	66.8	15.6	—	4.62	1.3	3.7	—	12.7	—
492															
493	.57	.07	15.7	.12	824.	.45	57.1	14.3	—	4.60	1.1	7.0	—	12.3	—
494															
495															
496	—	—	—	—	—	—	—	—	—	—	—	—	—	—	—
497															
498	.44	.07	15.6	.12	876.	.33	65.8	14.2	—	5.33	1.3	5.3	—	12.2	—
499															
500	.44	—	—	—	874.	.45	64.4	12.8	—	5.16	—	5.9	—	—	—
501															
502															
503															
504	1.85	.08	41.6	5.91	4177.	10.43	481.2	118.1	—	46.56	37.6	98.6	—	.0	—
505															
506	4.02	—	—	—	—	—	—	—	—	—	—	—	—	—	—
507															
508	—	—	—	1.72	—	33.33	322.7	334.7	—	—	41.6	6.9	—	—	—
509															
510															
511															
512	—	.01	106.7	1.20	3129.	25.00	537.8	89.1	—	31.70	47.7	6.7	—	—	—
513															

(4) energy feeds; (5) protein supplements; (6) minerals; (7) vitamins; (8) additives.

TABLE 30

AMINO ACID COMPOSITION OF SOME COMMON DOG FEEDS

Line Number	SCIENTIFIC NAME / National Research Council Name (NRC) / American Feed Control Name (AAFCO) / Canada Feed Act Name (CFA) / Other Names	International Reference Number	Dry Matter (%)	Arginine (%)	Cystine (%)	Histidine (%)	Isoleucine (%)	Leucine (%)	Lysine (%)	Methionine (%)	Phenylalanine (%)	Threonine (%)	Tryptophan (%)	Tyrosine (%)	Valine (%)
1	ALFALFA. *Medicago sativa*														
2	-aerial part, dehy grnd, mn 15% protein, (1)	1-00-022	93.1	.64	.18	.32	.73	1.18	.64	.21	.86	.64	.43	.43	.75
3	-aerial part, dehy grnd, mn 17% protein, (1)	1-00-023	93.0	.75	.34	.43	.75	1.40	.86	.21	.86	.86	.43	.54	.97
4	-aerial part, dehy grnd, mn 20% protein, (1)	1-00-024	93.1	.97	—	.43	.86	1.61	.97	.32	1.18	.97	.54	.75	.11
5	ANIMAL. Scientific name not used														
6	-blood, dehy grnd, (5)	5-00-380	91.0	3.85	1.53	4.62	1.10	11.32	7.58	.99	6.70	4.07	1.21	1.98	7.14
7	Blood meal (AAFCO)														
8	Blood meal (CFA)														
9	-blood, spray dehy, (5)	5-00-381	91.0	3.63	—	5.27	1.21	11.65	9.01	1.10	6.15	3.96	1.10	2.20	7.91
10	Blood flour														
11	-carcass residue, dry rendered dehy														
12	grnd, mx 4.4% phosphorus, (5)	5-00-385	93.5	3.96	.64	1.18	2.03	3.74	4.06	.86	2.03	1.93	.32	.96	2.78
13	Meat meal (AAFCO)														
14	Meat scrap														
15	-carcass residue w blood, dry or wet														
16	rendered dehy grnd, mx 4.4%														
17	phosphorus, (5)	5-00-386	92.0	3.91	—	2.07	2.07	5.54	4.34	.87	2.93	2.61	.76	—	4.57
18	Meat meal tankage														
19	Digester tankage														
20	-carcass residue w bone, dry rendered dehy														
21	grnd, mn 4.4% phosphorus, (5)	5-00-388	94.0	4.26	.64	.96	1.80	3.30	3.72	.74	1.91	1.91	.21	.85	2.55
22	Meat and bone meal (AAFCO)														
23	Meat and bone scrap														
24	-liver, dehy grnd, (5)	5-00-389	92.6	4.43	.97	1.62	3.67	5.83	5.18	1.40	3.13	2.81	.65	1.84	4.54
25	Animal liver meal (AAFCO)														
26	Animal liver meal (CFA)														
27	Liver meal														
28	-bone, steamed dehy grnd, (6)	6-00-400	95.0	—	—	—	—	—	—	—	—	—	—	—	—
29	Bone meal, steamed (AAFCO)														
30	-bone phosphate, precipitated dehy,														
31	mn 17% phosphorus, (6)	6-00-406	99.0	—	—	—	—	—	—	—	—	—	—	—	—
32	Bone phosphate (AAFCO)														
33	ANIMAL—POULTRY.														
34	-fat, heat rendered, mn 90% fatty acids														
35	mx 2.5% unsaponifiable matter														
36	mx 1% insoluble matter, (4)	4-00-409	99.5	—	—	—	—	—	—	—	—	—	—	—	—
37	Animal fat (AAFCO)														
38	BARLEY. *Hordeum vulgare*														
39	-grain, (4)	4-00-530	89.0	.60	.20	.30	.60	.90	.60	.20	.70	.40	.20	.40	.70
40	-grain, Pacific coast, (4)	4-07-939	89.0	.48	.25	.25	.45	.67	.34	.16	.54	—	.15	—	.52
41	-malt sprouts w hulls, dehy, mn 24%														
42	protein, (5)	5-00-545	93.0	—	—	—	—	—	—	—	—	—	—	—	—
43	Malt sprouts (AAFCO)														
44	BEET, SUGAR. *Beta saccharifera*														
45	-molasses, mn 48% invert sugar mn 79.5														
46	degrees brix, (4)	4-00-668	77.0	—	—	—	—	—	—	—	—	—	—	—	—
47	Beet molasses (AAFCO)														
48	Molasses (CFA)														
49	-pulp, dehy, (4)	4-00-669	91.0	.33	—	.22	.33	.66	.66	—	.33	.44	.11	.44	.44
50	Dried beet pulp (AAFCO)														
51	Dried beet pulp (CFA)														
52	BLOOD—see ANIMAL														
53	BONE—see ANIMAL														
54	BREAD.														
55	-dehy, (4)	4-07-944	95.0	—	—	—	—	—	—	—	—	—	—	—	—
56	BREWERS—see GRAINS														
57	BUTTERMILK—see CATTLE														
58	CALCIUM PHOSPHATE, DIBASIC														
59	-commercial, (6)	6-01-080	96.0	—	—	—	—	—	—	—	—	—	—	—	—
60	Dicalcium phosphate (AAFCO)														
61	CALCIUM—also see LIMESTONE														
62	Calcium Carbonate, CaCO$_3$														
63	-commercial mn 38%														
64	calcium, (6)														
65	CASEIN—see CATTLE														
66	CATTLE. *Bos* spp														
67	-whey, dehy, mn 65% lactose, (4)	4-01-182	94.0	.43	.32	.21	.96	1.49	1.17	.21	.43	.85	.21	.32	.74
68	Dried whey (AAFCO)														
69	Whey, dried														
70	-whey low lactose, dehy, mn	4-01-186	91.0	.55	.38	—	—	—	1.43	.24	—	—	.24	—	—
71	lactose, declared, (4)														
72	Dried whey-product (AAFCO)														
73	-buttermilk, condensed, mn 27% total														
74	solids w mn 0.055% fat mx 0.14% ash														
75	per 1% solids, (5)	5-01-159	29.0	—	—	—	—	—	—	—	—	—	—	—	—
76	Condensed buttermilk (AAFCO)														
77	Buttermilk, concentrated														
78	Buttermilk, condensed														
79	Buttermilk, evaporated														
80	-buttermilk, dehy, feed gr mx 8% moisture														
81	mx 13% ash mn 5% fat, (5)	5-01-160	93.0	1.18	.43	.97	2.90	3.66	2.58	.75	1.61	1.72	.54	1.08	3.01
82	Dried buttermilk, feed grade (AAFCO)														
83	Buttermilk, dried														
84	-casein, milk acid precipitated dehy,														
85	mn 80% protein, (5)	5-01-162	90.0	3.78	.33	2.78	6.33	9.56	7.78	3.00	5.11	4.22	1.11	5.22	7.56
86	Casein (AAFCO)														
87	Casein, dried														
88	-lips, raw, (5)	5-07-940	30.0	—	—	—	—	—	—	—	—	—	—	—	—

(1) dry forages and roughages; (2) pasture, range plants, and forages fed green; (3) silages; (4) energy feeds; (5) protein supplements; (6) minerals; (7) vitamins; (8) additives.

(From No. 8, Nutrient Requirements of Dogs, Revised 1974, National Academy of Sciences, NRC, pp. 52–57, Table 7.)

TABLE 30 (CONTINUED)

AMINO ACID COMPOSITION OF SOME COMMON DOG FEEDS

Line Number	SCIENTIFIC NAME / National Research Council Name (NRC) / American Feed Control Name (AAFCO) / Canada Feed Act Name (CFA) / Other Names	International Reference Number	Dry Matter (%)	Arginine (%)	Cystine (%)	Histidine (%)	Isoleucine (%)	Leucine (%)	Lysine (%)	Methionine (%)	Phenylalanine (%)	Threonine (%)	Tryptophan (%)	Tyrosine (%)	Valine (%)
89	-liver, raw, (5)	5-01-166	26.0	—	—	—	—	—	—	—	—	—	—	—	—
90	Beef liver														
91	-lungs, raw, (5)	5-07-941	20.0	—	—	—	—	—	—	—	—	—	—	—	—
92	-milk, dehy, feed gr mx 8% moisture														
93	mn 26% fat, (5)	5-01-167	93.7	.96	—	.75	1.39	2.67	2.35	.64	1.39	1.07	.43	1.39	1.81
94	Dried whole milk (AAFCO)														
95	Milk, whole, dried														
96	-milk, skimmed dehy, mx 8% moisture, (5)	5-01-175	94.0	1.28	.53	.96	2.45	3.51	2.98	.85	1.60	1.49	.43	1.38	2.34
97	Dried skimmed milk, feed grade (AAFCO)														
98	Milk, skimmed, dried														
99	-spleen, raw, (5)	5-07-942	25.0	—	—	—	—	—	—	—	—	—	—	—	—
100	Cattle, melts, raw														
101	-udders, raw, (5)	5-07-943	25.0	—	—	—	—	—	—	—	—	—	—	—	—
102	CHICKEN. Gallus domesticus														
103	-broilers, whole, raw, (5)	5-07-945	68.0	—	—	—	—	—	—	—	—	—	—	—	—
104	-cull hens, whole, raw, (5)	5-07-950	70.0	—	—	—	—	—	—	—	—	—	—	—	—
105	-day-old chicks, whole, raw, (5)	5-07-946	24.4	—	—	—	—	—	—	—	—	—	—	—	—
106	-eggs w shells, raw, (5)	5-01-213	34.1	—	—	—	—	—	—	—	—	—	—	—	—
107	-feet, raw, (5)	5-07-947	47.0	—	—	—	—	—	—	—	—	—	—	—	—
108	-gizzards, raw, (5)	5-07-948	69.0	—	—	—	—	—	—	—	—	—	—	—	—
109	-heads, raw, (5)	5-07-949	33.0	—	—	—	—	—	—	—	—	—	—	—	—
110	-offal w feet, raw, (5)	5-07-951	31.0	—	—	—	—	—	—	—	—	—	—	—	—
111	-offal wo feet, raw, (5)	5-07-952	27.0	—	—	—	—	—	—	—	—	—	—	—	—
112	CITRUS. Citrus spp														
113	-pulp wo fines, shredded dehy, (4)	4-01-237	90.0	.22	.12	—	—	—	.22	.09	—	—	.07	—	—
114	Dried citrus pulp (AAFCO)														
115	Citrus pulp, dried														
116	COCONUT. Cocos nucifera														
117	-meats, mech-extd grnd, (5)	5-01-572	93.0												
118	Coconut meal, mechanical extracted (AAFCO)														
119	Copra meal, expeller (AAFCO)														
120	Coconut meal, hydraulic														
121	Copra meal, hydraulic														
122	-meats, solv-extd grnd, (5)	5-01-573	92.0	2.93	.33	.61	.72	1.62	.70	.32	.98	.71	.22	.61	1.07
123	Coconut meal, solvent extracted (AAFCO)														
124	Solvent extracted copra meal (AAFCO)														
125	CORN. Zea mays														
126	-grain, flaked, (4)	4-02-859	97.0	—	—	—	—	—	—	—	—	—	—	—	—
127	Flaked corn (AAFCO)														
128	Corn grain, flaked														
129	-grits byproduct, mn 5% fat, (4)	4-02-887	90.6	.55	.20	.22	.44	.88	.44	.20	.33	.44	.11	.55	.55
130	Hominy feed (AAFCO)														
131	Hominy feed (CFA)														
132	-distillers grains w solubles, dehy,														
133	mn 75% original solids, (5)	5-02-843	91.0	1.10	.44	.66	1.00	2.97	.66	.66	1.32	1.04	.22	.88	1.43
134	Corn distillers dried grains with														
135	solubles (AAFCO)														
136	-distillers solubles, dehy, (5)	5-02-844	95.5	1.20	.42	.66	1.31	2.76	.99	.52	1.36	1.08	.31	.99	1.46
137	Corn distillers dried solubles (AAFCO)														
138	-germ wo solubles, wet milled solv-extd														
139	dehy grnd, (5)	5-02-898	93.0	1.29	.34	—	—	1.83	.97	.38	.86	.97	.32	1.61	1.40
140	Corn germ meal, solvent extracted,														
141	(wet milled) (AAFCO)														
142	-gluten, wet milled dehy, (5)	5-02-900	91.0	1.54	.66	1.10	2.53	8.35	.88	1.10	3.19	1.54	.22	1.10	2.42
143	Corn gluten meal (AAFCO)														
144	Corn gluten meal (CFA)														
145	CORN, DENT YELLOW. Zea mays indentata														
146	-grain, (4)	4-02-935	86.0	.58	.10	.23	.47	1.28	.23	.20	.58	.47	.12	—	.47
147	-grain, grnd cooked, (4)	4-07-953	88.0	—	—	—	—	—	—	—	—	—	—	—	—
148	CORN, FLINT. Zea mays indurata														
149	-grain, (4)	4-02-948	89.0	—	—	—	—	—	.30	.20	—	—	.10	—	—
150	CORN, WHITE. Zea mays														
151	-grits by-prod, mn 5% fat, (4)	4-02-990	89.9												
152	White hominy feed (AAFCO)														
153	White hominy feed (CFA)														
154	Hominy, white corn, feed														
155	Corn, white hominy feed														
156	COTTON. Gossypium spp														
157	-seed w some hulls, mech-extd grnd, mn 41%														
158	protein mx 14% fiber mn 2% fat, (5)	5-01-617	94.0	4.52	.90	1.17	1.70	2.66	1.81	.69	2.50	1.54	.69	.74	2.18
159	Cottonseed meal, 41% protein														
160	-seed w some hulls, pre-press solv-extd														
161	grnd, 41% protein, (5)	5-07-872	92.5	4.59	.92	1.19	1.73	2.70	1.84	.70	2.54	1.57	.70	—	2.22
162	Cottonseed meal, pre-press solvent														
163	extracted, 41% protein														
164	-seed w some hulls, solv-extd grnd, mn 41%														
165	protein mx 14% fiber mn 0.5% fat, (5)	5-01-621	91.5	4.64	.93	1.20	1.75	2.73	1.86	.71	2.57	1.58	.71	.77	2.24
166	Cottonseed meal, solvent extracted,														
167	41% protein														
168	-seed wo hulls, pre-press solv-extd grnd,														
169	mn 50% protein, (5)	5-07-874	92.5	5.14	1.08	1.35	2.00	3.03	2.27	.86	2.97	1.84	.76	.86	2.22
170	Cottonseed meal, pre-press solvent														
171	extracted, 50% protein														
172	CRAB. Callinectes sapidus, Cancer spp														
173	Paralithodes canschatica														
174	-processed residue, dehy grnd, mn 25%														
175	protein salt declared above 3%														
176	mx 7%, (5)	5-01-663	93.0	1.83	—	.54	1.29	1.72	1.50	.54	1.29	1.08	.32	1.29	1.61

(1) dry forages and roughages; (2) pasture, range plants, and forages fed green; (3) silages; (4) energy feeds; (5) protein supplements; (6) minerals; (7) vitamins; (8) additives.

TABLE 30 (CONTINUED)
AMINO ACID COMPOSITION OF SOME COMMON DOG FEEDS

Line Number	SCIENTIFIC NAME / National Research Council Name (NRC) / American Feed Control Name (AAFCO) / Canada Feed Act Name (CFA) / Other Names	International Reference Number	Dry Matter (%)	Arginine (%)	Cystine (%)	Histidine (%)	Isoleucine (%)	Leucine (%)	Lysine (%)	Methionine (%)	Phenylalanine (%)	Threonine (%)	Tryptophan (%)	Tyrosine (%)	Valine (%)
177	Crab meal (AAFCO)														
178	DISTILLERS—see CORN														
179	FAT—see ANIMAL														
180	FISH.														
181	-livers, extn unspecified dehy grnd,														
182	salt declared above 4%, (5)	5-01-968	93.0	—	—	—	—	—	—	—	—	—	—	—	—
183	Fish liver meal (CFA)														
184	-soluble, condensed, mn 30% protein, (5)	5-01-969	51.0	4.71	3.33	4.90	3.14	4.90	5.29	1.96	2.75	2.35	1.57	.98	3.14
185	Condensed fish solubles (AAFCO)														
186	-stickwater soluble, cooked dehy, mn														
187	60% protein, (5)	5-01-971	92.0	2.61	—	2.83	1.85	2.93	3.26	.98	1.41	1.30	.76	.76	2.07
188	Dried fish solubles (AAFCO)														
189	Fish solubles, dried														
190	FISH, ALEWIFE. *Pomolobus pseudoharengus*														
191	-whole, raw, (5)	5-07-964	26.0	4.04	.99	1.34	2.87	5.01	5.30	1.82	2.68	2.88	—	2.13	3.29
192	-whole or cuttings, cooked mech-extd														
193	dehy grnd, (5)	5-09-830	91.0	—	—	—	—	—	—	—	—	—	—	—	—
194	Fish meal, alewife														
195	FISH, ANCHOVY. *Engraulis* spp														
196	-whole or cuttings, cooked mech-extd														
197	dehy grnd, (5)	5-01-985	93.0	4.80	1.08	1.98	3.66	7.54	5.81	2.35	2.67	3.27	.86	1.90	3.81
198	Fish meal, anchovy														
199	FISH, CARP. *Cyprinus carpio*														
200	-whole, raw, (5)	5-01-986	22.0	—	—	—	—	—	—	—	—	—	—	—	—
201	-whole or cuttings, cooked dehy grnd, (5)	5-09-831	90.8	4.64	—	1.46	2.67	4.98	5.75	1.71	2.60	2.97	—	1.99	2.87
202	Fish meal, carp														
203	FISH, CATFISH. *Ictalurus* spp														
204	-whole, raw, (5)	5-07-965	17.5	—	—	—	—	—	—	—	—	—	—	—	—
205	-whole or cuttings, cooked mech-extd dehy														
206	grnd, (5)	5-09-835	93.9	4.45	—	1.21	1.84	3.55	4.03	1.10	1.93	2.32	—	1.35	2.47
207	Fish meal, catfish														
208	-whole or cuttings, cooked mech-extd														
209	press cake, (5)	5-09-834	47.1	8.36	—	2.72	4.03	6.30	7.41	2.12	4.29	5.03	—	3.29	5.05
210	-whole or cuttings, cooked pasteurized, (5)	5-09-833	39.9	4.96	—	1.35	2.43	3.98	4.21	1.30	2.56	2.88	—	1.68	3.13
211	-whole or cuttings, raw, (5)	5-09-832	42.2	3.60	—	1.40	2.65	4.57	4.83	1.14	2.56	2.96	—	1.30	3.36
212	FISH, FLOUNDER. Bothidae (family),														
213	Pleuronectidae (family)														
214	-whole, raw, (5)	5-01-996	17.0	—	—	—	—	—	—	—	—	—	—	—	—
215	FISH, HADDOCK. *Melanogrammus aeglefinus*														
216	-whole, raw, (5)	5-07-966	18.0	—	—	—	—	—	—	—	—	—	—	—	—
217	FISH, HAKE. *Merluccius* spp. *Urophycis* spp														
218	-whole, cooked, (5)	5-07-967	30.0	—	—	—	—	—	—	—	—	—	—	—	—
219	-whole, cooked acidified, (5)	5-07-968	25.0	—	—	—	—	—	—	—	—	—	—	—	—
220	-whole, raw, (5)	5-07-969	19.0	—	—	—	—	—	—	—	—	—	—	—	—
221	FISH, HERRING. *Clupea harengus harengus*,														
222	*Clupea harengus pallasi*														
223	-whole, raw, (5)	5-01-999	26.0	—	—	—	—	—	—	—	—	—	—	—	—
224	-whole or cuttings, cooked mech-extd														
225	dehy grnd, (5)	5-02-000	92.0	4.34	1.74	1.41	3.48	5.54	7.93	2.17	2.83	2.83	.98	2.28	3.48
226	Fish meal, herring														
227	FISH, MACKEREL ATLANTIC *Scomber scombrus*														
228	-whole, raw, (5)	5-07-971	32.0	—	—	—	—	—	—	—	—	—	—	—	—
229	FISH, MACKEREL PACIFIC. *Scomber japonicus*														
230	-whole, raw, (5)	5-07-972	31.0	—	—	—	—	—	—	—	—	—	—	—	—
231	FISH, MENHADEN. *Brevoortia tyrannus*														
232	-whole or cuttings, cooked mech-extd														
233	dehy grnd, (5)	5-02-009	92.0	4.34	1.02	1.74	4.46	5.43	5.76	1.96	2.93	3.15	.65	1.74	3.91
234	Fish meal, menhaden														
235	FISH, REDFISH. *Sciaenops ocellata*														
236	-whole, raw, (5)	5-08-113	19.8	—	—	—	—	—	—	—	—	—	—	—	—
237	Drumfish, whole, raw														
238	Ocean perch, whole, raw														
239	-whole or cuttings, cooked mech-extd dehy grnd, (5)	5-07-973	94.2	—	—	—	—	—	—	—	—	—	—	—	—
240	Fish meal, drum														
241	Fish meal, redfish														
242	FISH, ROCKFISH. *Sebastodes* spp														
243	-whole, raw, (5)	5-07-974	32.0	—	—	—	—	—	—	—	—	—	—	—	—
244	FISH, SALMON. *Oncorhynchus* spp. *Salmo* spp														
245	-whole, raw, (5)	5-02-011	35.0	—	—	—	—	—	—	—	—	—	—	—	—
246	-whole or cuttings, cooked mech-extd														
247	dehy grnd, (5)	5-02-012	93.0	5.59	.75	—	—	—	8.17	1.72	—	—	.54	—	—
248	Fish meal, salmon														
249	FISH, SARDINE. *Clupea* spp, *Sardinops* spp														
250	-whole or cuttings, cooked mech-extd														
251	dehy grnd, (5)	5-02-015	93.0	2.90	.86	1.94	3.55	5.05	6.34	2.15	2.80	2.80	.54	3.23	4.41
252	FISH, SMELT. *Asmerus* spp														
253	-whole, raw, (5)	5-07-975	21.0	—	—	—	—	—	—	—	—	—	—	—	—
254	FISH, SOLE. Soleidae (family)														
255	-whole, raw, (5)	5-07-976	19.0	—	—	—	—	—	—	—	—	—	—	—	—
256	FISH, TUNA. *Thunnus thynnus*														
257	-process residue, (5)	5-07-977	44.0	—	—	—	—	—	—	—	—	—	—	—	—
258	-whole or cuttings, cooked mech-extd														
259	dehy grnd, (5)	5-02-023	87.0	8.03	—	—	—	7.11	1.95	—	—	1.03	—	2.53	
260	Fish meal, tuna														
261	FISH, TURBOT. *Psetta maxima*														
262	-whole, raw, (5)	5-07-978	27.0	—	—	—	—	—	—	—	—	—	—	—	—
263	FISH, WHITE. Gadidae (family), Lophiidae														
264	(family), Rajidae (family)														

(1) dry forages and roughages; (2) pasture, range plants, and forages fed green; (3) silages; (4) energy feeds; (5) protein supplements; (6) minerals; (7) vitamins; (8) additives.

TABLE 30 (CONTINUED)

AMINO ACID COMPOSITION OF SOME COMMON DOG FEEDS

Line Number	SCIENTIFIC NAME / National Research Council Name (NRC) / American Feed Control Name (AAFCO) / Canada Feed Act Name (CFA) / Other Names	International Reference Number	Dry Matter (%)	Arginine (%)	Cystine (%)	Histidine (%)	Isoleucine (%)	Leucine (%)	Lysine (%)	Methionine (%)	Phenylalanine (%)	Threonine (%)	Tryptophan (%)	Tyrosine (%)	Valine (%)
265	-whole or cuttings, cooked mech-extd														
266	dehy grnd, mx 4% oil, (5)	5-02-025	92.0	3.80	.98	1.63	3.37	4.89	5.33	1.85	2.72	2.72	.76	2.17	3.48
267	White fish meal (CFA)														
268	Fish, cod, meal														
269	Fish, cusk, meal														
270	Fish, haddock, meal														
271	Fish, hake, meal														
272	Fish, pollock, meal														
273	Fish, monkfish, meal														
274	Fish, skate, meal														
275	FISH, WHITING. *Gadus merlangus*														
276	-whole, raw, (5)	5-07-979	23.0	—	—	—	—	—	—	—	—	—	—	—	—
277	FLAX. *Linum usitatissimum*														
278	-seed, mech-extd grnd, mx 0.5% acid														
279	insoluble ash, (5)	5-02-045	91.0	—	—	—	—	—	—	.77	—	—	—	—	—
280	Linseed meal, mechanical extracted (AAFCO)														
281	Linseed meal (CFA)														
282	Linseed oil meal, expeller extracted														
283	Linseed oil meal, hydraulic extracted														
284	Linseed meal, old process														
285	-seed screenings, mech-extd grnd, (5)	5-02-054	91.0												
286	Flaxseed screenings meal (AAFCO)														
287	-seed, solv-extd grnd, mx 0.5% acid														
288	insoluble ash, (5)	5-02-048	91.0												
289	Linseed meal, solvent extracted (AAFCO)														
290	Solvent extracted linseed meal (CFA)														
291	Linseed oil meal, solvent extracted														
292	GRAINS.														
293	-brewers grains, dehy, mx 3% dried														
294	spent hops, (5)	5-02-141	92.0	1.41	—	.54	1.63	2.50	.98	.43	1.41	.98	.43	1.30	1.74
295	Brewers dried grains (AAFCO)														
296	Brewers dried grains (CFA)														
297	-distillers grains, dehy, (5)	5-02-144	92.5	1.19	.22	.65	1.08	3.24	.65	.54	1.30	.97	.22	.86	1.41
298	HOMINY FEED—see CORN														
299	HORSE. *Equus caballus*														
300	-meat, raw, (5)	5-07-980	24.0	—	—	—	—	—	—	—	—	—	—	—	—
301	-meat w bone, raw grnd, (5)	5-07-981	36.0	—	—	—	—	—	—	—	—	—	—	—	—
302	LARD—see SWINE														
303	LIMESTONE.														
304	-grnd, mn 33% calcium, (6)	6-02-632	100.0	—	—	—	—	—	—	—	—	—	—	—	—
305	Limestone, ground (AAFCO)														
306	LINSEED—see FLAX														
307	LIVER—see ANIMAL														
308	MAIZE—see CORN														
309	MALT—see BARLEY														
310	MEAT—see ANIMAL														
311	MILK—see CATTLE														
312	MILLET. *Setaria spp*														
313	-grain, (4)	4-03-098	90.0	—	—	—	—	—	—	—	—	—	—	—	—
314	MOLASSES—see BEET, SUGAR, see SUGARCANE														
315	OATS. *Avena sativa*														
316	-hulls, (1)	1-03-281	93.0	.22	.06	.11	.22	.32	.22	.11	.22	.22	.11	.22	.22
317	Oat hulls (AAFCO)														
318	Oat hulls (CFA)														
319	-cereal byproduct, mx 4% fiber, (4)	4-03-303	91.0	.77	.26	.33	.60	1.10	.11	.22	.71	.53	.22	1.00	.82
320	Feeding oat meal (AAFCO)														
321	Oat middlings (CFA)														
322	-grain, (4)	4-03-309	89.0	.80	.20	.20	.60	1.00	.40	.20	.70	.40	.20	.60	.70
323	-grain, gr 1 US mn wt 34 lb per bushel														
324	mx 2% foreign material, (4)	4-03-313	91.0	—	—	—	—	—	—	—	—	—	—	—	—
325	-grain, gr 2 heavy US mn wt 36 lb per														
326	bushel mx 3% foreign material, (4)	4-03-315	89.5	.89	.25	.22	.59	1.01	.55	.20	.67	.45	.18	.59	.78
327	Oats, grain, heavy														
328	-grain, gr 2 US mn wt 32 lb per bushel														
329	mx 3% foreign material, (4)	4-03-316	89.0	—	—	—	—	—	—	—	—	—	—	—	—
330	OATS. *Avena sativa*														
331	-grain, gr 3 US mn wt 30 lb per bushel														
332	mx 4% foreign material, (4)	4-03-317	91.0	—	—	—	—	—	—	—	—	—	—	—	—
333	-grain, gr 4 US mn wt 27 lb per bushel														
334	mx 5% foreign material, (4)	4-03-318	91.2	—	—	—	—	—	—	—	—	—	—	—	—
335	Oats, grain, light														
336	-groats, (4)	4-03-331	91.0	—	—	—	—	—	—	—	—	—	—	—	—
337	Oat groats (AAFCO)														
338	Oat groats (CFA)														
339	Hulled oats (CFA)														
340	-groats, grnd cooked, (4)	4-07-982	91.0	—	—	—	—	—	—	—	—	—	—	—	—
341	OATS, WHITE. *Avena sativa*														
342	-grain, Can 2 CW mn wt 36 lb per bushel														
343	mx 3% foreign material, (4)	4-03-378	86.5	.58	—	.22	.37	.74	.42	.03	.52	.16	—	.17	.59
344	-grain, Can 2 feed mn wt 28 lb per														
345	bushel mx 22% foreign material, (4)	4-03-379	86.5	.54	—	.17	.25	.68	.31	.12	.46	.32	—	.27	.36
346	-grain, Can 3 CW mn wt 34 lb per bushel														
347	mx 6% foreign material, (4)	4-03-380	86.5	.59	—	.18	.28	.69	.34	.12	.49	.34	—	.27	.42
348	OYSTERS. *Crassostrea spp, Ostrea spp*														
349	-shells, fine grnd, mn 33% calcium, (6)	6-03-481	100.0	—	—	—	—	—	—	—	—	—	—	—	—
350	Oyster shell flour (AAFCO)														
351	PEA. *Pisum spp*														
352	-seed, grnd, (5)	5-03-598	91.0	1.54	.19	.79	1.21	1.98	1.76	.34	1.43	1.03	.26	—	1.43

(1) dry forages and roughages; (2) pasture, range plants, and forages fed green; (3) silages; (4) energy feeds; (5) protein supplements; (6) minerals; (7) vitamins; (8) additives.

TABLE 30
AMINO ACID COMPOSITION OF SOME COMMON DOG FOOD INGREDIENTS

Line Number	SCIENTIFIC NAME / National Research Council Name (NRC) / American Feed Control Name (AAFCO) / Canada Feed Act Name (CFA) / Other Names	International Reference Number	Dry Matter (%)	Arginine (%)	Cystine (%)	Histidine (%)	Isoleucine (%)	Leucine (%)	Lysine (%)	Methionine (%)	Phenylalanine (%)	Threonine (%)	Tryptophan (%)	Tyrosine (%)	Valine (%)
353	PEANUT. *Arachis hypogaea*														
354	-kernels, mech-extd grnd, mx 7% fiber, (5)	5-03-649	92.0	5.10	—	1.09	2.17	3.37	1.41	.65	2.50	1.52	.54	—	2.39
355	Peanut meal, mechanical extracted (AAFCO)														
356	Peanut meal (CFA)														
357	Peanut oil meal, expeller extracted														
358	-kernels, solv-extd grnd, mx 7% fiber, (5)	5-03-650	92.0	6.41	.65	1.30	2.17	4.02	2.50	.43	2.93	1.63	.54	1.96	3.04
359	Peanut meal, solvent extracted (AAFCO)														
360	Groundnut oil meal, solvent extracted														
361	Peanut oil meal, solvent extracted														
362	PHOSPHATE ROCK														
363	-defluorinated grnd, mx 1 part fluorine														
364	per 100 part phosphorus, (6)	6-01-780	99.8	—	—	—	—	—	—	—	—	—	—	—	—
365	Phosphate, defluorinated (AAFCO)														
366	Defluorinated phosphate (CFA)														
367	POTATO. *Solenum tuberosum*														
368	-tubers, dehy grnd, (4)	4-07-850	90.3												
369	Potato meal														
370	POULTRY.														
371	-feathers, hydrolyzed dehy grnd, mn 75%														
372	of protein digestible, (5)	5-03-795	94.0	6.28	3.79	—	—	—	2.13	.64	—	—	.53		
373	Hydrolyzed poultry feathers (AAFCO)														
374	POULTRY FAT—see ANIMAL														
375	RICE. *Oryza sativa*														
376	-bran w germ, dry milled, mx 13% fiber														
377	CaCO₃ declared above 3% mn, (4)	4-03-928	91.0	.55	.11	.22	.44	.66	.55	.32	.44	.44	.11	.75	.66
378	Rice bran (AAFCO)														
379	-grain w hulls, grnd, (4)	4-03-938	89.0	.60	.11	.10	.30	.60	.30	.19	.30	.20	.11	.67	.57
380	Ground rough rice (AAFCO)														
381	Ground paddy rice (AAFCO)														
382	-groats, grnd, (4)	4-03-935	89.0	—											
383	Ground brown rice (AAFCO)														
384	Rice grain without hulls, ground														
385	-groats, polished, (4)	4-03-942	89.0	.40	.10	.20	.51	.80	.30	.30	.60	.40	.10	.70	.60
386	Rice, white, polished														
387	-polishing, dehy, (4)	4-03-943	90.0	.55	.11	.11	.33	.56	.56	.30	.33	.33	.11	.70	.93
388	Rice polishings (AAFCO)														
389	Rice polish (CFA)														
390	RYE. *Secale cereale*														
391	-grain, (4)	4-04-047	89.0	.60	.20	.30	.60	.80	.51	.20	.70	.40	.10	.30	.70
392	SESAME. *Sesamum indicum*														
393	-seed, mech-extd grnd, (5)	5-04-220	93.0	5.16	.65	1.18	2.26	3.66	1.40	1.51	2.37	1.72	.84	2.15	2.58
394	Sesame oil meal, expeller extracted														
395	SEAWEED. Laminariales (order), Fucales														
396	(order)														
397	-entire plant, s-c grnd, (1)	1-04-190	89.4	.32	—	.10	.27	.48	.36	.07	.27	.31	—	.15	.39
398	SHRIMP. *Pandalus* spp, *Penaeus* spp														
399	-process residue, dehy grnd, salt declared														
400	above 3% mx 7%, (5)	5-04-226	90.0	—	—	—	—	—	—	—	—	—	—	—	—
401	Shrimp meal (AAFCO)														
402	SODIUM PHOSPHATE, MONOBASIC														
403	-technical, (6)	6-04-288	96.7	—	—	—	—	—	—	—	—	—	—	—	—
404	Monosodium phosphate (AAFCO)														
405	SODIUM TRIPOLYPHOSPHATE														
406	-commercial, (6)	6-08-076	96.0	—	—	—	—	—	—	—	—	—	—	—	—
407	Sodium tripolyphosphate (AAFCO)														
408	SORGHUM, GRAIN VARIETY. *Sorghum vulgare*														
409	-grain, (4)	4-04-383	89.0	.40	.20	.30	.60	1.60	.30	—	.51	.30	.10	.40	.60
410	SORGHUM, MILO. *Sorghum vulgare*														
411	-grain, (4)	4-04-444	89.0	.40	.20	.30	.60	1.60	.30	.10	.51	.30	.10	.40	.60
412	SOYBEAN. *Glycine max*														
413	-oil, (4)	4-07-983	100.0	—	—	—	—	—	—	—	—	—	—	—	—
414	-seed, mech-extd grnd, mx 7% fiber, (5)	5-04-600	90.0	2.89	.67	1.22	3.11	4.00	3.00	.89	2.33	1.89	.67	1.56	2.44
415	Soybean meal, mechanical extracted (AAFCO)														
416	Soybean meal, expeller extracted														
417	Soybean meal, hydraulic extracted														
418	Soybean oil meal, expeller extracted														
419	Soybean oil meal, hydraulic extracted														
420	-seed, solv-extd grnd, mx 7% fiber, (5)	5-04-604	89.0	3.60	.75	1.24	2.80	3.82	3.26	.67	2.47	1.91	.67	1.57	2.70
421	Soybean meal, solvent extracted														
422	(AAFCO)														
423	Soybean meal, solvent extracted														
424	Soybean oil meal, solvent extracted														
425	-seed wo hulls, solv-extd grnd, mx 3%														
426	fiber, (5)	5-04-612	89.8	4.23	.89	1.34	2.90	4.23	3.56	.81	3.01	2.23	.72	2.23	3.01
427	Soybean meal, dehulled, solvent														
428	extracted (AAFCO)														
429	Soybean oil meal, dehulled, solvent														
430	extracted														
431	SUGARCANE. *Saccharum officinarum*														
432	-molasses, dehy, (4)	4-04-695	96.0	—	—	—	—	—	—	—	—	—	—	—	—
433	Cane molasses, dried														
434	Molasses, cane, dried														
435	-molasses, mn 48% invert sugar mn 79.5														
436	degrees brix, (4)	4-04-696	75.0	—	—	—	—	—	—	—	—	—	—	—	—
437	Cane molasses (AAFCO)														
438	Molasses, cane														
439	SUNFLOWER. *Helianthus* spp														

(1) dry forages and roughages; (2) pasture, range plants, and forages fed green; (3) silages; (4) energy feeds; (5) protein supplements; (6) minerals; (7) vitamins; (8) additives.

TABLE 30 (CONTINUED)
AMINO ACID COMPOSITION OF SOME COMMON DOG FOOD INGREDIENTS

Line Number	SCIENTIFIC NAME / National Research Council Name (NRC) / American Feed Control Name (AAFCO) / Canada Feed Act Name (CFA) / Other Names	International Reference Number	Dry Matter (%)	Arginine (%)	Cystine (%)	Histidine (%)	Isoleucine (%)	Leucine (%)	Lysine (%)	Methionine (%)	Phenylalanine (%)	Threonine (%)	Tryptophan (%)	Tyrosine (%)	Valine (%)
440	-seed wo hulls, mech-extd grnd, (5)	5-04-738	93.0	4.52	.86	1.18	2.58	3.23	2.15	1.72	2.58	1.72	.65	–	2.58
441	Sunflower meal (AAFCO)														
442	Sunflower oil meal, without hulls,														
443	expeller extracted														
444	-seed wo hulls, solv-extd grnd, (5)	5-04-739	93.0	3.76	.75	1.08	2.26	2.80	1.83	1.61	2.37	1.61	.54	–	2.47
445	Sunflower meal (AAFCO)														
446	Sunflower oil meal, without hulls,														
447	solvent extracted														
448	SWINE. *Sus scrofa*														
449	-lard, (4)	4-04-790	100.0	–	–	–	–	–	–	–	–	–	–	–	–
450	TANKAGE—see ANIMAL														
451	TOMATO. *Lycopersicon esculentum*														
452	-pulp, dehy, (5)	5-05-041	92.0												
453	Dried tomato pomace (AAFCO)														
454	TURKEY. *Meleagris gallapavo*														
455	-offal mature birds, raw, (5)	5-07-984	28.0	–	–	–	–	–	–	–	–	–	–	–	–
456	-offal young birds, raw, (5)	5-07-985	35.0	–	–	–	–	–	–	–	–	–	–	–	–
457	-meat, raw, (5)														
458	WHEAT. *Triticum* spp														
459	-bran, dry milled, (4)	4-05-190	89.0	1.12	.34	.34	.67	1.01	.67	.11	.56	.45	.34	.45	.79
460	Wheat bran (AAFCO)														
461	Bran (CFA)														
462	WHEAT. *Triticum* spp														
463	-flour, coarse bolted, feed gr mx 2%														
464	fiber, (4)	4-05-199	89.0	.44	–	.33	.67	1.00	.33	.12	.67	.33	.12	.22	.56
465	Wheat feed flour, mx 1.5% fiber (AAFCO)														
466	Feed flour, mx 2.0% fiber (CFA)														
467	-flour byproduct, coarse sifted, mx 7%														
468	fiber, (4)	4-05-201	90.0	1.07	.22	.36	.79	1.35	.79	.20	.79	.56	.22	.45	.87
469	Wheat shorts, mx 7% fiber (AAFCO)														
470	Shorts, mx 8% fiber (CFA)														
471	-flour byproduct, fine sifted, mx 4%														
472	fiber, (4)	4-05-203	89.0	1.11	.22	.44	.78	1.33	.67	.11	.56	.56	.22	.56	.89
473	Wheat red dog, mx 4.0% fiber (AAFCO)														
474	Middlings, mx 4.5% fiber (CFA)														
475	-flour byproduct, mill run, mx 9.5%														
476	fiber, (4)	4-05-206	90.0	–	–	–	–	–	–	–	–	–	–	–	–
477	Wheat mill run (AAFCO)														
478	-grain, (4)	4-05-211	89.0	.80	.20	.30	.60	1.00	.51	.20	.70	.40	.20	.51	.60
479	-grain, Pacific coast, (4)	4-08-142	89.2	–	–	–	–	–	–	–	–	–	–	–	–
480	-grain screenings, (4)	4-05-216	89.0	–	–	–	–	–	–	–	–	–	–	–	–
481	-grits, cracked fine screened, (4)	4-07-852	88.0	.68	.34	.34	1.25	1.93	.45	.23	.68	.45	.34	–	.68
482	Farina														
483	Wheat endosperm														
484	-germ, grnd, mn 25% protein 7% fat, (5)	5-05-218	90.0	1.78	.56	.56	1.33	1.22	1.78	.33	.89	.89	.33	–	1.22
485	Wheat germ meal (AAFCO)														
486	WHEAT, DURUM. *Triticum durum*														
487	-grain, (4)	4-05-224	89.5	–	–	–	–	–	–	–	–	–	–	–	–
488	-grain, Can 4 CW mn wt 56 lb per bushel														
489	mx 2.5% foreign material, (4)	4-05-225	86.5	–	–	–	–	–	–	–	–	–	–	–	–
490	WHEAT, HARD RED SPRING. *Triticum aestivum*														
491	-grain, (4)	4-05-258	86.5	.63	.20	.20	.80	1.10	.40	.20	.90	.40	.20	.90	.80
492	WHEAT, HARD RED WINTER. *Triticum aestivum*														
493	-grain, (4)	4-05-268	89.1	.79	.28	.34	.79	1.01	.51	.22	.79	.47	.20	.67	.67
494	WHEAT, RED SPRING. *Triticum aestivum*														
495	-grain, Can 4 No mn wt 56 lb per bushel														
496	mx 2.5% foreign material, (4)	4-05-282	86.5	–	–	–	–	–	–	–	–	–	–	–	–
497	WHEAT, SOFT. *Triticum aestivum*														
498	-grain, (4)	4-05-284	90.0	.44	.22	.22	.44	.67	.33	.14	.44	.31	.13	.44	.44
499	WHEAT, SOFT RED WINTER. *Triticum aestivum*														
500	-grain, (4)	4-05-294	89.1	.40	.20	.10	–	–	.90	–	–	–	.30	.40	–
501	WHEY—see CATTLE														
502	YEAST. *Saccharomyces cerevisiae*														
503	-brewers saccharomyces, dehy grnd, mn														
504	40% protein, (7)	7-05-527	93.0	2.37	.54	1.18	2.26	3.44	3.23	.75	1.95	2.26	.54	1.61	2.47
505	Brewers dried yeast (AAFCO)														
506	-petroleum saccharomyces, dehy grnd, (7)	7-09-836	92.0	2.22	.50	.97	2.70	3.92	3.90	.89	2.41	3.26	.45	1.93	2.89
507	-primary saccharomyces, dehy, mn 40%														
508	protein, (7)	7-05-533	93.0	2.80	.54	6.02	3.87	4.00	4.09	1.08	2.69	2.69	.43	–	3.44
509	Dried yeast (AAFCO)														
510	Primary dried yeast (AAFCO)														
511	YEAST, TORULOPSIS. *Torulopsis utilis*														
512	-dehy, mn 40% protein, (7)	7-05-534	93.0	2.79	.65	1.51	3.12	3.76	4.09	.86	3.23	2.80	.54	2.26	3.12
513	Torula dried yeast (AAFCO)														

(1) dry forages and roughages; (2) pasture, range plants, and forages fed green; (3) silages; (4) energy feeds; (5) protein supplements; (6) minerals; (7) vitamins; (8) additives.

TABLE 31

FAT AND FATTY ACID (FA) COMPOSITION OF FEED INGREDIENTS [47]

SCIENTIFIC NAME National Research Council Name (NRC) American Feed Control Name (AAFCO) Canada Feed Act Name (CFA) Other Names	International Reference Number	Dry Matter (%)	Ether Extract[48] (%)	Saturated Fat[49] (%)	Unsaturated Fat[49] (%)	Linoleic Acid[50] (%)
ALFALFA. *Medicago sativa*						
-aerial part, dehy grnd, mn 17% protein, (1)	1-00-023	93.0	2.5	33.6	66.4	0.43
-leaves, dehy grnd, mn 20% protein mx 18% fiber, (1)	1-00-136	93.1	3.1	26.1	73.9	0.56
ANIMAL						
-carcass residue, dry rendered, dehy grnd, mn 9% indigestible material mx 4.4% phosphorus, (5) Meat meal (AAFCO)	5-00-385	93.5	10.6	46.7	53.3	0.36
ANIMAL						

-carcass residue w blood, dry or wet rendered dehy grnd, mn 9% indigestible material mx 4.4% phosphorus, (5)
  Meat meal tankage (AAFCO)
  Tankage, digester
	5-00-386	92.0	8.8	49.4	50.6	0.30

BARLEY. *Hordeum vulgare*						
-grain, (4)	4-00-530	89.0	2.1	29.6	70.4	0.27
BEEF TALLOW—see CATTLE						
CATTLE. *Bos* spp						
-whey, dehy, mn 65 lactose, (4) Dried whey (AAFCO)	4-01-182	94.0	0.9	63.6	36.4	0.01
-tallow, (4)	4-08-127	100.0	100.0	47.6	52.4	4.30
-milk skimmed dehy, mx 8% moisture, (5) Dried skimmed milk, feed grade (AAFCO)	5-01-127	94.0	1.0	36.2	63.8	0.01
COCONUT. *Cocos nucifera*						
-oil, (4)	4-09-320	100.0	100.0	90.3	9.7	1.10
CORN. *Zea mays*						
-grain, (4)	4-02-879	87.0	4.5	19.0	81.0	2.05
-oil, (4)	4-07-882	100.0	100.0	12.3	87.7	55.40
-distillers solubles, dehy, (5) Corn distillers dried solubles (AAFCO)	5-02-844	95.5	9.5	21.0	79.0	4.80
-gluten, wet milled dehy, (5) Corn gluten meal (AAFCO)	5-02-900	91.0	8.4	18.0	82.0	4.21
-yellow, grits by-product, mn 5% fat, (4) Yellow hominy feed (AAFCO)	4-03-011	90.5	7.2	16.0	84.0	3.71
CRAB. *Callinectes sapidus*						
-process residue, dehy grnd, mn 25% protein salt declared above 3% mx 7%, (5) Crab meal (AAFCO)	5-01-663	93.0	1.9	27.0	73.0	0.35
FISH						
-stickwater solubles, condensed, mn 30% protein, (5) Condensed fish solubles (AAFCO)	5-01-969	51.0	12.8	44.3	55.7	0.39
FISH, MENHADEN. *Brevoortia tyrannus*						
-menhaden, oil from whole fish, (7) Menhaden oil (AAFCO)	7-08-049	100.0	100.0	40.0	60.0	2.70
-whole or cuttings, cooked mech-extd dehy grnd, (5) Fish meal, menhaden	5-02-009	92.0	8.4	56.8	43.2	0.12
FLAX. *Linum usitatissimum*						
-oil, (4)	4-14-502	100.0	100.0	8.2	91.8	13.90
-seeds, solv extd grnd, mx 10% fiber, (5) Linseed meal, solvent extracted (AAFCO)	5-02-045	91.0	1.9	20.9	79.1	0.41
HOMINY FEED—see CORN, yellow						

(From No. 8, *Nutrient Requirements of Dogs*, Revised 1974, National Academy of Sciences, NRC, pp. 38–39, Table 5.)

TABLE 31 (CONTINUED)
FAT AND FATTY ACID (FA) COMPOSITION OF FEED INGREDIENTS

SCIENTIFIC NAME National Research Council Name (NRC) American Feed Control Name (AAFCO) Canada Feed Act Name (CFA) Other Names	International Reference Number	Dry Matter (%)	Ether Extract[48] (%)	Saturated Fat[49] (%)	Unsaturated Fat[49] (%)	Linoleic Acid[48] (%)
LARD—see SWINE						
LINSEED MEAL, solv extd—see FLAX						
LINSEED OIL—see FLAX						
MEAT MEAL—see ANIMAL						
MILO (sorghum grain)—see SORGHUM						
OATS. *Avena sativa*						
-grain, (4)	4-03-309	89.0	5.1	23.5	76.5	1.67
PEANUT. *Arachis hypogaea*						
-kernels, mech extd grnd, mx 7% fiber, (5)	5-03-649	92.0	7.3	23.9	76.1	1.36
Peanut meal, mechanical extracted (AAFCO)						
PECAN. *Caya illinoensis*						
-oil, (4)	4-14-503	100.0	100.0	6.9	93.1	30.60
POULTRY						
-viscera w feet w heads, dry or wet rendered dehy grnd, mx 16% ash 4% acid insoluble ash, (5)	5-03-798	93.4	12.5	36.0	64.0	1.98
Poultry by-product meal (AAFCO)						
-offal fat, (4)	4-09-319	100.0	100.0	39.1	60.9	22.30
RICE. *Oryza sativa*						
-oil from bran	4-14-504	100.0	100.0	18.5	81.5	36.50
SAFFLOWER. *Carthamus tinctorius*						
-oil, (4)	4-14-505	100.0	100.0	10.5	89.5	72.70
SKIM MILK—see CATTLE						
SORGHUM, MILO. *Sorghum vulgare*						
-grain, (4)	4-04-383	89.0	3.2	21.0	79.0	1.20
SOYBEANS. *Glycine max*						
-seeds, (5)	5-04-610	90.9	20.0	16.4	83.6	8.66
-flour by-product, grnd, mn 13% protein mx 32% fiber, (5)	5-04-594	89.4	6.8	19.5	80.5	3.29
Soybean mill feed (AAFCO)						
-seeds, solv extd grnd, mx 7% fiber, (5)	5-04-604	89.0	1.1	27.6	72.4	0.61
Soybean meal, solvent extracted 44% protein						
-seeds wo hulls, solv extd grnd, mx 3% fiber, (5)	5-04-612	89.8	0.9	28.8	71.2	0.39
Soybean meal, solvent extracted 49% protein						
SWINE. *Sus scrofa*						
-lard, (4)	4-04-790	100.0	100.0	35.9	64.1	18.30
TANKAGE, DIGESTER—see ANIMAL						
WHEAT. *Triticum* spp						
-bran, dry milled, (4)	4-05-190	89.0	4.6	20.3	79.7	2.53
-grain, (4)	4-05-211	89.0	1.9	21.4	78.6	0.65
-flour by-product, mx 9.5% fiber, (4)	4-05-205	88.9	5.2	20.2	79.8	2.79
Wheat middlings (AAFCO)						
WHEY, DEHY—see CATTLE						
YEAST. *Saccharomyces cerevisiae*						
-brewers saccharomyces, dehy grnd, mn 40% protein, (7)	7-05-527	93.0	1.1	22.7	77.3	0.05
Brewers dried yeast (AAFCO)						

[a] Data adapted from Edwards (1964).
[b] Expressed as percent (by weight) of the ingredient on a dry basis (100% dry matter).
[c] Expressed as percent (by weight) of the total fatty acids in the ingredient as fed. Fatty acids comprise about 95% of the weight of triglycerides, assuming the average triglyceride contains one glycerol, one 16-carbon fatty acid and two 18-carbon fatty acids.

5
Kennels (Houses) and Equipment

Chapter 5
Space Requirements	264
Single Doghouses	264
Indoors or Outdoors	267
Style and Design	267
Location	267
Requisites	268
Warm in Winter	268
Dry	268
Soft Bed	268
Light	268
Sanitation	268
Doghouse Materials and Plans	269
Loose or Tied	269
Wire Run	269
Kennel Run	269
Equipment	270
Multiunit Kennel	270
Requisites	273
Environmental Control for Dogs	276
Location	276
Zoning	277
Layout	277
Site	277
Floor Plan	278
Space Requirements	279
Kitchen	279
Office and Record Room	280
Trophy and Showroom	280
Grooming Room	280
Feed Room and Storage Area	280
Drainage Water	281

(Continued)

Plans, Specifications, and Construction   *281*
    Style   *281*
    Exterior Materials   *281*
    Interior Walls   *282*
    Water   *282*
    Cleaning   *282*
    Plumbing   *282*
    Heating   *282*
    Insulation   *283*
    Vapor Barrier   *283*
    Ventilation   *283*
    Flooring   *283*
Outdoor Runs   *284*
    Size of the Run   *285*
    Surface   *285*
    Fence   *285*
Interior Furnishings   *286*
    Pens   *286*
    Cages (Crates)   *287*
    Whelping Boxes   *288*
    Automatic Waterers   *288*
Equipment   *289*
Other Kennel Pointers   *289*

Fig. 235. Happy, a German Shepherd female owned by the author, and her single doghouse. Note kennel fence, also.

KENNELS (HOUSING) AND EQUIPMENT[1]

The effects of technological progress in buildings and equipment are evident everywhere—in our homes, and in the facilities that we provide for farm animals. But altogether too many dog owners continue to house their pets as their ancestors did at the time canines were domesticated; simply allowing them to sleep wherever convenient and use whatever is available. Also, there is a paucity of experimental work pertaining to the basic requirements of dog kennels (houses). The most glaring deficiencies pertain to (1) labor-saving devices, (2) stress control—including temperature, (3) proper ventilation, (4) method of handling excrement, (5) sanitation, (6) safety of animals and caretakers, (7) fire-resistant construction, (8) materials, and (9) cost.

From the standpoint of intended use, dog kennels are generally designed either to serve the one- or two-dog owner who wishes to house his dogs outdoors, or the dog breeding establishment, which maintains a number of dogs and may board and train dogs in addition to conducting a breeding program. A discussion of the kinds and plans of kennels needed for each of these is presented in this section.

---

[1] The author acknowledges with thanks the authoritative review accorded this chapter by: Mr. Herbert N. Holmes, Gunsmoke Kennels, 1541 East Lake Shore Drive, Springfield, Illinois 62705.

SPACE REQUIREMENTS

One of the first, and frequently one of the most difficult problems confronting the dog owner who wishes to construct a kennel or other item of equipment, is that of arriving at the proper size or dimensions.

Space requirements for kennels and kennel runs depend on the size of the dog. Where separate sleeping quarters are being constructed, the following procedure is recommended: project the size of the dog at maturity. Then construct the sleeping quarters of such size that the dog can lie down in it when fully stretched out. Make the door high enough to permit the dog to enter when standing up and without hitting his back.

In addition to size of dog, climate should be considered. In climates where dogs can spend much time outdoors, the need for spacious indoor quarters is less than in climates with long periods of rain, snow, or cold that keep dogs inside for days. In areas having severe winter weather, individual quarters need to be larger and facilities for indoor exercise, or covered outdoor runs, should be provided.

SINGLE DOGHOUSES

Where one or two dogs are kept, they may either be kept in the house with the owner and family or placed in separate doghouses. By a sin-

Fig. 236. A ring arrangement that will allow the dog unimpeded exercise around an elevated tie-out box. (Courtesy H. N. Holmes, Gunsmoke Kennels, Springfield, Ill.)

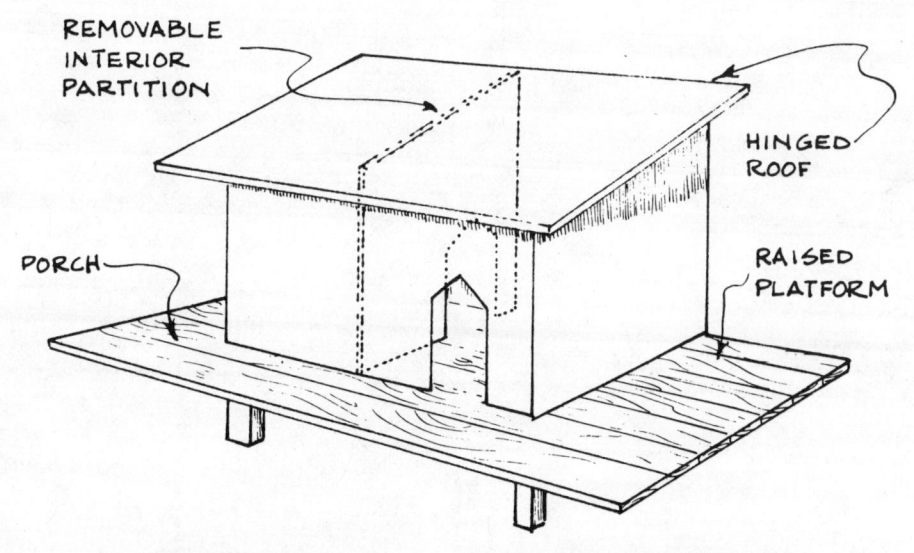

Fig. 237. Single doghouse. (Drawing by J. L. Medeiros)

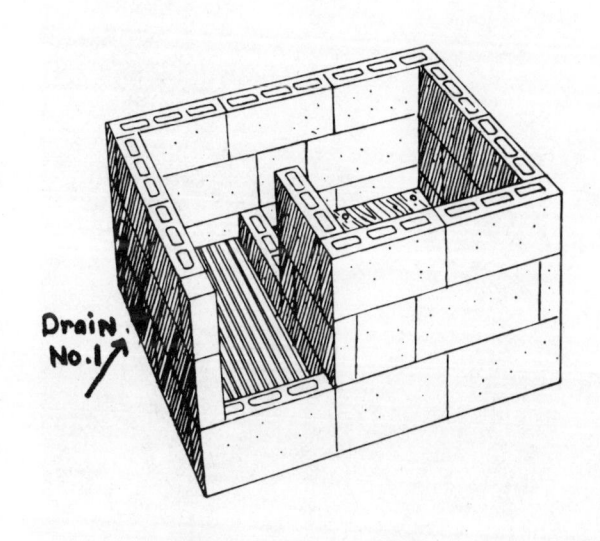

Fig. 238. Individual doghouse, which is easy to build and inexpensive.

The house measures 48″ wide, 40″ deep, and 24″ high. It is built of cinder blocks—thirty 4″ x 8″ x 16″, plus four half-blocks (used in the center of each wall—see picture) and two 4″ x 4″ x 8″ blocks. Cinder blocks are arranged as illustrated on a concrete slab or foundation, then cemented together for performance. The interior of the doghouse measures 24″ x 32″ in the sleeping quarters and 12″ x 32″ in the entryway, with the two areas separated by partition blocks as shown. Of course, a larger house can be built, simply by using more blocks.

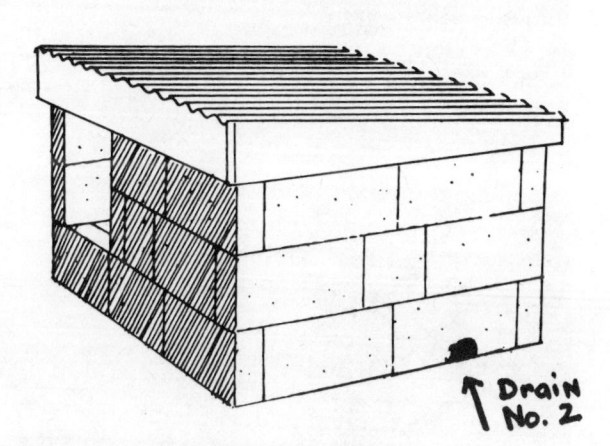

Wooden flooring is elevated 4″ from the slab to keep it dry and protect the dog from dampness.

For easy cleaning of the interior, the roof (constructed of metal over a wooden frame) is designed to be removable, with edges that extend beyond the cinder block walls and several inches down the sides.

Two 2″ pipe openings (one in each compartment) are included for drainage purposes when cleaning, flushing with a hose, and disinfecting.

(Courtesy F. J. Bartos, Kennel Manager, Carnation Farms Kennels, Carnation, Washington)

Fig. 239. Individual-unit kenneling and tree-shaded runs for Basset Hounds and Beagles. Haven Kennels, Lynn Haven, Florida, owned by Robert and Ruby Cox. (Courtesy Gaines Dog Research Center, White Plains, N.Y.)

gle doghouse, we refer to a specially constructed doghouse for keeping a dog outdoors. A soundly constructed unit of this type will keep the dog dry and comfortable in all kinds of weather. It should have runs to prevent the dog from straying, becoming a nuisance to the neighbors, being hit by a car, or getting stolen.

Frequently two friendly bitches may be housed together, or a dog may be housed with a bitch. But unless one is sure of male friendships, it is seldom safe to house two adult male dogs together. Actually, it is far better, if possible, to provide a separate house for each mature dog. Where there are two dogs, it is possible to build a two-unit doghouse with a wire divider in the middle. In this manner, the dogs can have companionship without fighting.

Night barking of dogs kept outdoors can be controlled by confining them to their individual doghouses.

Fig. 240. Tie-out boxes. (Photo by State of Illinois, Dept. of Conservation. Courtesy H. N. Holmes, Gunsmoke Kennels, Springfield, Ill.)

INDOORS OR OUTDOORS

Every dog owner will have to decide whether to keep his dog or dogs indoors or outdoors. The special circumstances of each individual owner will affect the decision. Many dogs, of course, are kept as house pets and share living accommodations with their masters. Others are provided separate outdoor houses, even though they may be permitted in the home of the master at times. Each system, indoors vs. outdoors, has its advocates.

Those who favor keeping dogs in the home argue that dogs do better if they are allowed to live and grow up in the house. They acquire better manners, they are happier, and they learn faster than dogs kept in the yard. For these reasons, so the argument goes, even if you want to have a hunting dog, you should plan to keep him in the house.

The other school of thought, which the author favors, is that the dog should be kept outside part of the time; that is, unless he is a small toy dog or house dog. Providing the dog with his own outdoor quarters then allowing visitation privileges in the home with the family is more as nature intended. Moreover, the owner has more freedom because the dog can be left in his kennel when no one is at home. Also, keeping the dog outside most of the time lessens the housekeeping problems of the owner.

STYLE AND DESIGN

Dogs are not sensitive to aesthetic considerations in the place in which they are kept; they have no appreciation of beauty. Nevertheless, the master and the master's friends do have an eye for beauty. Hence, if a single dog unit is to be used, consideration should be given to its style and beauty. It should enhance, rather than detract from the rest of the facilities of which it is a part. This means that it should be of the same general style as the house and the other buildings, and it should be attractive.

Usually the owner designs and constructs the doghouse. Sometimes, he merely uses what happens to be readily available—a barrel, a crate, or whatnot. Some of these improvised facilities work very well insofar as serving the dog is concerned, but few of them do anything to enhance the premises.

Commercially built doghouses are also available. Unless the dog owner is a "do-it-yourselfer," this may be the best bet. Such doghouses are usually well constructed; and there is a choice of sizes and styles.

LOCATION

Most single doghouses are portable; hence, they may be located wherever the owner wishes to have them. When locating the doghouse, consideration should be given to the following points:

1. *Accessibility*—The doghouse should be adjacent to a sidewalk or paved drive, thereby mak-

ing it easily accessible in all kinds of weather.

2. *Runway*—It should be so located that an adjacent runway can be provided.

3. *High and dry*—It should be on high ground, with drainage away from it, thereby making for dryness.

4. *Convenient to water and electricity*—Water should be available, and electricity should be in near proximity.

5. *Watchdogs*—The house for watchdogs should be so located that the dog will be able to alert the homeowner when the occasion demands; yet, it should be so situated that the dog can be confined when desired so that he will not interfere with guests or wanted visitors.

6. *Attractiveness*—The doghouse should be located so that it will enhance and fit into the scheme of all of the facilities of which it is a part.

REQUISITES

There are certain general requisites of all doghouses that should be considered. Among the most important ones are: warmth, dryness, softness of bed, light, and sanitation. Because of the importance of each of these requisites, they will be treated separately.

WARM IN WINTER

For dogs that are kept outdoors, single kennels are available that are heated electrically. Of course, provision for heating homemade kennels can be made, also.

Adult dogs with long hair require artificial heat in only the coldest of climates, if they are provided with tight boxes placed under shelter. However, puppies, even if they have long hair, need heat in cold weather up until weaning time, and even thereafter if they are not permitted to sleep together. When puppies are snuggled up together in a tight doghouse, with shredded paper bedding, they can withstand much cold without discomfort. During cold weather, all dogs without artificial heat should have an increase of their rations—especially as pertains to fat content.

Whatever artificial heat is provided for dogs, should be safe, foolproof, and dog-proof. Special caution should be exercised to make sure that electric wiring is not exposed, that whatever heaters are provided cannot be tipped over, and that sparks from electrical wiring or from heating equipment cannot ignite the premises. Many doghouses have been burned as a result of defective wiring and heating apparatus, or careless handling of it, resulting in the death of the inmates.

DRY

It is important that the quarters for the dog should be dry and that they should be warm. A damp, drafty doghouse is the cause of much disease and indisposition. It will do no harm to permit a dog to go out in inclement weather on his own choice, provided he has a sheltered bed to which he may return and dry himself. Dryness is best assured by having the doghouse on high ground and slightly raised, by having a roof that will turn water away, and by having overhanging eaves that prevent rain from beating in.

SOFT BED

Dogs like soft beds of sufficient thickness to protect them from the coldness of floors. The bed should be secluded. During mild weather, it may be placed in an open box. But, during most of the year, it needs to be in a covered doghouse.

The cushion, or bed, may be a burlap bag stuffed with shredded paper, wood shavings, or excelsior. Straw, hay, or grass should not be used because many dogs are allergic to fungi found on vegetable matter.

LIGHT

Except for a dark place in which to retire, the kennel should be relatively light. If sunshine is available for at least a part of the day, so much the better.

SANITATION

By sanitation is meant the measures that should be taken to keep the dog free from diseases and parasites. Excreta should be removed from the run daily, or, even better, twice daily; bones should not be permitted to accumulate in the dog's bed or run; feeding utensils should be cleaned after each feeding; and boxes and doghouses should be thoroughly scrubbed and disinfected at frequent intervals. Persistent filth in kennels can be counted on as a source of illness sooner or later. It is one of the axioms of keeping dogs that their quarters must be sanitary, or disease and parasites are sure to ensue.

The facilities for the dog should be constructed with sanitation in mind. The doghouse should have a hinged roof, thereby permitting it to be opened for easy cleaning. All dog boxes should be portable, so that they can be taken out and scrubbed. Runs should be easily accessible so that excreta can be removed at frequent intervals.

For information relative to disinfectants, see Table 38 in chapter 8.

DOGHOUSE MATERIALS AND PLANS

Exterior plywood is suitable building material for a doghouse, with the thickness determined by the climate in which the house is to be used. The wood can be treated with weather-resistant finishes. Insulation between double walls and floors gives added comfort in hot and cold weather.

The size of the doghouse should, of course, be adequate for the dog.

Two compartments are recommended, with separation by a removable partition. With this arrangement, the dog can enter, turn into the end of the box, and bed down in the second compartment. This keeps the direct wind off him. This is important because drafts make for illness. The panel should be removed in hot weather for maximum coolness. Also, the house can be constructed with removable hinged front and/or back walls, thereby converting it into an open shed, or a shade, that is airy, yet providing shelter from rain. A hinged roof also makes for ease of cleaning.

The following additional features should be incorporated in the individual doghouse:

1. It should be provided with a door sill, three inches or higher, to reduce drafts.

2. It should be raised three or four inches, or more, off the ground in order to prevent water from running in or moisture from rotting the floor.

3. It should have an overhanging roof above the door to prevent rain from beating in.

4. In very hot areas, it may be well to provide for sufficient overhang to the roof so that it may serve as a shade in the summertime.

5. A shed-type roof, with a slight slope, is recommended; it will turn water away, and it will serve as a sundeck for the dog.

LOOSE OR TIED

A provision must be made for a place of exercise and relief at frequent intervals for dogs kept in the house with the family. Of course, dogs may be exercised on a leash, but, this is not always convenient. Also, an enclosed yard may be used, but, here again, such facilities are not always available. Just turning a dog out isn't the answer either, for there is the ever present danger of cars running over him or of him becoming a nuisance to the neighbors. Hence, it is usually best to provide a wire run or a kennel run, even for house dogs.

WIRE RUN

Sometimes it is too expensive to have a fenced run. This is particularly true where dog owners are renting. In such cases, and for house dogs as well, a wire run will work very well. This consists of stringing wire between two objects; for example, from the back porch to a tree out in the yard. Then a ring is put on the wire and a leash is fastened to this. The other end of the leash is fastened to the dog's collar. When these are all hooked together, the dog can run back and forth from one end of the wire to the other, between the two objects. Also, he can be taught to relieve himself at one end of the run.

When leaving a dog on a wire run (tethered), make sure that he has water and can reach shade in hot weather, and that he can reach shelter in inclement weather.

KENNEL RUN

It is important that the doghouse open into a kennel run. This gives the dog an opportunity to get frequent respites from captivity, to obtain needed exercise, and to relieve himself. Such runs need not be too large, but they should be of sufficient size to relieve them of the aspect of cages. Where concrete is used, a 5' x 12' kennel run will suffice; with gravel, a 10' x 20' run is recommended.

The kennel run should be enclosed with fencing that is strong enough that dogs cannot tear it with their teeth and that is high enough that dogs cannot jump or climb over it. A galvanized steel fence of chain-link type or storm fencing is recommended. It should be 6 feet high, which is high enough to prevent most dogs from climbing over it. If jumping or climbing is encountered, construct in-turning flanges of wire netting at the top of the fence. If digging under is encountered, extend fencing inward at the bottom

Fig. 241. Puppy kennel, showing concrete surfaced, outdoor runs, with steel fencing. (Courtesy P. Bernard Smith Company, Kensington, Md.)

of the fence and cover it with soil as directed in a later section in this chapter.

The gates, hinges, latches, and other hardware of the outdoor kennel must be trustworthy; otherwise, the primary purpose of having such quarters to confine dogs will be useless. When you put a dog in a kennel, you want to be sure that he will be there when you return. For this reason, an improvised kennel made of old chicken wire will not suffice; you can never depend on it.

Unless a hard surface is provided, any small runway will become a mud hole during inclement weather. Everything considered, probably the best surface material for the one- or two-dog run is medium-sized, round gravel. Paved runs are easy to keep clean, but they are expensive and hard on the dog's feet. Hence, when dogs are confined on concrete or asphalt, or other hard surface, for long periods of time, they are prone to spread in their shoulders and become sore and/or flat-footed. If concrete runs are used, they should be constructed so that there is a slope of one-fourth inch to the foot, in order that the excreta can be flushed away more efficiently. Also, because concrete is cold in the winter and hot in the summer, a low platform of wood, large enough to enable the dog to sprawl out on it full length, should be provided.

Where a gravel arrangement is used, it is well that it be located on well-drained soil.

EQUIPMENT

A one- and two-dog owner has need for a few items of basic equipment with which to provide food, sanitation, and first aid for the dog. A list of the minimum equipment necessary follows:

1. Two dishes; one for food, the other for water—preferably, these should be of stainless steel
2. Cleaning tools, including a broom, a shovel, and a bucket
3. Disinfectant
4. Bedding
5. Grooming kit
6. First aid kit
7. Food.

The dishes are in constant use and are usually left outside. The food is usually stored in the kitchen pantry. The rest of the items of equipment are usually stored in the garage or in a separate service building.

MULTIUNIT KENNEL

Multiunit kennels are kennels that house a number of dogs, either in a central type house or by having a number of single dog units. Such

Figs. 242–251. Aranwood, elegant boarding kennel on a 200-acre estate, near Mahwah, New Jersey, 45 minutes from metropolitan New York. (Pictures courtesy of Arthur L. Sachs, owner)

Fig. 242. Exterior view of the kennel, nestled in the foothills of the Ramapo Mountains.

kennels are usually owned and operated as a business, with professional management in charge. Most of them are breeding establishments; and many of them also train and/or board dogs. For these establishments, especially designed buildings and equipment are necessary.

Fig. 243. Registering at Aranwood Kennels, A detailed fact sheet is made out, giving the dog's individual diet and eating habits, and the owner's grooming choice. A guest chart is maintained for each dog, detailing eating, exercising, and general demeanor.

Fig. 244. Living quarters at Aranwood. The owners of canine guests can choose between an Efficiency Apartment, a Studio, an Executive Suite, a Master Suite, or a Family Suite. Rates start at $7.50 and go to $19.50 per day. And there's a choice of room colors —blue, yellow, green, aquamarine, red, or rust.

Fig. 245. A Family Suite, 6' x 13', the largest room available at Aranwood. The rate, $19.50 per day.

Fig. 246. Efficiency Apartment, a 4' x 5' room, at Aranwood. The rate $7.50 per day.

Fig. 247. One of the exercise runs at Aranwood. Note the lounge deck, so that the dog does not have to lie on the cold concrete.

Fig. 248. Ultramodern kitchen, where all individual menus are displayed and meals are prepared. It is equipped with (1) stainless steel feeding bowls, which are mechanically washed and sterilized by an industrial dishwasher, and (2) full restaurant refrigeration and freezing, to insure the freshest and purest of foods. The dog is fed whatever, and as much as, the owner requests. Among Aranwood's food requests have been steaks, grass, and cornflakes topped by bananas and strawberries; occasionally teeth must be brushed after each meal.

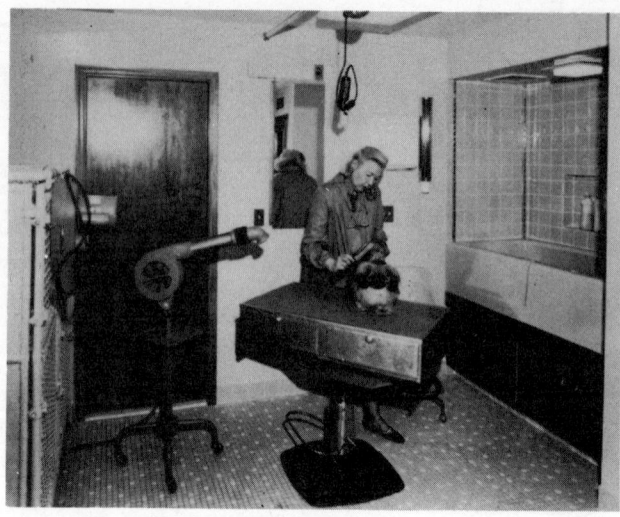

Fig. 250. The grooming salon, showing the wash area for small dogs.

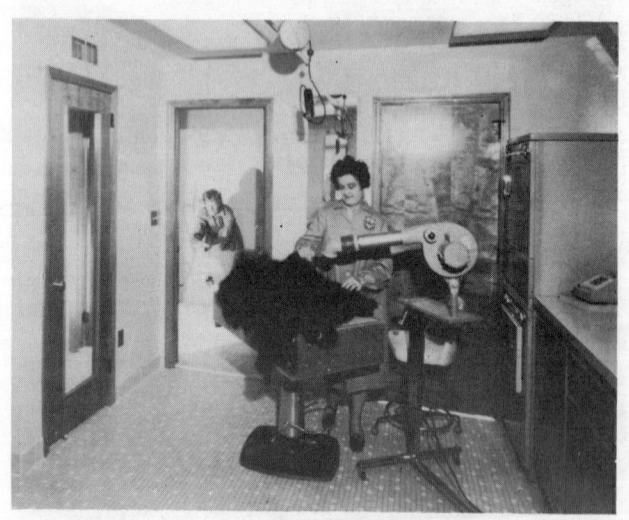

Fig. 249. The grooming salon at Aranwood. Note the large walk-in wash area for large dogs, to the left and rear. If desired by the owner, the dog is bathed, brushed, groomed, and trimmed according to instructions; and at no extra charge. Also, the grooming salon accepts outside (nonboarding) dogs by appointment.

Fig. 251. The office at Aranwood, where dogs are signed out and bills are paid.

Because of the increasing importance and sophistication of dogs, more and more modern, multiunit kennels will evolve; and more and more of these will meet the best requisites in building designs employed for other classes of animals.

Fig. 252. Multiunit kennel building, with well-fenced, concrete outdoor runs. (Courtesy H. N. Holmes, Gunsmoke Kennels, Springfield, Ill.)

REQUISITES

Each kennel is different, and the type and size of buildings will vary accordingly. Among the factors determining the type and size of buildings are: (1) the breed of dog, (2) tenant or owner operation, (3) personal preference, (4) climatic conditions of the region, and (5) storage requirements. Thus, the specific requisites of kennels will vary according to the needs of the region, state, community, and individual kennel. There are, however, certain general requirements of kennels that should always be considered; and it is with these that the ensuing discussion will deal. Once buildings are constructed, there is a definite limit to the changes that can be made in remodeling. Consequently, it is most important that very careful consideration be given to their initial design. The following points are pertinent thereto:

1. *Reasonable construction and maintenance cost*—The word *reasonable* is used herein, because, as is true in homes for people, low-cost buildings of durable construction are a thing of the past. However, if buildings are to be practical and economical, there must be reasonable construction and maintenance costs. In the first place, they cannot be built if the necessary capital is not available. Secondly, commercial kennels must be paid for out of the enterprises they house, if desirable economic relationships are to be maintained.

In addition to the practical aspects, however, certain intangible values accrue from having good buildings, such as the pride and satisfaction derived in caring for animals under such circumstances, reduced hazards, and, in the case of purebred dogs, the advertising value to accrue from an attractive set of buildings.

2. *Flexible design*—In order that buildings may be adapted to changes in a changing world, they should be as flexible in design as possible. This needed flexibility can best be achieved by constructing a one-story building with the maximum of movable partitions and equipment.

At the present time, it is impossible to predict the kind and extent of changes that will come with further mechanization and environmental control. It is obvious, however, that they will materially affect cleaning, and that one will not be able to take full advantage of these and other developments unless maximum flexibility in building design exists.

3. *Reduce labor*—Because of the high cost of labor, now and in the future, labor requirements must be held to a minimum. To this end, and to the extent that it is practical, all possible labor-saving considerations and devices should be a part of building construction.

4. *Utility value*—Buildings should have utility value; that is, they should be designed so that they will best serve their intended purpose—breeding, showing, training, or boarding; or any combination of two or more of these.

5. *Provide protection from the elements*—Kennels should provide protection from rain, snow, sun, and wind. Short-haired dogs have less resistance to weather changes than long-haired dogs. It is especially important, therefore, that their quarters provide a desirable temperature.

6. *Provide protection for newborn animals*—Puppies are "canine babies" and must be protected as such. Suitable buildings make it possible to save more newborn animals.

7. *Attractiveness*—Any structure that has utility value and is erected in good proportions and in harmony with the natural surroundings will add to the value of the kennel and the general enjoyment of living. Attractive buildings also add materially to the sale value of property.

8. *Durability*—Kennels should be adequately durable to stand firm against wind and weather and to last for a sufficient span of time without excessive maintenance cost, but they need not be so expensively or permanently constructed that there is danger of their becoming obsolete before being worn out. Thus, it is noteworthy that, with the mechanization of farms and ranches, many a draft horse barn throughout the country is either idle or has been remodeled, after a fashion, for the storage of the tractor.

Income tax authorities recognize the need for replacing farm buildings with new and modern structures. Thus, a barn depreciated at the rate of four percent annually is entirely written off the books in twenty-five years.

9. *Dryness*—Buildings should be constructed to assist in providing a dry bed for dogs. This means that the kennel should be located on high ground with drainage away from the building and that, except in dry areas, large buildings should be provided with eave troughs and down spouts that empty into a tile line draining away from the building. Proper ventilation and direct sunlight also aid materially in providing dry bedding. In individual type houses, it is important that the kennel be elevated and that there be overhanging eaves in order to assure dryness.

10. *Well ventilated*—Ventilation refers to the changing of air—the replacement of foul air with fresh air. Kennels should be well ventilated, but care must be taken to avoid direct drafts. Dogs cannot do well in poorly ventilated kennels. If a choice must be made between warmth and ventilation, secure the latter. The primary purposes of ventilation are to remove excess moisture and foul odors. A desirable ventilation system accomplishes these objectives with a minimum temperature variation inside the building.

Ventilation may be secured by various systems. The simplest method usually consists of open doors, or windows that open inwardly from the top. A more complete method of ventilating tight buildings consists of a system of intake and outtake flues operated on the basis of either gravity or forced ventilation. Whatever the system, proper ventilation is one in which the foul air is drawn off and harmful humidity conditions are eliminated without excess heat loss or creation of drafts.

11. *Well lighted*—Proper lighting is essential for visibility and the convenience of caretakers. A well-lighted building may be obtained in the following ways: (a) through an open door arrangement, (b) by providing adequate windows or plastic materials designed to let light through, (c) by artificial lights, or (d) through a combination of the previous three ways, as is usually the case.

12. *Direct sunlight*—Direct sunlight is a good germicide, and arrangements should be made to obtain its benefits.

13. *Sanitary*—Sanitation is essential for disease prevention and parasite control. This means that kennels should be constructed so that they may be easily cleaned, thoroughly disinfected, and free from vermin. Sanitation is also promoted structurally by providing for direct sunlight and elimination of moisture. Smooth walls and hard-surfaced or wire floors (a floor made of wire) are the most satisfactory from this standpoint.

14. *Easily cleaned*—A kennel that is arranged so that it may be easily cleaned is more likely to be kept in a sanitary condition. Construction that will permit mechanical disposal of excreta,

Fig. 253. A gutter flushing system, with trapdoor. This system may be employed for drainage of either interior pens or outdoor runs. (Courtesy F. J. Bartos, Kennel Manager, Carnation Farms Kennels, Carnation, Wash.)

in addition to such things as smooth walls and floors, is an asset from the standpoint of ease in cleaning.

15. *Proper provision for excreta disposal*—The excreta disposal system should be adapted to the particular conditions. Whatever the method, it should dispose of the excreta efficiently and as intended; and it should make for the maximum degree of sanitation with a minimum amount of odor, flies, and complaint from the neighbors.

16. *Convenient*—Kennels should be constructed to furnish the greatest possible convenience, which makes for fewer steps and man-hours. This means that attention should be given to the most convenient arrangement for feeding, watering, and bedding the dogs, and for cleaning the kennel. Among the most important points to be considered are the locations of the water, feed room, driveways, feed alleys, doors, and windows, and the arrangement for removing excreta with a minimum of labor. Greater convenience usually means that one man can and will care for more dogs, and this means greater profits. It is significant to note that an hour saved each day is equivalent to eliminating a full month's work in a year.

17. *Adequate space for animals*—Kennels should be of adequate size to accommodate the existing number of dogs, expected young, and any contemplated early expansion in operations. In general, too little space may jeopardize the health and well-being of animals; whereas too much space may make the buildings and equipment more expensive than necessary.

18. *Adequate space for food and bedding storage*—In arriving at the space needs for food and bedding storage, consideration should be given to (a) the size of dog, (b) the management practices, and (c) the frequency of food and bedding delivery.

19. *Minimum fire risk*—The principal causes of fire losses in kennels are smoking, spontaneous combustion, lightning, defective flues, sparks on roof, faulty wiring, ignition caused by accidents with equipment, trash fires, gasoline, and matches. The structural safeguards against fire include tile-lined flues, spark arrestors on chimneys, fire-resistant or fireproof shingles, masonry construction, approved wiring that is inspected at intervals, approved installations of equipment, lightning protection in those areas where thunderstorms are frequent and intense, and "no smoking" signs that are observed. In addition to these precautions, exit doors should be provided so that dogs may be removed from the building quickly in case of fire.

20. *Safety*—In the construction of kennels, it is important that safety features be given consideration. For example, doors should have adequate height and width; door sills should be low or omitted; and paved areas should not be dangerously smooth and slick.

21. *Rodent control*—Kennels, especially the food storage parts thereof, should be constructed to provide the maximum protection against rats, mice, and other rodents. This is important both from the standpoint of food conservation and disease prevention. New buildings may be rat-proofed as follows:

    a. By installing a concrete curtain wall around the foundation. This prevents rats from burrowing under the buildings.

    b. By using hardware cloth around the feed room and/or kitchen.

22. *Adjacent and suitable runs*—Kennels should be provided with adjacent, well-drained, safe, durably fenced, and attractive runs. Where land area is very restricted and in muddy areas, it may be necessary to resort to pavement. If the entire corral or lot is not surfaced, it will be helpful at least to pave a strip in front of the entrance to the quarters. It is recommended that runs be fenced with six-foot galvanized steel, cyclone-type fence, on steel post set in concrete.

23. *Water*—It is important that kennels have plenty of water, conveniently located for use in

Fig. 254. Kennel runs at Waiterock Ranch Kennels, noted dog-breeding establishment, Lafayette, California. Each run has its own water faucet (copper plumbing) and a metal pail kept under the shade next to the building and filled with water at all times. (Courtesy Juanita W. Howard, Waiterock Ranch, Lafayette, Calif.)

watering the dogs and in flushing and cleaning the kennel. Water is also important from the standpoint of providing fire protection. For the latter purpose, there should be adequate volume and pressure.

24. *Modify extreme temperatures*—Good kennels should make for uniform temperature, thereby assuring greater comfort to both man and dog. In order to accomplish this requisite, buildings in northern areas are constructed for warmth in the winter; whereas in the South they are made cool for summer. Fortunately, nature has provided warm coats for long-haired dogs, and it is not necessary that they have exceedingly warm buildings, although such shelter is needed for short-haired dogs and all puppies. In no case should warmth of a building be obtained at the cost of poor ventilation.

25. *Keep proper humidity*—Humidity refers to the amount of moisture in the air. The air inside kennels picks up moisture from respiration and excrement. When the humidity of a building is high, it causes a sensation of warmth in the summer and coldness in the winter. When there is a difference of several degrees between inside and outside temperatures, the moisture condenses on the cold surfaces. In freezing weather, this condensation forms frost. Condensation on the walls or other surfaces is evidence of unsatisfactory moisture conditions. Such condensation is objectionable because it is harmful for dogs to go from a moist, warm kennel into the cold outside air and because the excess moisture causes the structure to decay or deteriorate.

26. *Properly insulated*—Proper insulation, which slows up the passage of heat, is desirable in the summer as well as in the winter. In the winter, it helps to hold the heat within the building, while in the summer it tends to prevent the heat from entering the structure.

27. *Adapted to present and future needs*—In building a kennel, the owner should give consideration to present needs and future plans, the present and potential production, and the various uses for which the building is needed now and in the future. Thus, in constructing a kennel, it is desirable that it be of a size that will meet the existing conditions and be so built as to permit the erection of additions without disturbing the convenient arrangement or without tearing down any part of the structure.

28. *Protect animal health*—Kennels should provide healthful indoor living conditions for the occupants. This is most important, for healthy animals are the profitable ones for the commercial kennel operator.

ENVIRONMENTAL CONTROL FOR DOGS

Man achieves environmental control through clothing, vacationing in resort areas, and air-conditioned homes and cars. In the wild, dogs achieved environmental control in their dens, which were warm in the wintertime and cool in the summer. Also, they grow a heavier coat in the winter—this is particularly true of the long-haired breeds.

Limited basic research with farm animals has shown that they are more efficient—that they produce and perform better, and require less feed—if raised under ideal conditions of temperature, humidity, and ventilation. There is reason to believe that the same situation applies to dogs. The primary reason for having kennels, therefore, is to modify the environment. Properly designed kennels can be used to approach the environment desired. Naturally, the environmental control facilities must be balanced against the expected increased return; and there is a point beyond which further expenditures on environmental control will not increase returns sufficiently to justify the added cost. This point of diminishing returns will differ between sections of the country, between dogs of different ages (higher expenditures for environmental control can be justified for puppies than for adult animals), and between operators. Labor and food costs will enter the picture, also.

Because there is a paucity of experimental work on environmental control for dogs upon which to base recommendations for kennels, confinement systems in use for other classes of animals were studied by the author as a means of evolving with the recommendations given in Table 32.

It is hoped that these recommendations will be helpful guides until such time as more experimental work on the environmental control of dogs has been researched.

LOCATION

The kennels should be located so as to be:

1. *Accessible*—The kennel should be on an all-weather road, thereby facilitating accessibility of both people and services.

TABLE 32

ENVIRONMENTAL CONTROL FOR DOGS

Dogs	Temperature Comfort Zone (°F)	(°C)	Temperature Optimum (°F)	(°C)	Humidity Acceptable (%)	Humidity Preferred (%)	Drinking Water Winter (°F)	(°C)	Drinking Water Summer (°F)	(°C)
Adult dogs:										
Long haired	35–65	2–17	50	10	50–75	60	50	10	65–75	15–24
Medium haired	45–75	7–24	60	15	50–75	60	50	10	60–75	15–24
Short haired	60–80	15–27	70	21	50–75	60	50	10	60–70	15–24
Puppies	70–80[2]	20–27	75	24	50–75	60	60	15	60–75	15–24

[2] From birth to the fifth day of age, puppies should be kept in 85–90° F temperature.

2. *High and dry*—It should be on high ground, with pervious soil, and with drainage away from it, insuring dryness.

3. *Expandable*—There should be provision for easy expansion, if and when the time comes. Often a building can be expanded in length provided no other structure or utilities interfere.

4. *Convenient to water and electricity*—Water should be available and plentiful and electricity should be in near proximity.

ZONING

In the present era of environmental concern and protest, zoning consideration is most important. For this reason, prospective kennel owners should investigate local laws before starting construction. Often zoning ordinances prohibit a kennel operation, or limit the number of dogs that can be owned. Also, building codes may restrict certain types of structures.

LAYOUT

Prior to acquiring the site and starting construction, the kennel owner may avoid much subsequent difficulty and expense by first doing some paper-and-pencil planning. He should decide on the specific kind of enterprise—breeding, showing, training, and/or boarding; and he should decide on the size of the enterprise. Then, he should sketch out the buildings and equipment required to meet these needs in the most efficient and economical manner. In particular, the preliminary layout of the kennel should include the following:

1. *The management system*—The management system will greatly affect the kind, size, and amount of buildings and equipment. For example, the kennel owner must first decide whether he will rely on a multipurpose building or have a bunch of individual, single-unit doghouses; or perhaps a combination of the two. Also, he should decide whether he intends to buy commercial dog food, or do home mixing and cooking.

2. *Plans for the flow of materials*—Next, the kennel owner should develop detailed plans for the flow of all materials, with primary consideration given to maximum automation and minimum labor and expenses. These plans should include provision for (a) delivering the food to the dogs at the desired time and place, (b) providing a sanitary water supply, (c) removing excrement, and (d) the sale of dogs. All of these considerations, and more, enter into the handling of materials to, within, and from buildings.

The above information, constituting the layout of operations, should first be put on paper by the owner. From this, the architect can design, or recommend, buildings and equipment that most effectively and economically meet the production requirements of the planned enterprise.

SITE

Over most of the United States, a south or southeast exposure is best for a kennel; and usually an area that is square or rectangular works best. Consideration should be given to the following pertinent points when selecting the specific site:

1. Any houses in the immediate area of the kennel should be on the windward side, so that odors blow away from them, rather than toward them. The area should be protected from strong winds by a hill, by trees, or by buildings.

2. There should be a maximum of sunshine in the winter.

3. There should be a maximum of shade and of breezes in the summer.

4. The site should be in an attractive area, which is important, both from the standpoint of the caretakers and visitors.

FLOOR PLAN

The following two basic floor plans are used in multiunit kennels:

1. *Double row*—For very large kennels, the double-row house is standard construction. It is designed with pens of dogs on either side of a center aisle. Each pen opens into an individual run. Kennels of this design are usually located with the long axis north-south, so that the pens or stalls on either side may receive direct sun-

Fig. 255. A sanitary double-row kennel—one that may be easily cleaned and thoroughly disinfected, and that is free from vermin. Note the smooth walls and hard-surfaced floors. (Courtesy The Seeing Eye, Inc., Morristown, N.J.)

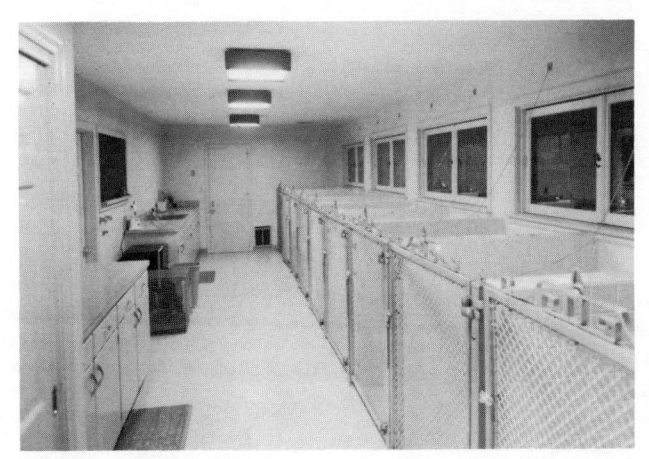

Fig. 256. Pens or stalls on one side of kennel. (Courtesy Mrs. Charles R. Anderson, Cedwood Puli Kennels, Bristol, Conn.)

Fig. 257. Stainless steel dishes and dish washing facilities. In a kennel, dishes should be washed daily to protect the health and well-being of the dogs. (Courtesy Leader Dogs for the Blind, Rochester, Mich.)

light during a part of the day.

2. *Single row*—Single-row kennels are generally used where it is desired that all pens or stalls have a south exposure, and where the kennel is of medium to small size. It consists of one row of pens or stalls along the south side of the building with a side aisle along the north. Here again, each pen opens into an individual run.

With either type of building—double row or single row—the kitchen, storage area, record room, grooming and showroom, and trophy room may either be located at one end of the building, or near the center.

SPACE REQUIREMENTS

The space requirements for the pens will depend primarily on the size of the dog and the weather conditions of the area. Generally speaking, dogs of the large breeds should have pens about 6' x 8' in size; small breeds or medium-sized breeds should have pens about 4' x 4' in size. In climates where dogs can spend much time in the outdoor runs, the need for spacious indoor quarters is less than in climates with long periods of rain, snow, or cold that keep dogs indoors for long periods. In cold areas, either each individual pen should be larger or facilities for indoor exercise or covered runs should be provided.

KITCHEN

All multiunit kennels should be equipped with a modern kitchen, with the size of the kitchen

Fig. 258. Feed room–kitchen. (Courtesy Claude H. Miller, Miller's Valley Redbones, Annville, Pa.)

and the size of the equipment therein dependent upon the number of dogs to be maintained in the kennel and whether or not feed is home mixed and cooked. It goes without saying that a larger kitchen area and larger equipment will be required if it is the intent to prepare dog foods at the kennel.

The kitchen should be equipped with the following basics: stove, refrigerator, sink, cupboards, and table area. The floor should be covered with linoleum or tile, and the interior of the kitchen should be finished. All in all, it should look much like the kitchen in any home, and it should be just as easy to keep clean.

OFFICE AND RECORD ROOM

The best way to assure that the business affairs —correspondence and records—of the kennel will be well kept is to provide a separate office and record room. It need not be large or elaborate, but it must be orderly. It reflects how the business is conducted. The office should be equipped with a desk, chairs, filing cabinets, a table for magazines and the like, and a typewriter if the person in charge can type.

It's exceedingly important that all registrations, transfers, birth records, and correspondence be handled with promptness and accuracy.

Fig. 259. A reception room. Note trophies and books. (Courtesy Mrs. Charles R. Anderson, Cedwood Puli Kennels, Bristol, Conn.)

TROPHY AND SHOWROOM

A trophy and showroom is an essential part of a kennel. In the smaller kennels, a combination trophy-showroom and office is usually used, for practical reasons. In larger kennels, the trophy room is frequently the showplace of the establishment. As such, the owner takes great pride in showing it off.

Ribbons and trophies are on permanent display in this room. Additionally, many kennels use the trophy room as a place for displaying puppies that are for sale. By doing so, it is possible to show them off to prospective buyers, without allowing visitors to wander through the main kennel. This is good procedure from the standpoint of disease control.

The trophy and showroom should be floored, rodent-proof, bird-proof, and sealed over.

GROOMING ROOM

The larger kennels have a separate grooming room, equipped with a grooming table and a tub. In smaller kennels, the grooming facilities may be combined in an all-purpose workroom.

The grooming table should be of adequate size for the dogs normally trimmed on it; and, preferably, it should have an adjustable height arrangement, so that it may be raised or lowered as the size of the dog necessitates. Also, it should be equipped with a nonskid surface and an attachable grooming rod to hold the dog in place. Professionals will want a large mirror hung a few feet from the table and at a height so that they can see the dog's reflection in it while they work.

The tub should be set up so that the person doing the work does not have to bend over too far to work comfortably.

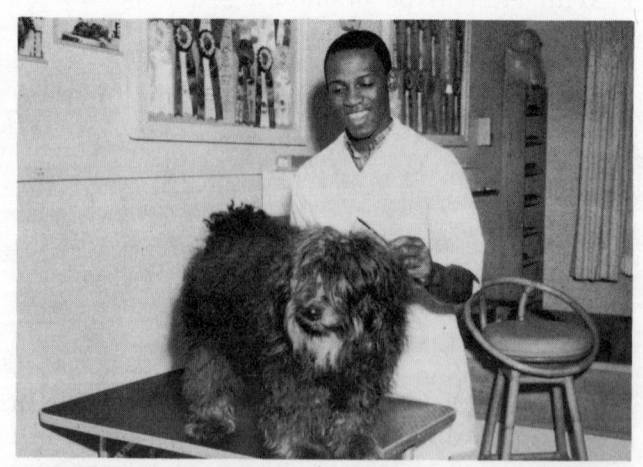

Fig. 260. Grooming room, with grooming table. (Courtesy Mrs. Charles R. Anderson, Cedwood Puli Kennels, Bristol, Conn.)

FEED ROOM AND STORAGE AREA

The larger and more modern kennels usually try to have a separate feed room; smaller kennels may combine the feed room with an all-purpose room, storage room, or some other room.

Whatever the arrangement, feed should never be stored in open containers, because of possible contamination by rodents whose excreta can transmit leptospirosis or other infections.

The size and nature of the feed room will be dependent upon the number of dogs and whether or not commercial food is used.

DRAINAGE WATER

Drainage water accrues from rainfall, excrement, and washing the house and runs. In these days of environmental control consciousness, it is important that drainage water be disposed of properly. Hillside drainage will facilitate movement. If properly constructed, any one of the following methods of disposing of drainage water will be satisfactory: a sewage line, a septic tank, or a lagoon.

PLANS, SPECIFICATIONS, AND CONSTRUCTION

Because of variations in climatic conditions, sizes and types of kennels, and systems of management, no attempt will be made here to present detailed building and equipment plans and specifications, or to suggest construction procedure. Rather, it is the intent merely to convey suggestions regarding some of the desirable features in use by kennels in various parts of the country. For detailed plans and specifications, the dog owner should study successful kennels, and visit with folks who have been successful in operations similar to what he intends to develop. Next, he should call upon a local architect. Before taking the latter step, however, it should be realized that the architect probably knows nothing about a kennel. Thus, it will save you time and expense, as well as expedite matters, if you will assemble information relative to the following before going to the architect:

1. A topographic map of the area
2. The space requirements
3. The size unit desired
4. The management systems that you plan to follow
5. The flow of materials
6. The style that you feel you want.

Generally speaking, it is best to engage the services of an architect and to contract with a construction man to build a kennel. They know, and will comply with, the building codes of the area. Also, they are familiar with the building materials that are available.

Of course, one of the very first things that a person planning to build a kennel wants to know is, "How much will it cost me?" Once you have decided on the size unit and the type of material, most local building contractors will be able to give you a good approximation on the basis of cost per square foot.

STYLE

An attractive kennel makes for, as Edgar Guest said, a "heap of living" for the owner, the caretakers, and the visitors. Besides, it enhances the sale value of the property. A kennel that has utility value, is in good proportions, and is in harmony with natural surroundings, will have aesthetic value. Good design is never achieved by indulgence in fads, frills, or highly ornamental features.

Fig. 261. Front view of Waiterock Ranch Kennels, Lafayette, California. Waiterock has bred English Springer Spaniels and American Cocker Spaniels since 1935, and red English Cocker Spaniels and Cavalier King Charles Spaniels since 1967. (Courtesy Juanita W. Howard, Waiterock Ranch, Lafayette, Calif.)

EXTERIOR MATERIALS

Technology has evolved with new building materials and forced the improvement of old ones. In selecting dog building materials, consideration should be given to (1) initial cost, (2) durability and minimum maintenance, (3) attractiveness,

(4) fire resistance, and (5) building codes.

Among the materials available and being used are:

1. Masonry, including concrete, concrete blocks, cinder, pumice block, brick, and stone
2. Metal
3. Plastics
4. Wood, including plywood.

INTERIOR WALLS

The interior walls of a kennel are subjected to considerable moisture, as a result of the excreta, and from washing the house out. Also, sanitation, or ease of cleaning, is paramount in a kennel. Thus, the two most important requisites of the interior walls are: (1) that it be water resistant and not absorb moisture, and (2) that it be easily cleaned. Without doubt, concrete masonry, of all building materials, most nearly meets these requisites. However, many other types of interior wall materials can be, and are, used.

For the office and record room, and the trophy and showroom, plywood paneling is commonly used. It is available in mahogany, knotty pine, cypress, and many other wood-type veneers. Such paneling is very attractive, and if properly stained and preserved, will withstand frequent cleaning.

WATER

Dogs need a supply of clean, fresh water. Thus, water should be readily available both inside and outside the kennel. This will minimize the carrying of water to the dogs.

In regions where temperatures drop below freezing, outside hydrants should be of the self-drainage type, shutting off on the outside.

CLEANING

The kennel floors should be cleaned with water under pressure. For the latter purpose, a minimum pressure of 75 pounds per square inch and 500 gallons of water an hour are necessary.

The kennel should be cleaned once, and preferably twice, daily. Modern cleaning involves maximum automation. But, there is no one best way in which to dispose of the excrement and other materials flushed out of a kennel; rather, there is a matter of designing and using that system which will be most practical for a particular set of conditions. The three most common methods of disposal are:

1. A sewage line
2. A large septic tank
3. The use of a lagoon.

PLUMBING

In any type of construction—whether it be a home, office building, or a kennel—plumbing is expensive. In recognition of this fact, one of the rules of building construction is always to keep the plumbing centralized in one location. Hence, in planning a kennel, it will minimize plumbing costs if the office, kitchen, laboratory facilities, and grooming room are located adjacent to each other.

Because of the quantity of hair and soap, drainage is a special problem in kennels. To lessen the problem as much as possible, all drains and sinks should have openings so that pipes and traps can be reached easily for cleaning.

HEATING

In northern climates, artificial heating may be necessary. Every effort should be made to keep the temperature near the comfort zone given in Table 32. In particular, heat may be necessary for puppies, for short-haired dogs, and for the office and grooming room.

Where heat is needed, it may be supplied by a wide variety of devices and methods, among them, the following:

1. *Space heaters*—These may be heated by gas, oil, or electricity. If properly and strategically located in the kennel, they work very well.
2. *Infrared lamps*—In this method, infrared lamps are suspended above the floor. These lamps do not heat the surrounding air, but they warm the dogs in the same manner as direct rays from the sun. Generally, 250-watt infrared bulbs are used.
3. *Central heating*—Several different kinds of central heating systems are available. Most of them are highly automated, thermostatically controlled, and fueled by oil, gas, or electricity. Central heating units may provide warmth through either hot water (pipes or radiant heating) or hot air (direct or indirect).

In addition to providing heat within the kennel, in the northern areas where there is considerable snow consideration should be given to providing heating beneath outdoor runs as a means of alleviating the shoveling of snow.

Any type of heating device can cause a fire, so heaters should be installed carefully.

INSULATION

The term *insulation* refers to materials that have a high resistance to the flow of heat. Such materials are commonly used in the walls and ceilings of kennels. Proper insulation makes for a more uniform temperature—cooler houses in the summer and warmer houses in the winter—and makes for a substantial fuel saving when heating the kennel.

You should rely on the local architect or contractor to advise you relative to the kind and amount of insulation to use in your area.

VAPOR BARRIER

There is much vapor in kennels; it comes from the excrement, the respiration of the dog, and water containers. When the amount of water vapor in the kennel is greater than the outside air, the vapor will tend to move from inside to outside. Since warm air holds more water vapor than cold air, the movement of vapor is most pronounced during the winter months. The effective way to combat this problem in a kennel is to use a vapor barrier with insulation. It should be placed on the warm side, or inside, of the kennel. Here again, it is well to rely on your local architect or contractor to advise you relative to the vapor barrier to use.

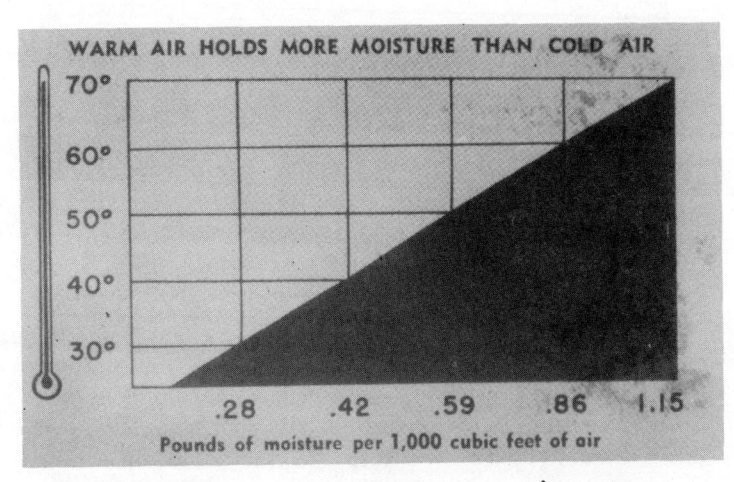

Fig. 262. Influence of air temperature on its water holding capacity. (From Washington State University Extension Bulletin, *No. 529, 1961)*

VENTILATION

Ventilation refers to the changing of air—the replacement of foul air with fresh air. Kennels should be well ventilated, but care must be taken to avoid direct drafts and coolness. Good kennel ventilation saves feed, and helps insure healthy dogs.

Three factors are essential for good ventilation: (1) fresh air moving into the kennel, (2) insulation to keep the kennel temperature warm, and (3) removal of moist air. Of course, the water-holding capacity of air increases with rising temperature (see Fig. 262).

A professional engineer should always be engaged to design the ventilating system. He will know best about the size and number of units to use, the placement of fans, and how to avoid drafts on dogs.

More and more kennels are being air conditioned. Air conditioning is especially important in hot climates, and in veterinary and boarding kennels.

During the summer, in areas that do not get too hot, a satisfactory ventilating system can usually be achieved by opening kennel doors, and high up walls, hinged panels, that swing down.

In kennels that are kept clean, and in which the bedding is renewed often, there is very little odor provided they are kept properly ventilated and floor drains are kept clean. Various deodorizing products can be, and are, used; but these can not substitute for a clean kennel that is well ventilated.

FLOORING

Wooden floors are warm to lie upon, but they are absorbent and unsanitary, they often harbor rats and other rodents, and they lack durability.

Concrete, if properly constructed, is the most practical floor for kennels, all factors considered—it is durable, and easily cleaned. However, it is very important that concrete slab be made warm and dry. This can best be achieved by the use of wooden platforms and wooden boxes, which can be taken out and scrubbed from time to time. Additionally, concrete can be made warmer and drier, provided the following construction details are observed:

1. Lay the floor on a well-drained site.
2. Build edge insulation of 2 inches of rigid, weatherproof material and extend it 24 inches under the floor as a border.
3. Prepare a 6-inch gravel or crushed rock fill under the floor.
4. Provide a waterproof barrier (commonly known as a paper-proof barrier) over the fill to prevent any rise of moisture from the ground

into the floor slab. Among such materials are: duplex paper with an asphalt center, sheets of plastic film, or a rigid asphalt board.

5. Place 4 to 6 inches (6 inches where a truck is to pass over it) of concrete in one pour; make it flat and even, but do not finish so smoothly that it becomes slippery when wet.

6. Floors of the inside pen should slope at the rate of one-fourth inch per foot toward a gutter. Floors of outside runs should have the same slope, but they should be 2 to 3 inches lower than floors inside the house. The slope is very necessary in order to facilitate flushing out excrement. To facilitate cleaning, do not place curbs across doorways or at partition lines.

The location of gutters is a matter of preference. Generally, inside gutters are located in the service alley, whereas gutters for outside runs are located at the outside edge—away from the house. Gutters should have flat bottoms, at least 15 inches wide, to facilitate cleaning, and they should slope at the rate of one-fourth inch per foot toward a disposal drain.

OUTDOOR RUNS

Outdoor runs are a very important part of any kennel. They provide a bit of exercise in fresh air, give the dog an opportunity to relieve him-

Fig. 263. Concrete-surfaced runs, with ample shade and sun for the English Springer Spaniels. Sililyn Kennels, Troy, Michigan, owned by Mrs. Julia Gasow. (Courtesy Gaines Dog Research Center, White Plains, N.Y.)

self outside, and insure the general health and happiness of the dog.

SIZE OF THE RUN

The size of the run will be determined by the size of the dog and the amount of other exercise, if any, provided. Under average conditions, a 4' x 10' run is adequate for medium-sized breeds; and a 4' x 24' run for large breeds. Some owners of hunting dogs insist on runs being 5 to 6 feet wide, rather than 4 feet. Their argument is that the extra width safeguards against injuries being incurred when dogs bang their tails against run fencing.

Some dog owners and kennel operators fence in large areas so that the dogs can have runs on natural footing. Although there is nothing quite like exercise on the "good earth," particularly on grass, it is recognized that considerable parasite hazard accompanies such an arrangement; hence, a rigid parasite control program should be a part thereof.

Fig. 264. Concrete runs (far) and large gravel area (near) at Sililyn Kennels (mostly English Springer Spaniels), Troy, Michigan, owned by Mrs. Julia Gasow. Also, note Plexiglass patio awning, which cuts glare inside kennels and helps keep runs partially shady. (Courtesy Gaines Dog Research Center, White Plains, N.Y.)

SURFACE

Concrete is the most commonly used surface material for runs. It is easy to clean, durable, and dogs cannot dig in or under it. However, it does have certain disadvantages: the initial cost is rather high; it may be slick when it is wet; it is cold in the winter and hot in the summer; it may rub off hair and make for abrasions on hocks and elbows as a result of dogs lying on it; and it may cause the dog's feet to spread and splay. Despite all the disadvantages, concrete is still the best material for an outdoor run, with the possible exception of a wire floor under certain circumstances.

When concrete is used, it should be reasonably rough finished so as to give the dog better footing and lessen the possible hazard of dogs damaging their running gear. Also, it should be constructed according to the specifications given in this chapter under the section entitled "Flooring."

The use of raised wood platforms and wood boxes on concrete runs will give relief from the temperature situation inherent in concrete and lessen the hazard of hair loss and abrasions.

Kennels are making increased use of wire runs, both in permanent construction and in portable pens. Where wire runs are part of a permanent multikennel, they are usually placed on raised platforms over concrete. The feces drop through the wire where they can be flushed out. As a result, wire runs are clean at all times, and there is better disease control than can be achieved with any other type of surface, including concrete. The main disadvantages to wire flooring are: wire rusts, and heavy wire and strong supports must be used, otherwise the wire sags and bends.

Wire runs are particularly suited for use in conjunction with single dog units, especially where both the individual doghouse and the wire run are elevated off the ground. When used in this manner, it is important that the area underneath the wire run be cleaned at frequent intervals and sprinkled with lime.

Portable wire runs are frequently used as temporary exercise yards for puppies and for grown dogs of the smaller breeds. These runs can be moved from place to place as desired.

FENCE

Strong, secure fences in dog runs are of the most importance. Kennel dogs must be prevented from climbing, jumping, hurting each other when fighting through a fence, or tearing or digging their way out; and roaming dogs from the outside must not be able to get in.

In a boarding establishment, good fences are doubly important. Nothing is quite so embarrassing, or will lose customers faster, than to have to tell a boarding dog owner that his dog escaped.

Despite all precautions, accidents do happen; if nothing else, someone may fail to close a gate. So, in addition to fencing the runs properly, as herein described, a high, outside fence around the entire kennel area is in the nature of good protection. It will keep roaming dogs from getting anywhere near the kennel, thereby lessening the disease and parasite problem. Also, if one of the kennel dogs gets out, he will not be able to go beyond the property, with the result that he can be returned quickly to his quarters.

Six-foot, chain-link fence, attached to steel posts, makes the most satisfactory fence for outdoor runs. This type of fencing is expensive, but it will last indefinitely; and, if properly constructed, it will not sag and become unattractive.

Other types of fencing material may be used. But usually they are unsatisfactory for two reasons: (1) they generally have to be replaced rather often, and (2) there is more hazard of dogs getting out. Above all, do not trust chicken wire; dogs easily chew through it, and it sags.

Many kennels have resorted to using masonry walls—cinderblock, concrete block, or brick—in the partitions between runs. Usually, the masonry construction is used for the first 2 or 3 feet, then fencing extends on above this. Masonry partitions have two advantages: (1) they prevent contamination from one pen to the other, thereby lessening the disease hazard, and (2) fighting dogs find it difficult to do battle while standing on their hind legs. Also, masonry should be used on the side of a kennel that faces a busy thoroughfare. This prevents dogs from seeing outside activities that may excite them and cause them to bark.

Gates should always swing in and the latches should be trustworthy. The doors between the outside runs and the inside pens can be operated by pulleys from inside the kennel. Other types of doors in use by some kennels include hinged doors, and flaps, made of burlap and canvas and weighted at the bottom.

Digging out of runs is no problem where a heavy fence is fastened to steel posts sunk in concrete. However, where gravel or dirt runs are used, dogs will usually dig out unless unusual precautions are taken. Gravel-type runs can be made tunnel-proof against most dogs by attaching about 3 feet of wire at ground level, then extending it underground and toward the inside of the run. The wire may be attached at ground level by means of hog rings, then it should be covered with a layer of soil. Most jumpers and climbers can be discouraged by extending inward 12 to 18 inches of wire at the top and letting it overhang at a 45° angle.

Some kennels put a roof over outside runs, for the purpose of providing shade in the summer and/or lessening snow shoveling in the winter. Also, many kennel owners consider it good business to enclose runs with screening against flies that torment dogs' ears, the heartworm-transmitting mosquito, and other biting insects.

INTERIOR FURNISHINGS

The interior furnishings of the kennel vary according to the ideas of the owner and the use to which the kennel is to be put. A brief discussion of each of the most common interior furnishings will follow.

PENS

The most common, and perhaps the most satisfactory of all arrangements in large kennels, con-

Fig. 265. Kennel runs at Waiterock Ranch Kennels, noted dog-breeding establishment, Lafayette, California. Runs are 15 feet long, surfaced with concrete, and divided by 1-foot high concrete partitions, then sheet metal panels about halfway up, and finally steel-mesh fencing. The concrete dividers allow each run to be cleaned without waste water spilling into adjacent runs and the metal panels prevent the dog's arguing or fence-fighting. (Courtesy Juanita W. Howard, Waiterock Ranch, Lafayette, Calif.)

Fig. 266. Clean, airy runs at Gaines Research Kennels, Kankakee, Ill., where more than 300 dogs of various breeds are on nutritional studies. (Courtesy Gaines Dog Research Center, White Plains, N.Y.)

sists of a center hall or alleyway with pens or stalls on each side, connected with individual outdoor runs. This type of arrangement requires the maximum outlay in building and fencing costs on a per dog basis, but it gives the dogs as much access to exercise and the outdoors as is possible to accord in a restricted but secure environment. Also, it minimizes labor, in comparison with the cage system.

The fences for pens or stalls are very similar to those described above for outside runs. The partitions may be wire or solid, or a combination of the two. Where solid pen or stall divisions are used, the masonry is usually about waist high, with wire extending above.

When pens or stalls are used, sleeping boxes should be provided, especially in unheated kennels. Single unit boxes can be either homemade or purchased commercially. Fiberglass boxes cannot be chewed and are completely immersible for cleaning.

CAGES (CRATES)

Instead of pens, some kennel owners prefer to use cages for kenneling dogs in a central building. Where cages are used, they are usually banked against the wall, one on top of the other. Cages may be homemade or purchased; made of wire, wood, or other materials; and movable or

Fig. 267. 4' x 4' steel cages in a kennel. (Courtesy Leader Dogs for the Blind, Rochester, Mich.)

unmovable. Suggested cage sizes follow:

For large breeds: 43" long x 25" wide x 30" high

For medium-sized breeds: 36" long x 22" wide x 26" high

For small breeds: 26" long x 18" wide x 19" high

When cages are used as permanent quarters for dogs, it is essential that dogs be put in either outdoor or indoor runs for exercise.

In addition to being used in some kennels, cages find special use for the following purposes:

1. *In veterinary hospitals*—For this purpose, cages are usually constructed of stainless steel, so as to permit ease in cleaning and disinfecting.

2. *In moving show dogs*—For this purpose, collapsible wire cages are particularly popular. They come in various sizes, are lightweight, and can be folded flat when not in use.

3. *For shipping dogs*—The use of crates for this purpose is fully covered in chapter 10; see the section therein entitled "Kennel (or Crate)."

4. *For nervous, excitable dogs*—Sometimes crates promote quietness in dogs that have a tendency to be nervous and excitable. This is particularly true in some of the smaller breeds.

Whether or not crates or cages are used as the permanent quarters for dogs in kennels, it is well that all dogs be accustomed to cages at an early stage in life. It prepares them for times when they may be crated for plane shipment or other travel, or for confinement in the veterinary hospital.

WHELPING BOXES

Special whelping boxes should be provided for bitches at whelping time, with the number of boxes needed by a kennel determined by the number of bitches due to whelp at the same time.

The whelping box should be large enough for the bitch to lie down full length, and to move about comfortably; and it should be deep enough to contain the puppies until they are moved to a regular pen. It is preferable that it have a hinged cover, as it will provide greater privacy. It should be made of solid material in order to keep out drafts from the bitch and her litter, but one side should be lower than the others in order to afford the bitch ingress and egress.

An inner railing, placed about 6 inches from the floor and extending out from the sides of the box 3 to 4 inches, will prevent the bitch from accidentally crushing or smothering a puppy against the sides of the box.

Fig. 268. Puli puppies in a puppy box, their second home following the whelping box. (Courtesy Mrs. Charles R. Anderson, Cedwood Puli Kennels, Bristol, Conn.)

Flat sheets of newspaper make good bedding for the whelping box. However, many breeders prefer to use toweling or ribbed rubber matting so as to give the pups better footing. Above all, do not put newborn pups in deep, loose bedding that might smother them.

AUTOMATIC WATERERS

More and more kennels are coming to the use

of automatic waterers, primarily as a means of saving labor. Dogs learn to operate automatic waterers readily. The only drawback to this use is that some dogs like to play with them, with the result that they may keep the water running.

Where buckets are used for watering, pails should either be suspended from hooks on the wall or fitted into wood stanchions.

EQUIPMENT

Generally speaking, kennel equipment refers to those things other than buildings used in the care and management of dogs. The following items of equipment are usually available and used in the operation of the dog kennel:

1. *Cleaning tools*—The most commonly used cleaning tools are: straight-handled broom, push broom, scoop shovel, mop, pail, hose, and stiff-bristled brush.

2. *Food containers*—Stainless steel dishes are recommended for feeding and watering purposes; they are durable, and they are easily cleaned. For mixing food, large buckets or bowls, and large spoons are needed.

3. *Carts*—Transport carts (similar to the tea carts used in restaurants) and feedwagons are commonly used in carrying food and dishes about the kennel. A creeper, or dolly, of the type used by garage mechanics to slide under cars, comes in handy for transporting cleaning equipment, large bags of dog food, bales of bedding, or other heavy and unwieldy materials and items.

4. *Food storage containers*—Food should always be stored in rodent-proof containers. If special metal bins are not available, tightly covered galvanized garbage cans can be used.

OTHER KENNEL POINTERS

In addition to the foregoing, successful kennels give attention to safety, sanitation, and bedding. Pointers pertinent to each of these follow:

1. *Safety*—In addition to the usual safety precautions taken to avoid injury to dogs or caretakers, and to prevent the escape of dogs, two other safety measures are particularly important in kennels: fire prevention and poisons.

  a. *Fire prevention*—Wiring and fuses should be considered as carefully as in the home. Make sure that dogs never have access to exposed cords. Also, detach electric appliances

Fig. 269. Roading machine for conditioning dogs, or keeping them in shape. Such a device may be used for brood matrons or for dogs in training. This particular machine is 32 feet in diameter and runs at 8 miles per hour. (Photo by State of Illinois, Department of Conservation. Courtesy H. N. Holmes, Gunsmoke Kennels, Springfield, Ill.)

Fig. 270. Roading device on truck, another method of conditioning dogs. This particular unit will accommodate eight dogs at a time. The dogs are usually worked one or two hours. (Photo by State of Illinois, Department of Conservation. Courtesy H. N. Holmes, Gunsmoke Kennels, Springfield, Ill.)

(including driers, clippers, and other grooming tools) when they are not in use. Bedding, especially flammable material like straw and shavings, should be stored away from stoves and other danger areas. All fuels should be stored in tightly enclosed metal containers, preferably some distance from the main kennel. "No smoking" signs should be prominently displayed, and observed.

Even with all precautions, the confinement of a large number of dogs in a mechanically controlled kennel does entail considerable fire risk. To guard against such a happenstance, an emergency warning signal should be installed.

b. *Poisons*—Every precaution should be taken in the use and storage of rodent poisons, insecticides, and disinfectants. Despite all precautions, however, accidents do happen. When one does, immediately administer the proper antidote if it is known or if you can find such information on the container. Otherwise, you should call your M.D. or one of the Poison Information Centers. Although they are for human beings, centers have been established in various parts of the country where doctors can obtain top, up-to-date information on treatment of poison cases. Local medical doctors have information relative to "Poison Information Centers" in their area, along with some of the names of their directors, telephone numbers, and street numbers. When calling any of these centers, one should ask for the "Poison Information Center." If this information cannot be obtained locally, call the U.S. Public Health Service at Atlanta, Georgia, or at Wenatchee, Washington. Even though these Poison Information Centers were established for human beings, they will usually accommodate a dog owner in distress; and the same antidotes that are used for a human apply to dogs.

2. *Sanitation*—Proper sanitation in every kennel is essential for the dog's health and for the control of external and internal parasites. Special care needs to be given to the following in the operation of a kennel:

a. *Care of pens*—Pens are commonly flushed out with a hose; it's quick and effective, but it does leave the pens wet. For the latter reason, many caretakers prefer to use a semidry mop. Also, a wet vacuum cleaner is excellent for cleaning and drying; the floor is first scrubbed with a brush and soap and water, then the vacuum is used to remove loose dirt and soapy liquid.

b. *Care of runs*—Concrete and other hard surface runs should be cleaned frequently; feces should be removed twice daily, and surfaces should be washed down several times a week and routinely disinfected. The use of hot water, such as is provided by a steam jenny, is excellent for cleaning hard-surfaced runs. In addition to removing most germs, it will kill round worm eggs, also.

Gravel and dirt runs should be cleaned at least twice a year, more often in warmer climates. Such runs may be made sanitary in either of the following ways: (1) remove all top soil to a depth of at least 3 inches, then replace with clean soil and/or gravel; or (2) treat the area with sodium borate (or borax) in a solution of 2 pounds per gallon of water, poured over the surface of the gravel or dirt run at the rate of 2 gallons per hundred square feet. Gravel and dirt runs can also be sanitized by spading in lime.

c. *Disinfectant*—The subject of disinfectants is fully covered in chapter 8 and Table 38, Handy Disinfectant Guide. Thus, repetition at this point is unnecessary; only a few pertinent matters will be mentioned:

(1) *The phenols (carbolic acid)*—These are nonspecific disinfectants. An important advantage possessed by these disinfectants for kennel use is that they are not inactivated by soap, anionic detergents, or organic matter. Some phenols may be irritating to the skin, some cannot be used in hard water, and all have strong odors.

(2) *Q.A.C. (quarternary ammonium compounds)*—Most of these compounds are odorless and nontoxic in the dilutions used. In securing Q.A.C. products for kennels use, check the label, because some of them cannot be used with soap, whereas others are corrosive to certain metals.

(3) *Hyperchlorites*—Sodium hyperchlorite is a common household bleach. These disinfectants lose their lethal properties rapidly in the presence of nitrogenous material. Hence, the kennel should be scrubbed first with soap and water, then the hyperchlorite should be used as a rinse.

(4) *Lime or whitewash*—These products inhibit most bacteria and kill eggs of some parasites. Surfaces must be clean, however, for the wash to be effective.

Two cautions are in order relative to the use of disinfectants:

(a) Always read and follow the directions on the label.

(b) Remember that germs, spores, and

the eggs of parasites survive in corners, cracks and any place that can be reached by dog's urine or by parasites. Remember, too, that the use of disinfectants should be preceded by thorough cleaning.

3. *Bedding*—The most commonly used bedding materials are: newspaper, cedar shavings, or pine shavings. Sometimes, clean, bright straw is used for bedding, especially for bird dogs. Bird dog fanciers sometimes object to the use of strong-odored, fragrant cedar shavings because they believe that such odors affect the dog's scenting abilities. Hay should never be used for dog's bedding because frequently (a) it is dusty, and (b) it contains weeds to which some dogs are allergic.

Newspaper makes an excellent bed, and it may be either used in shredded or flat sheets (flat sheets or liners are sometimes used for puppies). The ink on newspaper doesn't affect most dogs. There are two exceptions to the latter point, however: (a) sometimes light colored dogs are discolored by ink, and (b) occasionally puppies will develop sores on their bellies as a result of printed newspaper used as bedding. Thus, for the light colored breeds and puppies, it is well to secure unprinted newspaper, such as the printer has left over from the ends of newsprint rolls.

6
Training

Chapter 6
Dog Behavior and Psychology *294*
   Memory *294*
   Confidence and Fear *294*
   The Dog Cannot Reason *295*
   Association of Ideas *295*
   Willingness *295*
   Attention *295*
   Age and Intelligence as Factors *295*
   Rewards *295*
   Punishment *296*
Caring for the New Puppy *296*
   Your First Days *296*
   Your First Night(s) *297*
   Housebreaking *297*
   Feeding the New Puppy *299*
   Basic Commands *299*
      "No" *299*
      "Come" *299*
Obedience Training *299*
   Equipment for Training *299*
   Ten Training Guides *299*
   Basic Obedience Commands *300*
      Heel *300*
      Sit *301*
      Down *302*
      Sit-Stay *302*
      Down-Stay *303*
      Stand-Stay *303*
      Come *304*
Tricks *304*
   Sit Up *305*
   Carry *305*

(Continued)

Fetch	*305*
Catch	*306*
Shake Hands	*306*
Roll Over	*306*
Jump	*306*
Through the Hoop	*307*
Don't Touch It	*308*
Vices (Bad Habits)	*308*
Begging	*308*
Jumping Up On People	*308*
Jumping On Furniture	*309*
Garbage Pails and Wastebaskets	*309*
Chewing	*309*
Barking Excessively	*310*
Growling; Biting; Nipping; Unnecessary Roughness	*310*
Mailman—Deliveryman—Serviceman Phobia	*311*
Chasing Cars	*311*
Cat Chaser	*311*
Digging	*311*
Running Away From Home	*312*
Prevent Vices From Forming	*313*
Be a Good "Dog Neighbor"	*313*
Some "Do's" of Being a Good Dog Neighbor	*313*
Some "Don'ts" of Being a Good Dog Neighbor	*314*

Fig. 271. Two dogs being taught to sit-stay. (Courtesy The Seeing Eye, Inc., Morristown, N.J.)

DOG BEHAVIOR AND PSYCHOLOGY

The dog has whims and ideas of his own. Always, however, the trainer should be the boss, with the dog promptly carrying out his wishes. With the experienced trainer, this relationship is clear-cut, for he is able to relay his feelings to the dog instantly and unmistakably.

A well-mannered dog may be said to be the combined result of desirable heredity, skillful training, and vigilant control. Once conception has taken place, it is too late to change the genetic makeup of the animal. However, the eventual training and control of the dog are dependent upon how well the trainer understands canine mental facilities as well as methods of utilizing these facilities so that the desired performance may be obtained.

For complete control and a finished performance, the dog should have a proud and exalted opinion of himself; but, at the same time, he should subjugate those undesirable traits that make an animal difficult to handle. Complete control, therefore is based on mental facilities rather than muscular force. The facilities of the dog that must be understood and played upon to obtain skillful training and control at all times are summarized briefly in this section.

TRAINING[1]

Training is teaching and drilling, accompanied by rewards and punishments. With both a child and a dog, it's easiest and most effective if started early in life. An old adage puts it this way: "As the twig is bent, so the tree grows." And the Good Book says, "Train up a child in the way he should grow and when he is old he will not depart therefrom" (Prov. 22:6). Indeed, this same thought applies to the molding and shaping the life of a dog.

Much has been written about the training of dogs, but very little of it has been read, and still less of it has been put into actual practice. The reason: most dog owners are not professional trainers. They keep dogs because it's fun; hence, they want the training procedure to be a pleasant experience. This chapter is designed to provide for this.

MEMORY

To a considerable degree, the dog's aptitude for training is due to his memory; for he remembers or recognizes the indications given him, the manner in which he responded, and the rewards or punishments that followed his actions. These facts must be taken into consideration both in training the puppy and in retaining control of the trained dog.

Discipline and reward must be administered very soon after the act (some competent trainers say that it should be within three seconds) in order for the dog to associate and remember.

CONFIDENCE AND FEAR

In the wild state, the dog was his own protector; and his very survival was often dependent upon the use of his teeth or the rapidity of escape. But in the domesticated dog, it is necessary that confidence in the trainer or owner replace fear of man. He should be spoken to in

---
[1] The author acknowledges with thanks the authoritative review accorded this chapter by: Mrs. Lee Watts, Show Secretary, North Shore Kennel Club of B.C., 1840 Mathers Avenue, West Vancouver, B.C.

a calm, but firm, voice and should be patted by using the hands without exciting him.

When the dog is frightened, the trainer must utilize the means by which the dog will be calmed. However, when the dog is voluntarily and knowingly disobedient, the proper kind and degree of punishment should be administered immediately.

THE DOG CANNOT REASON

The most important single factor to remember in training your dog is that he cannot reason things out. A dog's mind functions by intuition, not logic. Moreover, he has no conscious sense of right and wrong. When training, it is one of your tasks to teach him the difference between right and wrong—between good and bad. Your dog cannot utilize pure reason, but he can remember, and he has the ability to use the memory of one situation as it applies to another.

ASSOCIATION OF IDEAS

Dogs are creatures of habit; for example, when the kitchen door is opened regularly at six o'clock for feeding, the dog may begin to anticipate his food. For this reason, the training of a dog should be handled by the same person, allowing the animal an opportunity to associate the various repeated commands with the desired responses. A well-trained dog may become confused and ill-mannered when poorly handled by several persons.

WILLINGNESS

A willing performer is to be desired. Some dogs submit to the trainers subjugation with little trouble and hesitation, whereas others offer resistance to the point of being stubborn. Complete control over the dog at all times is achieved through the judicious employment of rewards and punishments.

ATTENTION

Remember that your dog has a one-track mind. No matter how smart you may think he is, he cannot harbor two ideas at the same time.

Remember, too, that in order for him to learn something new, existing thoughts must be driven out. The latter is accomplished by "shock."

The simplest form of shock is a snap or jerk of the leash. This temporarily "clears" his brain, gets his attention, and affords an opportunity to introduce a new idea. Remember that a dog can't learn anything while he is thinking about where he buried a choice bone in the yard, or the petite French Poodle next door.

AGE AND INTELLIGENCE AS FACTORS

Some of the more difficult training exercises should not be attempted until your dog is at least five or six months old. However, even the young puppy can be taught good behavior patterns. At a very early age, he should be taught the meaning of, and be expected to respond to, the commands "no" and "come."

You should also keep in mind that the level of intelligence of dogs varies, just as it does in people. Some dogs are smarter than others. If your dog is on the slow side, it doesn't mean that he can't learn. It simply means that it will take longer, and that you will have to repeat the process more often. Remember that the dog learns by rote, or repetition; therefore, if he is a bit slow, you will simply have to repeat the training step more often.

REWARDS

The two most common rewards given dogs are a praising voice and a gentle stroking with the hand. Satisfying the dog's greediness for some choice tidbit is also effective, but this may make for great disappointment if the reward is not available at all times. To be effective, rewards must not be given promiscuously but only when deserved. It is also important that the same words or hand strokings always be used for the same thing and that the trainer means what he says.

In the matter of rewards, the word that is spoken is within itself unimportant, but the tone of the voice is—it should be a praising, happy, and lighthearted voice. Something like, "Good dog!", can be an exciting sound to the dog.

In stroking the dog with your hand, do not pat him on the head. A warm pat on the shoulder is much better. Run his ear through your hand, or move your hand affectionately along the side of his head. Then pat him on the shoulder. These are the gestures of affection he will understand.

PUNISHMENT

The two most common types of canine punishment are:

1. A sharp tug on the collar, accompanied by a quick jerk on the leash.

2. A verbal reprimand in a disapproving tone of voice—such as, "Bad dog!"

Striking with an object or losing your temper are useless. So, don't use rolled up newspapers to hit him; don't strike the dog with your hand; and don't use the leash as a whip.

Punishment should be administered only when the trainer is certain that the dog is being disobedient; and not when the dog lacks sufficient training, has not understood some command, or has done something wrong because of the trainer. When necessary, however, the punishment should be administered promptly, so that the animal understands why it is given; and it should be given justly, with the trainer retaining a cool head at all times. Following punishment, the animal should be made to carry out the original command that he failed to follow, and then he should be properly rewarded.

CARING FOR THE NEW PUPPY

A good start, beginning with the ride home and the all-important first few days in the new home, will set the pattern for the dog's entire life, and make him feel comfortable from the first. Remember that everything is new to him. Remember, too, that you and other members of your family are replacing his mother and litter mates, and that your home and his crate or box will become as much a sanctuary to him as the cave was to his prehistoric ancestors.

YOUR FIRST DAYS

The following points are pertinent to caring for the new puppy during those all-important first days:

1. *Have box ready*—Before bringing a new puppy home, you should have his box and bed

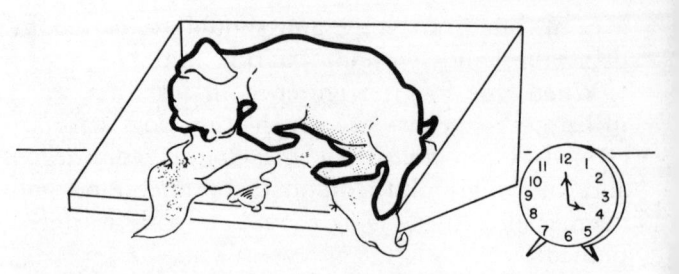

Fig. 272. First nights. (Drawing by R. F. Johnson)

ready (see Fig. 272). Any clean carton or box will make a good bed for a puppy, so long as it is large enough to allow him to stretch out. One side should be cut low enough to allow him to get in and out easily. If the dog is not housebroken, the box may be bedded with newspapers and covered with a small mattress or rug. This box should be placed in a draft-free room that is neither too hot nor too cold.

2. *Get him on Saturday morning*—Most puppies are brought into a new home when they are from six to twelve weeks of age. This means that your entire program should be geared accordingly.

If you are a professional person and away from the home from Monday through Friday, it is recommended that you obtain the puppy on Saturday morning. Then the two of you will have a long weekend together in which to get acquainted.

3. *Have a pleasant trip home*—If you have a long drive, ask the breeder not to feed the puppy the morning that you are going to pick him up, since he might become car sick en route.

On the trip home, either hold the puppy on your lap or place him on a blanket or in a box on the seat next to you. Calm him from time to time by speaking softly and patting him on the shoulder. Also, let him have an opportunity to sniff you; remember that dogs have "nose brains." Hence, it is advantageous to each of you that the puppy's nose tell him as soon as possible that you are his master. You should have with you a large bath towel, just in case the puppy gets sick.

4. *Pick him up properly*—Never pick a puppy up by the legs or ears. Neither should you use the nap of the neck. Instead, pick him up by placing your hand under his chest; that is, just back of the front legs. In this manner you may lift him up in your arms and cradle him so that his body lies along your arm.

5. *Don't wear him out*—Practically everyone will want to play with the new puppy. In time, he will want to play, too. But don't force attention upon him too quickly. Let him get acquainted with the family gradually. Gain his trust and still his fears. Speak quietly, gently, and avoid unnecessary noises. Also, and most important, remember that puppies tire quickly and want to rest and sleep a great deal. So put him in his box for frequent naps.

On the first day, forget about the, "No, no!" This will come in another few days.

6. *Register him*—If you receive the registration papers for your puppy at the time of taking delivery, as you should, do not file them away and forget them. Instead, send them directly to the registry association. In that way, they won't be misplaced, and the dog will not go unregistered for years. Remember that thousands of dog owners are *about to register their dogs.*

YOUR FIRST NIGHT(S)

In preparation for the first night, do not water the puppy in the evening. Also, at your own bedtime, take him out for an opportunity to relieve himself. Don't just put him out, take him out, preferably on a lead so that he cannot get away from you. Then wait until he has relieved himself.

Puppies are cuddlers, first to their mother's warm side, then to their brothers and sisters. Also, they're sociable creatures; hence, the puppy will miss the companionship of his own family. In order to give the puppy something warm to which to cuddle, a hot water bottle, carefully covered to prevent burning and tightly corked to remove any damage of scalding, should be put in the puppy's box. Also, an old shoe, especially one that is yours, is nice to snuggle up to. The ticking of an alarm clock in the puppy's bed gives him a sense of companionship.

Despite all of the above preparation, the puppy may howl and howl. But ignore him; he'll soon cry himself to sleep. Never, never, give in! If you do, you're well on the road to ruin—and so is your pup. The same thing applies when he awakens early in the morning. If you can't stand the howling any longer, and if you feel the neighbors can't either, roll a newspaper and slap it loudly against the box. This will usually shock him sufficiently to be quiet.

HOUSEBREAKING

The puppy has to learn to control his kidneys and bowels as well as his loneliness. So, here again, if once you give in, the job gets harder and harder—and finally impossible. By using the housebreaking system outlined herein, a puppy of 6 to 8 weeks of age can be housebroken in a week or less. That is, any accidents the dog may have after a week of following the program given here will be your mistakes and not the dog's. Contrary to what some people think, it is not necessary to wait until a dog is 7 or 8 months old before starting housebreaking; rather, it can begin about 6 to 8 weeks of age.

Housebreaking of a dog comes relatively easy when it is understood that it is based upon the age-old instinct of den dwellers to keep their beds clean. By contrast, other domestic animals—like the horse, cow, sheep, and pig—are not den dwellers; rather, in the wild state they roved over the prairies or through the forest, eating and sleeping on clean ground, and bedding down at a new site each night. They did not use dens, and there was no need for them to be "den broken." Since they were not housebroken in their natural habitat, they cannot be housebroken under domestication. But, as den dwellers, dogs can be easily housebroken. You simply make use of their age-old instinct and create a den for them. The box serves this purpose.

The following points and procedures are pertinent to housebreaking a dog:

1. *Box is nature's way*—As indicated above, the box is used for the purpose of imitating a den. Then, by instinct, the dog keeps his new "den" clean. The box should be fully enclosed, with a door or lid, but with adequate ventilation holes for aeration. It should be big enough for the puppy to turn around in, and even lie down at full length. It is a good idea to have the box larger than needed at first, so as to allow for growth of the puppy. A flexible arrangement can be secured by means of grooves in the side of the box and the use of a partition. In time, the partition can be inserted in new grooves further back in order to enlarge the puppy's bed. A show crate may be used as a housebreaking box, also.

Disposable bedding for the box can be made by using plain newspaper laid flat. A blanket or a pad may be used if you prefer, but there is always the hazard of the puppy scratching and chewing up other bedding. Besides, any cloth material that is to be used for any length of time must be laundered.

2. *Accidents do happen*—In the excitement of the first day and night, more than likely a puppy will get caught and relieve himself in the house or in his box. So, until he is housebroken, confine him to the kitchen where the inevitable accident will cause the least distress. Mop up a first mistake, then take the rag to the spot that you wish to have the puppy use as his place for relieving. Anchor the rag on a stake there. When you take the puppy out, he smells where he has been before, or thinks he has been before, and gets the idea immediately.

Remember that the puppy has a "nose brain." He can smell one part of urine in sixty million parts of water. Thus, if he smells urine odor in the house or box where he made his first mistake, he will likely want to use that spot again. It is important, therefore, to wash this spot with soap and water several times. Then, you should sprinkle a drop or two of nicotine sulphate solution or ammonia solution on the wet spot and rub it about. This will discourage the puppy from using this spot again.

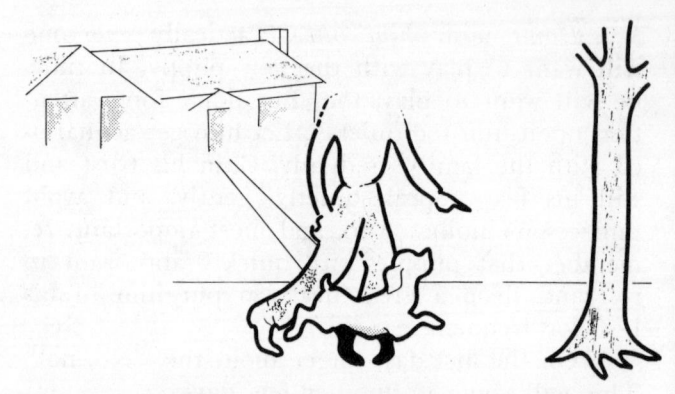

Fig. 274. Accompany the puppy to the spot. (Drawing by R. F. Johnson)

3. *Keep him regular*—You should assist your puppy in applying rigidly regular habits. To this end, you should take him to the outside "spot" for relieving himself (a) right after he wakes up, (b) after each meal, and (c) always at night. While he is very young, it is a good idea to do likewise immediately after a nap.

When your pup is young, you must never just put him out. Instead, you must take him to the spot, preferably on a lead, then wait for him to accomplish his purpose. Everything looks so wonderful to him, and there are so many things to divert his mind. But don't bring him back indoors until the purpose of his visit has been accomplished. When he does, compliment him.

4. *The weather's no excuse*—Despite all the instructions given herein, sometimes dog owners decide that the weather is too cold, or that it is too rainy, or too slick or too muddy. Usually they are making excuses for themselves, for dogs are equipped to take considerable disagreeable weather.

5. *Toy breeds may use paper*—Because toy breeds are kept in the house, and their stools are very small, it is quite alright to use paper for them if you so desire. But remember that if you start a dog on paper, you must continue it. Hence, be sure that you wish to follow this procedure, once you have initiated it. Training to use a newspaper is relatively simple. When you notice the puppy getting into a squatting position, pick him up quickly and put him on the newspapers that you intend that he use. Since your puppy has to "go" frequently, you must be on the alert. Scold him if he relieves himself anyplace but on the paper. Praise him when he visits the paper on his free will.

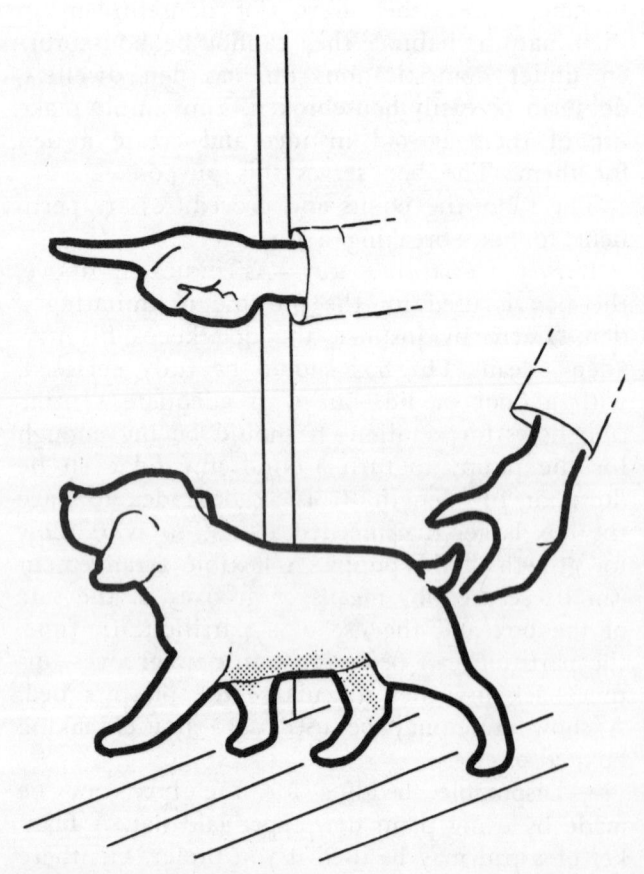

Fig. 273. Keep the puppy regular. (Drawing by R. F. Johnson)

FEEDING THE NEW PUPPY

During the first day or two after the new puppy arrives, when he is under heavy stress from moving to the new location, the diet should not be changed; that is, follow the same schedule and use the same food that the puppy was used to at his previous home. For this reason, it is wise to write down his schedule and diet at the time you pick him up. Following the first day or two, you may gradually shift your puppy to the new feeding program that you have selected (see chapter 4, Feeding).

Also, at the outset, it is best that the puppy have his very own dish. This should be constructed so that it is easy for him to eat from it, yet so that he will not spill his food. Also, weighted dishes are available, which cannot be picked up, carried around, and chewed.

Fig. 275. Obedience! The Dalmatian does his thing in an obedience training course. (Courtesy The American Humane Association, Denver, Colo.)

BASIC COMMANDS

Serious obedience training is usually not started until the puppy is four to nine months of age. However, two basic commands—"no" and "come"—should be started very early in life.

"NO"

The most needed, and the most easily understood, command, is "No!" It should be spoken in a sharp, disapproving tone, and accompanied with a shaking finger. At first, speak the dog's name, followed by the "No!"—as "King, no!" This should be repeated each time that the puppy commits an act that causes your displeasure.

"COME"

The puppy should be taught to come to you upon command, whether indoors or out. Let him go ten or more feet away from you. Then speak his name followed at once with "Come!"—as "King, come!" In order to lure the dog to you, crouch, clasp your hands, pick up a stick, or bounce a ball, or create any other attractive diversion. Then, when he comes, praise him and pat him effusively. As with all commands and exercises, repeat the lesson until the dog always comes to you when called.

OBEDIENCE TRAINING

A well-mannered dog makes for a proud owner. A canine delinquent makes for embarrassment, destroys property, and may make for accidents to children and other dogs. The latter unnecessary disadvantages can be eliminated by simple obedience training. Obedience training is, for the dog, the learning of a new language. Simple commands of one word each make it possible for him to associate the command with the lesson that he is learning.

EQUIPMENT FOR TRAINING

A lightweight metal chain collar, along with a leash, are best for training a grown dog, particularly one of the larger breeds. (See Fig. 276). An adjustable leather collar may be used for a young puppy, or a nylon choke collar may be used for a small, short-haired dog. A choke collar of any kind should never be left on the dog when he is free, as it may catch on something and strangle him. However, it is the best means of control when training, for it is gentle but firm.

TEN TRAINING GUIDES

The trainer should, at all times, exercise great

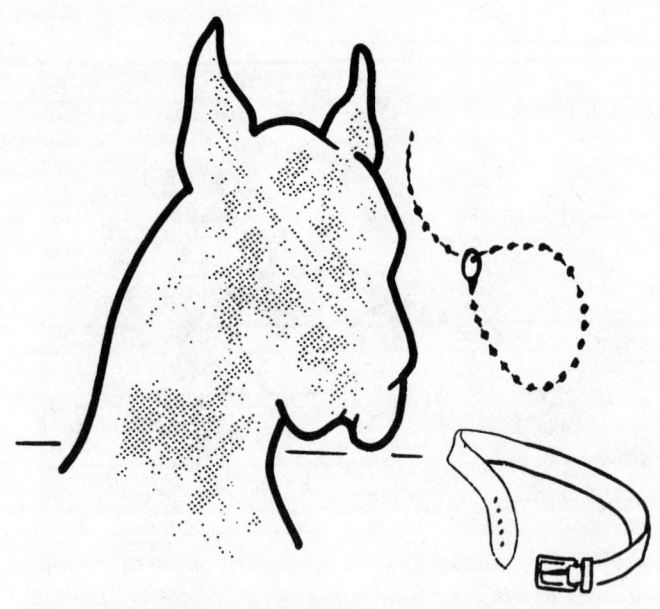

Fig. 276. A lightweight-metal chain collar, along with a leash, are best for training a grown dog. An adjustable leather collar may be used for a young puppy. (Drawing by R. F. Johnson)

patience, gentleness, and firmness. Although there are about as many training regimens as there are trainers, and each expert trainer may follow slightly different guidelines, each training program is designed to achieve the same end result —a well-trained dog, whose companionship you will enjoy.

With some slight variations here and there, most master trainers follow these ten guidelines:

1. *Have the dog relaxed and ready*—This may be accomplished by exercising the dog before each lesson begins and giving him an opportunity to relieve himself. Some trainers go a step further; they apply what is sometimes referred to as "flexion and relaxation," which is achieved by placing the dog on a table and massaging and working his limbs.

2. *Conduct two daily sessions*—Two daily sessions, each ten minutes, conducted at a regular hour, and in a businesslike manner, will usually suffice.

3. *Get his attention*—Effective training involves getting the dog's complete attention. To this end, the lesson should be conducted in strict privacy, without distractions.

4. *Review and praise*—Each lesson should begin with a review of one or more of the previous lessons, thereby giving the dog an opportunity to earn praise right from the start, and putting both you and the dog in a good mood.

5. *Be clear and firm*—In order to communicate effectively, you must be definite, clear, and firm.

6. *Don't lose your temper*—Never lose your temper or become impatient when you're training a dog. Do not scold, nag, or punish harshly.

7. *When things are not going well*—There will be days when training will not go well— when the relations between you and your dog become a bit strained. When this happens, it's a good idea to switch to a review of an earlier lesson for a few minutes in order to give you an excuse to praise and pet the dog before resuming the tougher task. Such an interlude will make both of you feel much better.

8. *Never let a command be ignored*—Once you have given a command, make sure that the dog complies. If the dog gets by with ignoring you just once, he will feel that he can do it again. So, see that your dog realizes that obeying you is the only thing. Your command must be law and order to him.

9. *End each lesson on an encouraging note*— Always end each lesson with praise. If you're working on one of the harder routines, switch to something simple at the end, so that you can let the dog feel successful. Remember that the dog must always succeed. If he fails to merit praise, keep on until he does accomplish his goal, even though the performance is not up to your standards. Quitting on a note of praise and success does wonders for the dog's morale, just as it does for people.

10. *One thing at a time*—Give one lesson at a time, and make sure that the dog understands and masters it before going to the next one.

BASIC OBEDIENCE COMMANDS

Each house dog should know and obey a few basic obedience commands. Seven of these basic commands are presented here. With some minor variations, as is inevitable between trainers, the methods that follow are just like those used by most professional trainers. You can use them to train your own dog at home.

HEEL

At the command *heel* (see Fig. 277), the dog should walk, without force or urging, at his handler's side, with the right side of his head about

"Duke, heel!"

Fig. 277. Heel. (Drawing by R. F. Johnson)

well trained to heel until he will walk quietly at the heel without a leash.

SIT

At the command *sit* the dog assumes a sitting posture, squarely on both hips (see Fig. 278). When properly trained, he must sit on command, even with the handler's left knee. If on a leash, the leash hangs loose. If off the leash, the dog walks equally well in the same position.

To execute the *heel,* hold the end of the leash in your right hand and use your left hand to hold the leash fairly close to the dog's neck. Then, command in a firm voice to "heel" and start walking forward, with the dog on your left side. During the first lesson, don't pay too much attention to the manner in which he goes—you're winning if he goes with you at all. Use the word "heel" often. In succeeding lessons, keep him fairly well in the correct position. If he pulls too far ahead, use a wrist action to give a series of quick jerks to bring him back to heel. If he lags behind, the same short jerks will bring him forward. But do not bring him to you by sustained pulling on the leash. Keep at this, all the while repeating "heel," lesson after lesson, until your dog heels in the correct position without tugging at the leash. Also, the dog must adapt himself to your changes of pace and direction, all the while he must maintain his position at your left side.

After the dog has mastered heeling on the leash, he should be taught to heel even when not on a leash. Heeling off the leash is best taught by starting each lesson with five minutes work on the leash. Then, take the leash off and proceed as instructed above, where the leash is being used. But be ready to grab the dog if he gives any indication of "taking off." If the dog gets away from you, catch him, but do not scold him. Instead, immediately put him back on the leash for a little extra work. When he responds, try him off the leash again. Your dog is not really

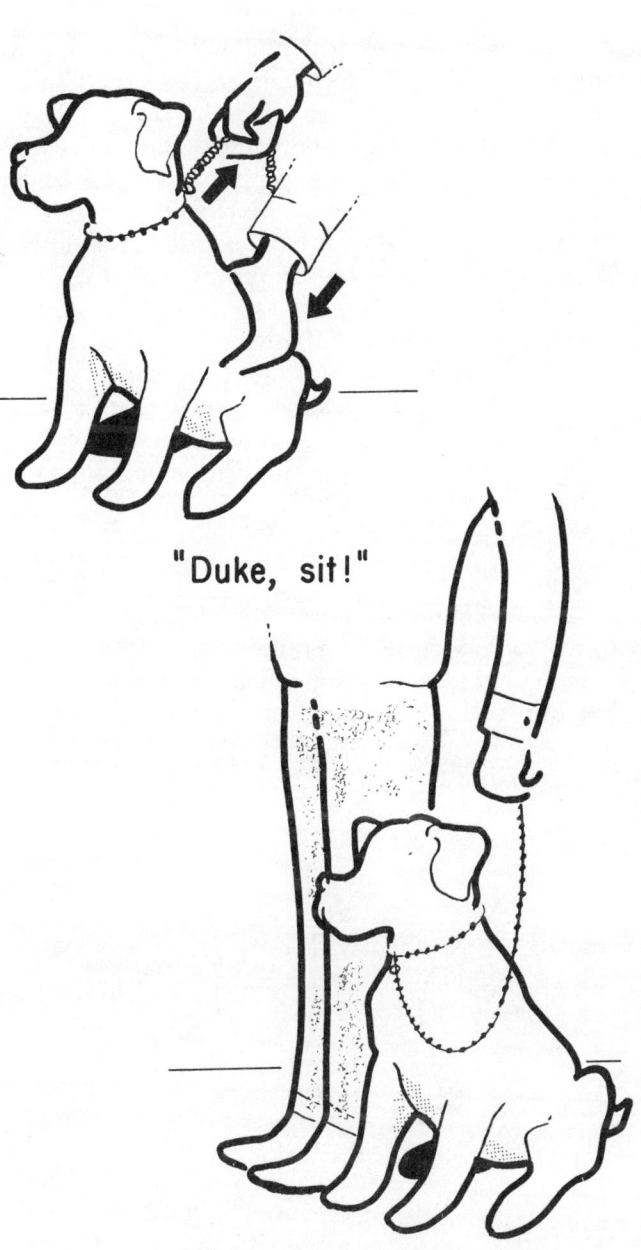

"Duke, sit!"

Fig. 278. Sit. (Top) Giving an assist by pulling back on the dog's collar and pushing down on his rump. (Bottom) Proper form at the sit—facing in the same direction as the handler, with his head even with or slightly ahead of the handler's knees, and with about six inches separating knees and head. (Drawing by R. F. Johnson)

301

whether at the time of the command he is heeling, running, or lying down.

To execute the sit, give the command, "sit." Simultaneously, pull back on the dog's collar and push down on his rump. If necessary, wiggle his rump in order to throw him off balance so that he has to sit. Hold him in this position, repeating the command, "sit." Then praise him by saying "good dog" and by patting him on the shoulder.

While the dog is learning what is meant by the word "sit," you need not be concerned about his form—that is, if he sits, you're doing alright. Once he knows and obeys the command, however, you can teach him proper position—facing in the same direction as his handler, with his head even with or slightly ahead of his handler's knees, and with about six inches separating the head and the knees.

Once the pupil has mastered the sitting routine on a tight leash, the same procedure should be applied on a loose leash. Then, when perfect results are obtained on a loose leash, the dog is ready to graduate to working the same command without a leash.

DOWN

At the command *down* the dog immediately drops to a lying down position. He must do this whether, at the moment of the command, he is heeling, sitting, standing, running, or walking.

There are several ways in which to teach a dog "down." One way is to have the dog sitting, then give the command, then shove down on the shoulders, while at the same time wobbling him off balance. This will work with most dogs.

The second method is to place the leash between the sole and the heel of your shoe. Give the command "down," then pull up on the leash. This pulls his neck down and forces him to go down. Also, if necessary, you can pull his legs forward until he goes down. Of course, when you see that he is starting to go down, compliment him.

It helps to give the verbal command repeatedly, even during the time the dog is actually down. Remember that he can't hear it too often while he's learning.

After executing this command, as well as after executing the sit, unless you order the dog to stay, he must instantly get up and heel when you start to walk away.

In teaching a dog to execute the "down," you should vary the routine—that is, do not give the various commands in the same order. This is imperative if you want this command to be obeyed instantly no matter where the dog is or what he is doing.

This exercise has a depressing effect on most dogs; hence, it is well not to require that they keep it too long at any one time. Also, be sure to praise the pet generously when he does a good job of "down." But do not say anything to him or pet him when he is down, for he will immediately want to get right back up.

Fig. 279. Down. (Left) One way to teach a dog down: *Have him sitting. Then give the command, shove down on the shoulders, and, at the same time, wobble him off balance. (Right) Another method is to place the leash between the sole and the heel of your shoe. Give the command* down, *then pull up on the leash. (Drawing by R. F. Johnson)*

SIT-STAY

The command *sit-stay* is given while the dog is in a sitting position, and when it is desired that he remain in this position.

This exercise is executed by first having the dog sit as directed above. Then, while placing the palm of your left hand against his face, give the command "stay"; keep commanding "stay"; and slowly walk away from the dog. If he gets up, force him back into the sit position at exactly the same spot from which he got up. The dog should hold the sit-stay position until you release and praise him.

Eventually he will sit-stay while you walk to the other end of the leash, while you walk around him, or even while you jump over him. Then, try turning your back on him and moving farther and farther away. All the while give the

Fig. 280. Sit-stay. First have the dog sit. Then, while placing the palm of your left hand against his face, give the command stay; and slowly walk away from him. (Drawing by R. F. Johnson)

Fig. 281. The down-stay assumes that the dog is already down. The command down-stay is given to make him remain in this position. (Drawing by R. F. Johnson)

command "stay" and hold the palm of your left hand toward him.

Next, place the dog in the sit-stay position and command him to stay while you walk out of sight. Return at intervals, with the intervals spaced farther and farther apart.

After the dog is well trained, you can feel free to walk away for 10–15 minutes to do a bit of housework or gardening, or even to visit with the neighbors.

The ultimate in a sit-stay exercise is a dog that will hold the position in the presence of other dogs. You can have your neighbors bring over their dogs for a testing session.

DOWN-STAY

The *down-stay* command assumes that the dog is already down, and the command is given to make the dog remain in this position. This is not difficult if the dog has already mastered the "down" position and the "sit-stay" position. Simply start with the down position, then teach the dog to remain in that position while you walk around him, over him, and away from him. If he starts to get up, say "No!" and see that he returns to the down position. You should see that he stays down until he is released and praised.

STAND-STAY

At the command *stand-stay* the dog should stand in position without moving (see Fig. 282).

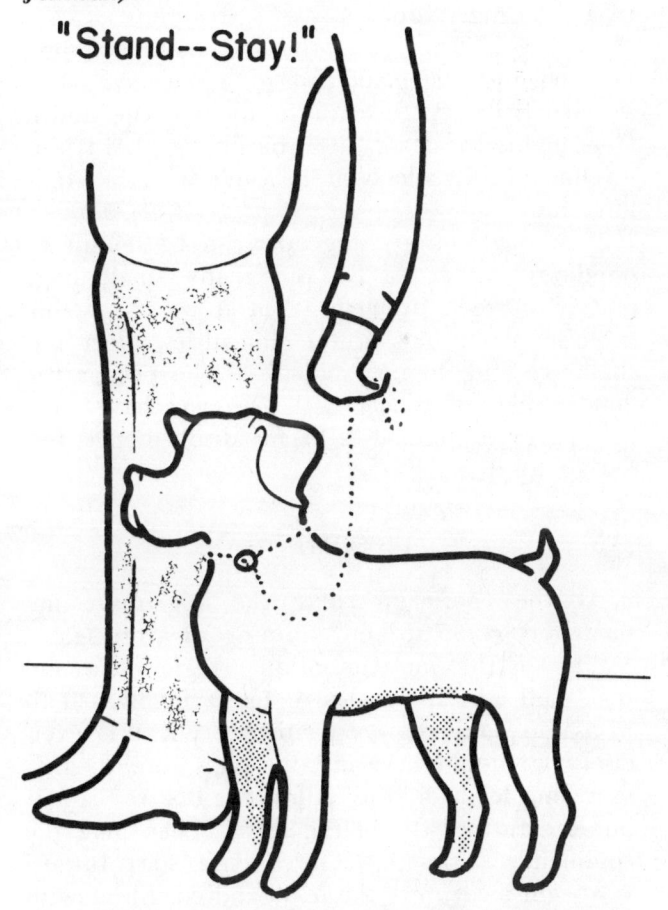

Fig. 282. Stand-stay. At the command stand-stay, the dog should stand in position without moving. He may be taught to execute the stand-stay (1) from the heel, (2) at the end of the heeling exercise, or (3) by placing him in a standing position manually. (Drawing by R. F. Johnson)

This is a more difficult exercise than either the sit or down, which are really negative responses. The stand-stay requires that the dog do something—that he use his muscles, balance, and intelligence to stay in a standing position on command.

The stand-stay has several practical applications: You can brush and groom him easier in this position, he can be shown off to better advantage, and the veterinarian can examine him more easily.

Perhaps the quickest and easiest way to teach this exercise is to give the "heel" command and start walking. Then, after a few steps, when the dog is well balanced on his feet, and as your left foot is swinging forward, swing your left hand over the front of his nose and give the command "stand." Another method is to make him stand at the finish of the heeling exercise. Still another method is to place him in a standing position manually; that is, simply lifting him into a standing position.

Once you have gotten the dog in the standing position, then command him to "stand-stay." Give a sharp little jerk if he starts to sit or lie down. If he fights the leash, just continue to hold him up until he decides that he can't win. It won't hurt him.

Most medium to large dogs can be taught to stand-stay rather easily. But many small dogs present quite a problem when it comes to this exercise. Regardless of the difficulties, meet the challenge and do not give in. If the pet proves that he has a stronger will than you have, you will have to contend with his disobedience the rest of his life.

COME

At the command *come* the dog must immediately come to you, running or trotting.

This is the most important single command that your dog has to learn, for it involves both his safety and your convenience. For this exercise, you should have the dog on a forty to fifty-foot long leash or cord. Allow the dog to wander out the full extent of the leash. Then give the command, "Come!" If he doesn't start toward you right away, jerk the leash and coax him with praise to come to you. If necessary, reel him in, praising him all the way. Pet him, then allow him to wander out again, and repeat this same exercise, praising him extravagantly with your voice and patting him on the shoulder when he obeys.

Fig. 283. Come. When starting this exercise, the dog should be on a 40- to 50-foot leash or cord. Then give the command come! *If he doesn't respond, jerk the leash, and, if necessary, reel him in. Next, remove the leash, but leave it on the ground, unattached to his collar. Finally, work the dog without any leash at all. (Drawing by R. F. Johnson)*

Next, leave the long leash stretched along the ground, but not actually attached to his collar. Call him as before. If he is slightly hesitant, go so far as to pull in the leash. Even though it isn't attached to the dog, he will think that it is.

Finally, work the dog without using any leash at all. If he continues to come the moment he is called, do not return to the leash. However, if he ignores the command, get the leash back on him again for a little concentrated review.

In time, to make this exercise a finished performance, have the dog come to you and "sit-stay." Sitting obviates any tendency that the dog might have to jump on you.

Your dog should come to you without delay when called, with head up and on the run. If he's slow, pull and jerk him on the long leash.

Never punish or scold your dog after he has come to you—even though he has done it the wrong way. If you punish him when he arrives in front of you, he will become confused—thinking the punishment was for coming to you, rather than for the manner in which he came.

TRICKS

Tricks are fun to teach, and fun for your dog to learn. The following basics are used in all trick training: (1) get the dog's attention, (2) give him a signal, and (3) practice using the same signal until the dog responds quickly. As is true in obedience training, keep the lessons short. Just ten to fifteen minutes once a day is enough. Never punish your dog for being a slow learner and always end each lesson with praise.

SIT UP

To teach a dog to *sit up*, sit him in a corner with his back close to the wall. This will prevent him from falling over backwards until he acquires balance. Now, lift his forepaws with your hands and help him balance while giving the command "sit up." Hold him up for only a few seconds at first. Repeat this exercise several times until you are certain that he has the idea and will sit up on command. Then, take your hands off him and give him the command again. If he does not obey, help him up again.

A dog can be induced to sit up and to hold the position by dangling a bit of food above his nose. However, this technique should be used only as a last resort for two reasons: (1) you don't want the dog to get the idea that he needn't sit up unless you have the reward ready, and (2) the reward takes his mind off the training.

After the dog is able to sit up in the corner, try him in other places. Each time, use the command "sit up." After responding, dismiss him by saying "all right" or "okay"; then praise and pet him.

CARRY

Because holding a hard object is a strain on teeth and jaws, you should use a newspaper, a piece of hose, an old shoe, or anything soft for this training exercise. For purposes of this discussion, we shall use a newspaper. Roll a newspaper and fasten it with a rubber band or string. Kneel beside the dog and give the command "carry." At that moment, force the dog's mouth open by pressing his lips against his teeth, then put the newspaper into his mouth. At first, he will try to spit it out. But don't let him do so. Hold it in his mouth firmly and repeat the command, "carry." But don't overdo it. After a few moments, say "all right" or "okay" to let him know that the lesson is over. Then praise and pet him. Repeat this exercise until he will open his mouth on command and hold the paper.

Once the dog has learned to hold the newspaper, you are ready to teach him to carry it. Put him in the corner of a room and fasten the leash to his collar. Command him to "carry," then begin to walk forward. If he tries to drop the

Fig. 284. Carry. (Drawing by R. F. Johnson)

paper, use your commanding voice, and, simultaneously, use your right hand to force him to hold the paper. When he does what you ask of him, praise and pet him generously. Usually it will require only one or two lessons to teach a dog to carry. After that, he will walk at heel and probably carry his object.

During these lessons, never let the dog drop the article before you tell him that he can. He must always give it directly into your hand. If you allow him to get away with dropping it, even once, you will never be able to depend upon him.

Most dogs take great pride in carrying. It fulfills their age-old desire to cooperate with and please man.

FETCH

After a dog has learned to hold and carry, it's usually relatively easy to teach him to fetch. The dog can be taught to bring your slippers, his leash, his bone, a ball, or a newspaper.

Practically any dog will chase a ball or a stick. The well-trained dog will not only chase a thrown object, but he will bring it back directly to your hand. Moreover, he should sit down in front of you before delivering it to your hand.

The training procedure for teaching a dog to "fetch" is very similar to that followed in teaching the dog to "carry." Put him in the corner of a room, kneel beside him, show him the object, but don't give it to him. Instead, throw it a few feet away. Then, command "fetch." If he doesn't respond, lead him to the object, draw his head down to it, force him to open his mouth, and if necessary lift the object into his mouth. Again, repeat the command "fetch" and make him carry the object back to his corner.

Once the dog has the idea, he'll chase and fetch with as much pride as he carries. But, be sure and praise and pet him for each accomplishment. For a more finished performance of the "fetch" procedure, you can teach your dog to find and fetch. Simply hide his dish, or an old shoe, or whatever article you wish to have him fetch, in another room. Gradually, you can teach him to go into another room and get such articles. Once the dog has learned to find and fetch, he'll enjoy it and beg you to hide things for him.

CATCH

To teach your dog to play catch, use small tidbits of food to start with. Place the dog in a sit position in a corner of a well-lighted room. Secure his attention, then toss the food at his face and say "catch." In all probability he won't budge and the food will fall to the floor. But don't let him eat it; grab it before he does. Put him back into position and tell him to stay. Be sure he is watching your hand, then toss the food and repeat the command "catch."

You may have to repeat this exercise a half dozen times. Eventually, however, the dog realizes that he must catch the food in the air; otherwise he won't get it. When he does, praise him and repeat the exercise so he gets more food.

Next, you are ready to try the same procedure with a ball or other objects. Once you have taught the dog to catch, it is a simple matter to teach him to retrieve the object.

SHAKE HANDS

A dog should be taught not to jump on people. Shaking hands is a more pleasant way for him to greet guests. It's an easy trick to teach. Put your dog in a normal sitting position and kneel in front of him. Tap the back of his foreleg with your hand. When he lifts his paw, take it gently in your hand and say "shake hands" or "shake." Smile and tell him that he's a "good dog."

ROLL OVER

To teach your dog to "roll over," first have him "lie down." Then swing your arm in a circular motion, while commanding "roll over." Push him over with your hand to show him how it's done

Fig. 285. Shake hands. (Drawing by R. F. Johnson)

for the first few times. He'll soon catch on. Sometimes it helps if you yourself roll over, to show him how it's done. Of course, praise the dog, even though you forcibly roll him over.

JUMP

Jumping is fun for a dog, and good exercise, too. You can build a low jump by placing a stick or broom handle across two or three piled up bricks. Put your dog on a leash, then have him walk at the heel as the two of you proceed toward the jump. You should jump over the object, the dog should follow you. At the proper moment, you should give the command, "jump," then jerk slightly on the leash. Repeat this trick over and over, with the stick or broom handle raised higher and higher until the dog can jump twice his shoulder height.

After the dog has learned to jump along with you, ask that he jump alone as you bypass the jump to the right. Next, make the dog jump without your trotting along and bypassing the object. Station him on one side of the object, or hurdle, by giving the command "stay." Then, you should proceed to the opposite side of the hurdle; tug slightly on the leash and command "jump," and make the dog jump toward you.

After the dog has learned to (1) jump over the hurdle with you, and (2) jump over the hurdle toward you when you are on the other side, both on and off the leash, then you are ready for the more finished jumping performance. For the latter, place the dog in front of the hurdle, while you stand aside. Give the command

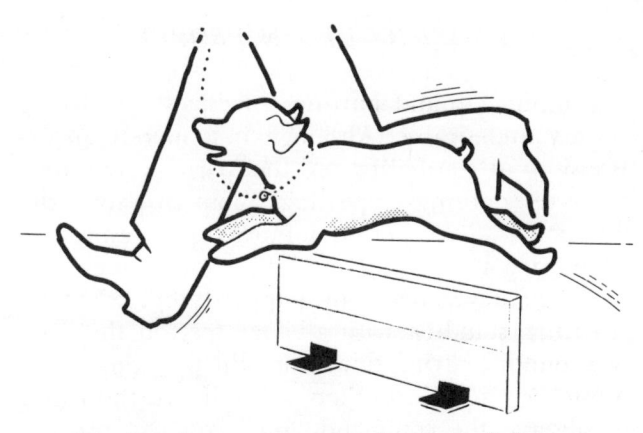

Fig. 286. Jump. (Drawing by R. F. Johnson)

"jump." If the dog does not respond, make him do so. If he starts to bypass the hurdle, reprimand him and make him jump as ordered. Within a very short time, the dog will jump on command from any position.

Once the dog has been taught to jump over the hurdle, you can have fun out of teaching him to jump over a friend who is kneeling on the ground or even to jump over another dog.

THROUGH THE HOOP

Once the dog has learned to jump over a bar, it's relatively easy to teach him to jump through the hoop.

Fig. 287. Dog trained to broad jump up to nine feet. (Courtesy Metropolitan Police Department, City of St. Louis, St. Louis, Mo.)

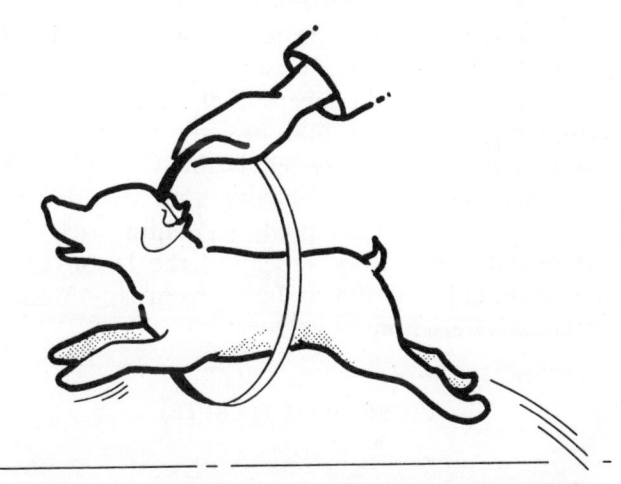

Fig. 289. Through the hoop. (Drawing by R. F. Johnson)

Fig. 288. Dog trained to scale a wall. (Courtesy Metropolitan Police Department, City of St. Louis, St. Louis, Mo.)

Fig. 290. Dog trained to go through a hoop. (Courtesy Metropolitan Police Department, City of St. Louis, St. Louis, Mo.)

At first, place the hoop on the floor and allow the dog to pass through it. Then, gradually raise the height of the hoop from the floor and ask the dog to jump through it, all the while giving the command "jump." After a jump, praise and pet the dog. Very soon, he will go through the hoop with the greatest of ease.

DON'T TOUCH IT

You should teach your dog not to touch food offered him by strangers, for the same reason that most mothers teach their children not to accept food offered to them by people whom they do not know.

This exercise is taught by placing a piece of food on the floor, then letting your dog approach it. Just as he reaches the food, say "no" and jerk him by the leash. Of course, your dog should already understand the meaning of "no." He'll very quickly get the idea that he isn't to touch anything that you have ordered him not to touch.

Next, try him out by having your friends offer him food. If he's tempted, jerk him back and command "no." Keep repeating the lesson until he automatically draws back from anything a stranger offers him.

VICES (BAD HABITS)

Vices, or bad habits, are difficult to detect for they are often present in the most handsome and lovable dog. Some vices are vicious and dangerous to man and other animals; others inflict punishment upon the offender himself; and still others merely use energy wastefully. Regardless of the type of vice, it is undesirable and to be avoided.

BEGGING

Puppies will beg when the family is at meals. When this happens, the puppy should be scolded and put into his box bed. He will learn very quickly that begging doesn't pay.

Above all, never start the habit. If you have some choice tidbits to give to the dog, or a prize bone, save them until after the meal is finished and the dog is outside.

JUMPING UP ON PEOPLE

Jumping up and putting front paws on people is very undesirable. Although it is merely an expression of cordiality on the part of the dog, there is nothing appealing about it from the viewpoint of the person jumped upon, especially if the dog is wet and muddy.

If you never pet your puppy except when he is sitting, standing with all four feet on the floor or ground, or lying down, he will probably never jump on you, or on others. Also, if you train him to observe the command "no," you can prevent him from jumping on others. However, if he already has this bad habit, it can be cured with a little patience. Either of the following cures will work like a charm:

1. *Make him walk backwards*—When the dog jumps on you, or on another person, grab his forepaws and walk him rapidly backwards for six to ten feet, scolding him as you go.

2. *Gently step on his hind toes*—When the dog jumps up, take his front paws in your hands, then gently step on his hind toes, applying just sufficient pressure to be effective without injuring him. While doing so, use the command "no."

Fig. 291. Jumping up on people is a bad habit. One way to break it: Gently step on the dog's hind toes. (Drawing by R. F. Johnson)

JUMPING ON FURNITURE

Usually, all members of the family are responsible for this bad habit. They carry the puppy around and sit with him on their laps while he is small. When he grows up, he still wishes to be up off the floor.

The following techniques may be used to break the jumping on furniture habit:

1. When the dog is seen jumping on furniture, use the "no" command and throw a rolled up newspaper at him.
2. Provide the dog with his own scatter rug as a comfortable substitute.
3. Designate one chair that he can lie in.
4. Set on chairs or couches a few mouse traps (without bait), then cover them with a layer of paper. This procedure will usually work if everything else fails. When the dog jumps up on furniture on which the mouse trap is set, he soon gets the message that he is not supposed to be there (and no harm is done); and he is none the wiser that you were the villain that set the trap.

GARBAGE PAILS AND WASTEBASKETS

All puppies love to get into garbage pails and wastebaskets. They're enticed by food odors, by the pleasure of scattering papers and boxes, and by tearing up things.

This vice, or habit, is easily broken by means of mouse traps. Simply set a few mouse traps in each garbage pail or wastebasket. Set them unbaited under a sheet of paper. When the dog makes his next call, the traps go off and startle him. After having this happen a couple of times, the puppy soon gets the idea that this is forbidden territory; and there is no more problem.

Mouse traps are too small to hurt puppies, except for those of the toy breeds; and the latter are too small to get into trouble in the first place.

CHEWING

Puppies chew on things to develop their teeth, whereas older dogs do so to exercise their jaws and for the pure joy of chewing. The best way to live with this instinctive habit is to provide something made for chewing, such as a piece of rawhide that stores have available for this purpose, rubber bones with built-in smell, and actual soup bones. Above all, don't let a dog chew on an old shoe or slipper. His mind is not able to distinguish between "his shoe" and yours—he'll not be able to understand why he can chew one shoe but not the other.

A grown dog that chews the furniture or a corner of the rug while you're at home should be no problem, because you can stop him with a command, or, if necessary, punish him. But the dog that chews things only when he is unobserved is a problem.

Most instances of chewing (including pulling down drapes and upsetting tables) are simply protests against being left alone. Usually this occurs with badly spoiled dogs, particularly those lacking the security that good training gives them.

In addition to providing the dog with something for his chewing, your best hope is to try to impart to the dog understanding of what pleases and what displeases you.

Fig. 292. Jumping on furniture is a bad habit. One way to break it: Set a few mouse traps (without bait), then cover them with a sheet of paper. (Drawing by R. F. Johnson)

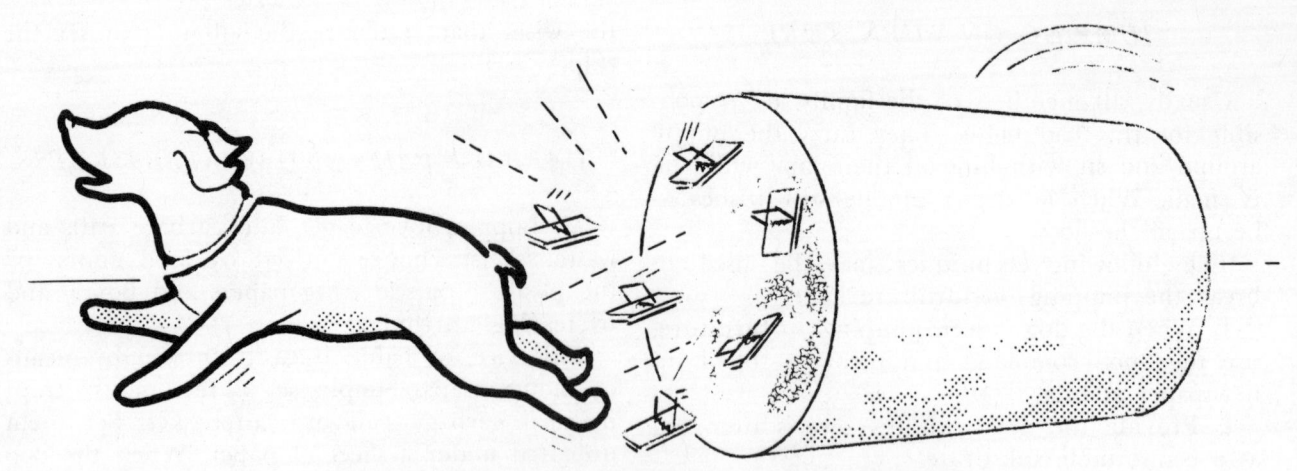

Fig. 293. Getting into garbage pails and wastebaskets is a bad habit. One way to break it: Set a few mouse traps in each garbage pail or wastebasket. (Drawing by R. F. Johnson)

If everything else fails, there is one last resort to the problem dog that chews things up while the owner is away: Either (1) put him in a crate, provided he has been trained to accept crate confinement early in life, or (2) put him in a bathroom or kitchen where there is nothing for him to chew. Usually such problem dogs—those that chew up things while the owner is away—can be alleviated by training the young dog to accept confinement in a pen a short time each day, with the result that confinement and being left alone are no shock or stress, even when the master is away.

BARKING EXCESSIVELY

Some barking, providing the dog exercises discretion, and doesn't bark excessively, is good, for there may be a time when a barked warning will be mighty important to you. However, excessive barking can become a nuisance; instead of being sweet music it may be disturbing to your neighbors.

Dogs are gregarious; hence, when left alone, they suffer boredom and loneliness. To offset this, they will sometimes do a lot of barking. Also, the barking gives them something to do, and it's a way of attracting company.

Excess barking can be stopped in a number of ways. First, set up conditions under which you know the puppy will bark. Then, apply one of the following techniques:

1. Give the command "no." If the dog has been obedience trained, he will likely comply.
2. Shake the dog while saying, "no," "no," "no."
3. Bomb the dog with empty tin cans. (Frozen orange juice cans or soup cans are ideal for this purpose.)
4. Hose the dog with cold water if he is out in the yard.

GROWLING; BITING; NIPPING; UNNECESSARY ROUGHNESS

Most biting dogs are spoiled dogs. They began by growling, which they got away with. Next, they tried nipping, which they also got away with, then they made the first bite.

Nipping, or biting at the heels, was bred into shepherd dogs—dogs used for driving cattle and sheep. So, when dogs nip at the heels of people, they are merely practicing an age-old instinct, for which they have not been disciplined. Once a dog has learned that he can bite or nip a human being, he can no longer be trusted. He'll bite again and again.

To alleviate biting or nipping, it is best to set up the conditions. A good way in which to do this is to take the puppy's food dish away from him while he is eating. If he growls, pick him up by the scruff of the neck, so that his front feet are off the ground, then slap upward under the chin. All the while, scold him severely. Then, return his food to him, along with some comforting words and a few pats. Repeat this process again and again until he knows that he should never growl or bite under any circumstances.

Often, romping or playing with a puppy will cause him to get too rough. If, in the excitement, this happens you should scold him severely and slap him under the chin, while holding his front legs off the ground. After disciplining him, make up with him immediately and play again. If he starts to get rough again, repeat the disciplinary measures; and continue this treatment as long as necessary.

Sometimes puppies need to be taught to be gentle with children, who often excite them by running and yelling and by their high-pitched voices. Admonish both puppy and children to be more quiet.

Teething puppies will pull and chew on most anything, including children's clothes and hands and legs. However, you can and should discourage this kind of playing, because it will be a nuisance when the puppy grows up. Give the command "no" when you see the puppy tugging or nipping at a child, then divert his attention to something else to do.

MAILMAN—DELIVERYMAN— SERVICEMAN PHOBIA

It should be a point of shame to dog owners to know that every year 100,000 dogs bite mailmen, deliverymen, meter readers, and garbage collectors. Both the folks bitten and dog owners must assume responsibility for this uncontrolled vice. Part of the fault lies in the fact that the people bitten do not take the time to get acquainted with dogs and to assure them that they are on the premises for good reason. But it's the dog owners fault, too, because he hasn't taught his pet to understand.

The dog owner should introduce his dog to the mailman, deliveryman, serviceman, etc. He should accompany the dog to meet these people; using encouraging words and urging the dog to be friends, and assuring him that nothing is wrong. Ask the stranger to pet the dog and tell him the pet's name.

Of course, if your dog is kept indoors or within an enclosed backyard, there is no hazard to those who deliver to or service the home.

CHASING CARS

Many dogs love to chase cars. Perhaps they fancy themselves indulging in either some prehistoric wolf chase, or driving sheep or cattle. Whatever the cause, a dog that chases cars is a menace to himself and to automobile drivers. A dog can be cured of the habit, although the "cure" may have to be repeated several times before it takes. The most common and effective measures to break a dog of chasing cars are: (1) have a friend bomb him with empty tin cans as he plies his vice; (2) have a friend dose him with cold water, released from a water pistol, a bucket, or a plastic bag; or (3) have a friend bring his car to a screeching halt, then lash the dog with a whip.

In the first place, car chasing would seldom happen if people kept their dogs home where they belong.

Whatever the method you use, it should be repeated until the dog learns not to chase. Repeat it as many as a dozen times in a week. When once the puppy stands quietly and watches a car go by without chasing it, praise him profusely.

The same techniques outlined above for the chasing car vice may be used in breaking a dog from the habit of chasing bicycles.

CAT CHASER

Some dogs love to chase cats. They probably don't hate them; it simply gives them something to do—besides, cats will run from them and give them an opportunity to chase.

The best cure for the cat chaser is to use the chain, or bomb with empty cans, along with the command "no," "no," "no." If all else fails, give the cat the opportunity to bury his claws in the dog—this will usually break him.

DIGGING

Most dogs like to dig. The terriers are particularly partial to it. Soft earth is an inviting spot for a nap or a great place to bury a bone. If possible, you should provide a dirt area where your dog can indulge in this inherited instinct.

Basically, there is no foolproof method to stop the dog from digging. If space is available, perhaps the best solution is to prepare a dog run

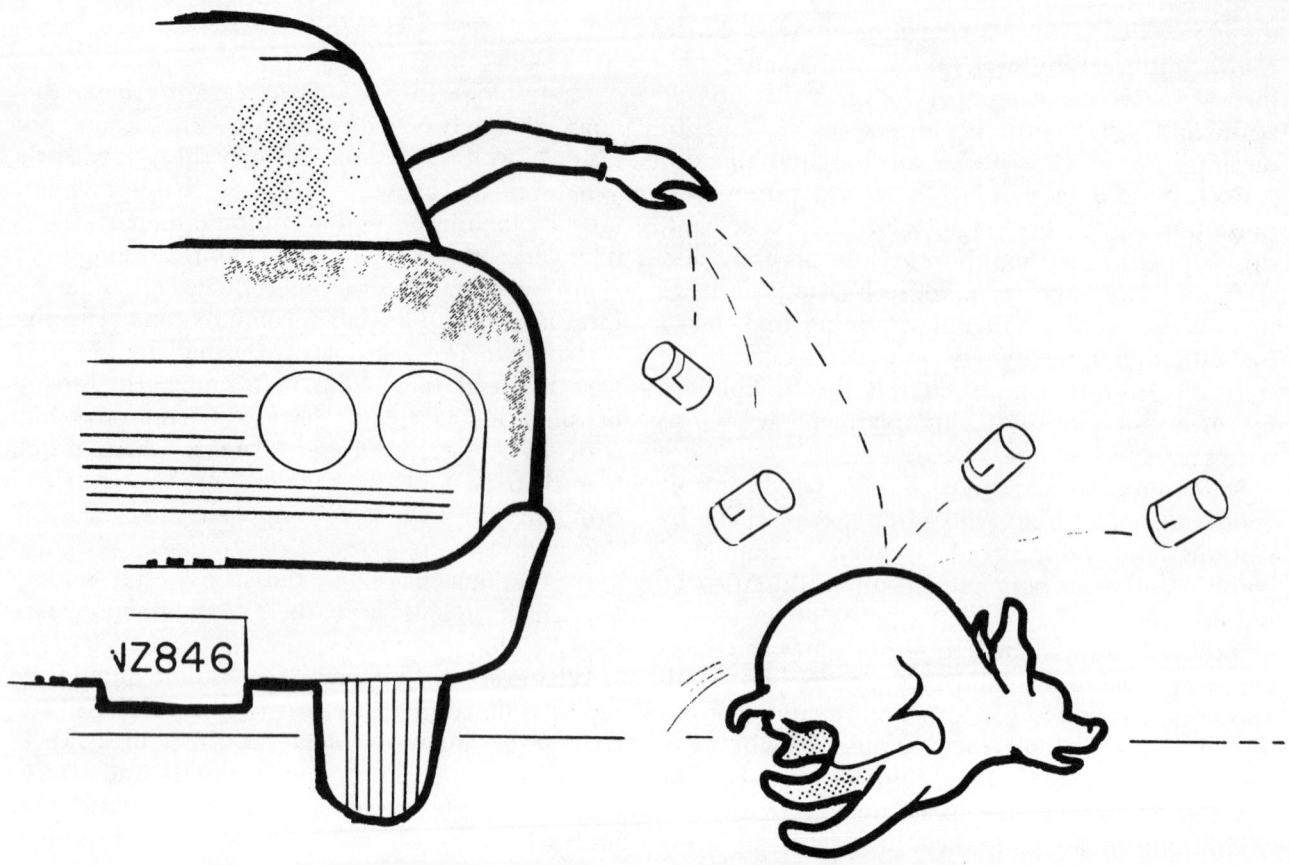

Fig. 294. Chasing cars is a bad habit. One way to break it: Bomb him with empty tin cans. (Drawing by R. F. Johnson)

Fig. 295. No cat chaser here! A puppy that grows up with a kitten seldom becomes a cat chaser later in life. (Courtesy The American Humane Association, Denver, Colo.)

that is underlaid with wire beneath the surface. Generally, this will discourage future digging. Of course, keeping the dog penned on concrete, or other hard surface, which he cannot get his claws into, may discourage him, and in time he might forget about digging altogether.

RUNNING AWAY FROM HOME

There are four main causes for dogs running away from home—

1. The dog does not feel wanted and is unhappy.
2. The dog is bored and feels the urge for more excitement and companionship.
3. The dog hears children playing at a distance and yearns for the excitement of their company.
4. The search for a mate (spring fever!).

Generally, it is not difficult for the owner to decide which of these factors is motivating the dog to run away from home. To cure a runaway dog, you must either remove the cause or build an escape-proof dog run for him to stay in.

PREVENT VICES FROM FORMING

Remember that just one bad habit may make the difference between a good dog and a neighborhood nuisance. Remember, too, that a bad habit can cause you to have your dog destroyed. So, try to prevent bad habits from forming.

Never permit your dog to growl over anything; then he'll never bite. Teach him his own place in the house, which is on the floor. Don't let him become a neighborhood "bum." And introduce him to the mailman, the deliveryman, and the serviceman; teach him not to bark at them.

Once vices, or bad habits, have formed, you can correct them—provided you outthink the dog. Where possible, use such devices as mouse traps to break a bad habit.

BE A GOOD "DOG NEIGHBOR"

As a dog owner, you must recognize that being a good "dog neighbor" involves certain responsibilities on your part; and the neighbors do not love your dog as you do—and they won't tolerate a spoiled brat, in either a child or a dog. Failure to recognize these basic facts, and to respect the feelings of others, prompts squabbles with the neighbors, gives rise to complaints to police departments and newspapers, and even makes for bitter lawsuits.

Here are some "do's" and "don't's" of being a good "dog neighbor."

SOME "DO'S" OF BEING A GOOD DOG NEIGHBOR

1. Either take your dog on an escorted walk, or have a fenced yard or wire run.
2. Teach your dog to use certain portions of your yard. If he insists on relieving himself in a forbidden area, discourage him by spraying the area with a commercial deodorant or a solution of nicotine sulfate. If you must rely on escorted walks entirely, use a back alley as a place for the dog to relieve himself.
3. Pick up stools regularly if you use a fenced area. Either dispose of them in the street sewer or spread them on your own garden.
4. Teach the dog not to bark by—
   a. Escorting him for a walk the first thing in the morning and the last thing at night; when doing so, stop him if he barks.
   b. Scolding him or bringing him in the house if he barks needlessly during the day.
   c. Throwing empty tin cans at him every time he barks when there is no real danger.
5. Chase off intruding dogs that try to pick a fight with your dog, either when you're walking him on a leash or when he's in a fenced area or on a wire run; by throwing empty tin cans. Two or three repeats will discourage the intruder.
6. Teach your dog to accept the mailman and service people. Let him perform his "doggie duty" by giving an initial warning—one bark. Then, discourage further barking, and possible biting, by scolding him or throwing empty tin cans at him. Also, and most important, introduce the dog and the mailman and other servicemen. Tell these folks the name of your dog and pass along to them a cookie, or other tidbit, for their use as a token of friendship. Teach the dog that these folks are good fellows, who have the right to come there and who will do no harm. If everything else fails, bring the dog in the house ahead of the time that these people usually make their rounds.
7. Avoid odors from stools and urine. If a small exercise pen must be used, concrete it and wash excrement into the sewer twice daily, and/or put up a windbreak to protect your neighbors.
8. If the dog howls needlessly, particularly when he's alone, substitute the security of a crate. The latter consists of securing a dog crate (like those used in transporting dogs to shows and field trials); putting the dog in the crate for about an hour each morning, following his walk; insisting on silence while in the crate; and repeating this ritual for a few days, with and without your presence in the house. With persistence, and insistence on quietness when the dog is in the crate, generally he'll accept the crate as his permanent home and a place of security, and remain quietly therein.
9. Where you cannot build fences or a wire run, teach the dog that anything beyond the borders of your yard is off limits. This is best done as follows:

a. Equip the dog with a choke chain and a long, trailing leash cord.

b. Purposely "bait" the dog to go out-of-bounds, by having someone call him, or walk another dog by.

c. When the dog reaches the yard border, grab the long leash and jerk hard enough to upset him—and simultaneously cry, "No!"

d. Remove the rope once the dog understands the yard limits. Repeat the "baiting." When he respects the don't-cross-the-border rule, praise him warmly with a pat and "good dog."

10. Use the empty-tin-can cure if your dog chases cars or bicycles. Also, you can use the same long leash technique as outlined in point No. 9 above. The psychology is to have the object being chased "fight back," and also to use the element of surprise.

11. Alleviate the female problem by having a female spayed, unless, of course, you plan to raise puppies. Otherwise, you'll have a pack of male dogs calling twice a year (bitches come in season twice a year). Spaying is best done before the first heat, at about six to seven months of age.

The alternatives to spaying your female are to put her in a boarding kennel twice each year, when she's in season, or keep her in the house during the heat periods. When house confinement is used, put your female in the car and drive to a vacant lot to allow her to relieve herself—but never let her off the leash.

SOME "DON'TS" OF BEING A GOOD DOG NEIGHBOR

1. Don't let your dog roam. He'll get into trouble if you do.

2. Don't allow your dog to soil your neighbor's shrubbery or lawn, or tear up his flower garden.

3. Don't allow your dog to fight the neighborhood dogs.

4. Don't let your dog chase cars, youngsters, or bicycles.

5. Don't let your dog bark needlessly at or bite mail carriers or service people.

6. Don't let your leashed dog jump at or on people or other dogs who pass by.

7. Don't leave your dog alone in a yard or on a wire run for most of the day.

8. Don't allow your dog to relieve himself on the "tree lawn" (the area between the sidewalk and the street).

9. Don't let your dog howl when you're away.

Remember that good neighbors have good neighbors. Remember, too, that every poor dog neighbor makes it difficult for all dog owners; they're the ones that cause apartment owners to refuse pets and town ordinances to be passed.

7
Grooming

Chapter 7
Groom the Puppy	*316*
Grooming Place and Frequency	*317*
Grooming Equipment	*317*
Coat Care	*318*
Combing and Brushing	*318*
Shedding	*320*
Matted Hair	*320*
Trimming	*320*
Do Not Give a Summer Haircut	*321*
Bathing	*321*
Toenails	*322*
Dewclaws or Dog Thumbs	*322*
Ears	*322*
Eyes	*323*
Teeth	*323*
Other Helpful Grooming Hints	*324*
Special and Show Grooming	*324*
Grooming Checklist	*325*

Fig. 296. Bath time! (Courtesy The American Humane Association, Denver, Colo.)

GROOMING[1]

"Trifles make perfection, but perfection is no trifle" is an old and well-known adage to which all dog owners who desire attractive pets should subscribe. This philosophy is particularly appropriate to good grooming.

Dogs like to be clean. In the wild state, they kept their dens clean, and they seldom befouled themselves as they roved over a wide area. They groomed themselves by rolling in the grass, particularly when shedding, and by licking themselves with their tongues.

Under domestication, proper and regular grooming is necessary (1) to make and keep the dog attractive, (2) to maintain good health and condition, and (3) to prevent doggy odors. Grooming cleans the hair, keeps the skin functioning normally, lessens skin diseases and parasites, and improves muscle tone. Also, it imparts pride of ownership to the dog's master. When it comes to showing, custom decrees certain types of grooming in some cases.

Many people are adverse to dogs (they won't have one of their own, and they object to their friends' dogs) because of what they may refer to as a "doggy odor." Of course, almost every living thing—whether it be animal or plant—emits a characteristic odor. So, the dog does have a certain amount of a characteristic odor, otherwise he would not be a dog. However, when that odor becomes too strong and obnoxious, it's a sure sign that the grooming has been neglected. The odor may be coming from the coat, the teeth, or clogged anal glands. In any case, proper grooming will rectify the situation. Before going further, it should be emphasized that correct and adequate nutrition will enable the clean and healthy skin to produce the live, lustrous coat that the dog is capable of growing; and that no amount of artificial grooming can replace this over a long period of time.

GROOM THE PUPPY

Early in life, the puppy should come to know that grooming is a pleasant experience. He is easy to handle at that stage, and, besides, in a few months, he will need regular grooming.

Lift the puppy onto the table; later he can be trained to jump up if he is big enough. Never leave him alone on the table until he has become used to it and learned the command "stay."

The first grooming session should be short. Brush the puppy, keeping one hand on him for reassurance and to prevent him from jumping down. Praise him and pat him, then put him down. Repeat this puppy grooming daily. Soon he'll react to it as a pleasant time when he receives special attention; and he'll enjoy the brushing.

Also, accustom the puppy to having his mouth open for inspection, and to having his ears handled. Pick up one foot at a time, and handle the paws. Then, later on, when his teeth need cleaning, when his ears must be cleaned, or when his nails must be clipped, he won't resent this care. Also, your veterinarian will benefit, for such training will make the dog easier to handle when he has to go for a checkup.

Remember that your dog is not thoroughly

---

[1] The author acknowledges with thanks the authoritative review accorded this chapter by: Mrs. Lee Watts, Show Secretary, North Shore Kennel Club of B.C., 1840 Mathers Avenue, West Vancouver, B.C.

Fig. 297. Dogs like to be clean. They groom themselves, and each other, by licking. (Happy Family. Courtesy Smithsonian Institution, Washington, D.C.)

groomed if you've only brushed his back and upper body. So, train him to lie on his side, especially if he is of a long-coated breed. Matted and tangled hair, which more frequently forms on the chest and the inside of the legs, can be more easily reached if the dog is on his side, rather than standing.

GROOMING PLACE AND FREQUENCY

The dog should have a regular grooming place. This may be a table, bench, chair, or even the top of his house if it is level. Also, grooming stands are manufactured for this purpose. The main requisites are that the grooming place be sturdy, that it be of adequate size, and that it be of sufficient height so that you can work on the dog without bending or stooping. Put a rubber mat on the top of the grooming area or fasten thick toweling to it to give the dog a secure footing.

It's best to set a definite schedule for the grooming period, then it will not be overlooked. Short-coated breeds should be groomed two or three times a week. Long-coated dogs should be groomed daily. Puppies should have their faces cleaned daily until they learn to eat without sticking their faces in food. Each grooming session will take only a few minutes if it is done regularly. If it is neglected, however, the dog owner faces the tedious ordeal of getting a messy coat back into shape.

GROOMING EQUIPMENT

The number of articles, and the type, of grooming equipment will depend on the breed to be groomed. The following are suggested:

Fig. 298. Attachable grooming stand. (Drawing by J. L. Medeiros)

1. *Brush*—A short or long-bristle brush, depending on the length of the coat
2. *Comb*—With wide teeth for long-haired or wirehaired dogs
3. *Stripping knife or wool comb*—Stripping knife for wirehaired dogs; wool comb for long-haired dogs
4. *Scissors*—Regular barber type
5. *Nail clippers*—Get nail clippers made especially for this purpose; an electric nail-grinding tool, equipped with sandpaper discs, is both effective and easy on the dog
6. *Grooming guide*—Obtain a grooming guide for your particular breed
7. *Hound glove*—These are available in most pet shops or stores

See Fig. 299 which shows articles of grooming equipment.

COAT CARE

The coat is the dog's complexion; and its care will greatly influence his general appearance. In order to grow a handsome coat, it is essential that the dog be well fed and in good health. If these conditions have been met, grooming of the coat is next in importance so far as appearance is concerned.

Normally the coat sheds out twice each year, spring and fall, although some shedding goes on all the time. Heavy shedding between seasons may be caused by lack of strength, as following illness, while dryness may result from too much washing or an overheated apartment. A temporary faded look may merely mean that the old coat is on the wane, since the hair loses its vigor and color just before it is shed.

COMBING AND BRUSHING

Each breed varies somewhat in regard to hair coat and the best method for caring for it. Short-haired dogs should be brushed; terrier-type dogs require a periodic plucking to remove their dead hairs and give them a trim appearance, with careful brushing and combing between pluckings; long-coated dogs are usually combed, after which they may be brushed to give added sheen or lustre to their hair. A blunt-edged steel comb is best. Use a fine comb for short-haired dogs and a comb with widely spaced teeth for the long-haired, medium-haired and wirehaired dogs. Also, use a brush with the correct bristle length—short for medium- and short-haired dogs, long bristles for long-haired dogs.

Combing of long-haired dogs should be done as frequently as necessary to keep the coat in good condition. Animals should be taught from puppyhood to stand or lie on a table, or, in the case of a large dog, on the floor. They should expect and enjoy combing. Short-haired animals need less combing, but a fine comb even for them is more efficient than a brush.

Running brushes over the outside of a long-haired animal's coat accomplishes little in the way of loose hair removal. So, when grooming your dog, be sure to get the brush all the way down to the skin, as the massaging action stimulates circulation of the blood, which is beneficial. This massaging also helps loosen and remove flakes of dandruff.

A flannel cloth or a hound glove will give an incomparable finish where the coat is required to lie flat to the body. This will not only lay the hair in place, but it will add greatly to the luster or gloss of the dog's coat by polishing. A hound glove may be obtained in almost any pet shop or from any pet supply store.

If you can, comb and brush your dog daily.

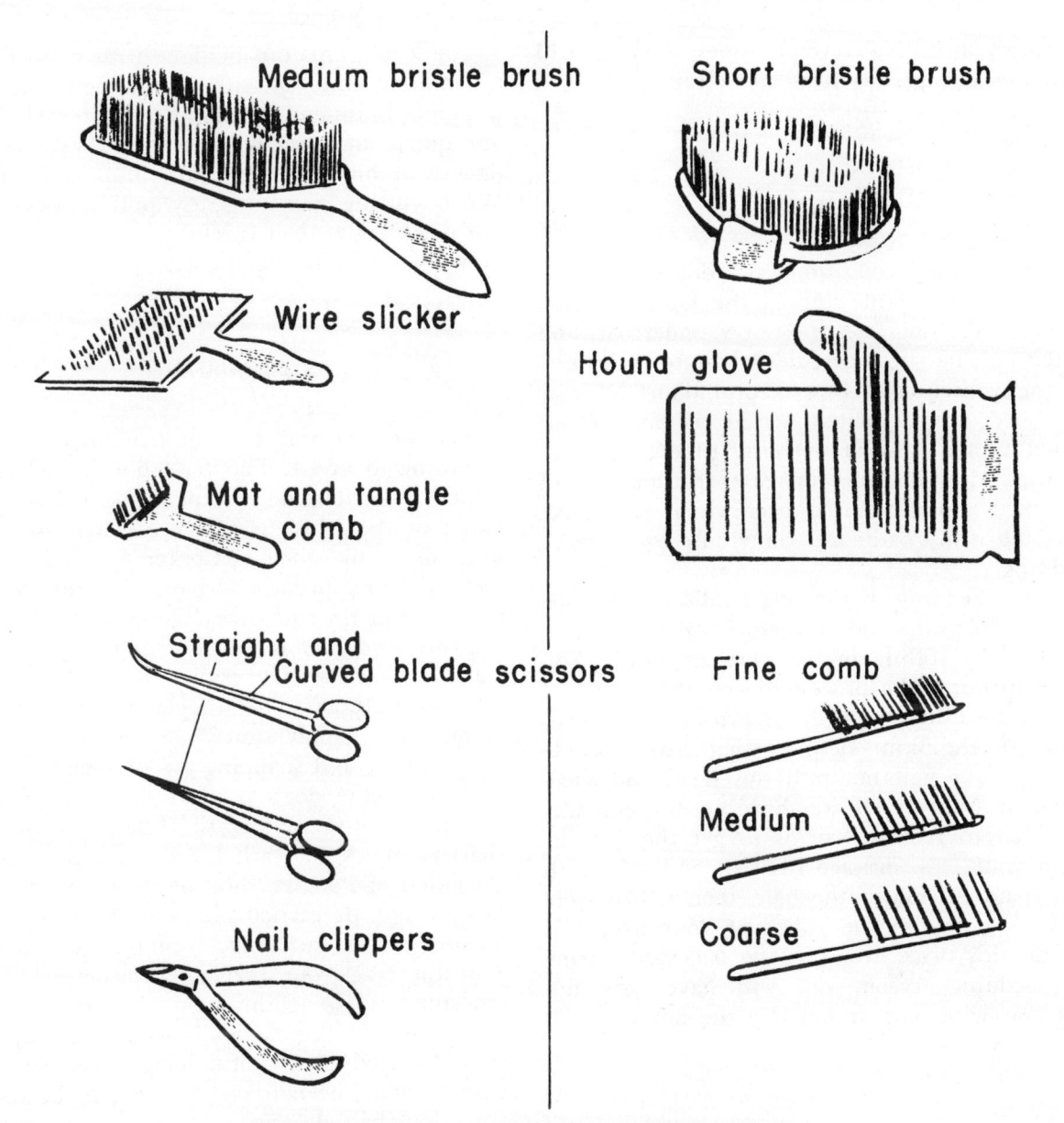

Fig. 299. Grooming equipment. (Drawing by R. F. Johnson)

Fig. 300. Daily grooming is important. (Courtesy The Seeing Eye, Inc., Morristown, N.J.)

319

However, brushing several times a week will keep the average dog neat and clean.

SHEDDING

Under natural conditions, the dog sheds twice a year—in the spring and in the fall. In spring shedding, the dog loses his heavy undercoat; and in the fall, he sheds dry, dead hair to make way for the winter coat. Dogs kept indoors all year may shed over a longer period of time. Overheated rooms, lack of exercise, illness, and unbalanced diet all will increase the amount of hair shed and the period over which it is shed. Also, too many baths can contribute to excessive shedding.

When shedding, if the dog is allowed outside, he will do as he did in nature—give shedding an assist by rolling in the grass or brush. You can help hurry the process during the period of natural shedding by vigorous brushing and massaging of the skin. Despite what many people think, combs will not pull out dead and shedding hair. When dogs are shedding, the best way in which to remove hair is to get the dog between your legs, massage his coat and skin with your hands to loosen the hair, then stroke from head to foot with the palms of your hands. If you do this twice a day in the backyard during the shedding season, you will have very few problems with hair dropped in the house.

MATTED HAIR

If you have a short- or smooth-haired dog, you will not have to worry about matted hair. But medium- and long-haired dogs do get tangled or matted hair from burrs, paint, tar, chewing gum, or even food. Matted hair is not only unsightly, but it can pinch and irritate a dog. Hence, it needs to be removed or unsnarled.

Avoid pulling or yanking on the matted tuft; that will hurt. If the hair is not too snarled, try combing it. Do this *gently*. Hold the matted hair or tufts in one hand, and gently comb it. Tar, paint, and other sticky or gummy matter can be softened with acetone (nail-polish remover) and then combed out.

If the hair is too tightly matted, you will have to cut it off. This can be done with scissors, with a trimming knife, or with a plucking razor. With puppies, blunt-end scissors are preferred. They are quick and wiggly, but there is very little danger of hurting them with blunt-end scissors. When cutting a mat, gently pull it away from the dog's body, then carefully cut the hair from between the skin and the mat or tuft.

TRIMMING

The amount and kind of trimming will vary according to breed. The very short-haired breeds require no trimming, except an occasional shortening of the whiskers and eyebrows. Dogs with long, fine hair—such as Cocker Spaniels, Setters, and Afghans—need to have the dead hair removed from time to time. The process of removing this dead hair is called *stripping;* and a special tool called a *stripper* or a *dog dresser* is used for this purpose. This gadget can be obtained at most pet supply stores.

Trimming and stripping are necessary to shape or balance the dog's coat. It must be done according to breed standards. Most pet shops have charts in stock for each breed, with the possible exception of Poodles, showing how the trimming process may be carried out, step by step. If you do not wish to tackle the trimming job yourself, you can take your dog to a professional who specializes in doing this kind of work.

Long-haired breeds don't need trimming, but they do need plenty of buffing. Also, you may wish to trim the hair on or between the toes of your long-haired dogs as well as the hair or feathering below the hocks on the hind legs. But be sure to check the breed standards before you start to do any snipping or trimming.

Terriers accumulate dead hair in their coats which requires trimming. However, they must be trimmed according to breed specifications.

Poodles are in a class to themselves when it comes to trimming. There are various Poodle trims and styles, all requiring some experience if the dog is to look its best. So, if you wish to take care of your own Poodle, it's best to let a professional show you how to do it. Watch how it's done for a time or two, then you can try it yourself. But don't expect perfection on your first few attempts; it takes time and skill to turn out a perfectly groomed and trimmed Poodle. That's why the beauty treatment of a Poodle costs so much.

DO NOT GIVE A SUMMER HAIRCUT

Do not clip a dog's hair close to the skin in the summer. His hair serves as an insulator against heat and protects him against insects. Thus, when you give him a crew cut, you expose him to sunburn and the bites of flies and other insect pests. Also, the short hairs will prick and itch every time he moves. Thus, you will not be doing your dog a favor by shaving him close, no matter how hot he looks.

BATHING

Dogs should be bathed when they look dirty or have a strong doggy odor; and this applies to dogs under one year of age, too.

Among many dog owners, there is strong prejudice against bathing the dog, particularly a young dog. Perhaps most of this thinking stems from the use of old-fashioned, harsh, strong soap, with flea-killing elements, that tended to irritate the dog's skin. Today, there are dozens of kinds of soaps and shampoos, many of which are as gentle as those used by humans. Also, flea-killing soaps are mild. Thus, the kind of soap, and how the bath is given, are more important than any concern over the frequency of bathing.

For dogs, there are specially made shampoos (including those in aerosol containers), dry baths, and plain bar soap. Also, you may use a soap made for humans which is both bactericidal and deodorant.

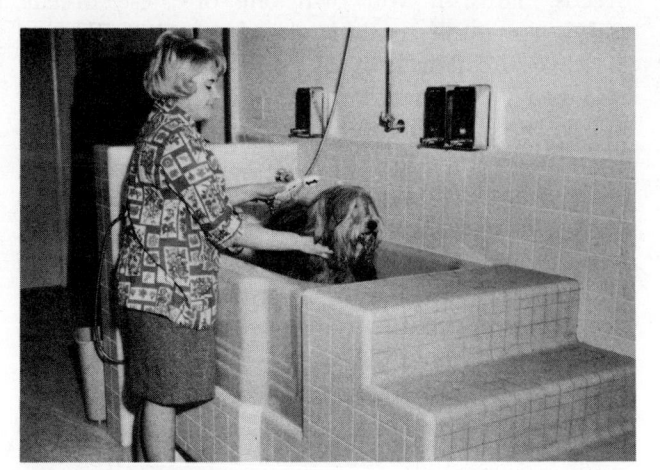

Fig. 301. Bathtub, of right height and with built-in steps. (Courtesy Mrs. Charles R. Anderson, Cedwood Puli Kennels, Bristol, Conn.)

The dog's fur holds heat in or keeps it out; in other words, it is an insulator against rapid changes in weather. When you bathe a dog, you temporarily destroy this insulating blanket, with the result that the dog shivers. This is why proper water temperature and drying are so important when bathing the dog.

You should bathe your dog in water at a temperature of about 100° F., which is close to his body temperature. Test the water with your elbow; if it's too hot for you, it's too hot for your dog. Fill the tub (a bathtub or any other receptacle) with water to the level of the dog's elbow. Put a rubber mat in the bottom for secure footing. Put cotton in the dog's ears, and a little mineral oil or eye ointment in his eyes to protect them. A small amount of bluing in the water brings out the sparkle in a white dog's coat.

Wash the dog's face with clean water and a sponge. Then, use your fingers for lathering and scrubbing the dog down to the skin. Although a brush may be used for lathering, fingers are far better. Never try to comb a wet coat.

Proper rinsing is very important. Leaving soap not only dulls the coat, but it may irritate the skin and cause scratching. A few drops of vinegar added to the final rinse water help to remove the soap; and a tablespoonful of glycerine in the rinse water makes smooth coats glossier.

After you have rinsed the soap off the dog, lift him out of the tub onto some newspapers. If possible, let him shake himself; he'll do a good job of getting off excess water. Then towel him dry, paying particular attention to his chest and undercoat. If possible, put him under a heat lamp or use a home hair dryer. Keep him indoors for two or three hours after the bath, or even longer if the weather is cold. Otherwise, he may catch cold, or, if it is warm, he may roll in dirt and destroy the results of the bath.

Like a spoiled child, the dog may object to a bath. But, be gentle and firm, and make the process as short as possible, and he will submit to what he knows to be inevitable.

There are times when it is best to avoid the use of soap and water, as when it is extremely cold, when the puppy is very young, when the dog is ill or convalescing, or when a bitch is near the end of pregnancy. Under such circumstances, one of the commercial foam or dry dog shampoos may be rubbed into the coat and then brushed out. Also, cornmeal, cedar sawdust, or fuller's earth may be used in this manner. When properly used, these products are nearly as effective as a wet bath.

Prescribed routines should be followed when preparing certain breeds for show. Hence, be sure to check your breed requirements.

TOENAILS

Most dogs resent work on their toenails more than any other part of grooming. Yet, this is important; and if you start this phase of grooming when the puppy is young, he will accept it.

Some dogs keep their nails short by digging and friction. As a result, their nails require little attention. However, it is best to check the nails about every two weeks.

The nails should be kept short and blunted, right down to the quick—never into the quick. If this is not done, the toes may spread and the foot may splay into a veritable pancake. Also, shortening of the toenails is very important with dogs that have flat feet; it won't alleviate the condition, but it will make the best of a fault. Moreover, long nails are undesirable because they make the dog slip-prone and interfere with his traction on smooth or glazed floors; and sharp nails may put holes in your stockings, trousers, skin, and furniture.

Nail clippers, made especially for this purpose, are available. After using them, the sides of the nails should be filed away as much as possible without touching the quick. When carefully done, this causes the dog no discomfort. But, once the quick of the dog's nail has been injured, he may forever after resent and fight having his feet treated or even having them examined.

The obvious horn of the nail can be removed, after which the quick will recede to permit the removal of more horn the following week. This process may be repeated until the nail is as short and blunt as it can be made, following which nails will need attention only at intervals of about six weeks.

DEWCLAWS OR DOG THUMBS

Dewclaws or dog thumbs are extra claws that are found on the inside of the dog's legs, just above the paws. They are vestigial claws, once having served as thumbs during the early evolution of the dog. In young puppies, the dewclaws are attached rather loosely to the leg by cartilage. Later, they become more firmly fastened to the leg bone. They are useless and should be removed by the veterinarian while the puppy is still young. The operation is a comparatively simple one. In two breeds, the Great Pyrenees and Briard, dewclaws are considered desirable and characteristic of the respective breeds. Thus, if you own one of these breeds, and if you wish to show the dog, you will need to leave the dewclaws on.

If you have an older dog with dewclaws, they should be clipped and trimmed along with the other nails. In doing so, remember that dewclaw nails also have quicks. Occasionally, dewclaw nails grow backward and into the surrounding skin. When this happens, they may become a source of pain and infection; and it may be necessary to remove them surgically.

EARS

Check your dog's ears at least once each month. Long-eared dogs should have their ears

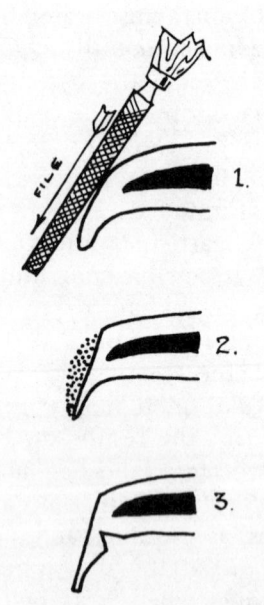

Fig. 302. Shortening the toenails. The method here illustrated is to take a sharp file and stroke the nail downwards in the direction of the arrow, as in step 1. Continue filing until the nail assumes the shape shown in step 2, the shaded portion being the part removed. A three-cornered file should then be used on the underside just missing the quick, as in step 3. The operation is then complete; and the dog running about quickly wears the nail to the proper shape. (Drawing by J. L. Medeiros)

checked more frequently, as they are more prone to ear trouble. Look for dirt, cuts, scratches, swellings, parasites, or discharge. Clean off wax deposits carefully with a cotton-tipped swab dipped in mineral oil, sesame oil, or baby oil. But never probe into the inner ear as this may injure it. If wax has dried and hardened, use a very little eye-and-ear-ointment to soften it before you remove it. If you come across dried blood, scabs, or a thick discharge, clean the ear, apply mineral or sesame oil, and watch the ear for a day or two. If the condition persists, consult your veterinarian.

On long-haired breeds, such as setters and spaniels, the heavy growth of hair on the underside of the ear should be kept trimmed. Thick hair growth on the inside of the ear prevents ventilation and holds moisture, both of which are undesirable.

On some breeds, such as Poodles, the inside of the ears needs to be kept free of excess hair. They should be checked monthly, at which time any excess hair should be removed.

You should always be on the alert for possible ear trouble as evidenced by the dog shaking his head, rubbing his head on the floor or ground, or scratching on his ears. Also, mats behind the ear are a sure sign that the dog has been scratching. If these signs appear, look for inflammation or an unpleasant odor, but don't be misled if there are no obvious signs and yet the dog acts uncomfortable. Infections often settle deep inside the ear canal. In addition to being very painful to the dog, when neglected, conditions of this sort can lead to long and involved treatment or possible deafness.

EYES

When all is well, the dog's eyes will be clear and bright, free from discharge and inflammation. But eyes are vulnerable and can easily get something into them. Pekingese, Pugs, Boston Terriers, and other breeds with prominent eyes are particularly susceptible to eye injuries and should have extra care in this respect. Sometimes eyelashes growing inward, or overlong facial hair, will rub against the eyeball, and, if not trimmed, will irritate and cause ulceration.

If the dog gets something in his eye, you can remove it with a handkerchief, in the same manner that an object is removed from a human eye. Eyes from which objects have been removed, or eyes that are gummy, should be cleaned with a soft cloth or cotton soaked in boric acid or mild saline solution. Applying one percent yellow oxide of mercury salve to hunting dogs' eyes is soothing and helpful in preventing infection from scratches caused by briars and rough cover.

White dogs, and dogs with white face markings, may have unsightly stains caused by tearing, unless their eyes are kept scrupulously clean.

Continuous eye weeping may be caused by ingrown eyelashes, eye disease, or deformity.

When in doubt as to the severity of the condition, or injury, or if the trouble persists for more than a few days, you should seek professional advice.

TEETH

It is always well to glance at the teeth whenever you groom your dog, because you might turn up a potentially troublesome condition.

Puppies are born without any teeth. They begin to cut their first teeth when they are about 3 to 4 weeks of age. When the puppy is 6 or 7 weeks old, he will have a full set of temporary or *milk teeth*—32 of them. These temporary teeth are satisfactory for the pup at this stage of his life. He can chew and gnaw objects that are not too hard, but he lacks the tooth strength and jaw power of the older dog. Moreover, his milk teeth can be broken if subjected to a bit of strain.

At 4 to 5 months of age, the milk teeth begin to loosen and fall and the second or permanent teeth appear. This process takes about a month or 6 weeks' time. If the puppy is unusually destructive at this stage, he is probably trying to soothe sore, achy gums by massaging them. Help him out by giving him a nonsplintering bone, such as a beef knuckle, or you may give him a tough leather or rawhide toy to chew on. Occasionally, a milk tooth fails to yield the right of way to an incoming permanent tooth. The result is that the new tooth may come in crooked. When this occurs, the milk tooth should be extracted to allow for the normal growth of the permanent tooth. This is best done by the veterinarian, who has all the tools for the job.

Tartar begins to form on the dog's teeth after a year. The molars are mostly affected. Feeding the dog hard biscuits or an occasional knuckle bone or shin bone will help the tartar from forming on the teeth. Heavy deposits of tartar cause mouth odors and should be scraped off by your veterinarian.

Don't mistake so-called *distemper teeth* for dirty teeth. Distemper, and certain other illnesses causing fever, will discolor and sometimes pit a dog's teeth. These should be kept clean, but don't try to scrape off the color, which is in the enamel.

Head shaking or facial swelling are signs of an infected tooth. This is painful to the dog. You shouldn't waste any time getting your dog to a veterinarian if you suspect tooth trouble; and this is particularly true with an older dog.

OTHER HELPFUL GROOMING HINTS

In addition to the matters already covered, the following points may be pertinent on occasion:

1. *Hunting dogs*—If you have a hunting dog, check him after each workout for burrs between the toes, in the armpits, or about the inner hindquarters. Also, check for weed seeds in the eye pockets. In warm weather, even dust from plants can cause eye irritation. Treat the eyes with boric acid solution or get a bland solution from your veterinarian.

2. *Removal of foreign substances*—Burrs will come out more easily if they are first saturated with vaseline, mineral oil, or olive oil. Turpentine may be used to remove paint, but be sure not to get it on the dog's skin, for it will burn. Nail-polish remover will take out tar and chewing gum. After using any of these substances, wash the area immediately in order to remove any last traces of the foreign substance and the cleaner.

3. *Thin long-haired coats in summer*—Although dogs should never be clipped or shaved in the summer, for reasons that have been emphasized earlier in this chapter, long-haired dogs will be more comfortable during hot weather if their coats are thinned. Normally, shedding will take care of this, but it is always well to give nature an assist when grooming. In addition to the added comfort to accrue from thinning in hot weather, skin parasites are more easily found and removed when there is not a thick undercoat.

4. *Check for external parasites*—When grooming your dog, check for ticks, fleas, and lice. This is best done by brushing his coat upwards so as to expose pests on the skin surface. Black specks are an indication of fleas, even though you may miss the adults that hop away from exposure. Skin parasites itch and are uncomfortable, deplete the dog's strength by feeding on him, and transmit tapeworms. So, eliminate them with a good commercial powder, spray, or dip. Your veterinarian may recommend one of the new orally administered internal insecticides. Remember that you should pay special attention to your pet's skin health during the summer months, for parasites and skin diseases thrive during hot, damp weather. Use a flea collar only on the advice of your veterinarian.

5. *Use suntan lotion when necessary*—Some suntan lotions should be applied to short-haired dogs if they are to be out in the strong sun for any length of time. Rub it on the back and sides; apply it to the short-haired face of long-haired breeds such as the Collie, which are particularly susceptible to sunburn on the nose.

6. *Remove salt water*—Salt water will irritate the skin. So, after spending a day at the beach, you should rinse the dog with clean, warm water.

7. *Trim the paws if necessary*—Occasionally, long-haired dogs need hair trimmed from between their pads. If it's profuse, it can splay the toes, mat, and carry dust and dirt into the house. So, excessive hair on the paws should be trimmed back to the paw's shape.

8. *Straggly hairs*—Straggly hairs may spoil the dog's outline and need a little judicious trimming on all breeds (but do read your breed standard first). Blunt-nosed scissors should be used for this purpose.

9. *Use of scissors*—Always keep scissors pointed away from the dog's face.

SPECIAL AND SHOW GROOMING

Normally, grooming is done in order to enhance the comfort and health of the dog. With certain breeds, and with show dogs, vanity and glamour are involved. Custom decrees that certain breeds be trimmed or clipped in a certain way. Some owners may prefer to turn their pet over to a professional groomer, while others may enjoy this aspect of coat care and, with practice, may become very expert at it.

The following guidelines may be helpful to the owner who wishes to trim his own dog:

1. *Equipment*—Secure adequate equipment, and know how to use it.

2. *Accustom dog to grooming*—Have the dog used to a grooming routine. Nothing ruins a trimming job faster than a restless, unhappy animal; it's not unlike a youngster going to the barbershop for the first time.

3. *Know your style*—You should become thoroughly familiar with the breed standard of the particular breed upon which you are going to work.

4. *Take lessons from a professional*—It's always well to watch the work of a professional groomer first. In fact, you may wish to have him do the job once or twice, while learning from him.

5. *Order of grooming*—Always follow a specific order in grooming and trimming. This may differ according to individual preference. Whatever the order, however, it will assure that the dog will be groomed thoroughly and that no body part will be missed.

6. *Don't overtrim*—Always proceed with caution; you can remove more hair later if you so desire. However, it will take weeks, even months, for hair to grow back.

7. *Don't panic*—If your first efforts look rather "chewed up" or "henpecked," don't panic; hair *does* grow back. Hence, trimming mistakes are not permanent.

Special breed styles have as their primary objective making the animal as attractive as possible. When dogs are to be shown, trimming has an additional objective—that of accentuating strong points and minimizing weaknesses. Some folks object to the latter objective, on the basis that it disguises animals and encourages deception. On the other hand, it must be recognized that the experienced judge is able to ascertain the true merits of the individual by handling and is not misled by fancy trimming or expert showmanship. Grooming and trimming, therefore, are an accepted art designed to make the dog appear more attractive in the show-ring or when inspected by prospective buyers. Thus, the dog showman should know the art, and this can be mastered through long and patient practice with a bit of an assist from a professional.

GROOMING CHECKLIST

The following checklist may be used as a means by which to evaluate the grooming job, whether plied by yourself or a professional:

Fill in

( ) 1. *Condition of coat*—Indicate good, fair, or poor
( ) 2. *Feet and toenails*—Long and untrimmed; trimmed
( ) 3. *Ears*—Clean; infected
( ) 4. *Eyes*—Clear; mattery
( ) 5. *Gums*—Clean and healthy; pale and anemic
( ) 6. *Teeth*—Clean and white; stained.

8
Diseases, Parasites, and First Aid

Chapter 8
Signs of Good Health	328
Signs of Illness	329
Disease	329
Causes of Disease	329
Bacteria	329
Viruses	330
Fungi	330
Protozoa	330
Parasites	330
Disease Prevention	330
Immunity	330
Vaccination	331
Biologics	331
Vaccines	331
Bacterins	331
Serums	332
Toxoids	332
Other Artificial Protection Mechanisms Against Disease	332
Diagnostic Agents	332
Drugs	332
Some Infectious Diseases of Dogs	333
Dog Parasites and Their Control	339
Internal Parasites of Dogs	339
General Signs	339
General Preventive and Control Measures	339
Common Internal Parasites	339
External Parasites of Dogs	361
General Signs	361
General Preventive and Control Measures	361
Common External Parasites	361
Common Health Problems	371
Older Dog Ailments	376

(Continued)

A Program of Dog Health, Disease Prevention, and Parasite Control   *377*
    Disinfectants and Their Uses   *378*
Dog Diseases and Parasites Transmissible to Farm Animals   *379*
Dog Diseases and Parasites Transmissible to Man   *383*
First Aid   *384*
    First Aid Kit and Medicine Chest   *384*
    How to Give Medicine   *385*
    Tying the Mouth Shut   *385*
    First Aid Chart   *385*

Fig. 303. To love and to be loved! (Courtesy The American Humane Association, Denver, Colo.)

DISEASES, PARASITES, AND FIRST AID[1]

In the wild state, dogs roved over the broad prairies or through virgin forests, and gleaned the foods provided by nature. Finally, as civilization advanced and dogs were domesticated, they were placed in restricted areas. Under unnatural conditions of close confinement, greater numbers, and eating in close contact with their own body discharges, the control of diseases and parasites became of paramount importance.

It is hoped that the information presented in this chapter will be of special value in assisting dog owners in the prevention of diseases and parasites. Although final diagnosis of disease and prescribed treatment should be left in the hands of a veterinarian, a well-enlightened dog owner will (1) be in a better position to carry out a program designed to assure dog health, (2) more readily recognize any serious outbreak of disease and promptly call a veterinarian, (3) prevent unnecessary suffering of sick animals, (4) be better qualified to assist the veterinarian in administering treatment, and (5) be more competent in carrying out a program designed to bring the disease under control with a minimum spread of the infection.

SIGNS OF GOOD HEALTH

In order that dog owners may know when animal disease strikes, they must first know the signs of good health; any departure from which constitutes a warning of trouble. Some of the signs of good health are:

1. *Contentment*—Healthy dogs appear contented; they stretch on rising and look completely unworried when resting.

2. *Alertness*—Healthy animals are alert and bright eyed and will prick their ears up on the slightest provocation.

3. *Eating with relish*—In healthy animals, the appetite is good and the food is attacked with relish (as indicated by eagerness to get to the food).

4. *Sleek coat and pliable and elastic skin*—A sleek, oily coat and a pliable and elastic skin characterize healthy animals. When the hair coat loses its luster and the skin becomes dry, scurfy, and hidebound, there is usually trouble.

5. *Bright eyes and pink eye membranes*—In healthy animals, the eyes are bright; and the membranes—which can be seen when the lower lid is pulled down—are pink in color and moist.

6. *Normal feces and urine*—The consistency of the stool varies with the diet. But they should be firm and not dry. And there should not be large quantities of undigested food. The urine should be clear. Both the feces and urine should be passed without effort, and should be free from blood, mucus, or pus.

7. *Normal temperature, pulse rate, and breathing rate*—Table 33 gives the normal temperature, pulse rate, and breathing rate of dogs. In general, any marked and persistent deviations from these normals may be looked upon as a sign of animal ill health.

Every dog owner should provide himself with a thermometer (either a human rectal thermometer, or an animal thermometer). The temperature is measured by inserting the thermometer full length in the rectum, where it should be left a minimum of three minutes. While the temperature is being taken, the dog should be supported so that it won't sit down.

In general, infectious diseases are ushered in with a rise in body temperature, but it must be remembered that body temperature is affected by kennel or outside temperature, exercise, excitement, age, feed, etc. It is lower in cold weather, in older animals, and at night; but in no case should it be below normal.

The pulse rate indicates the rapidity of the heart action. The pulse of dogs may be taken by holding the hand on the inside of the thigh where the femoral artery comes in close proximity to the skin or over the heart area; and counting the impulses of the heart beat. In general, the pulse rate varies with the size of the dog, with the smaller breeds having a more rapid pulse than the larger ones. For example, a Great Dane has a resting pulse of about 80, whereas toy breeds have a resting rate of about 120. Also, the younger and the more nervous the animal, the higher the pulse rate; and the pulse rate in-

---

[1] The author acknowledges with thanks the authoritative review accorded this chapter by: Gerald V. Ling, DVM, School of Veterinary Medicine, Department of Clinical Sciences-Medicine, University of California, Davis, California; and Richard H. West, DVM, 6493 E. Sierra, Clovis, California. But the review by these eminent authorities does not imply either full approval or full agreement of the reviewers and the author on the contents of this chapter.

The material presented in this chapter is based on factual information believed to be accurate, but is not guaranteed. Where the instructions and precautions given herein are in disagreement with those of your veterinarian or reputable manufacturers, always follow the latter two.

TABLE 33

NORMAL TEMPERATURE, PULSE RATE, AND BREATHING RATE OF DOGS

| Normal Rectal Temperature || Normal Pulse Rate | Normal Breathing Rate ||
Average	Range		Average	Range
(degrees F)	(degrees F)	(rate/min)	(rate/min)	(rate/min)
101	100.5–102.5	70–120	18	10–30

creases with exercise, excitement, digestion, and high outside temperature.

The breathing rate can be determined by placing the hand on the flank, by observing the rise and fall of the flanks, or, in the winter, by watching the breath condensate in coming from the mouth and nostrils. Rapid breathing due to recent exercise, excitement, hot weather, or stuffy buildings should not be confused with disease. Respiration is accelerated in pain and in febrile conditions.

SIGNS OF ILLNESS

Just as there are signs of good health, there are signs of illness. An observing master can tell whether his dog is ailing slightly, or is coming down with something serious. The signs of illness are:

1. Loss of appetite, or refusal to eat
2. The lower eyelids may hang down slightly, showing the red membrane
3. The coat may have a harsh feel and a dead texture, both to the eye and the hand
4. Mucus and traces of blood in the stool
5. A potbelly and thinness
6. Lack of interest in what's going on around him
7. Hiding in dark places
8. Discharge from the nose and eyes.

DISEASE

Disease is defined as any departure from the state of health. There are many degrees of ill health, but by far the largest loss is a result of the diseases that are due to a common factor transmitted from animal to animal. These disorders are classed as infectious, contagious, and parasitic diseases and are considered theoretically controllable. Today, with the modern rapid transportation facilities and the dense dog population centers, the opportunity for dogs to become infected are greatly increased compared with a generation ago.

CAUSES OF DISEASE

Any agent that may bring about an abnormal condition of any or all tissues of the body is a disease-producing entity. Among the chief causes may be listed infectious agents, such as bacteria, viruses, fungi, protozoa, and parasites; and noninfectious agents, including chemicals, poisons of various types, faulty nutrition, and injuries. In addition to the actual causative agents, any of the following conditions may predispose disease: overwork (as sometimes happens in hunting and racing), exposure to cold, and long shipments—especially in cold weather.

The infection of a tissue and the production of a disease by a living agent is not always easily accomplished. The agent must first gain entrance to the animal by one of the body openings (respiratory, digestive, or genital tract) or through the skin. It then usually multiplies and attacks the tissues. To accomplish this, it must be sufficiently powerful (virulent) to overcome the defenses of the animal body. The defenses of the animal body vary and may be weak or entirely lacking, especially under conditions of a low nutritional plane and poor management practices.

BACTERIA

Bacteria are one of the smallest and simplest known forms of life. They possess just one cell, vary in size and shape, multiply by transverse fission, and possess no chlorophyll. Bacteria are exceedingly numerous in nature, and the majority of them are beneficial; for example, those that create the fermentation processes used in the manufacture of vinegar and the ripening of cheese. The few that cause disease are referred to as pathogens. Among the latter is *Leptospira*, which causes leptospirosis.

Bacteria are classified by various distinguishing features. In shapes, they are either rods (bacilli), spheres (cocci), or spirals (spirilla). Some bacteria will grow only on special types of media in varying amounts of oxygen. Some are motile, whereas others lack the power of locomotion. Then there are those bacteria that under certain conditions form spores that are highly resistant to destruction and may live for years. Some also possess the ability to elaborate toxic products within themselves or in the media in which they grow, as does, for example, the fatal and relatively common toxin that causes botulism poisoning.

VIRUSES

Viruses may be defined as disease-producing agents that (1) are so small that they cannot be seen through an ordinary microscope (they can be seen by using an electron microscope), (2) are capable of passing through the pores of special filters that retain ordinary bacteria, and (3) propagate only in living tissue. They are generally classified according to the tissues they invade, although this is a very arbitrary method, as some viruses invade many tissues.

Viruses cause several dog diseases, including distemper, hepatitis, and rabies—all of which are highly contagious. Virus diseases are often complicated by the presence of secondary bacterial infections.

FUNGI

Fungi are a division of plants whose members are devoid of chlorophyll or any pigment capable of photosynthesis; they are unable to synthesize protein or other organic material from simple compounds, and are therefore parasitic. Ringworm of dogs is caused by a fungus.

PROTOZOA

Protozoa are the simplest form of animal life; they consist of only a single cell. There are many classifications of protozoa depending upon their method of reproduction and locomotion and general shape and structure. Since most of them are free-living (occurring in the soil, water, etc.), only a few concern human and animal health. Malaria and amoebic dysentery are examples of devastating human parasitic diseases caused by microorganisms known as protozoa; and coccidiosis is the best known and most widely distributed disease of dogs caused by protozoa.

PARASITES

Broadly speaking, parasites are organisms living in, on, or at the expense of another living organism. They include worms (helminths), insects (fleas, lice, flies), mites, and ticks.

Any animal that serves as a residence for a parasite is referred to as a host. In order to complete their life span (cycle), some parasites require only one host while others need more.

While in residence, parasites may seriously affect the host, but there are notable exceptions. Among the ways in which parasites may do harm are: (1) absorbing food, (2) sucking blood or lymph, (3) feeding on the tissue of the host, (4) obstructing passages, (5) causing nodules or growths, (6) causing irritation, and (7) transmitting diseases. These may result in death of the affected animal; or they may cause stunted growth, lowered production, general unthriftiness, and emaciation.

DISEASE PREVENTION

Although modern science has conceived many artificial protective mechanisms against disease, there is no substitute for sanitation and disease prevention. The artificial achievements, valuable as they are, are merely an adjunct to a high state of natural health that is built around a program of improved feeding and management of dogs.

IMMUNITY

When a dog is immune to a certain disease, it simply means that it is not susceptible to that disease.

The animal body is remarkably equipped to fight disease. Chief among this equipment are large white blood cells, called *phagocytes,* which are able to overcome many invading organisms.

The body also has the ability, when properly stimulated by a given organism or toxin, to produce antibodies and/or antitoxins. When an animal has enough antibodies for overcoming particular (disease-producing) organisms, it is said to be *immune* to that disease.

When immunity to a disease is inherited, it is referred to as a *natural immunity*.

Acquired immunity or resistance is either active or passive. When the animal is stimulated in such manner as to cause it to produce antibodies, it is said to have acquired *active immunity*. On the other hand, if an animal is injected with the antibodies (or immune bodies) produced by an actively immunized animal, it is referred to as an *acquired passive immunity*. Such immunity is usually conferred by the injection of blood serum from immunized animals, the serum carrying with it the substances by which the protection is conferred. Passive immunization confers immunity upon its injection, but the immunity disappears within three to six weeks.

In active immunity, resistance is usually not developed until after one or two weeks; but it is far more lasting, for the animal apparently keeps on manufacturing antibodies. It can be said, therefore, that active immunity has a great advantage.

It is noteworthy that puppies secure a passive immunity from the colostrum (first milk) that they obtain from the mother for the first few days following birth.

VACCINATION

Vaccination may be defined as the injection of some agent (such as a bacterin or vaccine) into an animal for the purpose of preventing disease.

In regions where a disease appears season after season, it is advised that healthy susceptible animals be vaccinated before being exposed and before there is a disease outbreak. This practice is recommended not only because it takes time to produce an active immunity but also because some animals may be about to be infected with the disease. The delay of vaccination until there is a disease outbreak may increase the seriousness of the infection. In addition, a new outbreak will "reseed" the premises with the infective agent.

In vaccination, the object, as has been previously pointed out, is to produce in the animal a reaction that in some cases is a mild form of the disease.

It is a mistake, however, to depend on vaccination alone for disease prevention. One should always insure its success by the removal of all interfering adverse conditions. It must also be said that varying degrees of immunity or resistance result when animals are actively immunized. Individual animals vary widely in their response to similar vaccinations. Heredity also plays a part in the determination of the level of resistance. In addition, nutritional and management practices play an important part in degrees of resistance displayed by animals.

BIOLOGICS

Biologics may be defined as medicinal preparations made from microorganisms (bacteria, protozoa, or viruses) and their products. They include various vaccines, bacterins, serums, and similar preparations. These agents are among the most valuable contributions to animal health, and they are constantly being improved. They are used essentially for rendering animals immune to various infections.

It is noteworthy, however, that not all attempts to confer immunity by biologics are successful. In some cases, it seems impossible to create an immunity against infection. The common cold is a case in point. In other cases, the animal may die from the disease or its complications, in spite of an inoculation because of a biologic of poor quality, infection before the treatment is begun, improper administration of the biologic, or inability of the animal to form proper immunity.

Vaccines

Usually vaccines are defined as suspensions of live microorganisms (bacteria or virus) or microorganisms that have had their pathogenic properties removed but their antigenic properties retained. As pointed out previously, vaccines are purposely administered to produce a mild attack of disease, thus stimulating the resistance of that animal to that specific disease, often resulting in permanent immunity. Vaccines are employed mainly in the prevention rather than in the curing of disease. Great care must be used in their preparation, storage, and administration. Since the improper use of vaccines may result in disease outbreaks, it is strongly recommended that a veterinarian be consulted about their use.

Bacterins

Bacterins are standardized suspensions of bacteria (and their products) that have been killed by heat or chemical means and are unable to produce disease. When introduced into the body, they stimulate the production of protective antibodies that act against subsequent attacks of organisms of the kind contained in the bacterin. They produce an active immunity.

Theoretically, bacterins should be useful in the prevention of every infectious disease in which

Fig. 304. Inoculation of eggs for the production of vaccine. Some vaccines are made by growing virus on chick embryos. For this process, the two main constituents are fertile chicken eggs and a stock culture of virus. (Courtesy Dr. Salsbury's Laboratories, Charles City, Iowa)

the causative agent is known. Unfortunately, they do not always give the desired results, especially in diseases of a chronic nature.

Often a product may be a mixed bacterin; that is, it may contain more than one organism. This usually includes secondary invaders when the true causative agent is unknown.

Serums

Serums, also known as *immune blood serum* or *immune serum,* are obtained from the blood of animals (often horses) that have developed a solid immunity from having received one or more doses of infectious organisms. They do not contain any organisms, either dead or alive. Serums are used for the protective nature of the antibodies that they contain, which stop the action of an infectious agent or neutralize a product of that agent. They give a passive immunity. Among the serums that have proved successful are those for tetanus and anthrax.

Toxoids

A toxoid is a "tamed" toxin. Some bacteria, such as those that cause tetanus, produce powerful poisons or toxins. These are the substances that actually cause the damage; the bacteria themselves may produce only very mild symptoms. The same toxin is formed when the bacteria are grown in the laboratory, but it is then treated chemically. It loses the poisonous or toxic properties but still retains the power to stimulate the body cells; they form the appropriate antibody (antitoxin). Among toxoids is tetanus toxoid.

Other Artificial Protective Mechanisms Against Disease

In addition to the vaccines, bacterins, serums, and toxoids, the following products are employed for the protection of animals against disease: sensitized vaccines, sensitized bacterins, germfree extracts, natural and artificial aggressins, and bacterial filtrates. Although these products are prepared differently, they all serve to provide protective substances against corresponding infections.

Diagnostic Agents

Other biological products are used solely for the diagnosis of diseases. Tuberculin is an example of such an agent. Any dog suspected of being tubercular can be tested very easily by injecting a tiny amount of tuberculin into the skin and observing the reaction (an enlargement at the site of the injection) seventy-two hours later.

DRUGS

Drugs, or medicinal agents, are substances of mineral, vegetable, or animal origin used in the relief of pain or for the cure of disease. Much superstition cloaks the reasons for the recommended use of many drugs that have been employed for centuries. An example of this is liverwort, which was heralded as a sure cure for liver disorders only because it was shaped like a liver. Unfortunately, there is no known cure-all for a large number of diseases or for the relief of a great number of different parasitisms.

Lacking the knowledge of limitations of drugs and the nature of disease, many dog owners have been sold worthless products. There is a flourishing business in various cure-alls that are sold under such names as "tonic," "reconditioner," "worm expeller," "liver medicine," "mineral mixture," "mineral and vitamin mix," "regulator," and numerous others. It is poor practice to disregard the advice of reputable veterinarians and experimental workers and to rely on claims made by unscrupulous manufacturers of preparations of questionable or fraudulent nature. Most of these patent drugs are sold for fantastic prices, considering their actual cost, and most of their ingredients are never indicated. To avoid being swindled, purchases should be limited to preparations of reliable firms and then confined to those recommended by the local veterinarian. Fortunately, the Food and Drug Administration has been very vigilant and has been instrumental in the disappearance of many misbranded drugs and remedies from interstate channels.

Fig. 305. Classical canine distemper. (Courtesy Dr. J. H. Reed, D.V.M., Ph.D., Ontario Veterinary College, University of Guelph, Guelph, Ontario, Canada)

SOME INFECTIOUS DISEASES OF DOGS

Every dog owner knows that keeping dogs healthy is a major responsibilty. In Table 34, Infectious Diseases of Dogs, the author presents a combination of practical and scientific information relative to the most important diseases affecting dogs. It is emphasized that it is intended that this should enhance the services of the veterinarian; for the dog owner can do a better job of preventing and controlling diseases if he has enlightened information at his disposal. Effective dog health programs call for full cooperation between the dog owner and the veterinarian. Perhaps it is a fair statement of fact to add that superstition, myth, and secret formulae are used more extensively in treating the diseases of dogs than in treating ailments of any other class of animals.

Fig. 306. Puppy distemper. (Courtesy Dr. J. H. Reed, D.V.M., Ph.D., Ontario Veterinary College, University of Guelph, Guelph, Ontario, Canada)

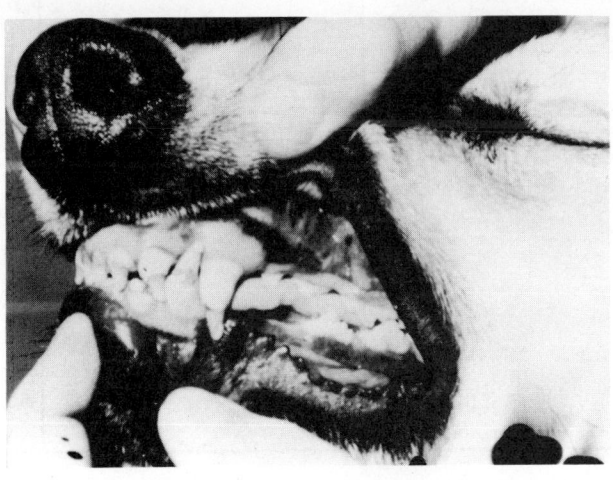

Fig. 307. Stained and pitted teeth, due to distemper. (Courtesy Dr. George Mather, College of Veterinary Medicine, University of Minnesota)

TABLE 34

Disease	Cause	Signs	Distribution and Losses Caused by
Distemper	A virus	The first signs are elevated temperature, lack of appetite, and evidence of depression. These initial signs will be followed by discharge from the eyes and nose, vomiting, diarrhea, pneumonia, or convulsion attacks	Distemper occurs worldwide

About 30% of the dogs that develop distemper die

In addition to dogs, many kinds of wild animals, (foxes, wolves, coyotes, skunks, raccoons, and mink) become infected with distemper and may transmit the disease to dogs |
| Hepatitis | A virus | Hepatitis, as the name implies, primarily affects the liver

It is most severe with puppies, but dogs of all ages are susceptible

The initial signs are: sudden rise and fall in temperature; loss of appetite; and depression. Also, there may be evidence of pain when pressure is applied to the abdomen, vomiting, enlargement of the tonsils, and redness of the mucous membranes of the mouth cavity. The abrupt onset of and prolonged bleeding suggests hepatitis | About 80% of all dogs over one year of age have been exposed to hepatitis |

INFECTIOUS DISEASES OF DOGS[2]

Treatment	Control and Eradication	Prevention	Remarks
Supportive treatments include: antibiotics (for limiting secondary bacterial invasion), electrolyte solutions, protein hydrolysates, dietary supplements, antipyretics, nasal preparations, analgesics, and anticonvulsants Once the disease appears in an unvaccinated animal, there is no uniform and effective treatment Good nursing will help Distemper often runs 6 weeks	The virus of canine distemper is universally present in dog populations. Hence, vaccination constitutes the only effective control	Several different types of vaccines that will prevent distemper are on the market. The choice of the product and the program should rest with the veterinarian. The latest of these developments was the discovery that measles vaccine produces a temporary immunity to distemper in dogs The puppy should receive several inoculations, ending at 4 months of age Vaccination gives good immunity for about a year. Thus, a yearly booster shot should be given for maximum protection	The virus of distemper is voided in the urine With few exceptions, it is short-lived outside the host animal A dog that has recovered from distemper will have antibodies and be immune Puppies develop a temporary immunity through the colostrum obtained from their distemper-immune mothers during the first 24 hours of their lives. This immunity lasts from a few weeks up to 14 weeks. During the time of this immunity, a vaccination won't take. There is a blood test, used by some veterinarians, which makes it possible to measure the amount of the distemper antibody and thus the degree of immunity carried in the dog's blood. However, the test is impractical and not widely used
Blood transfusions of 80 to 200 ml, depending on size of dog, given every other day, or 200 to 500 ml given once to seriously ill dogs In addition, 5% dextrose in physiological salt solution plus 5% protein hydrolysate in an amount of 250 to 500 ml daily should be given, preferably I.V. A broad spectrum antibiotic should be given if the disease is prolonged	A regular vaccination program will control the disease	Hepatitis can be prevented by giving the vaccine at the same time as the antidistemper vaccine A passive protection is transferred from an immune bitch to her puppies Over 80% of puppies become immune to infectious canine hepatitis when vaccinated at 9 weeks of age	The virus of hepatitis is voided in the urine. Virus-containing urine from recovered animals appears to be the usual means of spreading the disease

[2] Always follow the directions of your veterinarian or products manufacturers in the treatment, control, and prevention of disease.

(Continued)

TABLE 34 (CONTINUED)

Disease	Cause	Signs	Distribution and Losses Caused by
Leptospirosis — an acute, infectious disease	Infections with a rod-shaped spirochete (a bacterium) of either *Leptospira canicola* or *L. icterohaemorrhagiae*	The disease begins with a sudden rise in body temperature, weakness, refusal to eat, and vomiting; signs which are similar to distemper and hepatitis. After one or two days, there is usually a sharp drop in temperature, breathing is labored, and there may be evidence of stiffness—especially in the hind legs. The mouth cavity may show some dry necrotic patches and bleeding; the stools may be quite firm and blood tinged; urination is frequent; and, if the infection is of a type acquired from rats, there may be signs of jaundice	Widespread
Rabies	A virus transmitted through the bite of a rabid animal	In dogs, there are two forms— 1. The furious form, or the classical "mad dog" form, in which the animal becomes irrational and agressive 2. The paralytic form, characterized by early paralysis of the throat, profuse salivation, inability to swallow, and dropping of the lower jaw	Worldwide, except for Australia, New Zealand, New Guinea, and Oceania, although certain other countries have eradicated the disease
Ringworm	Fungi, or microscopic molds In dogs, about 70% of ringworm is caused by *Microsporum canis;* 20% by *M. gypseum;* and 10% by *Trichophyton mentagrophytes*	Circular scaly patches with broken stubs of hair within the lesions Mild itching usually accompanies the disease	Widely scattered. *M. canis* is transmissible to man; hence, it is not uncommon for the owner and his dog to have similar lesions

Treatment	Control and Eradication	Prevention	Remarks
Early and adequate use of certain antibiotics will usually alleviate the severity of symptoms and reduce death losses	Follow a vaccination program To reduce the chances of exposure, keep dogs leashed when in places frequented by other dogs. During an outbreak of the disease, owner should confine his dog(s) to his premises	Two to three initial shots of bacterin at two week intervals, followed by a booster at 3 to 4 month intervals	Leptospirosis is spread through contact of the mouth or nasal mucous membranes with the urine of infected dogs or rats The incubation period is 5 to 15 days
None	An outbreak of rabies can be controlled by— 1. Mass vaccination of dogs 2. Elimination of stray dogs 3. Reduction of excess wildlife vectors	Vaccination is recommended Consult your veterinarian as to the age at which to start this vaccination program There are four different types of antirabies vaccines available for dogs	This disease may be transmitted to man by the bite of a rabid animal. Hence, it is a public health problem. For this reason, dogs are subject to regulations governing movement, quarantine, and vaccination programs
Griseofulvin is the usual treatment	Isolate affected animals Spread of the infection to other parts of the body or other dogs or man can be reduced or alleviated by the use of an antifungal dip, such as (a) 1:200 solution of 45% captan or (b) iodine shampoos; applied to the whole body on the seventh and fourteenth days of griseofulvin therapy	Avoid contact with dogs, cats, or people that have ringworm	

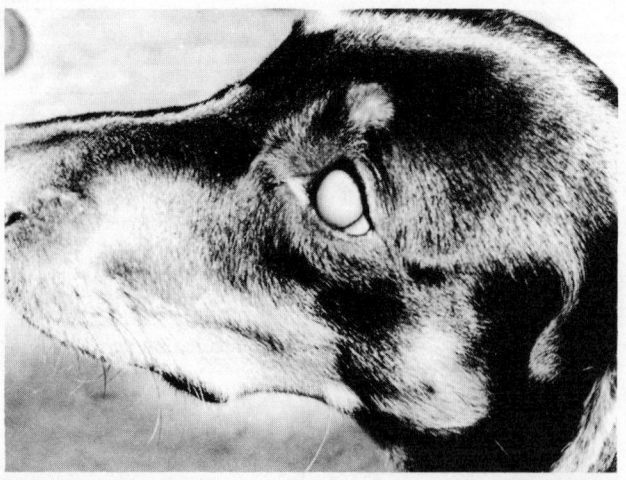

Fig. 308. The "blue eye" of infectious canine hepatitis. Edema of the cornea develops approximately ten days after the initial signs. (Courtesy Dr. J. H. Reed, D.V.M., Ph.D., Ontario Veterinary College, University of Guelph, Guelph, Ontario, Canada)

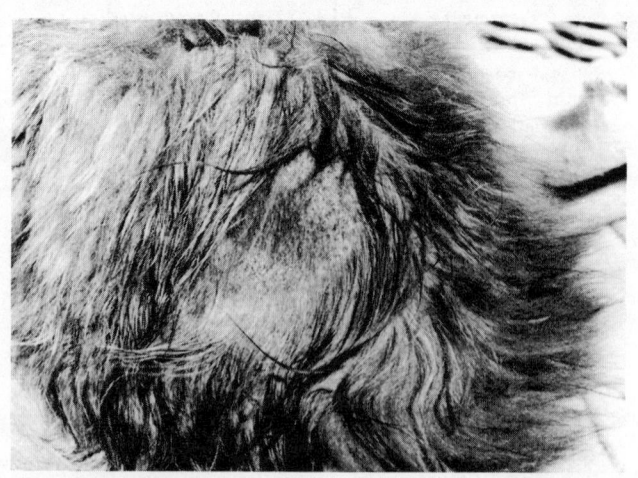

Fig. 310. Ringworm. Note the circular lesion with broken hair and scaly skin. (Courtesy Dr. J. H. Reed, D.V.M., Ph.D., Ontario Veterinary College, University of Guelph, Guelph, Ontario, Canada)

Fig. 309. Rabies. The dog is depressed, the eyes have a peculiar stare, the tongue may hang out of the mouth and excess salivation may occur. (Courtesy Dr. J. H. Reed, D.V.M., Ph.D., Ontario Veterinary College, University of Guelph, Guelph, Ontario, Canada)

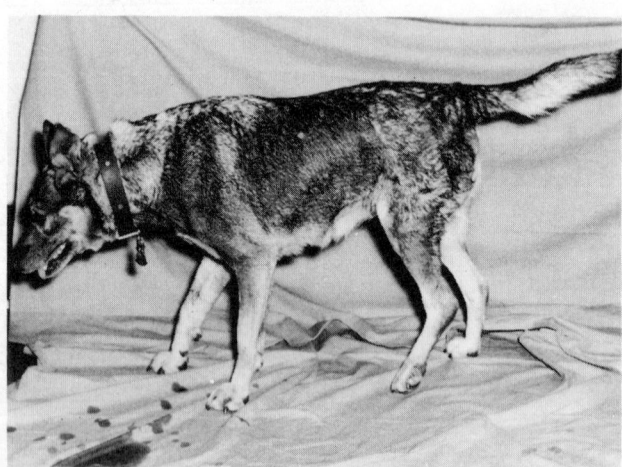

Fig. 311. Tetanus. Note the straight tail and the stiff appearance of the animal. (Courtesy Dr. J. H. Reed, D.V.M., Ph.D., Ontario Veterinary College, University of Guelph, Guelph, Ontario, Canada)

DOG PARASITES AND THEIR CONTROL

The term *parasite* refers to a form of animal life that lives in or on the body of the host animal, deriving its food therefrom. Those that live in the animal are known as *internal parasites*, whereas those that live on the body of the animal are known as *external parasites*. Parasites kill some dogs, but, by and large, the main damage is insidious and results in lower efficiency—i.e., something less than the best performance a dog is capable of giving—whether it be as a watchdog, work dog, hunting, racing, show dog, or household pet.

INTERNAL PARASITES OF DOGS

Many different kinds of parasites infect dogs throughout the world. Probably no individual animal is ever entirely free of them. Although dogs are not unique among animals in their susceptibility to parasitism, they do harbor many diverse species of pests. Probably this can be attributed to the fact that dogs, perhaps more than other domestic animals, have been transported widely as pets of their owners. Fortunately, comparatively few of these parasites inflict serious damage upon their hosts; but those few can be extremely harmful and even deadly.

As would be expected, the kinds of parasites and the degree of infection in dogs vary in different parts of the world, and also among individual dogs. Then, too, some of the parasites are distributed more or less regionally, primarily because of differences in developmental cycles.

The internal parasites may be located in practically every tissue and cavity of the body. However, most of them locate in the intestinal tract, lungs, body cavity, or bloodstream. Those that inhabit the digestive system usually become localized in specific parts of it. Still others are migratory or wandering in their habits, traveling throughout different parts of the body.

GENERAL SIGNS

Usually the signs of parasitism are marked by a slowly progressive chain of events that the dog owner may overlook entirely or confuse with other conditions. The general signs of parasitic infections in the dog are: weakness, unthrifty appearance and emaciation, tucked up flanks, distended abdomen ("potbelly"), rough hair coat, paleness of the membranes of the eyes and mouth, in some cases frequent digestive upsets and diarrhea, and stunted growth and development in puppies. Affected animals may eat well, and the temperature may remain normal; but there is always a loss in the functional efficiency of the individual as a working unit.

GENERAL PREVENTIVE AND CONTROL MEASURES

Most parasitic infections of dogs may be attributed to the fact that, under domestication, dogs (as well as all other animal species) have been forced to run and eat in close proximity to their own feces—being either confined and fed in a kennel or allowed only within a certain area. By contrast, in the wild state dogs roved over vast areas, seldom eating or traveling in the same spot.

As the feces of the dog are the primary source of infection of internal parasites, it should be obvious that the most important requisite of successful control measures is that they be designed to separate the animal from its own excrement. The following control measures are recommended to dog owners:

1. Provide good sanitary measures and a high level of nutrition.
2. Provide for a greater area per animal, thus lessening the degree of exposure to contamination.
3. Use concrete where several animals must occupy the same area. Also, a wire floor will work well.
4. Pick up the stools and dispose of them in such manner that they will not infect dogs.
5. Treat infected animals prior to turning them into a new area.
6. Follow rigid kennel sanitation in order to prevent fecal contamination of feed and water. This requires clean quarters and sanitary food and water containers.
7. Consult your veterinarian as to treatment, dosage, interval between treatments, and method of fecal examination; then treat all dogs regularly and precisely as directed.

COMMON INTERNAL PARASITES

Because there are so many kinds of internal parasites, only the most common and damaging ones are summarized in Table 35. It is emphasized, however, that other kinds of internal parasites are capable of producing severe injury on occasion and generally contribute to the overall picture of parasitism wherever they occur.

TABLE 35

Parasite	Life Cycle	Signs and Damage Inflicted
Coccidiosis, a parasite disease, caused by microscopic protozoan organisms known as *coccidia*; (three species commonly found: *Isospora bigemina*, *I. rivolta*, and *I. felis*; also, occasionally *Eimeria canis*)	Infected dogs eliminate in their feces coccidia in the resistant oocyst stage (See Fig. 312). Under favorable conditions of temperature and moisture, coccidia sporulate to maturity in three to five days. The oocyst then gain entrance into an animal by being swallowed with contaminated feed or water. In the intestine, the outer membrane of the oocyst, acted on by the digestive juices, ruptures and liberates the sporozoites. Each sporozoite then attacks and penetrates an epithelial cell, ultimately destroying it. While destroying the cell, however, the parasite undergoes sexual multiplication and fertilization with the formation of new oocysts. The parasite (oocyst) is then expelled with the feces and is again in a position to reinfest a new dog

(*Note:* *I. bigemina* is unique in that sporulation may occur within the intestine of the dog, and only in acute infestations are unsporulated oocysts discharged) | Coccidiosis usually causes little effect in an adult dog. If the dam is a carrier, it may be seen in puppies when they are 3 to 4 weeks of age. It starts with diarrhea, which may become mucoid and bloody. Puppies may become dehydrated and emaciated. The oocysts can be detected by microscopic examination of the feces |
| Esophageal worm (*Spirocerca lupi*) They are usually found in nodules, or tumors, in the walls of the esophagus, stomach, trachea, or aorta; the worms are 1 to 3 in. long, bright red, and generally coiled in a spiral | The eggs are embryonated when deposited by the female worms and are passed in the feces or vomitus of the host. Thence they are swallowed by the dung beetle, the intermediate host. The larvae develop to the infective stage and encyst in the body cavity of the beetles. The dog becomes infected by eating either (1) infected dung beetles, or (2) transport hosts (chickens, birds, frogs, snakes, mice, rats, or other small mammals), which are not harmed by the larvae, but which transport the larvae to the dog provided they (the transport animal) are consumed by the dog. Following ingestion by the dog, the larvae are liberated in the stomach, penetrate the stomach wall, and either stimulate nodule formation there or migrate to the aorta, esophagus, or trachea before doing so | In mild infestations, difficulty in swallowing may be the only sign. With severe infestation, the symptoms are: esophageal obstruction, vomiting, excessive salivation, cough, labored breathing, dehydration, and loss of weight

Diagnosis is made by the signs, examination of the esophagus with a gastroscope or by X rays, or by finding the eggs in the feces |

INTERNAL PARASITES AND THEIR CONTROL [3]

Distribution and Losses	Treatment	Prevention and Control	Remarks
Widespread throughout the U.S., but particularly prevalent in the South Heavy infections of young animals commonly end in death unless recognized and treated	*Eimeria canis:* no treatment known *I. bigemina, I. rivolta,* and *I. felis:* intestinal sulfonamides (sold under various trade names) given by mouth for 10 to 14 days are the usual treatment and very effective	Strict cleanliness Where coccidiosis exists, frequent and scrupulous cleaning of living quarters and disposal of feces are a must to prevent reinfestation	Coccidiosis generally develops under crowded, unsanitary conditions
Worldwide, especially in the tropical areas It occurs most frequently in outdoor dogs, including farm dogs	No highly effective drug is available	Sanitation; prevention of infection In areas where esophageal worms are troublesome, do not feed raw chicken scraps	

(Continued)

[3] The authoritative "Treatment" recommendations given herein are the methods of Gerald V. Ling, DVM, School of Veterinary Medicine, Department of Clinical Sciences-Medicine, University of California, Davis, California; and/or Kenneth S. Todd, Jr., Associate Professor of Veterinary Parasitology, College of Veterinary Medicine, University of Illinois, Urbana, Ill.

Always follow the directions of your veterinarian and product manufacturers in the treatment, prevention and control of internal parasites. Dosage and interval of treatment of all drugs should be made on the advice of a veterinarian or the label on the product.

TABLE 35 (CONTINUED)

Parasite	Life Cycle	Signs and Damage Inflicted
Heartworm (*Dirofilaria immitis*), a deadly parasite The worms are long, slender, and whitish; 6 to 12 in. long; and generally located in the right ventricle of the heart and the adjacent blood vessels (See Fig. 313)	The female heartworm produces active embryos, known as *microfilariae*, which are discharged into the blood stream, where they may remain active up to a year or more. The microfilariae are removed from the bloodstream by the bloodsucking intermediate host—various mosquito species. Within the mosquito, development from the microfilariae to the third-stage (infective) larva is completed in about 2 weeks. The infective larva escape from the mouth of the mosquito while it is feeding on a dog. Thence the immature stages develop and grow in the subcutaneous tissue, muscle, and adipose tissue of the dog and begin arriving in the right ventricle 3 to 4 months after infection. An additional 2 months are required for the worms to reach maturity; hence, microfilaria first appear in the peripheral circulation about 6 months after infection	Usually noticed in hunting dogs, and in other working dogs They are: fatigue, even after light exercise (for example, the dog may refuse to hunt); labored breathing; and there may be a gasping cough and excess nervousness. Other signs include rough hair coat and loss of weight Positive diagnosis of heartworm infection can be made by finding the active microfilariae in the blood. Because of the length of time required to complete the life cycle, heartworms are seldom found in dogs under 6 months of age. It generally affects dogs 3 to 6 years of age

INTERNAL PARASITES AND THEIR CONTROL

Distribution and Losses	Treatment	Prevention and Control	Remarks
Heartworm was once limited to the Atlantic seaboard and Gulf Coast. Although less frequent than in the Southeast, it is now found throughout the U.S. If not removed by proper treatment, heartworms cause poor heart function and eventual death	For adult worms: Caparsolate sodium (thiacetarsamide sodium) injected intravenously in several injections, followed by strict confinement (cage rest) for 2 to 3 weeks For microfilariae: first give above treatment for adult worms. Then, about 6 weeks later, Dizan (dithiazinine iodide) tablets should be given by mouth for several days	Periodic blood examinations, and treatments where necessary; in warmer, heavier infested areas two per year. In the rest of the U.S. one per year will suffice Control of mosquitoes House dogs and kennel dogs may be given some protection by keeping them in the house during evenings and nights when mosquitoes are feeding Caracide (R) (American Cyanamide) may be given as a preventive; beginning one month before the mosquito season and extending one month past the mosquito season	

(Continued)

TABLE 35 (CONTINUED)

Parasite	Life Cycle	Signs and Damage Inflicted
Hookworm (three kinds: *Ancylostoma caninum*, *A. braziliense*, *Uncinaria stenocephala*) *A. caninum* is the chief parasite involved in canine hookworms. In the Southern states, *A. braziliense* occurs frequently. In Northern U.S. and Canada, the fox hookworm, *U. stenocephala*, is most common. *A. caninum* is slightly larger than the other two. Hookworms are white or grayish roundworms about ½ to ¾ in. long and about the thickness of an ordinary straight pin. The front end is bent slightly upward to give a hooklike appearance, and the mouth is provided with teeth or cutting plates. Hookworms are generally attached to the lining of the small intestine, but in heavy infestations they may also be found in the cecum, colon, and rectum	Adult females produce many eggs, which pass out with the feces. When temperature and moisture are favorable, wormlike larvae hatch from the eggs in a few days. In about a week, the young larvae molt twice and are transformed into the infective stage. Dogs become parasitized by (1) swallowing the infective larvae in contaminated feed or water or (2) getting them off balls, rubber bones, or other objects. Thence, these swallowed larvae pass directly to the intestine. In pregnant females, hookworm larvae may pass by way of the circulatory system to the developing young (See Figs. 314, 315, and 316). Infected larvae may also penetrate the skin of dogs. Thence, they are carried with the blood to the lungs, where they escape to the air passages. They are coughed up and swallowed and pass to the intestine, where they develop to maturity	Anemia, manifested by extremely pale mucous membranes, marked depression, and a reluctance to move about. Diarrhea, with blood and mucus. The worms have a tendency to migrate to new areas of the small intestine, but the abandoned sites continue to bleed for some time; hence, the bloody discharge becomes progressively worse
Intestinal threadworms, or Strongyloides (*Strongyloides stercoralis*) This is a small, slender worm about 1/10 in. long which, when fully mature, is buried in the mucosa of the front half of the small intestine	The parasitic worms are only females (the males not occurring in the parasitic stage) which is unusual among nematodes. The female worm deposits eggs in the intestinal mucosa. The eggs embryonate rapidly and hatch before they are evacuated in the feces. Under proper conditions of warmth and moisture, the third larvae (or infective) stage may be achieved in little more than a day. The larvae then infect the dog either by skin penetration, or ingestion. Thence they migrate by way of the circulation and lungs to the small intestine, where they develop to maturity in a few days. Progeny may be shed in the feces within 7 to 10 days after infection	The disease is characterized by blood-streaked, mucoid diarrhea; emaciation; and stunted growth. Usually the appetite is good and there is no temperature. Positive diagnosis is made by finding the larvae in fresh fecal samples

Distribution and Losses	Treatment	Prevention and Control	Remarks
Ancylostoma caninum is widely distributed throughout the U.S. *A. braziliense* is limited particularly to the Southern states *Uncinaria stenocephala* occurs in more northerly areas Puppies are severely affected very early in life, and there is a high mortality rate. As dogs grow older and are subjected to repeated infestations they develop partial immunity Hookworms are especially severe in dogs maintained in a relatively small area where there is moisture and poor sanitation	Canopar (Thenium closylate), given by tablet DNP (Disophenol), given by subcutaneous injection and repeated in three weeks, is the treatment of choice Task (Dichlorvos), given by mouth in capsule or in food In 1973, the U. S. Department of Agriculture licensed a new vaccine for preventing hookworms in dogs—the first hookworm vaccine to be marketed anywhere in the world. It is not recommended that this vaccine replace other hookworm treatments; rather it should be used to increase immunity in puppies that have been treated for hookworm infection	Puppies may become infested (1) prenatally (before birth), (2) through nursing, (3) by ingestion, or (4) by larvae penetrating the skin Sanitation is extremely important. The following prevention and control measures are recommended: 1. Worm the bitch prior to breeding, and keep her in a clean place; thereby preventing the larva from passing by way of the circulatory system to the fetus 2. Whelp the puppies in a clean, dry place (preferably on wire) 3. Raise the puppies on wire or concrete. Keep floors clean, dry, and exposed to sunlight as much as possible 4. If dogs are kept on the soil, apply sodium borate (10 lb/100 sq. ft.) several times during spring and summer to kill the larvae. But do not use on grass because it is a herbicide 5. Have puppies checked regularly, beginning soon after birth; and follow the deworming program recommended by your veterinarian. Heat and cold will kill both the eggs and larvae	Forty hookworms may withdraw as much as an ounce of blood every 24 hours. With 1,000 worms, that's 25 ounces, or more than 1½ lb, of blood lost per day The infective larvae of *A. braziliense* occasionally penetrate the skin of man and produce a condition known as creeping eruption, characterized by tortuous burrows in the superficial layers of the skin
Intestinal threadworms are most common in Southeastern U.S., although they are on the increase nationwide When infection persists, death may occur in puppies	Dizan (Dithiazanine iodide), given in tablet Thiabendazole, given by mouth as directed by a veterinarian	Prevention of reinfestation is essential for the success of any control program. This calls for strict sanitation, isolation of dogs with intestinal threadworms, and sunny, dry quarters	(Continued)

TABLE 35 (CONTINUED)

Parasite	Life Cycle	Signs and Damage Inflicted
Roundworms, or ascarids (the dog is parasitized by two species: (1) *Toxocara canis*, and (2) *Toxascaris leonina*). *T. canis* occurs principally in young dogs, whereas *T. leonina* is found in older animals. Adult roundworms are round and whitish or yellowish in color, 2 to 8 inches long, and may be coiled up (Hence, they are sometimes called "spool worms")	Numerous eggs pass in the feces of the host dog. Under favorable conditions, the embryo develops in 2 weeks. The infective eggs are swallowed in contaminated feed or water and hatch in the small intestine. Thence the larvae burrow into the wall of the digestive tract, penetrate capillaries, and pass to lungs via the blood stream. They escape from the blood vessels and enter the alveoli of the air passages, grow and molt, and migrate up the trachea to the pharynx. Thence, they are swallowed and develop to maturity in the small intestine within a few weeks Infection with *T. leonina* can be direct by swallowing eggs, with the larvae developing in the intestinal wall (See Figs. 317, 318, and 319)	The most common signs of roundworms in puppies are: marked enlargement of the abdomen (potbelly), unthriftiness, digestive disturbances, and listlessness When infection is heavy, large numbers of worms may be seen in the feces or in the vomitus Coughing may be noted when larvae are passing through the lungs Diagnosis of infection is by detection of eggs in the feces As dogs grow older, they become more resistant to roundworms
Salmon poisoning The disease complex is the result of two etiological agents, *Neorickettsia helminthoeca* and the Eskimo fluke fever agent. The transmitting vector is a small fluke, *Nanophyetus salmincola*, with a snail-fish-dog life cycle	The first intermediate host of *Nanophyetus salmincola* is a snail, and the second intermediate hosts are fish of the salmon family. Dogs acquire the infection by eating these fish.	The signs of salmon poisoning resemble distemper, except that the temperature is much higher—106° to 107° F. The dog shows great thirst, refuses food, and has an eye discharge. In some dogs, there is a swelling of the face. The stools become liquid and bloody

INTERNAL PARASITES AND THEIR CONTROL

Distribution and Losses	Treatment	Control and Eradication	Remarks
Roundworms are the most commonly found worms in puppies and grown dogs They rob the dog of the food that he has eaten and harm the digestive system	Caricide (Diethylcarbamazine), given in tablet Piperazine compounds (sold under a variety of trade names), in tablet or powdered form (available in capsules or packets for individual weights). Repeat in 10 to 14 days Task (Dichlorvos), given in capsule or in food	Prenatal infection is quite common; hence, heavy infections may be present in young puppies. For this reason, bitches should be treated before breeding The two primary control measures are: (1) keeping dogs away from fecal contamination, and (2) having your veterinarian examine the feces regularly Collect and burn the feces during the suckling period; keep the dogs in clean quarters and on clean ground; and use only clean utensils for feed and water Puppies should be treated before eggs appear in the feces, particularly if there are children in the household It is recommended that the first treatment of both the pups and the bitch be made when the puppies are 2 weeks old One treatment may not be sufficient. Have fecal examinations made at intervals and follow advice of your veterinarian	The dog roundworm may affect people, especially children under 3 years of age. Hence, every effort should be made to prevent exposure of children to infective eggs of roundworms
In the Pacific Northwest of the U.S., and in southwestern Canada The mortality is less than 10%	Chlortetracycline, or other broad spectrum antibiotics, given intravenous or subcutaneous. Supportive treatment to correct and maintain fluid and electrolyte balance Good nursing	There are no prophylactic measures Do not feed raw or smoked salmon or trout to dogs	

(Continued)

347

TABLE 35 (CONTINUED)

Parasite	Life Cycle	Signs and Damage Inflicted
Tapeworms At least 14 species are known to infest dogs in the U.S., but the double-pored tapeworm is the most common one The following five parasites are all in the tapeworm genera: 1. *Dipylidium caninum* 2. *Dibothriocephalus latus* 3. *Taenia pisiformis* 4. *Echinococcus granulosus* 5. *Multiceps multiceps* Each is explained separately (see below)	The life cycles of tapeworm vary according to species	Tapeworms do not seriously affect the health of dogs, but they are difficult to eradicate The appetite of the dog is usually good, but it may appear unthrifty and nervous, have digestive disturbances, and lose weight Segments of tapeworms in the rectum and around the anus may cause the dog to assume a sitting position and drag itself around over the ground or rug Diagnosis is usually based on finding tapeworm segments in the feces and below the tail of the dog
The five types of tapeworms follow:		
1. *Dipylidium caninum* (Double-pored tapeworm) This species is 6 to 30 in. long and is often reddish yellow when freshly removed from the intestine of the host. Its segments are shaped like cucumber seeds	1. *Dipylidium caninum*—The intermediate hosts are the dog flea, cat flea, and the dog louse. The segments (gravid proglottids) pass out with the dog's feces. The larvae of the fleas eat the eggs, which then develop into an intermediate stage known as a *cysticercoid*. Dogs become infected by eating the infected fleas or lice. Thence, the larva travels to the small intestine of the dog where it develops into an adult worm by the growth of segments. With reproduction, a new life cycle is started (See Figs. 320 and 323)	1. The adult worm causes little trouble in the dog, but they are difficult to eradicate
2. *Dibothriocephalus latus* It is sometimes called the fish tapeworm, broad tapeworm, or Russian tapeworm. It varies from 1 to 7 in. in length and it may be $\frac{1}{4}$ to $\frac{1}{2}$ in. wide. The head is usually shaped like a club, but it may be lancet shaped or spoon shaped. The head does not have hooks or suckers as do other tapeworms; instead, there are narrow, deep grooves	2. *Dibothriocephalus latus*—It requires two successive intermediate hosts; the first is a small freshwater crustacean, and the second a freshwater fish. The dog becomes infected by eating the second intermediate host—the fish. The eggs pass in the feces of dogs (or other hosts) and must reach water. Thence, in succession, they must enter the two intermediate hosts—the freshwater crustacean and the freshwater fish. Inside the fish, it develops to the third infective larval phase. Thence, the dog is infected by eating fish (See Fig. 324)	2. The presence of *D. latus* in the dog has little effect, although it may cause an obstruction—especially when drugs are given to kill tapeworms

INTERNAL PARASITES AND THEIR CONTROL

Distribution and Losses	Treatment	Prevention and Control	Remarks
About 50% of all dogs have tapeworms The chief importance of dog tapeworms concerns their transmissibility to man and other animals	Varies, depending on the species of tapeworm. Hence, see the specie treatments that follow	Control of tapeworms is dependent upon controlling the intermediate host	See the specific tapeworm explanations that follow
1. It is found in the small intestine of the dog, cat, fox, and man	1. Nemural (Drocarbil), administered by tablet Scoloban (Bunamidine hydrochloride), administered by tablet Yomesan (Niclosamide), administered by tablet, is the treatment of choice	1. Control of fleas is necessary to rid any dog of this tapeworm permanently	
2. This species of tapeworm is parasitic in the small intestine of dogs, cats, polar bears, sea lions, and man It occurs in dogs in Florida and in the Great Lakes region of the U.S.	2. Nemural (Drocarbil), administered by tablet Scoloban (Bunamidine hydrochloride), administered by tablet Yomesan (Niclosamide), administered by tablet, is the treatment of choice	2. Cook fish properly	2. The presence of *D. latus* in the dog indicates that he ate raw or insufficiently cooked fish

(Continued)

349

TABLE 35 (CONTINUED)

Parasite	Life Cycle	Signs and Damage Inflicted
3. *Taenia pisiformis* It may be 80 in. long	3. *Taenia pisiformis*—The intermediate hosts are rabbits, hares, and certain other rodents. The segments (gravid proglottids) and eggs are passed in the feces of dogs. Thence, the eggs are ingested by rabbits, in which they migrate about and mature. Then the dog becomes infected by eating infected rabbits (See Figs. 321, 322, and 325)	3. This species of tapeworm usually causes little trouble in dogs
4. *Echinococcus granulosus* It is small, only 1 to 3½ in. long; and it has no more than 4 segments	4. *Echinococcus granulosus*—It has many intermediate hosts, including domesticated animals, wild animals, and man The segments (gravid proglottids) are passed in the feces. The eggs are ingested by the intermediate host and the embryos in them are carried in the bloodstream all over the body of the intermediate host. They develop into a bladderworm, larval phase called a *hydatid cyst,* inside which many tapeworm scolices arise. The hydatid cyst is then eaten by the dog and the scolices become adult tapeworms (See Fig. 326)	4. Normally, tapeworms do not cause serious symptoms in dogs. However, one or more of the following symptoms are sometimes observed: the appetite may be erratic—either ravenous or poor; a tendency to eat dung; harsh coat; emaciation; diarrhea or constipation; rubbing the abdomen on the ground or biting it; rubbing the anus on the ground; and fits and convulsions
5. *Multiceps multiceps* It varies from 16 to 40 in. in length	5. *Multiceps multiceps*—The segments (gravid proglottids) are passed by the dog (or other host) in the feces. The intermediate hosts—sheep, goats, horses, etc.—swallow the eggs. Embryos hatch, enter the bloodstream, and settle in the brain and spinal cord and develop into *coenuri.* Then the dog infects itself by eating the coenurus, which contain numerous tapeworms (See Fig. 327)	5. The adult tapeworm is not particularly harmful to dogs
Whipworms (*Trichuris vulpis*) A white or gray colored worm, usually found in the cecum. It is 1½ to 2½ in. long, and it resembles a whip	Dogs swallow embryonated eggs in feed or water. The eggs hatch in the small intestine, thence migrate to the cecum and colon where the adult worms attach themselves to the mucosa. There the female lays eggs that are eliminated with the feces of infected dogs (See Fig. 328)	Abdominal pain; diarrhea and/or constipation; vomiting; depression; and loss of weight Diagnosis by a veterinarian is easily made by finding the eggs on fecal examination

Distribution and Losses	Treatment	Prevention and Control	Remarks
3. It is found in the small intestine of the dog, fox, wild carnivores, and occasionally the cat	3. Nemural (Drocarbil), administered by tablet Scoloban (Bunamidine hydrochloride), administered by tablet Yomesan (Niclosamide), administered by tablet, is the treatment of choice	3. Prevent dogs from eating rabbits or rabbit meat infected with *Taenia pisiformis*	
4. It is found in the small intestine of the dog, fox, and wild carnivora	4. Arecoline hydrobromide (sold under various trade names), in tablet or powdered form	4. Prevention and control depends upon (1) treatment of dogs for the removal of the adult tapeworm, and (2) prevention of the infection of the dog by removing all contacts between dogs and tissues of the intermediate hosts likely to contain hydatid cysts	
5. Found in the small intestine of dogs, foxes and jackals	5. Nemural (Drocarbil), administered by tablet Scoloban (Bunamidine hydrochloride), administered by tablet Yomesan (Niclosamide), administered by tablet, is the treatment of choice	5. Do not allow dogs to have access to carcasses of sheep, cattle, or other intermediate hosts that may contain coenuri Periodical treatment of farm dogs is recommended, to remove tapeworms and prevent infection of intermediate hosts	5. The coenurus causes *gid,* which is particularly serious in sheep. "Giddy" sheep show defects of vision and disturbances in movements
A common and widespread parasitic disease of dogs	Milibis-V (Glycobiarsol), in tablet form, given daily by mouth for 5 days Task (Dichlorvos), given by mouth (in capsule or in food) Whipcide (Phthalofyne), given oral or by intravenous injection	Prevention and control is based on keeping dogs away from fecal contamination; having the veterinarian examine the feces from time to time; and administering a drug if necessary The eggs are destroyed by drying; hence, keep premises clean and dry	

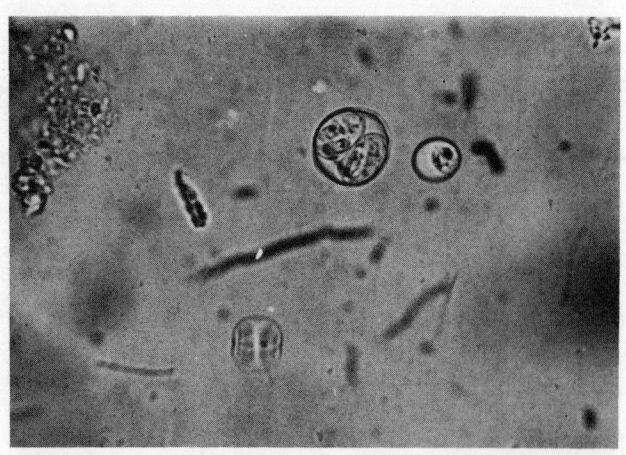

Fig. 312. Coccidia oocysts. (Picture prepared by Dr. Kenneth S. Todd, Jr., Associate Professor of Veterinary Parasitology, College of Veterinary Medicine, University of Illinois, Urbana, Illinois; supported by a grant from the Merck and Company Foundation)

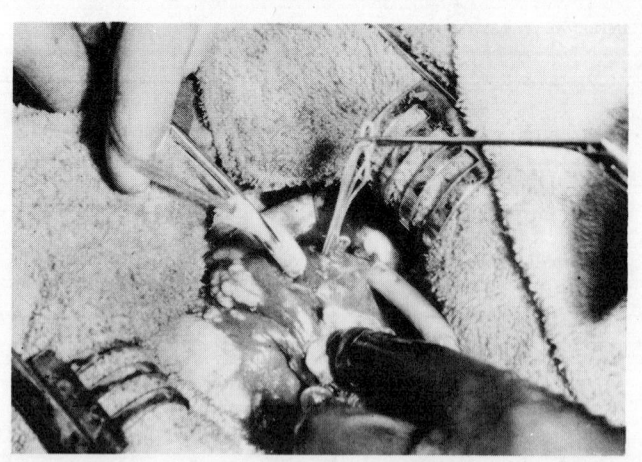

Fig. 313. Heartworms in long forceps being removed from the pulmonary artery. (Courtesy Dr. J. H. Reed, D.V.M., Ph.D., Ontario Veterinary College, University of Guelph, Guelph, Ontario, Canada)

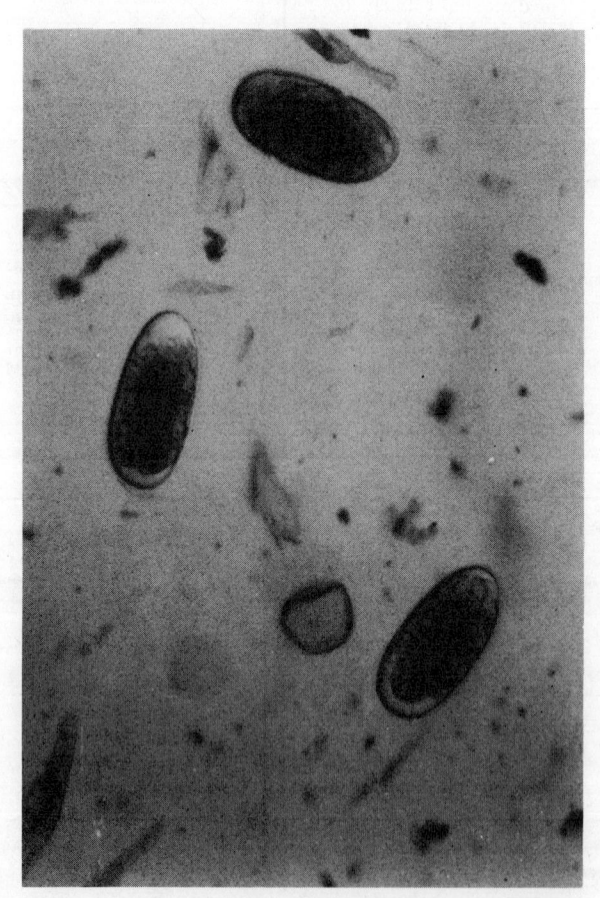

Fig. 314. Hookworm eggs. (Picture prepared by Dr. Kenneth S. Todd, Jr., Associate Professor of Veterinary Parasitology, College of Veterinary Medicine, University of Illinois, Urbana, Illinois; supported by a grant from the Merck and Company Foundation)

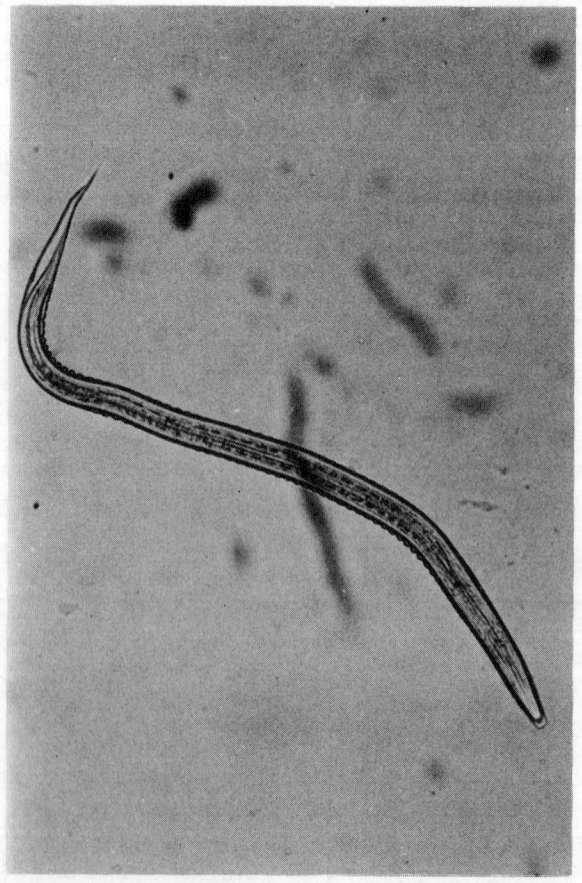

Fig. 315. Hookworm larva (Ancylostoma canium). (Picture prepared by Dr. Kenneth S. Todd, Jr., Associate Professor of Veterinary Parasitology, College of Veterinary Medicine, University of Illinois, Urbana, Illinois; supported by a grant from the Merck and Company Foundation)

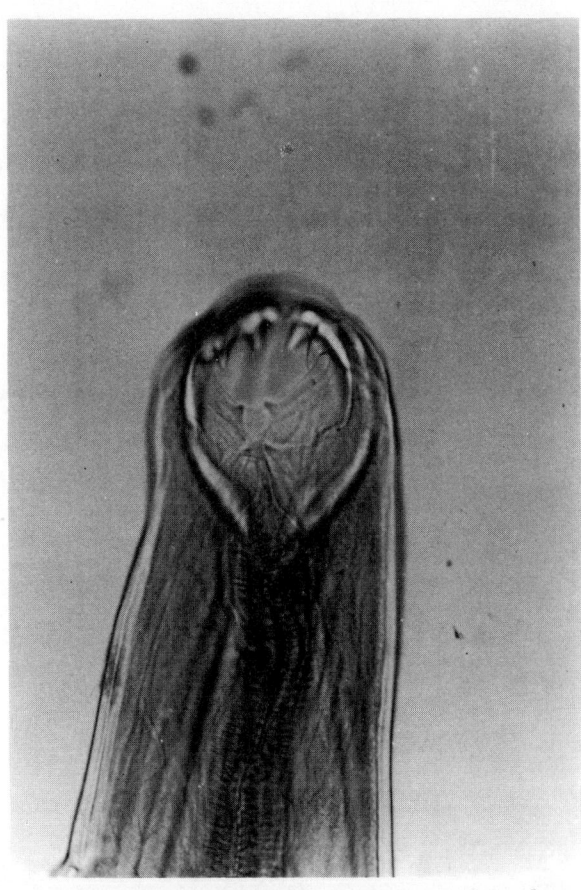

Fig. 316. Hookworm. Note the teeth or cutting plates. (Picture prepared by Dr. Kenneth S. Todd, Jr., Associate Professor of Veterinary Parasitology, College of Veterinary Medicine, University of Illinois, Urbana, Illinois; supported by a grant from the Merck and Company Foundation)

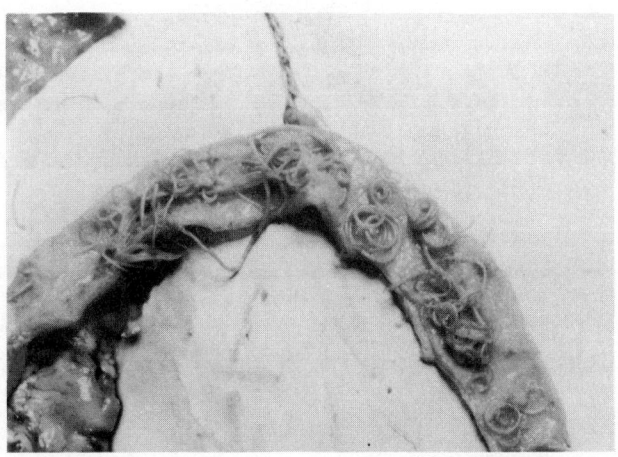

Fig. 317. Roundworms in the small intestine. (Courtesy Dr. J. H. Reed, D.V.M., Ph.D., Ontario Veterinary College, University of Guelph, Guelph, Ontario, Canada)

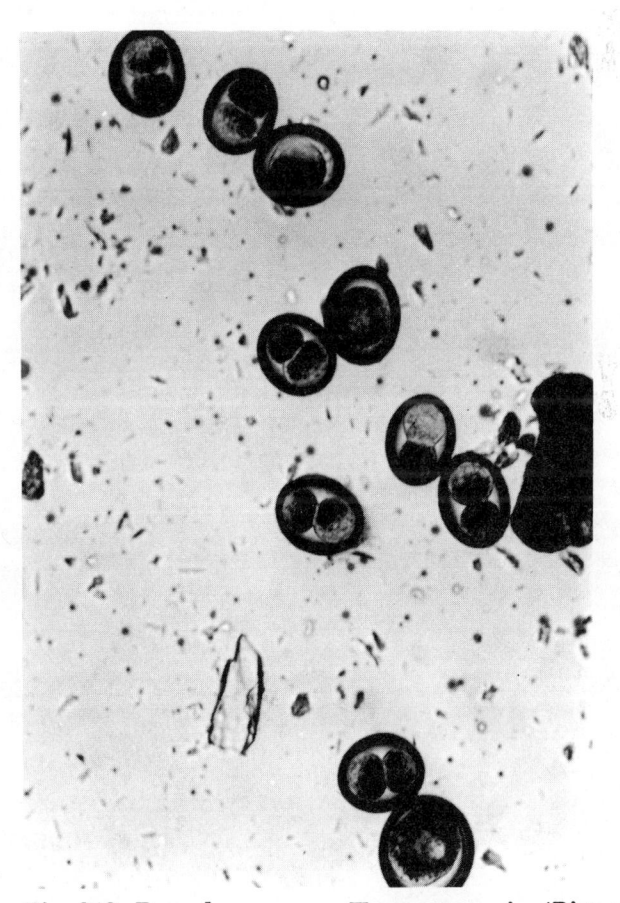

Fig. 318. Roundworm eggs, Toxocara canis. *(Picture prepared by Dr. Kenneth S. Todd, Jr., Associate Professor of Veterinary Parasitology, College of Veterinary Medicine, University of Illinois, Urbana, Illinois; supported by a grant from the Merck and Company Foundation)*

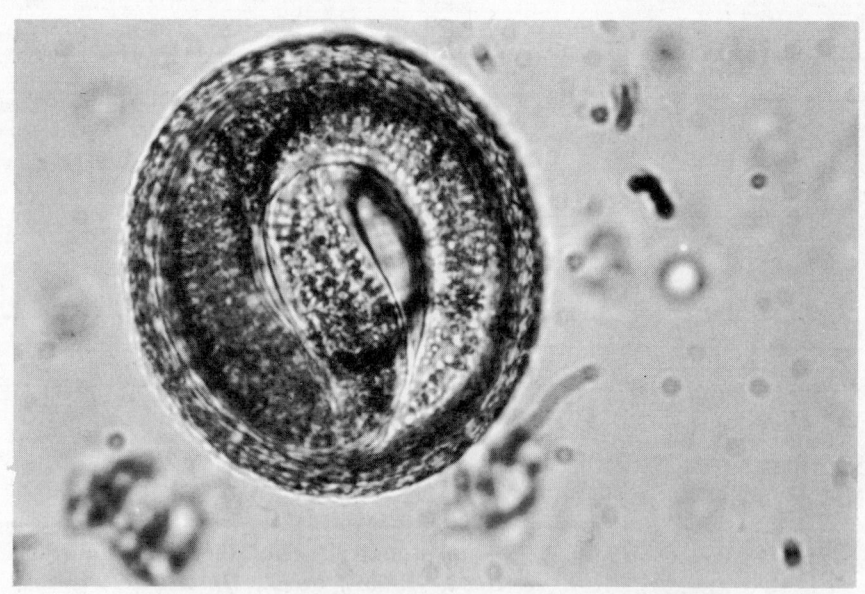

Fig. 319. Roundworm egg (embryonated), Toxocara canis. *(Picture prepared by Dr. Kenneth S. Todd., Jr., Associate Professor of Veterinary Parasitology, College of Veterinary Medicine, University of Illinois, Urbana, Illinois; supported by a grant from the Merck and Company Foundation)*

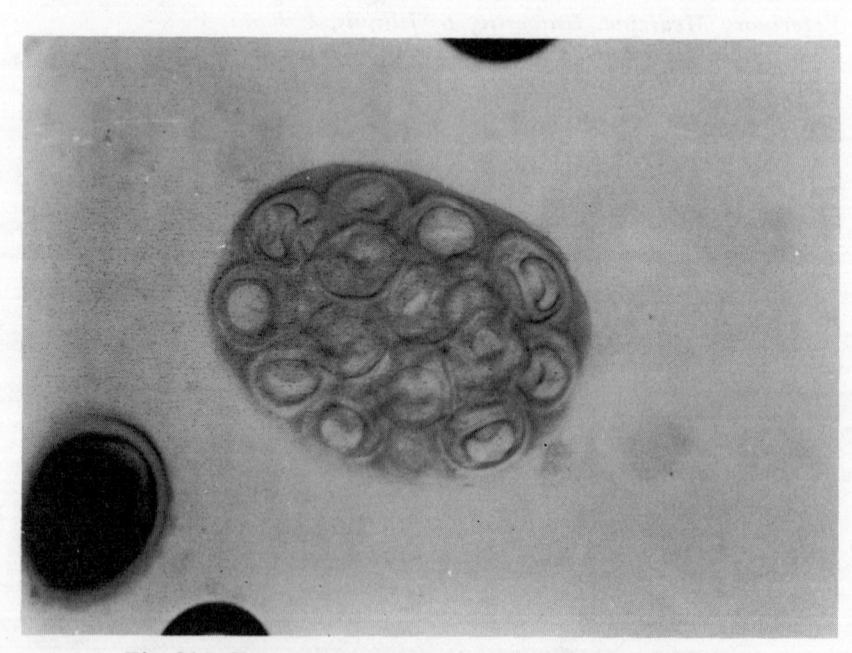

Fig. 320. Tapeworm egg packet, Dipylidium caninum. *(Picture prepared by Dr. Kenneth S. Todd, Jr., Associate Professor of Veterinary Parasitology, College of Veterinary Medicine, University of Illinois, Urbana, Illinois; supported by a grant from the Merck and Company Foundation)*

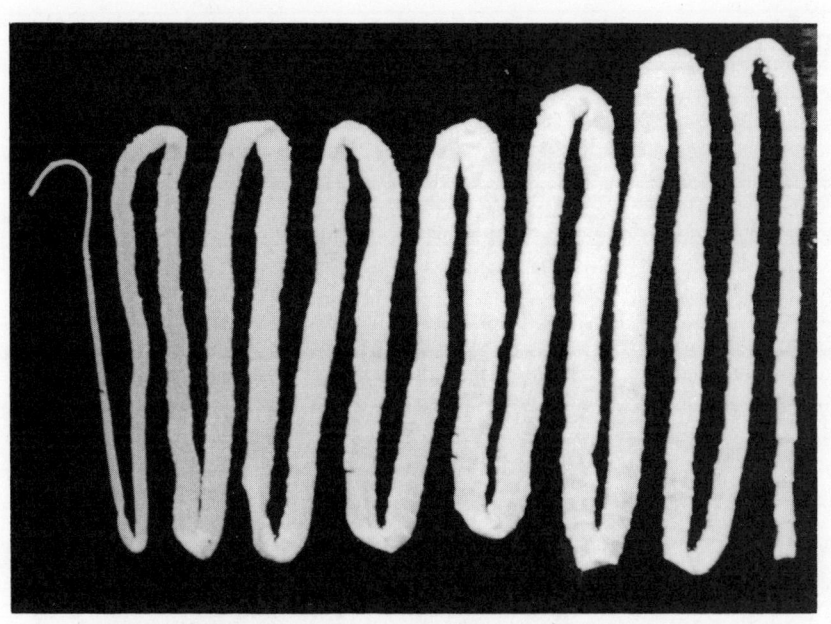

Fig. 321. Tapeworm, Taenia pisiformis. (Picture prepared by Dr. Kenneth S. Todd, Jr., Associate Professor of Veterinary Parasitology, College of Veterinary Medicine, University of Illinois, Urbana, Illinois; supported by a grant from the Merck and Company Foundation)

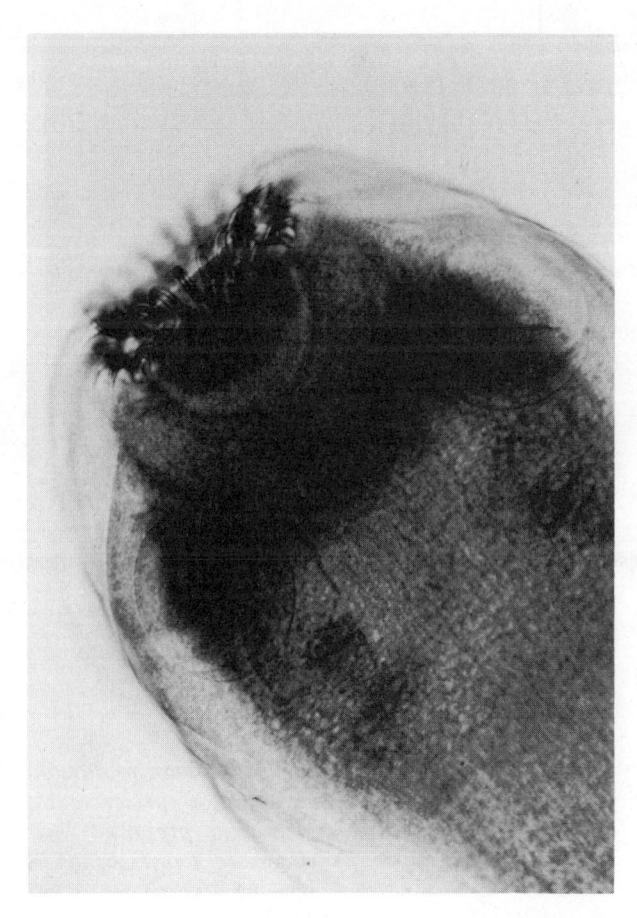

Fig. 322. Tapeworm, Taenia pisiformis. (Picture prepared by Dr. Kenneth S. Todd, Jr., Associate Professor of Veterinary Parasitology, College of Veterinary Medicine, University of Illinois, Urbana, Illinois; supported by a grant from the Merck and Company Foundation)

Life Cycle of Dipylidium caninum

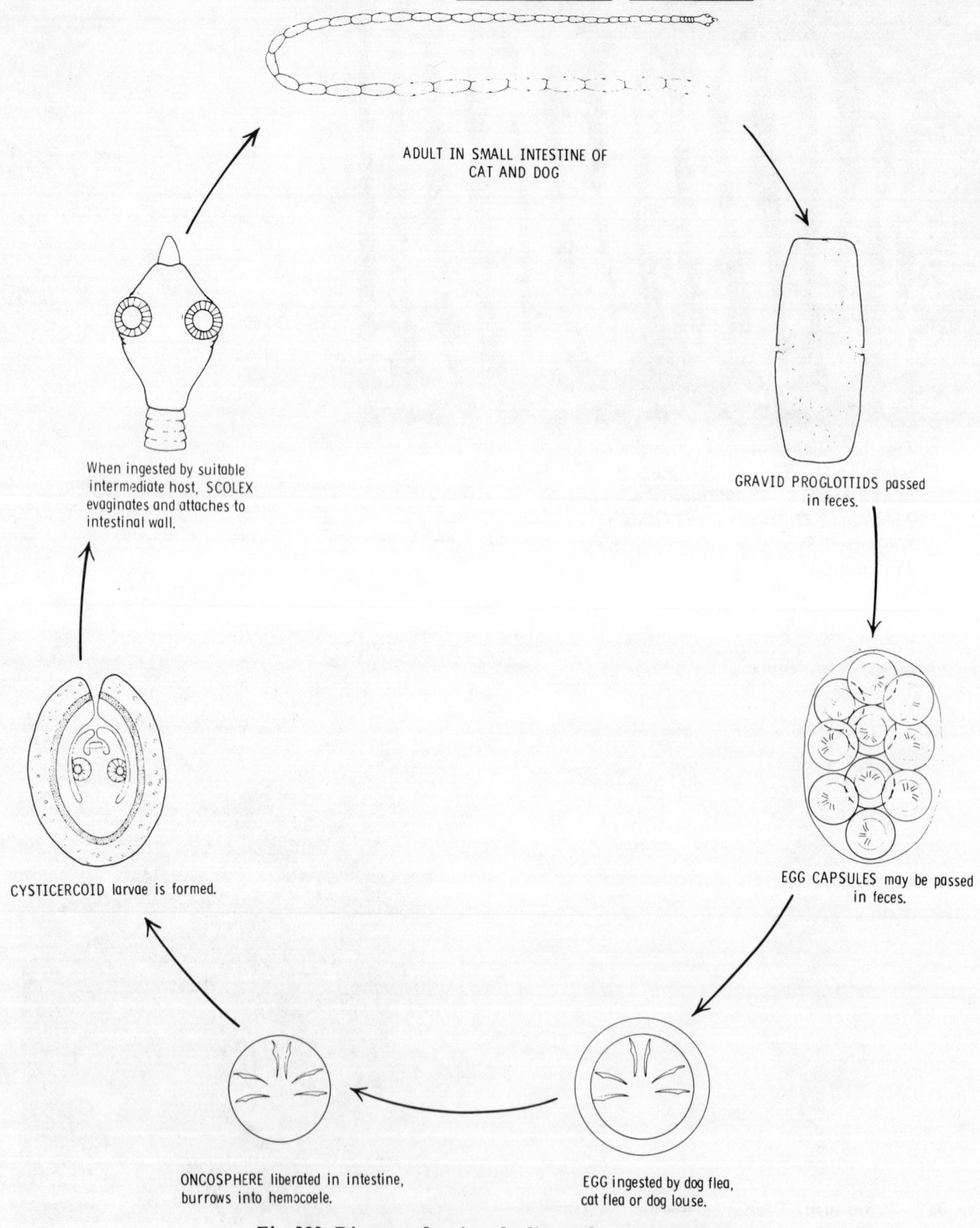

ADULT IN SMALL INTESTINE OF CAT AND DOG

GRAVID PROGLOTTIDS passed in feces.

When ingested by suitable intermediate host, SCOLEX evaginates and attaches to intestinal wall.

EGG CAPSULES may be passed in feces.

CYSTICERCOID larvae is formed.

ONCOSPHERE liberated in intestine, burrows into hemocoele.

EGG ingested by dog flea, cat flea or dog louse.

Fig. 323. Diagram showing the life cycle of Dipylidium caninum, *a species of tapeworm. Also, see Table 35. (Drawing prepared by Dr. Kenneth S. Todd, Jr., Associate Professor of Veterinary Parasitology, College of Veterinary Medicine, University of Illinois, Urbana, Illinois; supported by a grant from the Merck and Company Foundation)*

Life Cycle of Dibothriocephalus latus

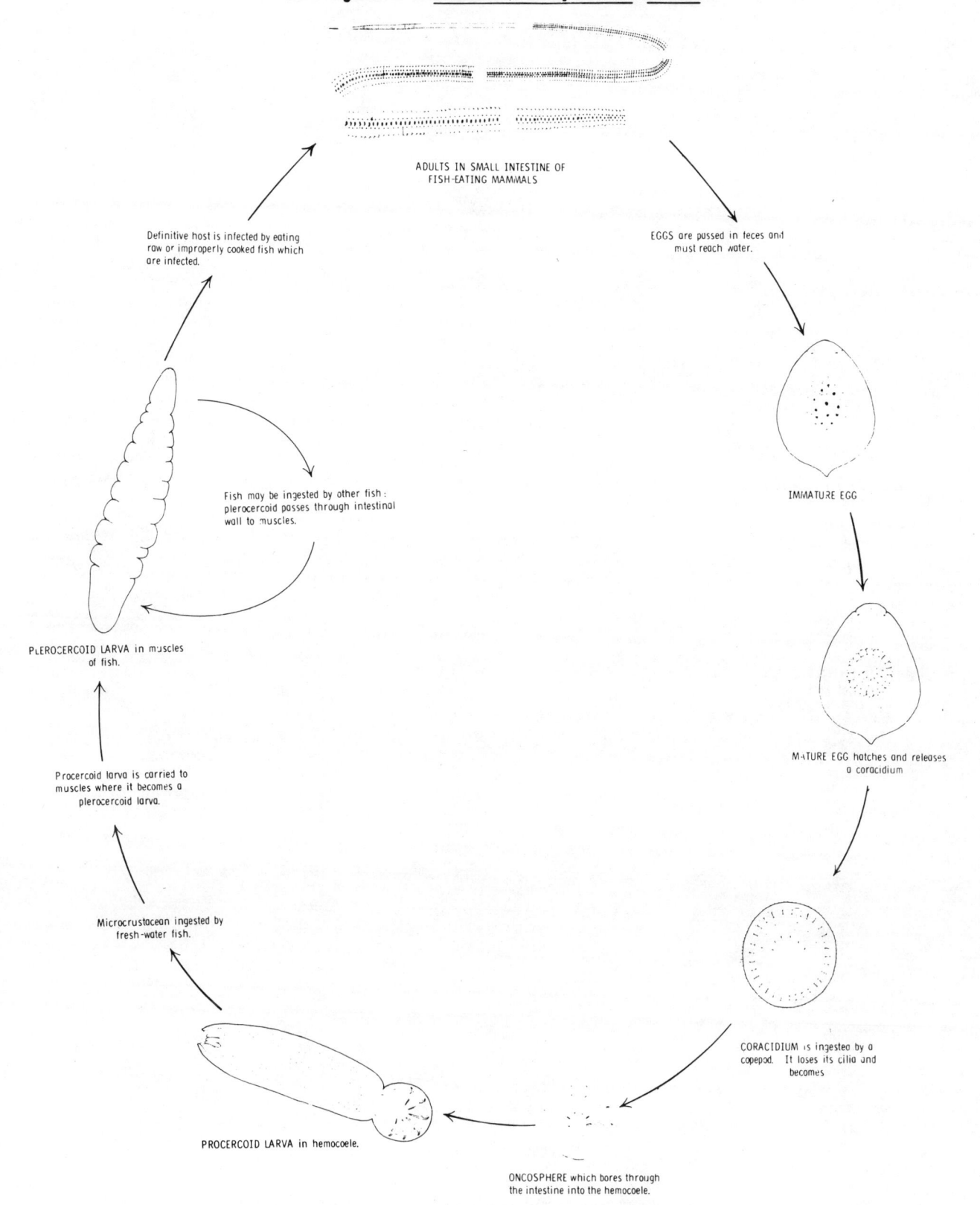

ADULTS IN SMALL INTESTINE OF FISH-EATING MAMMALS

EGGS are passed in feces and must reach water.

Definitive host is infected by eating raw or improperly cooked fish which are infected.

IMMATURE EGG

Fish may be ingested by other fish; plerocercoid passes through intestinal wall to muscles.

MATURE EGG hatches and releases a coracidium

PLEROCERCOID LARVA in muscles of fish.

Procercoid larva is carried to muscles where it becomes a plerocercoid larva.

Microcrustacean ingested by fresh-water fish.

CORACIDIUM is ingested by a copepod. It loses its cilia and becomes

PROCERCOID LARVA in hemocoele.

ONCOSPHERE which bores through the intestine into the hemocoele.

Fig. 324. Diagram showing the life cycle of Dibothriocephalus latus, *a species of tapeworm. Also, see Table 35. (Drawing prepared by Dr. Kenneth S. Todd, Jr., Associate Professor of Veterinary Parasitology, College of Veterinary Medicine, University of Illinois, Urbana, Illinois; supported by a grant from the Merck and Company Foundation)*

Life Cycle of Taenia pisiformis

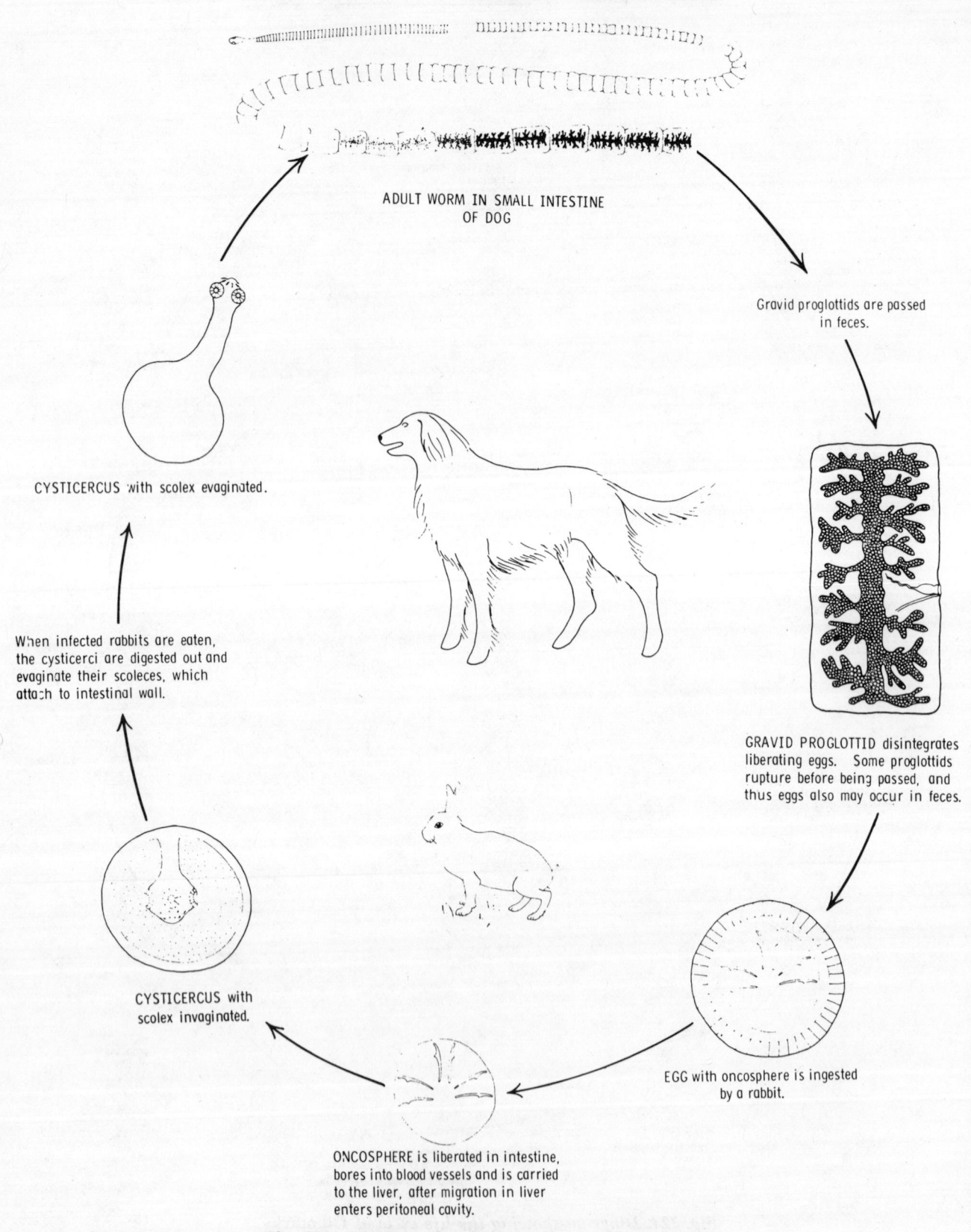

ADULT WORM IN SMALL INTESTINE OF DOG

Gravid proglottids are passed in feces.

GRAVID PROGLOTTID disintegrates liberating eggs. Some proglottids rupture before being passed, and thus eggs also may occur in feces.

EGG with oncosphere is ingested by a rabbit.

ONCOSPHERE is liberated in intestine, bores into blood vessels and is carried to the liver, after migration in liver enters peritoneal cavity.

CYSTICERCUS with scolex invaginated.

When infected rabbits are eaten, the cysticerci are digested out and evaginate their scoleces, which attach to intestinal wall.

CYSTICERCUS with scolex evaginated.

Fig. 325. Diagram showing the life cycle of **Taenia pisiformis**, *a species of tapeworm. Also, see Table 35. (Drawing prepared by Dr. Kenneth S. Todd, Jr., Associate Professor of Veterinary Parasitology, College of Veterinary Medicine, University of Illinois, Urbana, Illinois; supported by a grant from the Merck and Company Foundation)*

Life Cycle of Echinococcus granulosus

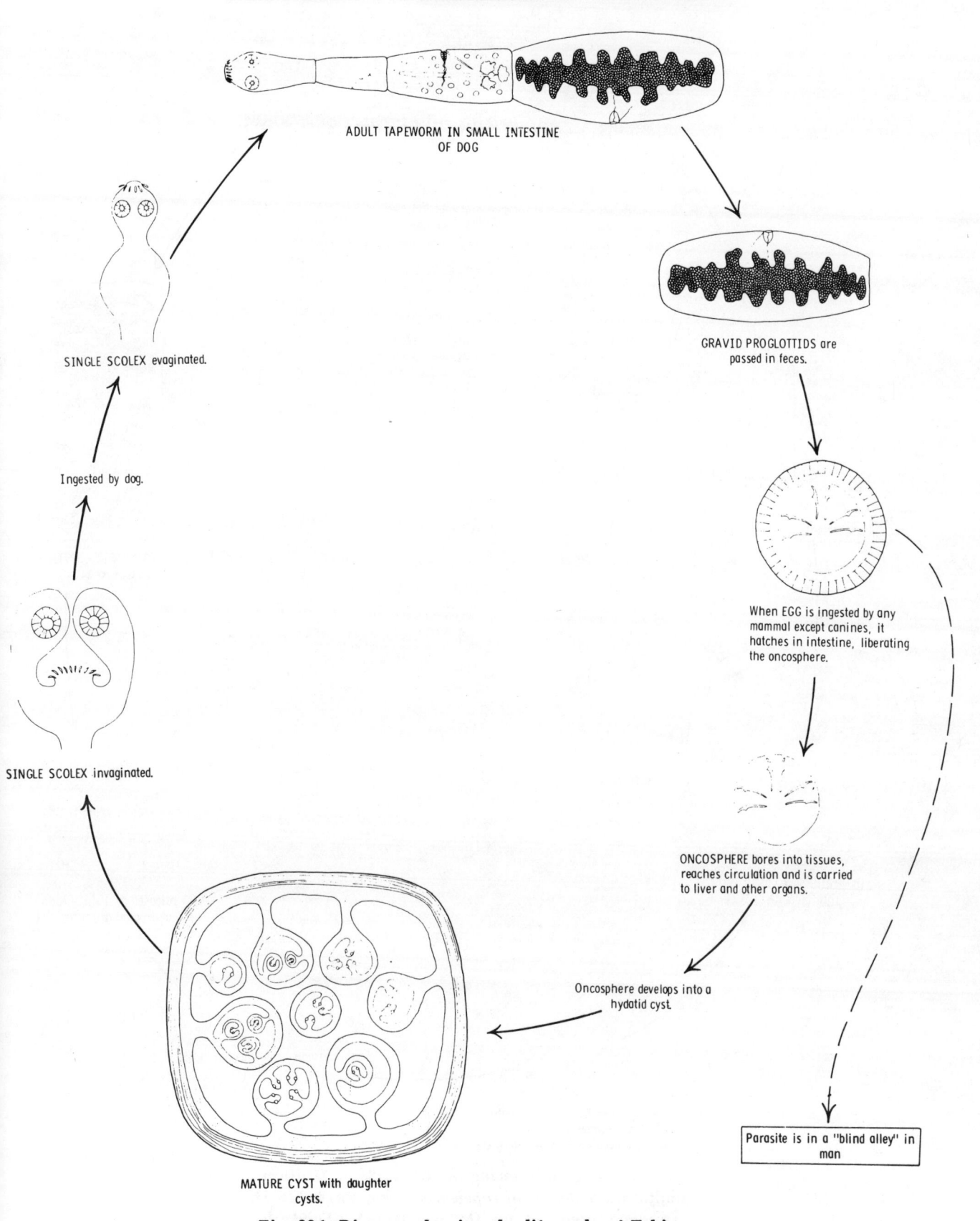

ADULT TAPEWORM IN SMALL INTESTINE OF DOG

SINGLE SCOLEX evaginated.

Ingested by dog.

SINGLE SCOLEX invaginated.

MATURE CYST with daughter cysts.

GRAVID PROGLOTTIDS are passed in feces.

When EGG is ingested by any mammal except canines, it hatches in intestine, liberating the oncosphere.

ONCOSPHERE bores into tissues, reaches circulation and is carried to liver and other organs.

Oncosphere develops into a hydatid cyst.

Parasite is in a "blind alley" in man

Fig. 326. Diagram showing the life cycle of Echinococcus granulosus, a species of tapeworm. Also, see Table 35. (Drawing prepared by Dr. Kenneth S. Todd, Jr., Associate Professor of Veterinary Parasitology, College of Veterinary Medicine, University of Illinois, Urbana, Illinois; supported by a grant from the Merck and Company Foundation)

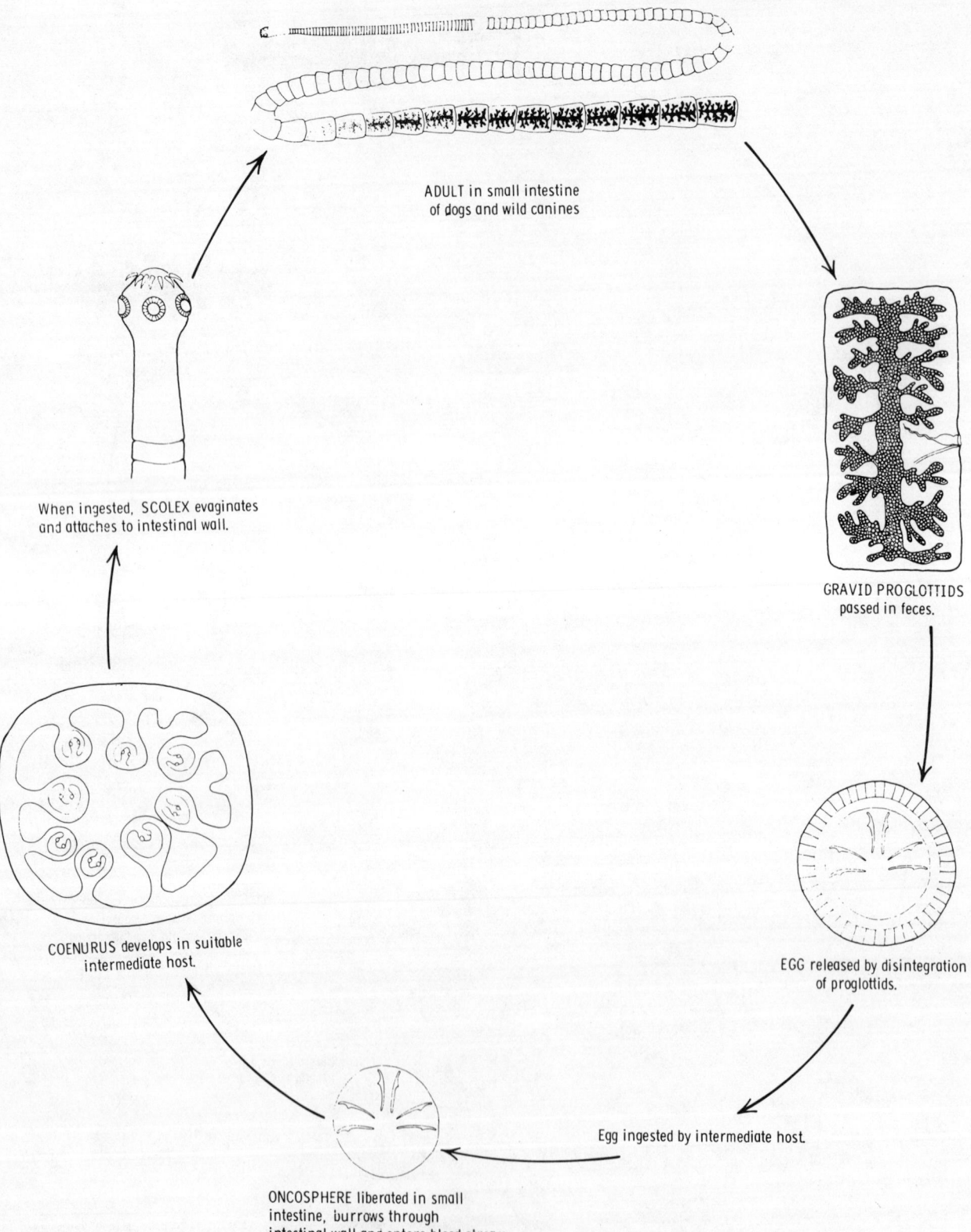

Life Cycle of Multiceps multiceps

ADULT in small intestine of dogs and wild canines

When ingested, SCOLEX evaginates and attaches to intestinal wall.

GRAVID PROGLOTTIDS passed in feces.

COENURUS develops in suitable intermediate host.

EGG released by disintegration of proglottids.

Egg ingested by intermediate host.

ONCOSPHERE liberated in small intestine, burrows through intestinal wall and enters blood stream.

Fig. 327. Diagram showing the life cycle of Multiceps multiceps, *a species of tapeworm. Also, see Table 35. (Drawing prepared by Dr. Kenneth S. Todd, Jr., Associate Professor of Veterinary Parasitology, College of Veterinary Medicine, University of Illinois, Urbana, Illinois; supported by a grant from the Merck and Company Foundation)*

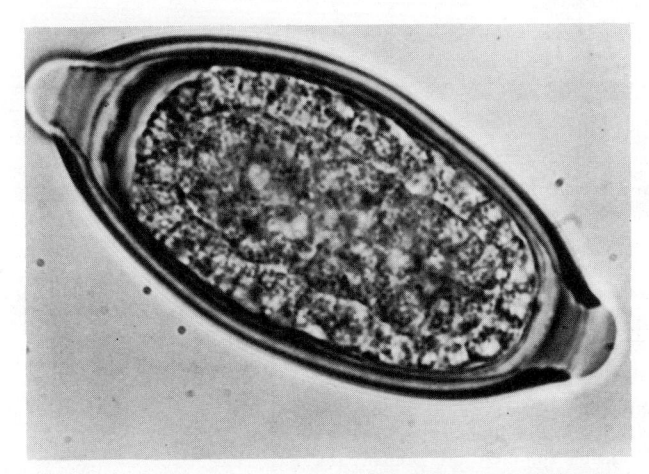

Fig. 328. Whipworm egg. (Picture prepared by Dr. Kenneth S. Todd, Jr., Associate Professor of Veterinary Parasitology, College of Veterinary Medicine, University of Illinois, Urbana, Illinois; supported by a grant from the Merck and Company Foundation)

EXTERNAL PARASITES OF DOGS

Dogs are subject to attack by a variety of external parasites; among them, fleas, lice, mites, and ticks. In addition to the harm that they themselves inflict, fleas are a threat to dogs because they carry and spread tapeworms.

GENERAL SIGNS

A heavy infestation of common external parasites may result in severe irritation, restlessness, rubbing, loss of hair, and an unthrifty condition.

GENERAL PREVENTIVE AND CONTROL MEASURES

Sanitation, good grooming, avoiding too heavy concentration of dogs, spraying or dusting, and the use of "flea collars," are the common measures employed in preventing and controlling external parasites of dogs.

COMMON EXTERNAL PARASITES

Table 36 lists the most common external parasites of dogs, along with control measures.

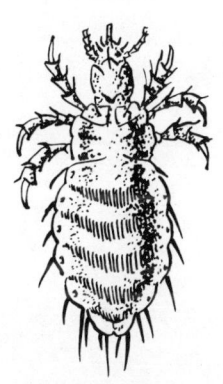

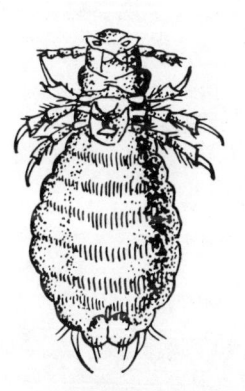

Fig. 329. Lice, enlarged twenty times. Blood-sucking louse (left); biting louse (right). (Drawing by J. L. Medeiros)

TABLE 36

Parasite	Life Cycle	Signs and Damage Inflicted
Fleas 　Several species of fleas infest dogs. The most common ones are: the dog flea, *Ctenocephalides canis;* the cat flea, *C. felis;* the human flea, *Pulex irritans;* and the sticktight flea, *Echidnophaga gallinacea.* Fleas are small, wingless, bloodsucking, external parasites. The first three listed above are active and run through the hair when disturbed. The sticktight flea attaches itself permanently to the less hairy parts, such as around the ears and eyes	All fleas pass through 4 stages—the egg, the larva, the pupa, and the adult. The female lays the eggs on the dog, and they drop to the ground, where they hatch in a few days into wormlike larvae. The larva live on organic matter in the dust or soil. In about 2 weeks, the larva becomes full grown and spins a tiny cocoon, in which it transforms to the pupa. Then the pupa changes to an adult flea in about 5 days under favorable conditions Fleas often breed in great numbers in quarters where dogs are kept. The larva proceed with their development even when the dog(s) is taken away. If no dog (or cats) are present, the fleas become annoying to people	Fleas irritate the dog. The animal becomes restless, and bites and scratches A careful examination will reveal the fleas in the hair, especially around the head, rump, and tail head

EXTERNAL PARASITES AND THEIR CONTROL[4]

Distribution and Losses	Treatment	Prevention and Control	Remarks
Fleas are found wherever there are dogs They are a threat to animals Fleas carry and spread tapeworms They also help irritate summer skin diseases, and cause poor coats	Any commercial flea spray or powder that is labeled for use on dogs may be used. Among them, are the following: 1. Chlordane—Dip or spray 0.5% to 2% solution. Available as emulsifiable concentrate, wettable powder, and dust. Sold under multiple trade names 2. Dichlorvos (Vapona)—Used as flea collar or flea medallion. Sold under various trade names. Do not use in conjunction with other organophosphate or chlorinated hydrocarbon insecticides. Multiple companies sell medallions and collars 3. Lindane (g-Benzene hexachloride)—Apply to dog as 0.03–0.06% dip or spray, as 1.0% dust. Available as emulsifiable concentrate, wettable powder, and dust. Multiple trade names 4. Malathion—Apply as 0.5% dip or 4–5% dust. Available as dust, emulsifiable concentrate, wettable powder, oil solution, and aerosol. Sold under many trade names 5. Methoxychlor—Apply as 0.25–1.0% dip, 0.5–1.0% spray, or 15–50% dust. Available as wettable powder, emulsifiable concentrate, dust, and aerosol. Sold under multiple trade names 6. Pyrethrins—Applied together with 10 times as much of various synergists, as 0.025–0.1% oil solution, 0.025–2.0% dust, 0.025–0.5% spray, 0.2% aqueous dip. Synergists used include Bucarpolate, MGK264, MGK R-11, MGK R326, Piperonyl cyclonene, sesame oil, sesamin, sesoxane, sulfoxide. Available as concentrated pyrethoum extract, emulsifiable concentrate, and aerosol. Sold under many trade names 7. Ronnel—Orally and externally on dogs. Orally 50 mg/#. External 0.5–1.0% (aqueous suspension of emulsion) dip, 5.0% dust or smear. Do not use on sick, stressed, lactating animals. Do not re-treat within 2 weeks systemically or generally. Available as emulsifiable concentrate, wettable powder, dust, petroleum-base solution, and tablets. Sold under multiple trade names Also, Carbaryl and Hepatachlor may be used according to the manufacturers' directions	Clean the bed of the dog frequently To control fleas, both the dog and its quarters must be treated frequently. If the dog stays in the home, any area where it spends considerable time (like a favorite chair or rug) must be cleaned regularly	Use flea collar or flea medallion only on your veterinarian's advice

(Continued)

[4] The authoritative "Treatment" recommendations given herein are the methods of Gerald V. Ling, DVM, School of Veterinary Medicine, Department of Clinical Sciences-Medicine, University of California, Davis, California; and/or Kenneth S. Todd, Jr., DVM, Associate Professor of Veterinary Parasitology, College of Veterinary Medicine, University of Illinois, Urbana, Ill.

Always follow the directions of your veterinarian or product manufacturers in the treatment, prevention and control of external parasites. Choice of insecticide and interval of treatment should be made on the advice of a veterinarian or the label on the product.

When using insecticides, always follow the directions and heed all precautions on the labels.

TABLE 36 (CONTINUED)

Parasite	Life Cycle	Signs and Damage Inflicted
Lice 　Three species may be found on dogs: (1) *Linognathus piliferus*, a blood sucker; (2) *Trichodectes canis*, a biting louse; and (3) *Heterodoxus longitarsus*, another biting louse. Lice are small, flattened, wingless parasites (see Fig. 329)	Although sucking lice and biting lice are quite different in structure and feeding habits, their life cycles are similar. All pass through the egg stage, several nymphal stages, and the adult; and they spend their entire life cycle on the dog's body. The eggs are fastened to the hair of the host. The nymphs are similar to the adults in appearance except for size and lack of sexual organs. The entire life cycle may be completed in a few weeks	Intense irritation and severe scratching The hair may be rough and lack luster Lice are apt to be most plentiful around the body openings, where they gather to find moisture Lice, and eggs or nits, may be seen with the naked eye

Distribution and Losses	Treatment	Prevention and Control	Remarks
Dog lice are not common in the U.S.	Usually one treatment of one of the following products will suffice: 1. Co-Ral (Coumaphos)—Apply as 0.375% dip, 0.25–0.5% spray, or 0.5–5.0% dust. Do not apply in conjunction with oral medications or on sick animals. Available as wettable powder and as dust. Sold under various trade names	Animals become inflected by direct contact. Hence, keep lice-infested dogs isolated Also, maintain separate grooming equipment for dogs that have lice	Abrasions made by scratching pave the way for secondary infections

    2. Lindane (g-Benzene hexachloride)—Apply to dog as 0.03–0.06% dip or spray, as 1.0% dust. Available as emulsifiable concentrate, wettable powder, and dust. Multiple trade names
    3. Malathion—Apply as 0.5% dip or 4–5% dust. Available as dust, emulsifiable concentrate, wettable powder, oil solution, and aerosol. Sold under many trade names
    4. Methoxychlor—Apply as 0.25–1.0% dip, 0.5–1.0% spray, or 15–50% dust. Available as wettable powder, emulsifiable concentrate, dust, and aerosol. Sold under multiple trade names
    5. Pyrethrins—Applied together with 10 times as much of various synergists, as 0.025–0.1% oil solution, 0.025–2.0% dust, 0.025–0.5% spray, or 0.2% aqueous dip. Synergists used include Bucarpolate, MGK264, MGK R-11, MGK R326, Piperonyl cyclonene, sesame oil, sesamin, sesoxane, sulfoxide. Available as concentrated pyrethoum extract, emulsifiable concentrate, and aerosol. Sold under many trade names
    6. Ronnel—Orally and externally on dogs. Orally 50 mg/#. External 0.5–1.0% (aqueous suspension of emulsion) dip, 5.0% dust or smear. Do not use on sick, stressed or lactating animals. Do not re-treat within 2 weeks systemically or generally. Available as emulsified concentrate, wettable powder, dust, petroleum-base solution, and tablets. Sold under multiple trade names
    7. Rotenone—Apply as 0.03–0.12% (aqueous suspension) spray or dip, 2.0–2.57% dust. Sold under multiple trade names
    8. Sevin (carbaryl)—Multiple trade names. Apply as 0.5% aqueous spray (aerosol) or as dust. Do not dust animals more often than once every 4 days. Available as dust or powder

(Continued)

TABLE 36 (CONTINUED)

Parasite	Life Cycle	Signs and Damage Inflicted
Mites (Mange) Two types: (1) *Sarcoptes scabiei canis*, which is related to human scabies, and (2) *Demodex canis*, which causes demodectic, or red, mange of dogs. Mange is an unsightly and painful skin condition A third type of mite affects the ear. It is known as the ear mite, *Otodectes cyanotis* (see Figs. 330 and 331).	*Sarcoptic mange:* The female mite burrows in the upper layers of the skin, where she lays 20 to 40 eggs. After 3 to 7 days, the eggs hatch and produce larvae. The larvae grow to nymphs by molting—shedding the skin—and the nymphs grow to adults in the same manner. The entire life cycle requires 2 to 3 weeks. The larvae, nymphs, and males do not burrow into the skin, but live under crusts or scales on the surface *Demodectic Mange:* The complete life cycle is not known; and the method of its transmission is obscure. Transmission of the parasite from bitch to offspring occurs before and just after birth; otherwise, it does not appear to be transmitted from dog to dog	*Sarcoptic mange:* It usually appears on the head first, but it may occur on any part of the body. Red spots appear and develop into small blisters. The scratching of the dog causes the reddish area to spread. The burrowing of the female causes the skin to exude serum, which dries in crusts or scabs. The infected part of the skin becomes dry and covered with crusts, the hair may come out, and the skin may thicken and become wrinkled. Itching is intense (see Fig. 332) *Demodectic mange (red mange):* The first sign of demodectic mange is usually the appearance of bald areas, from which the hair has been lost. Itching becomes pronounced as the spots spread and area becomes reddened. Bacteria invade the affected areas, the infection becomes pustular, the skin thickens, and a disagreeable odor is produced (see Fig. 333) Mange can be diagnosed positively only by a microscopic examination of scrapings from the diseased parts *Ear Mite:* The characteristic symptoms include scratching of the ear, head shaking, and a foul odor to the external ear. Diagnosis is based on observing the mites in the external ear or by microscopic examination of exudate from the ear canal

EXTERNAL PARASITES AND THEIR CONTROL

Distribution and Losses	Treatment	Prevention and Control	Remarks
Sarcoptic mange (scabies) occurs in all ages, but it is most frequent in young dogs Demodectic mange is primarily a disease of young dogs Ear mites may produce damage to the lining of the ear canal	*Sarcoptes scabiei canis:* Use any of the following treatments once weekly for 3 weeks: 1. Lindane (g-Benzene hexachloride)—Apply to dog as 0.03–0.06% dip or spray, as 1.0% dust. Available as emulsifiable concentrate, wettable powder, and dust Multiple trade names	Do not permit dogs to come in contact with dogs that have sarcoptic mange All animals in a household must be treated at the same time in order for ear mite treatment to be effective	Sarcoptic mange of dogs is related to human infection called *scabies;* hence, humans as well as dogs, can become infested with it Demodectic mange is not contagious to other pets or to people

    2. Malathion—Apply as 0.5% dip or 4–5% dust. Available as dust, emulsifiable concentrate, wettable powder, oil solution, and aerosol. Sold under many trade names

    3. Ronnel—Orally and externally on dogs. Orally 50 mg/#. External 0.5–1.0% (aqueous suspension of emulsion) dip, 5.0% dust or smear. Do not use on sick, stressed, or lactating animals. Do not re-treat within 2 weeks systemically or generally. Available as emulsifiable concentrate, wettable powder, dust, petroleum-base solution, and tablets. Sold under multiple trade names

    4. Rotenone—Apply as 0.03–0.12% (aqueous suspension) spray or dip, 2.0–2.57% dust. Sold under multiple trade names

    5. Sevin (carbaryl)—Multiple trade names. Apply as 0.5% aqueous spray (aerosol) or as dust. Do not dust animals more often than once every 4 days. Available as dust or powder

Demodex canis: No completely effective treatment. Among the treatments commonly used are: Canex, Ectoral, and Goodwinol ointment

Otodectes cyanotis: One dropper of mineral oil in each ear daily for 2 weeks will drown the mites and is very effective

(Continued)

TABLE 36 (CONTINUED)

Parasite	Life Cycle	Signs and Damage Inflicted

Ticks
  Several species infest dogs, including—
1. The brown dog tick, *Rhipicephalus sanguineus* (see Fig. 334)
2. The American dog tick, *Dermacentor variabilis*
3. The Rocky Mountain spotted fever tick, *D. andersoni*
4. The Pacific Coast tick, *D. occidentalis*
5. The gulf coast tick, *Amblyomma maculatum*
6. The blacklegged tick, *Ixodes scapularis;* and a closely related species, *I. pacificus*
7. The lone star tick, *Amblyomma americanum*
	1. *Brown dog tick*—The life cycle is as follows:
	  a. The females become engorged with blood, release their hold on the dog, and seek a nearby hiding place (roof of kennel, ceiling of porch, bark of trees, shrubs, grass, etc.). They lay 1,000 to 3,000 eggs, which hatch after 19 to 60 days into tiny, 6-legged larvae, or seed ticks
	  b. The larvae attach to a dog and fill with blood from 3 to 6 days, after which they drop and hide like the females. In 6 to 23 days, they molt their skins and become 8-legged, reddish brown nymphs
	  c. The nymphs attach to dogs and become engorged in 4 to 9 days. They drop, hide, and molt to eight-legged, sexually mature males and females; a stage which requires from 12 to 29 days
	  d. The adult ticks attach to various parts of the dog; and the female becomes engorged, drops off, and lays eggs as outlined in "a" above—thereby starting a new cycle
	2. *Other ticks*—The other ticks that infest dogs also infest other animals; thereby differing from the brown dog tick, which feeds almost exclusively on dogs. Also, they live outdoors and won't live very long in dry, heated buildings; whereas the brown dog tick is "domesticated." However, all species of ticks that infest dogs pass through the same stages—egg, larvae, nymph, and adult—but all stages do not always have the same host
		The brown dog tick—When fully mature and engorged with blood, the female is about one-third inches long and bluish gray. Both males and females attach to dogs. They cause irritation and loss of condition. Pulling them off leaves open wounds, which may become infected
		
		The American dog tick, the *Rocky Mountain spotted fever tick*, the *Pacific Coast tick*, and the *gulf coast tick* as adults, are reddish or dark brown in color and marked conspicuously with one or more patches of white
		
		The blacklegged tick posses a smoky black shield. The body of the female behind the shield is yellow or light brown

Distribution and Losses	Treatment	Prevention and Control	Remarks
The brown dog tick, which occurs mostly in the warmer regions of the U.S., is important because— 1. It feeds almost exclusively on dogs 2. It is a carrier of *canine babesiasis,* a protozoan infection of dogs 3. It has adapted to life in kennels, houses, and apartments 4. It is a drain on the vitality of dogs and a source of great irritation *The American dog tick* is the most widely distributed of all tick species. The rest of the species of ticks occur in certain areas, which, due to space limitations, cannot be given here *The American dog tick* and *Rocky Mountain spotted fever tick* may cause paralysis of dogs or children if the females attach and engorge at the base of the skull or along the spinal column	Among the treatments that may be used for control are the following: 1. Co-Ral (Coumaphos) —Apply as 0.375% dip, 0.25–0.5% spray, or 0.5–5.0% dust. Do not apply in conjunction with oral medications or on sick animals. Available as wettable powder and dust. Sold under various trade names 2. Rotenone — Apply as 0.03–0.12% (aqueous suspension) spray or dip, 2.0–2.57% dust. Sold under multiple trade names 3. Sevin (carbaryl) — Multiple trade names. Apply as 0.5% aqueous spray (aerosol) or as dust. Do not dust animals more often than once every 4 days. Available as dust or powder	The first control measure consists in treating the yard, or premises, of the dog. Among the products that may be used are: 1. Dusts containing 5% Sevin or 2% Dieldrin, applied at the rate of 2 to 3 lb per 1,000 sq ft of yard 2. A spray of Diazinon, applied at the rate of 5 tablespoons of 25% Diazinon in 10 gals of water per 1,000 sq ft If ticks are in the house or other buildings, spray with either (1) 0.5% Diazinon in a diluent that will not stain furniture; or (2) 1% Baygon in oil. Repeat all treatments for several months based on reinfestation as determined by visual inspection of the dog and its living quarters	The American dog tick, Rocky Mountain spotted fever tick, and lone star tick may carry Rocky Mountain spotted fever and tularemia. Dogs do not show signs of these diseases, but people may become infected by picking infected ticks from dogs

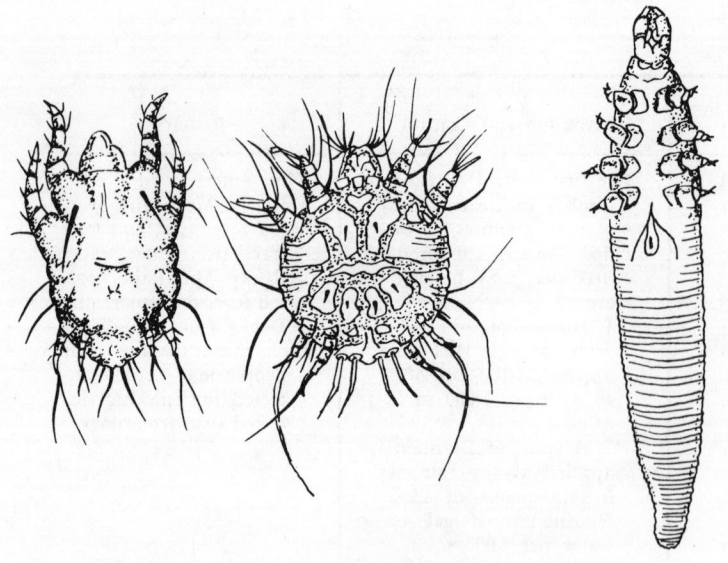

Fig. 330. Mites, all greatly enlarged. Ear mange mite (left); sarcoptic mange mite (center); demodectic mange mite (right), also called red and follicular mange mite. (Drawing by J. L. Medeiros)

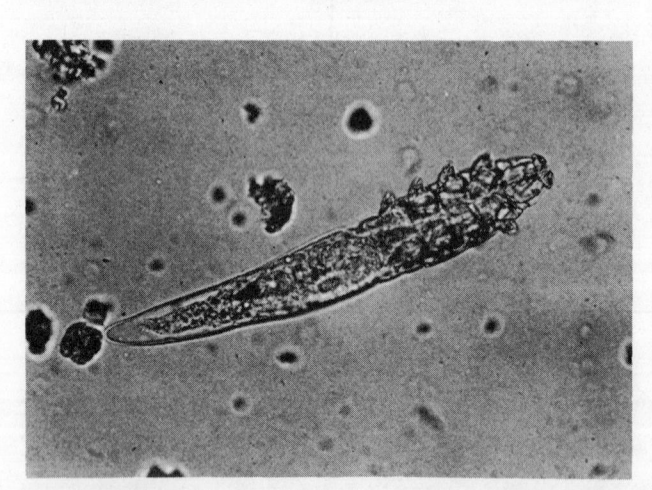

Fig. 331. Mange mite, Demodex canis. (Picture prepared by Dr. Kenneth S. Todd, Jr., Associate Professor of Veterinary Parasitology, College of Veterinary Medicine, University of Illinois, Urbana, Illinois; supported by a grant from the Merck and Company Foundation)

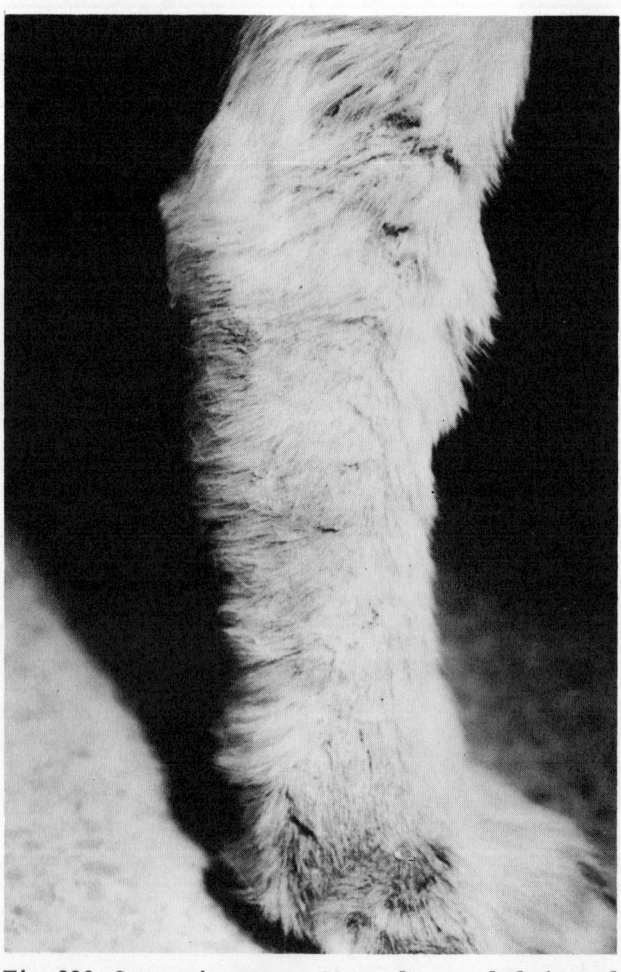

Fig. 332. Sarcoptic mange. Note the rough hair and the collection of sebum on the hair. (Courtesy Dr. J. H. Reed, D.V.M., Ph.D., Ontario Veterinary College, University of Guelph, Guelph, Ontario, Canada)

Fig. 333. Demodetic mange. An advanced case of the squamous form. (Courtesy Dr. J. H. Reed, D.V.M., Ph.D., Ontario Veterinary College, University of Guelph, Guelph, Ontario, Canada)

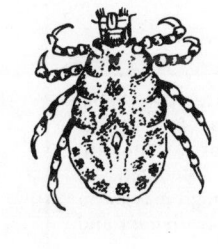

Fig. 334. Dog ticks, enlarged six times. Adult female before feeding (left); adult male (right). (Drawing by J. L. Medeiros)

Fig. 335. A dog dipping vat. (Courtesy H. N. Holmes, Gunsmoke Kennels, Springfield, Ill.)

COMMON HEALTH PROBLEMS

Illness in dogs is usually less frequent than in people. But when it occurs, it is just as natural.

Table 37 is a summary of some health problems, and what to do about them.

TABLE 37

COMMON HEALTH PROBLEMS

Problem	Cause; signs	Treatment
Appetite; decreased or depraved	Appetite is usually a good barometer of your dog's health. A sudden decrease in appetite is usually indicative that a dog is sick. A depraved appetite—eating such things as sticks, stones, grass, paper, leather, etc.—may be indicative of boredom, or some nutritional deficiency	A persistent lack of appetite or a depraved appetite is indicative of trouble. Hence, you should see your veterinarian
Breath, bad (Halitosis)	Bad breath may be caused by excess tartar, decaying teeth, a digestive upset, infected tonsils, or a mouth infection	Your veterinarian can scale off the excess tartar from the teeth. Likewise, he can treat the other conditions that may be causing bad breath. So, it is always well to let your veterinarian examine your dog if bad breath persists
Constipation	Constipation may result from the diet, from lack of exercise, or from more serious problems in the intestinal tract	Improve the diet and increase the exercise. If the constipation continues, give milk of magnesia—1 tsp for every 10 lb of body weight. If these measures do not rectify this situation, see your veterinarian
Convulsions (see fits)		
Cough	Coughing may result from the dog being chilled in a draft, or it may be the first symptom of a wide range of possible ailments—worms, laryngitis, distemper, or bronchitis. Within itself, a cough may mean very little, perhaps it is only temporary and will clear up shortly	If the cough is combined with a fever, running nose, hoarseness, a lot of blinking or sensitivity to light, and abnormal breathing, it may be indicative of a severe illness. Therefore, it should be attended to by a veterinarian without delay
Diarrhea	Diarrhea may be caused by any one of a number of things; among them, spoiled or moldy food, overfeeding, frequent and indiscriminate use of laxatives and worm medicines, and violent exercise in warm weather. Also, uncooked starches may cause diarrhea	Do not feed fluid foods like milk or broth. Give Kaopectate, 1 tsp per 10 lb of dog
Dragging rearquarters	Intense itching surrounding the anal glands on both sides of the rectum causes the dog to drag his hindquarters on the floor or ground. Sometimes, although rarely, dragging of the hindquarters is caused by tapeworm infestation	The signs described are not usually an indication of worms Your veterinarian can easily empty the anal glands by squeezing them. This will relieve the itching

(Continued)

TABLE 37 (CONTINUED)

COMMON HEALTH PROBLEMS

Problem	Cause; signs	Treatment
Ear trouble (ear infection, ear canker, ear mites)	Dust, dirt, and other foreign matter may become lodged in the ear. Also, wax may accumulate. As a result of such accumulations, along with possible injury or other causes, the ear canal may become infected. Accordingly, it is well to look at the dog's ears occasionally to be sure that there is no infection, burrs, or other sources of irritation. Also, it is advisable to learn the smell of your dog's normal ear and to check its odor frequently. Any change of smell may indicate infection	If needed you can clean your dog's ears by gently washing them with a mild soapy solution, using a small amount of cotton on the end of your finger. But leave the ears dry when you are through If the ear is foul-smelling, or if a discharge is present, do not attempt home treatment. See your veterinarian Ear mites move around in the ear canal and are sometimes responsible for cankers in the ears. Ear mites can be smothered by the use of certain oils, used under the direction of your veterinarian
Fits (convulsions)	Fits are characterized by chattering of the jaws, foaming at the mouth, rapid breathing, with the dog lying on its side "paddling." Fits are indicative of some disturbance, usually in the nervous system or of epilepsy, distemper, or similar diseases, and fright	Try to get the dog in a place where he cannot injure himself; and, if possible, cover him with a towel or blanket. When the fit ends, consult your veterinarian as to the underlying cause and recommended treatment
Frothing at the mouth	Within itself, frothing is not an ailment. However, it may accompany an ailment or it may be the dog's way of reacting to fright or anger. Also, frothing will sometimes occur during a fit. Motion sickness may bring it on with some dogs, even a short car ride	It is always well to determine the cause, then to apply the proper treatment
Gas (flatulence)	This refers to an accumulation of gas in the stomach or intestines of the dog, which may make him pass more wind than normal. Gas can result from large amounts of proteins like hard boiled eggs, meat, and cheese; from strong-flavored vegetables like cabbage, turnips, cauliflower; and from nervousness; and from old age	If the excess gas condition persists and becomes offensive, you should consult your veterinarian. He can recommend an anti-flatulent
Jaundice	Jaundice occurs when some growth blocks the bile duct or some disease interferes with the normal function of the liver. The signs are orange urine and yellowish coloring of the skin and the whites of the eyes	Like all other liver ailments, jaundice requires professional care

(Continued)

373

TABLE 37 (CONTINUED)

COMMON HEALTH PROBLEMS

Problem	Cause; signs	Treatment
Lameness	A dog may become lame if a foreign object becomes lodged in his paw. If this happens, your dog will whimper, whine, and hop on three feet; and the injured paw may bleed and swell Also, dogs may become lame from muscle and stone bruises, broken bones, and bone tumors. Several diseases of young dogs may cause lameness	If the lameness is due to a foreign object and not from a leg fracture, remove the object gently after first restraining the dog with a mouth tie. Make sure you get the entire object out. Use tweezers or pliers for pulling glass, thorns, nails, tacks, sharp splinters, etc. Wash the part thoroughly with mild soap and warm water. If the dog wishes to lick the area, let him do so. If there is swelling, apply warm compresses. Minor cuts will heal without further treatment If the cut seems to need further attention—that is, if there is continued swelling, pus, failure to heal—check with your veterinarian If there is no apparent cause of lameness, do not let it persist. See your veterinarian
Skin troubles (allergy, dandruff, distemper pustules, eczema, mange, ringworm) At the first sign of skin trouble, you should consult your veterinarian. He can determine the nature of the condition, then prescribe proper treatment. Remember that skin infections can be serious. Remember, too, that there are now available effective treatments for most skin ailments	1. *Allergy*—Allergies may be due to a number of things; new food, an insect dust, pollen, a particular plant or flower, certain chemicals in the soil or paint, even the dog's bedding. Also, some dogs are allergic to vaccines, serums, milk products, and even to their own bodies An allergy may be apparent in the same way as any of the other skin ailments; with inflammation, swelling or puffiness around the face, itching, hives, pus-filled pimples, irritation, thickening of the skin, flaking or scaling, perhaps loss of hair	1. *Allergy treatment*—As is true in human allergies, the important thing is to find what's causing the allergy, then remove the cause. Usually this means that you should call upon your veterinarian. Some allergies will disappear with time, whereas others will persist until the cause is removed. In the meantime, an allergy should be treated by washing the affected areas with mild soap and warm water and applying the treatment recommended by your veterinarian
	2. *Dandruff*—Dandruff in dogs is a dry scaliness, much like dandruff in man. Brushing will raise many dusty, little scales. It may be caused by too much washing that dries the coat's natural oil or it may be caused by not enough rinsing following the bath. As a result, the soap that remains, dries and irritates the skin	2. *Dandruff treatment*—A little cocoanut oil, olive oil, or caster oil, massaged into the skin will usually help. The larger dog may be rubbed all over with a dressing made especially for dogs
	3. *Distemper pustules*—Often during the course of distemper, little pustules appear on the abdomen. Usually, they will disappear when the disease has run its course	3. *Distemper pustule treatment*—Until pustules disappear, they should be kept moist with vaseline

(Continued)

TABLE 37 (CONTINUED)

COMMON HEALTH PROBLEMS

Problem	Cause; signs	Treatment

Skin troubles (cont.)	4. *Eczema*—Eczema is one of the most serious skin troubles afflicting dogs. It may be caused by any one of a number of things; external parasites, dirty bedding, overheating, excessively strong soaps, etc.
	
	Eczema may be classed either as dry or moist. In dry eczema, which is the most common form, the skin looks scaly and the hair may fall out in patches. Constant biting and scratching makes the condition spread. A moist eczema is usually due to improper diet or constipation. In this type, the skin is red and flushed and there is intense irritation and itching
	
	5. *Mange*—There are two types of mange, each caused by a particular parasite. *Sarcoptic mange* produces severe itching, causing the dog to bite and scratch. It spreads rapidly and strips the skin of hair. *Follicular mange* is less itchy but more serious. It causes the hair to fall out and pustules to dot the skin
	
	6. *Ringworm*—Ringworm is caused by a fungus. It appears as round, rough, and scaly patches protruding slightly above the normal level of the skin. The spots may be either dry or moist, and may discharge pus. You should always wear gloves when handling ringworm-infested dogs
		4. *Eczema treatment*—The following treatments are used in dry eczema, with varying degrees of success:
		  a. Add 1 to 2 tbs of corn oil to the daily diet of the dog
		  b. Apply externally, a homemade mixture made of 7 oz. of alcohol, 1 oz. of balsam of Peru, and a tsp of creolin, for the purpose of relieving the itching
		  c. Apply a patent soothing lotion to ease the itching and irritation; a number of such products are on the market
		
		Moist eczema should be treated by improving the diet, if necessary, and giving a purgative to alleviate constipation (see "Constipation" above; give milk of magnesia as directed)
		
		With moist eczema, it is very important to prevent the dog from biting or scratching. To this end, the use of the Elizabethan collar is recommended. An Elizabethan collar can be made from cardboard. When in place it looks something like a lampshade worn around the neck
		
		5. *Mange treatment*—The first step in mange control is to have your veterinarian take skin scrapings and examine them under the microscope, in order to determine which kind of mange the dog has. Then treatment should be as directed in Table 36, under "Mange"
		
		6. *Ringworm treatment*—As soon as ringworm has been positively identified, you should treat it as directed in Table 34 of this book, under *Ringworm*

Tooth troubles	The most common tooth problem is the formation of tartar, a yellowish, hard deposit, on one or more teeth. If not rectified, it may push into the gum and break the seal, which is the tooth's main defense against infection Although the dog suffers in silence when he has a toothache, he will let you know that the problem exists by rubbing his jaw on the affected side along the floor or perhaps pawing it. Also, he may eat gingerly, and he may drool	*Tooth treatment*—Requires professional aid. The veterinarian can easily remove tartar, and he is qualified to handle such other problems as may exist with the teeth Most tooth troubles can be prevented by the owner doing two things: (1) giving the dog knuckle bones daily, which stimulate the blood supply as they rub over the gums—they are the dog's toothbrush; and (2) by wiping the dog's teeth regularly and daily with a damp cloth dipped in salt or baking soda. This will stimulate the gums and clean the teeth

(Continued)

375

TABLE 37 (CONTINUED)

COMMON HEALTH PROBLEMS

Problem	Cause; signs	Treatment
Trembling (shivering)	Trembling may be caused by a number of things; among them, becoming chilled as a result of being in a draft, consuming some poisonous substance or, in the case of a pregnant or nursing bitch, it may be due to eclampsia, a disorder caused by severe calcium deficiency	If the trembling or shivering is due to exposure to a draft, it will usually rectify itself in short order. However, if it is due to consuming a poison, prompt attention is very necessary. If at all possible, determine what poison was eaten, then administer the proper antidote and seek help If trembling is due to eclampsia, your veterinarian can rectify the condition by the immediate injection of calcium
Vomiting	Dogs vomit easily and at will. Thus, it is not uncommon for them to vomit when given some medicine or food that they dislike. Other causes of vomiting are: heavy exercise on a full stomach, car sickness, overeating, eating of spoiled food, eating foreign matter such as grass, string, etc., and various illnesses	If the dog continues to vomit for a period of time, or if blood or bile (green colored fluid) is vomited, his condition may be considered serious and you should secure prompt professional help. Milk of bismuth or milk of magnesia, given in teaspoonful doses for larger dogs, will frequently help settle the stomach. If the car sickness is a problem and you wish to have your dog travel with you a great deal, you should talk to your veterinarian. He may prescribe Dramamine or Bonamine to overcome car sickness. A sedative, sodium bromide (3–5 grains), given before starting and periodically during the trip, may help to control drooling and vomiting
Weight loss	When your dog loses weight, worms may be suspected. Weight loss may be, and usually is, due to some significant illness. If it persists, seek professional help	When there is a loss of weight, feed more. Also, if worms are present, administer the proper vermifuge (see Table 35 in this chapter)

OLDER DOG AILMENTS

The older dog, who has served his master long and well, merits the best. He should be fed properly, on a well-balanced, easily digested diet; kept regular in bowel movements; provided with a warm, soft bed—because he is more brittle of bone and more sensitive to cold; kept out of drafts; thoroughly dried each time when exposed to rain or snow; and checked periodically by your veterinarian.

Among the ailments common to older dogs that may need special attention are the following:

1. *Constipation*—The older dog may become constipated. Usually, this is caused by lack of exercise that can be rectified by forcing the dog to take regular, although mild, exercise. However, it may be caused by a faulty diet, in which case this should be rectified. Whatever the cause, a gentle laxative may be necessary to get the digestive tract back into normal elimination.

2. *Deafness*—Deafness may be frustrating to the older dog, as well as to his master. Some cases of poor hearing can be rectified by proper treatment and care. Inflammation of the ear canal, ear mites, foreign material, and accumulation of ear wax often causes pain and loss of function.

3. *Exercise*—Exercise is good for the older dog. It improves the circulation, aerates the lungs, improves the elimination, and helps keep down body weight. For the older dog, exercise should be less strenuous and in smaller doses than for

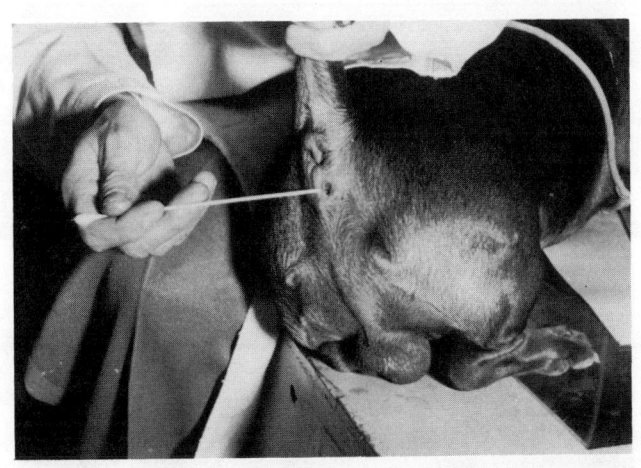

Fig. 336. Anal sac fistula. A common sequela to anal sac abscessation. (Courtesy Dr. J. H. Reed, D.V.M., Ph.D., Ontario Veterinary College, University of Guelph, Guelph, Ontario, Canada)

younger dogs; and there should be shorter periods of play and longer periods of rest.

4. *Nephritis* (kidney damage)—Nephritis is a common ailment in older dogs. It generally develops gradually and over a period of years as the result of various diseases suffered by the dog. The best assist for kidney damage is to provide the dog with a constant supply of cool, fresh water to help the kidneys function in elimination of waste material.

5. *Rheumatism*—Lameness or stiffness, particularly when it follows a period of rest, is generally evidence that the older dog is suffering from rheumatism. Rheumatism may be caused by a muscular spasm, arthritis, or boney disturbances.

Muscular rheumatism is most likely to occur when the dog lies on concrete surfaces or damp ground. Arthritis, which affects the joints, may be the result of infections elsewhere in the body—the teeth, kidneys, or any chronically infected organ. Bony disturbances, such as fragile bones, result from the poor use by the older dog of the calcium supplied in the diet.

Rheumatism in the older dog may be lessened by (a) keeping him dry and out of drafts, (b) supplying him with a soft bed in a sheltered area, and (c) feeding a diet that is adequate in calcium, phosphorus, and vitamin D, with each of these nutrients in proper proportion or balance.

6. *Sight*—The dimming of vision is very frequently the first sign of old age. Correct feeding may help to preserve the sight of your dog. But if this does not happen, you may just have to face the fact that your dog no longer sees well. Frequently, the older dog loses his sight entirely.

Bathing the eyes and putting in ophthalmic ointments, obtained from your veterinarian, can ease a dog's eye trouble when ulcers or other infections cause fading vision.

7. *Teeth*—The teeth of older dogs need regular attention. They should be kept free from tartar, and loose and defective teeth should be removed.

Your veterinarian can advise you on what to do to keep your older dog well, contented, and healthy. So, let him—a trained medical man—examine your older dog at frequent intervals, then prescribe a program for you to follow.

A PROGRAM OF DOG HEALTH, DISEASE PREVENTION, AND PARASITE CONTROL

In order to reduce the possibility of diseases and parasites, the owner must adopt certain management practices relative to the environment of the dog. It has been said that domestication and increased dog numbers imply a sort of contract. Man, in fulfilling his obligation for the service rendered, must protect his pet from the elements, parasites, and diseases, and furnish him sanitary quarters and suitable rations.

Dogs require sanitary quarters. In the wild state, they had access to plenty of fresh air, clean feed, and area over which to travel. They naturally have clean habits, and, if given the choice, will not voluntarily lie in filth.

The program that follows is, by necessity, general in nature. It may be adapted to an individual kennel, or to one dog, with the help and counsel of your veterinarian.

1. *Provide good housing and ventilation*—Although housing and close confinement predispose dogs to disease, they are often very necessary; to facilitate handling, to combat the elements, and/or to furnish protection when young are arriving.

Proper drainage, dryness, ventilation, adequate space, and good lighting are among the requisites of good housing. In addition, dog quarters must be of such construction as to facilitate proper cleaning, disinfection, and maintenance of sanitary conditions. The latter implies suitable floors, adequate waste disposal, and proper absorbent bedding.

2. *Provide for proper excreta disposal*—Situations that compel dogs to live in close contact with their own body excreta may be very injurious to physical well-being. Urine, feces, exhalations, and nose and mouth discharges may often contain disease-producing agents and furnish an ideal medium for the growth of microorganisms.

The importance of removing excrement frequently from the immediate surroundings can not be stressed too much. The method of disposal of the stools is also most important. As the feces may contain a variety of parasites and eggs, proper disposal offers an excellent opportunity for breaking the life cycle of these parasites. On the other hand, if left in an accessible place for dogs, stools can be a rich, never-ending source of disease and parasitism.

3. *Provide suitable and clean feed containers*—Avoid feeding the dog off the ground because of the hazard of spreading diseases and parasites. Instead, provide a suitable container, and keep it clean at all times.

4. *Control and exterminate rodents*—Rodents may spread diseases and parasites to dogs. Hence, they should be controlled, and eliminated if possible.

5. *Isolate new animals*—Where many dogs, such as in a kennel, are involved, it is important that the following procedure be adhered to when adding new animals to the kennel: (a) secure a health certificate signed by the veterinarian where the animal originated, and (b) isolate the new animal in separate quarters for a minimum period of three weeks, and arrange for a separate caretaker, as well as separate equipment for food and water, during this period.

Thoroughly clean and disinfect the isolation quarters after each animal is removed and before a new animal is placed therein.

6. *Use caution in showing*—Despite all the virtues of showing dogs, there is a disease hazard in exhibiting.

7. *Use your veterinarian*—Effective dog health programs call for full cooperation between the dog owner and his veterinarian, with the former calling upon the latter in exactly the same manner as well-informed people call upon the family doctor when human ill health is encountered.

8. *Use disinfectants*—Under ordinary circumstances, proper cleaning of the dog's quarters will remove most of the microorganisms, along with the filth, thus eliminating the necessity of disinfection. In case of disease outbreak, however, the premises must be disinfected. Also, a

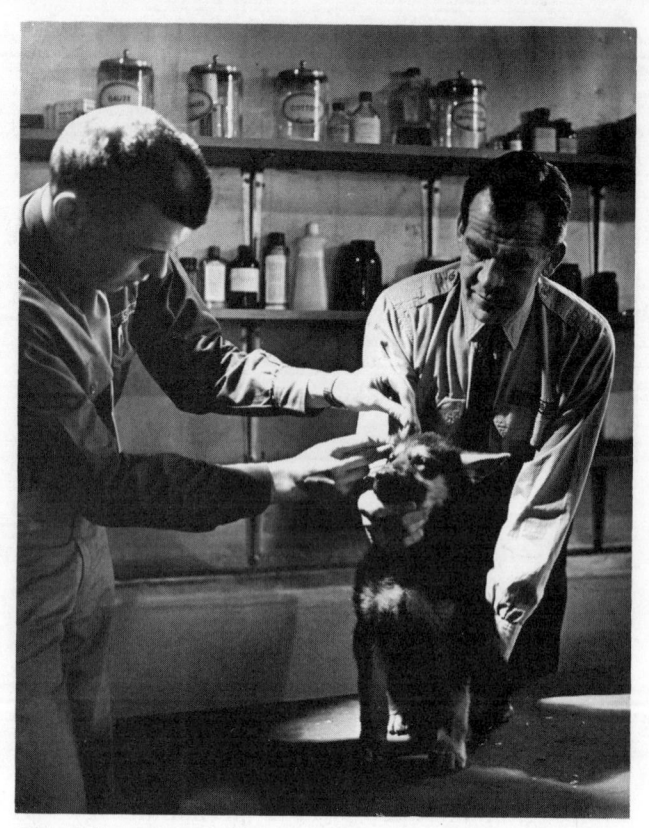

Fig. 337. Dog being physically examined. (Courtesy The Seeing Eye, Inc., Morristown, N.J.)

regular disinfection program is advisable where there is a concentration of dogs, such as in a kennel.

9. *Condition*—Avoid either an overfat or a thin, emaciated condition.

10. *Exercise*—Provide plenty of exercise, either by walking on a leash or by allowing the run of a large kennel area.

11. *Check feces for parasites*—At regular intervals, have your veterinarian examine a stool for parasites.

12. *Follow a regular vaccination and parasite treatment program*—Such a program should be set up by your veterinarian, then you should follow it without deviation therefrom.

DISINFECTANTS AND THEIR USES

A disinfectant is defined as any biological, physical, or chemical agent capable of exerting changes in environment unfavorable for the continued survival of microorganisms.

Under ordinary conditions, proper cleaning of

the dog's quarters removes most of the microorganisms, along with the filth, thus eliminating the necessity of disinfection. In case of disease outbreak, however, the premises must be disinfected.

Effective disinfection depends on the following five conditions:

1. Thorough cleaning before application;
2. The phenol coefficient of the disinfectant, which indicates the killing strength of a disinfectant as compared to phenol (carbolic acid). It is determined by a standard laboratory test in which the typhoid fever germ often is used as the test organism;
3. The dilution at which the disinfectant is used;
4. The temperature; most disinfectants are much more effective if applied hot;
5. Thoroughness of application, and time of exposure.

Disinfection must in all cases be preceded by a very thorough cleaning, for organic matter serves to protect disease germs and otherwise interferes with the activity of the disinfecting agent. This includes the burning of all inflammable refuse. All walls, ceilings, and woodwork must be brushed down and also washed down with water and scrubbed. Having accomplished this cleaning, one is ready to choose the disinfectant.

Unfortunately, there is no one best germ killer, nor is there anything like a general disinfectant that is effective against all types of microorganisms under all conditions. This stems partially from the fact that not all disease-producing bacteria are susceptible to the same chemical agents. A few bacteria—such as those that cause tetanus—possess the ability of forming seedlike spores that can remain dormant for years and resist destruction. Others, like those organisms causing tuberculosis, are resistant to oxidizing disinfectants such as the chlorine compounds. The organisms that cause distemper, and some other diseases are, fortunately, very readily killed by almost any disinfectant that reaches them.

Sunlight possesses disinfecting properties, but it is variable and superficial in its action. Heat and some of the chemical disinfectants are more effective. Table 38 gives a summary of the usefulness, strength, and limitations of some of the common disinfectants. (See pp. 380–382.)

DOG DISEASES AND PARASITES TRANSMISSIBLE TO FARM ANIMALS

Both dog owners and stockmen should be aware that some diseases of dogs may be transmitted to other farm animals. Additionally, the dog may be a mechanical carrier of many other livestock diseases such as brucellosis and anthrax, and many other contagious and infectious diseases of livestock, even though the dogs themselves do not actually contract the disease. These diseases may be carried on the feet of dogs or in their droppings when they have fed on dead animals that have died of one of these infectious diseases.

Among the diseases and parasites that may be transmitted by the dog to other farm animals are the following:

1. *Distemper*—This disease may be transmitted from the dog to commercially raised foxes or mink. Thus, all dogs should be vaccinated, and care should be taken to keep dogs from running in the areas where mink or fox are kept for commercial production.

2. *Fleas*—Fleas are the most common and easily recognized parasites of the dog. They not only cause the dog excessive irritation, but they may be transmitted to hogs, cattle, poultry, and other domestic livestock. Fleas are capable of transmitting many of the diseases of the bloodstream and septicemias of animals. Hence, they should be controlled on the dog.

3. *Gid in sheep*—This disease is due to the cystic form of *Coenurus cerebralis*, one of the common tapeworms of dogs that locates in the brain of sheep. The life cycle is completed when such a sheep is slaughtered or dies and the dog has access to the head of the sheep with which he swallows the cystic form of the tapeworm, which develops into a mature tapeworm in the intestinal tract of the dog. Then, the tapeworm eggs are voided by the dog, or other carnivorous animals, and are consumed by sheep. After the eggs are ingested by sheep, the embryos emerge and make their way into the bloodstream, with a few of them finally reaching the central nervous system where they occur as large cysts, or bladders, each the size of a hen's egg or larger. Prevention consists in the elimination of stray dogs; the examination and proper anthelmintic treatment, when necessary, of all dogs that must come in contact with sheep and goats; and the proper disposal of all carcasses or parts of carcasses coming from infected sheep or goats.

TABLE 38

HANDY DISINFECTANT GUIDE

Kind of Disinfectant	Usefulness	Strength	Limitations and Comments
Alcohol	Effective against the less resistant disease germs provided there is adequate exposure	70% alcohol — the content usually found in rubbing alcohol	Limited application. Not recommended for general use. Often used as a local antiseptic in obtaining blood samples or making hypodermic injections. Not reliable for sterilization of instruments
Bichloride of Mercury (mercuric chloride; corrosive sublimate)	Destroys less resistant bacteria under favorable conditions. Tends to prevent growth rather than actually destroying bacteria. Organic mercurials, sometimes used as local antiseptics, are less poisonous and more reliable	Tablets used in a dilution of 1 to 1,000	Unreliable as a germ killer in the presence of organic matter. For kennel disinfection, bichloride of mercury is inferior to iodine, lye, saponified cresols, and the cationic bactericides
Boric Acid (sometimes loosely classed as a disinfectant but actually an antiseptic and practically useful only on living tissue)	As a wash for eyes, and other sensitive parts of the body	1 oz in 1 pt water (about 2.2% solution)	It is a weak antiseptic. It may cause harm to the nervous system if absorbed into the body in large amounts. For this and other reasons, antibiotic solutions and saline solutions are fast replacing it. *Boric acid is toxic if given by mouth*
Cationic Bactericides (many commercial products available, including Q.A.C., i.e., quarternary ammonium compounds)	Primarily detergents but some are actively bactericidal. Often used in sanitizing dairy or other equipment and utensils. Use only as recommended by competent sanitarian	Concentration varies with different products and under different conditions. Follow authoritative recommendations	They have only a slight toxicity and are nonirritant and odorless. They are neutralized by soap, anionic detergents, and even by mineral content of some waters. Superior to chlorine compounds in the presence of organic matter. They are not effective against TB organisms and spores
Cresols (many commercial products available)	A generally reliable class of disinfectant	According to the directions found on the container	Cannot be used where odor may be absorbed, and, therefore, not suited for use around milk and meat

(Continued)

TABLE 38 (CONTINUED)

HANDY DISINFECTANT GUIDE

Kind of Disinfectant	Usefulness	Strength	Limitations and Comments
Heat (by steam, hot water, burning, or boiling)	In the burning of rubbish or articles of little value, and in disposing of infected body discharges. The steam "Jenny" is effective for disinfection if properly employed—particularly if used in conjunction with a phenolic germicide	10 min. exposure to boiling water is usually sufficient	Exposure to boiling water will destroy all ordinary disease germs but sometimes fails to kill the spores of such diseases as anthrax and tetanus. Moist heat is preferred to dry heat, and steam under pressure is the most effective. Heat may be impractical or too expensive
Hypochlorites (chlorine compounds)	For deodorizing manure, sewers, and drains	200 parts available chlorine per million of water. Unstable: replace solution frequently as recommended	Excellent for disinfection, but with following limitations: not effective against the TB organism and spores. Its effectiveness is greatly reduced in presence of organic matter, even in small quantities. Hypochlorites deteriorate rapidly when exposed to air
Iodine (sometimes loosely classed as a disinfectant but actually an antiseptic and practically useful only on living tissues)	Extensively used as skin disinfectant, for minor cuts and bruises	Generally used as tincture of iodine 2%	Never cover with a bandage. Clean skin before applying iodine
Iodophor (iodine complexed with a detergent, which releases free iodine at a controlled rate)	For disinfecting food and water utensils and for area disinfection where large quantities of organic soil are not present	75 parts available iodine per million is minimum under ideal circumstances — 150 ppm is recommended for most practical uses. Unstable—replace solution frequently	An excellent disinfectant but with the following practical limitations: Germicidal agent rapidly consumed by organic matter necessitating frequent replacement. Functions best in a highly acid range. Solution strength must be increased to get necessary available iodine when mixture is made with alkaline water. Iodine slowly volatilizes from solution. Considerable control should be exercised
Lime (quicklime, burnt lime, calcium oxide)	As a deodorant when sprinkled on stools, and animal discharges; or as a disinfectant when sprinkled on the floor or used as a newly made "milk of lime" or as a whitewash	Use as a dust; as "milk of lime"; or as a whitewash, but use fresh	Not effective against organisms of TB and the spore formers. Wear goggles when adding water to quicklime

(Continued)

TABLE 38 (CONTINUED)

HANDY DISINFECTANT GUIDE

Kind of Disinfectant	Usefulness	Strength	Limitations and Comments
Lye (sodium hydroxide, caustic soda)	On concrete floors; against microorganisms of brucellosis and the viruses	1 can (13 oz) to 12 to 15 gal water. To prepare a 5% solution, add 5 (13 oz) cans to 10 gals water	Damages fabrics, aluminum, and painted surfaces. Be careful, for it will burn the hands and face. Not effective against most spores. When used in kennels, lye should be mixed with hot water, as the heat of the water will destroy the worm eggs. *Diluted vinegar can be used to neutralize lye* Do not allow dogs in area that has been freshly treated with lye. First, wash area thoroughly with water and let it dry before using. Otherwise, the dog will be burned
Phenolic Germicides, Synthetic (those containing odorless nontoxic phenols such as orthobenzyl parachlorophenol)	A very reliable class of disinfectants effective against all disease-producing fungi and bacteria including the TB organism, but not the spores of tetanus	Varies with different formulations; follow directions on manufacturer's label	Excellent for disinfection. They are not inactivated by soap, anionic detergent, hard water, or organic matter. *Cats and foxes cannot stand phenol derivatives, but they are satisfactory for dogs*
Sal Soda	It may be used in place of lye against certain diseases	10½% solution (13½ oz to 1 gal. water)	
Soap	Its power to kill germs is very limited. Greatest usefulness is in cleansing and dissolving coatings from various surfaces, including the skin, prior to application of a good disinfectant	As commercially prepared	Although indispensable for sanitizing surfaces, soaps should not be considered as disinfectants. They are not regularly effective, staphylococci and the organisms that cause diarrheal diseases are resistant
Soda Ash (or sodium carbonate)	It may be used in place of lye against certain diseases	5% solution (1 lb to 3 gal water). Most effective in hot solution	Commonly used as a cleaning agent, but has disinfectant properties, especially when used as a hot solution

4. *Hepatitis*—Infectious canine hepatitis, which is a serious disease of dogs, can be transmitted to commercially reared foxes and mink. For this reason, fox farms and mink farm operators should be discouraged from raising dogs or cats.

5. *Leptospirosis*—This disease of dogs is very important to stockmen since leptospirosis may be transmitted from dogs to other domestic animals, particularly to cattle, hogs, and even to foxes and cats. Thus, care should be taken to prevent the spread of leptospirosis by being sure that the dog is immune to this disease.

6. *Rabies*—Probably the most serious of all diseases of dogs transmitted to other animals is rabies. Cattle, sheep, hogs, horses, cats, and all other warm-blooded animals are susceptible to this disease and may be infected through the bite of a rabid dog. Fortunately, this disease can be readily controlled by immunizing all dogs and regulating the licensing, quarantine, and transportation of dogs. Although wild animals—skunks, foxes, etc.—also transmit rabies, the control of the disease in dogs is the best way in which to eliminate it.

7. *"Sheep measles"* (*Cysticercus ovis*—the larval stage of the tapeworm or bladder worm which causes it)—This species of bladder worm infects sheep and goats in many parts of the United States, especially in the West. The animals ingest the eggs voided on pastures by dogs or other carnivores. The developing embryos penetrate through the wall of the intestine, reach the liver by way of the bloodstream, enter the veins, thence travel to the heart, diaphragm, and muscles. No specific symptoms have been attributed to infection with these parasites, and it seems unlikely that many sheep die because of the presence of "sheep measles." The chief economic loss occurs at slaughter. Infected carcasses are trimmed or condemned, according to the degree of infection. It is to be noted, however, that the parasite is not transmissible to man, the removal or condemnation of affected carcasses merely being done because of the unattractive appearance. There is no known anthelmintic for the removal of *Cysticercus ovis* from sheep or goats. Frequent treatment of dogs offers the best hope of control.

DOG DISEASES AND PARASITES TRANSMISSIBLE TO MAN

The book *Diseases Transmitted From Animals to Man,* by Dr. Thomas G. Hull, lists sixty-five diseases of dogs that may be transmitted either directly or indirectly to man. Thus, it is necessary for the dog owner to understand the importance of such diseases and to know how they can be controlled or eliminated. Among these diseases and parasites are the following:

1. *Fleas*—Dogs may be infested with dog fleas, cat fleas, and human fleas. All of these types of fleas will attack humans, also. Where fleas are found, both children and adults can become contaminated with them. In addition to being irritating, fleas may transmit diseases of the bloodstream and septicemic infections from one person to another in the family. Additionally, fleas are a serious menace to people because they spread tapeworms and bubonic plague. It is most important to remember that the intermediate hosts of the double-pored tapeworm *(Dipylidium caninum)* are the dog flea, cat flea, and the dog louse.

Dog tapeworm eggs that may contaminate food or other material, or toys of children, may be taken into the mouth and thus develop into the intermediate cystic form in some organ of the human body.

2. *Hookworms*—In humans, hookworms are responsible for "creeping eruptions" of the skin. Hookworms lay eggs in the digestive tract of the dog. Then the eggs pass out with the feces. In about a week, the young larvae molt twice and are transformed into the infective stage. These infective larvae may penetrate the skin of people and produce a condition known as "creeping eruption," characterized by tortuous burrows in the superficial layers of the skin.

3. *Hydatid cyst*—The dog (or coyote) is a link in the life cycle of this smallest known tapeworm. It does no harm to the dog, but the eggs pass out through the droppings and may be picked up by man (or sheep) where they may form cysts in the liver, lungs, or brain. The cyst starts out about pea size, then grows like cancer to the size of an orange. In people it develops, eventually, to the size of a soccer ball. It is resistant to all germicidal insecticides and may or may not respond to surgery. In 1972, it was recorded that, up to that year, a total of ninety-four operations had been performed in California to remove cysts. It would appear, therefore, that the disease is on the increase for it was unknown in California until 1966.

4. *Leptospirosis*—this disease may be contracted by human beings from affected dogs, as well as

from affected rats or farm animals. It is advisable, therefore, to vaccinate all dogs for this disease and to be sure that the dog is not a healthy carrier of the infection.

5. *Rabies*—without doubt, rabies is the best known of the diseases transmitted by dogs to man. Also, it is the most deadly of all such diseases. Fortunately, the disease may be prevented in dogs by vaccination. Control programs instituted by state and local governments for the prevention of introduction or the elimination of rabies have practically eliminated the disease in the United States. If the disease appears in an area, vaccination is the major program to follow in prevention.

6. *Ringworm*—*Microsporum canias* is transmissible to man; hence, it is not uncommon for the owner and his dog to have similar lesions. For this reason, ringworm in dogs should be controlled, and people with dogs should avoid handling their dogs with their bare hands if they have ringworm.

7. *Visceral larva migrans*—this is the name given to the syndrome caused by larvae of *Toxocaris canis* (roundworm), which emerge from eggs when swallowed by children, either in dirt or as a result of close contact with infected dogs, primarily puppies. The syndrome is especially important in young children in whom the larvae migrate to the liver, lungs, and other organs, including the brain or eye, where they eventually perish. The signs include eosinophilia, pneumonitis, cough, dyspnea, enlargement of the liver, and hyperglobulinemia.

Diagnosis of visceral larva migrans requires demonstration of the parasite in specimens obtained by biopsy or necropsy. There is no specific treatment. In a majority of cases, there is complete recovery.

Control consists in ridding dogs of intestinal parasites at frequent intervals in order to safeguard young children from contracting roundworm infections normally occurring in dogs.

FIRST AID

John Steinbeck, the Nobel Prize-Winning author, in *Travels With Charley In Search of America*, lamented the lack of a good book on home dog treatment. Charley, of course, was the aged Poodle that accompanied his illustrious owner-author on the motor trip of America.

A dog owner should have some knowledge of basic first aids, just as everyone should know how to rescue and revive a drowning person. When applying first aid, however, one should never forget the old proverb that "A little knowledge is a dangerous thing." Remember that it is important to recognize your own limitations in knowledge and ability, and that you should not try to be an amateur practitioner. Remember, too, that you should follow up most first aid treatments with a visit to your veterinarian.

First aid may save a dog's life, but extensive damage may have been done that the untrained eye will fail to recognize. For example, a dog can be seriously hurt internally from a fall or being struck by a car and yet fail to show it until later when he will begin to hemorrhage. Thus, when such accidents happen, a checkup by your veterinarian is important.

FIRST AID KIT AND MEDICINE CHEST

The dog's first aid and medicine chest should contain those things most frequently needed by the owner, particularly during an emergency, when their availability and knowing how to use them may mean the difference between life and death of your pet. The author's recommendations for the First Aid and Medicine Chest follow:

1. *Instruments*—

Pliers	Tablespoon
Razor blades	Teaspoon
Rectal thermometer	Tweezers
Scissors (straight)	(large size)

2. *Dressings*—
   Adhesive tape
   Cotton (sterile)
   Gauze, 2" or 3" (for bandage)

3. *Medicines*—
   Activated charcoal (antidote for poisoning)
   Antiseptic dusting powder
   Aromatic spirits of ammonia (for shock)
   Aspirin
   Bicarbonate of soda
   Boric acid (for an eye wash)
   Dramamine or Bonamine (for car sickness)
   Flea and lice powder
   Hydrogen peroxide (an antiseptic)
   Kaopectate (for diarrhea)
   Metaphen or iodine
   Milk of bismuth
   Milk of magnesia or mineral oil (laxatives)
   Rubbing alcohol (a disinfectant)
   Salt (to induce vomiting)

Snake serum (in snake country)
Soap (germicidal)
Tannic acid ointment, or other burn ointment
Vaseline

HOW TO GIVE MEDICINE

Many times your veterinarian will give you medicines or pills to give to your dog. So you should know how to administer them. Instructions follow.

1. *How to give liquid medicines*—most veterinarians will give you a vial holding the exact amount of liquid that they wish to give. However, the method shown in Fig. 338 may be used for either a vial or a spoon. It is what is known as the *lip pocket method*. It consists in making the dog sit first. Then pull out his cheek to make a pouch. Put the vial or spoon into the cheek pouch and let the medicine drain into the throat. Be sure and keep the dog's head horizontal to the floor until he swallows.

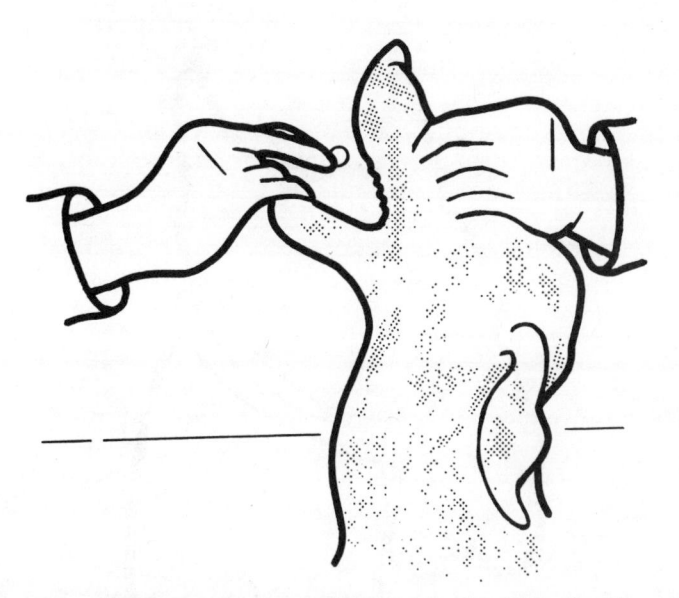

Fig. 339. How to give a pill or capsule. (Drawing by R. F. Johnson)

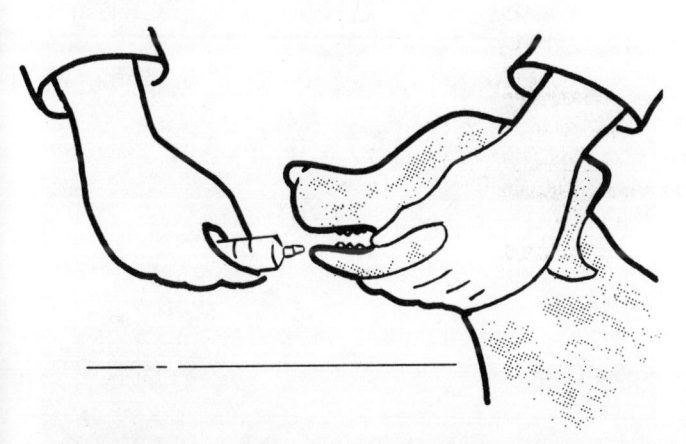

Fig. 338. How to give liquid medicine from a vial. (Drawing by R. F. Johnson)

2. *Pills*—Fig. 339 shows how to give a pill or capsule. First, make the dog sit. Then grasp his upper jaw with the left hand and press his lips against the teeth until the dog opens his mouth. With your right hand, pull his lower jaw down and extend your two longest fingers to push the pill down over his tongue, toward his throat. Close the mouth quickly and hold it shut until he swallows, then wait a few minutes to make sure that he doesn't regurgitate it.

TYING THE MOUTH SHUT

Although your dog may be your best friend and as docile as he can be, when frightened and in great pain, he may not recognize you, and he may bite you. So, any time that you are handling an injured or panic-stricken dog, use some means of restraint, or wear leather gloves, to keep him from biting you while you are trying to help him.

Fig. 340 shows a dog with his mouth tied shut. A bandage or strip of cloth about two feet long may be used (a necktie, cloth belt, or even a rope may be used in an emergency). First, wrap the material around the muzzle, then tie it under the chin, thence, bring it back of the ears and tie it again. The dog will be unable to get this off. Don't leave the mouth tied shut any longer than necessary, because a dog perspires through his tongue.

FIRST AID CHART

Table 39 lists many of the mishaps that may befall dogs and gives the first aid steps appropriate for each. It should be remembered that these are emergency measures only and that where medical treatment is required it is always wise to contact your veterinarian.

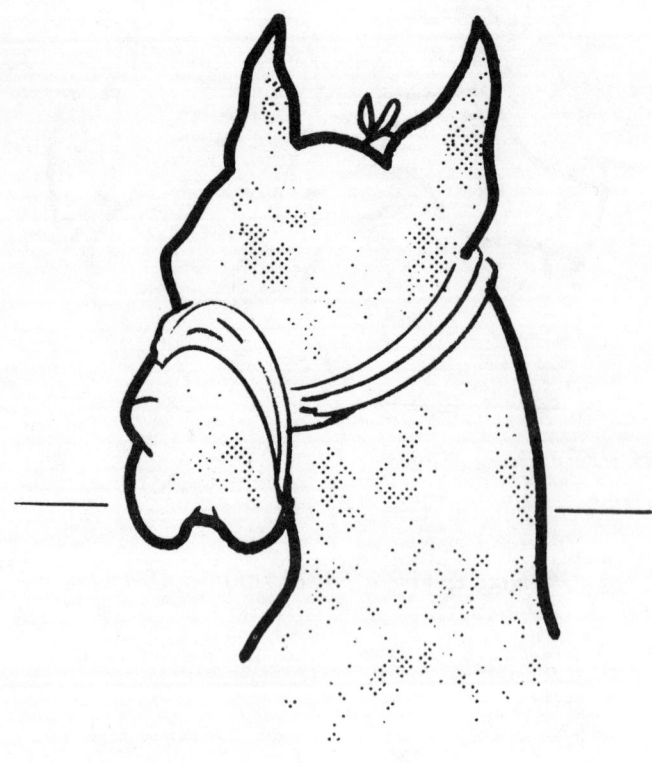

Fig. 340. Dog with his mouth tied shut. (Drawing by R. F. Johnson)

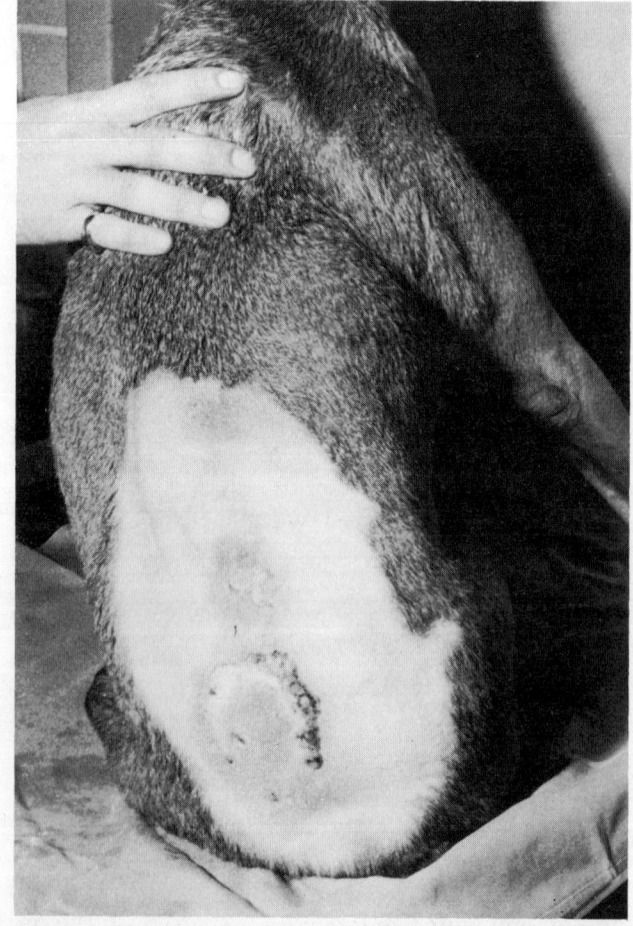

Fig. 341. A burn of the skin caused by a hot-water bottle. (Courtesy Dr. J. H. Reed, D.V.M., Ph.D., Ontario Veterinary College, University of Guelph, Guelph, Ontario, Canada)

TABLE 39

FIRST AID CHART

Problem or Injury	Signs	First Aid
Auto accident	More dogs are killed by motor cars than by disease. If the dog survives, the signs will usually be unmistakable and will vary in severity and location according to where the dog was hit and how hard	Don't move the dog. Apply restraint; check bleeding, and, if there is arterial bleeding (spurting) apply a tourniquet between the cut and the heart; and cover with a blanket. Then call the veterinarian
Bee sting (or other insect sting)	The dog gives evidence of shock and considerable pain. Occasionally, a dog is allergic to an insect sting, much like some people. In the latter case, he may be experiencing difficulty in breathing and appear to be passing out	Restrain the dog with a mouth tie. Then put a cold compress on the bite to help relieve the pain from the sting. If there is considerable swelling, apply a warm compress. If the dog appears faint, which is indicative of an allergy, take him to your veterinarian
Bites, dog	Dog bites result from dogs fighting other dogs. Puncture wounds result	Do not try forcibly to separate dogs. Throw a pail of cold water on them; rap each combatant on the rump with a strap; or throw a heavy towel or blanket over the head of the aggressor Treat as follows: Apply mouth tie; clean the wounds with soap and water; and then irrigate with a good antiseptic. Deep puncture wounds should receive veterinary attention

Bleeding	1. *Severe or deep cuts*—
	  a. Severed artery—Blood is bright red and flows in spurts
	  b. Severed vein—Blood is dark red and flows steadily
	2. *Internal bleeding*—As evidenced by weakness, prostration, and pale gray gums
		Apply mouth tie. If an artery is severed, apply tourniquet between the wound and the heart. If a vein is severed, apply the tourniquet on the other side of the wound—farthest from the heart. A pressure bandage may be used if a tourniquet is not possible, but the pressure should be released every 15–20 minutes, and this applies either to tourniquets or pressure bandages

Bruises	A bruise is actually a closed wound. Small blood vessels are ruptured and the soft tissue beneath the skin is damaged. The most common signs are pain, swelling, heat, and discoloration	Apply a cold compress and bandage the part firmly to limit the area of swelling. If the swelling has already developed and pain is great, apply a cold compress to relieve the pain
Burns, chemical	With severe burns, the dog will likely go into shock. In any event, there will be evidence of great pain, with the severity of the pain dependent upon the extensiveness of the burns	1. *Acid burns*—Apply alkaline solution: 1 pint warm water and 1 tbs of baking soda, or washing soda; or wash with milk of magnesia 2. *Caustic (alkali)*—Apply vinegar

(Continued)

TABLE 39 (CONTINUED)

FIRST AID CHART

Problem or Injury	Signs	First Aid
Burns, fire or hot water	Same as above for chemical burns	If more than a small area is involved, take the dog to your veterinarian. In the meantime, do not apply greases, ointments, or other home remedies
		If the burn is relatively minor, clip the hair from the area, apply lukewarm tea (for its tannic acid content) or cold water. Keep the dog warm if he seems to be in shock
Burrs	Burrs show up in the coat, especially on long-haired dogs that are allowed to roam in the country	Work the burrs out by hand, using the thumb and forefinger
Car sickness	Drooling and vomiting	Try to prevent car sickness by withholding the dog's food for an hour before starting on a trip, by limiting the amount of water that he drinks while in transit, and by giving him frequent opportunities to relieve himself during the travel. If these methods fail, consult your veterinarian, who may give your dog a Dramamine tablet or other motion-sickness pill. The latter should be given about an hour before starting a trip
Chewing gum	Matting of the hair by the gum	Remove from coat with a cleaning fluid of the carbon tetrachloride type, or harden with ice then break out
Cuts, scratches, and wounds	Generally, there will be bleeding, with the amount of bloodletting dependent upon the severity of the wound	Apply restraint. If slight, clean with soap and water, then apply an antiseptic. If the cut or wound is deep, follow the procedure indicated under "Bleeding" above
Dislocations (bones)	Intense pain Inability to stand or use legs	Immobilize the dog; carry on a stretcher. Take to your veterinarian
Drowning	Drowning will be unmistakable	Hold the dog by his hind legs to drain the water from the breathing passages. Then lay him on the side and resuscitate by pressing ribs in and out slowly every 2 seconds. If the dog is unconscious, try to revive him with spirits of ammonia under his nose. Keep him warm

(Continued)

TABLE 39 (CONTINUED)

FIRST AID CHART

Problem or Injury	Signs	First Aid
Electric shock	This usually happens as a result of a dog chewing an electric cord	Don't touch the dog, unless you are wearing rubber gloves, until the wire is detached from him. Protect your hand with a rubber glove or a thick dry towel, then pull the cord from the socket. If the dog has collapsed, hold ammonia under his nose, then apply artificial respiration as follows: Place the dog on his side with his head low, press on abdomen and rib cage, releasing pressure at 1–2 second intervals. Keep dog warm. Seek professional help
Eye trouble	Inflammation, cuts, or scratches	Wash the eye either with boric acid solution or a mild solution of salt water Plain water may be irritating to the eyes. Apply yellow oxide of mercury (1%), or similar eye ointment
Falls	Dog may be unconscious or in pain, depending upon the severity of the fall	Keep dog quiet. If bones are broken or there appears to be internal damage, do not move the dog except on a stretcher
Fighting (see Bites)		
Fish hooks	Usually, the dog will paw at the area where the hook is embedded. Generally fish hooks are lodged in the lip, mouth, or foot	If the hook is implanted, the easiest way to remove it is to push it through so that the barbed end of the hook is exposed. Then cut off the barbed portion with pliers and pull the shank of the hook out the same way it entered. Treat the wound with antiseptic
Food poisoning	Pain, trembling, and convulsions	Promptly induce vomiting by placing 2 tsp of salt on the back of the dog's tongue. When vomiting stops, give egg white
Foot troubles	Limping or chewing at the pad	Examine the dog's feet. Remove any burrs, grass, thorns, mud, rocks, or ice or snow that may be present
Foreign objects swallowed	If lodged in the throat, the dog will show signs of choking, coughing, pawing at the mouth, and shaking the head If lodged in the intestinal tract, there may be persistent vomiting	If the object is still in the mouth or throat, reach in and remove it. Objects that are small, smooth, or soft may not give any trouble if they have gotten past the throat Where the object is deeply embedded in the throat, or where it is sharp—even though it has been swallowed, veterinary attention is recommended

(Continued)

TABLE 39 (CONTINUED)

FIRST AID CHART

Problem or Injury	Signs	First Aid
Fracture (of bones)	Inability to stand or use leg or legs; intense pain; shock	Restrain and muzzle. Keep in position as well as possible; apply temporary splint to leg bones, if they are involved; immobilize—carry on stretcher; and take to your veterinarian. Until you reach the veterinarian, keep the dog warm and quiet
Frostbite	Because of the weather and the location of the dog, frostbite will usually be evident when it occurs	Bring the dog into a warm area and gradually thaw out the frozen part. If there is no warm area available, warm the frozen part with your hand, a blanket, or whatever soft object is available. *But do not rub the frozen area with snow or ice*
Grass seeds or awns in ear or eye	The dog will usually try to scratch the ear or eye, as the case may be, with his paw	Remove from the ear with tweezers or cotton swab Remove from the eye by blowing or with a cotton swab
Heatstroke (or sunstroke)	Staggering or lying prostrate; rapid breathing; rapid pulse; inability to focus eyes; and vomiting	Reduce the body temperature as quickly as possible. Put the dog in a quiet, cool spot. Apply cool wet towels or keep sponging with cold water
Nails (toe), broken	Lameness	Smooth any ragged edges with a file or emery paper. Tape if necessary
Nervousness	Excited	Remove the cause, or remove the dog from the site of the cause. Calm the dog
Porcupine quills	Presence of quills; dog in pain	Apply a mouth tie; apply vinegar to soften the quills; and, by means of tweezers or pliers, twist each quill one full turn and pull out. Apply hydrogen peroxide to bleeding wounds

Poisoning [common poisons of dogs include
  Antu (rat poison)
  Antifreeze
  Arsenic
  Chlorinated hydrocarbons
  Lead poisoning
  Phosphates, organic
  Red squill
  Strychnine
  Thallium
  Warfarin]
	Trembling, abdominal pain, drooling, convulsions, shallow breathing, eventual coma	Proceed with haste in the following order:
		1. If container of poison is handy, use recommended antidote printed thereon
		2. If information called for in step 1 is not available, induce vomiting by making a strong solution of household salt in water and forcing as much as possible into the dog's throat, using the lip pocket method
		3. Contact your veterinarian. If your veterinarian cannot be reached immediately, or if no other vet is available, try to get some advice from an M.D. or registered nurse

(Continued)

TABLE 39 (CONTINUED)

FIRST AID CHART

Problem or Injury	Signs	First Aid
Shock	Breathing is shallow, pulse is feeble, and gums are white	Let the dog sniff spirits of ammonia Lower dog's head Keep dog warm and quiet Call the veterinarian
Sprains	Tenderness and swelling at the joint, and evident pain when there is sudden pressure on it	The treatment followed is the same as recommended for fracture, because you may not be able to tell the difference. This means that you should restrain the dog, confine him, keep the affected joint immobilized by applying a splint, and call a veterinarian
Stomach upset	Nervousness, distress, and gas	Give milk of bismuth in following doses: body weight up to 10 lb, ¼ tsp; body weights from 10–25 lb, ½ tsp; body weights from 25–75 lb, 1 tsp; over 75 lb, body weight, ¾ tbs For more severe cases, brandy in the same doses indicated above, but diluted with an equal volume of water may be helpful
Sunstroke (see Heatstroke)		
Swallowing foreign objects (see Foreign objects)		
Skunk odor	The odor will be unmistakable Usually, the dog gets sprayed in the eyes; hence, he may be seen pawing at his eyes	Wash the eyes well with either (1) boric acid solution, or (2) a mild salt-water solution, of ½ tsp of salt to ½ glass warm water. Then apply an eye ointment To get the odor out of the dog's coat, wash him in tomato juice, followed by warm water and laundry soap. Then rinse with 5% solution of ammonia

(Continued)

TABLE 39 (CONTINUED)

FIRST AID CHART

Problem or Injury	Signs	First Aid
Snake bite	The venom of a poisonous snake travels quickly to the nerves of the dog and is followed by severe pain and swelling	Quick action is necessary Do not let the dog walk. Apply tourniquet. If veterinarian is not immediately available, proceed as follows: Slash wound with a razor blade or sharp knife; squeeze out blood, then suck wound with snake-bite suction cup or your mouth (if your mouth has no cuts or sores). Wash with full-strength hydrogen peroxide If a veterinarian is available, rush the dog to him for an antivenom shot
Tail injured	Depending on the seriousness of the injury, the dog evidences pain	If the tail is bruised, treat it with compresses soaked with boric acid or epsom salts (follow the directions on the label for the proper solution). If the skin is broken, wash out the area with peroxide or boric acid solution, then apply an ointment If the tail is broken, call upon the veterinarian to set it
Thorn in foot	Lameness; favoring the foot with the thorn in it	Remove the thorn with tweezers. Apply antiseptic
Thunder, fear of	Excited. Trying to get into the house. Seeking a dark place	Get the dog in a dark place. Upon the advice of your veterinarian, a mild sedative may be given
Unconsciousness (from concussion or stroke)	A concussion or stroke will result in the following signs: The dog will fall on his side, breathing will become slow and shallow, the pulse will be weak, the pupils enlarged, the body may feel cold and the inside of the lips may become pale and whitish	Keep the dog warm and quiet; call the veterinarian; but do not give stimulants
Wounds (see Cuts)		

9
Business Aspects of Kennels

Chapter 9
Capital	395
Credit	396
Types of Credit	396
Credit Factors Considered and Evaluated by Lenders	396
Credit Factors Considered by Borrowers	397
Helpful Hints for Building and Maintaining a Good Credit Rating	398
Calculating Interest	398
Budgets in the Kennel Business	399
How to Set up a Budget	399
How to Figure Net Income	399
Enterprise Accounts	399
Bookkeeping	402
Why Keep Books?	402
Kind of Record and Account Book	402
Kinds of Records to Keep	402
Summarizing and Analyzing the Records	403
Computers in the Kennel Business	403
Computers in Dog Breeding Operations	404
Management	404
Traits of a Good Manager	404
Incentive Basis for the Help	405
Indirect Incentives	406
Selling Dogs; Customer Relationships	406
Dog Owners and Income Taxes	409
Cash vs Accrual Method	410
Hobby or Business?	410
Capital Gain	410
In the Event of a Court Case	410
Insurance	411
Liability	411
Estate Planning	411
Inheritance and Partnerships	411

Fig. 342. The business aspects of kennels. (Drawing by J. L. Medeiros, Clovis, Calif.)

BUSINESS ASPECTS OF KENNELS[1]

In the present era, many kennels are owned and operated as businesses, with a profit motive—just as other animal producers have cattle, sheep, swine, or horse enterprises. These kennel owners must treat their operations as businesses and become more sophisticated; otherwise, they won't be in business very long. Others keep dogs as a hobby—for much the same reason that some folks play golf, fish, or go boating. When kept as a hobby, the cost should be looked upon much like that of any other hobby or an evening's entertainment; that is, decide in advance how much you can afford to spend, then stop when that amount has been reached.

There was a time when dog-hobbyists (like those who show, hunt, or race dogs, but who may also raise a few pups to sell) operated much like most fishermen, who do not wish to be reminded of the cost per pound of their catch. The guiding philosophy of these hobbyists was very similar to that of the story attributed to J. Pierpont Morgan, who once admonished an inquiring friend that, "If you have to ask what it costs to maintain a yacht, you can't afford it." But this attitude among dog-hobbyists has changed, primarily because of inheritance taxes making it increasingly difficult to pass wealth from one generation to the next, and closer scrutiny of tax write-offs. Also, even when dogs are kept primarily for the fun of it, most owners will derive more pleasure when the operation isn't too costly—it's a matter of pride and a challenge. For these reasons, more and more folks who keep dogs primarily for pleasure, like those who keep dogs for profit, are interested in improving the business aspects of their enterprises.

CAPITAL

Kennel owners who are in business to make a profit should never invest money, either their own or borrowed, unless they are reasonably certain that it will make money. Capital will be needed for land, buildings, equipment, dogs, feed, supplies, labor, and miscellaneous items.

Whether establishing or enlarging a kennel enterprise, the most common question, a two-pronged one, is: how much money will it take, and how much will it make? This information is needed by both kennel owners and lenders. Unfortunately, a simple answer cannot be given.

The following guides relative to costs, or capital needs, will be helpful:

1. *Land, buildings, equipment, and dog and labor costs*—Generally speaking, it is not too difficult to arrive at these costs.

The Kennel owner can easily determine the prevailing price of land in the area under consideration, either by inquiring of local land owners or reputable realtors. Where new buildings must be constructed, local architects or building contractors can quote approximate costs on a square foot basis. Likewise, dealers can give prices on major items of equipment.

Dog prices vary widely, by breed and age, and according to breeding and quality. Nevertheless, an established and knowledgeable kennel owner will usually give an assist to a newcomer in establishing the prevailing price for the breed, age, and quality desired. Also, going wages can usually be determined rather easily for a particular area.

2. *Food, veterinarian, and drug costs*—Ask other kennel owners for these figures, on a cost per dog basis. Usually, they'll be helpful, although, somewhat apologetically, they may admit that they do not keep very good records and, therefore, are estimating. However, if you are able to get several such estimates, even if they are from different sections of the country, then strike an average, the figure that you come up with will be pretty close. Of course, you can always make adjustments on food costs for different size dogs; for example, if you are going to breed Great Danes, you'll have to increase the estimated food costs of the kennel that breeds English Setters.

3. *Size of kennel enterprise*—Generally speaking, larger dog enterprises contribute to increased profits for the following reasons:

   a. They result in fewer hours of labor per dog.

   b. They are more apt to be used to capacity.

For example, if for an establishment producing 200 puppies per year, the depreciation, interest, repairs, insurance, and taxes run $6,000 annually, that's $30 per pup. If the same facilities were used to produce 400 pups per year, the cost would be lessened to $15

---
[1] The author acknowledges with thanks the authoritative review accorded this chapter by: Mr. Herbert N. Holmes, Gunsmoke Kennels, 1541 East Lake Shore Drive, Springfield, Illinois 62705.

per pup. This shows how increased numbers can reduce the building and equipment cost per pup.

CREDIT

Credit is an integral part of today's businesses of all kinds. Wise use of it can be profitable, but unwise use of it can be disastrous. Accordingly, kennel owners should know more about it. They need to know something about the lending agencies available, the types of credit, how to go about obtaining a loan, and methods of computing interest.

The common lending sources of credit are: commercial banks, production credit associations, federal land banks, individuals and other private lenders, life insurance companies, merchants and dealers, and the Farm Home Administration.

TYPES OF CREDIT

Following are the three general types of credit to consider, based on length of life and type of collateral needed:

1. *Short-term or production credit*—This is for up to one year. It is used for purchase of food and operating expenses.

2. *Intermediate credit*—This type of credit may be from one to seven years. It is used for the purchase of breeding stock, equipment, and semipermanent investments. Repayment is made from the profits over several production periods.

3. *Long-term credit*—This type of credit is used for land and major buildings, and for physical plant construction. Repayment is made over several years, from profits.

CREDIT FACTORS CONSIDERED AND EVALUATED BY LENDERS

Potential money borrowers sometimes make their first big mistake by going in "cold" to see a lender—without adequate facts and figures, with the result that they already have two strikes against them regarding their getting the loan.

When considering and reviewing loan requests, the lender tries to arrive at the repayment ability of the potential borrower. Likewise, the borrower has no reason to obtain money unless it will make money.

Lenders need certain basic information in order to evaluate the soundness of a loan request. To this end, the following information should be submitted:

1. *Analysis and feasibility study*—Lenders are impressed with a borrower who has a written-down feasibility study, showing where he is now, where he's going, and how he expects to get there. In addition to spelling out the goals, this report should give assurance of the necessary management skills to achieve them. Such an analysis of the present and projection into the future is imperative in big operations.

2. *The applicant, kennel, and financial statement*—It is the borrower's obligation, and in his best interest, to present the following information to the lender:

a. *The applicant:*

(1) Name of applicant and wife; age of applicant

(2) Number of children (minors, legal age)

(3) Partners in business, if any

(4) Years in area

(5) References.

b. *The kennel:*

(1) Owner or tenant

(2) Location; legal description and county, and direction and distance from nearest town

(3) Type of enterprise: breeding, training, boarding, or a combination.

c. *Financial statement:* This document indicates the borrower's financial record and current financial position, his potential ahead, and his liability to others. The borrower should always have sufficient slack to absorb reasonable losses due to such unforeseen happenstances as storms, diseases, and recessions, thereby permitting the lender to stay with him in adversity and to give him a chance to recoup his losses in the future. The financial statement should include the following:

(1) Current assets:

(a) Dogs

(b) Equipment

(c) Cash—there should be reasonable cash reserves, to cut interest costs, and to provide a cushion against emergencies

(d) Bonds or other investments

(e) Cash value of life insurance.

(2) Fixed assets:

(a) Real property, with estimated value

(b) Kennel property
(c) City property
(d) Long-term contracts.
(3) Current liabilities:
(a) Mortgages
(b) Contracts
(c) Open account—to whom owed
(d) Cosigner or guarantor on notes
(e) Any taxes due
(f) Current portion of real estate indebtedness due.
(4) Fixed liabilities—amount and nature of real estate debt:
(a) Date due
(b) Interest rate
(c) To whom payable
(d) Contract or mortgage.

3. *Other factors*—Shrewd lenders usually ferret out many things, among them:

a. *The potential borrower*—Most lenders will tell the potential borrower that he is the most important part of the loan. Lenders consider his:
(1) Character
(2) Honesty and integrity
(3) Experience and ability
(4) Moral and credit rating
(5) Age and health
(6) Family cooperation
(7) Continuity, or line of succession.

Lenders are quick to sense the "high-liver"—the fellow who lives beyond his income; the poor manager—the kind who would have made it except for hard luck, and to whom the hard luck has happened many times; and the dishonest, lazy, and incompetent.

In recognition of the importance of the man back of the loan, "key man" insurance on the owner or manager should be considered by both the lender and the borrower.

b. *Production records*—This refers to a good set of records showing efficiency of production. On a dog breeding establishment, for example, such records should show prices of dogs sold, pups per litter, replacement program, depreciation schedule, and other pertinent information. Lenders will increasingly insist on good records.

c. *Progress with previous loans*—Has the borrower paid back previous loans plus interest? Has he reduced the amount of the loan, thereby giving evidence of progress?

d. *Profit and loss (P & L)*—This serves as a valuable guide to the potential ahead. Preferably, this should cover the previous three years. Also, most lenders prefer that this be on an accrual basis (even if the kennel is on a cash basis in reporting to the Internal Revenue Service).

e. *Physical plant*—
(1) Is it an economic unit?
(2) Does it have adequate water?
(3) Is there adequate diversification; for example, in breeding, training, and boarding?
(4) Is the right kind of kennel enterprise being conducted?
(5) Are the right breeds being produced and handled; are approved methods of feeding, disease prevention, and parasite control being followed?
(6) Is the kennel neat and well kept?

f. *Collateral (or security)*—
(1) Adequate to cover loan, with margin
(2) Quality of security:
(a) Grade and age of dogs
(b) Type and condition of equipment.
(3) Identification of security:
(a) Tattoo on dogs
(b) Serial numbers on equipment.

4. *The loan request*—Kennel owners are in competition for money from urban businessmen. Hence, it is important that their request for a loan be well presented and supported. The potential borrower should tell the purpose of the loan, how much money is needed, when it's needed, the soundness of the venture, and the repayment schedule.

CREDIT FACTORS CONSIDERED BY BORROWERS

Credit is a two-way street; it must be good for both the borrower and the lender. If a borrower is the right kind of person and on a sound basis, more than one lender will want his business. Thus, it is usually well that a borrower shop around a bit, that he be familiar with several sources of credit and what they have to offer. There are basic differences in length and type of loan, repayment schedules, services provided with the loan, interest rate, and the ability and willingness of lenders to stick by the borrower in emergencies and times of adversity. Thus, interest rates and willingness to loan are only two of the several factors to consider. Also, if at all possible, all borrowing should be done from one source; a one-source lender will know more about the borrower's operations and be in a better position to help him.

HELPFUL HINTS FOR BUILDING AND MAINTAINING A GOOD CREDIT RATING

Kennel owners who wish to build up and maintain good credit are admonished to do the following:

1. *Keep credit in one place, or in few places*—Generally, lenders frown upon "split financing." Shop around for a creditor (a) who is able, willing, and interested in extending the kind and amount of credit needed, and (b) who will lend at a reasonable rate of interest; then stay with him.

2. *Get the right kind of credit*—Don't use short-term credit to finance long-term improvements or other capital investments.

3. *Be frank with the lender*—Be completely open and aboveboard. Mutual confidence and esteem should prevail between borrower and lender.

4. *Keep complete and accurate records*—Complete and accurate records should be kept by enterprises—breeding, training, boarding, etc. By knowing the cost of doing business, decision-making can be on a sound basis.

5. *Keep annual inventory*—Take an annual inventory for the purpose of showing progress made during the year.

6. *Repay loans when due*—Borrowers should work out a repayment schedule on each loan, then meet payments when due. Sale proceeds should be promptly applied on loans.

7. *Plan ahead*—Analyze the next year's operation and project ahead.

CALCULATING INTEREST

The total cost of using credit varies according to rate of and method of computing interest, and length of time the loan is needed. There are four commonly used methods of calculating interest, namely:

1. *Flat rate of interest (or simple interest) methods*—In which a specified rate of interest is paid on the original amount of the loan. For example, if $1,000 is borrowed for 12 months at 8% interest, the total interest will be $80.

2. *Added-on interest method*—In which the interest is added to the principal at the time the loan is made. Thus, if the loan at 8% interest is repaid in 12 equal monthly installments, the true interest rate will be 14.77%, because the interest is charged on the total original amount of the loan and does not decrease with each successive payment.

3. *Unpaid balance method*—In which interest is paid only on the amount that has not been repaid. Thus, if $1,000 is borrowed for 12 months at 8% interest, but half the original loan is repaid at the end of 6 months, 6 months' interest would be saved on $500. Hence, the interest on this $500 would be 4%, whereas the interest on the remaining $500 not repaid until the end of the 12 months would be 8%. Thus, the total interest cost would be $60.

4. *Points*—Points are a loan fee, paid in advance. Each point is 1% of the loan. For example, on a $1,000 loan at 8% and 3 points, the borrower will actually receive only $970 ($1,000 X .03 = $30. Then $1,000 — 30 = 970). Thus, the true interest rate on $970 would be 8.25% ($80÷970 = 8.25%). Also, if the borrower needs a minimum of $1,000, he must request a larger than $1,000 loan where points are required.

TABLE 40

TRUE INTEREST RATES ON A $1,000 LOAN, BY FOUR METHODS OF COMPUTING

Method of Computing Interest	Principal (12 mo.)	Interest @ 8%	Total to Repay	Effective Interest Rate
1. Flat rate of interest: paid in one sum at end of loan period....	$1,000	$80	$1,080	8%
2. Added-on interest: principal repaid in equal monthly installments..	$1,000	$80	$1,080	14.77%
3. Unpaid balance: $500 paid in 6 mos., $500 at end of 12 mos...	$1,000	$60	$1,060	8%
4. Points (3 points)	$1,000	$80	$1,000	8.25%

Table 40 shows the true interest rate of a $1,000 loan, with the interest computed by each of the above methods.

BUDGETS IN THE KENNEL BUSINESS

A budget is a projection of records and accounts and a plan for organizing and operating ahead for a specific period of time. A short-time budget is usually for one year, whereas a long-time budget is for a period of years. The principal value of a budget is that it provides a working plan through which the operation can be coordinated. Changes in prices, diseases, and other factors make adjustments necessary. But these adjustments are more simply and wisely made if there is a written budget to use as a reference.

HOW TO SET UP A BUDGET

It's unimportant whether a printed form (of which there are many good ones) is used or one made up on an ordinary ruled 8½" x 11" sheet placed sidewise. The important things are that (1) a budget is kept, (2) it be on a monthly basis, and (3) the operator be "comfortable" with whatever form or system is to be used.

An important part of any budget, or any system of accounting, is that there shall be a listing, or chart, of classifications or categories under which the owner wants the transactions accumulated. In a kennel operation that both breeds and boards, there may be twenty or more such classifications. From the standpoint of facilitating record keeping, each classification is usually given a number for identification purposes. Then the bookkeeper, or the kennel manager, codes or classifies each transaction into the proper category.

No budget is perfect. But it should be as good an estimate as can be made—despite the fact that it will be affected by such things as recessions, diseases, and many other unpredictables.

A simple, easily kept, and adequate budget can be evolved by using forms such as those shown in Tables 41, 42, and 43.

The Annual Cash Expense Budget should show the monthly breakdown of various recurring items —everything except the initial loan and capital improvements. It includes labor, food, supplies, insecticides and vermifuges, taxes, interest, utilities, etc.

The Annual Cash Income Budget is just what the name implies—an estimated cash income by months.

The Annual Cash Expense and Income Budget is a cash flow chart obtained from the first two forms. It's a money "flow" summary by months. From this, it can be ascertained when money will need to be borrowed, how much will be needed, and the length of the loan, along with a repayment schedule. It makes it possible to avoid tying up capital unnecessarily, and to avoid unnecessary interest.

HOW TO FIGURE NET INCOME

Table 43 shows a gross income statement. There are other expenses that must be taken care of before net profit is determined, namely:

1. *Depreciation on buildings and equipment*— It is suggested that the "useful life" of multiunit kennel buildings and equipment be as follows, with depreciation accordingly:
Buildings—25 years
Equipment—10 years.
Sometimes a higher depreciation, or amortization, is desirable because it produces tax savings and is protection against obsolescence due to scientific and technological developments.

2. *Interest on owner's money invested in kennel* —This should be computed at the going rate in the area, say 8%.

ENTERPRISE ACCOUNTS

When one has a diversified kennel—for example, when producing puppies for sale, training dogs, and boarding dogs—enterprise accounts should be kept; in this case three different accounts for three different enterprises. The reasons for keeping enterprise accounts are:

1. It makes it possible to determine which enterprises have been most profitable; and which least profitable.

2. It makes it possible to compare a given enterprise with competing enterprises of similar types, from the standpoint of ascertaining comparative performance.

3. It makes it possible to determine the profitableness of an enterprise at the margin (the last unit of production). This will give an indication as to whether to increase the size of a certain en-

TABLE 41

ANNUAL CASH EXPENSE BUDGET

For _____
(name of kennel)   (date)

Item	Total	Jan.	Feb.	Mar.	Apr.	May	June	July	Aug.	Sept.	Oct.	Nov.	Dec.
Labor hired													
Food purchased													
Stud fees													
Gas, fuel, grease													
Taxes													
Insurance													
Interest													
Utilities													
Miscellaneous													
Total													

TABLE 42

ANNUAL CASH INCOME BUDGET

_____
(name of kennel)

For _____
(date)

Item	Total	Jan.	Feb.	Mar.	Apr.	May	June	July	Aug.	Sept.	Oct.	Nov.	Dec.
200 puppies													
30 stud fees @ $100													
50 boarders													
Miscellaneous													
Total													

TABLE 43

ANNUAL CASH EXPENSE AND INCOME BUDGET (CASH FLOW CHART)

_____
(name of kennel)

For _____
(date)

Item	Total	Jan.	Feb.	Mar.	Apr.	May	June	July	Aug.	Sept.	Oct.	Nov.	Dec.
Gross income													
Gross expense													
Difference													
Surplus (+) Deficit (−)													

terprise at the expense of an alternative existing enterprise when both enterprises are profitable in total.

BOOKKEEPING

A modern kennel operation is more than a job; it is a business. Therefore, it should be conducted in a businesslike manner. This means that there should be adequate records and accounts; or bookkeeping.

WHY KEEP BOOKS?

The chief functions of kennel records and accounts are:

1. To provide information from which the kennel business may be analyzed, with its strong and its weak points ascertained. From the facts thus determined, the operator may adjust current operations and develop a more effective plan of organization

2. To provide a net worth statement, showing financial progress during the year

3. To furnish an accurate, but simple, net income statement for use in filing tax returns

4. To keep production records on dogs

5. To aid in making a credit statement when a loan is needed

6. To keep a complete historical record of financial transactions for future reference.

KIND OF RECORD AND ACCOUNT BOOK

A kennel operator or manager, can make his own record book by simply ruling off the pages of a bound notebook to fit his specific needs, but the saving is negligible. Instead, it is recommended that he obtain a copy of a farm record book prepared for and adapted to his area. Such a book may usually be obtained at a nominal cost from the agricultural economics department of each state college of agriculture. Also, certain commercial companies distribute very acceptable record and account books at no cost.

KINDS OF RECORDS TO KEEP

Most record and account books contain simple and specific instructions relative to their use. Accordingly, it is neither necessary nor within the realm of this book to provide such instructions. Instead, the comments made herein are restricted to the kinds of records to keep.

At the outset, it should be recognized that a kennel record should be easy to keep and should give the information desired to make a valuable analysis of the business. In general, the functions enumerated under the earlier section entitled "Why Keep Books" can be met by the following kinds of records.

1. *Annual inventory*—The annual inventory is the most valuable record that a kennel can keep. It should include a list and value of real estate, dogs, equipment, food, supplies, and all other property, including cash on hand, notes and bills receivable. Also, it should include a list of mortgages, notes, and bills payable. It shows the kennel owner what he owns and what he owes; whether he is getting ahead or going behind. The following pointers may be helpful relative to the annual inventory.

a. *Time to take inventory*—The inventory should be taken at the beginning of the account year; usually this means Dec. 31 or Jan. 1.

b. *Proper and complete listing*—It is important that each item be properly and separately listed.

c. *Method of arriving at inventory values*—It is difficult to set up any hard and fast rule to follow in estimating values when taking inventories. Perhaps the following guides are as good as any:

(1) *Real estate*—Estimating the value of kennel real estate is, without doubt, the most difficult of all. It is suggested that the kennel owner use either (a) the cost of the kennel, (b) the present sale value of the kennel, or (c) the capitalized rent value according to its productive ability with an average operator.

(2) *Buildings*—Buildings are generally inventoried on the basis of cost less observed depreciation and obsolescence. Once the original value of a building is arrived at, it is usually best to take depreciation on a straight line basis by dividing the original value by the estimated life in terms of years. Usually four percent or more depreciation is charged off each year for income tax purposes.

(3) *Dogs*—Dogs are usually not too difficult to inventory because there are gen-

erally sufficient current sales to serve as a reliable estimate of value.

(4) *Equipment*—The inventory value of equipment is usually arrived at by either of two methods: (a) the original cost less a reasonable allowance for depreciation each year, or (b) the probable price that it would bring at a well-attended auction.

Under conditions of ordinary wear and reasonable care, it can be assumed that the general run of equipment (except trucks and autos) will last about ten years. Thus, with new equipment, the annual depreciation will be the original cost divided by ten.

(5) *Food and supplies*—The value of food and supplies can be based on market price.

Two further points are important. Whatever method is used in arriving at inventory value (a) should be followed at both the beginning and the end of the year, and (b) should reflect the operator's opinion of the value of the property involved.

2. *Record of receipts and expenses*—Such a record is essential to any type of well-managed business. To be most useful, these entries should not only record the amount of the transaction, but should give the source of the income or the purpose of the expense, as the case may be. In other words, they should show the owner from what sources the income is derived and for what it is spent.

The following kinds and arrangements of record books are commonly used for recording receipts and expenditures:

a. Those that devote a separate page to each enterprise; that is, a separate page is used for the breeding enterprise, another for training, another for boarding, and so on.

b. Those that provide for a record of receipts and expenses on the same page, using one column for receipts and another for expenses. This type is easy to keep, but very difficult to analyze from the standpoint of any particular enterprise.

c. Those that combine the features of both "a" and "b" above. The latter are more difficult to keep than the others, and may be confusing to the person keeping the record.

Household and personal accounts should be kept, but should be handled entirely separate from kennel accounts because they are not kennel expenses as such.

3. *Record of animal production*—A record of the production and sale of puppies is most important, for the success of the kennel depends upon production. Such records help in analyzing the kennel business. They may be few or many, depending upon the wishes of the operator.

SUMMARIZING AND ANALYZING THE RECORDS

At the end of the year, the second or closing inventory should be taken, using the same method as was followed in taking the initial inventory. The final summary should then be made, following which the records should be analyzed. In the latter connection, the kennel owner should remember that the purpose of the analysis is not to prove that he has or has not been prosperous. He probably knows the answer to this question already. Rather, the analysis should show actual conditions of the kennel and point out ways in which these conditions may be improved.

Although the kennel owner or manager can summarize and analyze his own records, there are many advantages in having the services of a specialist for this purpose. Such a specialist is in a better position to make a "cold" appraisal without prejudice, and to compare enterprises with those of other similar operators. Thus, the specialist may discover that, in comparison with other operators, the dogs in a given kennel are requiring too much food, or that the enterprise is much less profitable than others have experienced. This may best be done by engaging the services of a consultant.

COMPUTERS IN THE KENNEL BUSINESS

Accurate and up-to-the-minute records and controls have taken on increasing importance in all businesses, including the kennel business, as the investment required to engage therein has risen. Today's successful kennels must have, and use, as complete records as any other business. Also, records must be kept current.

Big and complex enterprises have outgrown hand record keeping. It's too time consuming, with the result that it doesn't allow management enough time for planning and decision making. Additionally, it does not permit an all-at-once consideration of the complex interrelationships that affect the economic success of the business. This has prompted a new computer technique known as *linear programming*.

Linear programming is similar to budgeting, in that it compares several plans simultaneously and chooses from among them the one likely to yield the highest returns. It is a way in which to analyze a great mass of data and consider many alternatives. It is not a managerial genie, nor will it replace decision-making managers. However, it is a modern and effective tool in the present age, when just a few dollars per dog can spell the difference between profit and loss.

COMPUTERS IN DOG BREEDING OPERATIONS

In the past, the biggest deterrent to adequate records in kennel breeding establishments has been the voluminous and time-consuming record keeping involved. Keeping records as such does not change what an animal will transmit, but records must be used to locate and propagate the genetically superior animals if genetic improvement is to be accomplished. Also, records are requisite to good management.

Computerized records can be used for breeding record purposes—as a means of keeping management up-to-date and as an alert on problems to be solved or work to be done. Each animal must be individually identified. Reports can be obtained at such intervals as desired, usually monthly or every two weeks. Also, the owner can keep as complete or as few records as desired. Here are several of the records that can be kept by computer:

1. Pedigrees.
2. Records of dogs that need attention, such as:

    a. Dogs of a certain age that are unregistered

    b. Dogs ready for inspection or scoring

    c. Bitches that have been bred two consecutive times

    d. Bitches that have not conceived

    e. Bitches due to whelp in fourteen days

    f. Puppies five months of age that haven't been weaned

    g. Dogs that have not received their vaccinations; for example, that have not been vaccinated against rabies, leptospirosis, hepatitis, etc

    h. Dogs that have not been treated for parasites at the scheduled time.

3. A running or cumulative inventory of the kennel, by sex; including puppies born, litters due, and purchases and sales—in number of dogs and dollars.

4. The depreciation of purchased animals according to the accounting method of choice.

MANAGEMENT

Management is *the act, art, or manner of managing, or handling, controlling, directing, etc.*

Three major ingredients are essential to success in the kennel business: (1) good dogs, (2) a sound nutrition and health program, and (3) good management.

Management gives point and purpose to everything else. The skill of the manager materially affects how well dogs are bought and sold, the health of the animals, the results of the rations, the stresses of the dogs, the growth rate of puppies, the performance of labor, the public relations of the establishment, and even the expression of the genetic potential of the dogs. Indeed, a manager must wear many hats—and he must wear each of them well.

The bigger and the more complicated the kennel operation, the more competent the management required. This point merits emphasis because, currently, bigness is a sign of the times, and the most common method of attempting to "bail out" of an unprofitable kennel venture is to increase its size. Although it's easier to achieve efficiency of equipment, labor, purchases, and marketing in big operations, bigness alone will not make for greater efficiency, as some owners have discovered to their sorrow, and others will experience. Management is still the key to success. When in financial trouble, owners should have no illusions on this point.

In manufacturing and commerce, the importance and scarcity of top managers are generally recognized and reflected in the salaries paid to persons in such positions. Unfortunately, kennel operators as a whole have lagged; and altogether too many owners still subscribe to the philosophy that the way to make money out of the kennel business is to hire a manager cheap, with the result that they usually get what they pay for—a "cheap manager."

TRAITS OF A GOOD MANAGER

There are established bases for evaluating many

TABLE 44
MANAGER CHECKLIST

- ☐ **CHARACTER**
  Has absolute sincerity, honesty, integrity, and loyalty; is ethical

- ☐ **INDUSTRY**
  Has enthusiasm, initiative, and aggressiveness, is willing to work, work, work

- ☐ **ABILITY**
  Has dog know-how and experience, business acumen—including ability systematically to arrive at the financial aspects and convert this information into sound and timely management decisions, knowledge of how to automate and cut costs, common sense, and growth potential; is organized

- ☐ **PLANS**
  Sets goals; prepares organization chart and job description; plans work and works plans

- ☐ **ANALYZES**
  Identifies the problem, determines pros and cons, then comes to a decision

- ☐ **COURAGE**
  Has the courage to accept responsibility, to innovate, and to keep on keeping on

- ☐ **PROMPTNESS AND DEPENDABILITY**
  Is a self-starter; has "T.N.T." which means that he does it "today, not tomorrow"

- ☐ **LEADERSHIP**
  Stimulates subordinates and delegates responsibility

- ☐ **PERSONALITY**
  Is cheerful; not a complainer

---

articles of trade, including breed standards for each breed of dogs. Additionally, we chemically analyze foods and conduct nutrition trials. But no such standard or system of evaluation has evolved for kennel managers, despite their acknowledged importance.

The author has prepared the Manager Checklist given in Table 44, which employers may find useful when selecting or evaluating a manager, and managers may apply to themselves for self-improvement purposes. No attempt has been made to assign a percentage score to each trait, because this will vary among kennels. Rather, it is hoped that this checklist will serve as a useful guide to the traits of a good manager, and to what the boss wants.

INCENTIVE BASIS FOR THE HELP

Big kennels must rely on hired labor, all or in part. Good help—the kind that everyone wants—is hard to come by; it's scarce, in strong demand, and difficult to keep. And the kennel manpower situation is going to become more difficult in the years ahead. There is need, therefore, for some system that will give a big assist in getting and holding top-flight help and cut costs and boost

Fig. 343. A good incentive basis makes hired help partners in profit.

profits. An incentive basis that makes hired help partners in profit is the answer.

Many manufacturers have long had an incentive basis. Executives are frequently accorded stock option privileges, through which they prosper as the business prospers. Common laborers may receive bonuses based on piecework or quotas (number of units, pounds produced).

Also, most factory workers get overtime pay and have group insurance and a retirement plan. A few industries have a true profit-sharing arrangement based on net profit as such, a specified percentage of which is divided among employees.

No two systems are alike. Yet, each is designed to pay more for labor, provided labor improves production and efficiency. In this way, both owners and laborers benefit from better performance.

Family-owned and family-operated kennels have a built-in incentive basis; there is pride of ownership, and all members of the family are fully cognizant that they prosper as the business prospers. However, few commercial dog kennels, that have to rely on hired help, have evolved with an incentive basis for the help. They should give serious consideration to doing so.

Sometimes employers erroneously conclude that providing an incentive basis means that they are giving up a portion of their normal net. For a brief period of time, this may be true. But with the right kind of help, and over a period of time, it will make money for both owners and employees.

Many different incentive plans can be, and are, used. There is no best one for all operations. The various plans given in Table 45 are intended as guides only.

The incentive basis chosen should be tailored to fit the specific operation, with consideration given to kind and size of operation, extent of owner's supervision, present and projected productivity levels, mechanization, and other factors.

INDIRECT INCENTIVES

Normally, we think of incentives as monetary in nature—as direct payments or bonuses for extra production or efficiency. However, there are other ways of encouraging employees to do a better job. The latter are known as *indirect incentives*. Among them are: (1) good wages; (2) good labor relations; (3) an adequate house, plus such privileges as the use of the kennel truck or car, payment of the electric bill, and use of a swimming pool; (4) good buildings and equipment; (5) vacation time with pay, time off, sick leave; (6) group health; (7) security; (8) the opportunity for self-improvement that can accrue from working for a top man; (9) the right to invest in the business; (10) an all-expense paid trip to a short course, show, field trial, or convention; and (11) a year-end bonus for staying all year. Such indirect incentives will be accorded to the help of more and more establishments, especially the big ones.

SELLING DOGS; CUSTOMER RELATIONSHIPS

Most kennels breed and sell dogs. This means that they must attract customers, make sales, and give the buyer a good start. The following points are pertinent to this important aspect of kennel operation:

1. *Promotion and advertising*—Prospective customers must be made aware of the kennel. This is generally accomplished through advertising and shows and/or field trials.

   Advertising channels may include local newspapers, breed magazines (all-breed and/or specialty breed publications), show catalogs, and radio. Two "don'ts" are important in advertisements: (1) don't clutter ads with nonessential facts, and (2) never make a claim that cannot be substantiated.

2. *Answering inquiries*—Mail inquiries should be answered promptly, briefly, and in a businesslike manner. When describing a puppy, (1) be accurate, (2) emphasize that your statements apply to his present stage of growth and development, and (3) state that the full development of his genetic potential will be dependent upon his future environment—particularly his food, health, and training.

   Enclose a copy of the pedigree and a photograph, if the latter is good.

3. *Never ship on approval*—Sooner or later, those who ship dogs on approval encounter (1) nonpayment, and/or (2) the return of a dog, perhaps following exposure to disease and mishandling. So, never, never ship on approval. Also, it's best to sell on a cash basis.

4. *A good first impression of the kennel is important*—Most sales are made at the kennel. So, the first impression of the potential customer is that of the kennel as such, rather than of the dogs. The buildings should be attractive, well maintained, and painted; the surroundings should be neat and well kept; and the pens and runs should be clean and free of odors.

5. *Display sale dogs advantageously*—Sale dogs had best be shown to prospective customers in a quiet area, away from distractions. This might be in a special showroom, the trophy room, in the owner's home, or in some other similar room and area.

   Show off the puppy's dam, also. It's a good way in which to project the likely appearance and temperament of her offspring.

   If the visitors have come from another ken-

TABLE 45

INCENTIVE PLANS FOR KENNELS

Types of Incentives	Pertinent Provisions of Some Known Incentive Systems in Use	Advantages	Disadvantages	Comments
Bonuses	A flat, arbitrary bonus; at Christmas time, year-end, or quarterly, or other intervals	It's simple and direct	Not very effective in increasing production and profits	
	A tenure bonus such as: (1) 5% to 10% of the base wage or 2 to 4 weeks' additional salary paid at Christmas time or year-end, (2) 2 to 4 weeks vacation with pay, depending on length and quality of service, or (3) $3.00 to $20.00 per week set aside and to be paid if employee stays on the job a specified time			
Equity-building plan	Employee is allowed to own a certain number of bitches. These are usually fed without charge	It imparts pride of ownership to the employee	The hazard that the owner may feel employee accords his own dogs preferential treatment; suspected if not real	
Production sharing	$10 for every puppy sold above 6 per litter; $5 per month for every boarder above 20; $100 for every champion in specified major shows or field trials	It's an effective way to (1) achieve higher conception of bitches and survival of puppies, (2) secure more boarders, and (3) get more champions	Net returns may suffer If a high performance level already exists, further gains or improvements may be hard to come by	

(Continued)

407

TABLE 45 (CONTINUED)

INCENTIVE PLANS FOR KENNELS

Types of Incentives	Pertinent Provisions of Some Known Incentive Systems in Use	Advantages	Disadvantages	Comments
Profit sharing: 1. Percent of gross income in cash	1% to 2% of the gross, with each employee sharing on a prorata of salary basis	It's a good plan for a hustler	Percent of gross does not impart cost of production consciousness	There must be prior agreement on what constitutes gross or net receipts, as the case may be, and how it is figured Generally, a working owner should accord himself a salary as part of the operating expense of the business, just as he allows salaries to other help. Then, all operating costs, including interest on the owner's money, should be deducted as expenses
2. Percent of net income in cash	10% to 20% of the net after deducting all costs, with each employee sharing on a prorata of salary basis	It's an effective way to get hired help to cut costs	Controversy may arise (1) over accounting procedure; e.g., from the standpoint of the owner a fast tax writeoff may be desirable on new equipment, but this reduces the net shared with the worker; and (2) because some owners are prone to overbuild and overequip, thereby decreasing net There may not be any net some years	Books should not be opened up to all employees. Access to books should be limited to supervisory personnel and the bookkeeper. Most laborers do not understand accounting principles; hence, opening up the books to them may lead to gossip, suspicion, and distrust
3. Percent of net income as investment in the business	Giving employees an investment (stock) in the future growth and expansion of the business in an amount equal to 20% of the yearly net profit, with each employee sharing on a pro rata of salary basis	Employees stand to profit if the business grows and prospers		
4. Percent of net income placed in trust account	A certain percent (say 20%) of the net earnings placed in a trust account, and (1) divided among the employees on a pro rata of salary basis, and (2) paid to employees upon retirement or completion of a specified number of years' service	Provides for retirement income and encourages continuity of service. There is a considerable saving in income tax paid	Some employees do not wish to wait so long for their added compensation	

(Continued)

TABLE 45 (CONTINUED)

INCENTIVE PLANS FOR KENNELS

Types of Incentives	Pertinent Provisions of Some Known Incentive Systems in Use	Advantages	Disadvantages	Comments
Production sharing and prevailing price	On a kennel breeding establishment, the author recommends that profits beyond the break-even point (after deducting all expenses, including the salary of the owner) be split on an 80:20 basis. This means that every dollar made above a certain level is split, with the owner taking 80 cents and the employees getting 20 cents. Also, there is merit in an escalator arrangement, with the split changed to 70:30, for example, when a certain plateau of efficiency is reached	It embraces the best features of both production and profit sharing, without the major disadvantages of each It (1) encourages high productivity and likely profits, (2) is tied in with prevailing prices, (3) does not necessitate opening the books, and (4) is flexible—it can be split between owner and employee on any basis desired, and the production part can be adapted to a sliding scale or escalator arrangement	It is a bit more complicated than some other plans, and it requires more complete records	When properly done, and all factors considered, this is the most satisfactory incentive basis for a kennel selling puppies and/or boarding dogs. Also, it can be adapted to any other type of kennel; to showing and field trials, for example
Using a scorecard (rating)	The score is the basis for bonus, salary raise, and other considerations The score method involves the preparation of a scorecard listing desired traits and performance, with a numerical value assigned to each according to its relative importance	This method works well in an office in which the personnel are carefully selected		

nel or from a pet shop, it's in the nature of health protection to ask them not to touch your dogs, because of the possibility of transmitting disease. Usually, they accept such a "hands off" policy graciously, and it imparts confidence in your operation.

6. *Give (a) pedigree form and registration application and (b) health record*—Give the purchaser the pedigree form and registration application at the time that he takes delivery on the dog. Also, give the customer a written record of the puppy's immunizations and treatments for internal parasites.

7. *Instruct on dog care*—It's always well to give the purchaser pertinent instructions on future dog care, including printed literature. Also, it's good business to start him off with enough food (to which the puppy has been accustomed) to last a couple of days.

Remember that the kennel owner's responsibility is to his customers. Remember, too, that good customer relationships are built on the sale of well-bred, healthy dogs, of good temperament.

DOG OWNERS AND INCOME TAXES

In the discussion that follows, the author has directed his efforts specifically to kennel owners, so that they will be aware of the tax implications involved, and so that they may take steps to avoid certain pitfalls. Also, owners are admonished to consult a competent tax advisor before embarking upon any sizable kennel operation.

CASH VS ACCRUAL METHOD

There are two standard methods of reporting, the Cash Basis and the Accrual Basis. Most kennel owners use the Cash Basis, in which income is reported when it is actually received and expenses are recorded when actually paid. It does not include the value of dogs sold or services performed (boarding, showing, training, etc.) for which payment was not actually available during the taxable year. In addition to being simple and easy, the Cash Basis has the advantage of allowing the kennel owner partially to control his income for tax purposes by timing year-end payment of expenses.

From a management standpoint, however, the Accrual Basis is preferred because it more nearly reflects the income of a particular period. Under it, income is accounted for when it is earned and expenses are recorded when incurred rather than when paid. Also, the Accrual Basis necessitates that complete annual inventories be kept, with taxes paid on increases of inventory, and deductions made for any decreases in inventory.

In large kennels, it is recommended that both record systems be used—the Cash Basis for tax purposes, and the Accrual Basis for management purposes. A competent accountant can set up such a system with the same set of records simply by adding a few memo accounts that are removed at the end of the year when closing the books for tax purposes.

HOBBY OR BUSINESS?

The first real hazard, and one which should be avoided like the plague unless it really applies, is that participation in the dog business—whether in breeding, racing, training, field trials, and/or showing—may be regarded by the Internal Revenue Service (IRS), as indulgence in a hobby or diversion rather than a true business venture, with the result that any losses accruing therefrom are disallowed in their entirety. This should cause no concern to those who derive their entire living from the dog business or to those successful kennels who normally operate at a profit. Rather, it is the person of independent means, or one who is profitably engaged in another enterprise or other enterprises, who is likely to be challenged when he or she has an unbroken string of loss years accruing from breeding, boarding, training, racing, field trials, and/or showing operations. Also, IRS does not automatically take cognizance of the fact that breeding programs designed to develop a new breed of dogs, or even to build up a kennel, take many years. It is essential, therefore, that the kennel owner establish a profit motive and a reasonable chance of achieving this aim. Then, he must conduct his operations in a businesslike manner throughout, and refrain from anything that may cause his actions even to be suspected as pursuit of a hobby rather than the conduct of a business.

In the dog business—whether breeding, training, racing, showing, or competing in field trials—a fine line often separates a hobby from a business. Moreover, a hobby sometimes turns out to be a profitable venture to the point that the taxpayer may turn it into a business.

It is important to the taxpayer that the facts and circumstances support the premise that he entered into the activity with the INTENT of making a profit.

CAPITAL GAIN

Since capital gain is not taxed nearly so heavily as ordinary income, it behooves kennel owners to report the maximum thereunder permitted by law. For an individual kennel owner, with up to $50,000 long-term capital gain, the tax rate is 25%; for over $50,000 it is 35%. For corporations, capital gain tax is 30%.

IN THE EVENT OF A COURT CASE

In the event of a court case, it is usually advisable that the taxpayer appear in person and testify, rather than expect that his attorney and accountant handle the matter entirely. This is especially important from the standpoint of establishing intent, for no one knows the original intent better than the owner. Additionally, it is usually advisable that the testimony of recognized experts in the field be used to substantiate the fact that there was, or is, a reasonable expectation of making a profit. However, whether or not the taxpayer and/or experts testify in a particular case should be left to the decision of the lawyer, for nothing is worse for the taxpayer than not giving the lawyer free rein to develop the case.

INSURANCE

Most old-line insurance companies do not offer dog insurance. A few write it just as a sideline at varying rates, but they always exclude theft, straying, or mysterious disappearance.

The current rates of Harding & Harding, Livestock Insurance, 200 South Fourth Street, Geneva, Illinois, follow:

AGE LIMITS 4 MONTHS TO 6 YEARS

1 Year (Exc. Vehicular & Whelping Loss)
 . . . . . . $10.00 per $100.00
1 Year (Incl. Vehicular Loss)
 . . . . . . $13.00 per $100.00
1 Year (Incl. Whelping & Vehicular Loss)
 . . . . . . $15.00 per $100.00

(Certain breeds not acceptable for whelping risks)

Harding & Harding also make the following explanations and exclusions:

1. Vehicular loss refers to being run over by a car
2. The whelping exclusion applies to large-headed dogs, such as Boxers and Bulldogs
3. They will take puppies under four months of age under some circumstances, since, in recent years, the preventive inoculations are given earlier and are more successful.

LIABILITY

Most kennel owners are in such financial position that they are vulnerable to damage suits. Moreover, the number of damage suits arising each year is increasing at an almost alarming rate, and astronomical damages are being claimed. Studies reveal that about ninety-five percent of the court cases involving injury result in damages being awarded.

Several types of liability insurance offer a safeguard against liability suits brought as a result of injury suffered by another person or damage to their property.

Comprehensive personal liability insurance protects an operator who is sued for alleged damages suffered from an accident involving his property or family. The kinds of situations from which a claim might arise are quite broad, including injuries caused by animals, equipment, or personal acts.

Both workmen's compensation insurance and employer's liability insurance protect operators against claims or court awards resulting from injury to hired help. Workmen's compensation usually costs slightly more than straight employer's liability insurance, but it carries more benefits to the worker. An injured employee must prove negligence by his employer before the company will pay a claim under employer's liability insurance, whereas workmen's compensation benefits are established by state law and settlements are made by the insurance company without regard to who was negligent in causing the injury. Conditions governing participation in workmen's compensation insurance vary among the states.

ESTATE PLANNING

Human nature being what it is, most kennel owners shy away from suggestions that someone help plan the disposition of their property and other assets. Also, many of them have a long-standing distrust of lawyers, legal terms, and trusts, and, to them, the subject of taxes seldom makes for pleasant conversation.

If no plans are made, estate taxes and settlement costs often run considerably higher than if proper estate planning is done and a will is made to carry out these plans. Today, some kennel owners have well over $100,000 invested in land, buildings, equipment, and dogs. Thus, it is not a satisfying thought to one who has worked hard to build and maintain a good kennel during his lifetime to feel that his heirs will have to sell the facilities and dogs to raise enough cash to pay federal estate and inheritance taxes. By using a good estate planning service, a kennel owner can generally save thousands of dollars for his family in estate and inheritance taxes and in estate settlements costs. For assistance, owners should go to an estate planning specialist—an individual or company specializing in this work, or to the trust department of a commercial bank.

A requisite of any estate planning is that all dogs be properly identified, by tattooing or other means, without relying on the memory of family or kennel help.

INHERITANCE AND PARTNERSHIPS

Nothing pleases parents more than seeing their children succeed; and, generally speaking, having them take over the establishment makes for the ultimate in parental pride and satisfaction. Moreover, such an arrangement can provide a fine financial start in life for the young man who desires to carry on—provided, while the parents are still living, advantage is taken of the very considerable savings in federal inheritance taxes, as provided by law.

Frequently, even where it is the full intent and desire of the parents and the children that the latter continue with the kennel, the gift tax provision is not considered. Then, upon death of the parents, the heir(s) may be required to raise such a large amount of cash to pay the inheritance taxes that a part or all of the operation may have to be liquidated.

A sound logical step in this transfer is a partnership contract between the parents and their heir(s) recorded with the Clerk of Court in the county in which the kennel is located. Appropriate counsel should be consulted in the preparation and recording of this agreement. Where the partnership contract is between a father and the heir, a provision should be included permitting the heir to purchase the father's share of the partnership for a fixed amount. The amount stipulated will then go into the father's estate. This will provide for proper and uninterrupted operation of the kennel, because, upon the father's death, the partnership is legally terminated.

10
Traveling With Your Dog

Chapter 10	
Method of Travel	414
Preparation for Travel	415
Know Regulations of State or Country of Destination	415
See Your Veterinarian	415
Veterinary Health Certificate	415
Rabies Vaccination Certificate	417
General Travel Preparation and Information	417
Insurance	417
Kennel (or Crate)	417
Grooming	418
Lost Dog	418
Tips on Traveling by Car	418
Tips on Traveling by Air	420
Kennels for Rent	422
Kennels for Sale	422
Dog Guides for the Blind Free	422
ASPCA Animalport	422
Pets International, Ltd.	423
Requirements of the 50 U.S. States	424
Requirements of Countries Abroad	424

Fig. 344. Traveling with your dog can be fun. (The Little Trooper. Courtesy Smithsonian Institution, Washington, D. C.)

TRAVELING WITH YOUR DOG

More and more people are traveling today, and more and more people are taking their dogs with them, either when they travel in the United States or overseas. Also, every kennel that sells dogs to folks living at a distance is involved in their shipment.

Regardless of the method of travel or the objectives, all dog owners share in the desire to move their pets safely, with the maximum of comfort. Also, if they are taking the dog with them, they want the travel to be a pleasant experience for both of them. To this end, this chapter is presented.

METHOD OF TRAVEL

Dogs may travel by car, air, or train, and they may travel by bus if they are with a blind person. When they accompany their master, the method of transportation is generally the same as that chosen by the owners for themselves. When dogs travel alone, as often happens in the buying and selling of dogs, the choice may be made between air or train. Regardless of the method of transportation, the objectives are: to move them safely, with a maximum of comfort.

In summary form, a few pertinent facts pertaining to each method of transportation follow. Then, tips on traveling by car and by air—the two leading methods of transportation—are given later in the chapter.

1. *By car*—Each year, millions of vacationing families face the question of what to do with the dog—take him or leave him. If you leave him, you'll likely place him in a boarding kennel. If you take him, you will desire that he be happy—and that he not take all the pleasure out of the trip. It's not an easy decision, because your dog is virtually a member of the family.

2. *By air*—Today, the air transportation of dogs is big business. United Air Lines, just one line, reports that each year over 44,000 dogs and cats fly the "friendly skies of United."

Most airlines will let your dog travel with you on a plane. If it is a small dog, you may carry it aboard; if it is a large dog, usually it will be up front in the pilot's compartment. Also, dogs may be shipped by air freight or express.

3. *By train*—Most railways permit dogs to travel with their owners at no extra cost if the owner's ticket calls for a compartment or bedroom. Otherwise, a dog must travel in the baggage car, either as excess baggage at extra cost, or checked through on your ticket at no extra charge—depending upon the rules of the road on which you travel.

Dogs confined to baggage cars may be visited as often as the owner desires, and both the compartment dog and the baggage car dog may be exercised by the owner at stops. However, it is well to find out from the train conductor where the longer stops are to be made, so that you can arrange your exercise schedule accordingly.

Each year, fewer and fewer dogs are being shipped by Railway Express in the United States. In fact, with the coming of piggy-back transportation, Railway Express will not accept dogs for a greater shipping distance than 300 miles. With this limitation on mileage, it is obvious that most dogs traveling unaccompanied today are being sent by air.

4. *By bus*—Most states have laws against dogs traveling by bus; hence, bus companies are not permitted to have dogs aboard. There is one exception: a dog guide can accompany a blind person on a bus.

PREPARATION FOR TRAVEL

Dog travel must be preceded by proper preparation. This involves familiarizing yourself with the health regulations of your destination; conferring with your veterinarian, who will advise you on vaccinations, health certificate, and vaccination certificate; deciding on insurance; arranging for a kennel (or crate); deciding on food, water, and utensils enroute; and considering grooming, feeding, and watering prior to departure.

KNOW REGULATIONS OF STATE OR COUNTRY OF DESTINATION

In particular, anyone shipping a dog should, at the outset, familiarize himself with the health regulations of the state or country of destination. They vary widely from state to state, and from country to country. Some require rabies certificates, others ask for health certificates, and still others have quarantine rules.

The regulations, state by state and country by country, are reproduced at the close of this chapter. Because these regulations are subject to change, any person planning to ship a dog is admonished (1) to check with the State Department of Agriculture where interstate shipment is involved, or (2) where foreign shipment is involved, to check with the destination country's (a) Embassy in Washington, D.C., or (b) the health department of the consulate closest to you.

SEE YOUR VETERINARIAN

When planning travel for your dog, you should see your veterinarian. He can do much to help you. If you require health certificates, he will issue the proper ones after an examination of your dog. If you plan to cross a state or international border, in all probability you will need both a health certificate and a rabies certificate, with the latter showing rabies vaccination within a stated period of time. Also, your veterinarian will likely advise you to immunize your dog against distemper and hepatitis prior to going on a long trip.

Most veterinarians keep on file the current regulations of state and international laws regarding dogs. In any case, they can secure the information easily.

VETERINARY HEALTH CERTIFICATE

Where a state or foreign veterinary health cer-

TABLE 46
VETERINARY HEALTH CERTIFICATE (FROM: ASPCA BOOKLET, "TRAVELING WITH YOUR PET.")

VETERINARY HEALTH CERTIFICATE

Owner

Address

Animal   Rabies vaccination

Species   Breed   Sex   Age

Color   Date   Tag no.

Distemper vaccine

Date

I hereby certify that I have examined the above described animal and, to the best of my knowledge, find same to be free of any communicable disease or contact therewith except as noted in remarks. This animal has (not) been permanently immunized against distemper.

         (Place)   (Date)

(Signature of official veterinarian)

TABLE 47
RABIES VACCINATION CERTIFICATE (FROM: ASPCA BOOKLET, "TRAVELING WITH YOUR PET.")

RABIES VACCINATION CERTIFICATE

Owner

Address

Species   Breed   Age   Weight

Name of Animal   Color   Sex

Type of vaccine   Dosage   Manufacturer

I certify that the above described animal was inoculated as indicated herein with an approved rabies vaccine and that the above statements are true to the best of my knowledge and belief.

         (Place)   (Date)

(Signature of official veterinarian)

tificate is required, the form shown in Table 46 will usually meet these needs.

RABIES VACCINATION CERTIFICATE

Table 47 shows a rather standard rabies vaccination certificate.

GENERAL TRAVEL PREPARATION AND INFORMATION

Regardless of the method of travel for the dog—whether by car, by air, or by rail—the following points are pertinent.

INSURANCE

Before shipping, it is always advisable to check on the insurance provisions. Up to $50 valuation is usually included in the regular carrying charges. However, additional insurance is usually obtainable.

KENNEL (OR CRATE)

The kennel, or crate, may either be homemade, purchased, or rented. In any case, the specifications are the same.

The kennel should be large enough for the dog to stand, turn around, and lie down. Four of the most common custom sizes are given in Table 48.

The following construction specifications should be observed when making a kennel for shipment of a dog:

1. *Materials*—As follows:
  a. Plywood, ¼ inch 3-ply spruce or equivalent
  b. Sheet metal, 20 gauge
  c. Composition material, ¼ inch tempered Masonite or equivalent
  d. Framing, for wood or composition 1" x 2" dimension lumber, fir, or other close-grained wood.
2. *Cross ventilation*—The kennel must be provided with adequate cross ventilation.
3. *Floor of kennel*—The floor must be so constructed as to retain liquids and solids within the kennel during normal handling. This may be in the form of a permanent or disposable insert the full size of the floor extending upwards one inch or more on all sides.
4. *Door lock*—Doors must be equipped with positive locks, such as a hasp with harness snap.

The entire ensemble of the kennel should be such as to prevent escape of the dog in normal handling.

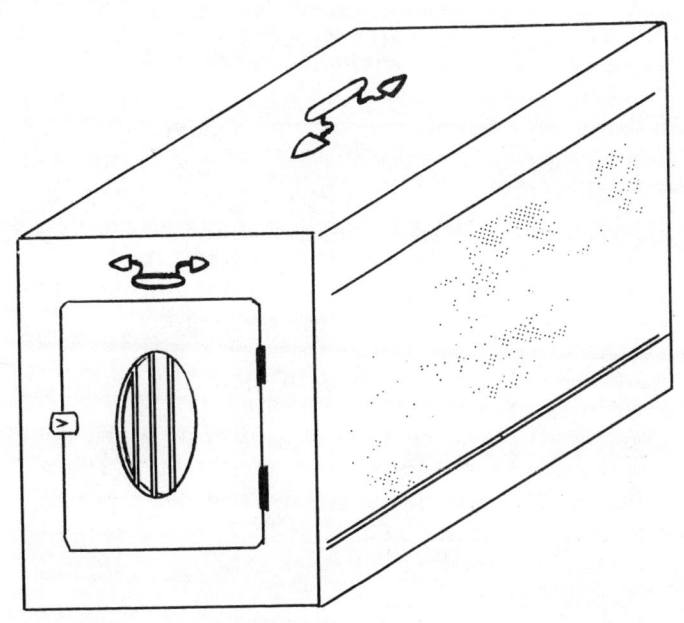

Fig. 345. A kennel (or crate), suitable for air or rail shipment. (Drawing by R. F. Johnson)

TABLE 48

FOUR POPULAR KENNEL SIZES

Size Dog	Size of Kennel Height	Width	Length	Approx. Kennel Wt.
	(in.)	(in.)	(in.)	(lb)
Small, under 20 lb	15	12	22	23
Medium, 20–35 lb	19	18	26	35
Large, 35–65 lb	26	22	36	60
Extra Large, 65–80 lb	30	25	43	65

GROOMING

Like people, dogs act sharp when they look sharp. So, your dog should be well groomed before starting on a trip. This involves bathing, combing, nail trimming, and any other grooming that will make your dog look and feel his best. Also, to make sure that he feels comfortable, and that you ride in peace, when you wash him, use a flea control remedy in the final rinse.

LOST DOG

One of the surest ways of recovering a lost dog is to be prepared for such an eventuality. Be sure that you attach to his collar your dog's license, and an identification tag, giving your name, address, and telephone number. Also, take along a snapshot of your dog.

In spite of the above precautions, your lost dog may not be immediately returned. Therefore, when a loss occurs, it is advisable to proceed as follows:

1. Report the loss to the police.
2. Contact the humane organizations in the area, as well as the local dog pound. Furnish a full description of your dog, preferably with pictures.
3. Contact the neighborhood children, local vendors, and deliverymen.
4. Advertise the loss in the newspapers.
5. Visit all animal shelters frequently to locate and identify your dog.

TIPS ON TRAVELING BY CAR

Most dogs enjoy traveling by car. To the end that it shall be a pleasant experience for both the dog and the people, the following tips are presented:

1. *Get him accustomed to short trips*—If possible, start the dog out on short drives near home when he's still a puppy. Gradually, (a) get him used to the motion of the car, and (b) teach him good car manners.
2. *Equipment*—When taking a long trip, the following equipment is recommended:

   a. *Traveling crate or bed*—If you are traveling in a station wagon, or if you have plenty of room in a large car, a traveling crate, such as shown in Fig. 346, may be used. A bed—the dog's own bed (his blanket or pad)—may be placed on the floor of the car or on the seat. The dog will feel more at home, and more secure, on his own bed.

Fig. 346. Traveling cages. Suitable for a station wagon or large car. Most steel cages fold flat and stack easily. (Courtesy Kennel-Aire Mfg. Co., St. Paul, Minn.)

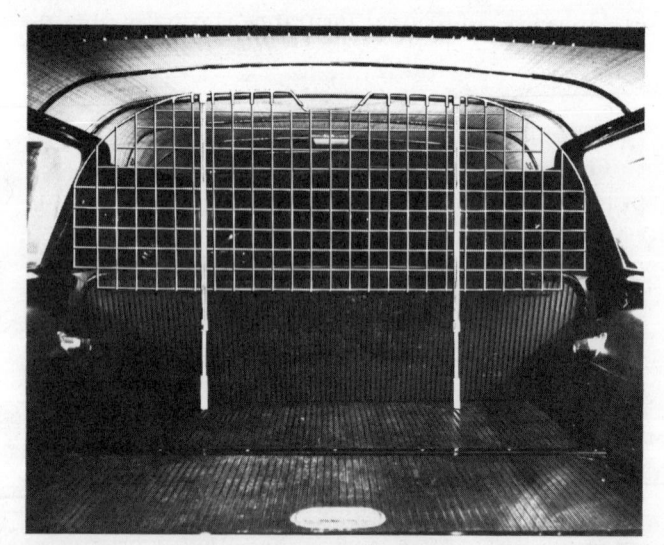

Fig. 347. Wagon barrier (partition). This type of equipment, which is available for virtually all station wagons, prevents dogs from annoying the driver and other passengers during travel. (Courtesy Kennel-Aire Mfg. Co., St. Paul, Minn.)

In addition to being used in the car, the crate or bed can be moved into the hotel or motel room at night.

   b. *Familiar toys*—Take along the dog's favorite toys. It will give him something to do and prevent boredom.

   c. *Two collars*—When traveling, the dog should wear two collars; a light chain-choke collar, and a leather collar, rolled or flat, as you prefer. Then you should put an identification tag on one collar, and the local dog license on the other. With this arrangement, even if the dog should lose one collar he can be identified.

d. *Leash*—A six-foot leash is desirable. Shorter leashes are more apt to be jerked out of your hand, particularly if the dog bounds off to meet another dog.

Where the dog is not accustomed to relieving himself while on a short leash, it is a good idea to take along a twenty-foot piece of strong, lightweight cord with a harness snap on one end and a loop on the other. By attaching this to your dog's collar before you take him out of the car to exercise, he has more freedom to sniff around at a distance. Yet, you have him under absolute control. This arrangement is suggested because you must never turn your dog loose in strange surroundings; the danger of being hit by a car or being lost is too great.

e. *Tie stake*—Many people who travel with dogs like to take along a tie stake, which is available at most pet shops. These can be shoved into the ground, and used for the purpose of staking the dog out. A swivel snap at the top makes it possible for the dog to go in a circle.

f. *His own bowl*—Take along the dog's own bowl. While traveling, the same bowl may be used for both watering and feeding.

g. *Flea powder*—Even though your dog may be free of fleas when you start the trip, he can pick up fleas along the way. Thus, you should take a can of flea powder along, and use it if necessary.

h. *Grooming equipment*—It is well to take along a comb and a brush, so that the dog can be freshened up when necessary.

3. *The car-sick dog*—Most dogs love a car ride. Occasionally, there are exceptions; some just don't like to ride in cars, and still others get car sick.

Veterinarians now have calming drugs (motion sickness pills or sedatives) for the excitable dogs and for those that just hate car riding. Thus, if your dog suffers from motion sickness, you should consult your veterinarian for a remedy. Usually such drugs will prevent motion sickness for as much as eight hours. Often dogs will overcome a tendency to car sickness after a few days of riding.

4. *Don't feed or water before travel*—Don't feed or water your dog for about two hours before the car trip. Also, allow him the time and opportunity to relieve himself beforehand.

5. *Car manners*—Make the dog observe good car manners. For the safety of everyone, he shouldn't be permitted to jump around in the car; he should sit or lie quietly and not annoy the driver. Neither should he be permitted to hang his head out the window. Flying objects from traveling cars may be driven into his eyes. Also, there is the hazard that the dog may get nasal and eye passage inflammation from the wind.

6. *Feeding, watering, and exercising enroute*— Any sudden change of food or water is apt to produce digestive upsets in the dog, even when he is at home. Thus, when traveling, you should always take along a supply of the food to which your dog is accustomed, or if you have been using a well-known brand, you can purchase some of it enroute.

Water is far more important for dogs than food, particularly in hot weather. If they have water, they can fast for many days without adverse effects. When traveling, the dog should have clean, fresh water at frequent intervals.

When traveling, dogs should be exercised and given an opportunity to relieve themselves at intervals. They'll ride better that way.

Like people, dogs will travel better if fed lightly, watered little and frequently, and exercised while enroute. The food allowance will vary with the individual dog and the amount of exercise accorded while traveling.

7. *Leaving the dog in a car*—When traveling, sometimes it is necessary to leave the dog in a car, either overnight or during a daytime stop. When you do, (a) leave the windows rolled down two inches on all sides for ventilation, and (b) lock the car.

Even some hotels, or motels that will not permit dogs in the rooms, have no objection to them being left in cars parked in their garages or parking lots. When this is done, the car should be parked in a spot where it won't have to be moved.

Also, dogs may be left in the car during the daytime, provided the weather is not exceedingly warm. The latter point is stressed, because there is no greater danger to your dog than leaving him in a closed car in hot weather. When the sun beats down on the roof of a standing car, the interior heats up rapidly (the heat in a closed car can reach well over 120° F), even though windows may be open an inch or so. Fresh oxygen-laden air cannot enter, and the dog suffocates. So, no dog should ever be left in a car unless it is in a completely shaded spot and the windows are left open sufficiently to permit fresh air.

8. *Hot weather driving*—Long trips in hot weather can be a real hardship to dogs. If you do not have a cool, air-conditioned car, you can keep your dog comfortable and cool if you will follow either of these plans:

a. Soak two large bath towels in cold water, then wring out the excess water and spread them on the car seat for the dog to lie upon. You may have to force him down the first time, but once he learns the comfort this brings him, he will readily stretch himself out on the towel. The cold water and evaporation lower the temperature and helps keep the dog cool, thereby preventing heat prostration.

b. An inner tube can be filled with water and frozen. This provides cooling for some hours without getting the dog wet.

9. *Motels and hotels*—When traveling with your dog, it is usually much handier to stay at a motel. However, it is noteworthy that more hotels than motels will permit dogs in the rooms. To be on the safe side, when you make your reservation be sure to mention that you will be traveling with your dog.

Automobile clubs, motel guides, and some dog food companies list hotels and motels that will accept dogs. With such guides, you can make your reservations in advance and plan your overnight stops. Although some states have laws that prohibit dogs from being admitted to hotel or motel rooms, the law is usually ignored.

The privilege of keeping your dog with you should not be abused. Unless the dog is housebroken, it should not be given the freedom of a hotel or motel room. Instead, it should be confined to a traveling crate. Likewise, a dog that chews rugs or bedding should be confined. Moreover, if damage is done, the owner should not only expect to pay for it, but should offer to do so. Remember that any time a hotel or motel refuses to accept dogs, it is usually the result of some thoughtless or irresponsible act on the part of a previous guest. Thus, you owe it to yourself and other travelers to be considerate.

Dog owners can keep their pets from causing damage or disturbing other guests by observing the following simple rules:

a. Dogs should always be kept on a leash when in public areas.

b. Dogs should not be taken into dining rooms.

c. Dogs should not be left alone in rooms.

d. Dogs' owners should expect to pay for any damage done by their dogs.

e. Untrained dogs should be confined to a crate or sleeping box while in the room.

f. Dogs should never be permitted to sleep on hotel or motel beds.

g. Dogs should not be permitted to bark.

h. Dogs should not be permitted to relieve themselves except in an alley or vacant lot.

It's good psychology, at the time you register at a hotel or motel, to offer the desk clerk a $10 deposit as a guarantee of the good manners of your dog and assurance that no damage will be done. Simply ask the motel or hotel keeper to retain the deposit until you leave, at which time you will be happy to have him make an inspection of your room. Chances are he won't even accept the deposit. Even if he does, it is an excellent way in which to build good will for all dog travelers.

TIPS ON TRAVELING BY AIR

Observance of the following tips will make for happier dog travel by air.

1. *Method of air travel*—Within certain limitations, there are four methods of air travel from which the dog owner may choose. These are:

a. *Carry on*—For puppies and small dogs, some airlines offer a free cardboard kennel that you can carry right on board with you. These kennels are about 21 inches long, 16 inches wide, and 8 inches high. The free "pet liner" kennel provided by United Air Lines is shown in Fig. 348.

The small carry-on type of kennel can be kept right with the owner; parked under the seat. The charge for the extra dog passenger is generally twice the excess baggage rate.

Usually, the following restrictions apply relative to carry-on kennels: You may carry only one on board, and your pet must stay in it at all times. Advance approval is required, because most airlines permit only one such compartment per plane. Also, the kennel must be stored at your feet or under the seat in front of you.

b. *Excess baggage*—When the dog is too large to carry on, excess baggage may be used. In this, you simply check your pet in at the passenger terminal, then claim him with your baggage at your destination. Dogs traveling

Fig. 348. Doggie bag: This Lhasa Apso pup peers out from a United Air Lines "Pet Liner" kennel that is provided free by the airline to passengers for the carrying of puppies or small dogs. (Courtesy United Air Lines)

as excess baggage must ride where the airlines specify. This may be in the cargo compartment, which is heated and pressurized; or it may be up front in the pilot's compartment.

Excess baggage cannot be used if your trip calls for transfer to another airline.

c. *Reserved Air Freight*—If your pet is flying solo (alone), or if transfer to another airline is involved, Reserved Air Freight is your best bet. You should allow a little more time for this method of transportation because you must deliver and pick up your pet at the air freight terminal rather than at the passenger terminal. Air freight shipment needing transfer to another airline must be in a kennel owned by the shipper, rather than a kennel rented from the airline.

In Reserved Air Freight travel, your pet travels in heated, pressurized comfort just like you. Travel charges by this method are based on the total weight of the animal and kennel.

When traveling Reserved Air Freight, advance arrangements must be made, so that the airline can smooth the way for your pet.

d. *Air Express*—Air Express with delivery service is also available for shipping dogs. Generally, delivery is made within a twenty-four-hour period.

2. *Call air reservations or freight office in advance*—The shipper should call the reservations or freight office of the airline that he wishes to use as far in advance as possible. They will help you decide the details of shipping.

3. *See your veterinarian*—Your veterinarian will advise you relative to health and quarantine problems. A health certificate and rabies inoculation are required by many states and countries. Even if they aren't required, your veterinarian may recommend them. Likewise, he may recommend that the dog receive distemper and hepatitis inoculations. Also, it is well to rely on the judgment of the veterinarian as to whether or not tranquilizers should be used.

4. *Age of puppy*—Puppies should not be shipped before they are six to eight weeks old—and only after weaning. They should have their distemper inoculation before shipment.

5. *Weather*—During the summer months, evening and night travel is easier on pets. Although air travel is in air-conditioned planes, it must be remembered that pets, especially long-haired pets, do not enjoy air-conditioned terminals as much as you do.

6. *Minimum of stops and transfers*—When shipping a dog, you should plan on a minimum of stops and transfers enroute.

7. *Kennel (or crate)*—Provide a sturdy kennel or crate with a leak-proof bottom. It should be large enough for the pet to stand, lie down, or turn around.

8. *Get acquainted with kennel*—If possible, you should let your pet get acquainted with his shipping kennel several days in advance.

9. *Kennel label*—On the outside of the kennel, clearly print (a) your name and address, and (b) the pet's destination. Also, add the pet's "call" name so that the attendant can talk to him, as he will be less lonesome that way. If the dog bites, that should be indicated, too.

10. *Collar identification*—Attach a tag with the owner's name and address and the pet's destination to a collar around the dog's neck. Then, if he should escape his crate, he can be identified.

11. *Withhold food and water prior to shipment*—Feed a light meal (about half the regular

allowance of one meal) six hours before shipment. Do not water within two hours of shipping, unless it is a very hot day.

12. *Exercise before shipment*—Exercise the dog, and give him an opportunity to relieve himself, prior to shipment. This might be done on the way to the airport.

13. *Check-in time*—When the dog is traveling "Excess Baggage," check him in forty-five minutes before plane departure. When he is traveling Reserved Air Freight, check him in two hours before departure.

14. *Never use escalator*—At the airport, never take a leashed dog on an escalator. Use stairs or an elevator instead.

15. *Place the dog in the kennel, and take him out*—For your dog's comfort and general safety, you must place him in the kennel at the airport, then either take him out or arrange for someone to do this at his destination.

16. *Bedding*—A shipper must provide a comfortable pad, or other adequate bedding material such as shredded paper.

17. *Give him toys*—A dog will be more at home if you put into his kennel a few of his favorite toys.

18. *Water dish*—Provide a water dish in the kennel so that attendants at stopovers can give him water. Attach the dish so that attendants can reach it without being bitten or without the pet escaping. Do not leave water in the dish during flight; it may spill and wet the crate.

19. *Food*—If the trip will take more than twenty-four hours, send food along. Dry food is best. If canned food is provided, send a can opener and a dish. Put the food in a cloth or mesh bag and attach it to the outside of the crate. Also, attach feeding instructions to the top of the crate.

20. *At the end of the journey*—When picking up a pet shipped by air freight, allow 45 minutes to 1½ hours after the flight has arrived. Also, it's a good idea for anyone receiving your pet to call the air freight office before going to the airport.

After the trip, help your pet to quiet down. Hold his food and water to a minimum for at least two hours.

KENNELS FOR RENT

Some airlines have kennels available for rent. Usually, they cost about $10 for one shipment; they come in different sizes, generally accommodating dogs up to 80 pounds in weight; and their use is restricted to the one airline only.

Of course, if your pet will be traveling a lot, or if your plans require changing airlines, you'll find it more convenient and economical to buy a kennel. Also, you must provide your own kennel if your pet is a big one—weighing over 80 pounds.

KENNELS FOR SALE

Several different companies have kennels for sale, including some of the airlines. Therefore, you may take your choice; either make it or buy it.

DOG GUIDES FOR THE BLIND FREE

Most major airlines make no charge for a dog trained to lead the blind that accompanies a passenger with impaired vision. However, the dog guide must be properly harnessed when aboard and must sit or lie at his master's feet.

ASPCA ANIMALPORT

The American Society for the Prevention of Cruelty to Animals (ASPCA) Animalport is a two-story brick building located at Kennedy International Airport, New York, and operated by the ASPCA. It is the first shelter in the Western Hemisphere catering exclusively to animal air travelers.

The address and phone number of the ASPCA Animalport follow:

The ASPCA Animalport
Air Cargo Center
Kennedy International Airport
Jamaica, New York 11430
Telephone: 656-6042 (Area Code 212)
Cable Address: Animalport

All you have to do to avail yourself of the facilities of ASPCA is to specify on the waybill that the dog be delivered to Kennedy Airport ASPCA Animalport upon arrival in New York. Then, if your pet arrives in New York before your plane does or if his plane leaves after yours, he can relax in the modern ASPCA Animalport. Here are

Fig. 349. Dog guide with blind master. Dog guides are allowed to ride the cabins of all major airlines. (Courtesy The Seeing Eye, Inc., Morristown, N.J.)

the pertinent details relative to the Animalport:
1. *Charges*—$7 per day, or part of day
2. *Hours*—It is open 24 hours a day, including Saturdays, Sundays, and holidays
3. *Services*—The services include—
  a. Examining, cleaning, feeding, watering, exercising, and caring for animals in transit
  b. Caring for pets during stopovers
  c. Providing veterinary service 24 hours a day by appointment with New York City Veterinary Medical Association
  d. Crating directions supplied and traveling crates when available
  e. Housing transient dogs any length of time
  f. Providing a scientific diet, including special diets on request.

Your pet will be fed, exercised in outdoor runs, and given veterinary care if necessary. He can stay a few hours, overnight, or several days.

The Animalport reports that its guest list has included over 140 species of animals. It handles anything from skunks, polar bears, and elephants to snakes and storks. Special attention is given to traveling pets.

PETS INTERNATIONAL, LTD

Pets International, Ltd, offers complete service to pet owners wishing to ship their pets either to other states or other countries, and from anywhere in the world back to the United States. They service anyone who comes to them; but their chief divisions of operations are: (1) military and government personnel services, (2) dog show exhibitor services, (3) international freight forwarders services, and (4) international organizations services (OAS, UN, World Bank, Shell Oil, etc.) Pertinent information about this organization follows:

1. *The address*—

    Pets International, Ltd
    2011 Eye Street, Suite 403
    Washington, D.C. 20006
    U.S.A.

2. *Charges*—This organization charges $30 for one pet, with a $5 charge for each additional pet. If permission cannot be obtained for entry to the point desired, a maximum of $5 will be charged to cover expenses for their efforts. Also, extra charges are made for consulate certification fees, import permits, stamp taxes, and veterinarian's examination at customs and transportation cost to the place of examination. However, they promise to hold these extra charges to a minimum.

3. *Travel arrangements*—All travel arrangements are made by Pets International.

4. *Kennels (crates)*—Kennels are available for purchase in four standard prices, ranging from $5 to $27. Pets International will advise you on the size kennel that you need, and make arrangements for the airline to have one available for sale if desired. Large kennels for large dogs (Great Danes, etc.) will be custom-made to order.

5. *Kennel care*—When it seems uncertain as to when you will be able to pick up your pet, Pets International have arrangements with kennels and veterinary service in most airports all over the world. They will meet your pet on arrival, take him through the necessary steps for entry into the country, and care for your pet until you are settled and have time to make arrangements for delivery. They will also be available for quarantine

restrictions, veterinary, and kennel services during layovers.

6. *Meeting documentary requirements and regulations*—Pets International, Ltd, is in constant touch with each country and keeps abreast of the frequent changes in their rules and regulations. They will process all forms to the government offices and, when necessary, arrange for the government officials to meet and inspect your pet at the plane to insure that your pet goes through swiftly. Also, they will forward to you all the necessary certificates, shot requirements, customs clearance forms, and (when necessary) they will obtain verification and approval by the Department of Agriculture on health certificates.

They will file for special permission when required, and they will have your forms certified by government consulates when necessary.

7. *Declared value*—The maximum value you may declare on your pet is $250. Of course, you can insure for more, but this is the amount for which the airlines will be responsible.

8. *Insurance*—The maximum allowable insurance for a dog is $2,500, at a rate of $1 to $3 per $100, depending on the final destination.

To obtain insurance, it is necessary that you do not have a declared value on your pet if the amount of insurance exceeds $250, and, the amount of insurance desired must be stated on the form provided.

REQUIREMENTS OF THE FIFTY UNITED STATES

In summary form, the requirements for traveling in the fifty states of the U.S.A. are given in Table 49 (From ASPCA booklet, "Traveling With Your Pet"):

REQUIREMENTS OF COUNTRIES ABROAD

In alphabetical order the requirements for traveling abroad follow (from ASPCA booklet, "Traveling With Your Pet").

Afghanistan
Rabies inoculation

Algeria
Health certificate and rabies inoculation for dogs

Argentina
Health certificate and rabies inoculation. Both must be validated by the senior U.S. Department of Agriculture veterinarian in the state of origin, usually located in the state capital, and legalized by the Argentine consulate for a fee

Aruba
Health and rabies certificates for dogs

Australia
Dogs may not enter except for those arriving from Britain, Ireland, or New Zealand. Animals from the United States must be taken to Great Britain or Ireland to undergo a 12-month quarantine there. The animal must then be brought to Australia by sea and not by air. After arrival in Australia the animal must remain in quarantine for 120 days, after which it will be released if it is in good health. If certain conditions of isolation are observed on the sea voyage to Australia, the quarantine may be reduced to 60 days. Animals that do not comply will be destroyed on arrival

Austria
No restriction on adult travelers taking not more than two dogs into Austria. In other cases specific authorization is needed from the Federal Ministry of Agriculture and Forestry in Vienna

Azores
Certificates of health and rabies vaccination (stating date and type of vaccine) issued by a qualified veterinarian and legalized by the Portugese Consulate for a fee. Veterinarian's signature must be notarized and notary's signature certified by county clerk

Bahamas
For dogs 6 months or older, rabies vaccination not less than 10 days nor more than 9 months before departure for the Bahamas. Health certificate signed by a veterinarian not more than 24 hours before departure. Dogs under 6 months are admitted only if the owner has a permit from the Bahamas Ministry of Out Island Affairs, Agriculture, and Fisheries at Nassau

Barbados
Dogs must be quarantined in Great Britain for 6 months before entering. Get import permit from the Ministry of Agriculture

Belgium
Rabies vaccination 30 days before entry. For dogs under 3 months the vaccine must

TABLE 49
REQUIREMENTS FOR TRAVELING IN THE FIFTY STATES OF THE U.S.A.

	Health certificate	Rabies inoculation	Within this time	Puppies	Other
Alabama	*	**	6 mo.	3 mo.	3, 6
Alaska	*	**	6 mo.	4 mo.	6
Arizona	*	**	1 yr. kv 3 yr. mlv	4 mo.	2
Arkansas	*	**	1 yr.	3 mo.	2, 6, 7
California	*	**	30 mo. mlv	4 mo.	
Colorado	*	**	1 yr.	3 mo.	6, 7
Connecticut	*	**	6 mo.		1, 2, 6
Delaware	*	**		4 mo.	2
Florida	*	**	6 mo.		11
Georgia	*	**	6 mo.	3 mo.	2, 6
Hawaii	120-day quarantine at owner's expense				
Idaho	*	**	6 mo. ntv 2 yr. cev	4 mo.	2, 6, 10

(continued)

Code definition
* — Health certificate required
** — Rabies inoculation required
Time — rabies inoculation must be given within the time listed
MLV — modified live virus vaccine
KV — killed virus vaccine
CEV — chick embryo vaccine
NTV — nerve tissue vaccine
Puppies — are exempt from rabies vaccination requirements up to age listed
Other
1 — show dogs exempt
2 — dogs from rabies quarantine area not admitted
3 — dogs with screwworms not admitted
4 — may be quarantined 60 days if from rabies area
5 — dogs from rabies quarantine area may enter with written permit
6 — not admitted if exposed to rabies or from an area where rabies exists
7 — cats require health certificate and rabies vaccination
8 — hunting dogs must receive rabies vaccination within 30 days of entry
9 — proof of ownership required
10—puppies under 4 months from a quarantine area need a permit from Bureau of Animal Industry
11—cats must be free from contagious disease
12—cats require a health certificate
13—dogs suspected of having rabies or being bitten by a suspected rabid animal may be quarantined 60 days

TABLE 49 (CONTINUED)

REQUIREMENTS FOR TRAVELING IN THE FIFTY STATES OF THE U.S.A.

	Health certificate	Rabies inoculation	Within this time	Puppies	Other
Illinois	*	**	6 mo. kv 1 yr. mlv	16 wks.	
Indiana	*	**	mlv or equal duration 1 yr.	3 mo.	7
Iowa	*	**	3 yr. mlv 1 yr. kv	6 mo.	1, 12
Kansas	*	**	1 yr.	3 mo.	
Kentucky	*	**	1 yr. kv 2 yr. mlv	4 mo.	1, 2, 6, 7
Louisiana	*	**	2 yr. cev 1 yr. ntv	2 mo.	
Maine		**			
Maryland	*	**	1 yr.	4 mo.	2, 6
Massachusetts	*	**	1 yr.	6 mo.	1
Michigan	*	**	6 mo. kv		1, 4
Minnesota	*	**	1 yr. kv 2 yr. mlv	6 mo.	6
Mississippi	*	**	6 mo.	3 mo.	2, 7
Missouri	*	**	2 yr. mlv 1 yr. kv	4 mo.	
Montana	*	**	2 yr. mlv	3 mo.	5
Nebraska	*	**	2 yr. mlv 1 yr. kv	4 mo.	
Nevada	*	**	2 yr. cev 1 yr. ntv	4 mo.	1, 2, 6
New Hampshire	*	**	3 yr. cev 1 yr. kv	3 mo.	2, 6
New Jersey	*				1, 2, 6
New Mexico	*	**	1 yr.	3 mo.	

(Continued)

TABLE 49 (CONTINUED)

REQUIREMENTS FOR TRAVELING IN THE FIFTY STATES OF THE U.S.A.

	Health certificate	Rabies inoculation	Within this time	Puppies	Other
New York	*				1
North Carolina	*	**	1 yr.	4 mo.	1, 5
North Dakota	*	**	3 yr. mlv	3 mo.	1, 2, 6, 8
Ohio		**	3 yr. cev 1 yr. other	6 mo.	
Oklahoma	*	**	1 yr.		2, 6
Oregon	*	**	2 yr. mlv 6 mo. kv	4 mo.	5, 12
Pennsylvania					9
Rhode Island	*	**	6 mo. kv 2 yr. mlv	6 mo. All Dogs	2, 6
South Carolina	*	**	1 yr.		2, 6
South Dakota	*	**	1 yr.		
Tennessee	*	**	1 yr.		2, 6
Texas	*	**	6 mo.		
Utah	*	**		4 mo.	7
Vermont	*	**	1 yr. mlv	4 mo.	2, 7
Virginia	*	**	1 yr.	4 mo.	2, 6, 7
Washington	*	**	2 yr. mlv 1 yr. kv	4 mo.	5, 7
West Virginia	*	**	1 yr.	6 mo.	1, 2, 6, 7
Wisconsin	*	**	3 yr. cev 1 yr. other	6 mo.	
Wyoming	*	**	2 yr. cev 1 yr. mlv	4 mo.	2, 6
District of Columbia		**	1 yr.	3 mo.	13

be the Flury-high-egg-passage vaccine. For other dogs the vaccine must be the inactivated nerve tissue vaccine, or the Flury-low-egg-passage vaccine or the inactivated tissue culture ERA strain. Health certificate filled out on a special form and signed by a licensed veterinarian and legalized by the senior U.S. Department of Agriculture veterinarian in the state of origin, usually located in the state capital

Belize (formerly British Honduras)

Certificate stating animal is in good health and has not been in contact with rabies. Obtain permit from Chief Agricultural Officer, Belmopan City, giving details of mode of travel and point of entry. Animal will be examined on arrival and quarantined if necessary

Bermuda

Import permit must be obtained from the Director of the Department of Agriculture and Fisheries, Point Finger Road, Paget, Bermuda. Applications must be received at least 10 days before the intended date of arrival. Animals without permit will be refused entry. Application forms (not permits) may also be obtained from any Bermuda tourist office

Animals must be accompanied by:

1. Import permit

2. A veterinary certificate issued within 10 days before arrival stating that the animal is free from all infectious and contagious disease and external parasites. Identify animal by breed, sex, age, and color

3. A certificate stating that the animal has not been exposed to rabies and has not been in a rabies quarantined area within the last 6 months

4. A certificate stating the animal, since reaching three months of age, has been vaccinated against rabies not less than one month or more than one year prior to arrival

Most hotels and guest houses do not permit dogs and cats. Those that do, accept only small, well-trained pets, and permission must be requested in advance.

Small dogs accompanying air passengers may be carried as excess baggage. Permission must be requested well in advance and may be impossible to secure. Animals must be in sturdy, leak-proof crates. Cunard Line ships carry pets one way, only if accompanied by the owner. Pets are not accepted on round trip cruises. Animals are not allowed in passengers' staterooms or public rooms. Kennels are available, and an attendant will feed them

Bolivia

Health and rabies vaccination certificates, stamped by the Bolivian Consulate

Brazil

Rabies vaccination and health certificates issued by a licensed veterinarian. Certificates must be certified by the Brazilian Consulate

Bulgaria

Health and rabies vaccination certificates signed by a veterinarian and notarized

Cambodia

Health certificate issued by the veterinary service in the country of origin. Antirabies vaccination certificate required for dogs

Cameroun

Rabies vaccination more than 1 month but less than 6 months old. Or an original certificate of health delivered 3 days before departure

Canada

Dogs over 3 months of age must be accompanied by a certificate signed by a licensed veterinarian certifying that the dog has been vaccinated against rabies during the preceding 12 months. The certificate must carry an adequate and legible description of the dog and date of vaccination and be initialed by the inspecting official at the Customs port of entry. Performing and guide dogs for the blind entering temporarily and kept under direct control are exempt

Canal Zone (Panama)

Immediately on arrival dogs and cats must be delivered to a representative of the Division of Veterinary Medicine. The animals will be quarantined for at least 30 days. A Health Bureau veterinarian will vaccinate the animal against rabies, regardless of previous vaccination, before the animal is discharged. At the discretion of the Health Bureau veterinarian the immunization requirement may be waived for animals less than 4 months old.

An animal found to be in poor health when admitted to the quarantine station will be quartined and treated at the owner's expense

Cayman Islands, B.W.I.

Veterinary health certificate. Six-month quarantine in the United States before shipping, to be certified by the U.S. Department of Agriculture

Ceylon

Health certificate for dogs. There is a duty for all dogs and an additional license fee

Chile

Rabies inoculations and health certificate authenticated by the senior U.S. Department of Agriculture veterinarian in the state of origin, usually located in the state capital. The certificate must be legalized by the Chilean Consulate at a fee

China, Republic of (Taiwan)

If the pet comes from a nonquarantine area, it must be accompanied by a health certificate and rabies inoculation certificate. It will be quarantined for 3 weeks in Taiwan at the owner's expense. If the pet is from a quarantined area, the owner must also file a special application for an entrance permit with the Health Administrative Dept., Taiwan Provincial Government, Taichung, Taiwan

Colombia

Rabies and distemper inoculations. A health certificate including a brief description of the dog should state that the dog is in general good health, is free of parasites, does not have hepatitis and has been vaccinated against rabies and distemper. The certificate must be authenticated by the Colombian Consulate at a fee

Costa Rica

Animal must be accompanied by:

1. Entrance permit signed by the Chief of the Veterinary Department of Health before arrival

2. A certificate not more than 30 days old, signed by the senior U.S. Department of Agriculture veterinarian in the state of origin, usually located in the state capital. The certificate must state the the animal is in good health and free of contagious diseases

3. Official certificate of stool test not more than 30 days old, stating that the dog is free of *Taenia equinococcus*

4. Certificate of rabies vaccination with a vaccine of avianizada, not less that 1 month and no more than 3 years before application. Six-month quarantine at the owner's expense if the animal comes from a country where rabies prevail

Cyprus

Six-month quarantine. Permission must be obtained in advance from the Chief Veterinary Officer

Czechoslovakia

Veterinary health certificate. Hotels charge a daily rate for pets. When making a hotel reservation, make a reservation for the pet, too

Denmark

If over 4 months of age, the animal must be inoculated against rabies not less than 4 weeks nor more than 12 months before entry. All animals must be examined immediately after arrival at the owner's expense and will be inoculated against rabies unless it can be proven that the animal was inoculated at a Danish border within the last 12 months.

The border veterinarian at the point of entry must be notified in advance of the date and hour of arrival so that he can be on hand. There are border veterinarians in Elsinore, Copenhagen, Gedser, Rodby Ferry, Padborg, Krusaa, Frederikshavn, and Elsbjerg.

Shipment of pets through the country is permitted if Danish customs authorities judge the crate to be secure. Pets accompanying passengers in through-cars of international trains may be kept in train compartments provided they have no contact with other dogs or cats.

The border veterinarian may permit dogs to enter in passenger cars or buses on condition that the dog be kept tied to the car, that the journey will not exceed 24 hours, and that the dog will be kept on a sturdy leash

Dominican Republic

A certificate of health signed by a veterinarian, a public notary, and the county clerk. The Dominican Consulate must then legalize it for a fee

Ecuador

No dogs admitted until further notice

El Salvador

Certificate of good health and inoculation against rabies. Certificates must be legalized at the Consulate of El Salvador

Fiji

No pets admitted from the United States. Animals may pass through if they do not leave the ship or plane. An animal may be transferred to a connecting air flight, but a maximum waiting period of 6 hours is normally allowed

Finland

Dogs must undergo a 4-month quarantine in a kennel approved by the Veterinary Department of the Finnish Ministry of Agriculture and Forestry, Ritarikatu 2.B., Helsinki, Finland. An import permit for dogs must be obtained from the department. There is a fee. No permit is required for dogs being transported between Sweden, Norway and Finland.

Also required are a health certificate not older than 14 days and a certificate showing the animal has been inoculated against distemper and is free of worms. The dog will be examined by a veterinarian

France

Vaccination against rabies more than 1 month and less than 6 months before entry. Or a certificate of health dated no more than 3 days before departure, stating the animal comes from a country free of rabies for at least 3 years and has lived in the country for the last 6 months (or since birth)

Germany (West Germany and West Berlin)

Dogs require a health certificate signed by a licensed veterinarian practicing in the area where the animal normally lives. The certificate, which must be in German or with a certified German translation attached, should indicate the name and address of the owner and identify the animal by breed, sex, age, color, type and pattern of fur.

The certificate, valid for 20 days, must state:

1. That the animal was examined and found free of contagious diseases and that no case of rabies has been officially recorded within 13 miles of where the animal lives within 3 months before the examination, or

2. That the animal has been vaccinated against rabies with a vaccine recognized by the U.S. Public Health Service (nerve-tissue or chicken-embryo vaccine) not less than 30 days or more than 12 months before entry. The date of the vaccination must be stated.

Exempt are pets used professionally by artists, pets in air transit if they do not leave the airport during change of planes, pets traveling through Germany by car or train if there is a reciprocal agreement with the neighboring country, pets on ships if they do not go ashore, Seeing Eye dogs, service dogs and dogs of the police, military forces or life saving agencies.

There is an import tax for animals brought in for commercial purposes

Ghana

Vaccination required. Vaccination certificate must be shown on request. On arrival in Ghana, animals must be examined by a veterinary inspector

Great Britain

Quarantine of 6 calendar months from the day of landing in approved kennels at the owner's expense. Accommodations must be reserved at one of the approved quarantine kennels, and an authorized carrying agent must be engaged to meet the animal, clear it through customs, and deliver it to the quarantine kennels.

All animals will be vaccinated twice with an inactivated antirabies vaccine while in quarantine, regardless of whether the animal has been vaccinated.

After written confirmations from kennel and carrier are received, write for import permit at least 6 weeks in advance to Ministry of Agriculture, Fisheries and Food, Hook Rise South, Tolworth, Surbiton, Surrey, England. In Scotland write to Department of Agriculture and Fisheries for Scotland, Chesser House, 500 Gorgie Road, Edinburgh, EH11 3AW, Scotland. In Ireland write to Ministry of Agriculture for Northern Ireland, Stormont, Belfast, Northern Ireland.

Lists of approved quarantine kennels and carrying agents may be obtained by writing to these addresses

Greece

Certificate of health and rabies inoculation, certified by the senior U.S. Department of Agriculture veterinarian in the state of origin, usually located in the state capital. Certificate must also be certified by the Greek Consulate for a fee

Guam

Except for military dogs and certified guide dogs for the blind, all dogs must undergo a 120-day quarantine at the owner's expense. They must also have a health certificate dated within 10 days of departure and a rabies certificate dated within 6 months. A letter confirming a reservation with the Animal Quarantine Station must be obtained from the Department of Agriculture, Government of Guam, Agana, Guam 96910

Guatemala

Certificate of health and rabies vaccination, legalized by the Guatemalan Consulate. If the animal is pedigreed, the pedigree should be submitted

Guyana

Permission must be obtained from the Principal Veterinary Officer, Ministry of Agriculture and Natural Resources, Brickdam, Georgetown, Guyana, South America. The animal must have a health certificate and must have been vaccinated against rabies at least 30 days before entry. The animal will be examined at Timehri Airport by a government veterinarian and at his discretion may be quarantined at a government quarantine station at the owner's expense

Honduras (Spanish)

Health and rabies vaccination certificates are required and before departure must be approved by the Consul General of Honduras, 290 Madison Ave., New York, N.Y. 10017, Room 603

Hong Kong

Health certificate. Six month quarantine in approved kennels. Write in advance for permit to the Senior Veterinary Officer, Agriculture and Fisheries Department, giving animal's type, age, color, sex, date, and time of arrival, whether by air or sea. Before release from quarantine a dog must be vaccinated and licensed

Hungary

Health certificate stating that the animal is healthy and that there is no rabies outbreak in the area where the pet lives. A rabies vaccination certificate issued at least 14 days, but no longer than 4 to 6 months before entering

Iceland

No animals admitted except in special cases. For permission write well in advance to Chief Veterinary Officer, Reykjavik, Iceland

India

A health certificate from a veterinarian stating that the dog is free from Aujossk's disease, distemper, rabies, leishmaniasis, and leptospirosis. Rabies vaccination more than 1 month, but within 12 months before embarkation with nervous-tissue vaccine or within 36 months of embarkation with chicken-embryo vaccine, both the vaccines having previously passed satisfactory potency tests. A certificate must contain a record of the vaccination, the vaccine used, brew of the vaccine, and the name of the laboratory

Indonesia

Animals may be imported only by special permission from the Department of Agriculture and after they have been examined and their entry approved by a veterinarian in Indonesia

Iran

Health certificate notarized by a notary public and legalized by the Iranian Consulate for a fee

Iraq

Inoculations against distemper and rabies. Certificate of inoculation must be legalized by the senior U.S. Department of Health veterinarian in the state of origin, usually located in the state capital, and authenticated by the Indian Embassy, Iraq Interests Section, 1801 P Street, N.W,. Washington, D.C. 20036

Ireland

Six-month quarantine at an approved quarantine kennel. Animal must be transported from the port of entry to the quarantine kennel by an approved carrying agent. Approved quarantine kennel for dogs is Wheatfield, Malahide, Co. Dublin. Approved carrying agents are: for Dublin—Coras Iompair Eireann, Transport House, Bachelor's Walk, Dublin 1; for Cork—Coras Iompair Eireann, Glanmire Station, Cork.

Write to kennel and carrying agents for confirmation of accommodations. Then send application for an import license to Secretary, Department of Agriculture (Veterinary Section), Upper Merrion Street, Dublin 2

Israel

Rabies vaccination and health certificate giving sex, age, color, and breed of dog, date of inoculation and stating that the animal is in good health, free of rabies, comes from a region free of rabies for at least 6 months and has not left it during that time. Certificate must also state that within 1 month before departure the animal had a blood test showing it to be free of leptospirosis

Italy

Certificate signed by a veterinarian stating breed, sex, color, and date of birth of the animal; name and address of the owner; that the animal has been vaccinated against rabies and vaccine used; that the animal does not show any clinical sign of disease; and that the animal comes from an area free of rabies for the last 6 months

Ivory Coast

Health certificate signed by a veterinarian in the country of origin and rabies vaccination

Jamaica

No dogs admitted

Japan

Dogs: Two-week quarantine. Health certificate and rabies inoculation certificate (at least 1 month old, but not older than 150 days). Both certificates must be endorsed by the senior U.S. Department of Agriculture veterinarian in the state of origin, usually located in the state capital

Jordan

Health certificate. Rabies inoculation not less than 1 month and not more than 1 year before departure. Rabies certificate must give date of vaccination, type of vaccine, number of the vaccine, control number, dose, and date of manufacture.

The animal must come from an area where there has been no rabies for 6 months. Six-week quarantine after arrival at the expense of the owner

Kenya

Rabies inoculation. Obtain import permit in advance from Ministry of Agriculture and Animal Husbandry, Veterinary Research Laboratory, P. O. Kabete, Kenya

Korea

Quarantine certificate must be obtained from the U.S. government health authorities. Dogs will be quarantined 21 days. The animal may enter only through the Port of Pusan, Suyong Airport, or Kimpo Airport (Seoul)

Kuwait

Certificate of health and rabies vaccination not less than 30 days or more than one year before entering

Lebanon

Rabies inoculation, and health certificate not more than a month old, signed by a veterinarian

Lesotho

Permit must be obtained from the Director of Veterinary Services, P. O. Box 24, Maseru, Lesotho. Rabies vaccination certificate validated by a state veterinary official stating that the animal was inoculated at least 30 days, but not more than 3 years before entering

Liberia

Certificate granting permission must be obtained from the Consulate or Diplomatic Mission. The owner must produce a veterinarian's certificate indicating that the animal has been vaccinated against rabies and is in good health

Libya

Health certificate, including a record of inoculations, should be shipped with the pet

Luxembourg

Rabies inoculation not less than 1 month or more than 3 months before entry. Official certificate must be signed by a veterinarian and legalized by the senior U.S. Department of Agriculture veterinarian in the state of origin, usually located in the state capital. Certificate must describe animal and indicate type of vaccine and serial number

Malawi

Get entry permit in writing from the Director

Malaysia

Not less than 30-day quarantine after rabies inoculation for animals from countries other than United Kingdom, Eire, Northern Ireland, Australia, and New Zealand

Mali

Rabies vaccination

Malta

Apply in advance to Principal Veterinary Surgeon, Public Abattoir, Department of Agriculture, Marsa, Malta. Dogs will be quarantined for a period determined by the Principal Veterinary Surgeon. All pets are liable to a 20 percent customs duty

Mauritius

Written permission must be obtained in advance from the Ministry of Agriculture and National Resources, Port Louis, Mauritius. Dogs are subject to a 6-month quarantine

Mexico

Inoculation against rabies and distemper. Health certificate in duplicate must be dated, bear the owner's name and address, a full description of the animal and tag number, and attest that it has been examined (giving date) and found free of any contagious disease, as well as having been immunized (giving date). The veterinarian's signature must be handwritten in ink. If it is illegible, the name must be typed under the signature. The certificate must be certified by the Mexican Consulate for a fee

Monaco

Vaccination against rabies more than 1 month and less than 6 months before entry

Morocco

Health and rabies vaccination certificates notarized by a notary public and legalized by the Moroccan Embassy or Consulate for a fee. Certificates must be less than 15 days old at time of entry

Nepal

A health certificate from a veterinarian stating that the dog is free from Aujossky's disease, distemper, rabies, leishmaniasis, and leptospirosis. Rabies vaccination more than 1 month before, but within 12 months of actual embarkation, with nervous-tissue vaccine or within 36 months of embarkation with chicken-embryo vaccine, both the vaccines having previously passed satisfactory potency tests. A certificate must contain a record of the vaccination, the vaccine used, brew, and name of laboratory

Netherlands

Rabies inoculation using an inactivated, nerve-tissue vaccine for dogs, or a weakened live vaccine of the Flury type (high egg passage for dogs under 3 months, low egg passage for dogs older than 3 months), or a tissue vaccine based on the E.R.A. strain.

Inoculation must be done at least 30 days, but not more than 6 months before entering for dogs younger than 3 months. At least 30 days, but not more than 1 year before entering for dogs vaccinated after 3 months with inactivated, nerve-tissue vaccine or the HEP vaccine. Or at least 30 days, but not more than 2 years before entry for dogs vaccinated after 3 months of age with LEP vaccine.

An inoculation certificate signed by a practicing U.S. veterinarian must state that the animal has been inoculated with one of the vaccines mentioned above, which has been inspected and approved in the country where manufactured. The certificate must show date of inoculation, type of vaccine and its expiration date, name of manufacturer, and serial number; description of animal, including sex, age, breed, color, type of hair and markings, and name of owner.

The certificate must be legalized and endorsed by the Animal Inspection and Quarantine Division, Animal Health Division, Agriculture Research Service, U.S. Department of Agriculture, Federal Center Building, Hyattsville, Maryland, or the Animal Health Division's field office, usually in the state capital

Netherlands Antilles (Anguilla, Aruba, Bonaire, Curacao, Nevis, St. Kitts, St. Maarten, Saba)

Same requirements as the Netherlands

New Zealand

Entry prohibited, except for animals kept in the United Kingdom for 12 months, 6 of which must have been in official quarantine. Additional requirements are a rabies vaccination and a permit from the Department of Agriculture, Animal Health Division

Nicaragua

Permit issued by the Nicaraguan Ministry of Agriculture and Livestock. A rabies vaccination not less than 30 days or more than one year before shipment.

A veterinary certificate stating that the animal was born in the United States and is free of contagious disease. The certificate must also give a complete description of the animal, date of vaccination, kind of vaccine used, lot number, and name and address of manufacturer

Nigeria

Dogs will be admitted with a health certificate stating that the animal is healthy and has not been exposed to rabies within 6 months. Get import permit from the Director of the Federal Department of Veterinary Research, Nigeria

Norway

Entry prohibited, but exceptions may be granted on application to the Royal Ministry of Agriculture, Veterinaerdirektoratet, Oslo, Norway. Applications must contain the name and address of the owner, kind and number of animals, means of transportation, and place and approximate time of arrival. If an import license is granted, a health certificate from a veterinarian is required, plus inspection by veterinary authorities on arrival in Norway. Four-month quarantine after arrival, followed by 2 months in which the animal must be constantly leashed

Okinawa

Examination by a licensed veterinarian no more than 10 days before shipment. Immunization against rabies by a licensed veterinarian more than 1 month, but not more than 12 months, before arrival in Okinawa, if a nervous-tissue vaccine is used; or more than 1 month, but not more than 36 months before arrival, if chicken-embryo vaccine is used. Valid health and rabies vaccination certificates, both in triplicate, must accompany each animal.

Limit 2 pets to a family. Animals must be older than 2 months. Pets under 3 months will be confined

Pakistan

Obtain permit from the Office of the Imports and Exports Control Organization at the point of entry. Application for permit should be accompanied by a health certificate. Rabies vaccination is recommended. If animal has not been vaccinated, it will be vaccinated on entry

Panama

Six-month quarantine for dogs. Health certificate and rabies inoculation required. Both must be legalized by the closest Panamanian Consulate. There is an admission fee and a daily fee

Paraguay

Health certificate

Peru

Inoculations against rabies and distemper. A certificate of inoculation must be signed by a veterinarian and legalized by the Consulate General at a fee. Animals that will stay in Peru also require a license from the Ministry of Agriculture

Philippines

Health certificate issued shortly before shipment by the senior U.S. Department of Agriculture veterinarian in the state of origin, usually located in the state capital. The certificate should state that the animal is free from, and has not recently been exposed to, any dangerous and communicable disease. If there is no health certificate, the Director of Animal Industry may place the animal in 10-day quarantine. If a disease appears in one or more of the animals, they must all be held in quarantine until 10 days after the disease has disappeared.

Rabies vaccination immediately before shipment

Poland

Rabies inoculation

Portugal

Certificate of health and rabies vaccination (stating date and type of vaccine) issued by a qualified veterinarian and legalized by the Portuguese Consulate for a fee.

Veterinarian's signature must be notarized and notary's signature certified by county clerk

Puerto Rico

Health certificate, dated not more than 10 days before departure, stating animal is free of disease. Rabies vaccination certificate dated not more than 30 days before departure. Statement that rabies has not been reported in the last 6 months within 50 miles of point of origin. This statement can be obtained from the U.S. Department of Agriculture, Bureau of Animal Husbandry in the state capital

Rhodesia

A health certificate signed by an official veterinarian within 14 days of departure stating that:

1. Animal is in good health, free from external parasites and contagious disease

2. If from an area where no case of rabies has been confirmed within 50 miles in the previous 6 months, it may enter if vaccinated against rabies not less than 30 days, but not more than 36 months before. If under 3 months (too young for vaccination), a dog's arrival must be reported to the nearest Government Veterinary Officer or Animal Health Inspector, and it must be presented for rabies vaccination on reaching 3 months

3. If the animal comes from within 50 miles of a confirmed case of rabies, in the previous 6 months, it may enter if:

a. It has been vaccinated against rabies more than 6 months, but not more than 36 months. If vaccination has expired, it will be admitted 30 days after revaccination

b. Dogs vaccinated less than 6 months before entry will be quarantined in an officially approved kennel at the owner's expense until the end of the 6-month period from date of vaccination. Animals liable to quarantine must be crated and consigned by rail, air, or public transport directly to the approved kennel. Quarantine accommodations must be reserved by the owner in advance. Duplicates of veterinary certificates issued to owners of animals for quarantine and dogs under 3 months from a rabies free area must be sent by the issuing authority to the Director of Veterinary Services, P.O. Box 8012, Causeway, Salisbury, Rhodesia. The certificate must state the name of the quarantine kennel

c. Animals under 3 months from a rabies infected area will not be admitted

Romania
Veterinary certificate

Rwanda
Rabies inoculation 3 months before entry

Santo Domingo
Certificates of health and rabies inoculation. A stamp must be purchased on entering at the International Airport of the Americas

Saudi Arabia
Rabies inoculation and immunization against other contagious diseases

Sierra Leone
Import permit stating age, sex, breed, and species must be obtained in advance from the Chief Veterinary Officer, Ministry of Agriculture and Natural Resources. Dogs need a health certificate, and depending on the country of origin and age of the dog, a vaccination certificate against rabies, hard pad disease, distemper, infectious canine hepatitis, and leptospirosis

Singapore
Health certificate. Animal will be examined and vaccinated against rabies on arrival and quarantined at least 30 days in the government quarantine station at the owner's expense. Apply at least 2 weeks in advance for an import license from the Director of Primary Production and to reserve quarantine accommodations. There is an import fee.

If the animal is less than 4 months old, it will stay in quarantine until old enough to be vaccinated against rabies and stay another 30 days after the vaccination. Pregnant dogs are not admitted.

If the animal does not accompany the owner, a commercial handler can be hired to transport the animal to the quarantine station

South Africa
Obtain entry permit from Director of Veterinary Services, Private Bag 138, Pretoria, Republic of South Africa. Give number and species of animals, approximate date, and port or airport of arrival. If permit is issued, animal may be admitted if accompanied by the permit and a health certificate dated not earlier than 21 days before departure, stating that:

1. The animal is in good health and free from external parasites and contagious disease

2. It was vaccinated with a strain of antirabies vaccine conforming to a potency standard recognized by the World Health Organization at least 60 days, but not longer than 36 months before arrival. Vaccination certificate must be on the special form provided by the laboratory that produced the vaccine. Age, date of vaccination, and batch number of vaccine must be included. An animal that does not have a rabies vaccination certificate will be quarantined 180 days in a government quarantine station at the owner's expense.

If the animal was inoculated less than 2 months before, it will be quarantined in the Republic of South Africa at owner's expense until the 2 months are up. Animals vaccinated before 6 months of age will be revaccinated before reaching 12 months

3. The animal has not been in contact with rabies-infected animals

4. The animal either did not come from an area where *T.evansi* (Surra) or *Babesia gibsoni* exist or was biologically tested for these diseases with negative results. Animals with a negative reaction to the first test for Surra must then be injected with Bayer 205 or Antrypol or Suramin and brought directly to the Republic for detention and further testing. Animals from areas where *T.evansi* (Surra) or *Babesia gibsoni* exist will, on arrival, be detained in the government veterinary quarantine station for up to six weeks and tested for these diseases.

Animals entering by air or ship must be crated and not leave the airport or any port en route. Animals will be examined by a South African government veterinary officer at port of entry. Unvaccinated dogs will be vaccinated at a government quarantine station at the airport

Soviet Union
No animals admitted

Spain
Health and rabies certificates legalized by the nearest Spanish Consulate for a fee. Waiting time: 24 hours

Sudan
Apply in advance for permission from the Ministry of Animal Resources in Khartoum, giving type of animal, age, sex, pedigree (where applicable), and number of animals. In emergency, permission may be obtained at the port of arrival.

All pets must be accompanied by a health certificate. Rabies and distemper inoculation not less than one month or more than three years from date of entry. Inoculation certificate must accompany application. On entry, animals must be examined by an official veterinary inspector. All animals must be in securely closed cages

Surinam
Same requirements as the Netherlands, plus a valid health certificate

Sweden
Obtain import permit from National Swedish Veterinary Board, Fack 10360, Stockholm 3, Sweden. The original copy must be shown to the Frontier Veterinary Surgeon and the customs officer. It will state the date before which the animal may enter.

There is a 4-month quarantine, and space must be booked well in advance. Affidavit dated within 10 days of departure must state that the animal is in good health with no signs of contagious disease and that it has undergone a blood test for leptospirae (spirochaete) within 10 days of departure. Signature of the veterinarian must be verified by a U.S. government agency or a Swedish diplomatic or consular mission for a fee.

At least 1 day before arrival the Frontier Veterinary Surgeon at the port of arrival must be notified as to the day of arrival and on what ship, train, or plane the animal is expected. On arrival the animal will be examined and quarantined.

A blood test made immediately must show that a dog is serologically free from signs of leptospirae infection. While in quarantine, if the animal shows signs of any contagious disease, it will be destroyed. Quarantine, examination, and tests are at owner's expense

Switzerland
Rabies vaccination not less than 30 days nor more than 1 year before entry. Rabies certificate must contain name and address of owner, description of animal (breed, sex, age, color), date of vaccination, type of vaccine, name of manufacturer, and serial number. The certificate, signed and stamped by a veterinarian, must state that the animal was clinically examined by the veterinarian before vaccination and found to be healthy.

These requirements are waived for animals passing through Switzerland by rail or air without staying

Syria
Veterinary certificate and rabies and distemper inoculations

Tanzania
Rabies and health certificates. Import permit

Thailand
Rabies vaccination. Obtain advance permission from the Department of Animal Husbandry, Paholyothin Road, Bangkok, Thailand, for a fee. A duty of 30% of the value of the animal is levied at the port of entry

Togo
Health certificate and rabies vaccination. Contact National Veterinary Dept. on arrival

Trinidad and Tobago
Health certificate certifying the animal is in good health and free from symptoms of contagious diseases. A minimum of 6 months quarantine. The animal must be presented for detention during the period specified, as kennel accommodations can be guaranteed only during that period.

On arrival, the animal must be confined in an escape-proof cage, have an import permit, and in the case of a dog, collar and lead. Twenty-four hours notice of the animal's arrival must be given the Veterinary Officer, North, c/o St. Joseph Farm, Trinidad. Telephone No. 94317

Tunisia

Health certificate no more than 15 days old

Turkey

A combined certificate of health and rabies vaccination in duplicate, signed by a veterinarian and notarized by a local county clerk. If the veterinarian is a member of the United States armed forces, no notarization is required. All certificates must be legalized by the Turkish Consulate for a fee by money order if the certificate is sent by mail

Uganda

Health and rabies certificate. Obtain import permit from Uganda veterinary authority. Alert airport in advance to arrange for animal's clearance. The captain of the aircraft must certify that animal has been isolated during the trip. An export permit must be obtained from veterinary authorities when leaving

United Arab Republic

Health certificate approved by the senior U.S. Department of Agriculture veterinarian in the state of origin, usually located in the state capital. Notification must be sent to the Veterinary Department in the U.A.R. Fees: observation fee and taxes, plus a license fee

United States

Must be inspected by a quarantine officer at port of arrival. Animals that do not appear to be in good health may be detained at facilities provided for and paid for by the owner. A healthy animal exposed to a sick or dead animal will be admitted only after tests or examinations show the animal is free of communicable disease. The quarantine officer will not admit animals in unsanitary containers until the containers are cleaned.

Dogs require a rabies vaccination with nerve-tissue vaccine more than 1 month, but not more than 12 months, before the dog's arrival, or with chicken-embryo vaccine more than 1 month, but not more than 36 months, before arrival. If a dog arrives without a valid certificate of vaccination, it will be vaccinated on admission and confined for at least 30 days (Confinement means restriction of an animal by the owner in a building or other enclosure isolated from other animals and people, except for contact necessary for its care. If it is allowed out of the enclosure, it must be muzzled and on leash).

If the vaccination was done less than 1 month before arrival, the dog will be confined until at least 30 days have elapsed since vaccination. Vaccination will not be recognized if performed on a dog less than 3 months of age. Such dogs will be confined, and the owner must certify that the dog will be vaccinated at 3 months and confined for at least 1 month following vaccination.

The rabies vaccination requirement is waived for dogs that for 6 months have been only in a country determined by the Public Health Service to be rabies-free. A current list of such countries may be obtained from the Chief, Foreign Quarantine Program, Center for Disease Control, U.S. Public Health Service, Atlanta, Georgia 30333, or from Public Health Quarantine Stations at United States Ports.

If a dog comes from a locality with a high incidence of rabies or under conditions indicating that a special hazard or rabies introduction is present, the medical officer in charge may take additional steps to prevent the introduction of rabies.

However, any such dog that has been vaccinated after the age of 3 months will be admitted after 30 days have elapsed since vaccination, if inspection of the animal after this period reveals no evidence of communicable disease.

Collie, Shepherd, and other dogs imported from any part of the world except Canada, Mexico, and countries of Central America and the West Indies must be quarantined at the port of entry if they are to be used for handling livestock. Such dogs will be detained for a sufficient period of time to determine their freedom from the tapeworm, *Taenia coenurus*. If found to be infested, they will be treated under the supervision of a veterinary inspector at the port of entry until they are free from infestation

Uruguay

Health certificate signed by a veterinarian. The veterinarian's signature must be authenticated by the senior U.S. Department of Agriculture veterinarian in the state of origin, usually located in the state capital. Certificate must be legalized by the Uruguay Consulate for a fee

Venezuela

Health, distemper, and rabies certificates for a dog. Certificates must be stamped and signed by the Venezuelan Consul

Vietnam

Send a letter describing pets, expected date and time of arrival, the name of the airline and flight number to the Animal Protection Service, Department of Agriculture, 29 Phan Dinh Phung Street, Saigon, Vietnam (Tel: 91745).

Enclose a health certificate issued not less than 15 days or more than 1 year before departure, stating that the pet has been vaccinated against rabies (specify type of vaccine used), is in good health and comes from an area free from rabies for more than 6 months and is located more than 12.5 miles from a rabies affected area. If traveling with your pet, carry a duplicate of the veterinary certificate.

(For exporting pets, present them to the Animal Protection Service three days before shipping. Same health documents as above)

Virgin Islands

Health certificate signed by a veterinarian stating that the animal is free from symptoms of infectious, contagious or communicable disease, and did not originate in an area under quarantine for rabies. Dogs more than 8 weeks of age must have been vaccinated against rabies within 6 months or not less than 2 weeks before shipment and must arrive with proper identification tag and certificate of rabies vaccination.

Health certificate must be prepared on the official interstate health certificate forms of the state of origin and must include the name and address of the consignor, the origin of the animal, and the consignee's name and address, with an accurate description of the animal. The health certificate must indicate the health status of the animal, including the results of required tests and dates of vaccination. Health certificates valid for 30 days

West Indies

Most of the islands do not admit dogs from the United States. See also Bahamas, Bermuda, Jamaica, Netherlands Antilles, Trinidad

Western Samoa

No animals admitted from the United States

Yemen

Dogs are not allowed in hotels, restaurants, buses, or planes. There are no veterinarians or veterinary hospitals

Yugoslavia

Rabies vaccination 15 days before entry and a health certificate signed by a veterinarian dated within 15 days of entry

Zaire

Rabies vaccination. A customs duty of 10 percent of the animal's cost must be paid on arrival

Zambia

Dogs must be vaccinated against rabies within 3 months of arrival unless already vaccinated. Veterinary health certificate must state that the animal is clinically healthy, free from external parasites and contagious diseases, and in a fit state to travel.

All animals require an import permit from the Director of Veterinary Services, P.B. RW 60, Lusaka, Zambia

11
People Need Pets

Chapter 11
For Inspirational and Spiritual Purposes   *440*
As a Civilizing Influence   *440*
As a Supplement to Man's Deficiencies and Sporting Instinct   *441*
As a Companion   *442*
In Child Development   *442*
In Pet-Facilitated Psychotherapy   *443*
They Also Serve   *444*
Famous Dogs and Famous People   *447*

Fig. 350. Gilles Payant and the Irish Setter star of the movie, Big Red. (Courtesy Walt Disney Productions, Burbank, Calif. © MCMLXI Walt Disney Productions)

PEOPLE NEED PETS

People need dogs and dogs need people. Both of them desire to love and to be loved. Since the first domestication of the dog, there has been no age and no religion, throughout the world, in which the dog has not taken his place at man's side—as hunting companion, guardian, general ally, and/or pampered pet. In flood and in fire, in war and in famine, dogs have been faithful to their masters unto death.

Many kinds of animals can be, and are, kept as pets; among them, crocodiles, snakes, fish, the young of various wild animals, birds, horses, cats, and dogs. As pets, all of them share some things in common: (1) they're generally kept for pleasure rather than utility; (2) they're treated with unusual kindness and consideration—they're cherished, indulged, fondled, endeared, and pampered; and (3) they're spoiled. But dogs are different! In addition to being without a peer as pets, some of them still perform important utilitarian functions—as watchdogs and guards, as police dogs, as leaders of the blind, as protectors and drovers of herds and flocks, as war dogs, and as sled dogs in the Far North. Moreover, they differ from all other pets in that they return in full measure the love and affection that is showered upon them—*they need people*. Because of these unique qualities, dogs outnumber all other pets—there are about twenty-six million of them in the United States.

The sections that follow point out the people-dog relationship—why and how they have contributed to each other with each advancing step in civilization.

FOR INSPIRATIONAL AND SPIRITUAL PURPOSES

The contribution of dogs has extended far beyond their utilitarian value. Prior to recorded history, they were accorded a conspicuous place in the art of the day and made one of the chief objects of myths. The Egyptians had a god that was a dog. Through the ages, therefore, dogs have contributed richly to man's inspirational and spiritual desires.

1. *The dog satisfies a deep-rooted want*—Animal companionship fills a deep-rooted want in man. On paved city streets and in apartment houses, dogs are kept by a surprisingly large number of people. This is true both in the districts inhabited by the wealthy and in the tenements of the poor. The poor may not be able to afford the handsome or striking bluebloods, but their mongrels sometimes have a greater capacity for affection, and often greater intelligence, than the "aristocrats."

2. *The dog satisfies an inner need*—The affectionate nature of dogs, along with some inner needs in ourselves for animal companionship, has led to the development of a great variety of toy dogs. Many of these are of no earthly use except to satisfy man's inner need for a pet; like the King Charles Spaniel and the Italian Greyhound, which may be recognized readily as dwarf races of some larger, useful breed.

3. *The dog provides a way to commune with nature*—People have an inherent need to get close to and commune with nature. That's why so many folks go to the country or the seashore for what they refer to as peace and quiet.

A dog revives our sense of kinship with nature. In a city apartment, a pet is often the only tie one can have to nature.

AS A CIVILIZING INFLUENCE

The first step towards civilization seen in even the most primitive tribes of men was the domestication of the dog. Savage hunters everywhere in

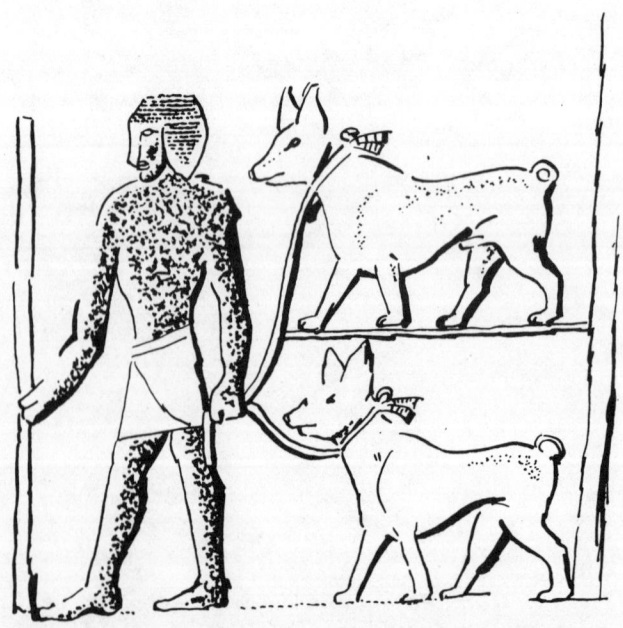

Fig. 351. Man with two dogs from tomb of Mereruka (Sixth Dynasty). Note exceptionally small, curled tails. (Drawing by J. L. Medeiros)

the world had dogs to help in their hunting and to guard their houses or tents at night. Among certain tribes, dogs were merely tolerated; among others there was an obvious fondness for animals, which plainly accelerated their domestication.

By the time the people living along the Tigris and Euphrates entered history, the dog was already serving them as a helper in hunting and a guardian of hearth and home.

Those of us who remember the last round of the barn at night—giving an ear of corn to one still-hungry cow, rearranging the hay for the favorite horse, taking a last look at some newborn pigs or lambs—are likely to think that animals have been among the most important civilizing influences in the evolution of our society. Whether we grew up on farms and hold fond remembrances of our animal companions, or whether we are city-bred and know them secondhanded, one of the most interesting things about the story of our species is the origin and history of this companionship. Sometimes the origin is fairly clear, as in the donkey and goat, whereas at other times it goes back into the dim period of prehistoric man, as with the dog and the horse.

1. *The dog helped establish permanent dwellings*—Only after the dog had placed his keen senses at man's disposal were the hunters able to move into permanent dwellings. Dogs guarded women and children and fended off predators. In return, the families granted the four-legged allies food and shelter, rewarding them for retrieving small game and seeking out large prey.

2. *The dog helped establish village settlements*—On the Nile and the Euphrates around 4000 B.C., and in Europe some 1,500 years later, many pastoral peoples gave up their roaming ways and established village settlements. They employed strong watchdogs whose task was to guard their homes and flocks. These animals have been named *Bronze Age dogs*. They were the forebears of many of our present-day races of dogs, such as the sheep dog and the German Shepherd Dog.

AS A SUPPLEMENT TO MAN'S DEFICIENCIES AND SPORTING INSTINCT

Without the help of the dog, man might not have made it—even with his superior intelligence. His sense of smell is so poor that he cannot trail game; he cannot outrun his quarry; and his necessity for sound sleep makes him an easy mark for predators. Thus, the "pact" that Stone Age man fashioned with the dog was truly one of the great events in human history.

1. *The dog provided scent*—Without a dog's nose, man would never have become the supreme master of the hunt. For although, by virtue of his reason, he knew how to make weapons, to use cunning, and to exercise patience, he lacked, to a large degree, the elementary ability with which all animals are endowed to a greater or lesser extent—he could not scent animals. This is a serious handicap. From the start, man seemed to have been aware of the dog's potential usefulness and wide range of talents, especially his keen sense of smell.

Fig. 352. Sculpture of ancient Egyptian dog with erect ears and heavy forelegs. Considered as related to the dog of Neolithic Anau in Turkestan. Perhaps used in hunting and related to our hounds. Roman period, sculptured in basalt, Louvre Museum. (Drawing by J. L. Medeiros)

2. *The dog permitted sleep*—It would appear that man was able to fight his way up from a state of nature to civilization much more easily with the aid of the dog. Man's high intelligence afforded him a formidable advantage in the struggle for existence. But the need for deep sleep, connected with intelligence, was a severe handicap in his contest with the great beasts of prey. The bond of friendship with the alert dog overcame this disadvantage.

3. *The dog served man's sporting instinct*—In

the Middle Ages, the sport of coursing developed. This consisted in the chase with large packs of hounds. The quarry was pursued until it either collapsed in exhaustion or came to a stop, panting and trembling, to be torn to pieces by the dogs or given the deathblow by the huntsmen. In following the trail of a proud stag, the lead-dog of the pack was the chief actor. The hunter depended on him to avoid a false scent. Mature stags were clever enough to double back and cross their own paths, then at the right moment they would break away from the younger stags of their herd and flee in another direction.

About 700 years after man and dog had leagued together for the hunt, the horse joined forces with them. Seated on the horse's back, the hunter could overcome the distance between himself and the fleeing game. Also, he could compensate for the limited range of his primitive weapons.

AS A COMPANION

Only very rarely is the dog eaten now, even by primitive tribes. Neither is he used as a draft animal. Instead, he serves a very special purpose, not met by any other animal. He is valued, above all else, as man's comrade and friend.

The dog is man's only real partner in the whole realm of animals. To the man-dog partnership the dog brought his strong natural instincts and highly developed senses to set against man's higher intelligence and imagination.

Today, the dog has his honored place in the home. He helps get the kids off to school in the morning, naps while they study, barks at strangers, romps with the children when they come home, and takes the warmest spot by the fireplace or sleeps on the warm-air register.

1. *The dog as a companion for children*—The companionship of children and dogs is well known. Both are happier when they're together. More than any other trait, this elevated the dog from living in or under the barn to living in the house, and from scavenging for food and eating leftovers to specially prepared diets formulated for his well-being.

2. *The dog as a companion for the elderly*—In urban areas, many elderly folks live alone. Their friends and world grow smaller and smaller. A dog gives them companionship and a reason to get out and make contact with other people.

3. *The dog as a companion for the businessman*—For the businessman, a dog is companion enough; he's always good humored, and he has no worries or business troubles to talk about.

4. *The dog as the companion for the whole family*—Owning a dog can be a very rewarding family experience. It gives the family a common interest and something to talk about. A dog makes a home livelier. Also, he'll get more pampering and loving than all the rest of the family put together. He's the family dog—all of him belongs to each one.

IN CHILD DEVELOPMENT

Every adult who was fortunate enough to own a dog while growing up is well aware of the contribution that his very own dog made to his development. Next to his parents, his pet was likely his closest attachment.

Boys and girls need a dog. It gives them an animal upon which to shower their love. Moreover, the dog is always ready to return affection. It never criticizes its young master, no matter how disappointing he may have been at school or at home.

1. *The dog occupies time*—A dog provides a youngster with an animate object to occupy his time, constructively; for the dog must be fed, cared for, trained, and petted. This is important in an era when many youngsters are getting into trouble simply because they have too little to do,

Fig. 353. Pekingese dog in imperial cloisonné enamel, Ch'ien Lung period, China, A.D. 1736-1795. This and similar Chinese effigies are probably symbolic of the lion, but actually represent Pekingese dogs. (Drawing by J. L. Medeiros)

too much time on their hands, and too much pent up energy. In the author's opinion, the great importance of dogs in occupying a child's time becomes apparent when one ponders the fact that few youngsters who have a pet ever become juvenile delinquents—busy boys and girls seldom get into trouble.

2. *The dog builds character*—Children build character through having a dog; automatically acquiring confidence, self-control, and patience—all through companionship with their good friend and companion, the dog.

It may take a long time and a few failures before the dog will do tricks. But he'll keep trying if he is not mistreated. In the process, a child can see that frailties and failures do not mean the end. Rather, he still loves his pet and the pet loves him, so eventually they'll make it. Out of this experience, the youngster learns to take setbacks and to find satisfaction in small achievements.

3. *The dog teaches kindness*—A dog teaches kindness. It won't tolerate abuse or neglect. The child learns that he cannot shout at or hit the dog —that such tactics accomplish nothing. Rather, gentleness and understanding do. Hence, it teaches its young master that to be loved, he must give love and kindness.

4. *The dog shows that love can be shared*—A child learns that the love of a pet may be shared by many. Thus, the dog cuddles up to all members of the family; he'll play just as eagerly with one as another. So, the child learns that he doesn't really lose anything when his pet loves others, too.

5. *The dog teaches responsibility*—Dogs help a child to accept responsibility. He learns that the pet needs to be fed, exercised, kept clean, and made comfortable. He feels a certain sense of gratification for doing something for someone else —his pet. Also, he sees what happens when these responsibilities are not fulfilled.

Parents should not be disturbed if a youngster does not immediately take total responsibility for taking care of a dog. Responsibility has to be learned, and there is bound to be considerable backsliding along the way. Thus, a young child should not be expected to take complete charge of a pet. On the other hand, an older child can learn to do this and get great satisfaction therefrom, provided he is praised and rewarded as he learns.

6. *The dog imparts pride of ownership*—A dog imparts pride of ownership. It gives status in the eyes of the youngster's playmates and friends. It's his very own dog.

7. *The dog aids in socialization*—A dog will give a big assist in socialization. It gives a youngster something to talk about to others. When he takes care of his dog, he is "the master." Children who tend to be bashful and withdrawn gain a feeling of confidence, security, and companionship from a dog. To his dog, he's big and important, and needed, too.

8. *The dog teaches animal behavior*—Ownership of a dog teaches animal behavior—and human behavior, too. Wolves, the Pariah dogs of the Orient, the Dingo of Australia, and even domestic dogs that are allowed to roam, live in highly organized societies. They live in packs and observe pack laws, which include helping each other. They take care of and protect the old and the young; and they take turns in running down their quarry.

Also, by having a dog, youngsters learn about sex in a very normal way. They observe estrus (heat) periods, breeding, and puppies being born—they learn how life begins.

9. *The dog teaches about death*—A child learns about death when he loses a very much-loved dog. The author vividly recalls the heart-rending experience when his six-year-old son lost his first dog. We had an elaborate graveside funeral, with flowers and all. While I buried the pet, Johnny sobbed his heart out. Thereupon, he raised the usual child's questions: Why did Sandy have to die? Whose fault was it? What will happen to him now? Will all of us have to die, someday, too? An open discussion of such perplexing and frightening questions will prevent the fear and fantasies of death. Moreover, it will put the youngster in the frame of mind to get another pet and go on from there.

IN PET-FACILITATED PSYCHOTHERAPY (PFP)

Research workers at Ohio State University used pet-facilitated psychotherapy on 16 hospitalized psychiatric patients who failed to respond favorably to traditional forms of therapy, including psychotherapy, drug treatment, electroshock therapy, and occupational and recreational therapy. Two of the 16 patients did not accept the particular pet (dog or cat). All the remaining 14 patients showed some improvement from pet-facilitated psychotherapy.

The Ohio research workers reported that the availability of a large assortment of well-trained dogs of different breeds made it possible to match the personality and the disorder of a given patient with a dog with which the patient could best interact. They concluded: "The results appear to be very encouraging, particularly since we selected patients who had reached a plateau of nonresponding to all traditional forms of therapy. The fact that none of the patients introduced to PFP exhibited unfavorable effects or a deterioration in their condition, would support the thesis that PFP may turn out to be a significant addition to the psychotherapeutic armamentarium."[1]

THEY ALSO SERVE

From very early times, man had domesticated the dog, using him to assist in his hunting and to provide protection by night. Perhaps even more important, the presence of the dog furnished animal companionship, thus filling a deep-rooted need that has always existed in human beings. Although these initial uses are still important, the services of the dog have been greatly expanded and varied in a number of curious ways through the ages, among them those which follow:

1. *In legend, myth, magic, art, religion, and superstition*—When Noah entered the Ark, he took with him two dogs. Legend has it that these were Afghan Hounds, and that the Ark sprang a leak which the dogs plugged with their noses. This, so the story goes, explains why a dog's nose is always cold and wet.

Primitive man throughout the world used the dog in magical rites. The belief prevailed that dogs were guides to the spirit world and messengers to the gods. When a man died, some Indian tribes sacrificed a dog to guide him safely on his journey to the other world. Also, dogs have been the object of many sacrificial offerings for the purposes of driving away evil spirits, curing illnesses, purifying places and people, and placating the gods. Dogs have been worshipped and ritually eaten by their worshippers.

---
[1] Corson, Samuel A. and Elizabeth O'Leary Corson, *Pet-Facilitated Psychotherapy*, Department of Psychiatry, College of Medicine, Ohio State University, Columbus, Ohio. Presented at "Pet Animals and Society," sponsored by The British Small Animal Veterinary Association, Jan. 30–31, 1974, London, England.

Fig. 354. An Egyptian statue of the Saite period, showing the jackal-headed Anubis, the god who conducted the souls of the dead to the presence of Osiris to be judged. (Drawing by J. L. Medeiros)

Man has always given dogs a conspicious place in the art of the day. Many of the great paintings of the world include a dog, or dogs, as an adjunct to a portrait or the object of a subplot to the main subject, thereby adding interest to the scene and often giving insight into the character of those portrayed.

Because of the dog's long and close association with man, it is only natural that he should have entered into the religious beliefs of many people and many periods. Among certain primitive people, it was believed that the dog was endowed with divine powers. Sometimes, they were served up as an offering to the deities.

444

The ancient Egyptians made a god of the desert dog. This point of history marks the time when the dog entered mythology.

Many interesting superstitions have evolved around dogs. Among them is the one to the effect that if you cut off a piece of your dog's tail and bury it under your front doorstep, he'll never run away and leave you. Another superstition is that white dogs possess supernatural powers as instruments for good. In Wales, the belief once prevailed that if a white dog came near the house of a dying person, the soul would be saved; but that if the dog was black, the soul was destined to everlasting torment.

2. *As a cure and comfort*—The belief that direct contacts with a dog will cure certain illnesses and bring comfort was widespread and long lasting. In England, during the fifteenth, sixteenth, and seventeenth centuries, small lapdogs, known as *comforters,* were carried about and were regarded as efficacious in relieving abdominal pains and in attracting the owner's fleas. The Aztec priests of Mexico used "pillow dogs," which were probably ancestors of the Chihuahua, as hot water bottles. The Tibetan lamas used dogs as foot warmers and carried them in the sleeves of their gowns. Even today, Australian aborigines use Dingo pups, carried across the hip or shoulder, to provide warmth on cold desert mornings.

3. *As motive power for wheels*—One of the earliest uses of dogs was to provide motive power for wheels. They have turned Buddhist prayer wheels in the Far East, water wheels in Scotland, butter churn paddles in Wales, and roasting spits all over Europe.

4. *For fighting*—Organized dog fighting, animal baiting, and bull-baiting, are now banned in most parts of the world. Exceptions exist in Hong Kong, where the Hong Kong Kennel Club recognizes the Chinese Fighting Dog—a dark, loose-skinned dog with curved teeth and a head resembling a hippopotamus. Dog fighting has long been popular in Japan, too. The Tosa, or Japanese Mastiff, is used for this purpose in Japan.

The origin of the Mastiff, Bulldog, Bull Terrier, and Staffordshire Bull Terrier are all closely associated with wild animal baiting, bull-baiting, and organized dog fighting. Yet, these fighting breeds have survived, with a transition to use as guard dogs.

5. *For bird lures and as scarers*—Ducks and geese swimming on water display a great deal of curiosity about the movements of predators, such as foxes, on the banks. In Europe, this behavior trait of ducks and geese has been used in luring them for ringing (marking), and in America it has been used to lure ducks within the range of sportsmen. The dog, which is fox-like in build, is trained to lure the curious water fowl into nets or within shooting range.

Dogs have been used as scarers in a number of ways and for a number of purposes, among them: to clear airport runways of birds (which is accomplished by the amplified bark of a dog being played over loud speakers); to clear airfields of stray dogs; and a railway in Wales once used dogs to "walk the rails" for the purpose of clearing the road of stray sheep and to warn the repair gang of an approaching train.

6. *For truffle (underground fungi) hunting*—In Italy, the scenting power of the dog is still used for hunting truffle, the edible subterranean fruity body of certain fungi; a great delicacy that is supposed to give the consumer increased sex drive and potency. Dogs are used to scent out and indicate where digging will uncover a truffle. Thereupon, the digger uncovers the luxury and gives the dog a tidbit as a reward.

7. *As mining prospectors*—The Russians have trained dogs as mining prospectors. Ore deposits have characteristic odors. It is reported that trained dogs can detect ore deposits to a depth of more than twenty feet.

8. *As foster mothers*—The best known story of an animal serving as a foster mother pertains to Romulus and Remus, who were suckled by a wolf. Romulus was the legendary first king of

Fig. 355. She-wolf suckling Romulus and Remus; bronze sculpture by Carl Milles, in Milles Garden, Stockholm, Sweden. (Photo by A. H. Ensminger)

Rome and the founder of the city. Anulius, who was on the throne of Alban, ordered a mother to be buried alive (because she had broken her vestal vows) and her two children to be thrown into the Tiber River. The legendary story goes on to say that the river received them kindly and bore them to a little bank, where they were cast ashore at the foot of a fig tree. Here they were found by a she-wolf, who cared for them until they were discovered by the shepherd Faustulus, who took them into his home and reared them.

Bitches with a strong maternal instinct and a placid nature make excellent foster mothers. The mothering instinct of some bitches is so strong that they will produce milk for orphans placed in their care, whether or not they have recently had a litter. There are records of bitches having raised rabbits, pigs, cats, and other animals.

In passing, it is also noteworthy that women have been known to suckle pups. During the eighteenth century, this sometimes occurred in Italy, where women suckled the pups of highly prized, delicate lapdogs. Eskimo women have also been known to rear orphaned Huskies with their own children, thereby pointing up the recognized importance of sled dogs in the Arctic from the standpoint of survival.

9. *In medical and space age research*—Dogs have contributed richly to both medical and space age research. They're monogastric (single-stomached animals) like man. Also, in comparison with rats and chicks, they are more nearly of comparable size to man. Hence, research conducted with dogs is more likely to be applicable to humans. For this reason, dogs are particularly valuable in medical research. A large number of dogs have lived and died helping man to find the cause of, and the means of preventing, diabetes, pellagra, and rickets. Dogs also preceded man in blood transfusions, in open heart surgery, and in testing radioactive substances. Likewise, dogs preceded man into outer space.

10. *In advertising*—Dogs have always been popular for use in advertising. Without doubt, the most famous trademark in the world is the painting by Francis Barraud, showing a dog listening to the sound emitted by a Gramophone (see

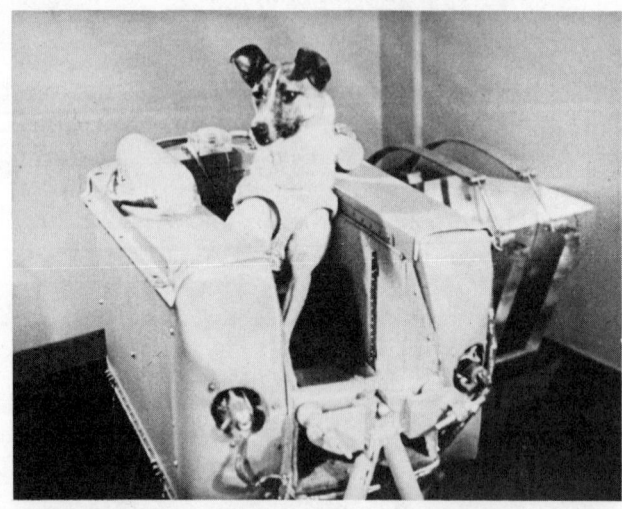

Fig. 356. The crossbred female, Laika, in the capsule of an artificial earth satellite, on November 3, 1957. This was the second artificial satellite launched by the Russians, but the first to contain an animal (or man). At the time of the historic flight, Laika was six years old and weighed 13.2 pounds.

The realization of man's age-old dream of flying off beyond the bounds of earth, to other planets, could not have been achieved without having a profound knowledge of the conditions existing in interplanetary space. Scientists first needed to know (1) the intensity of the various kinds of radiation that can exert a substantial influence on the living organism; and (2) how the living organism reacts to the conditions of cosmic flight.

The dog, the devoted friend of man, helped solve many riddles of the cosmos. The flight of the small canine astronauts in geophysical rockets and sputniks enabled scientists to obtain the necessary data on the adaptability of animals to the unusual conditions of the cosmos. (Courtesy The Soviet Embassy, Washington, D. C.)

Fig. 357. Dog and phonograph trademark. Trademark registered in the United States by RCA. Without doubt, this is the most famous dog trademark in the world. (Courtesy RCA, New York, N.Y.)

Fig. 357). Dogs are also used in many other less well-known trademarks and advertisements.

FAMOUS DOGS AND FAMOUS PEOPLE

Many famous people have been dog fanciers through the ages. The Egyptian Pharaohs often had sculptures or pictures of their favorite dogs placed in their tombs. Many of the rulers of the world, including U.S. presidents, have displayed great fondness for dogs; and many of their dogs have become famous as companions to their masters—George Washington rode to hounds.

Dogs became film stars right from the start of silent movies. Rin Tin Tin—a German Shepherd Dog born in a German trench during World War I, deserted by the retreating Germans, found in a dugout by Lt. Lee Duncan, an American officer, who nursed him through puppyhood and brought him home—became the first great canine star. At one time his name was as well known as that of any human star, and his salary compared favorably with theirs.

Soon after the phenomenal success of the film "Lassie Come Home," it was estimated that Hollywood had some 250 professionally trained dogs working in its studios. The use of dogs in movies and television has continued unabated. For big film parts, dogs nearly always have a double. In fact, there are usually several doubles, each good at a different thing; and they are changed according to the action.

Fig. 358. Washington's Last Meeting With His Mother, showing his dog standing beside him as he embraces his mother. (Courtesy General Services Administration, National Archives and Records Service, Washington, D. C.)

Fig. 359. Calvin and Mrs. Coolidge with Rob Roy, a white Collie. (Courtesy General Services Administration, National Archives and Records Service, Washington, D. C.)

Fig. 360. Herbert Hoover, with his dog, Pat, a German Shepherd. (Courtesy Herbert Hoover Presidential Library, West Branch, Iowa)

Fig. 361. Franklin D. Roosevelt and Fala, a Scottish Terrier. No White House dog was ever so close to his master as was Fala. (Courtesy Franklin D. Roosevelt Library, Hyde Park, N.Y.)

Fig. 363. Charlie, a Welsh Terrier (left), and Pashinka, a dog of mixed breeding, pets of President John F. Kennedy. (Courtesy John F. Kennedy Library, Waltham, Mass.)

Fig. 362. General Dwight D. Eisenhower, with his Scottish Terriers, Caacie (standing) and Telek. Picture taken in Algiers, North Africa, in 1943. (Courtesy Dwight D. Eisenhower Library, Abilene, Kan.)

Fig. 364. Blanco, a white Collie (left), and Him, a Beagle, with their master, Lyndon B. Johnson. (Courtesy Lyndon B. Johnson)

Fig. 365. President Richard Nixon shows his Irish Setter, King Timahoe, to Marian Scully, 18, of Timahoe County, Ireland. Miss Scully first met the President in 1970 when he landed in her father's field on his trip to Ireland. (Wide World Photos)

Fig. 366. Her Majesty, Queen Elizabeth II, of England, has always had Welsh Corgi (Pembroke) dogs. One of them is buried under a headstone with the inscription, "The Queen's faithful friend, Susan." The members of the royal family pictured above are, from left, Prince Philip, Princess Anne, Prince Edward, Queen Elizabeth, Prince Charles, and Prince Andrew. (Courtesy The Fresno Bee)

Fig. 367. President Eamon de Valera, of Ireland, shown on his ninetieth birthday with his Shetland Sheep Dogs (Collie in miniature), Bran (begging) and Nessa. In transmitting this picture to the author of this book, the President's personal secretary commented as follows: "The devotion between the President and his dogs is something wonderful. He frequently remarks that 'they are God's own creatures.'" (Courtesy Marie O'Kelly, Personal Secretary to the President, Dublin, Ireland)

449

Fig. 368. Lassie, Collie canine star. (Courtesy Champion Valley Farms, Inc., Camden, N.J.)

Fig. 369. The Incredible Journey, featuring: Bodger, the Bull Terrier; Tao, the Siamese cat; and Luath, the Labrador Retriever. (Courtesy Walt Disney Productions, Burbank, Calif. © MCMLXIII Walt Disney Productions)

Fig. 370. Little Skye Terrier, Bobby, steals this scene from veteran character actor Laurence Naismith by standing on his hind legs for the camera during filming of Walt Disney's Technicolor motion picture, Greyfriars Bobby, the tale of Scotland's famous dog who became immortal because of his faithfulness to his master. (Courtesy Walt Disney Productions, Burbank, Calif. © Walt Disney Productions)

Fig. 371. Darren McGavin with Boomerang, Dog of Many Talents. *(Courtesy Walt Disney Productions, Burbank, Calif.   © Walt Disney Productions)*

Fig. 373. Old Yeller, *in a movie of the same name. (Courtesy Walt Disney Productions, Burbank, Calif. © MCMLXXI Walt Disney Productions)*

Fig. 372. Johnny Whitaker and George Spell with Moreover, title star of the film, The Biscuit Eater. *(Courtesy Walt Disney Productions, Burbank, Calif. © MCMLXXI Walt Disney Productions)*

Fig. 374. Pluto and His Bone, with Cricket. *(Courtesy Walt Disney Productions, Burbank, Calif.   © Walt Disney Productions)*

451

Fig 375. Lady and the Tramp. *(Courtesy Walt Disney Productions, Burbank, Calif.* © *Walt Disney Productions)*

Fig. 376. Two hearts beat as one when a couple of canine cuties, Pongo and Perdita, discuss their coming parenthood in this scene from Walt Disney's Technicolor feature-length cartoon comedy One Hundred and One Dalmatians. *Adapted from the Dodie Smith novel, this is the hilarious story of an ultra-villainous woman who steals Dalmatians for the wonderful fur coats they make. Re-release is by Buena Vista. (Courtesy Walt Disney Productions, Burbank, Calif.* © *MCMLXI Walt Disney Productions)*

Fig. 377. Monument to Old Drum at Warrensburg, Mo.; by Reno Gustaldi. (picture on next page)

When Senator George Graham Vest paid his famous tribute to the dog in the old Court house in Warrensburg, Mo., in 1870, he appealed to the hearts of dog lovers everywhere when he said: "The one absolutely unselfish friend that a man can have in this selfish world, the one that never deserts him, the one that never proves ungrateful or treacherous, is his dog."

That eulogy of Senator Vest won the case for Charles Burden whose favorite hound, Drum, was shot by a neighbor, Leonidas Hornsby, who had sworn to kill the first dog that came on his place after he had lost a number of sheep. Though Hornsby had hunted with Drum, and acknowledged him to be one of the best hunting dogs he had ever seen, he stubbornly insisted on carrying out his threat when one dark night a dog was found prowling in his yard. That dog was Old Drum.

Immediately Burden sued Hornsby for damages and the trial became one of the strangest in the history of this section of the country. Each man was determined to win his case, and several appeals were made till Hornsby finally took it to the Supreme Court of Missouri. Burden, however, was awarded $50 damages for the loss of his favorite hunting dog, Drum. Vest's eulogy to the dog, which he made in his final appeal to the jury, won the case and became a classic speech.

When Senator Vest said: "Gentlemen of the jury, a man's dog stands by him in prosperity and poverty, in health and sickness," he touched a common bond of relationship in all dog lovers. (Courtesy The Warrensburg Chamber of Commerce)

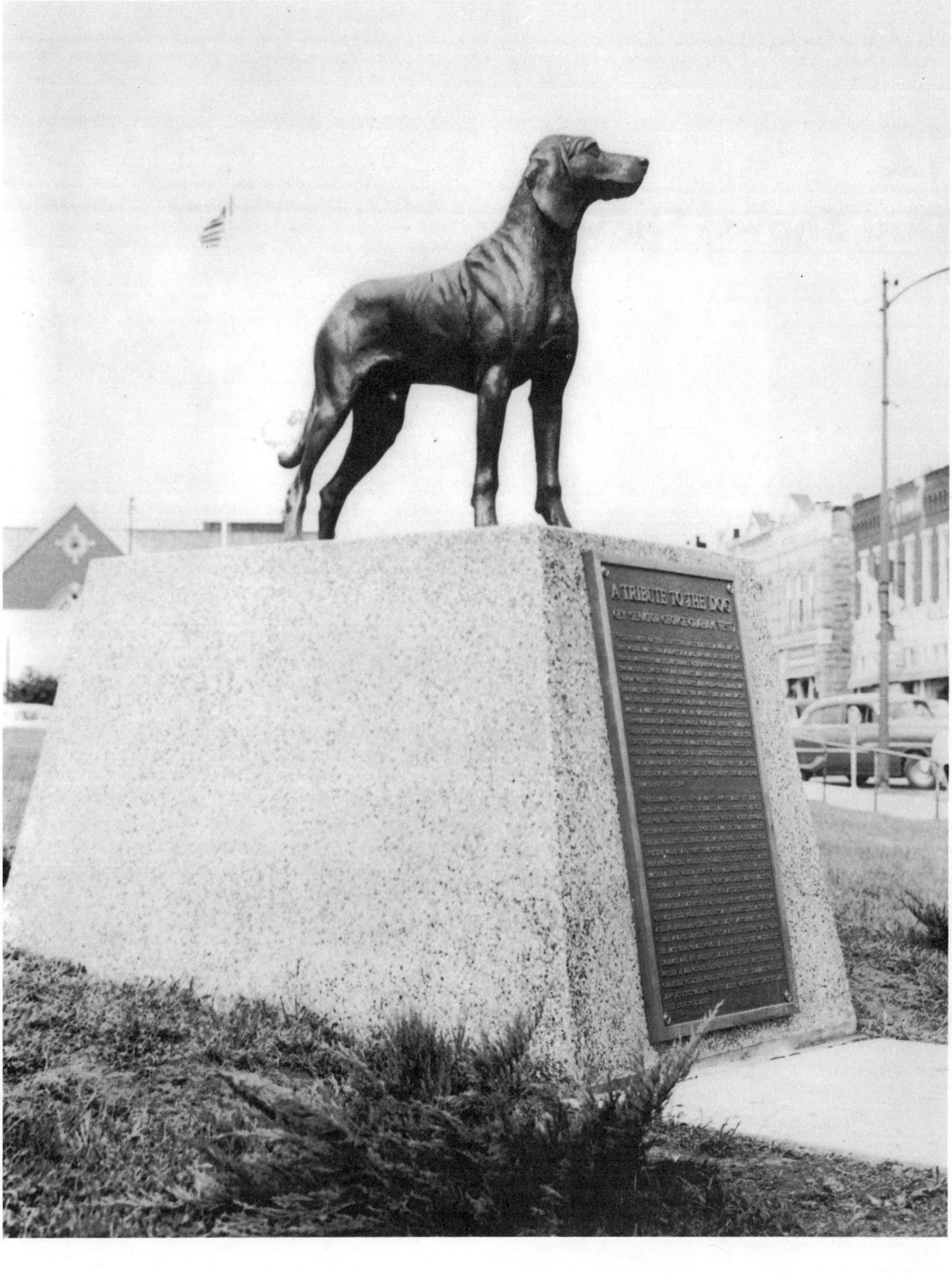
A TRIBUTE TO THE DOG

12
Dog Shows; Showing

Chapter 12
History   *457*
Present Popularity   *457*
Purposes of Shows   *457*
Dog Show Classes   *457*
    Championship Points   *460*
Obedience Trials   *461*
    Obedience Degrees   *461*
    Five Basic Classes   *461*
Kinds of Shows   *462*
    Match Shows   *462*
    Championship Shows—Benched or Unbenched   *463*
    Specialty Shows   *463*
Show Facilities and Personnel   *463*
    Facilities   *463*
        Benching Stalls   *463*
        Ring   *463*
    Personnel   *463*
        Superintendent   *463*
        Committee   *464*
        Judge   *464*
        Steward   *464*
        Veterinarian   *465*
        Professional Handlers   *465*
Premium List   *465*
Entry Blanks   *465*
Preparing Your Dog for the Show   *465*
    Conditioning   *465*
    Show Leash   *466*
    Gaiting   *466*
    Pose and Stance   *467*
    Teeth Examination   *468*
    Scrotum Examination   *468*

(Continued)

Examination by Strangers; Presence of Other Dogs	*468*
Grooming	*468*
The Art of Showing	*468*
The Art of Judging	*470*
Dogs Shows Abroad	*471*
Canada	*472*
Bermuda	*472*
Great Britain	*472*

Fig. 378. Best of Show, showing the six group winners competing for the top award at the Great Westminster Kennel Club, New York City—the oldest club in the U.S. with a continuous record of annual dog shows, going back to 1877. (Photo by William P. Gilbert, Flemington, N.J.)

DOG SHOWS; SHOWING[1]

Expert dog showmen are artists. Not artists whose tools are the clay and the marble of the sculptor. Not artists whose materials are the "green pastures and still waters" that have inspired musicians to capture their beauty in pastoral symphonies, and painters to reproduce their splendor in landscape designs. But artists whose materials are the living flesh and blood of dogs molded to perfection through heredity and environment.

The great dog shows throughout the world have exerted a profound influence in breed improvement. Here the exhibitor is afforded an opportunity to compare his dogs with those of his fellow breeders and to exchange ideas. There is no higher achievement than that of breeding and fitting a champion—an animal representing an ideal that has been produced through intelligent

---
[1] The author acknowledges with thanks the authoritative review accorded this chapter by: Mrs. Lee Watts, Show Secretary, North Shore Kennel Club of B.C., 1840 Mathers Avenue, West Vancouver, B.C.

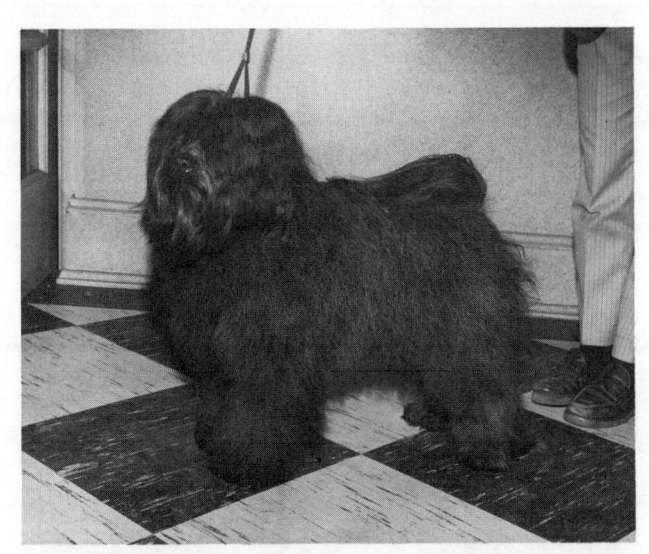

Fig. 379. Champion Cedwoods Pierre, a Puli properly presented for show. There is no higher achievement than breeding and/or fitting a champion. (Courtesy Mrs. Charles R. Anderson, Cedwood Puli Kennels, Bristol, Conn.)

breeding and then fitted and shown to the height of perfection.

HISTORY

The first dog show on record was held in England in 1859.

Dog shows in the United States had their beginning in the 1870s, with a half-dozen poorly regulated events. The oldest club in the United States with a continuous record of annual dog shows is the Westminster Kennel Club of New York City. Its first event was held in 1877.

Although dog shows have grown continuously since their inception, they have experienced their greatest growth since World War II.

PRESENT POPULARITY

In 1971, 2,802 dog shows were held under AKC rules in the United States, of which 586 were all-breed shows, 646 were specialty shows, and 1,570 were sanctioned show matches. From 10 to 3,000 dogs competed at each show, making for a total of 658,247 dogs at all-breed and specialty shows. Also, participating in these events were about 2,630 licensed dog show judges, and 1,200 licensed handlers who look to this sport as a major source of income.

PURPOSES OF SHOWS

The primary purpose of dog shows is the improvement of breeds. They afford the best medium yet discovered for molding breed type. For this reason, it behooves the American Kennel Club and purebred breeders alike to accept their rightful responsibility in seeing that the dogs winning top honors are those which most nearly meet the breed standards.

Today, 116 breeds of dogs are recognized by the American Kennel Club. There is no question but that dog shows have wrought great changes in the long-established breeds, as is evidenced by comparison of photographs of top winners of dogs of any of these breeds through the years. They have undergone great improvement in type, confirmation, and temperament, as a result of being subjected to the eyes of critical dog-show judges and discriminating fanciers.

Other purposes of dog shows are:

1. They provide an incentive to breed better animals, for the breeder can determine how well he is keeping pace with his competitors only after securing an impartial appraisal of his entries in comparison with others.

2. They offer an opportunity to study the progress being made within other breeds.

3. They serve as one of the very best advertising or promotional mediums for both the breed and the breeder.

4. They give breeders an opportunity to exchange ideas, thereby serving as an educational event.

5. They offer an opportunity to sell a limited number of breeding animals.

6. They set values for the animals back home, for such values are often based on the sale of show animals.

DOG SHOW CLASSES

Many people who go to a dog show for the first time are bewildered by the procedure and the many breeds and classes that they see. Others have never attended a dog show because they feel their lack of knowledge of showing and judging dogs would prevent them from enjoying it. Much of this chapter is provided for such people. Also,

TABLE 50

DOG SHOW CLASSES

REGULAR CLASSES .... *EACH BREED: (1) DOGS, AND (2) BITCHES* ....

All dogs competing for championship points are entered in one (or more) of the regular classes for their breed or variety, and by sex. A variety is a division within a breed based on height, weight, and/or color. Four ribbons are awarded for each class—blue for first, red for second, yellow for third, and white for fourth

PUPPY
For dogs under one year (may be divided 6–9 and 9–12 months)

NOVICE
For dogs not having won three firsts in novice, none in other classes (except puppy) nor any championship points

BRED BY EXHIBITOR
For dogs not champions owned wholly or partly by breeder; shown by him or his family

AMERICAN-BRED
For all dogs, except champions, born in the U.S.A., resulting from a mating which took place in the U.S.A.

OPEN
For any dog; if divided by color, height, or weight, it must be entered in the correct division

WINNERS CLASSES .... *WINNERS DOG and WINNERS BITCH* (and any other class) competes for Winners. He or she receives a purple ribbon

The first-place winner of each class (which has not been beaten in any other class) competes for Winners. He or she receives a purple ribbon and points proportionate to the number of entrants present

RESERVE WINNERS DOG and RESERVE WINNERS BITCH

The second-place animal from the Winners class competes with the animals remaining in the ring (unless he or she has already been defeated by one of them), for Reserve Winners. The RW receives a purple-and-white ribbon, and moves up to Winners if the Winners is for any reason disqualified

BEST OF BREED .... *BEST OF BREED*

The Winners Dog and Winners Bitch compete with any champions entered for Best of Breed (entries in this class are dogs or bitches that are champions, having acquired sufficient points in previous competition. If there are no champions entered, the Best of Winners is automatically Best of Breed. The other dog or bitch competing for Best of Winners is Best of Opposite Sex), and winners of nonregular classes such as Veteran, Local, or Field Dog (if they have not been previously defeated in a regular class), for Best of Breed, or for Best of Variety of Breed, if there are varieties. The winner receives a purple-and-gold ribbon

BEST OF WINNERS

If the Winners Dog or Winners Bitch is awarded Best of Breed or Best of Variety, it automatically is awarded Best of Winners; otherwise, the Winners Dog and Winners Bitch are judged together for Best of Winners. In addition to the blue-and-white ribbon, the BW may receive additional points if the opposite sex had an entry qualifying for higher points

BEST OF OPPOSITE SEX

Following selection of Best of Breed and Best of Winners, all individuals of the sex opposite to BOB remain in the ring. The Winners Dog or Winners Bitch (whichever is also of the sex opposite to Best of Breed) is judged in this class. From this group, Best of Opposite Sex is chosen. A red-and-white ribbon is awarded to the Best of Opposite Sex to Best of Breed (or of Variety)—BOS

amateur showmen should familiarize themselves with procedures and classes.

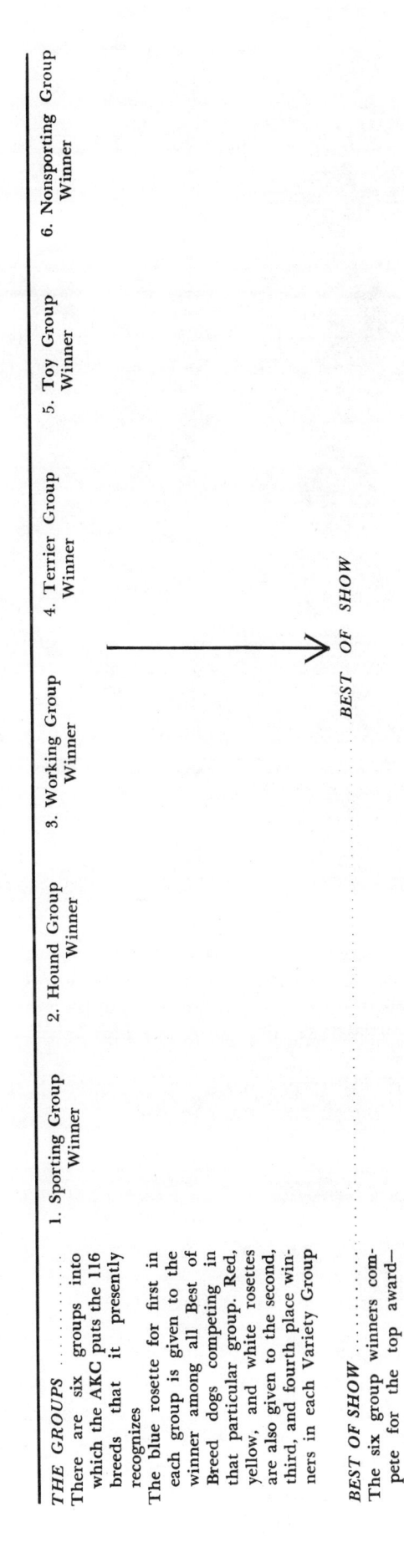

The dog show classes are set forth in Table 50. As shown therein, a dog show is actually an elimination contest. Thus, in a show that might have 2,500 dogs, each breed is first exhibited. Then, gradually through a process of elimination, the show progresses until a single dog is selected as Best Of Show.

The following facts are pertinent to Table 50: In the average dog show, there are 5 classes for dogs and 5 for bitches—Puppy (as shown in Table 50, the puppy class may be divided into (1) 6 to 9 months, and (2) 9 to 12 months), Novice, Bred by Exhibitor, American-Bred, and Open. There are 4 placings in each of the classes; a blue ribbon for first, red for second, yellow for third, and white for fourth. The first place winners of each class compete against each other, and a purple ribbon is given to the Winner. This means that the dog (or bitch) is the best male (or female) of all those competing in the classes that day. He (or she) receives points towards his (or her) championship; the number of points depending upon the number of dogs (or bitches) of the breed present and the part of the country in which the show is held. The second place winner receives a purple and white ribbon marked Reserve Winners Dog (or Bitch). The best male and the best bitch then both enter the Best of Breed competition class, together with all champions entered. If the male or bitch wins Best of Breed, he or she is automatically also Best of Winners, which earns a blue and white ribbon. But if neither wins the breed, the judge then decides between them.

Any number of champions may compete in the Best of Breed competition class, but only one will be Best of Breed. This may be either a dog or a bitch, and the ribbon is purple and gold. If there are varieties of the breed, as in Poodles, the winner is called Best of Variety. If the Best of Breed (or Best of Variety) winner is a dog, a bitch will be picked as Best of Opposite Sex and she does not necessarily have to be a champion. The ribbon is red and white. If a bitch should win Best of Breed (or Best of Variety), a male is selected to receive the red and white rosette.

All breeds recognized by the American Kennel Club are divided into 6 groups (See next paragraph for certain exceptions). So, all Best of Breed or Best of Variety winners have the opportunity to compete against the other breeds of dogs in their respective group. Again there are

TABLE 50 (CONTINUED)

THE GROUPS	1. Sporting Group Winner
There are six groups into which the AKC puts the 116 breeds that it presently recognizes	2. Hound Group Winner
The blue rosette for first in each group is given to the winner among all Best of Breed dogs competing in that particular group. Red, yellow, and white rosettes are also given to the second, third, and fourth place winners in each Variety Group	3. Working Group Winner
	4. Terrier Group Winner
	5. Toy Group Winner
	6. Nonsporting Group Winner
BEST OF SHOW	
The six group winners compete for the top award—Best of Show	→ BEST OF SHOW
A rosette, colored red, white, and blue or in the colors of the kennel club is given	

459

Fig. 380. All breed dog show and obedience trials, sponsored by the Sun Maid Kennel Club, Fresno, California, in which more than 3,000 dogs competed. (Courtesy The Fresno Bee)

4 placings, and the ribbons, although more elaborate, are the same colors as in the classes—blue, red, yellow, and white. The winning dogs of the 6 groups then compete against each other for Best of Show.

Certain breeds of dogs, though recognized by the American Kennel Club, have not as yet gained sufficient popularity to be represented at dog shows. Many times there will be only one exhibit of a breed. In such cases, the dog automatically receives Best of Breed and becomes eligible for competition in the group. The dog does not receive championship points because he has no competition, but if he should place first in the group, he will receive the maximum number of points awarded to any breed in his group that day.

A dog eligible in more than one class may be entered in each class, but it is usually wiser to enter him in one class only. For example, a puppy should, unless he is unusually precocious and mature, be placed in the Puppy Class; and it is unrealistic to expect so young a dog to defeat older dogs, although an exceptional puppy may receive an award in the Winners Class.

Anyone planning to enter a dog show should check the most recent Rule Book because the regulations change from time to time.

CHAMPIONSHIP POINTS

To become a champion, a dog must win 15 championship points. Such points are earned only by placing first in the Winners Class. However, the dog chosen Best of Winners is entitled to the highest number of points won in the 2 sexes. For example, if there were very few males competing and the Winner's dog won only one point, but beat the Winner' bitch, who had won 5 points because of more competition, then he (the dog) would also be entitled to 5 points.

Championship points are awarded on a scale drawn up by the American Kennel Club. The nation is divided into four areas. In each area, the points for each breed are figured on the basis of national registrations and previous show entries from that area. All show catalogs are required to carry the scale of points for all breeds in the section of the country where the show is held. This may vary for dogs and bitches of the same breed.

Five points is the largest number that can be won at one show. Rare breeds can combine the sexes for judging. This yields more championship points, but only one Winners Class instead of the usual two.

The German Shepherd Dog is one of the most popular breeds and the most often shown dog. So, it requires an average of between 50 and 60 males in actual class competition to yield 5 championship points, and 55 to 65 bitches of this breed must compete to gain 5 points, depending on location of show.

There is one other way in which a dog can win championship points. If he comes up through the classes, wins Best of Breed, then wins first of his group, he is entitled to the maximum number of points awarded to any other dog in the group.

"Cheap championships" are prevented by the provision that a dog must win two shows with 3 points or more under at least 2 different judges (these are called 3 point, 4 point, or 5 point "majors"). Thus, a dog must be shown in stiff competition before it can win the coveted title of "Champion."

OBEDIENCE TRIALS

Obedience trials have increased in popularity in recent years. More than half the American dog shows now have obedience trials in conjunction with them.

The principle value of obedience training work is that it brings home to the public the fact that it is a simple and easy matter to teach dogs to obey commands readily and willingly. After having witnessed an obedience trial, most spectators are convinced that anyone of even temper and reasonable patience can teach his own dog the exercises observed in obedience training programs. If there are no obedience training classes available in the neighborhood, a person can take advantage of good books on the subject. There is absolutely no reason why every dog owned by an intelligent person should not possess at least a reasonable amount of good manners.

OBEDIENCE DEGREES

Winning degrees is a little different from making your dog a Bench Show Champion. The four obedience titles offered by the American Kennel Club are:

1. C.D., or Companion Dog
2. C.D.X., or Companion Dog Excellent
3. U.D., or Utility Dog
4. T.D., or Tracking Dog.

The tracking test is held apart from dog shows. While the first three degrees are progressive, the tracking title may be won at anytime.

Dogs entered in this class are required to locate a missing object that shall be left at least 440 yards away from the starting point and on a trail that is at least 30 minutes old.

Each set of exercises carries a maximum possible score of 200 points, divided among the various exercises in proportion to their importance. Perfect scores are possible, but not often achieved. At least half of the points of each exercise and a total of 170 of the possible 200 must be scored for a "passing" score. After 3 qualifying scores under different judges with a minimum number of dogs (6 in combined Novice or Open classes and 3 in Utility) a dog will receive his degree.

FIVE BASIC CLASSES

Much like breed shows there are five basic classes in obedience, namely:

1. *Novice A and Novice B Classes*—Both Novice A and Novice B are for dogs over six months of age that have not won the C.D. title. Novice A must be handled by an amateur who has not previously shown or trained a dog that has won a C.D. title in the obedience ring, whereas dogs in Novice B may be handled by a professional. The exercise and points follow:

	Points
a. Heeling on leash	35
b. Stand for examination	30
c. Heel free	45
d. Recall	30
e. Long sit	30
f. Long down	30
Maximum total score	200

Fig. 381. Executing the 8-inch jump. (Courtesy McLaughlin Photography, Morrison, Colo.)

Fig. 382. Executing the 36-inch jump. (Courtesy McLaughlin Photography, Morrison, Colo.)

Fig. 383. Executing the broad jump. (Courtesy McLaughlin Photography, Morrison, Colo.)

2. *Open Class A (for amateur showmen) and Open Class B (for amateurs or professionals)*—Open Class A is for dogs that have won the C.D. title, but have not won the C.D.X.; whereas Open Class B is for dogs that have won either the C.D. or C.D.X. The exercises and points for open classes are:

		Points
a.	Heel free	40
b.	Drop on recall	30
c.	Retrieve on flat	25
d.	Retrieve over high jump	35
e.	Broad jump	20
f.	Long sit	25
g.	Long down	25
	Maximum total score	200

3. *Utility Class*—There are five exercises for the 200 points that count for perfection in the Utility Class. These are:

		Points
a.	Scent discrimination article No. 1	30
b.	Scent discrimination article No. 2	30
c.	Directed retrieve	30
d.	Signal exercise	35
e.	Directed jumping	40
f.	Group examination	35
	Maximum total score	200

In a speciality show that features only obedience, there may be additional classes such as Graduate Novice, Brace, Team, and Versatility. These last four increase the number of entries and make the show more interesting from the spectator's point of view, but they have no bearing on the dog's obedience degrees.

KINDS OF SHOWS

There are different kinds of dog shows. A brief discussion of each kind will follow:

MATCH SHOWS

Match shows are generally quite informal and are designed primarily for the pleasure of local club members and exhibitors. Young dogs frequently receive their first show experience at match shows. Match, or sanctioned shows, are excellent training and experience for regular bench shows. Entry fees are low, usually ranging from $.50 to $1, and are made at the show instead of in advance. Sanctioned shows are unbenched, informal affairs where the puppy may follow his owner about on the leash and become accustomed to strange dogs, behaving himself in the ring, and to being handled by a judge. For the novice exhibitor, too, sanctioned shows will provide valuable experience for the ring procedure followed at regular bench shows.

CHAMPIONSHIP SHOWS— BENCHED OR UNBENCHED

Championship shows, or point shows, are the top shows approved by the American Kennel Club. Such a show may be undertaken by a club only after it has satisfactorily conducted a series of match shows.

Each member club in the American Kennel Club is entitled to conduct at least one championship, or point show, each year. Such shows are known as *member shows*. Nonmember clubs which can qualify may obtain a license from the AKC to offer a show of the same general type as members. The latter shows are designated *licensed shows*.

Shows may either be *benched* or *unbenched*. In benched shows, the dogs must be left at the show for the duration of the exhibit. When not being judged, they are kept on an elevated platform, divided into stalls. Some exhibitors choose to sit by their dog's bench, but if he is securely chained he is likely to be safe in his owner's absence. The greatest danger is that the dog may grow nervous and insecure, so it is best that the owner return to the bench once in a while to reassure the dog of his security.

If the show is unbenched, dogs may be kept with the owner anywhere on the showgrounds. Your identification slip, received following your entry, may tell you that you need not be at the show until an hour before your breed is called for judging, and that you may leave as soon as you are no longer needed.

SPECIALTY SHOWS

A specialty show is one that is devoted to only one breed of dogs. Usually, a specialty show provides for more than the five basic classes shown in Table 50.

SHOW FACILITIES AND PERSONNEL

A successful dog show necessitates a combination of adequate facilities and experienced personnel.

FACILITIES

Facilities must include benching stalls for the dogs, a ring in which to exhibit, seating arrangement for the spectators, food service, and toilet facilities. Depending on the kind of show, certain special and additional equipment may be necessary; for example, jumps for dogs in obedience trials.

Shows may be held in permanent buildings, tents, or in the open.

BENCHING STALLS

Benching stalls are places for keeping dogs that are exhibited in a bench show. They are flat areas equipped with a ring on the bench with which to secure the dog. It is recommended that a bench chain be used to secure the dog; otherwise, he might chew his leather leash and escape. The bench chain is designed with a snap on each end—one to snap to the dog's collar, and the other to secure him to the ring on the bench. A familiar blanket or cushion for the bench makes the dog feel more at home.

RING

The ring(s) should be of sufficient size to accommodate the number of dogs that will be exhibited at the maximum; and there should be sufficient ringside seats to accommodate the maximum number of spectators that it is anticipated will be in attendance.

PERSONNEL

The staging of a successful dog show requires considerable manpower, particularly if it is a large show. Also, it goes without saying that the larger the show, the greater the demands on the personnel. Hence, for managing a large show, there is nothing like having experienced personnel.

SUPERINTENDENT

Some clubs appoint one of their own members

as their show secretary, then this person obtains a license from the American Kennel Club to handle a particular show. Other clubs, engage the services of a licensed superintendent. Some twenty organizations in the United States are licensed by the American Kennel Club to handle superintending problems. Some of these superintendents offer complete service to the clubs—ring equipment, benching, seating, and even tenting.

The rules of the American Kennel Club clearly define the duties and responsibilities of the superintendent of a show and hold him accountable for carrying out these responsibilities. Among other things, he prints the premium list and mails it out to the dog owners in the show area in advance of the show, furnishes the ribbons and prints the catalog that lists the dogs in their respective classes, and promotes the sale of tickets.

COMMITTEE

The committee shares responsibility with the superintendent in planning and conducting the show. Actually, they are in direct charge of the show. They engage the superintendent, they engage the judges, and they attend to all arrangements that are not assigned to the superintendent. Additionally, the AKC grants to the bench show committee some very broad disciplinary powers over the affairs of its own show. This committee must rule on many questions that are certain to arise at its show. Also, if major rule violations occur at the show, the committee is expected to sit as a court in a determination of such cases. The committee is empowered to suspend persons from all privileges of the AKC for conduct at its show that is found to be prejudicial to the best interest of dog shows.

JUDGE

The judge is the person chosen by the show-giving club to determine the relative merits of all dogs entered in the show. Judges are licensed, following investigation, by the American Kennel Club. However, each show must select its own judge or judges. Judges vary in their compensation; some serve without any pay whatsoever, others expect reimbursement for expenses, and still others expect a professional fee plus expenses.

Judging dogs is an art, the rudiments of which must be learned through patient study and long practice. The essential qualifications that a good judge of dogs must possess are as follows:

1. *Knowledge of the parts of a dog*—This consists of mastering the language that describes and locates the different parts of a dog (see Fig. 15). In addition, it is necessary to know which of these parts are of major importance; that is, what comparative evaluation to give to the different parts.

2. *A clearly defined ideal or standard of perfection*—The judge must be thoroughly familiar with the breed standards published by the AKC for the breed or breeds that he is judging. He must know what he is looking for; and he must have in mind an ideal or standard of perfection.

3. *Keen observation and sound judgment*—The good judge possesses the ability to observe both good conformation and defects, and to weigh and evaluate the relative importance of the various good and bad features.

4. *Honesty and courage*—The good judge must possess honesty and courage. For example, it often requires considerable courage to place a class of dogs without regard to (a) winnings in previous shows, (b) ownership, and (c) public applause.

5. *Tact*—In discussing a show-ring class, it is important that the judge be tactful. The owner is likely to resent any remarks that imply that his dog is inferior.

Having acquired the above knowledge and skill, long hours must be spent in patient study and practice in comparing dogs. Even this will not make expert and proficient judges in all instances, for there may be a grain of truth in the statement that "the best judges are born and not made." Nevertheless training in judging and selecting dogs is effective when directed by a competent instructor or experienced dog owner.

STEWARD

Each ring must have at least one steward. The steward's job is to help the judge. He sees that the exhibitors have the right arm bands, and that they bring their dogs into the right classes. The judge cannot look in the official dog show catalog. So the steward must check the dogs, the arm bands, and see that trophies are present and awarded.

Good stewards keep the ring running efficiently. Poor stewards can complicate and make more difficult a judge's assignment. Stewards work hard and are an important part of every well-run dog show.

VETERINARIAN

The veterinarian performs two important functions:

1. He may give each entry a once over as they come on the show grounds, just to make sure that they are healthy. Healthy dogs are quickly passed along.

2. If a dog is limping in the ring, the judge must disqualify him and mark his book, "Excused—lame."

PROFESSIONAL HANDLERS

Both the American Kennel Club and the Canadian Kennel Club license professional handlers, who will exhibit dogs for others on a charge basis. The granting of a handler's license indicates that the person is experienced and skilled at grooming and showing dogs and that adequate kennels are maintained in which to keep dogs between shows.

Usually, owners pay entry fees and board during the interim between shows. Handlers get any premium money the dog may win, but trophies go to the owners of the winning dogs.

The services of a professional handler are not essential, but it is recognized that an exhibitor without previous show experience is usually at a disadvantage. Thus, where the owner has a good dog that has a chance to win, it may be in the nature of a good investment for him to hire the services of a professional handler.

PREMIUM LIST

The premium list contains entry blanks, a list of the classes and prizes offered, information about judges, and the time of the show. Lists are usually distributed five to six weeks ahead of the show.

ENTRY BLANKS

If you decide to enter your dog in a particular show, you must fill out the entry blank, which is usually at the back of the premium list, and mail it, along with the required fee, so that it will reach the superintendent's office before the closing date.

Every dog entered in an approved show must be registered or in the process of being registered with the American Kennel Club. Remember that a sanctioned or licensed dog show is for purebred dogs only. Also, to be accepted the entry form must show the dog's individual registration number or the litter registration number. An eligible dog that is only litter registered may be shown no more than three times unless it has been given an indefinite listing privilege by the AKC.

In addition to the registry rule, other dog show rules with which you should be familiar are: A dog that is blind, deaf, or lame is automatically barred from competition. Cryptorchids, monorchids, castrated males, and spayed bitches may be shown in obedience trials but not in breed competition. On the other hand, bitches in season may be shown in breed competition, but not in obedience trials. In the breed ring, a dog's color or markings may not be changed by the use of any substance. Chalk may be used on a white dog for the purpose of cleaning his coat, but it must be brushed off thoroughly before the dog is exhibited.

Five to six days before the show, you will receive a receipt for your entry that will serve as identification which you must present for you and your dog to enter the show. If the show is benched (stalls provided in which the dogs must be kept during show hours), your identification will show your stall number and the deadline hour for getting your dog into the show. If the show is unbenched (dogs may be kept with you anywhere on the show ground), your identification slip may tell that you need not be at the show until half an hour before your breed is called for judging and that you may leave as soon as you are no longer needed.

PREPARING YOUR DOG FOR THE SHOW

If you have decided to exhibit your dog, many things must be done long before the show in order to get him ready. Each of the major points involved in preparing for the show will be discussed.

CONDITIONING

By conditioning we refer to the sum total of the things involved in getting the dog in show shape. This includes the following:

1. *Good nutrition*—The subject of nutrition

and feeding is fully covered in chapter 4 of this book, so needless repetition will be avoided at this point. The better grades of commercial dog foods, in either canned, dry, or soft-moist form, will take care of the nutritive needs. The main objective is to have a strong, healthy dog that is attractive in appearance. He should be full of life, his eyes should sparkle, and his coat, whatever the length or texture, should have a live, shining quality.

2. *Freedom from parasites*—At the beginning of show preparation, it is well to consider whether the dog is harboring either internal or external parasites. If so, the recommended treatment given in chapter 8 of this book should be applied.

3. *No skin trouble*—If there are any skin troubles, proper treatment should be given immediately. In the first place, a dog with skin trouble will not likely get past the show veterinarian who examines each dog when he enters the show. Secondly, skin trouble is a serious handicap in that no dog can look his best unless his coat is in healthy condition.

4. *Inoculations*—Since the dog must be over six months of age in order to compete at a major dog show, it is assumed that your dog will have been permanently inoculated against distemper and hepatitis prior to the time that you plan to show him.

Even an older dog, or one that has been inoculated, can, if he comes in contact with distemper or hepatitis, acquire the diseases. Hence, it it well to take extra precaution and give your dog booster shots annually.

Prior to showing, (1) study Table 34 of this book, and (2) confer with your veterinarian relative to the inoculations that he recommends prior to showing.

5. *Exercise*—Exercise is a part of conditioning. The dog needs to be brought to a moderate state of flesh, which is hard and firm. Merely turning a dog loose in an enclosure will not achieve this. Daily walks on the leash bring the best results.

6. *Good behavior*—A vicious dog, one that is known to bite people or fight other dogs, should not be in competition. Thus, it is important that the dog that is being prepared for show should be trained to be a gentleman at all times.

7. *Accustomed to crate and car*—More than likely the dog will have to be transported to the show in a crate and/or a car. Hence, training to accept these should be given very early in the conditioning process. Feed him in the crate occasionally, and take him for a car ride once in a while.

8. *Used to high stairs*—Train your dog to walk up and down stairs. More than likely, he will have to do this at the show. Hence, you should prepare him for it.

SHOW LEASH

Most people use a show leash, which serves as both a collar and a leash, at shows. It is important, however, that the dog become accustomed to the show leash well in advance of the show. Put the leash on the dog and tighten it so that it is firm about the throat, but does not choke. When in proper position, the collar should be at the end of the neck so that when the dog's head is raised the leash is just back of his ears. In some breeds, the dog is shown with the lead coming out from under the chin.

GAITING

The dog must be taught to walk or trot with his head up. Also, he must trot on a leash without breaking stride. Remember that the judge must check the dog for soundness of movement. Remember, too, that if the dog's head is down along the ground, soundness of movement cannot be checked because the dog will be spreading his legs slightly as he moves and his head will block the judge's view.

At dog shows, it is required that the judge check gait when the dog is moving straight away from him and when he is coming directly to-

Fig. 384. Trotting on leash. (Drawing by R. F. Johnson)

Fig. 385. A dog properly posed. (Drawing by R. F. Johnson)

ward him. Thus, you should train your dog to move in a straight line.

When you gait your dog, wad the leash into a ball and hold it in your left hand. Keep your elbows straight and the dog away from your body. Select the trot most suited to your dog—faster for German Shepherd Dogs, and slower for the smaller breeds. Above all, keep his nose off the ground.

Although most of the gaiting should be from the left side, it is well that you train your dog to gait on your right side, also. This is important should the judge switch over in order to obtain a side view of the action.

Some handlers make a wide right or left turn (the author prefers a right turn) at the end of the ring, thereby giving the judge a side view of the dog in motion. The judge may want this in the case of certain breeds that have a tendency to be swaybacked; hence, it is well that the dog receive advance training in executing such a turn.

Of course, if the dog has received proper obedience training (as outlined in chapter 6 of this book) gaiting the dog for the show-ring should pose no great problem. Likewise, teaching proper stance will be relatively simple.

POSE AND STANCE

Figs. 385 and 386 show a dog properly posed. The proper stance will vary slightly according to the breed; for example, German Shepherd Dogs are posed with one hind leg brought forward and the tail laid across the other, which is drawn far back. Chows are inclined to be straight in the stifles; hence, they should not be shown with the hind legs back. A good way in which to arrive at the correct pose for your breed of dog is to check books and magazines for pictures showing champions of your particular breed. They will be posed as you will wish to pose your dog in the ring. You should practice having the dog stand with his feet in proper position, with his head and back up. If necessary, slap him under the chin to remind him that he

Fig. 386. Waiterock Elmer Brown, American and Canadian Champion English Springer Spaniel, owned and exhibited by Waiterock Ranch, Lafayette, California. (Courtesy Juanita W. Howard. Waiterock Ranch, Lafayette, Calif.)

must obey and get his head up. If he slumps in the middle, slap him upward in the belly to remind him that he should get his back up and pose. Dogs with arched or roached backs should be trained so that they get their backs level when you stroke or touch the topline.

Place your dog's front feet by grasping them at the elbow; do not take hold of the paws. Pose the back legs by supporting the stifle joints.

Stroke your dog gently along his back or under his stomach while he is posing. This will calm him for a longer period of time.

If the dog becomes restless, hook the little finger of your right hand under the collar on the throat and rest his muzzle in your hand. The slight pressure of the collar on the back of his neck will prevent the dog from drawing back and getting out of hand.

TEETH EXAMINATION

Train your dog to permit examination of his teeth. Then, he will be prepared for the judge's examination. Usually judges examine the teeth for overshot or undershot jaws, or missing teeth. The latter is particularly important in the case of German Shepherd Dogs and Doberman Pinschers, where the premolars may be missing.

Some judges ask the owners or handlers to show the teeth. Even if they do not so request, you will be extending a courtesy to the judge if you show the dog's teeth to him. Thus, your dog should be trained to allow his teeth to be examined; either by you showing them off, or by the judge examining them.

SCROTUM EXAMINATION

All judges are required to check the scrotum of each male, to make sure that there are two normal testicles, and that both of them are descended into the scrotum. Unless trained, most dogs do not like this examination. So you should practice examining your dog's scrotum, so that he won't try to pull away or sit down when this is done.

EXAMINATION BY STRANGERS; PRESENCE OF OTHER DOGS

Since the judge will be a stranger to your dog, it is important that you get him accustomed to having strangers examine him. Call upon your friends to serve in this capacity.

Also, it is important that your dog get used to the presence of other dogs. He should stand calmly and quietly with other dogs next to him, without trying to lunge toward them or becoming nervous.

GROOMING

All dogs should be groomed regularly as discussed in chapter 7 of this book. But, if you plan to enter your dog in a show, you will have to give more care than usual to his coat. With some breeds, such as Terriers and Poodles, it is necessary to start months in advance in order to get the coat in prime condition by show time.

In order to groom a dog for the show-ring, you must have a mental picture of the ideal appearance of a member of the particular breed. Here again, it is a good idea to look over pictures of winners in various books and magazines. Then work toward the attainment of that ideal.

There are so many different "haircuts" and "hairdos" for the various breeds that space limitations will not permit discussing all of them in a book of this kind. However, the most common ones for Poodles are shown in Figs. 387 through 390.

It is good business to call upon a professional, or experienced showman, to give you an assist for the first few times in your efforts to groom your dog for show.

THE ART OF SHOWING

Expert showmanship cannot be achieved through reading any set of instructions. Each show and each ring will be found to present unusual circumstances; and there are some breed differences. However, there are certain guiding principles that are always adhered to by the most successful exhibitors. Some of these are:

1. Train the dog long before entering the ring.
2. Have the dog carefully groomed and ready for the parade before the judge.
3. Dress neatly for the occasion.
4. Enter the ring promptly when the class is called.
5. Keep one eye on your dog and the other

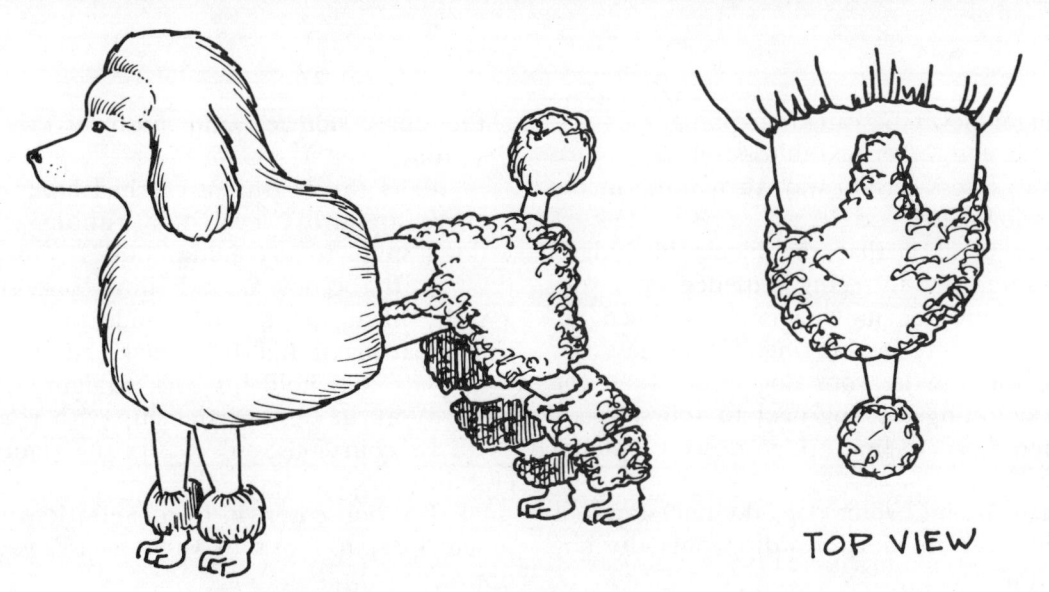

Fig. 387. Poodle. The English Saddle Clip. (Drawing by J. L. Medeiros)

Fig. 388. Poodle. The Continental Clip. (Drawing by J. L. Medeiros)

Fig. 390. Poodle. The Kennel Clip. (Drawing by J. L. Medeiros)

Fig. 389. Poodle. The Puppy Clip. (Drawing by J. L. Medeiros)

on the judge; never be caught napping.

6. Watch the other exhibitors; if they turn their dogs to face a certain way, turn yours in the same direction, also.

7. Never stand so that you block the judge's view; he's interested in seeing your dog—not you.

8. Keep your dog moving or in a posed position while you are in the ring. If the class is a large one, you can let your dog relax when the judge is examining the dog next to yours.

9. When asked to line up, go quickly but not brashly.

10. When posing your dog, do not stand or crouch too close to him; crowding puts the dog at a disadvantage.

11. When asked to pose your dog, do so with a minimum of fuss; the details can be worked out later.

12. Stroke your dog gently along his back or under the belly while he is posing. This will keep him quiet for a longer period of time.

13. If the dog becomes restless, hook the little finger of your right hand under the collar on the dog's throat and rest his muzzle in your hand. The slight pressure of the collar on the back of his neck will prevent him from drawing back and getting out of hand.

14. When you gait your dog—that is, when you move him so that the judge can see his style or trot—wad the leash in a ball and hold it in your left hand; keep your elbows straight and the dog away from your body; and step out in good stride without running. Select the trot most suited to your particular dog and breed—faster for some, slower for others.

15. If you find that you are hemmed in and that the judge cannot see your dog, move to another spot of vantage, unless, of course, the judge has asked you to hold your position.

16. Limit your grooming equipment in the ring to a brush or a comb for long-coated dogs; leave the rest of the grooming equipment on your grooming table.

17. Minimize your dog's faults. A few of the tricks of the trade follow:

a. If your dog has a double throat (loose skin on his throat), place the leash close behind his ears and hold it taut to keep the skin from sagging.

b. If the dog is "out at the elbows," show him on a tight leash to keep his weight off the front legs.

c. If the dog has flatfeet, whereas the breed standard calls for well-arched ones, lift up on the dog's stomach and push his weight forward.

d. If the dog has a roached back (one that curves upward), level it by rubbing along the dog's spine to make him pull it down.

e. If the dog has a hollow back, straighten it by lifting on the underside of the stomach and patting it lightly to make the dog hold it in place and hold his back straight.

18. Work in close partnership with your dog.

19. Be courteous and respect the rights of other exhibitors.

20. Do not enter into conversation with the judge. Speak to him only when he asks you a question.

21. Never question the judge.

22. Be a good sport, *win without bragging and lose without squealing.*

THE ART OF JUDGING

Judging is hard work and great responsibility. Not only does the judge pick the winners, but he leads or misleads many people. For better or worse, he may be the cause of changing breeding programs and affecting the quality of the entire breed.

The judge evaluates dogs against the standards of the particular breed, and he rates them against each other. He tries to pick those dogs that are nearest to the ideal type, and which are both physically and mentally sound.

In making his selections, the judge is guided by the standard of perfection of each breed (see chapter 2, Table 3 of this book for the standards in condensed form). The standard describes what is considered a perfect specimen of the breed, and often the relative importance of each detail. Also, it lists definite faults that are to be discouraged or penalized in the breed.

Sometimes folks wonder how a judge evaluates different breeds in the six variety groups and in the Best of Show competition. The answer is that the judge is guided by the Standard of Perfection. He does not compare one breed against another, but each dog against its breed standard. He looks for the dog that, in his judgment, most nearly fills the criteria set by the standard for its breed.

Of course, opinions differ and two equally competent judges may come out with different placings in a given class. The more faults the dogs have, the more judges' opinions will differ.

This is because they will evaluate faults differently.

The judge must study each dog carefully with his hands as well as his eyes; and with the dog in motion as well as standing. He checks on the texture of the coat, the firmness of muscle and bone, and the soundness of teeth. The way a dog moves is important to him, not only from the standpoint of beauty in motion, but as a test of body structure.

When officiating, most judges follow this sequence:

1. When the class is ready to enter the ring, the judge motions the handlers to circle the ring counterclockwise; and they do so with leashes held in the left hand.

2. The judge stands in the center of the ring and observes the circling dogs.

3. The judge calls a halt and asks that the dogs line up in tandem (one behind the other) along one side of the ring.

4. The handlers quickly arrange the dogs in proper show stance, so as to show their dog's conformation to best advantage.

5. The judge makes a personal inspection of each dog—he examines its head, teeth, ears, neck, shoulders, and front feet; then he steps back and runs his hand over the dog's back, feels its girth, examines its coat, continues back and makes an examination of its rear quarters; and he examines the scrotum of males to make sure that both testicles are normally descended. This same procedure is followed on each dog down the line.

6. After having examined each dog individually, the judge asks each handler to gait his dog across the ring and back. He may ask the exhibitor to make a second or a third trip until he is satisfied with the action.

7. Following this, the judge may elect to have the dogs lined up side by side, while he examines them from the front then from the rear. At that time, he may go over them again with his hands.

8. Finally, the judge evolves with a ranking of the dogs in the class, based on the nearness with which each approaches the Standard of Perfection, along with their merits and demerits.

9. The judge then signals four of the handlers to positions that are marked along one side of the ring—first, second, third, and fourth.

10. The rest of the entrants are excused from the ring.

11. The judge goes over to the judge's table and marks the judge's book with the ranking that he has decided to give to each dog.

12. The steward gives the judge the proper ribbons, the prize envelope, and perhaps a trophy; and the judge presents the awards to the four handlers.

13. The steward announces the next class. Then, class by class, this judging procedure is followed until the class winners in each of the male classes and the bitch classes are judged; and the procedure moves along as outlined in Table 50 of this chapter, finally ending with Best of Show.

DOG SHOWS ABROAD

Dog shows are held throughout the world. But they vary from country to country; in classes offered, and in the system of awarding championship points.

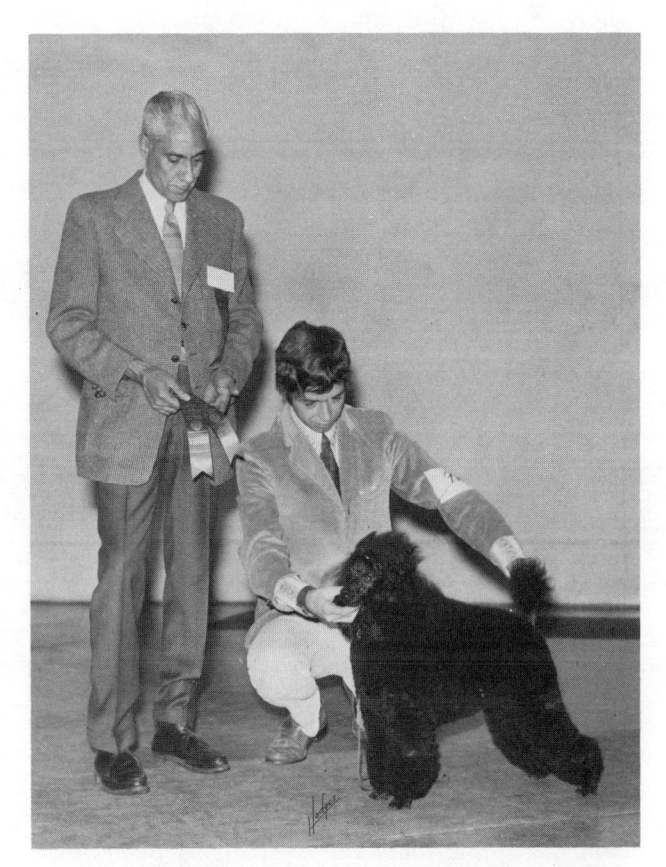

Fig. 391. Canadian Champion Danger Sign of Escapade, owned by Mrs. Lee Watts, Barbet Kennels, West Vancouver, B.C.; handled by Tim Brazier; judged by Mr. Ellsworth C. Gamble. (A Hodges Photo. Courtesy Mrs. Lee Watts)

CANADA

In Canada, the Best of Breed winners are required to compete in the Variety groups. The penalty for not doing so is the loss of ratings won earlier.

The system of awarding championship points in Canada is very similar to that used in the United States; that is, championship points are awarded on the basis of the number of dogs of each sex entered, and, this in turn, is based upon the popularity of the breeds. This means that the number of dogs competing must be measurably greater in the popular breeds than in the less popular ones. Thus, some breeds might require 10–15 males competing in order that the winner's dog be given 5 championship points, whereas only 8 competitors would suffice in a relatively rare breed.

There is one great difference in what makes a champion in Canada in comparison with the United States. In Canada, a dog must win only 10 championship points to become a champion, whereas 15 points are required in the United States. Also, in Canada no "majors" are required but the 10 points must be won under 3 different judges.

Fig. 392. Bermuda International Dog Show winner in the Best Brace category. Alike as two peas in a pod, these West Highland White Terriers are: Dancer's Eminence of the Rouge and Denisette Mandan of the Rouge. The people (left to right): Judge Louis Murr of Spring Valley, New York; owner L. G. Gignac, Ottawa, Ontario, Canada; and, presenting the trophy, the Rt. Rev. Erric J. Trapp, Lord Bishop of Bermuda. (Courtesy Bermuda News Bureau)

BERMUDA

In recent years, dog shows in Bermuda have become very popular. They attract entries from throughout the United States, Canada, and Europe. There are usually a series of three or more shows, all held within a period of one week, during the month of November.

Bermuda shows are held under the auspices of the Bermuda Kennel Club, whose rules apply.

GREAT BRITAIN

Great Britain has more large dog shows than any other area in the world. This is understandable when it is realized that the English originated more breeds of dogs than any other country. Also, the English have always been great animal breeders, with all classes of livestock. Another factor is the density of both human and dog population in the relatively small area. For the latter reason, dog shows are more accessible than in some other countries. The Cruft's Show, which is held in London each February, is the world's largest dog show. It is a two-day event, with an entry exceeding 7,000 dogs.

Because of the preeminence of dog shows in England, their system of awarding championships has been more widely copied than any other. It is based upon the awarding of Challenge Certificates. To become a champion, a dog must win three of these certificates; and these certificates are awarded regardless of the number of dogs competing. However, Challenge Certificates are limited in this way: They are available only in the 23 General Championship Shows; and, even here, the number of sets of Challenge Certificates (one for dogs and one for bitches) is determined by the registrations for the previous year.

Other all-breed shows in Great Britain than the 23 General Championship Shows are called *Open Shows*. In addition, the more popular breeds are permitted to hold Specialist Club Championship Shows, which are based on breed registrations for the previous year. Miniature and Toy Poodles, are each allowed 10 Specialist Club Championship Shows. German Shepherd Dogs (which are called Alsatians in Great Britain, and which are the most populous breed) and English Cocker Spaniels are permitted nine each.

In the United States, previous champions can usually enter in the open class. But they seldom do, since it is usually considered unsportsmanlike possibly to deny another dog points. Hence, champions most often enter a Special Class For Champions, usually called "Specials Only." This means that they are competing for special awards only—that is, for Best Of Breed and high honors. However, this is not the case at shows held in Great Britain. There, both champions and non-champions must compete together. Thus, the winner of the Challenge Certificate may have to defeat a dozen champions at that particular show.

13
Dogs as Hunters

Chapter 13
The Man-Dog Hunting Pact Through the Ages   *475*
Breeds of Hunting Dogs   *478*
Bird Dogs   *479*
   Pointers   *479*
   Spaniels or Flushing Breeds   *482*
   Retrievers   *482*
Hounds   *482*
   Beagles   *482*
   Foxhounds   *483*
   Coonhounds   *483*
Other Hunting Dogs   *484*
Training Hunting Dogs   *484*
   Training Bird Dogs   *485*
      Training the Gundog VS the Field Trial Dog   *486*
   Training the Spaniel   *486*
   Retriever Training   *487*
Some "Do's" and "Don'ts" of Training   *488*
Facts About Hunting Dogs   *488*

Fig. 393. Hunter and Retriever in shooting blind. (Courtesy Browning Arms Company, Morgan, Utah)

DOGS AS HUNTERS[1]

The numerous breeds of dogs used exclusively for hunting, and the development of special breeds for special kinds of hunting and for special kinds of game, show that this use of the dog must also have been one of the earliest.

The circumstances that render necessary the habitual pursuit of wild animals or birds, either as a means of subsistence or for self-defense, generally accompany a phase of human progress distinctly inferior to the pastoral and agricultural stages. Resorted to as recreation, however, the practice of hunting in most cases indicates a considerable degree of civilization and sometimes ultimately becomes the almost distinctive employment of the classes that are possessed of most leisure and wealth.

Prior to domestication, and for many years following domestication, the dog was a hunter through necessity. Early civilizations divided dogs into two classes; those that followed their quarry by sight and captured it by using great speed, and those that hunted by scent. Even today, the hunting instinct in most dogs is very strong, although some of them never have been seriously used for hunting.

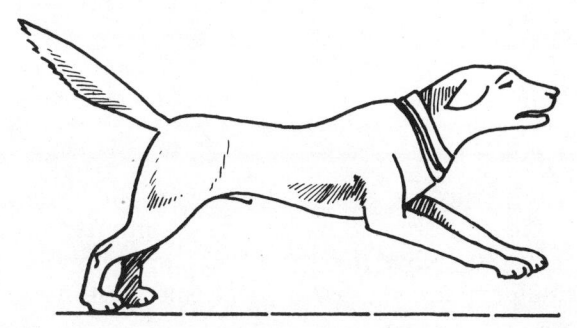

Fig. 394. A hunting dog of the Assyrians and Babylonians. (Drawing by J. L. Medeiros)

THE MAN-DOG HUNTING PACT THROUGH THE AGES

The "pact" that Stone Age Man fashioned with the dog was one of the great events in human history. In his remarkable essay "On Hunting," the Spanish philosopher Ortega y Gasset describes this alliance as "the only real advance in the art of the chase." Without it, man would never have become the supreme master of the hunt; in fact, he might never have made it. Although man, by virtue of his reason, knew how to make weapons, to use cunning, and to exercise patience, he is deficient in the elementary ability that all animals possess to a greater or lesser degree—man cannot scent animals. This is a serious handicap. From the beginning, man seems to have been aware of the dog's potential usefulness and his wide range of talents, particu-

Fig. 395. Powerful Lionhound with armored collar. Assyrian. (Drawing by J. L. Medeiros)

---
[1] The author acknowledges with thanks the authoritative review accorded this chapter by: Mr. Herbert N. Holmes, Gunsmoke Kennels, 1541 East Lake Shore Drive, Springfield, Illinois 62705.

larly in the hunt. So, since the first domestication of the dog, there has been no age and no region around the world in which the dog has not taken his place at man's side as hunting companion. Some historical points of interest relative to the man-dog hunting pact through the ages follow:

1. *Hunting dogs made possible man's permanent dwellings*—Only after the dog had placed his keen senses at the disposal of man, were the hunters able to move into permanent dwellings. Dogs guarded women and children and fended off predators. In return, the family granted their four-legged allies food and shelter, rewarding them for retrieving small game and flushing out large prey.

2. *Origin of hunting hounds*—The early-day hunting hounds probably arose out of the crosses between Bronze Age dogs and peat dogs with subsequent selective breeding. In the excavations of ancient settlements between Silesia and the Danube River, skeletons of such hounds have been found in the ashes of campfires and burned down huts. These hunting hounds were named Ash Dogs. They are regarded as ancestors of the Pointer, Setter, Spaniel, and Dachshund.

3. *Coursing developed in the Middle Ages*—During the Middle Ages, the sport of coursing developed; the riding to the chase with large packs of hounds. The quarry was pursued until it either collapsed in exhaustion or came to a stop, panting and trembling, to be torn to pieces by the dogs or given the death blow by the huntsmen who came dashing up on their horses. This type of hunting is scarcely practiced nowadays on the continent of Europe. Instead, it developed into fox hunting.

4. *The horseman's second companion in the hunt*—About 700 years after man and the dog had leagued together for the hunt, the horse joined forces with them. The participation of the horse in hunting represented a notable advance in the art. Seated on the horse's back, the hunter could overcome the distance between himself and fleeing game. He could compensate for the limited range of his primitive weapons. He could pursue his quarry over great stretches of countryside. His hunting territory thereby expanded. Above all, he was safer from the great predators who might be after him. The horse could also be made to draw his chariot or wagon. In terms of hunting, the latter meant that the pursuit of the quarry no longer involved much exertion and whole wagon loads of game could

Fig. 396. Assyrian Greyhound pursuing an Oryx Antelope (2000 B.C.). Wall painting from Thebes. (Drawing by J. L. Medeiros)

be brought back in triumph. Hunting had become a form of conspicuous consumption.

5. *The king must hunt*—In Thebes, the capital of Egypt under the Eighteenth Dynasty, hunting was viewed as a political event and governed by strict rules of protocol. The proper entertainment of sovereigns and envoys in ancient Egypt consisted of grand hunts, characterized by rich display.

The Assyrian kings were also eager to go down in history as "mighty hunters before the Lord." In contrast to the situation in Egypt, where hunting was the privilege of kings and princes, in Greece hunting was free to everyone. The entire people practiced it in keeping with tradition. Boar hunts, in particular, harked back to mythological origin. Homer described how Heracles caught a wild boar with a lasso and brought it home alive. The most famous hunt of all is Homer's account of the Calydomaian Hunt of Prince Meleager, which ended in a dispute over the boar's head. In 380 B.C., the sculptor, Scopas, represented this hunt in a frieze on the temple of Tegea.

6. *Roman cruelty to animals*—Although the Romans loved their dogs and horses, toward all other creatures of the wild they showed a callousness that exceeded that of any other civilized people. The cruel treatment of animals was sponsored by the government and formed the basis for vast spectacles in which the rulers reveled as much as the most base of their subjects. Animals were first captured at great risk in the

more remote parts of the Roman Empire. Then, they were brought to Rome by caravan and by ship. In the so-called "games," hundreds of animals were used as living sacrifices; none was given even a sporting chance to live. Elephants were favorite victims.

By the time of Nero, elephants and leopards were already in short supply. To obtain animals as performers in their bloody spectacles, Nero sent a hunting expedition to the game-rich regions of the Upper Nile, and as far as Ethiopia.

7. *Early bird hunting with firearms was hazardous*—Hunting birds with firearms was a risky affair in the beginning. Muskets, although heavy, could be aimed without support. But if they were raised above a certain angle of inclination, the priming charge slid backwards and either fell off the pan or blew up in the hunter's face. This danger was eventually conquered by the invention of an arrangement that enclosed the powder.

8. *Otto the Great proclaimed first closed season*—Of course, there can be no hunting if there is no game. In recognition of this fact, Otto the Great (636–73), the first Emperor of the Holy Roman Empire, instituted the first closed season. He proclaimed the first closed season for elk, which, in his time, was still plentiful all over Central Europe.

9. *Poachers were punished*—Anyone who hunted without permission, or who was merely suspected of intending to poach, was punished with severity and without respect to person. The oldest recorded account of the treatment of a poacher dates from A.D. 515. It describes a singularly cruel punishment dealt by a Frankish Duke, Guntram, who came upon his chamberlain, Chundo, who was cutting up a red deer in the forest. The Duke's fury was so great that he had the chamberlain seized and buried alive on the spot, under a mound of rocks.

A Bavarian law in 1663, provided that some mercy be shown a poacher who had committed his felony out of poverty.

In the eighteenth century, many enlightened lords substituted money fines for the traditional penalties. Even these were not easy. The fines were so high that poachers frequently lost their farms and were forced to hire themselves out as mercenaries.

The bans that forbade villeins and serfs to hunt, or even to enter the forests also ruled on their possession of dogs. Until the beginning of the modern age, peasants in Germany, France, and England were forbidden to keep any dogs other than the spitz, which is usually not suited to pursue game. In some regions, other dogs could be kept only on the gruesome condition that (1) one of the animal's four legs would be lopped off below the knee joint, or (2) the sinews of the hind legs were severed. This form of "licensing" was not abolished until the eighteenth century. Only the sheep dogs of herdsmen, the cart dogs of butchers, and the police dogs of watchmen were exempted from such cruelty. But even they had to be marked. In 1733, Ernst August of Saxony decreed that sheep dogs were to have their ears cropped and butchers' dogs their ears and tails cut off.

The common man, therefore, was not permitted to keep hunting dogs of his own. However, he had the dubious honor of boarding his lord's dogs for him, because the lord needed large packs of dogs for occasional hunts. Those to whom the dogs were assigned had to board them free; and they were also responsible for their welfare in all respects.

10. *American Indian had the dog*—The American Indian had the dog. It was their hunter, pack animal, draft animal, and frequently their source of food.

11. *Exclusive hunting privilege of aristocracy abolished*—The French Revolution of 1789 put an end to the exclusive hunting privileges enjoyed by the aristocracy. The fields and woods of France became common property; and those who were in need of food or amusement could hunt at will. The people took full advantage of the new freedom. For half a century, they were free to ravage the forests and the prairies of the animal life of the country, with telling results.

12. *Hunting licenses required*—Altogether too late, it was found that the freedom to hunt had senselessly and shortsightedly decimated the stock game of Europe. As a result, the hunting privilege in the form of a license came into being.

Today, hunting licenses are high all over Europe, and hunting is almost a luxury as it was in feudal times. In the early days, only wealthy nobles could afford the vast entourage and expensive trappings of the hunt. Nowadays, a hunter pays dearly for a single shot. Bank accounts, rather than nobility, determine who shall hunt. Indeed, things have not changed very much.

13. *Game preserves established*—Beginning about the middle of the last century, governments in all parts of the world began establish-

ing game preserves, to save imperiled animal life both from hunting and the inroads of civilization. The United States, the U.S.S.R., and Poland, have led the way in this movement. Native and transplanted wild animals and birds have found homes in these protected areas. These preserves, in most cases carefully marked and strictly overseen by rangers and game wardens, now extend over many parts of the world.

14. *Today, hunting dogs are essential for hunting enjoyment*—As game becomes more and more scarce in this country, a good hunting dog becomes more valuable. Even if no game is killed, he can provide thrills from watching him work. Moreover, no hunter can cover the amount of ground that his dog searches over, and no hunter possesses the nose of a dog. Finally, when the game is located and brought down, no hunter is as efficient in finding it and bringing it to bag as a good retrieving dog. So, for the greatest enjoyment in hunting, it is recommended that the hunter acquire a dog that is a specialist in hunting the particular game that he is interested in pursuing.

BREEDS OF HUNTING DOGS

Most breeds of dogs are hunters to some degree. In certain breeds, however, the instinct or trait has been developed through selection and controlled breeding.

Fig. 397. Washington (third from left) relaxing with fellow hunters, following the kill of a deer. Note presence of four dogs. (Courtesy General Services Administration, National Archives and Records Service, Washington, D. C.)

Fig. 398. Eisenhower on bird hunt in 1961. As the former President held his gun on ready, his hunting dog, Rap, was on point, in a field at Blue Springs Plantation, near Albany, Ga. Ike bagged the limit that day. (Wide World Photos, Inc., New York, N.Y.)

The breeds under two of the six groups used by the American Kennel Club are primarily hunters—the sporting breeds, and the hound breeds. The sporting breeds serve as hunters' assistants in finding and fetching game birds. This group includes the spaniels—the small, flushing breeds; the pointers—whose sensitive noses point toward a single bird or covey; and the retrievers—the strong, expert swimmers, specialists at recovering water fowl on land or water. There are two types of hounds: (1) the sight hounds—long-legged, slender-bodied, keen-visioned hounds, which follow their quarry by sight and capture it by using great speed; and (2) the scent hounds—medium-sized to small hounds, which track their quarry by scent and wear it down by their superior endurance. It should be noted, however, that certain breeds that are in other groups can be, and are, trained to hunt. Terriers, for example, come from a hunting background; and they can be trained to be marvelous hunters.

A full discussion of all the breeds is presented in chapter 2 of this book; hence, repetition at this point is unnecessary. Instead, the reader is referred to the first part of chapter 2 for a classification of dogs, noting in particular the breeds under Groups 1 and 2, which are usually used for hunting purposes. For a description of each of the breeds, see Table 3 of chapter 2.

BIRD DOGS

Bird dogs serve as hunters' assistants, mainly as finders and retrievers of birds. There are three basic types of bird dogs, divided according to their specialty and use. These types are: (1) Pointers, (2) Spaniels or Flushing Breeds, and (3) Retrievers. There are exceptions, of course, to this classification; for example, the Brittany Spaniel is the world's only pointing spaniel. Also, Irish and American Water Spaniels are used chiefly as retrievers.

POINTERS

Pointers have come up fast in recent years, their development and expansion paralleling the development of sporting firearms. Wing shooting came into popularity during the first decade of the eighteenth century, and from that period forward the rise of bird dogs was marked. The pointing breeds range far ahead of the huntsman—often out of sight. When they scent game, they do not immediately force the birds into the air. Rather, they stand immobile within a few feet of the game, their sensitive noses pointing toward the single bird or covey. They remain in this position until the hunter flushes and shoots the birds. A well-trained pointing dog will hold such a point for a minute to two hours, stand staunchly while the game is shot, and wait for the hunter's command to find and retrieve the killed game.

The pointing breeds are similar in many respects. Most of them weigh fifty to eighty-five pounds, are nearly square in body form, and are primarily bird hunters.

The best known of the pointers is the Pointer breed. But there is also the German Shorthaired Pointer and the Weimaraner. The Pointer's tail should reach only to the hock joints, whereas the other two should have docked tails. All are short coated.

Fig. 399. The Pointer, Champion Jester; a great bird finder, beautiful style on point, and he hunts with desire and purpose. (Courtesy H. N. Holmes, Gunsmoke Kennels, Springfield, Ill.)

Fig. 400. Burt, an English Setter, in action. (Photo by State of Ill., Department of Conservation. Courtesy H. N. Holmes, Gunsmoke Kennels, Springfield, Ill.)

Fig. 401. Six English Springer Spaniels at home overlooking Lafayette Reservoir on Waiterock Ranch, Lafayette, California. (Courtesy Juanita W. Howard, Waiterock Ranch, Lafayette, Calif.)

Fig. 402. A Labrador Retriever returning from mid-pond with a duck. (Courtesy Winchester-Western, Olin Corp., New York, N.Y.)

Fig. 403. Pointers in action. (Courtesy H. N. Holmes, Gunsmoke Kennels, Springfield, Ill.)

SPANIELS OR FLUSHING BREEDS

The spaniels or flushing breeds range the hunting ground just ahead of the hunter. Their task is to range back and forth over terrain selected by the hunter, but always close enough to the gunner that the charge from his shotgun can kill the game that the dogs flush. Thus, spaniels may be as close as twenty yards to the hunter, and they are rarely more than seventy-five yards away. The reason that spaniels must hunt close is that they give no warning upon finding game as do the pointing dogs, but immediately rout the game from the covey. A well-trained spaniel of this type hunts until he finds game, flushes the game, then immediately sits. For such a dog to chase flushed game is a serious hunting fault. If the game is killed, the spaniel is ordered to find the dead bird or animal and return it to the gunner.

The English, Irish, and Gordon Setters are long-coated dogs, with long tails.

Best known of the flushing spaniels are the American Cocker, English Cocker, and English Springer.

RETRIEVERS

The retriever breeds are specialists in the hunting of water fowl. In this type of sport, the retriever remains in the shooting blind until birds are killed. Then, he is ordered after the downed game. They retrieve equally well on land or water, but they're noted as strong swimmers.

As a whole, the retrievers are rather square in body form, and they're expert swimmers. Retrievers, more than any other group of hunting dogs, underline the slogan, "get that cripple and save game!"

The retriever breeds are: American Water Spaniel, Boykin Spaniel, Chesapeake Bay Retriever, Curly-Coated Retriever, Flat-Coated Retriever, Golden Retriever, Irish Water Spaniel, and Labrador Retriever.

HOUNDS

The hound group that serves the hunter is made up of two very different types of hounds—the sight hounds and the scent hounds. The sight hounds follow their quarry by sight and capture it by using great speed. They include such breeds as the Greyhound, Deerhound, Irish Wolfhound, Afghanhound and Saluki. These coursing hounds have a very ancient history in the Middle East where, in the clear desert air, a Saluki might sight a bird in flight half a mile away.

The second group of hounds are those that hunt by scent. These, too, probably came from the Middle East, but when they reached the cooler, moist, heavily vegetated lands further north, they were bred with a greater diversity of types for greater scenting ability. A temperate climate affords better scenting conditions than the Mediterranean one, and it is therefore not surprising that Europe was the cradle of the greatest number of hound breeds.

All hounds that hunt by scent have certain characteristics in common. They are nearly all short-coated dogs with pendulous ears and plenty of stamina and perseverance. They are slower than the coursing hounds, being bred to wear down their quarry by their endurance on the trail rather than to overcome it by superior speed. Coursing hounds run mute, needing all their breath for their physical exertion; whereas hounds bred to follow a scent give tongue while doing so. This enables the huntsmen to know where they are, and, based on the quality of their cry, to know how hot the line is that they are following and whether or not their prey is at bay. Most hounds have been bred for centuries to live in packs; hence, they are not particularly aggressive towards other dogs. But they are both independent and stubborn. These are invaluable qualities when hunting a cold line, but they're not always desirable in a pet.

The English country gentlemen of the Middle Ages were the prime developers of hound breeds, and the development of breeds paralleled the hunting fancies of the time. Stag hunting and hare hunting were popular long before fox hunting came in vogue; hence, Harriers and Beagles, which were followed on foot, are older breeds than the Foxhound. The latter breed probably was developed by crossing one of the old English hounds of the bloodhound type with a Greyhound to give speed in the pursuit of the fox in open country.

BEAGLES

The Beagle is the best known scent follower and tracking dog in America, and the most numerous of the hound breeds. Basically, they are hunting dogs, and the Beagle's popularity is due to its ownership by thousands of rural sportsmen for the hunting of rabbits. Single Beagles commonly are used for this type of hunting, but they may be hunted in braces or in packs.

FOXHOUNDS

The American Foxhound is racier in build than the English Foxhound. Moreover, great diversity in its use has led to great variation of type. The Foxhound in this country is used for four purposes, each of them quite different from each other, and each calling for hounds of different characteristics. These uses or purposes are:

1. Hunting a fox with a gun. Here a slow-trailing hound with a good voice is needed

2. Trail hounds, or drag hounds, which are raced or hunted on a drag, with speed alone counting

3. Hounds to hunt in large numbers (maybe fifteen to twenty or more) in a pack. This class is, of course, the type used by hunt clubs

4. The field trial hound, which is run competitively, at field trials where speed and a rather jealous nature are important.

The sport of "riding to hounds" is reminiscent of hunting in Old England and is very popular among many sportsmen and sportswomen.

COONHOUNDS

A severe case of nostalgia comes over the author at the mention of the word *coonhounds*, for some of the happiest recollections of his childhood were all-night coon hunts, with a pack of hounds in the Ozarks of Missouri.

For use in coon hunting, several different strains of hounds have been developed. Some of these have never been registered; others are registered in the United Kennel Club and other Stud Books; and a few are registered with the American Kennel Club.

The coonhound breeds recognized and registered by the United Kennel Club are:

1. American Black-and-Tan Coonhound

Fig. 404. **The First Gentleman of Virginia; Washington Following His Foxhounds,** *by John Ward Dunsmore. This shows Washington jumping over fence during fox hunt, with the dogs running before him. (Courtesy General Services Administration, National Archives and Records Service, Washington, D. C.)*

Fig. 405. Redbone Coonhound, with quarry treed. (Courtesy Moran's Midnight Kennels, Inc., Duquesne, Pa.)

OTHER HUNTING DOGS

Originally, both Basset Hounds and Dachshunds were used for hunting purposes. In fact, there are about ten packs of Basset Hounds hunting hare in Britain today. But, for the most part, members of these two breeds are used as house pets, and only occasionally for hunting.

In many areas, squirrel hunting is a popular sport. Many squirrel hunters prefer to still-hunt without dogs, whereas other squirrel hunters like a rather quiet dog to locate the squirrel.

Airedale, Fox Terriers, and Scotch Terriers were originally used for hunting purposes. However, according to the American Kennel Club classification, they do not come under either Sporting Dogs or Hounds. They are seldom used for hunting in this country anymore.

TRAINING HUNTING DOGS

There are about as many hunting dog training methods as there are hunters. However, the following basic facts apply to all hunting dogs:

1. They won't learn anything in the kennel.
2. Take them hunting often; otherwise, they forget what they've learned previously.
3. Don't overwork them when they are too young.
4. Reward them generously when they do what you ask of them.

2. Bluetick Coonhound
3. English Coonhound
4. Plott Hound
5. Redbone Coonhound
6. Walker (Treeing) Coonhound
7. American Black-and-Tan Fox-and-Coon Hound.

The Black-and-Tan Coonhound is also registered by the American Kennel Club.

Coonhounds work their trail with skill and determination, albeit not a particularly fast pace. They trail bloodhound-fashion, entirely by scent, with nose to the ground, "barking up," or giving voice, the moment quarry is treed. Despite the fact that they are known as coonhounds, they are proficient in hunting opossum, raccoon, and even deer, mountain lion, bear, and possibly other big game.

Fig. 406. Herb Holmes and trainees. To learn to hunt, puppies must be taken where game birds abound. (Photo by State of Ill., Department of Conservation. Courtesy H. N. Holmes, Gunsmoke Kennels, Springfield, Ill.)

TRAINING BIRD DOGS

The following points are pertinent to training a bird dog:

1. *Expose the young dog to field training early in life*—The only way a bird dog will ever learn to hunt is to take him out where game birds abound. Field work and introduction to the gun on game should begin when puppies are four months old. By the time they're five to six months of age, they should be well started in hunting and getting used to the gun.

2. *Use a whistle*—It is a good idea to train the dog with the whistle. A short, sharp double note can be used to indicate "go"; this same signal can be used to direct the dog to get busy or swing wider. The come-in signal is usually indicated by a longer whistle.

3. *Chasing livestock and rabbits*—Until the young bird dog learns what he is supposed to hunt, you may have to discourage him from chasing farm animals and rabbits. This can usually be done by commanding "no" in a firm voice. This form of disapproval will usually suffice.

4. *Hold on point*—The best way to accomplish this is to be near enough to the dog on first contact with game so that you can get your hands on him. Take hold of him and steady him for two

Fig. 408. Young Pointer returning downed bird. (Photo by State of Ill., Department of Conservation. Courtesy H. N. Holmes, Gunsmoke Kennels, Springfield, Ill.)

Fig. 407. Pointing dogs being trained. (Courtesy Browning Kennels, Morgan, Utah)

or three minutes. Stand him in proper position; with the body slightly forward, and the tail held proudly.

5. *Steadiness to wing and shoot*—For this step, you need a stout cord. Put it on the dog, rather loosely, but with the end of it firmly in your hand. Then either flush the birds yourself, or have someone do it for you. At that moment, as the dog moves forward, command "whoa." If the dog doesn't listen, which will probably be the case the first time, jerk him firmly, even to the point of causing him to turn a somersault. This will teach him that the word "whoa" means just that. The only exception to this step is that of allowing the dog to retrieve a bird that is killed.

6. *Get the dog used to the gun*—To avoid gun shyness, follow these simple rules: gain the dog's confidence; do not follow too closely to the dog; and never shoot except in the field when the dog is flushing or chasing or pointing game. Remember that gun shyness is never hereditary; it's man-made.

TRAINING THE GUNDOG VS. THE FIELD TRIAL DOG

The main difference between a gundog and a field trial dog is in the training.

A class gundog is one that hunts for you—not for him. He enjoys pleasing you rather than being afraid not to please you. He hunts with style and animation that's pleasing to watch, and he hustles about in a good, intelligent forward pattern. He points his game with style and intensity, locating it accurately, and exhibiting good manners in flushing and during the shooting of game. This is also the description of a good field trial dog —the requirements are the same.

A field trial dog's training is much more exacting than that of a gundog. You must concentrate on his pattern of hunting, his manners at flush and shot and, depending upon the type of trial you plan to compete in, his range. You need a dog with the physical attributes to give you a nice-appearing, attractive-moving individual, both hunting and on point. The field trial dog must be worked often; and how you work him makes a great deal of difference. Long, hard heats tend to make a dog pace himself and move a bit slower throughout the heat. Hence, short heats with adequate rest between workouts give better results. Champions, which are a real pleasure to hunt over, would not be flashy performers were they hunted in long, hard heats. It would tend to make them slower and their ground pattern would likely suffer, also.

Shooting dog stakes do not call for extremely wide-ranging dogs, though they may call for a dog to range wider than what some hunters would prefer. The type of country and personal preference govern the range the hunter wants to allow his dog.

You have to make a decision as to what you want from your dog. Proper training and development makes the difference in whether you have a gundog, a field trial dog, or one that is both. Of course, if you want the dog to win in top field trial competition, you can't make a "meat" dog out of him. The decision must be yours!

TRAINING THE SPANIEL

Perhaps it is fair to say that more is involved in training the Spaniel in hunting and in field-trial competition than is required of other hunting dogs; he must seek and find his game, flush it within the range of the gun, mark its fall and recover it for the gunner—regardless of whether it falls in water or on land.

The Brittany Spaniel is taught to point much like the pointer breed. Pertinent information and steps relative to training other spaniel breeds follow:

1. *Objectives*—A hunting spaniel must learn two things right away:

    a. To confine his flushing, and activity, within a range of forty yards from the gun.

    b. To retrieve or fetch.

2. *Start training early*—Take them to the field when they are 3 to 4 months old. However, don't expect them to get too serious until they are about 8 months of age. At this early age, you can teach the puppy to "come," "sit," "fetch," "heel," and "stay." Each of these exercises should be executed on command.

    Never walk in a straight line; take a zig zag pattern in areas where game is likely to be located. Never let the puppy range too far—never more than 40 yards and preferably within 25 to 30 yards of you.

3. *Train the dog to halt and mark fall*—First, the dog should acquire the desire for and love to hunt. Once this is firmly established, you should force him to halt while hot on a moving bird, or sit and mark a fall.

4. *Retrieving*—If you have taught the pup to "fetch" a newspaper, an old shoe, an old glove, or whatever object, retrieving is relatively simple. In addition to fetching the object, you should also train him to "drop." Then, having mastered the fetch-drop exercise, all that remains is to apply it to retrieving game on land or water.

Fig. 409. English Springer Spaniel puppy at seven weeks of age retrieving quail. (Courtesy Juanita W. Howard, Waiterock Ranch, Lafayette, Calif.)

5. *Get used to gun fire*—Many successful trainers like to use a .22 blank pistol for this purpose. While playing fetch with some dummy object, it is well to have an assistant fire off the .22 blank pistol at the time the object is tossed in the air. Soon, the puppy associates the fire of the gun with a pleasant experience of picking up the dummy and fetching it to you. The same technique is then transferred to the actual shooting of game, with the spaniel retrieving it following shooting.

RETRIEVER TRAINING

Most dogs, regardless of breed, take naturally to retrieving—to retrieving a ball, for example. So, it's a relatively simple matter to transfer their retrieving instinct to a duck. Additionally, most puppies of the spaniel and retriever breeds take naturally to water. Chesapeakes, Labradors, Goldens, Curly-Coated Retrievers, Flat-Coated Retrievers, Irish Water Spaniels, and American Water Spaniels are adapted by their warm coats to retrieve water fowl from icy water.

Step by step, the following procedure is usually used in training a Retriever:

1. *Teach to retrieve by use of the "force method"*—Many bird dog trainers refer to the common system used in training retrievers as the "force method." In reality, it's nothing more nor less than teaching the retriever to "fetch," which is a part of the obedience training received by many nonhunting dogs (see chapter 6, Training). As is true in any obedience training, the retriever must be forced to carry out any command, then generously praised for doing so.

Equipment for teaching "force" retrieving consists of a choke collar and leash for the dog, and several dummies. To begin with, dummies may consist of rolled up newspapers, corn cobs, pieces of rubber hose, or other similar objects. With this equipment ready, fetching is usually taught, step by step, as follows:

a. *Open mouth*—The dog must first be taught to open his mouth and get hold of the dummy. Each dog is an individual, so they differ in this regard. But, one way or another, get the dog to open his mouth and take hold of the dummy.

b. *Carry Dummy*—Train the dog to carry the dummy about.

c. *"Give"*—Train the dog to release the dummy on command.

d. *Lower head and fetch*—After the dog has acquired the technique of getting hold of the dummy with his head in a raised position, he is ready to be taught to lower his head as he goes after the dummy, then to fetch it.

e. *Throw Dummy*—Next, throw the dummy a short distance, and give the command, "fetch."

f. *Practice on dead bird*—After the dog has become fully efficient in handling an inanimate object, like a piece of hose or whatnot, teach him to fetch with a dead bird. Expect the same perfection that was required in the fetching of the earlier objects.

g. *Throw dead bird in bushes and the like*—This step is necessary in order to teach the dog to find.

h. *Carry dead bird*—Next, teach the dog to carry the dead bird about, and to release it on command. He should be schooled to carry dead birds steadily to heel.

Always insist that each and every command be carried out promptly and thoroughly, then reward the dog generously with a pat and your voice.

2. *Get used to water*—This step is best accomplished during very warm weather. It consists of getting the dog used to going in water, and feeling at home when doing so. This may best be accomplished by having an older dog that's fond of swimming lead the way. Also, it's not a bad idea for you to set the example by taking a swim, then asking the puppy to join you.

3. *Retrieve dead bird from water*—Next, teach the dog to retrieve a dead bird from the water. Toss it from the bank, gradually increasing the distance that it is tossed from the shore. Do not let the dog acquire the habit of stopping and shaking upon coming out of the water, then dropping the dummy. Insist on the dog holding the dummy and delivering it to your hands each time.

4. *Take directions*—Retrievers need to be taught to take directions. This is essential when the retriever has not seen the kill or properly marked the fall. Directions are given by several short blasts of the whistle; waving your hand in the direction that you desire that he move; and you yourself moving in the direction that you wish that he go. But don't make the mistake of overdirecting—always let the dog use his head as much as possible.

SOME "DO'S" AND "DON'TS" OF TRAINING

When training hunting dogs, the following do's and don'ts should be observed:

1. *Change the course*—A young dog worked in the same locale each time soon covers the territory like a city motorist weaving through downtown traffic. Hence, train your dog so that he will do his "stuff" anywhere you ask him to hunt.

2. *Well grounded in obedience training*—All hunting dogs should first be well grounded in obedience. If this fundamental training has been sound and well mastered, all he will need at the beginning of each further lesson is a touchup in certain respects.

3. *If you have used a professional, get instructions from him*—If you have had your dog trained by a professional, get instructions from him about handling the particular pupil; that is, use the same commands and signals that the professional did.

4. *Don't "cow" the dog by drastic training*—Remember that an overly drastic system of training is apt to "cow" a dog. So, always let the dog succeed.

5. *Don't train your dog to exceed his natural gait*—Don't drive the dog beyond what appears to be his natural gait. You can get the dog to accelerate his pace, but make sure that the speed achieved is accompanied by corresponding degrees of bird sense and nose.

6. *Don't train a dog unless you enjoy it*—Unless you like dogs, and like training them, never try to train a hunting dog.

When training a hunting dog (or doing any other assignment) it is well to remember the words of Phillips Brooks—

> It may be truly said that no man does any work perfectly who does not enjoy his work. Joy in one's work is the consummate tool without which the work may be done indeed, but without its finest perfectness. Men who do their work without enjoying it are like men carving statues with hatchets. A man who does his work with thorough enjoyment of it is like an artist who holds an exquisite tool which is almost as obedient to him as his own hand, and almost works intelligently with him.[2]

---
[2] Phillips Brooks (1835–1893), American clergyman and author.

7. *Never vary commands*—Always make commands the same, thereby precluding any confusion or uncertainty.

8. *Don't let your dog be spoiled by another dog*—Don't let your dog be spoiled by the poor dog(s) of your hunting partner(s). If you go with men whose dogs will spoil yours, leave them and hunt alone.

9. *Never lend your dog*—Never lend your dog to anyone—even your best friend, for if you do you're not apt to be friends anymore.

10. *Never allow your dog to roam*—If allowed to roam, a dog is apt to find bad company and become a tramp; so don't let it happen.

FACTS ABOUT HUNTING DOGS

The following facts about hunting dogs are pertinent:

1. *Number of* Pointers *vs* English Setters—The best, and most authoritative, figures on the subject are the registrations in the *Field Dog Stud Book*, in which most of the hunting, or field bred, Pointers and Setters are registered. Their 1970 and 1971 registration numbers were:

	1970 Reg. Nos.	1971 Reg. Nos.
Pointers	16,525	17,250
Setters	11,250	12,660

Thus, Pointers outnumber Setters by a considerable margin.

Fig. 410. An English Setter (front) and a black French Pointer. (Photo by State of Ill., Department of Conservation. Courtesy H. N. Holmes, Gunsmoke Kennels, Springfield, Ill.)

2. *Number of* Pointers *vs* Setters *in* bird dog field trials—There are more Pointers than Setters competing in most bird dog field trials today. The explanation appears to be that field-trial enthusiasts have come to prefer the Pointer over Setters because, (a) they are easier to train, generally speaking, and (b) with more and more scarcity of game in most areas, they are more useful in hunting over a wider area.

3. *Coat Advantages of* English Setter *over* Pointer *as a gundog*—Because of his heavier coat, the Setter has advantages over the Pointer in (a) cold weather, and (b) when hunting among burrs and heavy underbrush.

4. *Natural hunters; roamers*—Most breeds of hunting dogs are natural hunters; that is, given the opportunity they will go out and hunt on their own. But a word of caution is in order! When permitted to run loose, dogs of any breed —hunters and nonhunters—are apt to become incurable roamers.

5. *Breeds that point*—The Pointer is the best-known pointing breed, but the following sporting breeds can be taught to point birds, also: English Setter, Irish Setter, Gordon Setter, Wirehaired Pointing Griffon, German Shorthaired Pointer, Brittany Spaniel, and Weimaraner.

6. *Sight hound vs scent hound*—All hound breeds are classified either as sight hounds or scent hounds, depending on their manner of hunting. Hounds that use their eyes to follow their prey are called *sight hounds*. They seem to have much keener vision than other breeds. The Greyhound, the Afghan hound, and the Borzoi are examples of hounds that hunt by sight. Those that run down game by using their noses to follow the trail are called *scent hounds*. Beagles, Bloodhounds, and Foxhounds are three of the breeds that hunt this way.

7. *Best duck-hunting breed*—Most duck hunters prefer the Chesapeake Bay Retriever for duck hunting. They have great natural aptitude as swimmers and will plunge without hesitation into rough and icy water, displaying tremendous endurance and courage. Of course, there are exceptions; and many individuals of other breeds are excellent duck-hunting dogs.

8. *Best breed for use on pheasants*—The English Springer Spaniel is a specialist on pheasant, so most sportsmen prefer this breed above all others when it comes to hunting this crafty game bird.

9. *Hunting methods of* Spaniels *vs* Pointers— Spaniels and Pointers do not hunt in the same manner. Spaniels should hunt within range of the hunter's gun, find and flush birds, mark the spot where the shot birds fall, then retrieve them. Pointers, on the other hand, are expected to cover a wide range in seeking feathered game, to find and point birds, and then remain steady on point while the hunter shoots.

10. *Llewellin Setters*—Many of today's field trials winning English Setters are referred to as *Llewellin Setters*. Contrary to what some folks think, this is not a separate breed. Rather, it is a strain of English Setters whose pedigrees trace back to the original foundation stock of the breed owned by Mr. R. L. Purcell Llewellin of Pembrokeshire, South Wales.

11. *Irish Setters as bird dogs vs show dogs*—In recent years, fewer and fewer Irish Setters have been used as bird dogs, while more and more of them appear in dog shows. This frequently prompts the question, why? The answer is that Irish Setters have been the victims of their own good looks. The breed's handsomeness, gaiety, and personality make it an ideal show dog and pet. As a result, for many years breeders have entirely ignored the Irishman's hunting ability and concentrated almost entirely on producing specimens of great physical beauty.

12. *"Nonslip" retriever*—This is a hunting term. The term *nonslip retriever* refers to the work a dog has been trained to do in the hunting field or duck blind. The job of the nonslip retriever is to stay right with the handler, walking quietly at heel in the field or sitting in the duck blind, and to find and retrieve fallen game on order. Labrador, Chesapeake, and Golden Retrievers, along with some of the Spaniel breeds, are used in this way by hunters.

13. *Leading breed in retriever trials*—The Labrador has won more first places in retriever trials than all other breeds combined.

14. *Hunting dog vs pets*—Sometimes folks have the erroneous impression that making pets out of dogs spoils them for hunting purposes. Nothing could be further from the truth. The best way to get the most out of your dog for any assignment, hunting or whatnot, is to win his affection and gain his confidence and respect. The shortest cut to this is to make a pet of him. Further proof of the fact that a dog can be a pet and good hunting dog at one and the same time is found in the fact that many of the greatest field-trial winners have been house dogs who got plenty of affection and attention from their owners or handlers.

14
Field Trials

Chapter 14
Beagle Hound Field Trials 492
   History 492
   Present Popularity 492
   Objectives 493
   Method of Operating and Judging 493
      Championships and Championship Points ... 494
Bird Dog Field Trials 495
   History 495
   Present Popularity 495
   Objectives 495
   Method of Operating (Modus Operandi) 495
      Classification of Field Trial Stakes 496
         Puppy Events 496
         Derby Events 496
         Shooting Dog Events 496
         All-Age Events 496
         Open Stakes vs. Amateur Stakes 496
   Important Field Trials 497
   Judging Methods 497
      What Makes a Winner 497
   Winners As Practical Hunting Dogs 498
   Setters vs. Pointers 498
   The American Field 498
Foxhound Field Trials 500
   History 500
   Present Popularity 500
   Method of Operating and Judging 500
United Kennel Club-Licensed Nite Hunts 501
United Kennel Licensed Water Races 502

Fig. 411. The Redbone Coonhound, Grand Nite Ch. Moran's Midnight Magic, treeing coon at night. (Courtesy Moran's Midnight Kennels, Inc., Duquesne, Penn.)

FIELD TRIALS[1]

The primary object of field trials is to promote better dogs through the breeding of superior individuals. An owner may think that his dog is a champ on his own hunting terrain, but he can see for himself just how good the dog actually is when he meets the competition offered in a field trial. It's not unlike the situation relative to race horses, where the real test comes when the best are pitted against the best in a derby or stakes race.

Field trial enthusiasts are much like confirmed golfers—there is nothing in the world quite so important! Neither are field trials exclusively male affairs; more and more women are participating, and more and more families are making it a family project.

Also, field trials are a great boon to wild life conservation because the average field trial participant prefers to work his dogs on live game instead of actually hunting and killing it. His philosophy is: "You can have more fun with a live bird or rabbit than you can with a dead one." Thus, he is extremely interested in promoting conservation. Most bird dog clubs release game at their trials, and these birds are left as stock for the surrounding countryside. Beagle clubs release literally thousands of rabbits annually and keep them protected during the open hunting season. With the ever decreasing supply of game and shorter hunting seasons, field trials offer the hunter the opportunity of following his sport without decreasing the game supply.

Field trials promote good sportsmanship since the average dog owner must learn to take his defeat along with his wins, as only a small percentage of the dogs in each trial can be winners.

Neither is it necessary to have a dog entered in competition to enjoy a field trial. There are usually far more spectators present than there are contesting owners.

Dog owners are a universal society of friendly people. A visit to the club house at any field trial is the easiest and most pleasant experience you can imagine. There is always plenty going on, and a newcomer very quickly becomes an "old friend" through the very genuineness of the association. If you like people and enjoy dogs, you will like field trials.

[1] The author acknowledges with thanks the authoritative review accorded this chapter by: Mr. Herbert N. Holmes, Gunsmoke Kennels, 1541 East Lake Shore Drive, Springfield, Illinois 61705.

Fig. 412. Beagles returning from field competition performance at the Bay State Beagle Club Trials, Berkley, Mass. (Courtesy Morgan Wing, Jr., Pres., The National Beagle Club, Millbrook, N.Y.)

The field trial dog is judged by his ability to perform intelligently in the field under actual hunting conditions. The show dog, by contrast, is judged on his physical conformation as compared to the standard for his breed. It follows that many famous field trial winners would never win on the show bench, and, likewise, many dog show champions might not do well in a field trial.

BEAGLE HOUND FIELD TRIALS

Thousands of dog owners all over the United States keep a few Beagles and hunt them. The Beagle is universally recognized as a specialist in rabbit hunting.

HISTORY

The first Beagle field trial was held in 1888, at which time The National Beagle Club was formed. From that day forward, field trials carrying championship points sprang up rapidly all over the United States. Additionally, many more clubs sanctioned to hold informal trials evolved.

PRESENT POPULARITY

Beagle hound field trials are very popular in the United States; and they are growing in popularity. There are two primary reasons for this, namely:

1. *Cottontail rabbits are abundant*—The cottontail rabbit is the most prolific of our upland game animals. He is found in practically all sections of the country, and he seems to withstand hunting pressure better than any other species. Suitable terrain, well stocked with rabbits, is to be found in almost every section of the nation; hence, there is no shortage of Beagle hound field trial grounds. Thus, the Beagle is not confronted with the problems that beset the bird dog fancier in this respect. Moreover, this assures owners and dogs many opportunities for training over a long season each year.

2. *Beagle field trials are relatively inexpensive*—The usual fee at licensed Beagle hound field trials is $5. At sanctioned trials, the fee is usually $2 or $3. By contrast, entry fees in bird dog trials range from $5 to $150. Thus, the sport is the least expensive of any in the gundog field. Actually, the greatest single cost item attached to Beagle trials is transportation.

Fig. 413. A handler with four dogs, waiting his turn in a Beagle field trial. One of the judges is shown mounted on horseback. (Courtesy Hounds and Hunting, Bradford, Penn.)

OBJECTIVES

The stated purpose of Beagle hound field trials is the improvement of the field qualities of the breed, as well as improvement in type. Proof that the sport has served well in these dual objectives is found in the fact that field trial winners are frequently also winners of honors on the bench. Although good type and conformation are not necessary for the best field performance, it is noteworthy that good performing dogs are frequently found among good type dogs.

It can be said, therefore, that Beagle trials are of paramount importance to breeders of quality hounds. Such field trials provide a sound basis for intelligent, selective breeding.

METHOD OF OPERATING AND JUDGING

The pertinent points in operating and judging a Beagle hound field trial are:

1. *Height Divisions*—All Beagle Trial Stakes (except championship stakes, which embrace both height divisions) are divided by height into the following two divisions:
   a. Beagles under 13 inches in height.
   b. Beagles 13–15 inches in height.

2. *Sex divisions*—Whether or not a field trial is divided according to sex is left to the discretion of the sponsoring club.

3. *Under AKC*—Most Beagle field trials in America are held under the jurisdiction, license, or sanction of the American Kennel Club.

4. *Cottontail rabbits and braces; hares and a pack*—At all field trials run on cottontail rabbits, Beagles are run in braces; that is, the dogs are divided off in hunt pairs, and each pair is called a *brace*. Braces are formed by the simple procedure of drawing names out of a hat (or other receptacle); the first two dogs drawn constitute the first brace; the next two the second brace; and so on down the line. If there should not be an even number of entrants, the odd dog is run with a brace mate selected by the judges.

After all braces have run, the judges may call for whatever dogs they wish to run in a second series, and brace them in any manner that they like. The latter is important for a number of reasons; it gives the judges an opportunity to evaluate different braces. Moreover, one of the rules of Beagle trials is: Before the judges announce the winners in a class, the placed hounds must have beaten the hound placed directly beneath them.

When a Beagle trial is run on hare, all entries in a stake are run in a pack. Hares do not go to ground and spoil a hunt, and they give much longer, straighter, and faster runs. Hares have been imported from Germany with great

493

success. They make for splendid sport and thrive in this country.

5. *Beagle trials are not elimination affairs*—Judging of Beagle hound field trials is by what is known as the "spotting system." Thus, each brace does not constitute a race, with the loser being eliminated from further consideration.

6. *Quality more important than quantity*—Ability and desire to hunt are of paramount importance. The quality of the performance, rather than the quantity, should receive first consideration.

7. *Interference by one hound with his brace mate is penalized*—One brace mate may interfere with the other; and there are all kinds of interference, with all degrees of each. Such interference is penalized.

8. *Luck can be a factor*—Generally speaking, the best dog wins. However, it is realized that there is considerable luck in field trials; vagaries of scent are many, atmospheric conditions sometimes play havoc with the hounds' ability to travel a trail, and then there is the luck of the draw or the brace mate.

9. *Gallery walks*—At Beagle field trials the gallery walks behind the judges, who are often mounted. Members of the gallery are required to remain far enough back so that they will not interfere with the running; and when game is raised, they must stand fast.

10. *Releasing game*—In order to insure ample opportunities for game, field trial clubs generally release captured or pen-raised rabbits in advance of trials.

11. *Not all Beagles are good field trial competitors*—Although some Beagles do superior work on their home grounds, the stress of a field trial may be too great for them—stress due to change in environment, the presence of the gallery, the association with strange dogs, and so forth. Still other dogs rise to new heights when in competition.

12. *Great determination and independence necessary*—A good field trial Beagle must evidence more than a good nose, a properly used voice, and the desire to hunt. He must display great determination and independence.

CHAMPIONSHIPS AND CHAMPIONSHIP POINTS

Championship points for Beagles are awarded only to winners of open All-Age Stakes. These points are awarded on the following basis: one point (1) to the winner of first place for every hound started; one-half (½) point to the winner of second for each hound started; one-third (⅓) point to winner of third place for each hound started; and one-fourth (¼) point to winner of fourth place for each hound started.

At the present time, a hound of either sex must win a total of at least 120 points, which must include three first places in licensed or member trials, to be declared a Field Trial Champion of Record by the American Kennel Club.

It is noteworthy that, due to the large number of trials being held annually, a Beagle has

Fig. 414. Gallery at a Beagle field trial walking behind one of the judges, who is mounted. (Courtesy Hounds and Hunting, *Bradford, Penn.)*

a far better chance to gain the field trial champion than foxhounds and bird dogs. Yet, the acquiring of the necessary points—120 points, especially when three first places must be won, is certainly no mean accomplishment.

As long as there are rabbits, a bright future seems to be assured for Beagle field trials and millions of American sportsmen.

BIRD DOG FIELD TRIALS

Bird dog field trials are events wherein individual bird dogs are given the opportunity to display their field qualities in direct competition.

HISTORY

The first recorded field trial for Setters and Pointers took place near Stafford, England, in the spring of 1866. That initial event preceded Stud Books, but the competition gave birth to the idea of improvement of the bird dog breeds. Field trials in this country had their inception eight years later, in 1874. The first public trial in the United States was held at Memphis, Tennessee, on October 8, 1874.

PRESENT POPULARITY

From the beginning, the sport enjoyed a steady growth. Since World War II, the growth of this sport has been phenomenal. In 1971, there were about 500 recognized field trial clubs in the country sponsoring over 785 recognized trials, embracing 2,952 stakes (Open and Amateur), with about 43,642 starters. All in all, field trials have been fittingly described as the fastest growing recreational activity in the United States.

OBJECTIVES

The primary objective is the improvement of the bird dog breeds, which is accomplished through pointing up winning bloodlines and breeding systems. This knowledge, so essential if future bird dog generations are to measure up to the high standards of field performance, can best be obtained through the avenue of public competition provided in field trials. Field trial standards approach the ideal and the history of progress in American bird dog breeding is found in the annals of the sport.

Of course, the social side of field trials is one of their most attractive features. Many lasting friendships are formed. There is always a spirit of good fellowship and comradeship, and there is no class distinction among the devotees of the sport. Every field trial is a gathering of good sportsmen and sportswomen on common ground and in a common interest; no higher degree of sportsmanship is prevalent in any sport. Also, the sport provides a medium for the interchange of constructive thoughts and ideas concerning everything pertaining to the gundog.

Field trials make an outstanding contribution to game restoration and conservation programs. Many game management programs, beneficial to the entire countryside, have been launched on field trial grounds, with the resulting research proving of great value to wildlife resources in general.

METHOD OF OPERATING (MODUS OPERANDI)

With increased interest and the passing of time, it is only natural that there should be a number of changes in the method of operating bird dog field trials, among them the following:

1. *On horseback*—In the early days of bird dog field trials, all events were conducted on foot. But changes in conditions, the scarcity of game, and differences in standards made for

Fig. 415. Field trial dogs staked out, waiting to run. (Courtesy P. Bernard Smith Co., Kensington, Md.)

Fig. 416. Start of a brace of dogs (two dogs) at field trial, with mounted gallery. (Courtesy P. Bernard Smith Co., Kensington, Md.)

changes. Now, many who attend a major field trial follow the running from horseback. Professional handlers train from horseback almost exclusively. Of course, this does not apply to the shooting-dog stakes or the cover-dog trials in grouse country, where the handlers, and in some instances the judges, walk.

2. *Owner-handler stakes*—Several of the major clubs hold owner-handler stakes in which the competing dogs must be owned and handled by their owners. A number of these dogs are professionally trained for their owners. As a result, many of these owners are strangers to their own dogs.

3. *Amateur trials*—As is true in any sport—golf, baseball, football, or whatnot—the amateur is disadvantaged when in competition with professionals. To him, bird dog training is a hobby, and a source of pleasant recreation. Consequently, he cannot devote as much time to his dogs as the professional, who makes a business of it. Thus, amateur trials, for amateurs only, are available. These trials constitute the backbone of the sport. For the most part, the entries are made up from the ranks of shooting dogs, most of which are handled by their fond owners. The trophies that they win are highly valued as marks of achievement.

CLASSIFICATIONS OF FIELD TRIAL STAKES

In the sections that follow, the most common field dog trial stakes are listed, along with pertinent information on how each of them is judged.

Puppy Events

These are designed for puppies to compete against one another. They are judged on the dog's hunting pattern, range, style of hunting, and response to the handler. Puppy Events are designed for dogs about one year old, but they extend up to eighteen months of age.

Derby Events

These are designed for young dogs ranging from 1 year to 2½ years of age. These events are judged on much the same standards as Puppy Events, but with more emphasis placed on actual bird work. There are 2 types of Derby Stakes, with range being the difference, i.e., shooting dog Derby Events and wider ranging Derby Events judged along all-age range standards.

Shooting Dog Events

Several classes of events come under this category. They are:

a. Shoot to kill events that are unrecognized events designed for the fun of competing under the gun, testing a dog's responsiveness to handling, finding game, and retrieving.

b. Foot shooting dog events which are held for dogs run from foot only—the handler walks while handling the dog.

c. Shooting Dog Championship competition. These are events in which the handler rides horseback. The dog must be most responsive to its handler, show class in hunting, style and intensity in pointing game, with perfect manners to flush and shot. The range of this dog can vary considerably with the terrain. The dog should keep in touch with its handler, but it can range fairly wide where the terrain so dictates.

All-Age Events

These are stakes that are designed for a wide ranging dog—class, style, bird-finding ability and handling finesse are also important. The biggest difference between these events is the range of the dog.

Open Stakes vs. Amateur Stakes

Here the difference is the handler. An amateur handler cannot accept pay for working dogs or handling dogs for the public. He may compete in both amateur or open stakes. The professional handler is a person who works dogs for pay for the public. He can compete only in the open stakes, which are held primarily for the professional handlers. Under no condition can a professional trainer compete in an amateur event. In general, it is advisable for amateurs to compete in amateur competition and leave the open stakes for the professionals.

IMPORTANT FIELD TRIALS

There are many bird dog field trials, all of which are important and serve a purpose. But the two most important ones are:

1. *National Bird Dog Championship*—This event has grown in prestige and size. In recent years, there have been large fields in competition —sometimes over fifty starters; and the eligibility requirements have been made more stringent.

The National Bird Dog Championship is considered the acid test of the bird dog in field trials. The heats are of three hours' duration; and the dogs must handle to the gun. This field trial operates on the theory that the best field trial dog is nothing more than the shooting dog at his very best.

2. *National Free-For-All Championship*—Ranking next in importance to the National Bird Dog Championship is the National Free-For-All Championship. In this event, the qualifying heats are one hour in length and the finals three hours.

JUDGING METHODS

The "spotting system" of judging prevails today. Under this method, the judges are unhampered by red tape and unnecessary rules, and are left free to pick the winners from the performances recorded. All dogs are run in braces (paired off two at a time), with the running time of the first-series heat being stipulated in the rules of the club. Unless the judges are able to pick their winners at the end of the first series, they may request that their leading performers contend for a second time, with the judges bracing them in any manner that they like.

The first-series heat in a field trial are all the same duration, but the time allotted for second-series competition is, like the bracing, at the discretion of the judges.

WHAT MAKES A WINNER

The ideal bird dog has been described as one that looks the country over when he is led to the starting point, selects the most likely looking cover in the right place on the proper course and goes to it; that keeps the wind in his face and possesses a knowledge of where birds are likely to be in the morning, at noon, and in the late afternoon, with due consideration of weather conditions; and that is aristocratic in appearance and noble in expression.

Experienced judges are not carried away by a dog that runs fast and far, but mostly in straight lines. They seek out the dog that displays pace, range, bird sense, nose, stamina, and style; the contender that renders a balanced performance —that searches intelligently, exhibits bird-finding ability, manifests accuracy of location and intensity of point. In short, the genuine field trial dog must do more than merely get out and run in compliance with the whistle of his handler. Here are some of the points that experienced judges look for when judging Pointers in a bird dog field trial:

1. *Instinct to hunt*—A field trial dog should be fast and should range over a wide area of ground searching for the scent of game.

2. *Good nose*—Dogs locate game by scent and those with a good nose will locate birds accurately. When a dog with a good nose finds game and points, the handler or hunter should expect to find the game bird located in the direction the dog is pointed—not behind or to the side of him.

3. *Obedience*—The dog is subservient to his handler and responds to his signals.

4. *Bird sense*—Intelligence as shown by ability to go to the most likely game bird's cover with the least waste of time and effort.

5. *Stamina and physical development*—The dog should be able to take a strenuous workout.

6. *Style and action*—A stylish dog moves with grace and is pleasing to watch. He will carry his tail above the level of the back and keep it in motion until he gets the scent of game. Stylish dogs fairly glide over the ground—they're poetry in motion.

7. *Style in pointing*—A dog on point freezes into immobility in the exact position where he first locates the bird scent. The stylish dog points to the source of the scent with his head high and his tail well above the level of the back.

8. *Intensity of point*—On point, every mus-

Fig. 417. Dog on point. (Courtesy P. Bernard Smith Co., Kensington, Md.)

cle in the dog's body is tense. It is difficult to see any movement other than a possible quiver that is an indication of the thrill and excitement in finding a bird.

9. *Finish*—A dog perfectly trained (finished), points accurately and stays on point until his handler comes in to flush the bird. After the bird is flushed, the handler fires his gun, then gives the dog the signal to proceed.

10. *Honoring the point*—A finished hunting dog should always honor his brace mate's point if the brace mate is first to locate a bird. When he sees his brace mate point, he should either stop immediately on point or swing back of the other dog and point without disturbing the bird.

WINNERS AS PRACTICAL HUNTING DOGS

Arguments frequently wax hot on the subject of the ability of the dog developed for a field trial to adapt himself to the requirements of shooting. The fact that experienced dog breeders select winning dogs to use in their breeding operations gives ample evidence that, in their judgment, properly trained field trial winners can be used as shooting dogs in the type of country in which they have been developed. Also, it is noteworthy that the vast majority of the participants in owner-handler stakes and in amateur trials regularly use their dogs for hunting purposes.

SETTERS VS. POINTERS

Ever since we have had both Setters and Pointers, the question has been posed: "Which makes the best field trial dog, the Setter or the Pointer?" Actually, there is no one answer to all conditions. It all depends on the individual dogs, for there have been field trial winners and champions in both breeds. In the early days of this sport, the Setters held sway—primarily because there were more of them. Today, the Pointers hold the major portion of the field trial spotlight, for the reason that there are more Pointers entered than Setters.

Most professional dog handlers express the opinion that short-haired Pointers, as a breed, are a bit more precocious in their development than their long-haired rivals—the Setters. Because of this, the Pointer can be pushed in his training at an early age, whereas the Setter must be allowed to develop more slowly and naturally.

When all is said and done, however, there is no best breed. Rather, there is a best individual. In addition to all the other fine bird dog qualities, good field dogs must possess the competitive spirit—they surpass themselves when hunting in front of a gallery.

Although Pointers and Setters dominate field trials with respect to numbers, other breeds do participate. In 1971, a total of 43,642 starters participated in U.S. field trials (Open and Amateur), with a breakdown by breeds as follows:

Breed	No. Field Trial Starters in 1971
Pointer	27,728
Setter	8,043
Brittany	2,877
German Shorthair	3,198
Irish Setter	1,224
Other Breeds	572
Total	43,642

THE AMERICAN FIELD

The *American Field* is a weekly publication, with headquarters in Chicago, which devotes most of its editorial matter to field trial activities and matters pertaining to the gundog. Also, the publication (1) maintains the *Field Dog Stud Book*, and (2) sponsors the *American Field Futurity (run on quail)* and the *American Field Pheasant Futurity*.

Fig. 418. Field trial winners with judges. (Courtesy P. Bernard Smith Co., Kensington, Md.)

Fig. 419. English Setter hunting chukar partridge in New Jersey. (Courtesy Winchester-Western, Olin Corp., New York, N.Y.)

Fig. 420. Pointer in action. (Courtesy P. Bernard Smith Co., Kensington, Md.)

In conclusion, it may be said that bird dog field trials, like horse racing, can be regarded as a spectator form of sport, and a basis for data on which to conduct breeding operations. The principal objective of field trials is the promotion of high-class bird dogs, to provide competition of the highest caliber among hunting dogs, to stimulate enthusiasm among owners, and to act as a practical guide for breeders by setting a high standard of excellence.

FOXHOUND FIELD TRIALS

Foxhounds in this country are used for four purposes, all of them quite different from each other, thus calling for hounds of different characteristics. These uses are:

1. Field trials that are run competitively, and where speed and a rather jealous nature are important.
2. Hunting fox with a gun, where a slow-trailing hound with a good voice is needed.
3. Trail hounds, or drag hounds, that are raced or hunted on a drag, where speed alone counts.
4. For hunting in large numbers (say fifteen to twenty, or more) in a pack. The latter, is of course, the type used by hunt clubs.

In this section, we shall pursue the first use —Foxhound field trials.

HISTORY

Whenever two, or more, proud Foxhound owners put their individual hounds into a single pack, there is always competition, whether it's formal or informal. According to historical records, however, the first formal Foxhound field trial ever held in America was staged at Albany Hills, Maine, from November 11 to 15, 1889. Less than a month later, on December 2, 1889, the Interstate Fox Hunters Club held its first recorded trials at Waverly, Mississippi. Over the next few years, the sport grew slowly, but without guidance. In 1893, a group of fox hunting enthusiasts gathered at Waverly, Mississippi, and organized the National Foxhunters Association.

PRESENT POPULARITY

The present popularity of Foxhound field trials is best indicated by the number of state organizations which have held or continue to hold annual championship events. The list includes: Alabama, Arkansas, Connecticut, Florida, Georgia, Kentucky, Maryland, Minnesota, Mississippi, Missouri, New York, North Carolina, Ohio, Pennsylvania, South Carolina, Texas, Virginia, and West Virginia.

METHOD OF OPERATING AND JUDGING

The following points are pertinent to operating and judging Foxhound field trials:

1. *Painted dogs*—Special dog paint (available in white, red, black, yellow, orange, and blue) is used to mark the dogs. Each hound competing in a field trial is given a number at the time of entry. Then these numbers are painted on the sides of the dog, so as to give the judges their identification. In this manner, the judges may note faults or credits for each dog.

2. *How stakes are conducted*—The All-Age Stakes usually last at least four days. Each morning at dawn, the hounds are lined up for a roll call, following which they are cast away together. Then, the task of keeping up with them, which is no easy assignment, is the responsibility of the judges.

The standing of the hounds is generally posted after each day's running, along with a list of those that are scratched or disqualified.

3. *Judging*—The number of judges varies according to the importance of the stake and the number of the entries.

The dogs are judged on hunting and trailing, speed and driving, and endurance. They are faulted or scratched (disqualified) for the following: babbling (for throwing their tongue too much, either when they are not sure of the scent or when they are very far behind the leading hound), loafing, skirting or cutting (that is, running wide of the line or leaving the line and trying to head off the fox), refusing to run with the pack, or quitting.

Judging a Foxhound field trial is hard work. In addition to being knowledgeable of Foxhound field trials, the assignment calls for great physical stamina, for the judges must be in the saddle from dawn until the hunt is called off for the day, usually about noon. Of course, they must keep up with the hounds, otherwise they cannot score their performance.

4. *Important field trials*—The two most important Foxhound field trials are:

a. The annual trials of the National Foxhunters Association in the National Championship;

b. The United States Open, which ranks next to the National Championship. It is a hard-fought endurance race, the requirements of which test the merits of the best hounds in the country.

Foxhound field trials are reminiscent of Old England. The sport is loved and followed by both sexes, all ages, and all classes.

UNITED KENNEL CLUB-LICENSED NITE HUNTS

The UKC-Licensed Nite Hunts are very popular. They attract people of all walks of life, and old and young alike.

The UKC licenses these events under rules and regulations belonging to the UKC. Local clubs sponsor the events, judge them, and give the dogs their proper winning credit under a schedule of points for various placings. Dogs work toward the Nite Hunt Championship. Under special rules and regulations covering Grand Nite Champions, the dogs that have become champions go on and work toward Grand Championship degrees.

The complete Official Nite Hunt Honor Rules may be obtained from the UKC. Because of space limitations, only a few of the pertinent rules follow:

1. *One night only. All casts to hunt three hours*—Three or four dogs in cast, except Nite Champions and Grand Nite Champions, but not more than four. Dogs must prove to be open trailers. There must be one handler to each dog. Any handler unable to complete the hunt must pick up his dog. The scorekeeper may give permission for another handler to complete the hunt. All dogs, including Champions must hunt the entire hunt unless an emergency arises or the dog is scratched.

2. *Point system*—(a) 100 points for the dog that opens first; 75 points second; 50 points third; 25 points fourth. (b) 100 points for the dog declared treed first; 75 points second; 50 points third; 25 points fourth.

3. *Scorecards*—Scorecards must be finished in the woods and signed by each handler. Scorecards must be signed thirty minutes after presentation to the Master of Hounds or the dogs will be scratched. (Any changes must be made by the Master of Hounds with members of the entire cast present.) This rule must be strictly adhered to. The Club Secretary must keep scorecards and make them available to contestants or the UKC for one year.

4. *Winners*—(a) A dog must have a total score of plus points before he can receive Championship Points; (b) the 10 high point winners from different casts will be judged the first 10 winners. If there are not 10 cast winners with plus points, the placing will follow in order of total plus points.

5. *Nite Champions; Grand Nite Champions*—Each Nite Hunt must have a Champions' cast and a Grand Nite Champion cast. In order to receive credit, a Champion or Grand Champion must have a total plus score and hunt the entire hunt. At least one coon must be treed and seen in order for Champion or Grand Nite Champion to receive credit and a total plus score. This is to apply even if only one Champion or Grand Nite Champion is present to be entered in these casts. A Champion or Grand Nite Champion cannot hunt in open competition. These casts should be reserved for spectators, if any.

6. *Advertised*—UKC Nite Hunts must be ad-

Fig. 421. Enthusiastic Redbone Coonhound at tree during a field trial. (Courtesy the United Kennel Club, Inc., Kalamazoo, Mich.)

Fig. 422. The Walker (Treeing) Coonhound, Nite Champion Pfeisters Big Jim, at tree during a field trial. (Courtesy the United Kennel Club, Inc., Kalamazoo, Mich.)

vertised to the public and in at least one Coonhound Publication. Advertising must show whether clubs furnish hunting or nonhunting judges.

7. *Final report*—The final report form must be sent to United Kennel Club, Inc., 321 West Cedar Street, Kalamazoo, Michigan 49006, within 10 days if credit is to be given to top 10 winners. A fee of 25 cents for each UKC dog in the hunt must accompany the report.

UNITED KENNEL LICENSED WATER RACES

The UKC licenses these events under rules and regulations belonging to the UKC. Local clubs sponsor the events, judge them, and give the dogs their proper winning credit under a schedule of points for various placings. Dogs work toward their Water Race Championship. Under special rules and regulations covering Grand Water Race Champions, the dogs that have become champions go on and work towards grand championship degrees.

The complete Water Race Rules may be obtained from the UKC. Because of space limitations, only the pertinent rules follow:

1. Under UKC Rules dogs are run for trophies and points only. No money may be involved for prize money.

Fig. 423. The Plott Hound, Nite Ch. Brandenburgers Pioneer Jake, with coon treed. (Courtesy Pioneer Plott Hound Kennels, Millstadt, Ill.)

2. UKC registered Coonhounds and grade dogs are run separately. They never compete.
   a. Where possible, there are 5 or 6 dogs to a heat.

3. Each Water Race must have a Champion heat even if only 1 Water Race Champion is present.

4. All dogs must start from the starting line. The line must be established 15 to 25 feet from the water's edge, depending on the circumstances and conditions present. The stakes are to be set at water's edge and are 30 feet apart. All dogs must pass between these stakes or be disqualified.

5. A float is to be placed a uniform distance from shore for entire race. A live coon must be used on float and in tree.

6. Line flags are to be placed in swimming water 75 feet apart.

7. Dogs must tree within a 15-foot radius of

the tree inside a circle to qualify for **Tree Winner**.

8. Tree Dog: The tree dog declared Tree Winner within 5 minutes after first dog arrives at the tree. If no dog has qualified for a Tree decision, the Judge blows his whistle and declares the heat over.

9. To win a Line Decision, a dog must pass free and clear in swimming water, between line flags going in the direction of the home tree.

10. First Tree and First Line Winners advance to semifinals.

11. All semifinals will be run under the same set of rules.

12. Line Winners and Tree Winners will run separately in semifinals and finals.

13. Rules to Be Used for Small Entry: When the entry is 36 dogs or less, it is not large enough for semifinals. Use six dogs or less to the heat. Heat winners will advance to finals. Regular rules to be followed.

14. Point System for Small Entry:
Heat Winners:
    A dog winning First Tree receives——5 points
    A dog winning First Line receives——5 points
Grand Final Winners:
    A dog winning First Tree receives——15 points
    A dog winning First Line receives——10 points
If dog should win First Tree and First Line in the grand finals he will receive——25 points. No dog may receive over 35 points in any Water Race.

15. Regular Point System:
No Heat points are given.
Semifinals:
    A dog winning First Tree receives——10 points
    A dog winning First Line receives——5 points
Grand Final:
    A dog winning First Tree receives——15 points
    A dog winning First Line receives——10 points
If dog should win First Tree and First Line in the grand finals, he will receive——25 points.

No dog may receive over 35 points in any Water Race.

16. The requirement for UKC Water Race Champion is 100 Champion Points and must include one First Tree and First Line win in grand finals at least one time; this applies as of March 1, 1969.

17. The requirement for UKC Grand Water Race Champion is that the dog win three grand finals, including at least one grand tree final.

18. Fee due for Water Race Points: A fee of 25 cents for each UKC dog entered in a Water Race must be sent to United Kennel Club, Inc., with final Water Race Reports.

15
Coursing and Racing

Chapter 15
History of Dog Racing   505
Dog Racing Worldwide   505
Coursing in the United States   506
    The National Coursing Association   506
Development of the Artificial Hare   507
Greyhound Racing in the United States   508
    Speed and Training of Dogs   508
    Magnitude and Conduct of Dog Racing   510
Whippet Racing   511
The Greyhound Hall of Fame   512

Fig. 424. Racing Greyhounds coming round the first turn traveling at speeds in excess of 35 miles per hour. (Courtesy Biscayne Kennel Club, Miami, Fla.)

COURSING AND RACING

When held under natural conditions with live animals as the incentive, the sport of dog racing is called *coursing*. When held on an enclosed circular track, with the hounds pursuing a mechanical hare motivated by electricity, the sport is called *Greyhound racing*. Of course, coursing is the older of the two methods. As a sport, it antedates horse racing by at least 1,000 years, having been originated by the ancient Egyptians, who raced their Greyhounds in open fields with wild hare as quarry.

HISTORY OF DOG RACING

Coursing first took place in the Middle East, some 4,000 years ago, where the hounds that were used were of the same type as the Greyhound and the Saluki of today.

The group of breeds that were used for coursing, and later for racing, were known variously as gazehounds, sighthounds, or windhounds. The Arabs used them for coursing gazelles and the ancient Greeks used them for coursing hares. The Afghan Hound hunted deer and the smaller antelope in its native land. Arabian Greyhounds were taken to Russia in the seventeenth century and crossed with hardier Russian breeds to create the Borzoi, a dog used for hunting wolves. In Scotland, the Deerhound appears to have been in existence for as long as we have written records. Built to tackle large deer and travel across rough country, the Deerhound is the largest and heaviest of the group. The smallest member of the gazehounds is the Whippet, a comparatively modern breed created in the nineteenth century for racing, coursing, and ratting.

Greyhounds were used both for coursing and racing by ancient Egyptian nobility; and we are told that Cleopatra was a railbird.

History records that many pharaohs rated Greyhounds first among animals, both as pets and hunters. In that day and age, they chased hares in open fields.

Ovid (43 B.C.–A.D. 18), a celebrated Roman poet, wrote the first known description of coursing. It follows:

As when the impatient greyhound, slipped from far,
Bounds o'er the glade to course the fearful hare,
She in her speed does all her safety lie,
And he with double speed pursues his prey,
O'erruns her at the sitting turns; but licks
His chops in vain; yet blows upon the flix.
She seeks the shelter which the neighboring covert gives,
And, gaining it, she doubts if yet she lives.

Saxon tribal chiefs in England often were given Greyhounds as state gifts of honor. Early British laws forbade the ownership of Greyhounds by commoners, so racing was conducted only among the peers. Around 1700, this restriction was removed and commoners entered into the Greyhound racing picture.

The first written code for coursing was formulated in England. It followed organization, by the Earl of Orford, of the Swaffham Coursing Society in 1786. Lord Orford was a racing enthusiast to match the most dedicated racing fan of today. The story goes that, after spending years experimenting in breeding and training methods, he became mentally ill and was kept indoors. One day his favorite Greyhound, Czarina, was scheduled to race. Just preceding the race, Lord Orford broke out of his room, mounted a pony, and galloped off to the race. Ignoring friends' pleas to return home, he raced along behind his beloved Czarina as she won the trial. Then he fell dead from his pony.

In 1886, 100 years following the first written code for coursing and the organization of Lord Orford's Swaffham Coursing Society, the first simulated rabbit was used in Hendon, England. The *London Times* of September 11, 1876, described it as follows:

> For a distance of 400 yards in a straight line, a rail has been laid down on the grass. It has an apparatus like a skate on wheels. On this sort of shuttle is mounted an artificial hare. It is made to travel along the ground at any required pace and so naturally to resemble the living animal that it is eargerly pursued by the greyhounds. On Saturday afternoon at one-half past three, a trial was run of the new mechanical arrangement run by a windlass at West Harpen. When the hour came, all that was seen was the artificial hare bounding out, quite naturally, from its bag, and followed at once by the greyhounds. The new sport is undoubtedly an exciting and interesting one.

DOG RACING WORLDWIDE

Today, dog racing is worldwide. England leads the world with the greatest number of active tracks, and Ireland ranks second. Also, there is professional Greyhound racing in Australia,

Spain, and other countries. Although the rules and regulations differ slightly from country to country, in each the sport is controlled by a single authoritative body whose inspectors or stewards rigidly enforce the rules. This insures a fair return to the punter and helps explain the continued attraction of "going to the dogs."

COURSING IN THE UNITED STATES

Coursing began in the United States in 1878. Live hares were used for coursing in those states where rabbits were a severe and constant menace to crops. No one knows what the future of Greyhounds might have been if this mode had prevailed exclusively.

Owen Patrick Smith, known to this day as the Father of Greyhound Racing, visualized a nationwide network of coursing meets. In 1905, he first proposed this to George Sawyer, an expert on Greyhounds and a resident of Dorchester, Nebraska, who was attending a coursing meet being staged by Smith at Hot Springs, South Dakota. But Sawyer wanted no part of a national network of coursing meets, so he spurned Smith's invitation to join him in the venture. The resolute Smith went ahead with an Intermountain Coursing Association meeting at Salt Lake City in 1907. Once again, Smith and Sawyer met. Thereupon, concerned by public complaint over the slaughter of live hares, Smith told Sawyer that he wanted to substitute an inanimate lure for live rabbits. Sawyer reacted by saying, "Greyhounds will chase only live game." Sawyer was joined in this opinion by other men familiar with Greyhounds. Nevertheless, Smith was not easily discouraged, so later he went ahead with his idea—but this is another story to be presented later in this chapter.

THE NATIONAL COURSING ASSOCIATION (NCA)

The address:

Norman McAsey, Secretary-Treasurer
The National Coursing Association
RFD 3
Abilene, Kansas

In addition to being the headquarters of The National Coursing Association, it is noteworthy that Abilene, Kansas lays two other claims to fame:

1. It came into being in 1867, as an early-day shipping point for cattle. This end of the Texas cattle trail in eastern Kansas on the Kansas Pacific Railroad was established for the purpose of providing safe transportation to the East, unmolested by the Ozark outlaws.

2. It is the hometown of President Dwight D. Eisenhower, and the location of the Eisenhower Center, which was dedicated soon after President Eisenhower's death in 1969.

It was in Kansas where coursing on this continent first took root, and subsequently blossomed into a hub for coursing buffs throughout the nation. The National Coursing Association performs a whole host of services in the interest of dog racing. It maintains Greyhound Registrations; publishes an annual *Stud Book;* and publishes the monthly *Coursing News,* which provides members with records of breedings, meetings, litter registrations, and coursing meet results. Also, the Association acts as a storehouse of past records, pedigrees, and historical data for the many years Greyhounds have been included in the gamut of sporting events in America. Information on more than 400,000 Greyhounds pack the files of the NCA office building and the list of registered Greyhounds continues to grow at a fast rate.

Each spring and fall, the NCA sponsors the National Coursing Meet, which attracts coursing fans from all over the nation. Some 400 to 500 Greyhounds compete in various stakes during the one-week meets, with prize money and trophies going to the winners. Also, the NCA licenses coursing meets each fall in Texas, called the Lone Star Coursing Meets. These are conducted in identical fashion to the National Meets, but on a smaller scale.

A modern coursing field consists of a level, fenced area, 450 yards long and 150 yards wide. At one end of the sodded enclosure are caged (or penned) hares, which are driven onto the coursing field when a brace (two dogs) is ready for the chase. At the opposite end of the course, or park, are escapes into which the hares may run if they are fortunate enough to avoid being caught during the course. Fig. 425, which was taken at the Fall Coursing Meet in Abilene, shows just about all the active parts of a coursing event. It should be noted that the Greyhounds are held on a leash by a "slipper," who does not release them until the hare has about a 30 yard start on the dogs.

Fig. 425. Fall Coursing Meet in Abilene, Kansas. This picture shows most of the active parts of a coursing event: The man in the foreground is the "slipper"; the hare, which the Greyhounds are pursuing, is about 30 yards in front of the dogs; the Greyhound on the left wears a red collar, whereas the one on the right wears a white collar; the grandstand is to the left, and atop of the grandstand is the judges' stand; the persons on the left inside of the field are known as "shaggers," and their purpose is to keep the hare centered in the park to prevent the Greyhounds from going unsighted. Three judges decide which Greyhound gets the win, then the winner advances on elimination fashion, one step closer to the finals. (Courtesy National Coursing Association, Abilene, Kan.)

Coursing differs from Greyhound racing on a track in that the dogs are awarded points by a judge or judges, stationed either in towers alongside the field or on horseback. Points are allowed for speed (1, 2, or 3 points); the go-bye (2); the turn (1); the wrench (½); the kill (2); and the trip (1). The dog having the highest number of points is declared the winner of the course. In stake events, in which there are generally 35 to 65 entries (there can be any number), there are eliminations, with the winners meeting winners until the field is reduced to 2 finalists, who compete for the purse or prize. In case of a tie in points, the purse is divided.

Informal coursing events are also staged in the Midwest, using jackrabbits and coyotes as quarries, both of which are nuisances. These hunts are made without guns, the dogs are transported in the back of pickup trucks, confined to crates. When a coyote or jackrabbit is spotted, the hunter tries to overtake and pass it. Then, after the dogs spot the quarry out the back of the truck, they are released, hopefully to overtake the quarry.

DEVELOPMENT OF THE ARTIFICIAL HARE

In an earlier section, reference was made to the simulated rabbit that was first used in 1876 in a field near the Welsh Harp, Hendon, England. But the innovation—the mechanical rabbit—received insufficient encouragement to keep it "alive." It seems that the public's ideas of sport at the time were not satisfied by the mere racing of Greyhounds, for, when a year or two later, enclosed coursing was introduced, the objection was raised that it was more like racing than coursing, and it soon died out.

But the persistent Mr. Owen Patrick Smith, to whom we have made earlier reference, saw things differently. He had the vision to realize that the public, along with the humane societies, would not permit the continuing slaughter of live hares; and he had the tenacity to do something about it. He raised money to build a small circular track near Salt Lake City. Then he stuffed a rabbitskin, attached it to a motorcycle, and sent the affair whizzing around the track. The Greyhounds followed in pursuit. Thus was born the artificial lure in the United States, crude though it was, some thirty-one years after a similar apparatus appeared in England.

Nothing came of Mr. Smith's artificial rabbit for a very long time. Finally, in 1919, Messrs. Sawyer and Smith joined forces. Under the title of Blue Star Amusement Company, they built a dog track in Emeryville, California. By now, Mr. Smith had refined his original idea. In his new arrangement, a motor was mounted on four wheels resembling a railway handcar. This contraption chugged around a miniature track for three-sixteenths of a mile, carrying an artificial rabbit. It was supposed to stop in a brakehouse, but very often the carriage careened through the brakehouse or jumped the track before it got there.

An Emeryville stockholder, Mr. George Heintz, evolved with a folding arm that made the lure disappear at the end of a race, so the car would keep going and there was no need for a sudden stop, the lure having vanished and the Greyhounds having completed their race. But Mr. Smith refused to accept this innovation. Later, it was the subject of a long litigation.

No wagering was allowed at Emeryville, and expenses were high. Both Smith and Sawyer lost money on the venture, but at least the mechanical lure was on its way.

An English patent on the mechanical lure, installed within a circular track, was issued in 1880; and a Mr. J. A. Pinard was granted a patent by the U.S. Patent Office on a similar hand-operated lure in 1887. Records show that three other Americans received patents on lures of varying types preceding the time that Mr. Owen Patrick Smith made his application for an electrically-propelled lure in 1912. Nevertheless, Mr. Smith is recognized as the Father of Greyhound Racing in America, and his mechanical equipment, or improved variations thereof, is now employed universally in all tracks.

GREYHOUND RACING IN THE UNITED STATES

It is easy to understand the success of Greyhound racing. The Greyhound itself possesses beautiful lines, and there is an undoubted thrill in seeing him at full stretch in close competition with others. But, be that as it may, at any race the majority of the spectators are less interested in this aspect of racing than in the actual results of the races and the money that is to be won or lost in the betting. This, combined with the fact that most meets are held in the evening, when working people have leisure to attend, has been a large influence in attracting spectators. Moreover, Greyhound racing provided something entirely new to the public, both in conception and in presentation.

SPEED AND TRAINING OF DOGS

The speed of a running dog depends on the length and rapidity of the stride. The gait, which is similar to that used by nature's fastest

Fig. 426. Greyhound racing, the Sport of Queens. (Courtesy Biscayne Kennel Club, Inc., Miami, Fla.)

sprinters—the cheetah and some of the antelopes—can best be described as a series of extended leaps. The animal propels with his hindlegs and becomes fully extended in the air with the forelegs stretched out in front as far as possible. When the forelegs touch the ground, the hindlegs are still in the air and are drawn forward under the body to land in their turn in front of the forelegs, ready for another propulsive effort. The entire action, which is like a jackknife, depends on the back muscles, which expand and contract like a powerful spring.

Fig. 427. The trainer is trying to get Greyhound puppies used to running after a "lure," such as they will later encounter when they run at a track. (Courtesy Fabulous Flagler, Miami, Fla.)

Fig. 429. Hurdle jumpers must be specially trained. On practice hurdle tracks, the trainer actually runs with the dog, helping him make those first jumps. (Courtesy Fabulous Flagler, Miami, Fla.)

Fig. 428. After a dog has trained on the farm, he is moved to a training track that is equipped with a starting box and a mechanical lure. This time, the Greyhounds race against each other, maybe for the first time. It is on this type of practice track that the racers will begin to learn racing manners. (Courtesy Fabulous Flagler, Miami, Fla.)

Whippets travel at 33 to 34 miles per hour, and Greyhounds at about 37 miles per hour. Currently, the fastest Greyhound record stands at 38.67 miles per hour. Racing Greyhounds have a stride of about 18 feet.

A young Greyhound, called a *sapling*, is put into training when it is about 15 months old. The dog's desire to chase a mechanical hare is often kindled by allowing it to course a live one. Also, the dog must be accustomed to wearing racing colors and the cage muzzle, and to the use of starting traps. Training also involves building up the dog's muscular condition until it reaches the peak of physical fitness. Greyhounds can be as temperamental as any other star performer; hence, maintaining a fine edge on the dog's enthusiasm for racing is one of the hallmarks of a top trainer.

MAGNITUDE AND CONDUCT OF DOG RACING

Pertinent information relative to dog racing in America follows:

1. *Magnitude*—The following statistics indicate that U.S. dog racing is big business:

    Spectator Attendance (1971) 13,666,462
    Pari-mutuel turnover (1970) $730,000,000
    Revenue to states (1970) $53,000,000
    Monies distributed (1970) $6,000,000

2. *Standard U.S. Tracks*—Standard U.S. tracks resemble an up-to-date football field; they are oval in shape, with accommodations for spectators. The actual track is ¼ mile (oblong), with a racing surface 18 to 22 feet wide. It is brilliantly illuminated at night by means of powerful electric lights, while the rest of the ground is in semidarkness during the races. The dummy hare, which is electrically propelled, runs on rails circling the racing strip, either on the inside or outside. A racing official is stationed in the top of a tower, from which he can regulate its speed according to the pace of the dogs. At the end of the race, the hare is switched into a tunnel, which is closed to the dogs by means of a trapdoor. Common racing distances are 3/16 mile, ¼ mile, 495 yards (futurity), 5/16 mile, 3/8 mile, 7/16 mile, and ½ mile; with 5/16 mile being most popular in the United States. In England, the 525 yard distance is most popular. Dogs of average quality can cover the 5/16 mile distance in 32 seconds, traveling at the rate of about 37 miles per hour.

Fig. 431. The Paddock Judge checks the Greyhound prior to the race. (Courtesy Biscayne Kennel Club, Miami, Fla.)

Fig. 430. A view of the Biscayne Clubhouse and Grandstand area. (Courtesy Biscayne Kennel Club, Miami, Fla.)

The Multnomah Kennel Club at Portland, Oregon, with a seating capacity of 35,000, is the largest dog racing establishment in the United States. A record crowd of 35,000 people once filled the Multnomah Stadium.

Florida, with 13 dog tracks, leads the nation in number of race tracks.

Race track income is derived from commissions on pari-mutuel betting, with the rate ranging from 12½% in Oregon to 17% in Massachusetts and Florida. A modern racing establishment of normal size will cost $750,000. The big ones will cost more. Most track operators are satisfied if they make a net of one percent profit on gross wagering.

3. *Race*—A race usually consists of eight dogs, equipped with leather racing muzzles and numbered blankets. They start from enclosed barriers, or boxes, with double doors that open simultaneously. Races are electrically timed, with the finish photographed; most tracks have a camera that both times and photographs the dogs. The dogs follow an electrically-paced lure, which may

be either single or double replica of a rabbit skin stretched over a wire frame to give it a rabbitlike appearance. A single lure is most commonly used, although some tracks employ a double lure either on the outside or inside rail.

4. *Wagering*—Coursing was done for sport, but dog racing has always depended upon betting for spectator interest and financial support.

An evening's racing program, or nightly performance, consists of 10 contests, or races. The unit of wagering is $2. All U.S. tracks use the mutuel form of betting, and wagers are made on first, second, and third (win, place, and show), and daily double. In daily-double wagering, a single bet couples a contestant in each of 2 races and both must finish first to complete a winning transaction. Additionally, some tracks now have what are known as *Perfecta* and *Quiniela* betting. In Perfecta betting, the bettor is required to select 2 dogs that must finish either first or second in a race. In Quiniela betting, the bettor is required to select 2 dogs. If both finish either first or second, he wins.

5. *Purses*—In 1970, total purses of $6 million were paid in the United States. Purses paid winning dogs vary from $18 to $50,000; and, at the larger tracks, average $400 to $800 per race. A good racing kennel, with 20 to 30 dogs, can gross up to $75,000 annually. Average kennels probably do not gross over $15,000 to $20,000 annually.

6. *Kennels and dogs*—The most successful racing kennels own and maintain their own breeding farms, with most of these located in California, Florida, Kansas, Oklahoma, and Texas. The top establishments keep in reserve as many as 100 dogs.

The price of Greyhounds is as variable as the price of Thoroughbred horses. It is determined primarily by breeding and racing records; along with what a buyer is willing to pay, and a seller is willing to take. Pups of weaning age sell for about $500 each. Pups ready for racing, but untried, may bring as much as $1,000. Experienced dogs, with a good racing record, will bring from $1,000 up.

As is true of Thoroughbred horse breeders, most Greyhound breeders are not interested in dog shows. However, there are classes for Greyhounds in most bench shows, and a number of racing dogs have stood high both in dog shows, and on the track.

All dogs that are raced must be registered; identified by description detailed sufficiently to distinguish the animal without any possibility of mistake; and tattoed.

WHIPPET RACING

The Whippet, an English Greyhound in miniature, is the fastest domesticated animal, pound for pound; it is capable of speeds up to 30 to 35 miles per hour. A Whippet was timed in 18.7 seconds for 275 yards at Oregon's Multnomah Kennel Club in 1961. However, Whippets over the long haul have not compared in popularity with Greyhounds.

When bullbaiting, bearbaiting, and dog fighting began to lose favor in England, the sporting gentry of that period originated the Whippet for coursing rabbits in an enclosure. At first the breed was known as the *snap-dog,* and the sport was termed *snap-dog coursing.* This was because the dog that caught or snapped-up the greatest number of rabbits during a match was declared the winner. Later, this system of racing was outlawed as unsportsmanlike, and the Whippet was subsequently used for straight racing in England, where it acquired the nickname "The Poor Man's Race Horse." The standard course was 200 yards straightaway, and the method of racing was unique. Each dog had two attendants —a slipper and a handler. All dogs were held on their handicap marks by their slippers while their handlers trotted up the track and across the finish line, all the while yelling encouragement and frantically waving towels or rags (which the Whippets were trained from puppyhood to run to). At the "get-set" command of the starter, each slipper picked his dog up by the tail and the skin of the neck and when the pistol cracked, the animals were literally thrown into their stride. Then, they raced at top speed up the track and grabbed the waving rags of their handlers, who were some 20 yards behind the actual finish. Different-colored wool collars were worn to distinguish entries. The first dog to cross the finish line was declared the winner.

In these Whippet races, a rather elaborate system of handicapping evolved. It was based upon the fact that the heavier the dog, everything else being equal, the faster he should travel. The heaviest dog was at the back and his lighter opponents gained a yard for every pound. A good dog could cover the 200 yards in 12 seconds or less.

This old-style Whippet racing in England

died out in the 1920s, helped in its decline by the rise of Greyhound racing, with its better controls. Since the 1950s, there has been some revival of coursing, with handicapping on form, and the dogs starting with all four feet on the ground.

THE GREYHOUND HALL OF FAME

For years, Abilene, Kansas, has been the locale of the National Coursing Association, which, in turn, has staged National Coursing Meets each spring and fall since the turn of the century. It is only natural, therefore, that the Greyhound Hall of Fame should be located in Abilene.

Further, it was most fortunate for the NCA and the participating Greyhound race tracks that they purchased land for the Greyhound Hall of Fame directly across the street from the Eisenhower Center. The huge influx of traffic to the Center (now running at three-fourths of a million per year) will provide the bulk of the visitors to the Greyhound Hall of Fame.

In addition to telling the story of racing through various exhibits, films, and the like, the superstars of the sport, on the coursing field and at the racing oval, will be recognized and preserved for posterity.

16
Dog Guides for the Blind

Chapter 16

Needs and Facts	*514*
Dog Guide Organizations	*515*
The Seeing Eye, Inc.	*515*
Facts About Seeing Eye	*515*
Other Dog Guide Organizations	*518*
Eye Dog Foundation	*518*
Facts About Eye Dog Foundation	*519*
Guide Dog Foundation for the Blind, Inc.	*519*
Facts About Guide Dog Foundation for the Blind, Inc.	*519*
Guide Dogs for the Blind, Inc.	*520*
Facts About Guide Dogs for the Blind, Inc.	*520*
Guiding Eyes for the Blind, Inc.	*522*
Facts About Guiding Eyes for the Blind, Inc.	*522*
Leader Dogs for the Blind	*522*
Facts About Leader Dogs for the Blind	*523*
Master Eye Foundation	*524*
Facts About Master Eye Foundation	*524*
Pilot Dogs, Inc.	*525*
Facts About Pilot Dogs, Inc.	*525*

Fig. 432. A young Dumas, Texas, high school student walks with a new confidence with Wick, his German Shepherd dog guide received from Guide Dogs for the Blind, Inc., San Rafael, California. (Courtesy Guide Dogs for the Blind)

DOG GUIDES FOR THE BLIND

The history of dog guides for the blind in the United States begins with an article entitled, "The Seeing Eye," written by Dorothy Harrison Eustis, an American woman living in Switzerland, and published in *The Saturday Evening Post* of October, 1927. In this article, Mrs. Eustis described the work that she had observed in Germany, where German Shepherd Dogs were being trained to lead blinded German veterans of World War I.

During World War I, the Germans had trained many dogs as message carriers and in other occupations, so it was not difficult in the immediate postwar years to find men capable of training, and willing to train, intelligent German Shepherd Dogs to serve as guides for the blind. By 1923, there was formed in Germany the organization of Guide Dogs for the Civilian Blind, with headquarters in Potsdam. It was here that Mrs. Eustis (who had been breeding and training dogs for the Swiss Army) first saw the possibilities of such dogs being trained to aid American blind. Responding to the challenge of Morris Frank, a blind American to whom her article in *The Saturday Evening Post* had been read, Mrs. Eustis undertook, at her place in Switzerland, the development of a dog guide. The result was Buddy I, heroine of the book *First Lady of the Seeing Eye,* the first such dog trained by an American for use by a blind American.

Although the Germans must be credited with the first extensive training and use of dog guides for the blind, it is noteworthy that records of dogs leading the blind go back much earlier. In the archaeological ruins of Pompeii, which was buried by volcanic ash in the year 79 A.D., there is a painting that depicts a woman and her maid in the market place being approached by what seems to be a blind man with a staff being led by a small dog. An even more explicit depiction of a dog used as a guide is found in the Chinese scroll painting dated in the middle of the thirteenth century, a copy of which is now in the Metropolitan Museum in New York City. Other early historical records, in writings and in art, can be cited.

NEEDS AND FACTS

Today, there are approximately 450,000 blind persons in the United States; and the number of blind is increasing about 10 percent each year. Further, based on a study made by the Research Center of Columbia University and other sources, the following facts and figures relative to numbers and needs are noteworthy:

1. Of the 450,000 blind persons in the United States 2.5 percent want a dog now; that's 11,250 dogs. Of course, not all blind persons are qualified to use a dog guide.

2. There are approximately 6,000 guide dogs in use now, which means that fewer than 1 percent of blind persons of all ages use dog guides. Since the average life of usefulness is slightly more than seven years, 857 replacements are needed each year, just to replenish the dogs now

in use. Of course, as the number of dog guides increases, the needed replacements must increase, also.

3. Dog guides are not recommended for children under age sixteen, because the majority of such children are not yet mature enough to assume responsibility for a dog guide, and they lack the judgment to exercise control measures on which a reliable guide dog depends.

4. Blind people with well-trained dogs are accepted today on buses, planes, trains; in hotels and restaurants; on college campuses—almost everywhere. Well-trained dog guides are inconspicuous and temperamentally stable; in no way do they complicate functioning of public accommodations. Also, most states have reinforced this public acceptance through legislation, making it a legal right for a blind person to be accompanied by his dog guide in facilities serving the public.

5. It is the function of a dog guide to lead its owner with speed, efficiency, and safety to various points. In unfamiliar places, the dog guide user must ask directions, as would a person with good sight.

6. A dog guide is not inherently a badge of blindness; rather, it emphasizes independence, which, coupled with the social competence of the individual, opens up new horizons of community acceptance.

7. The blind owner of a dog guide has the same responsibilities for the care of his dog as any other owner; for his food, health, grooming, and other care.

8. It costs $2,000 to $4,000 to equip and train a blind person with a dog guide. This includes the cost of teaching the blind person to use the dog, the board and room during the four weeks that they are trained together, the equipment, and the breeding, rearing, and educating of the dog. But most philanthropic schools provide everything, either free or nearly so.

DOG GUIDE ORGANIZATIONS

There are eight philanthropic organizations serving the blind by providing dog guides and educating their blind masters. A brief about each of them follows.

THE SEEING EYE, INC.

The address:

The Seeing Eye, Inc.
Morristown, New Jersey 07960

The seeing Eye, Inc., is America's largest dog guide school. The "Seeing Eye" is a registered trademark.

Officially, The Seeing Eye came in existence on January 29, 1929, when it was incorporated at Nashville, Tennessee. However, its roots go back several years earlier to one woman's vision, to a magazine article she wrote in 1927, and to a blind young man who could see its possibilities and who did something about the situation.

The woman, of course, was Dorothy Harrison Eustis, of Philadelphia, who was then living in Switzerland.

FACTS ABOUT SEEING EYE

Pertinent facts about The Seeing Eye, Inc., follow:

1. *Organization*—The Seeing Eye is a philanthropic organization.

   a. *Purposes*—The stated purposes of The Seeing Eye are: (1) to train dogs to guide blind persons; (2) to obtain dogs for this purpose by purchase, gift, breeding, or raising; (3) to teach instructors the science and technique of training dogs as guides for blind persons; (4) to teach blind persons the proper use and handling of dogs.

   The aim of The Seeing Eye is to help blind men and women achieve independence through mobility. A secondary purpose is to support research being carried on in different fields of benefit to blind people.

   b. *A national philanthropic organization*—The Seeing Eye is a nationwide philanthropic organization. It has provided dog guides to blind people in all fifty states, the District of Columbia, Puerto Rico, and Canada.

   It has only one school, which is located at Morristown, New Jersey; there are no branch schools. The Morristown headquarters are located among rolling hills about 30 miles west of New York City. The staff consists of nearly 60 persons. Modern kennels on the grounds house 150 dogs, trained or in the process of being trained. To assure a sufficient supply of suitable dogs at all times, a breeding farm for German Shepherd Dogs is operated at nearby Mendham, New Jersey, under the direction of a graduate geneticist.

c. *Support*—The Seeing Eye is a philanthropy and is supported by income on capital funds composed mainly of legacies. It does not receive any government aid of any kind.

2. *The service*—The Seeing Eye has a record of distinguished service. Pertinent facts about the service rendered and the rules and regulations under which it operates follow:

a. *Who is eligible?*—Any blind person may apply, simply by writing in to The Seeing Eye, Inc., at the aforementioned address. In determining who should come to Morristown for a Seeing Eye dog, however, careful consideration is given to the following factors of the applicant: physical and mental fitness; degree of vision (generally applicants who are accepted are totally blind or have light perception only); age limitations (the usual limits are 16 to 55 years); character; and a desire for inde-

Fig. 433. Working in harness, Seeing Eye dogs learn to stop at every street crossing, letting their blind owners orient themselves by finding the curbs with their feet. The dogs are under constant observation for flaws of temperament or training and are periodically tested with the instructors blindfolded, as this photo depicts. (Courtesy The Seeing Eye, Inc., Morristown, N.J.)

pendence. There are no restrictions with respect to race, color, creed, economic status, or sex.

b. *Cost*—The Seeing Eye policy is based on the assumption that all self-respecting people, whether blind or sighted, rebel against support through charity. Accordingly, a modest charge is made for each dog, but, of course, it is far less than the cost of providing the dog and the training.

The blind person is asked to pay $150 for his first dog. This covers all equipment and a month's board and lodging at the training school for the new master. Subsequent dogs are supplied at $50 each. The blind person may make payments over a long period of time, or often in small monthly installments. Also, and most important, transportation costs to and from Morristown are paid by The Seeing Eye. No one has ever been denied a Seeing Eye dog because of lack of funds.

c. *Training man and dog*—For the blind person, the training takes four weeks, during which time he is seldom apart from his dog. He has to learn to adjust to his dog, and the dog has to adjust to him. In classes of not more than eight students each, the blind person learns how to direct his guide and how to interpret the signals that come back to him through the leather harness handle.

The method by which dog and man work together is relatively simple. It is based on the proper use of the dog's special leather harness and stiff U-shaped leather handle, which is held in the master's left hand. Through this communication system, the dog indicates movements to the master. Of course, the master gives verbal commands—"Left," "Right," "Forward." If there is an obstacle or potentially dangerous situation, the dog guide stops or moves to one side or the other, and the master knows instantly what he must do.

d. *Blind who have received Seeing Eye dogs*—More than 3,600 people have received Seeing Eye dogs. Some of them have returned for their second, third, fourth, and even fifth dogs.

Seeing Eye graduates are employed in all sorts of professions; by actual count, nearly 100 different occupations are involved. These blind persons have been taught how to use and control their dogs, both on the job and while traveling to and from work.

3. *The dog*—Of course, the dog is basic to the program itself.

Fig. 434. John Weagley, head of the Seeing Eye's Breeding and Procurement Division with one of the Breeding Farm's puppies. At least fifty percent of the Seeing Eye dogs placed in service with blind people are bred by The Seeing Eye itself. (Courtesy The Seeing Eye, Inc., Morristown, N.J.)

a. *Breed, sex, source*—German Shepherds predominate, but Boxers, Labrador Retrievers, and individual dogs of other breeds are used, also. Both males and females are used, although females predominate.

A great many of the German Shepherds are bred by The Seeing Eye. However, some additional Shepherds, along with dogs of other breeds, are purchased or are received as donations.

b. *Life span; replacement*—The average life span of Seeing Eye dogs is slightly more than 9 years. However, many Seeing Eye dogs have lived, and worked, to the ages of 12, 13, and even 14 years or longer. When a dog dies, a replacement can be obtained by payment of only $50.

4. *Training of Seeing Eye dog*—The training of Seeing Eye dogs is a specialty within itself.

a. *Who trains them; how are they trained?*

—Seeing Eye dogs are trained by sighted instructors, who have developed their skill as a result of serving a three-year apprenticeship at the school.

The fundamentals back of the training program used are based on the fact that dogs enjoy man's company and delight in pleasing him. So, they are trained primarily through a system of rewards and corrections; the rewards usually consisting of an affectionate pat and an appreciative voice. The dogs are first taught obedience. Then, they are taught "intelligent disobedience"; that is, to disregard the master's command if it would lead to danger. In short, the dog often has to use his own initiative in executing a command.

b. *Number of dogs trained to date*—Seeing Eye has trained more than 6,000 dogs to date.

c. *Age of dogs trained; length of training*—The dogs are trained when approximately fourteen months of age. The actual training period, which is intensive, takes about three months. Additionally, it takes about one month, or more, to adjust the blind master to his dog.

d. *Do Seeing Eye dogs see traffic lights?*—The answer is "no." Dogs are color blind. So, when it's time to cross the street, the master learns to judge the movement of traffic by ear and, at the appropriate time, commands his dog "Forward." Of course, the dog will refuse to carry out the command if it is unsafe to do so.

e. *How does the dog know where the blind master wants to go?*—The answer is that the master tells him. Generally, he knows the area in which he is walking, so he directs the dog by the commands of "right," "left," or "forward." In a strange city, the master does just as the sighted person would if not familiar with the area; he simply asks his way, then relays the directions and simple commands to his dog.

f. *What is the greatest difficulty that dog guide owners encounter?*—Public interference. When anyone takes hold of, or otherwise distracts, either man or dog, it leads to confusion and disrupts their smooth functioning as a team.

The best and most kindly way in which to assist a blind person using a dog guide is first to ask if assistance is necessary, then render only the kind of assistance required.

Fig. 435. A Seeing Eye graduate with his dog. (Courtesy The Seeing Eye, Inc., Morristown, N.J.)

OTHER DOG GUIDE ORGANIZATIONS

Since The Seeing Eye, Inc. is the largest of the several fine dog guide organizations, description of it was detailed. However, many of the stated purposes of, and principles employed by, the various organizations are much the same; hence, they will not be repeated. Instead, in the discussion that follows, mention will be made of primary differences between dog guide organizations.

The other seven organizations serving the blind are listed alphabetically in the discussion that follows.

EYE DOG FOUNDATION

The address:

Eye Dog Foundation
257 South Spring Street
Los Angeles, California 90012

Eye Dog Foundation is a nonprofit, charitable organization, incorporated in, and operating under, the laws of the State of California. It is the oldest guide training school in the West; it began training guide dogs for the blind in 1938. The Foundation is supported entirely by public contributions—bequests contained in wills, annual contributions from public-minded citizens, and proceeds of special events conducted by service clubs and community organizations.

FACTS ABOUT EYE DOG FOUNDATION

Pertinent facts about Eye Dog Foundation follow:

1. *Dogs*—

 a. *Breed, sex, and age*—Purebred German Shepherd females from 10 to 30 months of age are used.

 b. *Source*—To date, all the dogs used by the Foundation have been obtained as gifts. However, a breeding program is contemplated, so that, genealogically, the dogs trained will be ideally adapted to guide dog purposes.

 c. *"Project puppy"*—This is the name of the Foundation's puppy raising project. Boy and Girl Scouts, members of 4-H Clubs, Pathfinders, and other similar organized groups, "adopt" carefully selected German Shepherd female puppies and keep them in their homes until they are 10 to 14 months of age. Then they are turned over to the Foundation for intensive training as guide dogs.

 d. *Training the dog*—Each dog is put through an intensive 6-month training period by a state licensed trainer. The first step in the training of the dog is that she learn to obey simple obedience commands. Next, the dog is trained to guide the blind.

2. *The blind recipient*—

 a. *One-month training*—The blind person is trained with the dog for 1 month. Prior to intensive training, the blind person and the dog are matched in size and temperament.

 b. *Absolutely free*—The guide dog, harness, leash, and a supply of dog food for a few months, along with 30 days in-residence instruction on the care and handling of a guide dog, including board and room for the blind recipient, are provided free.

 c. *Qualification of the applicant*—To qualify, the blind applicant must demonstrate to a physician's satisfaction that he or she is physically and emotionally capable of handling a guide dog in such a manner as not to be a hazard to himself or herself, the public, or the dog.

GUIDE DOG FOUNDATION FOR THE BLIND, INC.

The address:

Guide Dog Foundation for the Blind, Inc.
109-19 72nd Avenue
Forest Hills, New York 11375

The Guide Dog Foundation for the Blind has been serving blind people since 1946. It is a nonprofit, nonsectarian organization incorporated under the Membership Corporation Laws of New York State. It is supported entirely by public contribution (gifts and bequests); it neither solicits nor receives government aid.

FACTS ABOUT GUIDE DOG FOUNDATION FOR THE BLIND, INC.

The Guide Dog Foundation for the Blind, Inc. program is very similar to the other fine organizations serving the blind; hence, only differences in programs and emphasis will be covered in the following brief.

1. *The dogs*—Pertinent facts about the dogs used follow:

 a. *Breeds*—Golden, Labrador, and Chesapeake Retrievers, and German Shepherds are the main breeds used. But the Foundation has also used Boxers, Weimaraners, and smooth-coated Collies.

 b. *Source*—Most of the retrievers are bred by the Foundation. German Shepherds are obtained from the Fidelco Breeders Association of Connecticut. Adult dogs are rarely accepted from outside sources.

 c. *Spayed females preferred*—Spayed females are preferred for training to become guide dogs.

 d. *Gift dogs*—A limited number of gift dogs are accepted provided they meet the following stipulations: 10 months to 2 years of age; females preferred, although a placid male will be considered; and minimum of 22 inches at the shoulder.

 e. *Foster homes*—The foster home program has proved invaluable in producing a better prepared dog of more predictable tempera-

Fig. 436. Blind student and Guide Dog crossing the street. (Courtesy Guide Dog Foundation for the Blind, Inc., Forest Hills, N.Y.)

ment. When the puppies are 6 to 10 weeks of age, they are placed in foster homes; where they remain until they're about 14 months of age.

f. *Training*—Dogs are put in serious training at about 14 months of age. Training embraces the following three stages, in order:

(1) *Stage 1*—Dogs introduced to crowds, traffic, cats, other dogs, and loud noises

(2) *Stage 2*—Obedience training

(3) *Stage 3*—Harness work.

2. *Blind student training*—Students receive four weeks' instruction at the Training Center in the care and handling of their dogs.

3. *All free*—Guide dogs, and training in their use and care, including board and lodging at the Training Center, are entirely free of charge as rehabilitation benefits. These services are available to all qualified applicants, regardless of race, creed, or national origin; from any part of the United States, as well as from all parts of the world.

GUIDE DOGS FOR THE BLIND, INC.

The address:

Guide Dogs for the Blind, Inc.
P. O. Box 1200
San Rafael, California 94902

San Rafael is located twenty miles north of San Francisco. The Guide Dogs for the Blind, Inc. covers eleven acres, which includes administrative offices, a student dormitory, and kennels.

California is the only state having laws governing the operation of a Guide Dog School. Both the school and the instructors must be licensed by the State Dog Board. Guide Dogs for the Blind, Inc. operates under License No. 1 from the California State Guide Dog Board. This school is not connected with any other training center and does not receive state or federal aid.

FACTS ABOUT GUIDE DOGS FOR THE BLIND, INC.

Guide Dogs for the Blind, Inc. operates very much like the other fine organizations that serve the blind. The following points are pertinent to it:

1. *Organization*—The school was founded in 1942, with its first location at Los Gatos, California; it was moved to its present location in 1947.

Fig. 437. Blind graduate working as typist, with Guide Dog at side. (Courtesy Guide Dog Foundation for the Blind, Inc., Forest Hills, N.Y.)

Guide Dogs for the Blind, Inc. is a nonprofit organization dedicated to giving highly trained guide dogs and training in their use to qualified blind men and women. It is supported entirely by private contributions, chiefly in the form of annual memberships from individuals, organizations, and business firms. Additionally, a trust and endowment fund has been set up for legacies received.

2. *The service*—The following rules and regulations apply to the trainee and services: Trainee must spend 28 days in residence at the school, working with his dog, under the supervision of a licensed instructor; there is no upper age limit on persons eligible for guide dogs, although they must be over 16 years of age; both men and women are eligible; and there is no charge to a blind person for either the dog or the 4 week in-residence training program, although normally transportation to and from the school is paid by the student.

3. *The dog*—The school owns its own breeding stock. Only a dog with an exceptional pedigree is accepted or added to the stock. The three breeds used are: German Shepherd, Labrador Retriever, and Golden Retriever. Both male and female dogs are used.

The training of a dog starts when he is 12

Fig. 438. Three Guide Dogs for the blind. From left to right: A Labrador Retriever, a German Shepherd, and a Golden Retriever. (Courtesy Guide Dogs for the Blind, Inc., San Rafael, Calif.)

to 15 months old. However, when a puppy is 3 months old, he is farmed out to 4-H Club boys and girls to be raised in a family atmosphere, and to be taught simple obedience. Then, at 12 to 15 months of age, they are returned to the school for completing their serious training as guide dogs. The latter training requires from 3 to 5 months of concentrated work.

4. *Training of Guide Dogs for the Blind*—Guide Dogs for the Blind are trained by qualified instructors who must serve a four-year apprenticeship and pass a rigid examination by the California State Guide Dog Board.

Each class is assigned two licensed instructors who work with the students for the entire four weeks of their stay. The instructor selects the dogs for the students, being careful to see that the dog and the master are matched according to temperament and size.

GUIDING EYES FOR THE BLIND, INC.

The address:

Guiding Eyes for the Blind, Inc.
106 East 41st Street
New York, N.Y. 10017

Guiding Eyes for the Blind, Inc. is a national service incorporated in the State of New York with its principal area of operation being the United States and its territorial possessions. It is voluntary, nonprofit, and supported through contributions. During its first fifteen year history, Guiding Eyes for the Blind graduated 1,200 units—dog and master.

FACTS ABOUT GUIDING EYES FOR THE BLIND, INC.

A few pertinent facts about Guiding Eyes for the Blind follow:

1. *The dogs*—A breeding program operated by the school provides dogs with the intelligence, temperament, and natural aptitude for a "career" as a guide dog.

a. *Breeds*—The majority of the school's dogs are of three breeds: Labrador Retrievers, Golden Retrievers, and German Shepherds. However, other breeds are also used, including smooth-haired Collies, Bouvier des Flandres, and Boxers.

b. *4-H Club observation and development*—In cooperation with the Agricultural Extension Service in New York, puppies are assigned as 4-H Club projects at eight weeks of age. They remain "farmed out" until about one year of age, at which time they are returned to the school for intensive training.

c. *Instructional period for the dog*—When 1 to 2 years of age, and prior to being placed with a blind student, the dog receives a minimum 3-month intensive training. During this period, the dog is taught 2 basic principles—obedience and disobedience. By "disobedience" is meant the ability to reject the master's command when there is impending danger, to make a choice between safety and accident. For example, the trained guide dog will never cross an intersection unless conditions are safe.

2. *Blind student training*—The sightless person and his selected guide dog receive individual instruction for a period of four weeks. During this period, the blind student is taught how to travel with his guide dog under all kinds of conditions—on busy city streets, on buses and trains, in restaurants and stores. He learns how to get to just about anywhere on his own.

3. *How much does it cost?*—The tuition fee is $150 for the first dog, and $50 for a blind person coming to Guiding Eyes for the Blind with previous guide dog experience. (However, where hardship exists, no acceptable candidate is denied a guide dog for financial reasons.) This small tuition fee is for the purpose of imparting pride to the blind person, rather than to defray the cost of the dog, training, and equipment. It costs Guiding Eyes for the Blind over $3,000 to place a dog with an individual.

Guiding Eyes for the Blind, Inc. estimates that it will cost the blind master about $12 per month to feed his dog, after returning home.

4. *The instructors*—All instructors must go through a three-year training course. This assures reliable training of the dogs.

LEADER DOGS FOR THE BLIND

The address:

Leader Dogs for the Blind
1039 Rochester Road
Rochester, Michigan 48063

Rochester is located about twenty-five miles north of Detroit, Michigan.

Leader Dogs for the Blind was founded in 1949 by a group of Michigan Lions, for the purpose of training dogs to lead blind persons and providing facilities and means whereby blind persons may obtain leaders. The school is supported entirely from voluntary contributions from the public; Lions Clubs, sororities, kennel clubs, various public-supported agencies, and private sources.

FACTS ABOUT LEADER DOGS FOR THE BLIND

The Leader Dogs for the Blind program is very similar to that of The Seeing Eye program. However, there are the following differences:

1. *The dogs*—All dogs are contributed, no dogs are purchased. The most commonly used breeds are: German Shepherd, Labrador Retriever, Golden Retriever, and Malamute. No sex preference of dogs is indicated, but dogs must be between the ages of one and two years and at least twenty-four inches high at the shoulder.

Leader Dogs for the Blind indicates that it costs them approximately $2600 to train and provide each dog to a recipient.

2. *The trainee*—After acceptance, the trainee must travel to the school at his own expense. Likewise, he must pay his return expenses. However, there is no charge whatsoever for the four-week training period. Neither is there any charge for the dog.

Fig. 440. Reward is important. The above dog is being told, "good girl." (Courtesy Leader Dogs for the Blind, Rochester, Mich.)

Fig. 439. Learning simple obedience commands is the first step in training Leader Dogs for the Blind. The above dog is being taught to "stay." (Courtesy Leader Dogs for the Blind, Rochester, Mich.)

Fig. 441. Leader Dogs are taught to stop at all curbs. (Courtesy Leader Dogs for the Blind, Rochester, Mich.)

Fig. 442. Leader Dogs are taught to clear parking meters. (Courtesy Leader Dogs for the Blind, Rochester, Mich.)

Fig. 444. Travel with a Leader Dog is unlimited. Pick up the harness of a well-trained Leader Dog and the man is in business to "go." Leader Dogs are furnished without cost, but the owner works for his partnership by training hard to be as efficient as his Leader. (Courtesy Leader Dogs for the Blind, Rochester, Mich.)

Fig. 443. The gate is wide open for the man who achieves graduation with a well-trained Leader Dog. A faithful Leader Dog will get his owner through any obstacle and all he expects is a "good boy" reward. (Courtesy Leader Dogs for the Blind, Rochester, Mich.)

MASTER EYE FOUNDATION

The address:

Master Eye Foundation
216 Produce Bank Building
Minneapolis, Minnesota 55403

FACTS ABOUT MASTER EYE FOUNDATION

The Master Eye Foundation was founded in 1926, by John L. Sinykin, whose hobby was breeding German Shepherd Dogs. He conceived the idea that these intelligent dogs, if properly trained, would be excellent guides for the blind. He reasoned that the German Shepherd had already proven valuable as guards of livestock, companions, and children, and, during World War I, they had proven invaluable for police and military duty. The first Master Eye dog ever trained by Mr. Sinykin was presented to the blind U.S. Senator from Minnesota, the late Thomas B. Schall.

1. *Organization*—The Master Eye Foundation is a charitable, nonsectarian organization; hence, all contributions to it are tax deductible.

2. *The service*—The service is available to any blind person who qualifies, without any cost whatsoever. The Master Eye dog, the training of the blind person, transportation from wherever the blind person lives to the training session in Minneapolis, including all expenses in Minneapolis, is presented as a gift. The training period of the man and dog, the period when they are required to work together in training, lasts for three to four weeks.

The Foundation spends an estimated $1,700 for each Master Eye guide dog given to a worthy blind person. The cost includes breeding, raising, and training the dogs, as well as all expenses for the blind recipient to travel to Minneapolis for a period of instruction with the selected dog.

3. *The dog*—All dogs are of the renowned LaSalle strain of German Shepherd.

4. *Training of Master Eye guide dogs*—There are no salaries or commissions paid to the staff of the Master Eye Foundation; their work is completely voluntary.

Training of the dog starts when he is about 15 months of age. At that time, a concentrated training program, requiring from 4 to 8 months, depending on the dog's ability to learn, is instituted. Even following this long period of training, not all dogs graduate. They may not have the temperament or disciplinary reactions to be calm Master Eye dogs.

PILOT DOGS, INC.

The address:

Pilot Dogs, Inc.
625 West Town Street
Columbus, Ohio 43215

Pilot Dogs, Inc., is a nonprofit organization that was chartered by the State of Ohio in 1950. It is supported entirely by public contribution. As of July, 1972, it had presented over 1,200 guides to graduates without charge, either for the dogs or the four-week in-residence training. The cost to Pilot Dogs, Inc., is approximately $1,800 a unit (master and guide dog).

FACTS ABOUT PILOT DOGS, INC.

A few pertinent facts about Pilot Dogs, Inc., follow:

1. *The dogs*—Pilot Dogs are obtained either through donation, or the agency's breeding program.

Donated dogs must be between 10 and 30 months of age; females preferred; weight 50 to 65 pounds; stand between 22 and 24½ inches at the shoulder; and be home raised (not kennel raised). Gift dogs are carefully screened—only 1 out of every 6 makes the grade as a Pilot Dog.

a. *Breeds and sex*—Four breeds are used: German Shepherd, Doberman Pinscher, Boxer, and Labrador Retriever. They can be male or female and need not be registered.

b. *Foster homes*—Selected pups are placed in foster homes until they are a year old, as home-raised dogs make better adjustment as guides than do kennel-raised dogs. They are raised by members of the 4-H Junior Pilot Club of Columbus, Ohio.

c. *Training the dog*—When between 9 and 24 months of age, Pilot Dogs are put through a basic training program of 3 to 4 months, following which they are ready to meet their new blind masters. Preliminary obedience training is done at the agency's kennel. Then advanced training is given in downtown Columbus, Ohio, involving the busiest streets, buses, revolving doors, escalators, elevators, and numerous other conditions.

2. *The blind recipient*—

a. *Dog and master training*—The blind person and the dog are trained together for an additional period of four weeks. Upon arrival, the blind student immediately begins to take care of his dog. This usually starts with the new master bathing the dog.

b. *There is no charge for this service to the blind*—Pilot Dogs, Inc., gives its trained animals to the blind at no charge. This includes the Pilot Dog, four weeks' room and board for the student, all equipment, and round trip transportation to the student.

17
Police Work

Chapter 17
Advantages of Dogs as Policemen   527
Breed of Dogs   528
Training Police Dogs   528
Qualifications of Officers Handling Dogs   529

Fig. 445. Bourbon, a bomb-sniffing German Shepherd, and his trainer-master, Officer Wm. D. Langlois. Bourbon's star reads: Bomb Dog No. 1, San Francisco Police Department. Instead of finding men, Bourbon finds bombs—live bombs. When he indicates that a suspicious package is an explosive, the bomb squad is called to dismantle it. Bourbon was the first dog in the U.S. to ferret out a live bomb. On Jan. 7, 1972, he sniffed out a live bomb in a safe deposit box at the Crocker Citizens Bank, 1 Montgomery Street, San Francisco. (Courtesy Officer Wm. D. Langlois, San Francisco Police Department, Crime Prevention Company, Bomb Dog Unit)

POLICE WORK

A new breed of policemen is arising all over America—in St. Louis, Philadelphia, Chicago, Los Angeles, San Francisco, Miami, Boston, Winston-Salem, Providence, Cincinnati, and Norfolk, to name some of the first cities to make use of him—he's a member of the K-9 Corps (canine corps); he's a dog. As a policeman, the dog is, according to Norfolk, Virginia, Police Department, "worth his weight in gold" when it comes to outrunning and locating a hidden suspect, dispersing an unruly crowd, tracking down a criminal, searching for evidence at the scene, and sniffing out "pot" (marijuana). Also, he's a fearless protector of the officer with whom he works. The St. Louis Police Department says of their *dope dogs*, "They're our secret weapon in this war on marijuana." Today, you'll find "marijuana dogs" along the Mexican border with U.S. Customs, and you'll find them working with the international police force all over Europe and the Far East, to stem the illegal traffic in and production of opium (raw material for morphine and heroin).

The Metropolitan Police Department of London, England, has used dogs since the close of World War II. Based on their success, in 1958 the St. Louis Metropolitan Police Department sent five patrolmen to London for a fourteen-week training course in the handling of dogs for police service. Upon their return, a similar program was initiated in St. Louis, where it has been highly successful. Other police departments across the country followed suit.

Dogs have been particularly outstanding in night work, for night is the dog's natural hunting time. They become very alert and inquisitive when on night patrol.

Of course, police dog training is not for house pets. It's highly specialized training involving an attack dog. Hence, police dogs must be kept under constant control by their master-officer.

The use of dogs as police is based on their natural protective instinct. Through specialized training, the protective instinct is encouraged and directed to a high degree.

Indeed, the guard dog of old is rising to a new and more important role in modern society —he's a policeman; in which work he has proven himself again and again. More and more dogs will be an integral and important part of modern police forces of the future.

ADVANTAGES OF DOGS AS POLICEMEN

Police Departments credit dogs with the following advantages when it comes to serving as policemen:

1. *Sight*—The keen sense of sight of dogs is well known. According to the Norfolk, Virginia, Police Department, a dog can see a moving object at ten times greater distance than a human.

2. *Smell*—The nose—the sense of smell—is perhaps the dog's most important weapon. A dog's sense of smell is much more highly developed than that of a human being. The Norfolk, Virginia, Police Department makes the statement that a dog's sense of smell is forty times greater than a human's. Scent can be used for tracking by the direct scent of the human body; by ground scent made from human sweat deposited on the ground from feet or through footwear; and by scent, which is more persistent, created by pressure on the ground of the human foot or of any heavy article. Consequently, a police

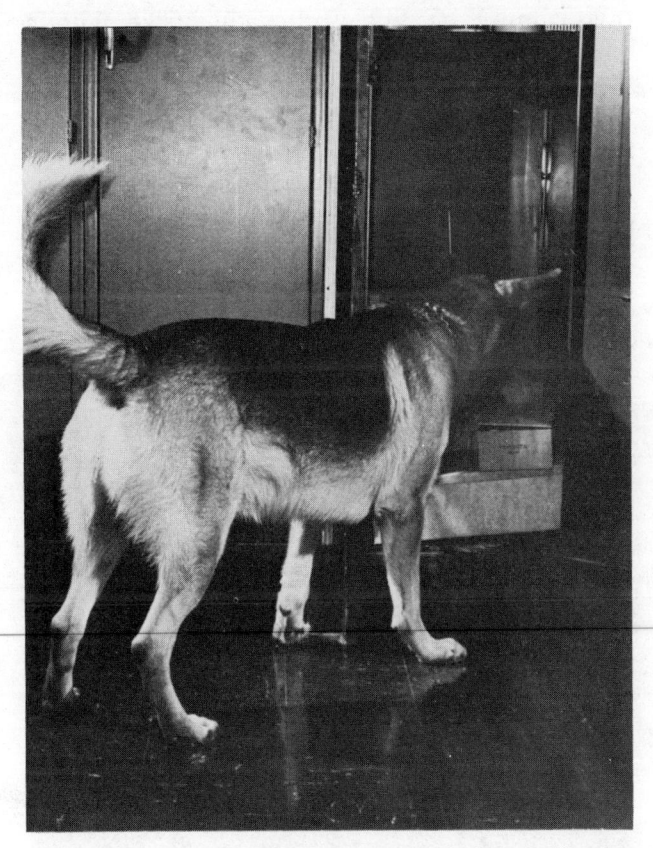

Fig. 446. St. Louis Police Department dog indicating to his handler that there is an explosive in the cigar box. (Courtesy St. Louis Post Dispatch)

dog brought to the scene of the crime can pick up and follow a ground scent, or can be trained to search a wide area quickly and discover persons hiding in the vicinity by picking them up by direct scent, even if they are concealed in dense vegetation or up a tree. Equally good results can be obtained in the search of large premises. Moreover, darkness is no handicap for this type of dog work.

As already indicated, the dog's keen sense of smell makes him invaluable in tracking down marijuana.

3. *Hearing*—Dogs have an acute sense of hearing, perceiving higher and fainter noises than the human ear. According to the Norfolk, Virginia, Police Department, the hearing of dogs is 20 times greater than that of humans.

4. *Speed*—Should a suspect be younger and in better physical condition than the officer, chances are that he'll outrun him and escape. But no man can outrun a German Shepherd Dog; they have been clocked at speeds of 35 to 38 miles per hour.

5. *Strike force*—According to the Norfolk Police Department, a 75-pound German Shepherd Dog running at full stride, will strike with a force of 300 pounds. This is adequate to knock a person down.

6. *Grab and hold*—The teeth of a dog allow him to grab and hold, which is his natural tendency. In criminal work, a dog is taught to chase and stop a man by gripping him by the arm.

Fig. 447. Nitro, German Shepherd in the Dog Patrol Unit, San Francisco Police Department, grabs a suspect. (Courtesy San Francisco Police Department)

7. *Psychological effect*—The mere sight of a large, well-trained dog being handled by a uniformed police officer has a terrific psychological effect. It aids at crime scenes, in dispersing crowds, and in crime prevention—a most important factor to any police agency or department.

Experience has shown that a crowd, which pays little heed to the line of police officers, quickly scatters at the sight of one or more canine teams. On other occasions, the dogs have cleared the way for an officer surrounded by menacing groups of people.

Of course, dogs are not supernatural, so no one should expect the impossible of them. When it comes to sniffing out bombs, dynamite, and black powder, some do and some do not. Neither will dogs be effective in locating refined heroin or cocaine, and only rarely will they work on LSD. These are acids and odorless. And there are two reasons for not using dogs in tracking down the worst drug of all—heroin—even after it does obtain a smell from being "cut" with milk sugar. First, the dog would stop anyone carrying a candy bar. Secondly, and more important, the Federal Bureau of Narcotics and Dangerous Drugs warns that by learning to sniff out heroin, dogs would become addicts themselves.

BREED OF DOGS

Both American and British Police Forces favor the German Shepherd Dog. First, he looks the part of the police dog—this produces an important psychological effect. Second, he can be trained to work eagerly with human scent, either tracking or searching. Further, the British experience indicates that the Bloodhound's nose is not any better than that of the German Shepherd. Third, he can be trained to control himself and deal with varying circumstances as they arise. He will bite without fear; yet he is prepared to hold the criminal by barking if that is all that is required. Fourth, and probably the most important, the German Shepherd seems to enjoy police work.

TRAINING POLICE DOGS

Generally speaking, dogs are put in the police training course when they are 18 to 24 months of age. Their training is divided into three main parts as follows:

Fig. 448. Richter, a bomb-sniffing German Shepherd, and his trainer-master, Officer Carl Jackson, of the San Francisco Police Department. (Courtesy San Francisco Police Department, Crime Prevention Company, Bomb Dog Unit)

1. *Obedience*—First, the dog is taught obedience. This gives the officer control of his dog. The dog is taught to heel properly, on or off the leash; to "sit down" and "stay" on command; to bark on command; to retrieve on command; and to jump on command.

2. *Scent*—Training in scenting consists of teaching the dog how to use his sense of smell to follow human scent or the disturbance of a natural scent, such as crushed grass or insects. A dog can be trained, by the use of his sense of scent, to search quickly over a wide area and discover persons in hiding. When on patrol, the dog uses his sense of smell to warn his handler of nearby persons whose presence would not otherwise be revealed. Then, with the assistance of his dog, the officer is in a position to investigate and make an arrest if necessary.

3. *Criminal work*—The dog is taught to jump hurdles from 2 to 5 feet high, crawl through an 18-inch pipe, climb ladders, climb over narrow planks that are elevated 6 feet from the ground, jump through windows, and walk a catwalk that represents the rafters of a building. The dog is taught not to back down from any type of weapon, such as a gun, knife, or a stick held in the hand. He is taught to attack; and when he can and cannot bite.

A large dog trained to go in hard when in pursuit of a criminal will almost invariably make a successful arrest. The dog is taught to stop the fleeing man by barking until his handler can arrive at the scene. However, if the criminal refuses to stop, the dog will then restrain him by gripping him by the sleeve whenever possible. This is usually sufficient to discourage any further effort to flee.

QUALIFICATIONS OF OFFICERS HANDLING DOGS

Police forces have discovered that not just any officer can handle a dog. Further, certain requisites other than liking a dog must be met. The following requirements must be met by officers desiring to become dog handlers in the St. Louis Police Department: Applicants—

Fig. 449. St. Louis police dogs are trained to: go over a fence. (Courtesy Metropolitan Police Department, City of St. Louis, St. Louis, Mo.)

1. Must be below the age of forty
2. Must have been a commissioned officer at least three years
3. If married, must have permission of wife to become a dog handler
4. If married, must have permission of wife to house dog at home
5. Cannot have another dog on the premises
6. Must own or be buying his home, or be renting from a relative with the assurance that he will not have to move
7. Must have permission of neighbors living adjacent to applicant's home.

Fig. 450. St. Louis police dogs are trained to: scale a wall. (Courtesy Metropolitan Police Department, City of St. Louis, St. Louis, Mo.)

Fig. 451. St. Louis police dogs are trained to: broad jump up to nine feet. (Courtesy Metropolitan Police Department, City of St. Louis, St. Louis, Mo.)

Fig. 452. St. Louis police dogs are trained to: walk on different types of steps. (Courtesy Metropolitan Police Department, City of St. Louis, St. Louis, Mo.)

Fig. 453. St. Louis police dogs are trained to: jump through a window. (Courtesy Metropolitan Police Department, City of St. Louis, St. Louis, Mo.)

Fig. 455. St. Louis police dogs are trained to: crawl through an eighteen-inch pipe. (Courtesy Metropolitan Police Department, City of St. Louis, St. Louis, Mo.)

Fig. 454. St. Louis police dogs are trained to: jump through a hoop. (Courtesy Metropolitan Police Department, City of St. Louis, St. Louis, Mo.)

Fig. 456. St. Louis police dogs are trained to: walk a pole, which represents the rafters of a building. (Courtesy Metropolitan Police Department, City of St. Louis, St. Louis, Mo.)

Fig. 457. Ptn. Robert Busch and his German Shepherd, Satan, a man-dog team of the canine unit, St. Louis Metropolitan Police Dept., leave the scout car to go on foot patrol. (Courtesy Metropolitan Police Department, City of St. Louis, St. Louis, Mo.)

Fig. 458. Home kennels that St. Louis Police Department places in each K-9 officer's home yard for the K-9s. (Courtesy Metropolitan Police Department, City of St. Louis, St. Louis, Mo.)

18
Dogs as Soldiers

Chapter 18
Breed Used   536
Behavior and Instincts   536
Training   536
Sentry Dogs   538
Patrol Dogs   538
Marijuana Dogs   539
Procurement of Military Dogs   539
Accountability   539
Military Dogs Cited   540
   Stubby   540
   York   541
   Nemo   541

Fig. 459. On guard. (Coast Guard Photo. Courtesy The American Humane Association, Denver, Colo.)

DOGS AS SOLDIERS[1]

Throughout the history of warfare, dogs have gone into combat or have been used in direct support of combat operations. Initially, entire formations of attack dogs, frequently equipped with armor and spiked collars, were sent into battle against the enemy. With the invention of gunpowder and the consequent change in military tactics, the value of dogs in combat diminished. However, their usefulness in other military activities increased.

During World War I, vast numbers of dogs were employed as sentries, messengers, ammunition carriers, scouts, sled dogs, and casualty dogs. It is estimated that Germany employed more than 30,000 dogs for such purposes, and approximately 20,000 dogs served with the French Army. The American Forces had no organized dog units, but they did borrow a limited number of dogs from the French and Belgians for casualty, messenger, and guard duty.

During World War II, dogs were used on a larger scale, with more than 250,000 dogs serving with the armies of the Allies and the Axis Powers. The U.S. Army recognized the need for large numbers of dogs in 1942 and established its Canine Corps (usually written K-9). This organization operated five War Dog Training Centers throughout the United States and trained approximately 10,000 dogs.

Fig. 461. Note plaque. (Courtesy Department of the Navy, Washington, D.C.)

Responsibility for military dog training was transferred to the U.S. Air Force from the U.S. Army in 1958, and the function was assigned to the Patrol/Sentry Dog Training Branch, Department of Security Police Training, 3275th Technical School (USAF) at Lackland Military Training Center near San Antonio, Texas.

While Air Training Command's Lackland AFB is the center of training in both programs for all the U.S. Armed Forces, sentry and patrol dogs are trained also at Kadena Air Base, Okinawa, and at Wiesbaden Air Base, Germany. Scout dogs, used primarily by the U.S. Army as an advance patrol, are trained at Fort Benning, Georgia.

The Air Force turned to its patrol dog concept in 1969; it is the sole Department of Defense user of patrol dogs. Prospective patrol dog handlers attend a 12-week course. Sentry dogs are used by the Army, Navy, and Marine Corps. Sentry dog handlers attend an 8-week training course.

In addition to the actual training with a dog, all handlers receive instruction in psychology of

Fig. 460. Armored dog. (Drawing by J. L. Medeiros)

[1] The author expresses grateful appreciation to Doug Moore, DAFC, Chief, Public Information Division, Department of the Air Force, for providing authoritative information and pictures for this section.

dogs, prevention of canine diseases, first aid and care of dogs, and principles of dog training.

BREED USED

The German Shepherd was selected as the breed best suited to the needs of the armed forces. This determination was based on the German Shepherd's demonstrated traits of keen sense of smell, endurance, reliability, speed, power, tracking ability, courage, and adaptability to almost any climatic condition.

The German Shepherd is a working dog; strong, agile, well-muscled, alert, and full of life. He is longer than he is tall, and has a deep body with an outline of smooth curves, rather than angular. The ideal male is 25 inches high and weighs between 75 and 85 pounds; the female is 2 inches shorter and approximately 15 pounds lighter. The German Shepherd has a distinct, direct, fearless, but not hostile, expression; a self-confident personality; and a certain aloofness that does not lend itself to indiscriminate friendship. His long effortless trot covers maximum ground with a minimum number of steps. The breed's intelligence is rated as comparable to that of a 7-year-old child and the dog is capable of learning about 100 commands.

BEHAVIOR AND INSTINCTS

The dog's world differs from the human's in specific ways. His vision is inferior to human vision although he can detect movement, however slight. He depends less on visual impressions than on his superior senses of hearing and smell. A dog's hearing ability is about twenty times better than man's. He can detect sounds above and below the frequencies a human is capable of hearing. If a dog wishes to examine an object, he moves downwind to take advantage of his keenest sense—smell—and then moves in close.

The one instinct that sets dogs apart from all other animals is their willingness to work for an intangible reward—the approval of the handler. Canine subjects usually become attached to a trainer who finds that a caress or praise can be an effective reward; a disappointed or disapproving word is a potent punishment. Even anticipation of such disfavor clearly controls the dog's behavior.

TRAINING

Once the handler-dog relationship has been established, there is brought into play that motivation which finds its roots in the sentimental attachment of canine and man. Concrete punishment and reward are still used, and are necessary on occasion, but to a large extent these may be abandoned. It is more pleasant and more convenient to rely upon the dog's eagerness to serve.

The entire training of dogs is based upon proper use and development of the natural instincts of the dog. They are:

1. The dog's instinctive companionship for man is turned into comradeship with his handler.

2. The dog's instinctive response to human attitudes is used as the basis of training; the dog is praised and encouraged when he does well and is corrected and reprimanded when he does badly.

3. The dog's instinctive urge for prey is heightened by agitation, and allowing him to pursue the agitator.

Vocal commands are given firmly and clearly. The tone and sound of voice, not the volume, are the qualities that will influence the dog. It is essential that the dog be made to carry out the same command over and over until the desired response is obtained without delay.

Patience is one of the prime requisites of a good dog handler, but it must be coupled with firmness. Obedience must be demanded if the dog is to be a prompt and accurate worker. The trainer must never lose patience or become irritated. If he does, the dog will become difficult to handle.

From the very beginning of training of a military dog, he is never permitted to ignore a command or fail to carry it out completely. He learns to associate the handler's command with his execution of it. He is never allowed to suspect that there is anything for him to do but obey. Laxity on the part of the handler may result in an attitude or mood of disobedience that means difficulty and delay in the training program.

A dog does not understand right and wrong according to human standards. Neither is he influenced by social, political, economic, or environmental considerations that often affect his human counterparts. Rewards and punishment are the means of teaching him the subject areas desired. Real punishment is inflicted as a last

Fig. 462. "Have faith." This Air Force security policeman seems to be telling his German Shepherd sentry dog partner to have faith in his leadership as the animal traverses a footbridge training device during obedience training at the sentry dog training program conducted for all the armed services at Lackland Military Training Center. The obstacle course is a refinement of obedience training and reinforces the dog's confidence in himself and his handler. (U.S. Air Force photo. Courtesy Lackland Military Training Center, Lackland AFB, Tex.)

Fig. 463. Togetherness. This German Shepherd sentry dog has overcome his instinctive dislike for confined places to crawl through a narrow culvert at his handler's command. Emerging, he flashes an "A-okay" look toward his waiting teammate who will respond with praise and affectionate thumps. The sentry dog training at Lackland Military Training Center depends heavily on these gestures to motivate the animal. A sharp jerk on the choke-type obedience collar and a harshly voiced reproof is used when the dog's attention wanders. (U.S. Air Force photo. Courtesy Lackland Military Training Center, Lackland AFB, Tex.)

Fig. 464. The attack! German Shepherd sentry dog attacking. (U.S. Air Force photo. Courtesy Lackland Military Training Center, Lackland AFB, Tex.)

resort and only for deliberate disobedience, stubbornness, or defiance. He is never punished for clumsiness, slowness in learning, or inability to understand what is expected of him.

The word "no" is used to indicate to the dog that he is doing wrong. "No" is the only word used as a negative command. If this form of reproof is not successful, the dog is muzzled, chained, or kenneled.

A dog is never slapped with the hand or struck with the leash. The hand is an instrument of praise and pleasure to the dog and he must never be allowed to fear it. Beating with the leash will make him shy of it and lessen the effect of its proper use.

SENTRY DOGS

A sentry dog team consists of the handler and his dog. Normally, the handler is drawn from security and law enforcement personnel of the armed service he represents. As a sentry dog handler, he does not lose his identity as a policeman, but rather, he receives additional training that qualifies him to utilize an item of special equipment—his sentry dog.

The sentry dog team is used to increase the security of such areas as distant perimeter posts and isolated radar sites. When on post, the sentry dog's primary function is that of a detection and warning device. This function has been performed when the sentry dog detects and alerts his handler to the presence of an intruder. The secondary function of the sentry dog is to pursue, attack, and hold any intruder who attempts to evade or escape from apprehension.

Designed as a defense against the possible saboteur or espionage agent, sentry dogs are trained to be hostile and aggressive toward all persons except their regular handlers. The dogs can be retrained, however, to accept a new handler when the original handler leaves the unit.

PATROL DOGS

To the uninformed, little distinction can be drawn between the sentry dog and a patrol dog. In both cases, the German Shepherd is chosen for its intelligence, size, strength, alertness, fearlessness, and adaptability to varying climates. The difference rests with the training.

The Air Force first became interested in the use of patrol dogs during tests at Andrews AFB, Maryland, in 1968, in conjunction with the Washington, D.C., Police Department. Later, 30 security policemen from Vandenberg and Castle Air Force Bases in California, and Davis-Monthan AFB, Arizona, completed a 14-week training course with patrol dogs at Lackland AFB.

Subsequent evaluation at the three Strategic Air Command bases proved the dogs far superior to the sentry dog in meeting Air Force security needs.

Initial classes for dogs and handlers began at Lackland AFB in August, 1969. Patrol dog and handler training takes twelve weeks. Continuing obedience training is provided the dog as well as practice in building and vehicle search and tracking after assignment to a Security Police unit.

Training objectives for the new patrol dog seek a composed, discriminating, controllable animal with all the capabilities of the sentry dog for detection of unauthorized intruders and for subsequent aggressive attack at the command of the handler, but with a wider range of responses to vocal or signal commands of the handler.

Fig. 465. One for all! A sentry dog and his U.S. Air Force air policeman handler show an easy, poised grace as they survey the situation while enjoying a water break (note canteen cup for the dog). The man and dog establish a firm association with each other during the training period and remain as a closely integrated team throughout the airman's service. The handler keeps the dog under control on training exercises with the long leather leash and choke collar shown here. (U.S. Air Force photo. Courtesy Lackland Military Training Center, Lackland AFB, Tex.)

The patrol dog is not disturbed by the approach of another person and discriminates between a definite threat and the acceptance of the person by the handler. He remains alert; but is not excited by strangers moving about him. He willingly enters vehicles with other persons and dogs without becoming hostile.

The patrol dog has the same degree of obedience when off the leash as on; he may be sent by his handler into an empty building to search for hidden persons or to cover an area to find a lost or concealed object. He will press an attack of another person at the command of his handler with the same aggressiveness as the sentry dog, but, unlike the sentry dog, he may be called off the attack at any point.

The German Shepherd's ability to follow a trail made by a human is developed during training. The animal will ignore game trails. His natural instinct is heightened during training by having a human decoy disturb the existing environment at the start of the track and by either allowing the decoy to be caught or leaving some object at the end of the exercise to be found by the dog.

Training methodology for the patrol dogs differs from sentry dog procedures. Basic obedience drills are continued daily, but other training aspects are introduced earlier and several training procedures may be practiced in a sequence. Agitation and attack drills, to build the dog's confidence and increase the biting power of his jaws (400–700 pounds per square inch), are important objectives of training.

Sentry dogs deemed eligible by criteria of health, temperament, and adaptability are being successfully retrained as patrol dogs.

MARIJUANA DOGS

The armed services are using trained dogs to sniff out marijuana. Unlike tracker dogs, which are buoyed by the excitement of the chase, detector work is often boring and the only reward is a pat on the shoulder and a loving hug from the handler. Detector dogs must possess high intelligence, high stability, and a high degree of willingness to work for praise from their master.

In addition to locating the stuff, the dogs have a tremendous psychological impact; they make a believer out of the guy who hasn't started—never to start smoking marijuana, for you will always get caught.

Training the marijuana detector dog and his handler is a thirteen-week course. The course begins with basic dog-handling skills—care and obedience. Five basic obedience techniques are taught: "Sit"; "stay"; "heel"; "down"; and "come." Following graduation, with his handler, from the basic detection course in "manners," the team advances to the basic detection portion of training—to detecting the scent of marijuana. Each dog has his own method of alert. With further training and experience, the dog learns to find the hidden drug, and not to be thrown off by masking agents, such as perfume, ammonia, or herbs.

PROCUREMENT OF MILITARY DOGS

There is a continuing requirement to recruit approximately 2,000 German Shepherds each year for sentry, scout, patrol, and marijuana dog duties. The San Antonio Air Material Area of Air Force Logistics Command manages the Department of Defense (DOD) Military Working Dog Program and recruits and procures dogs for all military services. About 50 dogs each month are assigned to the Air Training Command for its patrol dogs training program. After training, the dogs are then allocated to other Air Force commands for use.

The Air Force will pay up to $150 or accept donations of acceptable German Shepherd dogs. Eligible for evaluation are male or spayed female German Shepherds (they need not be pedigreed), 1 to 3 years old, weighing 60 pounds or more, and standing at least 23 inches at the shoulder. Females must have been spayed for at least 90 days. Pure white dogs are not accepted because they can be seen more readily at night and are more prone to skin disorders.

ACCOUNTABILITY

Dogs accepted by the Armed Forces, either through donation or purchase, remain the property of the U.S. Government. Whether serving overseas or in the United States, these dogs receive the best possible housing, nutrition, veterinary, and related care.

When a dog loses its handler, a new handler is retrained with the dog. There is no limit to the number of times a handler and dog can be rematched.

Dogs that are no longer needed in a particular command are first reported to command headquarters for redistribution. If a requirement exists, they will be reassigned to another base within the command. If no requirement exists within that command, dogs are reported to San Antonio Air Material Area (SAAMA) for reassignment. In the United States, excess dogs returned to Lackland are retrained and/or reassigned to fill other worldwide requirements.

In an overseas theater the same procedure applies except that excess dogs may be reassigned to another U.S. base within that theater or transferred to the host country as part of U.S. support to that country.

Most military working dogs serve long, useful careers; if dogs become too senile to perform effectively or incurably ill, directives specify humane disposition procedures, much like those used by reputable veterinary doctors in the civilian community.

MILITARY DOGS CITED

There have been many instances of dogs performing heroically in the face of danger. Stubby, York, and Nemo are but three of these.

Fig. 466. In tribute. A U.S. Marine scout dog at the Third Military Police Battalion compound west of Denang pays tribute to other scout dogs who have been killed while operating with Leatherneck units in the Republic of Vietnam. (Defense Dept. photo. Courtesy Dept. of the Navy, Washington, D.C.)

STUBBY

Stubby was the famous Mascot of the 26th Division during World War I. He saw nineteen months service overseas, including the battles of Champagne-Marne, Aisne-Marne, St. Mihiel, and Meuse Argonne. In combat, he was as discreet as any soldier; when shell fire got thick, he went

Fig. 467. Stubby. (Courtesy Smithsonian Institution, The National Museum of History and Technology, Washington, D.C.)

for a dugout. On at least one occasion, he saved a man's life by scurrying into a trench just ahead of a gas attack and rousing Sergeant John J. Curtin, who donned a mask. Stubby took it upon himself to administer to the wounded in his own peculiar way; he cuddled up to them, slept with them, and watched over them. When his master lay gravely ill in a hospital in Paris, the rules were waived to admit Stubby. His behavior in the hospital won a place in every medic's heart.

When the Armistice was signed, Stubby was smuggled aboard a return ship. Back in America, he led all the American Legion parades to which his little legs would carry him.

Stubby was decorated by General Pershing. He wore one wound stripe and three service stripes. His chamois coat, with the flags of the Allies, was made and embroidered by the women of Chateau-Thierry. He was made a life member of the American Red Cross, the Y.M.C.A., and the American Legion. President Wilson shook hands with him on Christmas Day, 1918; and he was officially received at the White House by President Harding in 1921, and by President Coolidge in 1924.

When he died in 1926, at the age of 10, Stubby was accorded a hero's burial. A plaster cast was made of his body, within which the ashes of his cremated remains were encased in an airtight metal container.

YORK

Army Scout Dog York was credited with leading 148 advanced combat patrols in Korea without loss of a single man due to enemy gunfire.

NEMO

On 5 December 1966, Nemo and his handler, A1C Robert A. Throneburg, were on a routine patrol at Tan Son Nhut Air Base, Republic of Vietnam. The base had been hit the previous day by a Viet Cong mortar attack. The main enemy force had been turned back, but four infiltrators eluded detection by earlier search parties and hid inside the base's perimeter. Airman Throneburg and Nemo were assigned to search for the intruders. Nemo detected the hidden Viet Cong and Throneburg commanded him to attack. The pair quickly killed two of the enemy, but before help could arrive both were wounded, leaving Nemo blind in one eye. Nemo was credited with saving the life of his handler and preventing further destruction of life and property at Tan Son Nhut.

19
Dogs in Harness; Sled Dogs

Chapter 19

Cart Dogs and Pack Animals	*543*
In Belgium	*543*
In Switzerland	*543*
In Britain	*544*
In Newfoundland	*544*
In Portugal	*544*
Other Work Uses	*545*
Sled Dogs	*545*
Gold and Mushers	*545*
The Nome Diphtheria Serum Run of 1925	*546*
About Dogs, Sleds, and Men	*546*
Sled Dog Musher's Hall of Fame	*547*
Sled Dog Races	*547*
Iditarod Trail Seppala Memorial Race	*547*
Nikki	*548*
Sled Dog Still King of the Trail	*548*

Fig. 468. Sled dog racing has grown steadily in popularity and competition over the past few years. Here, a fourteen-dog team, with double lead, is pouring on the speed. (Courtesy Morgan Wing, Jr., Pres., The National Beagle Club, New York, N.Y.)

DOGS IN HARNESS; SLED DOGS

The use of dogs for draft purposes was once very widespread. But the ancient practice has almost vanished in modern times. In his overland journey to the Far East, Marco Polo reported that he saw dogs used to draw sleds in mud and over ice too slippery for horse or wheeled traffic. Throughout Mongolia, Tibet, Northern China, and Manchuria, Mastiff-type dogs hauled loads over terrain unsuitable for hoofed animals. Later, the practice of using dogs for hauling spread to Europe and the Low Countries, where the dog was known as the "poor man's horse." Here again, the dogs that were used were Mastiff-like animals, with broad heads, blunt muzzles, and short- to medium-length coats. Farther north, in the countries bordering the Arctic Circle, Spitz-type dogs were used exclusively. Pricked ears, pointed muzzle, bushy tail, and dense coat are the common features of all the sled dogs of the North.

CART DOGS AND PACK ANIMALS

Except in the frozen North, dogs were usually harnessed and hitched to carts, with the main strain of the weight behind them taken by a broad band across the chest (a type of breast collar). Some carts were equipped with shafts; either in front with two dogs inside the shafts, or with the shaft at the back for the driver to hold. The shaft at the back enabled the dog(s) to seek shade when the cart was at rest, as well as to guard the load more effectively. Any dog that was big enough could be used for this type of work.

IN BELGIUM

Dogs were commonly used in Belgium during the nineteenth and early twentieth centuries for the purpose of taking farm produce to market. Draft dogs were, and in some sections of Belgium still are, used by milkmen, butchers, fruit and vegetable vendors, bakers, and coal dealers. The size of dog, type of harness, and weight of load were stipulated by law, and inspectors made spot checks on the dogs as they worked, and on the licenses of their owners. Dogs had to be 24 inches high, or more, at the shoulder. The load limit for a single dog was 300 pounds, and for a pair, it was 400 pounds.

The draft dog of Belgium was Mastiff-like in appearance, and mostly black or fawn in color with large white patches.

IN SWITZERLAND

In Switzerland, dogs were used for about the same purposes as in Belgium; and they were also used to bring cheeses and wicker work down from the Swiss Cantons (states). Three of the

Fig. 469. Two dogs attached to a wagon used for street cleaning in Belgium. (Courtesy The Bettmann Archive, Inc., New York, N.Y.)

543

four Swiss Mountain breeds were used for drayage—the Appenzell Mountain Dog, the Bernese Mountain Dog, and the Great Swiss Mountain Dog. All of these are believed to be descendants of the droving dogs brought over the Alps by the invading Roman armies.

IN BRITAIN

The custom of using dogs for draft purposes spread from the Low Countries to Britain, although it never got as far north as Scotland. By the early nineteenth century, dogs were pulling butcher's, baker's, and milkmaid's carts; they were hauling building supplies and knife-grinding machines; they were taking families for cart rides, and they were pulling baby carriages and children's carts. In the south of England, dogs were used to take fish from the ports to the rail heads. A team of four dogs pulled 300 to 400 pounds.

Eventually, the use of dogs for draft purposes in England was banned. But it was not done for humanitarian reasons. They were disliked in London because they were alleged to frighten horses, and to bark too much in the early morning hours. In 1839, the Metropolitan Police banned the use of all dogs in London. In 1854, the ban became general throughout England.

IN NEWFOUNDLAND

In Newfoundland, the most popular breed in the early 1800s was the Newfoundland. During the fishing season, the dogs hauled in the nets and took the catch from the boats to the drying sheds. They were also used as pack animals, taking mail to the outlying parts of the island. During the winter months, the dogs were used to haul wood. Sometimes they were hitched to sleds.

IN PORTUGAL

In Portugal, the Portuguese Water Dog accompanied the fishing fleet. This breed, which traces back to the fourteenth century, is believed to be closely related to the Poodle. The similarity between the two breeds is accentuated by the fact that the Portuguese Water Dog had its back, loins, hind legs, and tail clipped during the summer months. These dogs, which were powerful and enthusiastic swimmers, were expected to retrieve anything that fell overboard, help haul the fishing nets, and carry messages from boat to boat and from boat to shore. Although these needs no longer exist, and breed numbers have been greatly reduced, it is noteworthy that Portuguese Water Dogs are still bred and exhibited.

Fig. 470. A dog travois, a vehicle fashioned by the American Indians for drawing a load. (Drawing by J. L. Medeiros)

OTHER WORK USES

A few of the early settlers in Canada were known to have used dogs to pull the plow. Also, dogs were often used as pulling and pack animals by the American Indians. They fashioned a dog vehicle which they called a *travois*. It consisted of two trailing poles that served as shafts and carried a platform or net for the load.

SLED DOGS[1]

To most people, sled dogs and Eskimos are synonymous. There is no doubt about the history of sled dogs and their contribution deserving a well-merited position of prominence in the history of the Far North, including Alaska.

Dog mushing (traveling over snow by dog sled) is a vital part of the heritage of Alaska. Good dog teams were a necessity in the early days; and so were experienced mushers. Early Alaskans had to carry the mail in the winter by dog sled, deliver food and other supplies, and use the teams to run their traplines. Dog teams were used by medical doctors to transport medicine to the sick and to move those who needed more intensive care to hospitals. The U.S. Marshalls used dog teams to make their appointed rounds and bring justice to the far flung frontier. Census takers used this means of travel to count noses in the Far North. Dog teams were a necessary part of everyday living; they were used in the native villages to haul fish and game to the homes, to carry firewood, and to transport blocks of ice in the winter for fresh drinking water. They served as general freight and passenger carriers.

The early-day sled dog mushers of Alaska were the aristocrats of the unbroken trails. Their many feats and accomplishments have been recorded on the yellowing pages of the Northland's past.

GOLD AND MUSHERS

The roll of mushers in the development of Alaska first began to be publicized in the waning years of the last century. Gold in the Forty-Mile country, Dawson in the Yukon, the Tanana Valley in the interior, and later Iditarod and Nome, brought fortune seekers by the thousands to the North. When man came to open up a new territory, there were always trails to be blazed. During the long, cold winters, there was a need for a means of transportation from one sourdough roadhouse to another; a need to carry mail, mining, and building supplies; and a means of bringing out gold from the interior gold camps. Dogs were the only answer. Sled dogs, in-

Fig. 471. Mail and passenger haul, Iditarod Trail, Alaska. (Photo by Joe Redington, Knik, Alaska. Courtesy Mrs. V. S. Page, Wasilla, Alaska)

Fig. 472. Sled dog team in Alaska. (Photo by Tom Johnson, Wasilla, Alaska. Courtesy Dorothy Page, Wasilla, Alaska)

---

[1] The author expresses his grateful appreciation to the following person who provided much of the material and the pictures used in this section: Mrs. V. S. (Dorothy) Page, Wasilla, Alaska. Mrs. Page was a member of the committee of the Iditarod Trail Race, which was the richest and largest dog race ever held in Alaska.

cluding Siberians, Malemutes, half-wolf, and mixed breeds, were tried and tested on the trails. Likewise, the mushers who drove them were proved. They were an unbeatable combination in the Far North.

There were no railroads, so gold was hauled from the interior to the coast by "gold trains," using dog power. One train from Iditarod consisted of dog teams totaling 75 dogs, along with their drivers. The train carried 4,000 to 5,000 pounds of gold.

THE NOME DIPHTHERIA SERUM RUN OF 1925

The Nome diphtheria serum run—a race against death itself—stands as one of the great feats of history. It began at the Nenana Railroad Station on January 27, 1925, and ended at Nome. In the battle with the elements to haul diphtheria serum to Nome, the dog teams traveled in relays. They covered the run of 674 miles in 127½ hours. When the chips were down, the dogs came through against heavy odds.

Balto, the lead dog on the team that completed the memorable run to Nome, bringing antitoxin and hope to the people of Nome, became a symbol of the heroic northern sled dog. A statue of Balto was erected in New York City's Central Park. The inscription at the base of the statue reads—

"Endurance, fidelity, intelligence"—a fitting tribute to a Husky—or to a man.

ABOUT DOGS, SLEDS, AND MEN

Out of this ruggedness and need, Alaska developed its own strain of dogs and men. They were rough, understanding of the ways of wilderness, and able to meet the challenge of Alaskan winters, frozen trails, blinding blizzards, flowing rivers and lakes, and the isolation of wilderness travel. Some pertinent facts about dogs and sleds follow:

1. *Speed*—On the average, a dog team will travel 20 to 30 miles a day, over an uneven trail, in all kinds of weather.

2. *Dogs*—The typical Alaska sled dog may be described as having a wolfish appearance, great width of chest, being rather rangy; with heavy, but not long hair; and with feet particularly adapted to trail conditions. Today, there are four

Fig. 473. Sled dog team in Alaska. (Photo by Tom Johnson, Wasilla, Alaska. Courtesy Dorothy Page, Wasilla, Alaska)

Fig. 474. Malamute puppies in foreground; Siberian puppies in background. Notice the Siberian turned with his back to the camera. Puppies owned by Knik Kennels, Knik, Alaska. (Photo by Howard Lowery, Teacher, Wasilla Area High School, Wasilla, Alaska. Courtesy Mrs. V. S. Page, Wasilla, Alaska)

main breeds of Alaskan sled dogs. They are: the Samoyed, the Alaskan Malamute, the Greenland Dog, and the Siberian Husky. Of these, the Samoyed is recognized by the Kennel Clubs of America and Great Britain. A good lead dog is extremely intelligent and deft at picking up and following an indistinct trail. Also, he usually has an uncanny ability at sensing dangers, such as an overflow of water beneath a frozen crust of snow or thin ice incapable of supporting the weight of the team and sled.

3. *Number of dogs per team; handling*—The

Fig. 475. Nenana, Siberian puppy, owned by Knik Kennels, Knik, Alaska. (Photo by Howard Lowery, Teacher, Wasilla Area High School, Wasilla, Alaska. Courtesy Mrs. V. S. Page, Wasilla, Alaska)

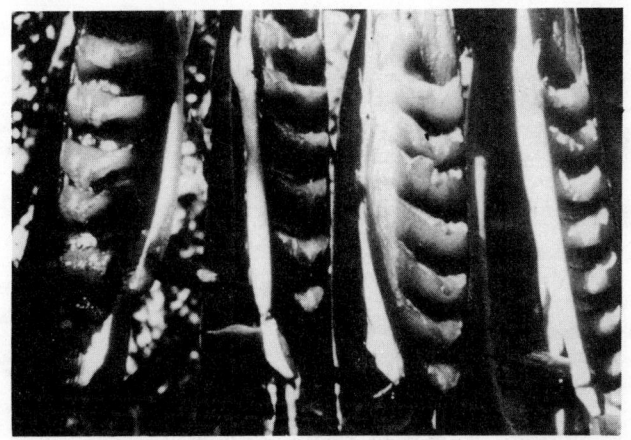

Fig. 476. Dog food drying. Dried fish was once the fuel of Alaskan dog teams. Today, commercial dog foods are used. (Photo by Joe Redington, Knik, Alaska. Courtesy Mrs. V. S. Page, Wasilla, Alaska)

average Alaskan dog team consists of 5 to 9 dogs, usually driven 2 abreast in tandem formation, with the leader either loose or in harness well out in front. The 2 dogs nearest the sled are called *the wheel dogs*. The long cable to which each pair is attached by means of collars and harness is known as the *tow line*. There are no reins; instead, the dogs are directed by the driver's voice. The command, "mush!" sets the team in motion; and the command "whoa!" brings it to a standstill—that is, as one sourdough musher put it, "sometimes it does." "Gee" and "haw" are the commands for right and left turns, respectively.

Larger teams make for less speed. However, it is noteworthy that some of the early-day mail teams contained as many as 21 dogs.

4. *Weight of dogs*—On the average, sled dogs weigh from 60 to 80 pounds each.

5. *Load*—Sled dogs are capable of pulling at least twice their own weight. Thus, a team of 7 dogs weighing 70 pounds each will normally pull about 1,000 pounds.

6. *Food*—When on the trail, sled dogs are fed about 2 pounds of dried fish per dog per day (today, many sled dogs are fed commercial dog foods).

7. *Sleds*—Sleds range from 5 to 16 feet in length, depending upon the intended use. The skid sled is most commonly used in the interior of Alaska. Its runners are usually about 20 inches apart. Freight sleds are generally from 15 to 22 feet in length. Most sleds are equipped with handles at the rear, which are located about the height of a man's hand, with which the driver keeps the sled on the trail.

SLED DOG MUSHER'S HALL OF FAME

In 1967, the Sled Dog Musher's Hall of Fame was started at Knik, Alaska. In it, mushers and their dogs, along with the stories of their feats, will be enshrined for posterity. This project is one of great historic and artistic significance.

SLED DOG RACES

In addition to being a necessity in the more isolated parts of Alaska, and even in the less isolated parts during times of severe storms, mushing eventually gained a degree of popularity and became a sport. Finally, in 1972, the Alaska State Legislature made sled dog racing "the official sport" of the state.

IDITAROD TRAIL SEPPALA MEMORIAL RACE

The Iditarod Trail Race was the richest and largest ever held in Alaska. The race was run at Knik, Alaska, in 1967, with $25,000 in prize money. There were 58 sled dog teams in the race, representing almost all of the native villages in Alaska. Also, entries came from outside the State. The stated purposes of the race were to encourage native mushers to continue to train

Fig. 477. Nikki, Wild Dog of the North. *(Courtesy Walt Disney Productions, Burbank, Calif.* © *MCM-LXXI Walt Disney Productions)*

Fig. 478. Kings of the Alaskan trail. Chinook and Frosty, freight team wheel dogs, owned by Knik Kennels, Knik, Alaska. *(Photo by Howard Lowery, Teacher, Wasilla Area High School, Wasilla, Alaska. Courtesy Mrs. V. S. Page, Wasilla, Alaska)*

their teams, through getting prize money high enough to be more in line with that offered in other sports, and to salute the great mushers who helped blaze the trails in Alaska.

NIKKI

Nikki, a dog whelped and trained in Fairbanks, was used by Walt Disney in the film *Nikki, Wild Dog of the North*. While shooting the film, it was necessary to use seven different dogs to depict Nikki in various sizes during the time period covered in the story of the film.

SLED DOG STILL KING OF THE TRAIL

The whirring wheels of progress—the automobile and the airplane—have lifted much of the burden from the sled dog of Alaska. However, he still occupies a place in the scheme of things from which he cannot be dethroned. When the blinding blizzards come, he is still king of the trail, and the one who is able to serve and give comfort to thousands of Alaskans who reside beyond the ranges of mountains that border the Pacific Coast.

20
Farm Dogs; Sheep Dog Trials

Chapter 20
Farm Dogs 550
   Uses and Breeds 550
   Working Border Collie 551
   Training the Stock Dog 552
   Housing 552
   Know the Whereabouts of Your Dog 552
   Some Farm Dog Problems 553
Sheep Dog Trials 553
   Origin 553
   Popularity 555
   How Conducted 555
   North American Sheep Dog Society 555

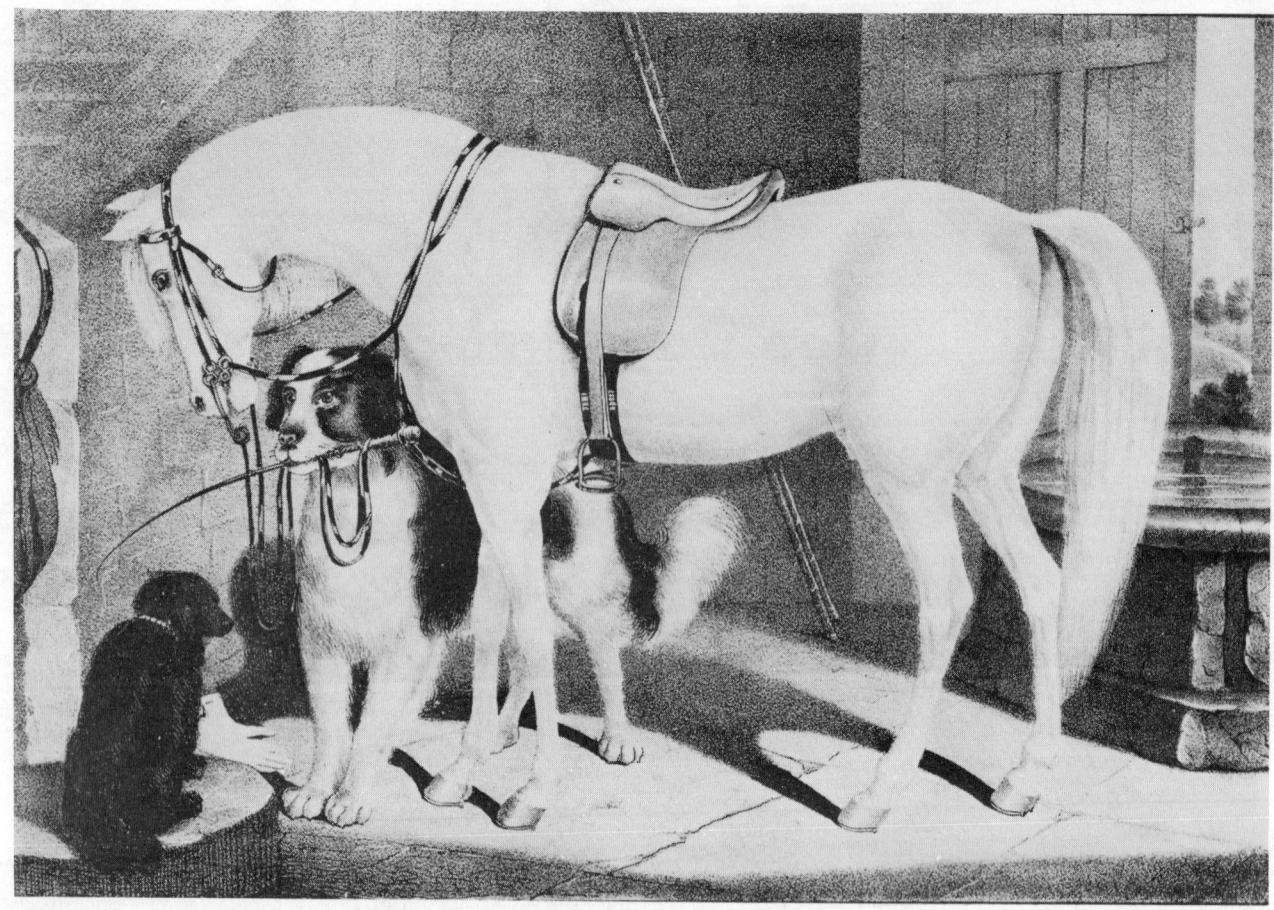

Fig. 479. Farm dogs. (The Favorite Horse. Courtesy Smithsonian Institution, Washington, D.C.)

FARM DOGS; SHEEP DOG TRIALS

In its long history as a servant of man, there can be little doubt that the most useful of all dogs has been, and still is, the farm dog, especially the sheep dog. Without sheep dogs, the production of lamb and wool would be an uneconomic proposition on the unfenced ranges of Western United States, as well as in Great Britain, Australia, New Zealand, and the U.S.S.R., and in parts of many other countries where sheep are kept.

FARM DOGS

Few American farms are without a dog; an estimated 76 percent of farmers own one or more dogs.

USES AND BREEDS

Many different uses are made of dogs on the farm, with the result that the choice of breed varies accordingly. The primary uses are: as stock dogs, to guard property, for hunting, and as ratters.

When it comes to working sheep, the Working Border Collie is without a peer. It is widely used for this purpose in the United States, the British Isles, New Zealand, and in other parts of the world. In Australia, the Kelpie (a Scottish word for water nymph), which appears to be descended from a mixture of various British dogs, along with the infusion of Dingo blood, is widely used. Also, in Australia, the Australian Cattle Dog is the cattleman's helper. In the south of England, where the sheep holdings are small, but where the winters are long and muddy, the bobtailed English Sheep Dog is used extensively. In Wales,

Corgis are famed for their ability to work both sheep and cattle.

On most U.S. farms, the most frequent livestock use of the dog is to bring in the cows, but dogs are also used, on occasion and on certain farms, to drive hogs, horses, and turkeys.

Without doubt, more farm dogs are used as watchdogs, or as guards, than for any other purpose. Even if the dog is not fully trained, he will usually bark when visitors or strangers approach the property, when stock or predatory animals wander near farm buildings, or when anything else out of the ordinary happens. As watchdogs, Collies and German Shepherds are commonly used on the farm. There is one precaution relative to using German Shepherds for this purpose, of which most farmers are aware. They cannot be permitted to roam over the countryside, because they are likely to become sheep-killing dogs. The Collie, on the other hand, has little tendency in this direction.

Some farmers keep one or two hunting dogs. Depending on the kind of game, these may be upland game dogs, like the Setter or Pointer, or dogs adapted to duck or goose hunting, like the Labrador. In some rural areas, hound dogs are popular for fox, 'coon, or 'possum hunting.

For a versatile, all-around, farm dog—one that is suited to helping with the stock, doing a bit of hunting, and even serving as a ratter—the Airedale Terrier is excellent.

Fig. 480. Toast, Working Border Collie, owned and trained by Guy W. Hilton, Kenton, Ohio. (Courtesy Mr. Hilton)

WORKING BORDER COLLIE

Despite the wide use of Working Border Collies for livestock purposes, particularly for sheep, they are not recognized as a breed by the American Kennel Club; hence, they are not listed in Table 3, chapter 2, of this book. For this reason, the breed will be discussed at this point.

Working Border Collies are found in every country of the world, wherever sheep are herded. The breed superiority for sheep work is due to its tremendous instinct to work—and to work in a certain way. As a wide-run, strong-eyed dog, they can control a flock of sheep with a quiet efficiency unknown in any other breed. At this point, it's worth remembering that the instinct that puts the Working Border Collie above all other dogs as a sheep dog stems from the wild dog's instinct to stalk and hunt his prey.

There is little doubt that the Working Border Collie has the same genetic background as the Collie in Scotland. They have the same general conformation and build. Through selection, and infusion of other breeding, Working Border Collies have been molded to meet the needs of shepherds and sheep. These needs are: vigor, intelligence, courage, initiative, and obedience. Type is quite varied in Border Collies. The ability to work is all that matters to breeders. The application for registry form used by The International Sheepdog Society of England has a space for size: "large, medium, or small." Also, it has a space for coat: "rough-coated, medium-coated, smooth-coated, or beardie." And there is no color bar. Black and white predominate, followed by tricolor (black, tan, and white), but blue, merle, slate blue, sable, and chocolate are found. Sometimes, white pups turn up, although they are very unpopular with shepherds because sheep do not respect a white dog as they do a black one, and lambs will usually run after it with apparent curiosity.

Without a dog, a shepherd or herder is helpless in handling a large flock or band of sheep. On the western range, a herder and one Border Collie can handle a thousand sheep under most conditions. Where larger bands are run, or where the terrain is broken and rough, more than one dog is used by the herder in working his band.

Although the Working Border Collie is preeminent as a sheep dog, it should not be overlooked that they can be, and are, trained to work cattle, swine, horses, and turkeys. Also, a Border Collie can be trained to distinguish different classes of animals; for example, to go out and get the cows, but to leave the sheep in the field.

Sheep dog trials—a type of public performance—have become the accepted means of performance testing dogs of the Working Border Collie breed. The concentration of the Border Collie makes him an ideal dog to perform before spectators. But the real value of the Working Border Collie lies in his ability to move and hold livestock with great efficiency, thereby saving his master's time and effort.

TRAINING THE STOCK DOG

Training a stock dog is not difficult. The first step consists in teaching the dog simple obedience. This is covered in chapter 6 of this book; hence, repetition at this point is unnecessary.

Once obedience training is mastered, work relating to the dog's duties on the farm may be undertaken. Such training is really not difficult. It is even simpler than training a child because, once the dog catches on, he is anxious to do everything possible to please his master. First, one must remember that the dog will not be able to understand many words. So, be sure to limit the commands you use to single words; and, if possible, always coordinate the words with some physical action, like waving of an arm in a directing movement. Hence, when the herder wishes to have his dogs circle wide around a band of sheep, he usually waves his arm as well as makes use of his whistle. In training the stock dog, it is necessary to be patient, but firm. You must never back down or give up on a project that you have started, because once the dog finds that you are not demanding an order, he will take advantage of you. When he carries out your instructions, reward him generously, with your voice and a pat on the shoulder.

HOUSING

When left to roam, the farm dog can find many places to bed down at night, or to rest where it is dry and warm. Areas out of direct wind, and where sufficient bedding is available, such as stables, barns, or sheds, may be used, or the dog may burrow in the hay or straw stored in buildings. However, these places are not as satisfactory as a box or house prepared especially for the dog. In the first place, you don't know where the dog is when he picks shelter at random. Secondly, such shelters frequently become infested with fleas; hence, a source of annoyance to the dog. So, a special box or house should be available for the farm dog. A box need not be elaborate, providing it is placed inside a building or shed, on a porch, or in some other area that will break the wind and possibly supply some heat if the weather is cold. A nest box in the garage is often satisfactory.

Where an outside doghouse is built, it should be designed to fit the dog. A rule of thumb is that the doghouse should supply thirty-six square inches of floor space in the nesting area for each inch in height of the dog at the shoulder. The roof of the doghouse should be high enough to allow the dog to sit up without bumping his head. Also, the roof should be so designed that it can be raised and lowered to (1) allow for easy cleaning, and (2) permit good ventilation during warm weather in warm climates. It is also a good idea to extend the roofline in front of the house so as to provide shade in hot areas. Double construction should be used if the house is outside and is to be used in the wintertime, especially in cold areas. The house itself should be raised off the ground about four inches, thereby assuring dryness.

KNOW THE WHEREABOUTS OF YOUR DOG

A good rule to follow with your dog, as well as with your child, is to know where he is at all times. Dogs that have the run of the farm and the community often develop undesirable traits; they may actually kill sheep or chickens or other animals. On the other hand, the supervised dog is usually a good dog. A fenced yard around the house can be used to confine a dog when he is not with you. If the yard is not fenced, a small enclosed dog run will suffice, or a wire run with leash attached to the dog's collar may be used. Sometimes, a shed, a back porch, or some other enclosure, can be used to confine the dog. Dogs that are allowed in the house can often be housed there. Be sure to keep the dog confined to a definite area at night. It is during the night that dogs on the loose tend to gang together, and it is these packs of dogs that get into trouble in the community.

SOME FARM DOG PROBLEMS

The ownership of a farm dog does not bring rewards without, at the same time, creating some problems. Some dogs will kill chickens or chase sheep. Others will bite neighbors or friends. Dogs may have fleas, and they are apt to have tapeworms if unusual care is not taken. Control of tapeworms is especially important, because tapeworms may cause sheep measles in carcasses (See chapter 8). Some dogs, if they are poorly trained, are too rough on animals. In roaming the fields, farm dogs collect much foreign matter in their coats; hence, a certain amount of grooming is always necessary.

SHEEP DOG TRIALS

Sheep Dog Trials are tests of the intelligence, talent and ability of sheep dogs. As such, they promote better breeding and better training. Also, they have evolved as a popular spectator sport.

ORIGIN

The first Sheep Dog Trial was held in Wales in 1873. It was won by a Scotchman with a strong-eyed dog. Without doubt, this was the beginning of the great invasion of Wales by this type of dog, which became known as the Work-

Fig. 481. Control! With quiet efficiency, and without fences, this Working Border Collie competing in the Worcester International Sheep Dog Trials, in England, has the flock under perfect control. With a good working dog in command, the shepherd has no fear that the flock will escape. (Courtesy Mr. J. Anderson, Hartrigge Gardens, Jedburgh, Roxburghshire, England, who is the competing shepherd in the picture.

OFFICIAL SHEEP DOG TRIAL COURSE
NORTH AMERICAN SHEEP DOG SOCIETY

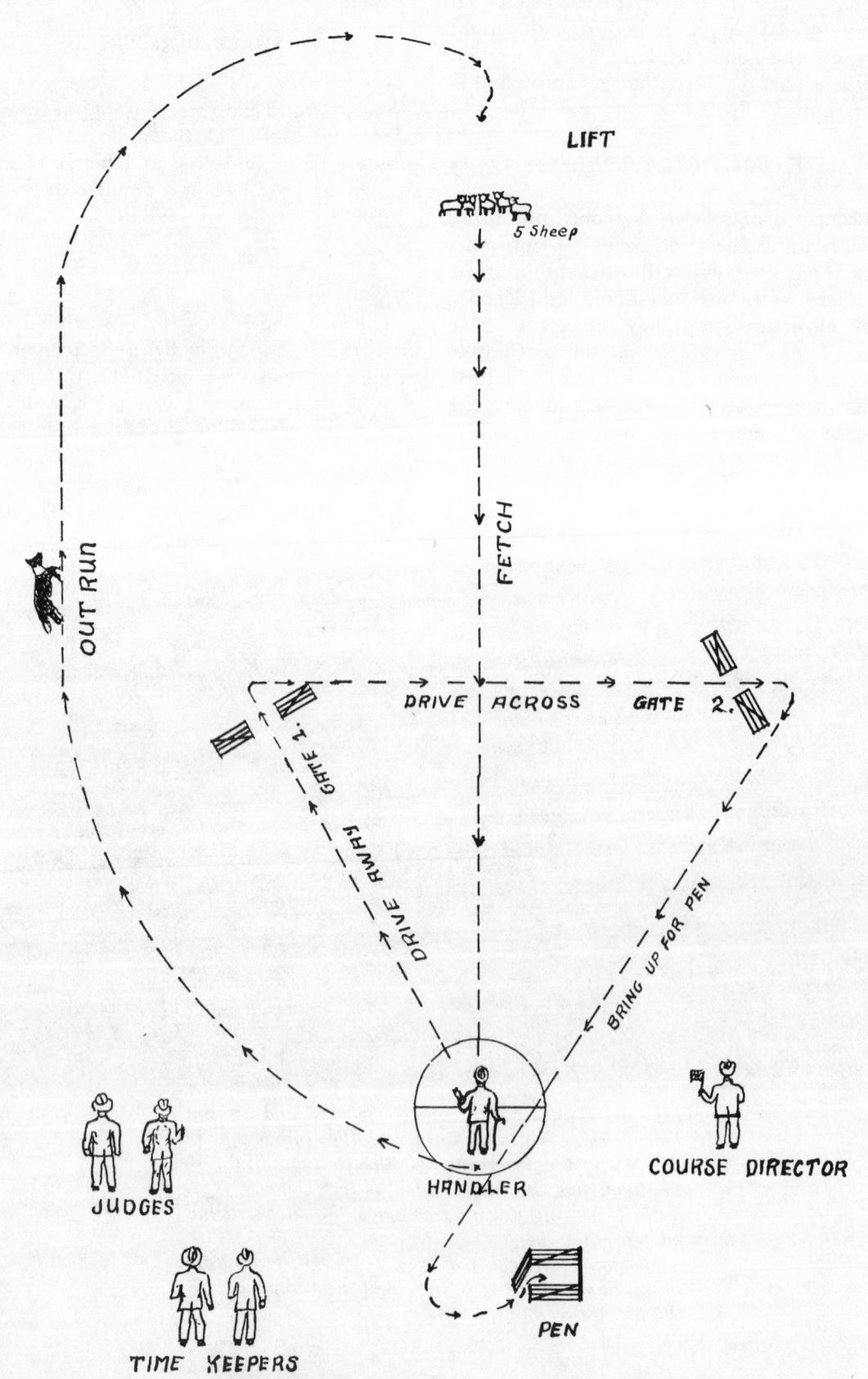

Fig. 482. Official course outline of North American Sheep Dog Society. (Courtesy North American Sheep Dog Society)

ing Border Collie. But, contrary to what some people think, Border Collies are not native to Wales. Even today, the majority of Welsh winners in Sheep Dog Trials are either imported from Scotland or bred from imported stock.

POPULARITY

Sheep Dog Trials first became popular throughout the British Isles. As they did, the demand for a strong-eyed dog, which could win such trials, increased. In 1910, the International Sheep Dog Society was formed and published its first Stud Book. Sheep Dog Trials soon became very popular with the general public, enabling them to be run at a profit. In turn, this meant that more and more of them were held, at which shepherds could see just what could be achieved by a well-bred, well-trained dog. Many of them would either buy a Border Collie pup or mate one of their own local strain bitches to a trial winner.

Today, Sheep Dog Trials are held in England, Scotland, Canada, Australia, New Zealand, and the United States. In this country, Sheep Dog Trials are held in conjunction with many of the leading livestock expositions, where the expert work of these fine dogs commands the warm applause of spectators. Occasionally, a Sheep Dog Demonstration is included as an added feature in one of the leading American Bench Shows.

HOW CONDUCTED

The conduct of a Sheep Dog Trial must, of necessity, vary somewhat according to conditions that prevail, particularly the size and kind of area available. The author first conducted a Sheep Dog Trial on the play field of a college campus.

The North American Sheep Dog Society adopted the Course Outline shown in Fig. 482. Additionally, the following rules, regulations, and scoring system are pertinent to the conduct of "official" trials:

1. *Course*—The minimum field area for holding official outdoor trials must be at least 250 yards long and 150 yards wide. Minimum distance for each phase of work shall be as follows:

   a. *Gather*—Not less than 150 yards from center of Shedding Ring to point of pick up

   b. *Drive*—Not less than 75 yards on diagonal from center of Shedding Ring to Gate No. 1 on left; and not less than 75 yards in the Drive Across from Gate No. 1 to Gate No. 2 on the right; both gates to be set with a 12-foot opening

   c. *Shedding Ring*—Not less than 20 yards in diameter

   d. *Pen*—Shall be 6' x 6' or 8' x 8' or any square dimension between these two—and shall be set not less than 10 yards outside of the above working field

   e. *Overage*—No fixed obstacle or point on the course shall be closer than 25 yards to any limiting fence (It is noteworthy that in England a larger area is favored; an open area 400 yards by 200 yards is used)

2. *Performance*—Dogs are required to perform 4 phases of work: gathering, shedding, driving, and penning

3. *Sheep*—Usually 5 sheep are used. However, no dog can be assigned fewer than 3 sheep

4. *Time*—Each dog is allowed 12 minutes

5. *Scoring*—Each dog is scored individually in each phase of work according to the following basis:

Assignment	Points
Gathering (divided into "out-run," 10 points; "lift," 5 points; and "fetch," 10 points)	25
Driving (7½ points on each drive)	15
Shedding	5
Penning	15
Single sheep	5
Total	65

Most dogs love performing before a crowd. However, this is not always true. Some dogs that are superb out on the range will not perform at all before a crowd. Others are unable to cope with the stress of strange surroundings, or working against time. Still others are not suited temperamentally to this type of work, whereas others take to it quite naturally.

NORTH AMERICAN SHEEP DOG SOCIETY

The address:

Bernard L. Minton, Secretary-Treasurer
210 East Main Street
McLeansboro, Illinois 62859

In 1940, the North American Sheep Dog Society was formed. The Society maintains its own *Stud Book* and provides the course outline, rules and regulations, and scoring system for the conduct of "official" Sheep Dog Trials.

21
Glossary of Terms

Fig. 483. Puli puppies. (Courtesy Mrs. Charles R. Anderson, Cedwood Puli Kennels, Bristol, Conn.)

A mark of distinction of a knowledgeable dog owner is that he "speaks the language"—he uses the correct terms and knows what they mean. Even though dog terms are used glibly by old-timers, often they are baffling to the newcomer.

Many terms that are defined or explained elsewhere in this book are not repeated in this chapter. Thus, if a particular term is not listed herein, the reader should look in the index or in the particular chapter and section where it is discussed.

A

ABERRATION—1. The act of wandering away or going astray. 2. A sport or mutation.
ACCRUAL BASIS—a method of reporting income taxes in which income is accounted for when it is earned and expenses are recorded when incurred rather than when paid.
ACQUIRED CHARACTERS—Attributes developed in the body that are of environmental origin, as opposed to being of genetic (germ-plasm) origin.
ACQUIRED IMMUNITY—An immunity from a disease, resulting either from vaccination or from a previous attack of that disease which renders the body resistant to it.
ACTION—the way in which a dog moves—walks, trots, or runs.
AGOUTI—a grizzled color of the hair consisting of the barring of each hair in several alternate dark and light bands, blackish blue or brown at the base and yellowish at the tip.
ALBINO—an animal that lacks normal pigmentation. An albino is characterized by a white coat, blue or gray eyes, and a flesh colored nose.
ALLELE—Mendelian characters are inherited in alternative pairs (or series). These alternative forms of a gene, which are located at the same point on each of a pair of chromosomes, are called alleles.
ALLERGY—a severe reaction, or sensitivity, which occurs in some individuals following the introduction of certain antigens into their bodies.
ALMOND EYES—eyes set in tissues shaped like almonds; that is, slanting, oval, and pointed at the end.
ALSATIAN—the English name for the German Shepherd Dog.
ALTER—to castrate (a male); to spay (a bitch).
AMERICAN KENNEL CLUB (AKC)—A nonprofit organization devoted to the advancement of purebred dogs.

ANAL GLANDS—a small pair of secretory organs located on either side of the anal opening.

ANEMIA, NUTRITIONAL—a condition in which the blood is deficient in either quality or quantity. A deficient quality refers to a deficiency in hemoglobin and/or red cells. Commonly, it is caused by an iron deficiency, but it may be caused by a deficiency of copper, cobalt, and/or certain vitamins (riboflavin, pyridoxine, pantothenic acid, and/or folic acid).

ANESTRUS—the prolonged period of sexual quiescence between the mating seasons of animals.

ANGULATION—the angle formed by meeting of two bones; it usually refers to the angle between the shoulder blade and the upper arm, or to the angle formed by the upper and lower thigh bones.

ANOREXIA—loss of appetite, especially when prolonged.

ANTHELMINTIC—a product for expelling or destroying parasitic worms, especially of the intestine.

ANTIBIOTIC—a chemical substance, produced by molds or bacteria, that has the ability to inhibit the growth of, or to destroy, other microorganisms. Based on the kind of bacteria attacked, antibiotics are classed as follows:
1. BROAD-SPECTRUM ANTIBIOTIC—an antibiotic that attacks both gram-positive and gram-negative bacteria, and that may also show activity against other disease agents.
2. MEDIUM-SPECTRUM ANTIBIOTIC—an antibiotic that attacks a limited number of gram-positive and gram-negative bacteria.
3. NARROW-SPECTRUM ANTIBIOTIC — an antibiotic whose activity is restricted to either gram-negative or gram-positive bacteria. For example, penicillin is active primarily against gram-positive organisms, whereas streptomycin attacks only gram-negative organisms.

ANTIBODY—a substance that opposes the action of another substance.

ANTIGEN—a foreign substance that, when introduced into the body, stimulates the formation of protective antibodies.

ANTISEPTIC—a compound that inhibits the growth of microorganisms, and that is usually applied to the skin.

ANUS—the posterior opening of the alimentary canal through which the feces are discharged.

APPETITE—the immediate desire to eat when feed is present. Loss of appetite in a dog is usually caused by illness. When a dog passes more than one feeding, he should be examined by the veterinarian to determine the cause.

APPETITE, DEPRAVED—see DEPRAVED APPETITE.

APPETIZERS—see TREATS AS REWARDS.

APPLE DOME OR HEAD—a rounded or domed skull; typical of the English Toy Spaniel and Chihuahua.

APRON—a frill of long hair that hangs below the throat and over the front of the chest. Characteristic of most Collies.

ARTHRITIS—an ailment of the joints, similar to rheumatism. It occurs fairly frequently in old dogs, where it usually develops very slowly. There is no known treatment.

ARTIFICIAL INSEMINATION (A.I.)—the deposition of spermatozoa in the female genitalia by artificial rather than by natural means.

ASH—the mineral matter of a feed. It is the residue remaining after complete burning of the organic matter.

ASTRINGENT—a drug, such as tannic acid, alum, and zinc oxide or sulphate, that causes contraction of tissues.

AUTOPSY—inspection, and partial dissection, of a dead body to determine the cause of death.

AVOIRDUPOIS WEIGHTS AND MEASURES—Avoirdupois is a French word, meaning "to weigh." The old English system of weights and measures is referred to as the *avoirdupois system*, or U. S. Customary weights and measures, to differentiate it from the *metric system*.

B

BABBLER—a hound that barks, or gives tongue, when not on the trail of game.

BACK-CROSS—the mating of a hybrid (F_1) back to one of its parents.

BACTERIA—bacteria are one of the smallest and simplest known forms of plant life. They possess just one cell, vary in size and shape, multiply by transverse fission, and possess no chlorophyll. Bacteria are exceedingly numerous in nature, and the majority of them are beneficial; for example, those that create the fermentation processes used in the manufacture of vinegar and the ripening of cheese. The few that cause disease are referred to as *pathogens*.

Bacteria are classified by various distinguishing features. In shapes, they are either rods (bacilli), spheres (cocci), or spirals (spirilla). Some bacteria will grow only on special types of media in varying amounts of oxygen. Some are motile, whereas others lack the power of locomotion. Then there are those bacteria that under certain conditions form spores that are highly resistant to destruction and may live for years. Some also possess the ability to elaborate toxic products within themselves or in the media in which they grow, as does, for example, the fatal and relatively common toxin that causes botulism poisoning. Bacteria are further classified as follows:
1. GRAM-NEGATIVE—those bacterial species that are decolorized by acetone or alcohol.
2. GRAM-POSITIVE—those bacterial species that retain a crystal violet color even when exposed to alcohol or acetone.

BACTERICIDE—a product that kills bacteria.

BACTERINS—standardized suspensions of bacteria (and their products) that have been killed by heat or chemical means and are unable to produce disease. When introduced into the body, they stimulate the production of protective antibodies that act against subsequent attacks of organisms of the kind contained in the bacterin. They produce an active immunity.

Theoretically, bacterins should be useful in the prevention of every infectious disease in which the causative agent is known. Unfortunately, they do not always give the desired results, especially in diseases of a chronic nature.

Often a product may be a mixed bacterin; that is, it may contain more than one organism. This usually includes secondary invaders when the true causative agent is unknown.

BACTERIOSTAT—a product that retards bacterial growth.

BADGER COLORED—grizzled-gray hair, like a badger.

BALANCE—a pleasing relationship of the parts to each other; no part is too big or too small for the whole body. Such an animal is said to be nicely balanced, or to possess symmetry and balance.

BALANCED RATION—a ration that provides an animal with proper proportions and amounts of all the required nutrients for a period of 24 hours. Needs differ according to age and use. (Also see RATION(S).)

BAND DOG—a watchdog kept tied by day and turned loose at night.

BARREL—the rib section of the body. When the rib section is rounded, the animal is said to be *barrel shaped*.

BARREN—a bitch that is not pregnant.

BAT EARS—erect ears that are shaped like the ears of a bat, as in the French Bulldog.

BAY—the voice of a hound when trailing or when the quarry is brought to a stand.

BEARD—profuse growth of hair on the muzzle and lower jaw; characteristic of the Belgian Griffon.

BEEFY—very heavy development through the hindquarters.

BELL EARS—ears that are blunt-tipped, rather than pointed.

BELTON—a type of color formed when two colors blend so closely so as to lose their individual identity; for example blue belton is a combination of black and white, whereas the orange belton is a combination of orange and white.

BENCH SHOW—a dog show at which all the dogs are "benched" or leashed on benches.

BEST IN SHOW—the dog show award signifying best of all breeds.

BEVY—a group of game birds, such as quail.

BIOLOGICS—medicinal preparations made from microorganisms (bacteria, protozoa, or viruses) and their products. They include various vaccines, bacterins, serums, and similar preparations. These agents are one of the most valuable contributions to animal health, and they are constantly being improved. They are used essentially for rendering animals immune to various infections.

It is noteworthy, however, that not all attempts to confer immunity by biologics are successful. In some cases, it seems impossible to create an immunity against infection. The common cold in humans is a case in point. In other cases, the animal may die from the disease or its complications, in spite of an inoculation; because of a biologic of poor quality, infection before the treatment is begun, or improper administration of the biologic.

BIRD DOG—any of the sporting breeds that are used as hunting dogs, usually Pointers or Setters.

BIRDS—to a hunter, this refers to game birds, i.e. quail, pheasant, grouse, woodcock, and prairie chicken.

BIRTH DATE—regardless of when a dog is born, its birth date is always considered as January 1 from the standpoint of showing or racing. Thus, a puppy whelped May 1, 1975, will be ten years old on January 1, 1985.

BISCUIT COLOR—the color of a biscuit (beige).

BITCH—the female of the dog species.

BITE—the position of the teeth when the mouth is shut. (See also LEVEL BITE, SCISSORS BITE, UNDERSHOT, OVERSHOT.)

BLAZE—a white mark running up the middle of the foreface and between the eyes; characteristic of many St. Bernards.

BLINDNESS—partial or complete loss of vision. Either or both eyes may be affected. A blind dog usually has very erect ears and a hesitant gait. Frequently, blindness also can be detected by the discoloration of the eye. Further and more certain verification can be obtained by moving the hand gently in close proximity to the eye.

BLINKER—a bird dog that points at birds and then leaves before they are flushed; often such a dog goes past the birds even when he knows their location.

BLOCKY—a square or boxlike head, as in the Boston Terrier.

BLOOD—the red fluid that is carried by arteries from the heart to all parts of the body, thence returns through veins, with the heart acting as a pump.

BLOODED—a dog of good breeding—pedigreed.

BLOOM—the gloss or sheen of the coat, indicative of good condition.

BLUE EYE—an unsound eye with a blue appearance; the sight may or may not be entirely gone.

BLUE MERLE—blue and gray mixed with black. Marbled.

BOARD—to feed, house, and care for a dog on a fee or charge basis.

BOBTAIL—1. A dog born tailless or on which the tail has been docked very short. 2. Often used as the nickname for the Old English Sheepdog.

BODY SCENT—the scent emanating from the bodies of animals and birds.

BOLT—to drive or scare an animal out of its earth or burrow.

BOLTER—a bird dog that goes out of control, without obeying his handler. One that goes hunting in any direction that he desires.

BONE—the relative size of a dog's leg bone.

BORB—abbreviation for bitch; used in most announcements of dog shows and on racing cards.

BOSSY—overdeveloped and thick through the shoulders.

BRACE—1. A pair of dogs. 2. Also, two dogs that are run together in the same heat in a field trial.

BREATHING RATE—normal breathing rate for the dog is 18 times per minute, with a range of 11 to 38; meaning that the animal inhales that many times per minute, and exhales a like number of times.

The breathing rate can be determined by placing the hand on the flank, by observing the rise and fall of the flanks, or, in the winter, by watching the breath condense coming from the nostrils. Rapid breathing due to recent exercise, excitement, hot weather, or poorly ventilated buildings should not be confused with disease. Respiration is accelerated in pain and in febrile conditions.

BREECHING—the tan marking at the back of the thighs of a black-and-tan dog, as in such breeds as the Manchester Terrier or Gordon Setter.

BREED (s)—a group of dogs having a common origin and possessing certain well-fixed, distinctive, uniformly transmitted characteristics that are not common to other dogs.

BREEDER—1. A person who breeds dogs. 2. Under AKC rules, the breeder of a dog is the owner (or if the dam was leased, the lessee) of the dam at the time she was bred.

BREEDY—exhibiting to a high degree the characteristics or qualities that distinguish the breed.

BRINDLE—a mixture of black hairs with hairs of a lighter color, usually tan, brown, or gray.

BRISKET—the forechest. The section of the body in front of the chest and between the front legs.

BROKEN COLOR—descriptive of a coat that is all one color (self color) except that it is broken by white or another color.

BROKEN-HAIRED—a roughed-up wire coat.

BROOD BITCH—a bitch kept for breeding purposes.

BRUSH—a tail with thick, bushy hair; characteristic of the fox, the Collie, and the Alaskan Malamute.

BULLBAITING—an ancient sport, now outlawed, in which the dog baited or tormented the bull.

BURR—the visible, irregular inside formation of the ear.

BUTTERFLY NOSE—a nose of two colors, usually dark brown or black, spotted with flesh color.

BUTTON EARS—ears that fold over to the front and are held close to the head, as in the Fox Terrier.

BYE—a field trial term applied to the odd dog remaining after the dogs entered in a stake have been paired in braces by drawing.

C

CAESARIAN SECTION—the surgical delivery of young by a section of the abdominal walls and uterus, used when normal birth is apparently impossible.

CALCIUM—an essential mineral element that is present in foods in varying quantities.

CALL-NAME—the name by which a registered dog is known and called at home or in the kennel; usually it is a shorter and easier name than the registered name.

CALORIE—a calorie (cal always written with a small c) is the amount of heat required to raise the temperature of one gram of water one degree centigrade. To measure this heat, an instrument known as the *bomb calorimeter* is used, in which the feed (or other substance) tested is placed and burned with the aid of oxygen. Briefly stated, the procedure is as follows: an electric wire is attached to the material being tested, so that it can be ignited by remote control; 2,000 grams of water are poured around the bomb; 25 to 30 atmospheres of oxygen are added to the bomb; the material is ignited; the heat given off from the burned material warms the water; and a thermometer registers the change in temperature of the water. For example, if one gram of material is burned and the temperature of the water is raised one degree centigrade, 2,000 cal are given off. Hence, the material contains 2,000 cal/gram.

CANINE—any animal of the family *Canidae,* including dogs, wolves, jackals, and foxes.

CANINE TEETH—long, strong, pointed teeth just behind the incisors; sometimes called *fangs,* corresponding to the eye teeth of humans.

CAPPED HOCKS—an enlargement at the point of the hocks, usually caused by bruising.

CARBOHYDRATES—the sum of the crude fiber and nitrogen-free extract.

CAROTENE—the yellow colored, fat soluble substance that gives the characteristic color to carrots and to butterfat (vitamin A is nearly a colorless substance). Carotene derives its name from the carrot, from which it was first isolated over 100 years ago. Although its empirical formula was established in 1906, it was not until 1919 that Steenbock, of the University of Wisconsin, discovered its vitamin A activity. Though the yellow color is masked by the green chlorophyll, the green parts of plants are rich in carotene and thus have a high vitamin A value.

CASTRATION—the operation in which the testes (or ovaries) are removed.

CAT FOOT—a short, compact, round foot with well-arched toes, which resembles a cat's foot; characteristic of a good English Foxhound.

CHARACTER—a combination of points of appearance, behavior, and disposition distinctive of an individual dog or of a breed.

CHEEKY—a heavy, pronounced development of the cheek, as in the Bulldog.

CHEST—that portion of the body behind the brisket and in front of the abdomen that is encircled by the ribs.

CHINA EYE—a clear, light blue eye.

CHISELED—well defined, clean-cut about the head.

CHOKE COLLAR—a collar made in the form of a noose, for the purpose of applying force in a humane manner.

CHOPS—the thick upper lip that hangs below the lower jaw; characteristic of Bloodhounds and Bulldogs.

CHOREA—a nervous disorder characterized by involuntary contractions of the muscles, usually affecting the face or legs. A frequent aftermath of distemper.

CHROMOSOME—gene-carrying body, arising from the chromatin of a dividing cell.

CLASS—a term denoting high quality performance.

CLIP—the method of trimming the coat in some breeds, especially the Poodle.

CLODDY—a low and very thick-set build.

CLOSE BREEDING—the mating of closely related animals; sire to daughter, son to dam, and brother to sister.

CLOSE-COUPLED—short in the loin area; that area from the last ribs to the hips.

COARSENESS—the quality or state of being coarse.

COAT—the dog's hair covering.

COAT, SINGLE—all the hairs of the coat are of about the same length—a single coat; there is an outercoat and an undercoat.

COBBY—compact and muscular in build. The word stems from the shortbacked, sturdy conformation of the cob horse.

COCCIDIOSIS—a parasitic disease of animals. Each class of animals harbors its own species of coccidia, and there is no cross infection. Afflicted animals show diarrhea and bloody feces, and pronounced unthriftiness and weakness.

COLLAR—1. The marking around the neck, usually white. 2. A leather or chain for restraining or leading the dog when the leash is attached.

COLOSTRUM—the milk secreted by the bitch for the first few days after whelping. It is nature's product, designed to give young a good start in life. Colostrum is higher than normal milk in dry matter, protein, vitamins, and minerals. Additionally, it contains antibodies that give newborn puppies protection against certain diseases.

COMMERCIAL FEEDS—feeds mixed by manufacturers who specialize in the feed business. Today, about 60 million tons of commercial feeds, for all classes of animals, are marketed each year.

CONCEPTION—the act of becoming pregnant.

CONDITION—the state of physical well-being, as evidenced by the coat, state of flesh, and general appearance.

CONFORMATION—body shape or form of a dog.

CONGENITAL—acquired during development in the uterus and not through heredity.

CORKY—compact, spirited, and alert; a term usually applied to Terriers.

CORPUS LUTEUM—a gland of the ovary that secretes progesterone. After the ovarian follicle ruptures and the egg is released, the cells within the follicular cavity change in character and function, forming a corpus luteum or yellow body in the cavity of the ruptured follicle.

COUPLE—a pair of hounds.

COUPLING—the loin area; that part of the body from the last rib to the hip bone.

COURSE—the area to be covered.

COURSING—hunting hares with Greyhounds.

COVEY—a group of game birds, generally a brood, such as quail. A bevy.

COW HOCKS, COW HOCKED—standing with the joints of the hocks bent inward, with the toes pointing outward. Presumably, like the hocks of a cow.

COW, TO—to subdue.

CRANK TAIL—a short tail that curves downward then away from the body; shaped like a crank.

CREST—the upper arched portion of a dog's neck.

CROPPED EARS—ears from which a portion has been cut in order to make them stand erect. In this country, Great Danes, Dobermans, and Boxers are always cropped. Cropping has been forbidden in England since 1895.

CROSSBRED—a dog whose sire and dam are of different breeds.

CROUP—that portion of the topline from the hips to the root of the tail; also called the *rump*.

CROWN—the highest part of the head. The top skull.

CRUDE FAT—the material that is extracted from moisture-free feeds by ether. It consists largely of fats and oils with small amounts of waxes, resins, and coloring matter. In calculating the heat and energy value of the feed, the fat is considered 2.25 times that of either nitrogen-free extract or protein.

CRUDE FIBER—the relatively insoluble carbohydrate portion of a feed consisting chiefly of cellulose. It is determined by its insolubility in dilute acids and alkalies.

CRUDE PROTEIN—the term used to designate the nitrogenous consistuents of a feed. The percentage is obtained by multiplying the percentage of total nitrogen by the factor 6.25. The nitrogen is derived chiefly from complex chemical compounds called amino acids.

CRY—the baying of hounds on the trail.

CRYPTORCHID—a male dog with one or both testicles retained in the abdomen. Such undescended testicles are usually sterile because of the high temperature in the abdomen. This condition appears to be heritable. Thus, it is recommended that animals so affected not be retained for breeding purposes.

CULOTTE—long, bushy, hair on the back of the thighs, as in Pomeranians.

CULTURE—the propagation of microorganisms, or of living tissue cells, in special media conducive to their growth.

CUR—a mongrel.

CUSHION—fullness of the upper lips and foreface, as in the Bulldog and Pekingese.

CUT UP—1. To divide into parts, as cut up in the flanks. 2. To clown or act boisterously.

CYNOLOGIST—a person who specializes in the care and training of dogs.

D

DAILY DOUBLE—a bet on two dogs to win races in a given day. The holder of a daily double ticket collects only if both dogs win.

DAM—the female parent.

DAPPLED—mottled marking of different colors; no one color predominating.

DEAD HEAT—a race in which two or more dogs tie—there is no single winner.

DEBILITATING—weakening.

DEFICIENCY DISEASE—a disease caused by a lack of one or more basic nutrients, such as vitamins, minerals, or amino acids.

DEPRAVED APPETITE (PICA)—a craving for and eating

of unnatural substances (dirt, hair, dung, etc.).

DERBY—field-trial competition for young, novice, sporting dogs, usually more than 18 months of age and under 30 months old.

DERMATITIS—inflammation of the skin, typically evidenced by reddening, swelling, oozing, crusting, or scaling.

DEWCLAW—the useless fifth claw or toe sometimes found on the inside of the hind leg. In most breeds, they are removed when the puppy is a few days old.

DEWLAP—the loose, pendulous skin under the throat.

DIAGNOSTIC AGENTS—biological products used solely for the diagnosis of diseases. Tuberculin, which is used in the diagnosis of tuberculosis, is an example of such an agent.

DIEHARD—the common nickname for the Scotch Terrier.

DISH FACED—when the nasal bone is such that the nose is higher at the tip than at the stop; a slight concaveness from the stop to the nose tip. This is characteristic of Pointers.

DISINFECTANT—an agent that is intended to destroy microorganisms on inanimate surfaces. It should be distinguished from an antiseptic, which is intended for destruction or reduction of microorganism populations on living tissue.

DISQUALIFICATION—a fault so serious that it disqualifies a dog from bench show competition, such as a German Shepherd with hanging hound-type ears.

DISTAFF SIDE—the female side of the pedigree.

DISTEMPER—a widespread contagious disease caused by a virus.

DISTEMPER TEETH—teeth that are marked, pitted, ringed, and often stained; caused by distemper or some other disease accompanied by high fever during the teething period.

DOCK—to shorten the tail by cutting. Cocker Spaniels and Fox Terriers are two of the breeds that are commonly docked.

DOG—1. A male dog. 2. Also, collectively to designate both male and female.

DOME—the rounded portion of the skull.

DOMINANCE—the power of one of a pair of genes to mask the affect of the other member of the pair.

DOUBLE COAT—two coats; an undercoat of soft, thick hair to warm the body, and an outercoat of coarse, strong hair to keep out dampness and cold. Retrievers, and certain other breeds, have double coats.

DOWN FACED—having a face that goes downward from the stop to the nose, as in Bull Terriers.

DOWN TAIL—a tail that is carried downward, like the tail of a Great Dane.

DRAG—a trail laid down by dragging along the ground a bag impregnated with a scent—usually an animal scent.

DRAG HUNT—a hunt staged on horseback with hounds following a laid trail, made by dragging a bag containing anise seed or litter from a fox's den.

DRAWING—the pairing of dogs in a field-trial stake.

DRENCH—a dose of medicine in liquid form that is put down the throat of a dog.

DROP EARS—soft, pendulous ears that hang flat to the head and cheeks.

DROPPERT—a crossbred produced by mating a Pointer and a Setter.

DROPPINGS—the dung or feces.

DRUGS—drugs, or medicinal agents, are substances of mineral, vegetable, or animal origin used in the relief of pain or for the cure of disease.

DRY MATTER—the amount of dry matter in a food is found by determining the percentage of water and subtracting the water content from 100 percent.

DUAL CHAMPION—a dog that has won championships in both a bench show and a field trial.

DUDLEY NOSE—a flesh colored nose.

DUNG—the excrement of an animal. Manure.

DUNG EATING—eating of dung or droppings. This vice can be prevented by the use of a muzzle; also, it can be lessened by increasing the exercise and attention given to the animal.

E

EARTH—the den of a burrowing animal.

EARTH DOG—a hunting dog that likes to go after game burrowed in holes in the ground. Dogs of the Lakeland Terrier breed are used as earth dogs.

ECLAMPSIA—a disease of bitches, occurring during late pregnancy or early lactation.

ELBOWS OUT—elbows that point away from the body, as in Bulldogs.

EMBRYO—the unborn organism, especially in the earlier stages of its development; the fetus.

ENDURANCE—the ability of a dog to withstand hardship and to perform under adverse conditions.

ENEMA—the injection of a liquid into the intestines by way of the anus.

ENTERITIS—inflammation of the intestines.

ENTROPION—a condition in which the eyelids are inturned so that the lashes rub against the eyeball. This occurs in several breeds of dogs and may develop at any age from early puppyhood onward.

ENVIRONMENT—see HEREDITY AND ENVIRONMENT.

ENZOOTIC—a disease confined to a certain locality.

ENZYMES—chemical substances that can produce reactions in other substances without themselves undergoing any change. Also, called *catalysts*.

EPISTASIS—the masking or covering up of the effect of one gene by another to which it is not allelic.

ESOPHAGEAL WORM—worms 1 to 3 inches long, bright red, and generally coiled in a spiral, found in nodules, or tumors, in the walls of the esophagus, stomach, trachea, or aorta.

ESTRUS—the estrus period is commonly called *heat*. During this period, the bitch can be bred.

EWE NECK—a concave curvature of the top neckline, giving a shape like that of a sheep's neck.

EXOPHTHALMOS—abnormal protrusion of the eyeballs.

EXPRESSION—the combination of various features of the head and face, particularly the size, shape, placement, and color of eyes, to produce a certain impression—the outlook.

EXUDATE—a fluid oozing from tissue.

EYE TEETH—same as canine teeth; the fangs; equivalent to the upper canines in people.

F

F_1—the first generation offspring of a given mating.

F_2—the second generation produced by intercrossing the F_1s.

FAKING—changing the dog's appearance by means of surgery, dyeing, chemicals, drugs, or cosmetics, with the object of improving the appearance of the animal.

FALL—long and loose hair hanging over the face; characteristic of the Skye Terrier and the Yorkshire Terrier.

FAMILY—the lineage of an animal as traced through either the males or females.

FANCIER—a person interested in the breeding and showing of dogs, usually of one particular breed.

FANGS—long canine teeth; eye teeth.

FATTY ACIDS—see POLYUNSATURATED FATTY ACIDS.

FEATHER IN EYE—a mark across the eyeball, not touching the pupil; often caused by an injury, it may be a blemish or some other defect.

FEATHERS, FEATHERING (FRINGES)—long fringes of hair on the ears, legs, tail, or body; characteristic of Setters, Spaniels, and Collies.

FEBRILE—of or relating to fever or temperature.

FEED—any product, whether of natural origin or artificially prepared, that is fed to animals.

FELTED COAT—a coat that has formed into dense mats and wads.

FERAL—a dog that has escaped from domestication and become wild, as contrasted to one originating in the wild.

FERTILITY—reproductive ability as indicated by offspring.

FETCH—1. To retrieve game or other objects. 2. Also, the command to do so.

FETUS—the unborn animal as it develops in the uterus.

FIDDLE FACE—an elongated, pinched foreface.

FIDDLE FRONT—crooked or bandy forelegs. The elbows turn out, the pasterns turn in, and the feet turn out in Charlie Chaplin style.

FIELD TRIAL—a competition held under natural conditions for testing the hunting ability of bird dogs or hounds.

FILM PATROL—the recording of a race on film.

FILTERABLE VIRUS—an organism so small that it is capable of passing through filters which will retain the ordinary bacteria.

FIRST AID FOR DOGS—the immediate and temporary care given in the case of accident or sudden illness, before the veterinarian arrives.

FITTING—the conditioning of an animal for show or sale, which usually involves a combination of special feeding plus exercise.

FIXING OF TRAITS—the obtaining of repeatability and uniformity of traits through breeding and selection.

FLAG—a long, bushy tail; characteristic of Setters and some Retrievers.

FLAT SIDES—sides with insufficient spring of ribs.

FLECKED—a coat that is marked with small spots of a darker shade; usually white with brownish orange or gray black flecks.

FLESH NOSE—pink or tan nose.

FLEWS—the pendulous inner corners of the lips of the upper jaw.

FLOP-EARED—having long pendulous ears.

FLUSH—to cause game birds to fly or take wing.

FLY EARS—semierect ears that point in opposite directions and look as if they were about to fly away. This is a fault when it occurs in Fox Terriers and German Shepherds.

FOLLICLE—a bubblelike structure on the ovary that contains an egg.

FOREFACE—the front part of the head—that portion from the eyes to the tip of the nose.

FOSTER MOTHER—a female that nurses young that are not her own.

FOUNDATION STOCK—1. The original bitches and dogs from which a kennel makes its start. 2. The original animals used in forming a new breed.

4-H CLUB DOG PROJECTS—the H's of the four-leaf clover stand for Head, Heart, Hands, and Health. Back in the 1890s and the early 1900s, many forces focused attention on farm boys and girls; among them (1) concern over the needs of adolescents, and (2) concern over the migration of farm youth to the city. The 4-H Club movement grew out of these concerns.

FOWLER'S SOLUTION—a tonic containing arsenic sometimes used by breeders for conditioning show dogs, particularly those breeds that have a very heavy coat. Poisoning can result from its continued use.

FOX HUNT—a hunt with hounds, staged on horseback, after a live fox. The fox may have been released from captivity or tracked and flushed out of hiding by the hounds.

FRATERNAL TWINS—two members of the same litter developed from different ova and spermatozoa but with the same parents, as distinguished from identical twins.

FRILL—long hair under the neck and on the forechest; characteristic of Collies.

FRINGES—see FEATHERS.

FROG FACE—a face with an extended nose, a receding jaw, and undershot teeth; characteristic of such short-faced breeds as the Bulldog, the Boxer, and the Boston Terrier.

FULL BROTHERS (OR SISTERS)—Dogs having the same sire and the same dam.

FULLER'S EARTH—a white or brown naturally occurring

earthy substance resembling potter's clay but lacking in plasticity.

FUNGI—certain vegetable organisms such as molds, mushrooms, and toadstools.

FURROW—an elongated depression or groove in the center of the skull extending from the occiput to the stop, especially marked in Dalmatians and Bulldogs.

FUTURITY STAKE—a dog show or field trial class for young dogs that were nominated at or before birth.

G

GAIT—the manner of walking, trotting, or running.

GAME—wild birds or animals that are hunted.

GAMETE—a mature sex cell (sperm or egg).

GAVAGE—introduction of material (as nutrients) into the stomach by means of a stomach tube.

GAY EARS—ears carried straight up.

GAY TAIL—a tail that is carried high. This is proper in some breeds, whereas in others it constitutes a fault.

GAZEHOUND—a term, now obsolete, for a hound that tracks game with the eyes rather than the nose. Now known as *sight hounds.*

GEE—the musher's term signaling a turn to the right. The musher is the driver of a sled dog team.

GENE—a unit of inheritance.

GENEALOGY—recorded family descent, family tree.

GENETICS—the branch of biology that deals with heredity, variation, sex determination, and related phenomena.

GENOTYPE—the hereditary makeup of an individual, as distinguished from the expression or manifestation of the genes—as how they look.

GENOTYPE SELECTION—selection of breeding stock not necessarily from the best appearing animals but from the best breeding animals, according to genetic makeup.

GERM CELL—a cell with the potential to form a zygote, i.e., a functional spermatozoon or ovum.

GERM PLASM—germ cells and their precursors, bearers of hereditary characters.

GESTATION—period of pregnancy. The normal period for the bitch is 63 days.

GET—progeny or offspring.

GID—a disease of sheep caused by the cystic form of the tapeworm, *Coenurus cerebralis,* the eggs of which are voided by dogs. "Giddy" sheep show defects in vision and disturbances in movements.

GIVING TONGUE—baying when on the trail of game.

GLASS EYED—term applied to an eye, the iris of which is devoid of pigment.

GOITER—an enlargement of the thyroid gland, due to a failure of the body to obtain sufficient iodine from which the thyroid gland can form thyroxine, an iodine-containing compound.

GONAD—an organ in either male or female in which reproductive cells are formed and developed; a testicle or ovary.

GOOSE RUMP—a sharply sloping rump.

GRADING UP—that system of breeding in which a purebred male of a given breed is mated to mongrel or grade females.

GRIZZLE—a bluish gray color.

GROOM—to brush, comb, trim, or otherwise make the coat neat. Grooming cleans the hair, helps keep the skin functioning naturally, lessens skin diseases and parasites, and improves the condition and fitness of the muscles.

GROUND COLOR—the base color. For example, the ground color of hounds is usually white, then it is marked with tan and/or black.

GROUPS—the six divisions into which the American Kennel Club has, for purposes of dog show competition, classified all recognized breeds.

GUARD COAT (GUARD HAIR)—the long coarse hairs that form a protective coating over the underhair of some breeds of dogs.

GUNDOG—a dog trained to work with its master in finding live game and in retrieving game that has been shot.

GUN SHY—a dog that is frightened by the sound of the gun being fired.

H

HACKNEY GAIT—a high-stepping gait like that of a Hackney horse; in excess it results in wasted effort and is undesirable.

HAIR BLINDEDNESS—complete, or partial, loss of vision due to hair protruding over the eyes.

HALF-BROTHERS—dogs out of the same dam but by a different sire.

HANDLER—a person who handles a dog at a dog show, field trial, or obedience test.

HAPLOID—one-half of the diploid number; the number of chromosomes and spermatozoa and ova after meiosis.

HARD MOUTHED—descriptive of retrievers that bite down on retrieved game; a serious fault.

HARE FOOT—a long, narrow, and close-toed foot, like that of the hare or rabbit.

HARELIP—an upper lip that is divided by a slit running from its front edge up to the nose. It is almost impossible to raise puppies that are born with this deformity, because they are unable to nurse.

HARLEQUIN—a combination of colors in patches on a solid ground, as in the coat of a Great Dane. Usually black on white.

HARNESS—a leather strap fitted around the shoulders and chest, with a ring at its top over the withers, or top of the shoulders.

HAUNCHES—the back portion of the thighs. The dog's "sitting surface."

HAW—1. The red membrane inside the lower eyelid that is often prominent in breeds having heavy-wrinkled faces which pull the eyelids down; characteristic of Bloodhounds and St. Bernards. 2. Mushers (drivers of sled dog teams) use the command "haw" to signal sled dogs to turn to the left.

HAZEL EYE—A light brown eye.

HEARTWORM—infection of dogs with the parasites, *Dirofilaria immitis* or *Dipetalonema reconditum*.

HEAT—1. A common term for the estrus period. 2. The length of the period in which the dog is hunted in training or field trials.

HEAT PERIODS—the estrus period; the period of ovulation.

HEELER—1. A dog that heels. 2. A dog that heels animals.

HEIGHT—the measurement from the highest point of the shoulders (the withers) to the ground.

HELMINTHS (OR WORM PARASITES)—helminths (or worm parasites) are many-celled parasites varying greatly in size, shape, structure, and physiology.

HEPATITIS—a contagious disease of dogs with signs varying from slight fever and congestion of the mucus membranes to severe depression, marked leukopenia and prolonged bleeding time.

HEREDITY—heredity refers to characteristics that are transmitted to offspring from parents and other ancestors.

HEREDITY AND ENVIRONMENT—a dog is the result of two forces—heredity and environment. Heredity may be thought of as the foundation, and environment as the structure. Heredity has already made its contribution at the time of fertilization, but environment works ceaselessly away until death.

HERMAPHRODITE—an organism that has the reproductive organs of both sexes.

HERNIA (RUPTURE)—refers to the protrusion of any internal organ through the wall of its containing cavity; usually it means the passage of a portion of the intestine through an opening in the abdominal muscle. Depending on location, hernias are designated as umbilical, scrotal, or inguinal.

HETEROSIS—the superiority over either or both parents of the progeny resulting of crossing strains, varieties, breeds or species, which is known as *hybrid vigor*.

HETEROZYGOUS—having unlike genes that can be present for any of the characteristics such as coat color, size, etc.

HIDEBOUND—having the hide tight over the body.

HIE ON—a command to urge the dog on; used in hunting or in field trials.

HIGH CONDITION—an animal that is fleshy or fat.

HOCK—the joint in a hind limb that corresponds to the ankle of man.

HOMOZYGOUS—having like genes in a dog, which can be present for any of the characteristics of the animal such as coat color, size, etc.

HOMOZYGOUS DOMINANT—a dominant character that produces only one kind of gamete.

HOMOZYGOUS RECESSIVE—a recessive character that produces two kinds of gametes; one carries the dominant gene, while the other carries the recessive gene.

HONORABLE SCARS—scars suffered in the line of duty—as a result of work.

HONORING—a hunting dog that recognizes and backs up the first dog to detect game.

HOOKWORM—the parasite that causes canine hookworm disease. Dogs may be infected with *Ancylostoma caninum, A. braziliense,* or *Uncinaria stenocephala*.

HORMONE—a secretion from any one of the ductless or endocrine glands.

HOUND—a dog commonly used for hunting by scent or sight.

HOUND COLORS (HOUND MARKED)—Black, tan, and white. The ground color is usually white, which means that it is marked with tan and/or black patches.

HOUND EARS—long low-set ears, like a hound.

HOUND JOG—the usual pace of the hound.

HUCKLEBONES—the top of the hip joint.

HUNT—pursuit of game. As used by horsemen, the term usually implies a hunt on horseback with hounds.

HYBRID—the offspring of two parents of unlike genetic makeup.

HYPERESTHESIA—1. Excessive or pathological sensitivity of the skin or of a particular sense. 2. Heightened perceptiveness of or response to the environment.

HYPERTROPHY—excessive growth of an organ or part.

HYPERVENTILATION—excessive ventilation; excessive rate and depth of respiration leading to abnormal loss of carbon dioxide from the blood.

HYPOSTASIS—converse of epistasis. A hypostatic gene is one masked by the action of another that is not its allele, a kind of nonallelic recessive.

I

IDENTICAL TWINS—litter brothers or sisters (always of the same sex) that developed from the same ovum and spermatozoon, as distinguished from fraternal twins.

IMMUNITY—when an animal is said to be immune to a certain disease, it means that it is not susceptible to that disease.

IMMUNITY, ACQUIRED—acquired immunity may be either active or passive. When an animal is stimulated in such manner as to cause it to produce antibodies, it is said to have acquired active immunity. If an animal is injected with the antibodies (immune bodies) produced by an actively immunized animal, it is referred to as an *acquired passive immunity*.

IMMUNITY, NATURAL—when immunity to a disease is inherited.

IMPORT—a dog brought from another country.

INBREEDING—the mating of closely related animals; for example, brother to sister, or sire to daughter.

INCISORS—the six small front teeth in each jaw between the canines or fangs, which are adapted for cutting.

INDEPENDENT ASSORTMENT (MENDELIAN)—segregation and independent assortment are two of the general laws of inheritance. Independent assortment refers to the fact that the chromosomes of the hybrid assort themselves at reduction into all possible combinations, with each germ cell necessarily having one member of each pair of chromosomes.

INGESTION—the taking in of food and drink.

INGUINAL CANAL—1. A passage in the male through which the testis descends into the scrotum and in which lies the spermatic cord. 2. A passage in the female accommodating the round ligament.

IN HEAT—a bitch's period of estrum. Same as IN SEASON.

INHERITANCE—see HEREDITY IN DOGS.

IN-SEASON—a female in heat, during which time she will accept a male.

INTESTINAL THREADWORM, OR STRONGYLOIDES—this worm, *Strongyloides stercoralis,* which is small, slender, and about one-tenth inch long, is buried in the mucosa of the front half of the small intestine.

IN THE MONEY—a race dog, show dog, or field trial dog that receives prize money is said to have been "in the money."

INTRADERMAL—into, or between, the layers of the skin.

INTRAMUSCULAR—within the substance of a muscle.

INTRAPERITONEAL—within the peritoneal cavity.

INTRAUTERINE—within the uterus.

INTRAVENOUS—within the vein or veins.

IN VITRO—occurring in a test tube.

IN VIVO—occurring in the living body.

IN WHELP—pregnant; as said of the bitch that has conceived.

IODINE DEFICIENCY (GOITER)—a failure of the body to obtain sufficient iodine from which the thyroid gland can form thyroxine, an iodine-containing compound.

IRIS—the colored portion of the eye.

ISABELLA—a fawn or light bay color.

J

JUDGE—the person officiating at dog shows, field trials, or obedience tests; the one making the decisions and awards.

K

KEEPING QUALITIES—the ease with which an animal is kept in condition by food.

KELPIE—a breed of Australian dogs, used for sheep herding. It is considered one of the best breeds for handling sheep.

KENNEL—1. The building, or house, in which a dog or dogs are kept. 2. All the dogs belonging to one kennel owner.

KINK TAIL—a short, bent tail; characteristic of Bulldogs and Boston Terriers.

KISSING SPOTS—contrasting marking on the cheeks; typical of several of the toy breeds.

KITCHEN MIDDENS—refuse heap, or mound, marking the site of a primitive human habitation.

KNUCKLING OVER—faulty structure of the carpus (wrist) joint, which causes it to double forward under the weight of the standing dog.

L

LAMENESS—a defect detected when the animal favors the affected foot when standing. The load on the ailing foot in action is eased and a characteristic bobbing of the head occurs as the affected foot strikes the ground.

LANDSEER—a Newfoundland that is not all black. Landseers are usually white with black or bronze.

LAXATIVE—a feed or drug that will induce bowel movements and relieve constipation.

LAYBACK—a receding nose with an undershot jaw; characteristic of many short breeds, especially the Bulldog.

LEADER—the head dog in a dog sled hitch.

LEATHER—the skin or flaps of the long pendulous ears of certain breeds; characteristic of Spaniels, Poodles, and some Hounds.

LEGGINESS—the quality or state of being leggy; long-legged.

LEGGY—long-legged.

LEPTOSPIROSIS—a disease affecting several species of animals, with transfer between species. It is caused by several species of corkscrew-shaped organisms of the spirochete group.

LETHALS—traits that cause death of the animal—either embryonically, at birth, or shortly after birth—are known as *lethals*. Those that cause death later in life are called *sublethals*. Many of these conditions are caused by undesirable genes. Any dog or bitch that possesses and transmits a lethal is a detriment to the species.

LETTING—same as leasing.

LEVEL BITE (LEVEL MOUTH)—the condition when the front teeth (incisors) of the upper and lower jaws meet exactly edge to edge.

LICE—these are small, flattened, wingless insect parasites.

LICENSE—1. The recording or registration of the ownership of a dog in a municipality. 2. the formal permission granted by the AKC to a nonmember club to hold a dog show, obedience trial, or field trial; or to a person to handle dogs in the show-ring for pay.

LINE BREEDING—the mating together of animals somewhat related, but less closely so than in the inbreeding, as, for example, a dog to his granddam or a bitch to her grandsire.

LINKAGE—the tendency for two or more characters to be transmitted together, because the genes are located in the same chromosome.

LINTY—like lint.

LIP POCKET METHOD—a method of giving liquid medicine to a dog. It consists in making the dog sit, pulling out his cheek to make a pouch, putting the vial or spoon containing the medicine into the cheek pouch, and letting the medicine drain into the throat.

LIPPY—the upper lip being more pendulous than is desired.

LITTER—all puppies brought forth by a bitch at one whelping.

LIVER COLOR—a dark, reddish brown color.

LOADED SHOULDERS—shoulders that are much too thick and heavy.

LOBULAR—of, relating to, or resembling a small lobe.

LOCI (LOCUS)—the place of a particular gene on its chromosome.

LOIN—that part of the topline between the last rib and the hips.

LOP EARS—ears that tend to flop forward and downward, or toward each side.

LUMBERING—an awkward gait.

M

MAD DOG—a rabid dog.

MAINTENANCE REQUIREMENT—is a ration that is adequate to prevent any loss or gain of tissue in the body when there is no growth, work, reproduction, or lactation.

MAMMALS—warm-blooded animals that produce their young alive and suckle them for a variable period on a secretion from the mammary glands.

MANAGEMENT—the act, art, or manner of managing, or handling, controlling, directing, etc.

MANE—long and profuse hair on the neck and throat.

MANTLE—the dark portion of the coat covering the shoulders, back and sides of the body of the animals of the St. Bernard breed.

MARCEL—a deep soft wave or series of waves made in the hair.

MASK—the dark part of the foreface and muzzle; characteristic of Mastiffs, Boxers, and Pekingese.

MASSAGE—the manipulation of tissues by rubbing or stroking with the hand.

MASTER OF FOXHOUNDS (MFH)—the "master" is the ruler. Where his pack is concerned, his word is law.

MATCH SHOW—an informal dog show where no points toward championships are awarded.

MATE—the copulation, or sexual union, of a dog and bitch.

MATS—thick wads of felty hair that occur in the coats of long-hair dogs due to lack of combing.

MEAT DOG—a hunting dog that can always be depended upon to find game, but whose work does not approach brilliancy.

MELANIN—the dark brown or black pigments of skin or hair.

MENDELISM—the theory embodied in the first and second laws of Mendel, which establishes that characters are inherited as entities and independently one of another due to segregation and the independent assortment of the genes.

MERLE—a blue gray color flecked with black.

MERRY—quick, snappy, lively, and attractive.

METABOLISM—refers to all the changes that take place in the nutrients after they are absorbed from the digestive tract, including (1) the building-up processes in which the absorbed nutrients are used in the formation or repair of body tissues, and (2) the breaking-down processes in which nutrients are oxidized for the production of heat and work.

MICROORGANISM—any organism of microscopic size; applied especially to bacteria and protozoa.

MILK—the natural, whitish, or cream colored secretion from the mammary glands of all mammals (warm-blooded, hairy animals that produce their young alive and suckle them for a variable period).

MILK TEETH—a puppy's first set of teeth.

MITES—these are very small parasites that cause mange (scabies, scab, and itch).

MOLERA—incomplete, imperfect, or abnormal ossification of the skull.

MONGREL—a dog of mixed ancestry.

MONOHYBRID—a hybrid that is heterozygous for one pair of allelic genes.

MONORCHIDISM OR MONOCHISM—the condition in which one of the testes has failed to descend into the scrotum.

MORBIDITY—sick rate.

MORTALITY—death rate.

MULE-EARED—having long, upright ears, like a mule.

MULTIPLE GENE INHERITANCE (QUANTITATIVE TRAITS)—relatively few characters are inherited in a simple manner like coat color. Rather, such characters as speed are due to many genes; hence, they are called multiple factor characters or multiple gene characters.

MUSIC—the baying of the hounds.

MUTATION (OR SPORT)—heritable germinal variation of an abrupt origin that is passed on to the progeny; it may be only a minor variation, or it may result in a trait much dissimilar from that of any ancestor.

MUTE—to run silent on the trail; i.e., to trail without baying or barking.

MUZZLE BANK (MUZZLE HEAD)—the white marking around the muzzle; characteristic of the Boston Terrier.

N

NATURAL INSTINCTS—the inborn qualities characteristic of certain breeds of dogs, such as the desire of hounds to hunt and the instinct of Pointers to point.

NAVEL INFECTION—an infectious disease of newborn puppies caused by several kinds of bacteria.

NECROSIS—death or dying of local tissue.

NICKING—successful nicking is due to the fact that the

right combination of genes for good characters are contributed by each parent, although each of the parents within itself may be lacking in certain genes necessary for excellence.

NITROGEN-FREE EXTRACT—consists principally of sugars, starches, pentoses, and nonnitrogenous organic acids. The percentage is determined by subtracting the sum of the percentages of moisture, crude protein, crude fat, crude fiber, and ash from 100.

NONSLIP RETRIEVER—the dog that walks at heel, marks the fall, and retrieves game on command; he's not expected to find or flush.

NOSE—1. Organ of smell. 2. The ability to detect by means of scent.

NOVICE CLASS—a dog show class for animals that have never won a first prize except in the puppy class.

NUCLEUS—the central body within the cell that contains the chromosomes.

NUTRITIVE NEEDS—to supply all the needs—maintenance, growth, fitting, reproduction, lactation, and work—the different classes of dogs must receive sufficient food to furnish the necessary quantity of energy (carbohydrates and fats), protein, minerals, and vitamins. These are the nutritive needs.

NUTRITIVE REQUIREMENTS VS ALLOWANCES—in ration formulation, two words are commonly used—"requirements" and "allowances." Requirements do not provide for margins of safety. Thus, to feed a dog on the basis of meeting the bare requirements would not be unlike building a bridge without providing margins of safety for heavier than average loads or for floods. No competent engineer would be so foolish as to design such a bridge. Likewise, knowledgeable dog nutritionists provide for margins of safety—they provide for the necessary nutritive allowances. They allow for variations in feed composition; possible losses during storage and processing; day to day, and period to period, differences in needs of animals; age and size of animal; stage of gestation and lactation; the kind and degree of activity; the amount of stress; the system of management; the health, condition, and temperament of the animal; and the kind, quality, and amount of feed—all of which exert a powerful influence in determining nutritive needs.

O

OBEDIENCE—response to the trainer's commands.

OCCIPUT—a bony projection at the top of the skull between the ears. It is particularly prominent in the Bloodhound.

OLFACTORY—of or pertaining to the sense of smell.

OPEN BITCH—a bitch that is not pregnant; a bitch that can be bred.

OPEN CLASS—a class at a dog show in which all dogs of a breed, both champions and imported, may compete.

OSTEOMALACIA—a bone disease of adult dogs caused by lack of vitamin D, inadequate intake of calcium or phosphorus, or an incorrect ration of calcium and phosphorus.

OTTER TAIL—a tail that is thick at the root and tapers gradually to the end.

OUT AT ELBOWS—having elbows that stand out from the body.

OUT AT SHOULDERS—with shoulder blades loosely attached to the body, leaving the shoulders jutting out in relief and increasing the breadth of the front.

OUTCROSSING—the mating of two dogs of the same breed but of different families.

OVARY—the female sex organ that produces eggs. There are two ovaries.

OVERHANG—a heavy or pronounced brow; characteristic of Pekingese.

OVERSHOT—Descriptive of a dog's mouth wherein the upper jaw protrudes beyond the lower jaw with the result that the front teeth do not meet properly.

OVULATION—the time when the follicle bursts and the egg is released.

OVUM—the female reproductive cell produced by the bitch; an egg.

P

PACE—1. A gait in which the legs on the same side move in unison; hence, the animal is supported alternately by the right and left sides and there is a rolling motion of the body. 2. The rate of speed at which a dog travels.

PACK—a group of dogs, usually hounds, that hunt together.

PAD—the cushionlike, tough sole of the foot.

PADDLING—walking or trotting with a swinging out motion of the front feet.

PALATABILITY—well liked; eaten with relish.

PALPATION—1. An act of touching or feeling. 2 Physical examination in veterinary diagnosis by pressure of the hand or fingers to the surface of the body.

PAPER FOOT—a foot that is thin, and that has a flattened pad.

PARASITES—broadly speaking, parasites are organisms living in, on, or at the expense of another living organism. They include fungi, protozoa (or unicellular animals), arthropods (or insects, ticks, and related forms), and helminths (or worms).

PARASITES, EXTERNAL—several kinds of external parasites attack dogs. These pests lower the vitality of dogs, damage the hair and skin, and produce a generally unthrifty condition. External parasites also are responsible for the spread of several diseases of dogs. Among the external parasites of dogs are fleas, lice, mites, and ticks.

PARASITES, INTERNAL—many different kinds of internal parasites attack dogs throughout the world and probably no animal is ever entirely free of them. Parasites may be located in practically every tissue and cavity of the body. However, most of them are in the alimentary tract, lungs, body cavity, or bloodstream. Those in the digestive system usually become localized there, but others travel throughout different parts of the body.

PARI-MUTUELS—This refers to machine-controlled pool betting. It was invented in France in 1865, by a perfume shop proprietor named Pierre Oller, who, embittered by a losing streak with the bookies, worked out the idea of the betting pool and began selling tickets over his store counter. His take was five percent; the rest was divided equally among the winners.

PARROT MOUTH (OVERSHOT JAW)—an hereditary imperfection in the way in which the teeth come together. In parrot mouth or overshot jaw, the lower jaw is shorter than the upper jaw.

PARTI-COLOR—a coat of two colors in equal proportions, generally red and white or black and white.

PARTURITION—the act of whelping or giving birth to young.

PASTERN—that part of the foot between the fetlock and the coffin joint.

PATHOGENIC—disease producing.

PATHOLOGICAL—diseased, or due to disease.

PEAK—an unusually prominent occiput.

PEDIGREE—a written record of the ancestry of a dog going back at least three generations.

PEDEGREE BREEDING—selection on the combined bases of the merits of the individual and the average merits of its ancestry.

PENCILING—markings consisting of thin black lines against a tan background, with these pencil marks running up each toe; characteristic of Manchester Terriers.

PENDENT (PENDANT) EAR—a hanging ear, as in Pointers.

PEPPER AND SALT—a coat color consisting of an even mixture of gray and black hair.

PHENOTYPE—the appearance or how an animal looks.

PHOSPHORUS—a major mineral required by dogs.

PICA—depraved appetite characterized by eating dirt, sand, hair, feces, etc.

PIED—having two colors in approximately equal proportions, usually in irregular patches.

PIG JAWED—an overshot jaw.

PIGEON-TOED—front feet that point inward toward each other.

PIG EYED—a small squinty eye that generally imparts an unattractive expression and often indicates a bad temperament.

PIGMENTATION—coloration, usually referring to the darkness of nose, eyerims, and toenails.

PILE—the thick undercoat of breeds having a double coat.

PINCER BITE—front teeth of the upper and lower jaws that meet at the edges rather than overlapping when the mouth is closed.

PLACE—finishing second in a race.

PLACENTA—the membrane by which the fetus is attached to the uterus. Nutrients from the mother pass into the placenta and then through the navel cord to the fetus. When the animal is born, the placenta is expelled. It is commonly called the *afterbirth*.

PLUCKING—removal of dead or superfluous hair of the coat with a trimming instrument. Terriers are usually plucked.

PLUME—a tail with long, soft hair; characteristic of Pomeranians, Pekingese, and Setters.

POACH—to trespass on private property when hunting.

POINT—the rigid stance that a hunting dog takes when he is showing the hunter the position of the game.

POINTS—1. Units of credit toward championship. 2. Color on face, ears, legs, and tail when correlated—they are usually white, black, or tan.

POLAR BODY—a small, nonfunctional cell cast off by the ovum after reduction division.

POLICE DOG—any dog that has been trained to do police work. Also, a common, but incorrect, name for a German Shepherd Dog.

POLYUNSATURATED FATTY ACIDS—the term *polyunsaturated fatty acid* is applied to fatty acids having more than one double bond. There is no experimental evidence that polyunsaturated fatty acids are either (1) required by dogs, or (2) superior to saturated fatty acids.

POMPON—the tufted hair left on the end of a Poodle's tail.

POOR DOER—a dog that is almost impossible to get into good condition; a poor keeper.

POP EYED—1. Refers to a dog whose eyes are generally more prominent or bulge out a little more than normal. 2. A dog that is "spooky" or attempts to see everything that goes on.

POSING—placing the dog in a standing position that will display him to the best advantage.

POST ENTRY—a last minute entry in a dog show or race. The term stems from racing, where, at one time, the entries were not named until going to the post.

POSTMORTEM—examination after death.

POST POSITION—refers to race starting position. Beginning with position No. One nearest the rail, dogs line up at the starting gate according to number.

POULTICE—a soft mass (such as bread, bran, flaxseed, or medicated clay), usually heated and spread on a cloth, for application to sores, inflamed areas, or other lesions. A poultice may be used for the purpose of supplying moist warmth, relieving pain, or acting as a counterirritant or antiseptic.

PREMIUM LIST—a printed brochure listing the prizes offered at a dog show, obedience test, or field trial, along with the classes, and naming the judges who will officiate.

PREPOTENT—said of an animal with an unusually strong tendency to pass its characteristics on to its offspring; probably due to the presence of many dominant alleles in the prepotent parent.

PRICK EARS—sharp, pointed ears that are normally directed to the front, and that give an alert and expectant appearance, as in the Scottish Terrier.

PROFESSIONAL HANDLER—a person licensed by the American Kennel Club to show dogs owned by others and to accept payment for these services.

PROGENITOR—an ancestor in the direct line.

PROGENY—offspring.

PROLAPSE OF VAGINA—turning outward of the vagina through the vulva.

PROPHYLAXIS—preventive treatment against disease.

PROTEIN—complex organic compounds made up chiefly of amino acids present in characteristic proportions for each specific protein. This nutrient always contains carbon, hydrogen, oxygen, and nitrogen; and, in addition, it usually contains sulphur and frequently phosphorus. Proteins are essential in all plant and animal life as components of the active protoplasm of each living cell.

PROTOPLASM—the vital substance of all plants or animal life.

PROTOZOA—the simplest form of animal life; they consist of only a single cell.

PROUD FLESH—the unhealthy tissue that sometimes forms around a wound. If allowed to remain, a large scar will result. For this reason, the veterinarian may prescribe something to burn off proud flesh so that the wound will heal more quickly.

PULSE RATE—indicates the rapidity of the heart action. Normal for the dog is 100 to 130 per minute.

PUMPKIN SEED—a tan (red yellow) coloration, like a pumpkin seed. Small pumpkin seeds appear over the eyes of American Black-and-Tan Coonhounds.

PUNISHMENT—the act of punishing; the infliction of a penalty, as with a whip.

PUPPY—a dog under 12 months of age.

PUREBRED—a dog whose parents are of the same breed, and who is either registered or eligible for registry.

PURGATIVE—a laxative.

PURSE—race prize money to which the owners of dogs in the race do not contribute.

PUT DOWN—generally used to denote a dog that did not place in competition.

Q

QUALIFYING SCORE—an obedience test score of 170 points or better.

QUALITATIVE TRAITS—traits that are governed by a small number of genes, like coat color.

QUALITY—refinement and fineness, particularly as denoted by the hair and bone.

QUANTITATIVE TRAITS—traits that are governed by many genes, such as the speed of a dog.

QUARANTINE—the segregation and confinement of one or more animals in the smallest possible area to prevent any direct or indirect contact with animals not so restrained.

QUARTERS—the two hind legs taken together.

R

RABIES—an acute infectious (virus) disease affecting all warm-blooded animals and man. The disease manifests itself in two forms: (1) paralytic form, and (2) furious form. Furious rabies represent the classical "mad dog syndrome" in which the animal becomes irrational and viciously aggressive.

RACINESS—the quality of being racy.

RACY—lean, long legs, and speedy looking in structure; characteristic of Greyhounds and Whippets.

RANGE—the distance a dog hunts from his handler.

RANGY—elongated and generally loosely put together.

RATION (s)—the amount of food supplied to a dog for a definite period, usually for a day. However, to most people the word *ration* implies the food fed to a dog or dogs without limitation to the time in which it is consumed.

RAT TAIL—a tail in which the root is thick and covered with soft curls and the tip is devoid of hair; characteristic of Irish Water Spaniels.

RECESSIVE—opposite of dominant; a gene that is masked by the dominant member of the pair.

RECESSIVE CHARACTER—a characteristic that appears only when both members of a pair of genes are alike.

REGISTRATION—the record of a dog's ancestry in a recognized *Stud Book*.

REPRODUCTION—puppies spring from preexisting forms of life through the process of reproduction. Females must mate with males, or be artificially inseminated, before they can produce young.

Reproduction in dogs, or the development of a new puppy, results from the union of an egg, or ovum, produced by the bitch and a spermatozoon produced by the dog.

REPRODUCTIVE CELLS—cells set aside in the development of the organism, the function of which is to reproduce it; the cells of the germ plasm as distinct from the somatoplasm.

REQUIREMENTS, NUTRITIVE — see NUTRITIVE REQUIREMENTS VS ALLOWANCES

RETRACTILE—capable of or exhibiting retraction; capable of being drawn back in the claws.

RETRIEVER—when a dog brings an object back to the handler, he is said to have retrieved. However, the term *retriever* is generally applied to the finding and fetching of dead or wounded game birds.

REWARDS—the training of a dog is based on a system of rewards and punishment. Rewards differ according to the circumstances. They may include a pat on the shoulder, or a word of praise. Sometimes it is well to give a tidbit of food as a reward or treat. It should be recognized, however, that feeding treats from the hand is apt to become a nuisance, and a disappointment to the dog if it is not available and forthcoming.

RICKETS—a bone disease characterized by enlargement of the knee and hock joints, and the animal may exhibit great pain when moving about. Irregular bulges (beaded ribs) at juncture of ribs with breastbone, and bowed legs. Rickets is a disease of young animals. The condition is caused by a lack of calcium, phosphorus, or vitamin D; or an incorrect ratio of the two minerals.

RIGOR MORTIS—stiffening of the body after death.

RINGER—a dog substituted for another dog that it closely resembles.

RING TAIL—a tail that curls into a circle.

RINGWORM—a contagious infection of the outer layers of skin caused by an infestation of microscopic fungi.

ROACH BACK—a back that arches over the spine from behind the withers to over the loins; characteristic of the Dandy Dinmont and the Whippet.

ROAN—a mixture of white with another color, usually blue or red, in equal proportions; hence, blue roans, orange roans, lemon roans, etc.

ROMAN NOSE—a foreface showing a convex line from the stop to the nose tip when seen in profile.

ROSE EAR—an ear that folds backward, exposing the inner ear; characteristic of the Bulldog.

ROUNDED—ears that have been shortened and trimmed to a round edge by cutting. Usually practiced only on Foxhounds for the purpose of preventing the ears from being cut and torn in briars and underbrush.

ROUNDWORM, OR ASCARIDS—the dog is parasitized by two species of roundworms, (1) *Toxocara canis* and (2) *Toxascaris leonina*. Adult roundworms are round and whitish or yellowish in color, two to eight inches long.

RUDDER—the tail.

RUFF—Thick, long hair on the neck and shoulders; characteristic of the Chow Chow and the Collie.

RUNT—an undersized specimen.

RUSSIAN WOLFHOUND—the Borzoi breed.

S

SABLE—a lacing of black hairs over a lighter ground color, as in the Collie.

SADDLE—a black marking over the back, resembling a saddle; frequently seen in Beagles.

SCENT—the odor (1) left by man or animal on the trail (ground scent) or (2) wafted through the air (airborne scent).

SCISSORS BITE—a bite in which the upper front teeth slightly overlap the lower front teeth.

SCRATCH—to withdraw a dog from a race.

SCREW TAIL—a short, kinky tail; characteristic of the Bulldog.

SCROTUM—the saclike pouch that suspends the testicles outside the male animal.

SCRUB—a low-grade animal.

SEASON—a bitch's period of heat or estrum.

SEED STOCK—superior animals for breeding purposes.

SEEING EYE DOG—the registered trademark of the Seeing Eye, Inc., which trains guide dogs for the blind.

SEGREGATION (MENDELIAN)—segregation and independent assortment are two of the general laws of inheritance. Segregation refers to the separation of the chromosomes and genes at the time the sex cells divide.

SELECTIVE BREEDING—planned mating in the hope that some, if not all, of the progeny will possess the traits of the parents.

SELF COLOR—of a single color, or of one color with lighter shadings of the same color.

SELF-FEEDING—self-feeding refers to the practice of keeping feed before animals at all times, as opposed to feeding given quantities at certain times of the day.

SEMEN—fluid containing innumerable spermatozoa that is produced by the generative organs of the male and by which impregnation is effected.

SEMIPRICK EARS—ears that are carried erect with the tips pointing down and forward; characteristic of the Collie.

SEPTICEMIA—invasion of the bloodstream by virulent microorganisms from a focus of infection marked by chills, fever, and prostration.

SEPTUM—the bone between the nostrils.

SERUM, BLOOD—the clear portion of blood separated from its more solid elements.

SERUMS—serums, also known as *immune blood serums* or *immune serums,* are obtained from the blood of animals that have developed a solid immunity from having received one or more doses of infectious organisms. They do not contain any organisms, either dead or alive. Serums are used for the protective nature of the antibodies that they contain, which stop the action of an infectious agent or neutralize a product of that agent. They give a passive immunity.

SET ON—the juncture of the tail and the body.

SEX CELLS—the egg and the sperm, which unite to create life. They transmit genetic characteristics from the parents to the offsyring.

SEX CHROMOSOMES—the X and Y chromosomes that carry the determiners for sex.

SHORT COUPLED—short from the last rib to the hips.

SHOULDER HEIGHT—height of the dog's body as measured from the withers to the ground.

SHOW—finishing third in a race.

SHOW CONDITIONING—fitting for the show, usually obtained through a combination of food and exercise.

SIBLINGS—progeny of the same parents, but not necessarily of the same litter.

SICKLE TAIL—a fairly long tail that is carried out and up in a semicircle.

SIGHT HOUND—a hound that tracks game with the eyes rather than with the nose.

SIRE—the father of a litter of puppies.

SLAB SIDES—flat sides with insufficient spring of ribs.

SLED DOGS—dogs that are usually worked in teams to draw sleds.

SLOPING SHOULDERS—a shoulder that is obliquely angulated and laid back.

SMOOTH COAT—a coat that is short, sleek, and close lying.

SNIPY—a pointed, narrow, weak muzzle.

SOFT MOUTHED—said of a dog that is able to carry retrieved game in the mouth without damaging it.

SOLID COLOR—having no white markings.

SOUNDNESS—the state of mental and physical health when all organs and faculties are complete and functioning normally.

SPAY—to render a bitch sterile by the surgical removal of her ovaries; to castrate a bitch.

SPEAK—to bark.

SPECIALTY CLUB—same as breed club; an organization to sponsor and forward the interest of a single breed.

SPECIALTY SHOW—a dog show confined to a single breed.

SPECIES—a group of animals (or plants) usually making up a subdivision next smaller than the genus, having certain characteristics that distinguish it from any other group, and that are usually inherited. The common criterion for a species is that its members are interfertile.

SPECTACLES—dark markings around the eyes, as in the Keeshond.

SPERM, SPERM CELL—male sex cell produced in the testicles.

SPERMATOGENESIS—the development of spermatozoa from the primary sex cells.

SPERMATOZOON—a male gamete; a single sperm.

SPIKE COLLAR—a nooselike training collar with small spikes next to the dog's flesh.

SPLASHED—having a colored coat with irregular patches of white, or a white coat with irregular patches of any color.

SPLAY FEET—feet with toes spread wide apart.

SPRING—to flush.

SPRING OF RIBS—the curvature or roundness of the ribs, indicative of heart and lung capacity.

SQUIRREL TAIL—a tail curving forward and over the back.

STAKE—designation of a class, used in field trial competition.

STANCE—the manner of standing.

STANDARD—the ideal as set forth for each breed.

STAND-OFF COAT—a rough, coarse hair that stands away from the body, as in the Chow Chow and Samoyed.

STERILE—a term used to designate a male or a female that is infertile.

STERILITY—the inability or failure to produce live gametes; barrenness; not to be confused with impotence.

STERN—the tail, but the use of the term should properly be limited to hounds or sporting dogs.

STEWARD—a person assigned as an assistant to a judge at a dog show or obedience trials.

STIFLE—the thigh joint in the hind legs, which is comparable to a man's knee.

STILTED—having a stiff, awkward way of moving.

STOP—a depression in front of the eyes between the skull and the muzzle. It may be deep as in Pugs or nonexistent as in Borzois.

STRAIGHT HOCKED—hocks that show no bend when viewed from the side.

STRAIGHT SHOULDERS—shoulder blades running almost straight up and down, without angulation.

STRAY—an animal that has wandered into a kennel, or that has wandered away; commonly referred to as a *stray dog*.

STRESS—refers to any physical or emotional factor to which the dog fails to make a satisfactory adaptation. Stress may be caused by excitement, temperament, fatigue, shipping, disease, heat or cold, nervous strain, number of dogs together, previous nutrition, breed, age, or management. Show, field trial, and race dogs are always under stress. Also, the greater the stress, the more exacting the nutritive requirements.

STRIDE—the leap of a dog while running.

STUD—male used for breeding purposes.

STUD BOOK—the registry in which each breed of dogs is recorded is known as the *Stud Book*.

STUD FEE—a fee paid to the owner of the male dog for the privilege of breeding a female to the dog.

STYLE—a term referring to the dog's general attractiveness.

SUBSTANCE—a combination of good bone, and width and depth of body.

SULFA DRUG (SULFONAMIDE)—a synthetic organic drug that has the ability to inhibit the growth of, or to destroy, microorganisms.

SWAY BACK—a sagging back.

SWEEPSTAKES—a race in which the winner takes all.

SYMMETRY—see BALANCE.

T

TALLYHO—a hunting term meaning the "game is in sight."

TDN—the accepted abbreviation of Total Digestible Nutrients. The TDN is the sum of all the digestible organic nutrients—protein, fiber, nitrogen-free extract, and fat (the latter multiplied by 2.25).

TESTICLE—a male gland that produces sperm. There are two testicles.

TETANUS (LOCKJAW)—chiefly a wound-infection disease caused by a powerful toxin, more than 100 times as toxic as strychnine, that is liberated by the bacterium *Clostridium tetani*.

THERAPY—treating disease.

THRIFTY—healthy and vigorous in appearance.

THROATY—having too much skin around the throat.

THROWBACK—a dog that does not resemble his littermates and whose physical traits and characteristics seem to be derived from distant ancestors rather than his parents or grandparents.

THUMB MARKS—round black marks around the pasterns.

TICKED—a coat with small splashes of a darker color against a white background. The splashes are known as *ticking*.

TICKS—several kinds may be found on dogs, including the brown dog tick, the American dog tick, the Rocky Mountain spotted fever tick, the Pacific Coast tick, and others.

TIMBER—another name for bone, usually referring to the bones of the legs.

TOEING IN—the toes turn in.

TONGUE—the noise made by hounds when on the trail of game.

TONGUE LOLLER—a dog whose tongue hangs out.

TONIC—a drug, medicine, or feed designed to stimulate the appetite.

TOPKNOT—a clump of long hair on the top of the head; characteristic of the Dandy Dinmont Terrier.

TOTE BOARD—an electrically operated board on which is flashed all parimutuel information before or after a race.

TOUT—a low-order con man who peddles tips, betting systems, etc. to the unwary racegoer.

TOXEMIA—a condition produced by the presence of poisons (toxins) in the blood.

TOXOIDS—a toxoid is a "tamed" toxin. Some bacteria, such as those that cause tetanus, produce powerful poisons or toxins. These are the substances that actually cause the damage; the bacteria themselves may produce only very mild symptoms. The same toxin is formed when the bacteria are grown in the laboratory, but it is then treated chemically. It loses the poisonous or toxic properties but still retains the power to stimulate the body cells; they form the appropriate antibody (antitoxin). Among toxoids is tetanus toxoid.

TOY DOG—one of the group of very small dogs.

TOYISHNESS—small, resembling a toy; also, fit for a plaything.

TRACTABLE—capable of being easily controlled or handled.

TRAIL—to hunt by following ground scent.

TRAINING COLLAR—a slip collar with a ring on each end. It is made so that it tightens on the dog's neck if he lunges forward.

TREATS AS REWARDS—the training of dogs is based on a system of rewards and punishment. This doesn't mean that the dog is fed a tidbit each time he obeys, or that he is beaten when he refuses or does something wrong. But it's best that he wants to do something, rather than have to be forced. Dogs appreciate a pat on the shoulder or a word of praise. Also, good results may be obtained by working on a dog's greediness—his fondness for certain foods.

TRICOLOR—three colors; black, white, and tan.

TRIM—to groom by clipping or plucking.

TUCKED UP—the sharp rise of the underline just back of the ribs and under the loin—in the region of the rear flank; characteristic of Greyhounds, Whippets and Borzoi.

TULIP EARS—ears that are carried erect with a slight forward curvature.

TYPE—those unique characteristics that distinguish a breed; the embodiment of breed standards.

U

UMBILICAL CORD—the cord that connects the fetus with its mother and through which it receives nutriment and oxygen (the navel cord).

UMBILICUS—a small depression in the middle of the abdomen where the umbilical cord is attached in the embryo.

UNDERSHOT—the condition in which the front teeth (incisors) of the lower jaw project beyond the upper front teeth; the opposite of overshot.

UNIDENTIFIED FACTORS—unidentified factors include those vitamins that the chemist has not yet isolated and identified. For this reason, they are sometimes referred to as the vitamins of the future. There is mounting evidence of the importance of unidentified factors for animals, including man. Unidentified factors appear to be of special importance during breeding, gestation, lactation, and growth. Some sources of unidentified factors are: liver meal, fish solubles, distillers' solubles, and antibiotic fermentation residues.

UPFACE—a foreface that tilts upward, as in the bulldog.

U. S. CUSTOMARY WEIGHTS AND MEASURES—the common system of weights and measures in the U.S., as differentiated from the metric system.

UTILITY—the quality or state of being useful or fit for some purpose.

V

VACCINATION—vaccination may be defined as the injection of some agent (such as a bacterin or vaccine) into an animal for the purpose of preventing disease. In vaccination, the object is to produce in the animal a reaction that in some cases is a mild form of the disease.

VACCINES—usually vaccines are defined as suspensions of live microorganisms (bacteria or virus) or microorganisms that have had their pathogenic properties removed but their antigenic properties retained. Vaccines are purposely administered to produce a mild attack of disease, thus stimulating the resistance of that animal to that specific disease, often resulting in permanent immunity. Vaccines are employed mainly in the prevention rather than in the curing of disease. Great care must be used in their preparation, storage, and administration. Since the improper use of vaccines may result in disease outbreaks, it is strongly recommended that a veterinarian be consulted about their use.

VAGINITIS—inflammation of the vagina.

VENT—1. Rectum. 2. Patch of light colored hair under the tail.

VERMIFUGE—a product used to destroy or expel parasitic worms, especially of the intestine.

VESTIGIAL—relating to a small and degenerate or imperfectly developed bodily part or organ that remains from one more fully developed in an earlier stage of the individual, in a past generation, or in closely related forms.

VETERINARIAN—one who treats diseases or afflictions of animals medically and surgically; a practitioner of veterinary medicine or surgery.

VIRUSES—disease-producing agents that (1) are so small that they cannot be seen through an ordinary microscope (they can be seen by using an electron microscope, (2) are capable of passing through the pores of special filters that retain ordinary bacteria, and (3) propagate only in living tissue. They are generally classified according to the tissues they invade, although this is a very arbitrary method, as some viruses invade many tissues.

VITAMINS—largely through the trial and error method, it was discovered that specific foods were helpful in the treatment of certain illnesses. In 1912, Funk, a Polish scientist working in London, first referred to these nutrients as "vitamines" (later the "e" was dropped; hence, the word vitamin). The actual existence of vitamins, therefore, has been known since 1912, and only within the last few years has it been possible to see or touch many of them in pure form. Previously, they were mysterious invisible "little things" known by their effects.

VITAMIN A DEFICIENCY (NIGHT BLINDNESS AND XEROPHTHALMIA)—night blindness, the first symptom of vitamin A deficiency, is characterized by faulty vision, especially noticeable when the affected animal is forced to move about in twilight in strange surroundings. Xerophthalmia develops in the advanced stages of vitamin A deficiency. The eyes become severely affected, and blindness may follow.

VITAMIN A POTENCY—the vitamin A potency (whether due to the vitamin itself, to carotene, or to both) of feeds or foods is usually reported in terms of I.U. or U.S.P. units. These two units of measurement are the same. They are based on the growth response of rats, in which several different levels of the test product are fed to different groups of rats, as a supplement to a vitamin A-free diet that has caused growth to cease. A U.S.P. or I.U. is the vitamin A value for rats of 0.30 microgram of pure vitamin A alcohol, or of 0.60 microgram of pure beta-carotene. The carotene or vitamin A content of feeds is commonly determined by colorimetric or spectroscopic methods.

VULVA—the exterior opening of the genital organs of the female.

W

WALLEYE—a parti-colored blue and white eye, often seen in Blue Merle Collies and in Harlequin Great Danes.

WEAVING—crossing of the front feet when walking or running.

WELL RIBBED UP—see SHORT COUPLED.

WELL SPRUNG—well-rounded ribs.

WHELPING—the act of giving birth to puppies.

WHELPS—newly born puppies.

WHIP TAIL—a tail that is carried stiffly, straight, and pointed, typical of the Pointer.

WHISKERS—long, stiff, down hanging hair on the foreface and jaws, as in the Miniature Schnauzer

WIND—to catch the scent of game.

WIREHAIRED—a harsh, crisp coat.

WITHERS—the ridge at the top of and between the shoulder bones.

WRINKLED—a loosely folded skin on the forehead and sides of the face in some breeds, as the Bloodhound and the Bulldog.

WRY MOUTH—a lower jaw that is not horizontal when viewed from the front; it is tilted from one side or the other and does not line up properly with the upper jaw.

Z

ZONARY DECIDUATE PLACENTA—a band of villi that interlocks the fetal and maternal tissue in such manner that a layer of maternal tissue is torn away at parturition and forms a part of the afterbirth.

ZONING—often zoning ordinances prohibit a kennel operation in a certain area, or limit the number of dogs that may be owned. Hence, in the present era of environmental concern and protest, it is very important that kennel owners be familiar with existing or proposed zoning ordinances.

ZOOLOGICAL CLASSIFICATION OF THE DOG—in the zoological scheme, the dog is classed as *Genus Canis* and species *familiaris;* hence, the zoological name is *Canis familiaris.*

Appendix

Appendix
Section I—Identifying Your Dog ... 575
    Lost Dogs ... 575
    Dog Identification Chart ... 576
Section II—Breeding and Health Chart ... 575
Section III—Dog License ... 578
Section IV—Dog Laws ... 578
    Sheep-Killing Dogs ... 578
Section V—Humane Organizations ... 579
    American Society for The Prevention of Cruelty to
       Animals (ASPCA) ... 579
       Origin ... 579
       Where the Money Comes From ... 579
       What It Does ... 580
    American Humane Association, The (AHA) ... 581

       Origin ... 582
       Where the Money Comes From ... 582
       What It Does ... 582
    Humane Society of the United States (HSUS) ... 583
       Where the Money Comes From ... 583
       What It Does ... 583
Section VI—Dog Books ... 585
Section VII—Dog Magazines ... 585
Section VIII—Colleges of Veterinary Medicine ... 585
Section IX—Metric System ... 585

LOST DOGS

Dogs become lost or stolen. When such a misfortune occurs, you should not have to rely solely on memory to describe the dog to the police, or in advertising him as lost. So, it is a good idea to fill out a chart, such as Table A-I, with full information about your dog. Also, include snapshots in the spaces provided. This record could prove very valuable in establishing ownership, should your dog become lost.

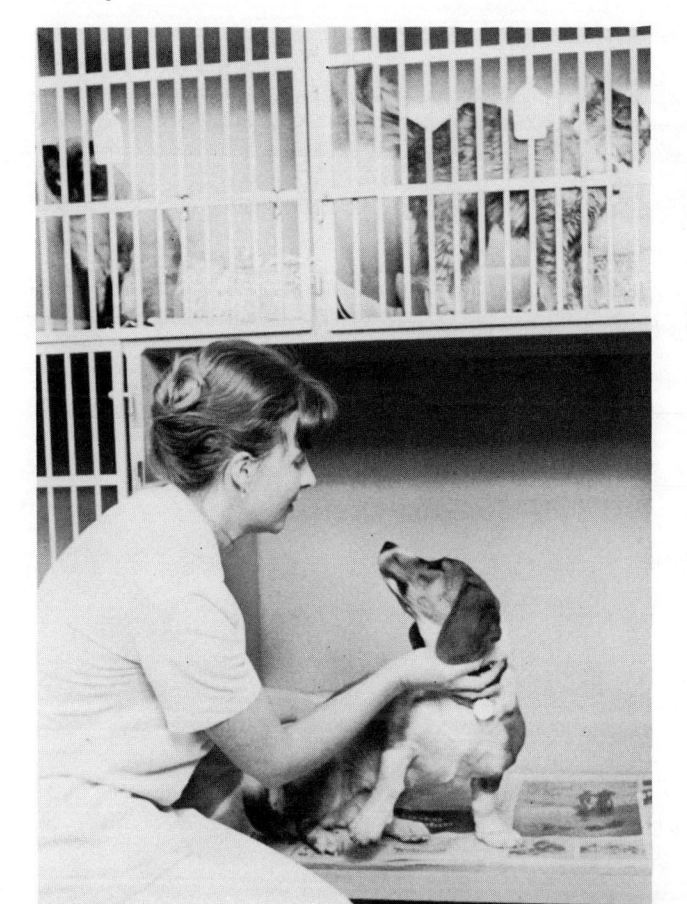

Fig. 484. Loving care! (Courtesy The Humane Society of the United States, Washington, D.C.)

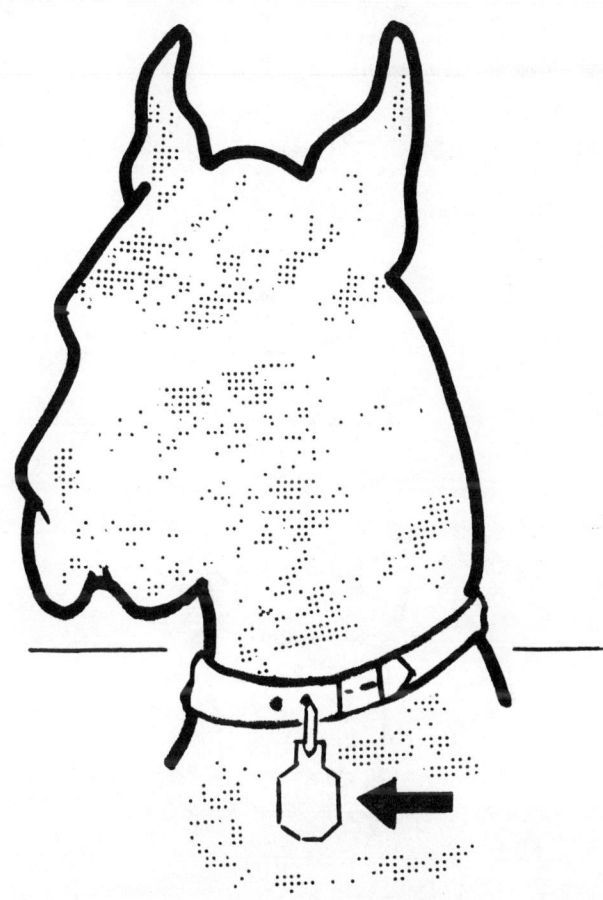

Fig. 485. Every dog should be identified, by means of a tag on the collar and/or a tattoo. (Drawing by R. F. Johnson)

SECTION I—IDENTIFYING YOUR DOG

Every dog should be identified, by means of a name tag on the collar and/or a tattoo. This is important from the standpoint of locating a lost dog. Moreover, in a breeding kennel, it is a means of ascertaining ancestry or pedigree.

In breeding establishments, it is never well to rely on the memory of one or more persons to identify dogs. If something should suddenly happen to that person, there is no way in the world to determine the ancestry of each dog.

SECTION II—BREEDING AND HEALTH CHART

It is a good idea to have a complete breeding and health record of your dog. The chart shown in Table A-II will meet this need.

TABLE A-1—DOG IDENTIFICATION CHART

Date this chart filled out: _____

Dog's call name (name he goes by): _____

Breed: _____ Sex: _____ Birth Date: _____

Collar: (1) License No. _____; (2) Owner's name, address, and telephone number _____

_____

Ear shape (sketch & describe): _____

Tail shape (sketch & describe): _____

Hair (check proper squares): ☐ Long ☐ Short

☐ Wiry ☐ Silky ☐ Rough

Height at withers, (in.) _____ Weight, (lb.) _____

Color and markings (show in drawings, then describe below):

RIGHT SIDE

LEFT SIDE

Description of color and markings (including any unusual scars or markings):

_____

paste snapshot here	paste snapshot here
Front view	Side view

576

TABLE A-II—BREEDING AND HEALTH CHART

Dog's registered name: _____ Dog's call name: _____
Registration No. _____ License No. _____
Breed: _____ Sex: _____ Birth date: _____
Sire: _____ Dam: _____
Special female record: If spayed, date: _____

Heat	Date	Date	Date	Date	Date	Date

	Date	Date	Date	Date	Date	Date
Bred						
Whelped						

Veterinarian (name, address, and phone No.): _____

Vaccinations and immunizations (also, indicate whether "permanent" or "booster"):

	Distemper	Hepatitis	Leptospirosis	Rabies (also, give kind of vaccine)
Date				
Date				
Date				
Date				
Date				
Date				

Worming:

Date	Product Administered	Dosage	Date	Product Administered	Dosage

Other illnesses and visits to Veterinarian:

Date	Nature of illness; treatment

SECTION III—DOG LICENSE

Dog licensing differs in each locality. If you are new to dog-keeping and unfamiliar with your town's dog ordinance, ask the town clerk exactly what the laws are and where you should obtain your license.

Most communities set six months as the legal age of a dog. In some cases, the license for a spayed bitch costs less than for an unspayed bitch. Many communities, however, make no distinctions, and the license generally costs from $2 to $5.

When you pay your license fee, you will receive a properly filled out printed form containing the dog's license number. Be sure that on his form, a copy of which is retained in safe keeping, you have written in the dog's call name, breed, markings, and sex. You should also attach the metal tag to the dog's collar, giving your own name, address, and telephone number.

As a result of licensing, you establish the identity of your dog, by a tag and by means of a written record. Second, part of the fee goes toward operating dog pounds, SPCA shelters, and other organizations that try to make life easier for the dog. Third, in many rural areas, the fee goes toward an indemnity fund for livestock killed or injured by dogs. One final caution: If an unlicensed dog roams free, he may be picked up and used for medical purposes in those states that permit vivisection, while the licensed dog will ordinarily be returned to the owner.

SECTION IV—DOG LAWS

Dogs do not recognize any man-made laws. As far as they are concerned, they are subject only to those natural laws dealing with food, mating, and self-preservation. Therefore, you are responsible for your dog's actions. As a dog owner, you are liable for any damage done by your dog to a person, property, or the welfare of the community.

In general, most laws involving dogs are restrictive and very few favor the dog. Under the law, your dog is regarded as a piece of property, a chattel. But he is unique property. Like a house or a car, the dog has monetary value. But, unlike them, he is alive and has emotional value. Yet, the dog laws usually ignore both the monetary value and the emotional aspect of owning a dog. In some sections of the country, the law states that your dog can be seized or shot on sight without your permission or without your being compensated for the loss of the dog. The latter happens in spite of the fact that the Constitution of the United States specifically states that no person can be deprived of property without his consent. The Constitution further provides that a person must receive due compensation for his property. Obviously, the law is a bit lopsided when it comes to dogs.

Most of the dog laws are vested in the state and are considered "police power." In turn, each state can job out the dog laws to various counties, towns, villages, or hamlets. This is usually done by the state legislature passing laws permitting counties or towns to control the licensing and keeping of dogs in their respective areas. It is simply a delegation of authority by the state to the county or government.

There are so many state, county, and local laws governing dogs, that it is impossible to reproduce them all in this book. Hence, the author merely proposes to make you aware that dog laws do exist and to admonish you on the fact that "ignorance of the law excuses no one."

SHEEP-KILLING DOGS

In many areas, one of the greatest causes for discouragement in sheep production is the problem of sheep-killing dogs. The problem is accentuated by the failure of dog owners to recognize that even the most lovable pet may roam the countryside at night, molesting and killing sheep and other domestic animals.

Unfortunately, from state to state, there is wide variation in laws pertaining to sheep-killing dogs. Few such laws are entirely satisfactory from the standpoint of the sheep owner, and most of them are not aggressively enforced. Most such state laws provide for one or more of the following forms of legal protection against dogs:

1. *That dogs must be licensed*—This provision has two objectives; namely, (a) to eliminate those dogs that the owner does not consider worthy of a license fee, and (b) to build up a county indemnity fund for payment to animal owners who suffer damage from dogs. Usually the maximum indemnity payment for various kinds of animals is stipulated by law, and claims must be presented through the township supervisor or other designated official.

2. *That it is a misdemeanor to allow a dog known to possess harmful tendencies to run at large*—Some state laws make it a misdemeanor to keep such a dog unless it is confined or chained. Also, these states usually make the owner an insurer for any and all damage inflicted by such a dog.

3. *That animal-molesting dogs may be killed*—Some state laws allow the owner of domestic animals the right to pursue and kill dogs not accompanied by their owners when they are discovered in the act of killing, wounding, or chasing domestic animals.

4. *That animal-molesting dogs may be poisoned*—Some state laws allow a sheep owner to put out poison for dogs on his own premises, provided it is done with reasonable care and good intentions.

5. That damages may be collected from the dog's owner—In some states, the law provides that the owner of animals killed or injured by dogs has a cause of action against the dog's owner for all damages caused by the dog.

Such laws as the above have done some good, but—regardless of the printed law—it is generally recognized that sheep-killing dogs make for much ill-feeling and that any damages collected seldom cover the actual losses. Under these circumstances, the best protection for a flock owner still consists of a dog-proof corral for lotting at night.

SECTION V—HUMANE ORGANIZATIONS

Throughout the ages, and all over the world, humane organizations have evolved to protect the welfare of animals, both domesticated and wild. In the United States, there are several fine humane organizations. Because of space limitations, however, only three of them will be detailed in the discussion that follows.

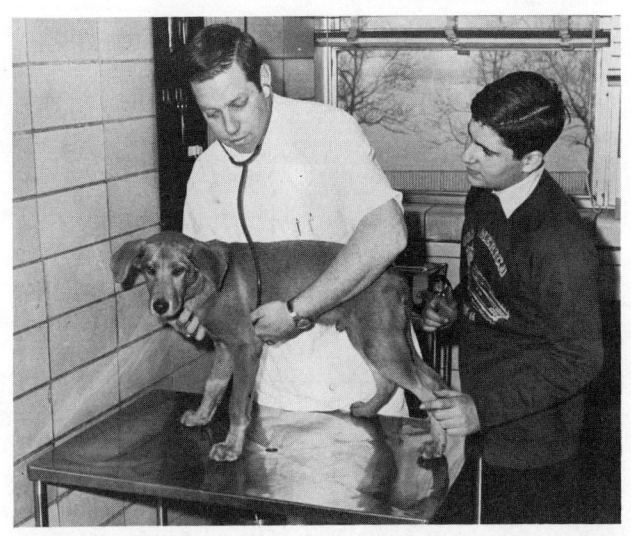

Fig. 486. ASPCA veterinarian examining dog at the Henry Bergh Hospital of The American Society for the Prevention of Cruelty to Animals, New York, N.Y. (Courtesy ASPCA, New York, N.Y.)

AMERICAN SOCIETY FOR THE PREVENTION OF CRUELTY TO ANIMALS (ASPCA)

The address:
The American Society for the Prevention of Cruelty to Animals
441 East 92nd Street
New York, N. Y. 10028

This is the oldest and most famous of U.S. humane societies. Contrary to what most people think, the ASPCA has no jurisdiction over the SPCAs (Societies for the Prevention of Cruelty to Animals) across the United States, all of which operate independently. The general aims of the ASPCA and the SPCAs are very much the same—to prevent cruelty to animals, to enforce all laws for the protection of animals, to provide adoption services, to maintain a shelter for lost or unwanted animals, and to dispense general information about the care of the dog, especially about laws and licenses. Some provide medical and surgical care.

ORIGIN

The ASPCA, oldest and largest humane society in the Western Hemisphere, was born in the nineteenth century, at a time when dog fighting and bearbaiting were popular. It all began with Henry Bergh, son of a wealthy American shipbuilder, born in 1813. In his travels throughout Europe, he was shocked to see circus horses abused, dogs stoned, bulls stabbed in the fight ring, and a tired, overburdened horse being beaten. He determined to do something about it. Newspapers ridiculed him; some animal owners, sportsmen, politicians, and businessmen called him a "mad man," and others simply referred to him as "the great medler." Despite the rebuffs, Bergh finally rallied sufficient support among his prominent New York friends to persuade the New York State Legislature to grant, on April 10, 1866, a charter to a new organization to be called The American Society for the Prevention of Cruelty to Animals. From that day forward, the tall, lanky Bergh pursued horse dealers all over New York City, invoking the new law; tangled with P. T. Barnum on cruelty to circus animals; raided dog fights; championed the substitution of clay discs for live pigeons in trap shooting; and battled against overloaded stage coaches, ill-ventilated stables, and overcrowded cattle trains.

By the time Bergh died on the day of the great blizzard of 1888, twenty-two years after founding the ASPCA, his idea that animals should be protected from cruelty had reached out and touched the hearts and conscience of the country. Kindness to animals had begun to take root as an accepted way of life. Humane Societies sprang up throughout the nation.

By 1900, the emphasis was shifting from horses to small animals. This trend was accentuated with the decline in draft horse and mule numbers.

WHERE THE MONEY COMES FROM

The ASPCA does not receive any funds from city, state, or federal government. Operating expenses are derived from dog licenses, supplemented by income from bequest money and trust funds. Also, nominal fees are charged for the hospital, animal port, and other minor services. However, services such as humane education, inspection of animal facilities, investigation of alleged cruelty, and charity work in hospitals, depend completely on gifts and contributions.

WHAT IT DOES

The ASPCA of New York, reported that, in 1972, in New York alone, it cared for 155,524 animals in its shelters; treated 37,826 patients in the hospital; found homes for 21,596 animals; made 9,953 inspections and investigations of alleged cruelty; and instructed 222,526 children and adults in humane education.

Point by point, here are some of the things that the ASPCA does in New York; similar programs are conducted by the SPCA's located throughout the nation:

1. *Preventing cruelty*—Special agents investigate nearly 10,000 reports of alleged cruelty each year. Also, they regularly inspect stables, circuses, pet shops, horse shows, dog shows, dude ranches, cattle farms, and roadside zoos to check for proper care. Offenders are warned and instructed, and, in flagrant cases legal action is taken.

2. *Help for the sick and injured*—The ASPCA Hospital, staffed with 15 veterinarians, treats approximately 30,000 patients per year in facilities that include medical wards, recovery rooms, a research laboratory, two surgery suites, a pharmacy, X ray and emergency rooms, and isolation wards for animals suffering from communicable diseases. Special programs are conducted in eye disease and heart disease in animals. Two out of every 5 patients belong to owners who cannot afford to pay, but no animal in need of care is ever turned away.

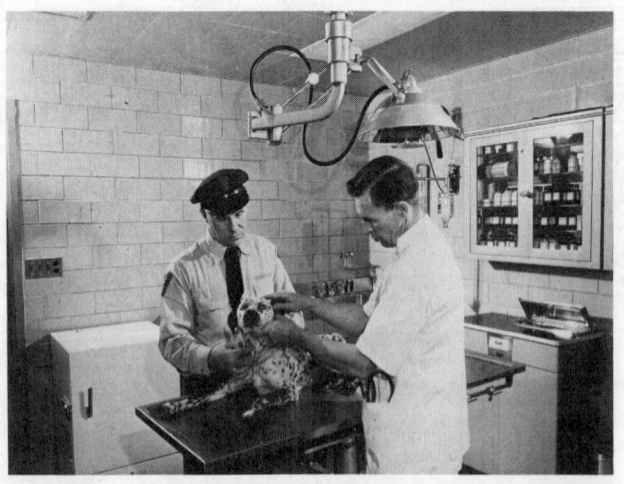

Fig. 487. Veterinarian examining dog at ASPCA Animalport, John F. Kennedy International Airport, New York, N.Y. (Courtesy ASPCA, New York, N.Y.)

3. *Unwanted animals*—More than 160,000 animals—strays, abandoned, and trapped—are cared for annually in the ASPCA's five shelters in New York City. The animals are brought to the shelters by their owners or are called for in the Society's ambulances. Animals too ill or too old to be placed in new homes are humanely put to sleep.

4. *Home for the homeless*—More than 22,000 animals find new homes each year through the free adoption service. Each adopted animal is entitled to free examination in the Society's hospital and a serum inoculation against communicable diseases. Voluntary spaying is encouraged to prevent the birth of surplus puppies.

5. *Education*—Education is the backbone of the ASPCA's multifaceted program.

Children from kindergarten to high school visit the ASPCA's classroom to learn first hand about animals in a two a day program that is booked months in advance. A miniature zoo used especially for classroom instruction enables the youngsters to see and touch many of the animals. Also, a traveling arkmobile visits schools, playgrounds, churches, day camps, settlement houses, and parks with a selection of animals.

But humane education calls for educating adults as well as children. Much of today's anticruelty work focuses on teaching prevention of cruelty to employees of pet shops, circuses, poultry markets, zoos, stables, stockyards, slaughterhouses, horse shows, and other places where animals are kept in numbers.

6. *Obedience training for dogs*—Obedience training courses, conducted in four locations in the New York area, help dog owners gain control over unruly dogs. The classes perform a public service by preventing ill-mannered dogs from becoming a hazard in traffic and a nuisance to neighbors.

7. *Animals in transit*—Although the ASPCA had its roots in the horse and buggy era, today it is as modern as the jet age. In fact, jets figure prominently in one of the society's most exciting activities.

The ASPCA Animalport, a two-story brick building in the cargo area of Kennedy International Airport, is the Western Hemisphere's only completely equipped stopping place for animal travelers. It houses, feeds, cleans, waters, nurses, and doctors animals entering and leaving the country by air. Zoo and farm animals, race horses, and pets belonging to servicemen have been among its 800,000 guests.

8. *Humane slaughter of food animals*—For a number of years, the ASPCA has been interested in more humane slaughter of food animals. In 1958, it was instrumental in the enactment of federal legislation known as the Humane Slaughter Act, which became effective on June 30, 1960. This law stipulates that unless a packer uses humane slaughter methods, he forfeits the right to sell meat to the government. The law lists the following two methods as humane:

Fig. 488. ASPCA Animalport, at John F. Kennedy Airport, New York, N.Y. (Courtesy ASPCA, New York, N.Y.)

a. By rendering insensible to pain by a single blow or gunshot or an electrical, chemical, or other means that is rapid and effective, before being shackled, hoisted, thrown, cast, or cut.

b. By slaughtering in accordance with the ritual requirements of the Jewish faith or any other religious faith.

AMERICAN HUMANE ASSOCIATION, THE (AHA)

The address:
The American Humane Association
P. O. Box 1266
Denver, Colorado 80201

The American Humane Association is a national federation devoted to promoting child and animal protection. At the national level, the AHA operates through its Denver headquarters, the address of which is given above. Additionally, it has offices in Hollywood, New York, and Washington, D.C.

The American Humane Association stands ready to represent local organizations at the national level and to assist regionally and locally whenever the need arises. Today, more than 1,000 humane organizations recognize the strength and experience accruing to their national organization after almost a century of

Fig. 489. The AHA comprises the world's largest field service of humane experts. As the sleeve badge indicates, this is Alaska. (Courtesy The American Humane Association, Denver, Colo.)

progress. All in all, the AHA comprises the world's largest field service of humane experts.

Although the AHA is primarily a United States federation, the Association also has valuable contacts and participates in action programs in Canada, Mexico, and throughout most of the free world. The AHA is an active, charter member of The International Society for the Protection of Animals (ISPA).

ORIGIN

The American Humane Association was founded in 1877. John G. Shortall, who was then President of the Illinois Humane Society, called the organizational meeting. The meeting was prompted to consider means for combating abuses that were then connected with cattle transportation.

Prior to the birth of the AHA, all of the humane organizations of the time were working toward a common goal—the alleviation of cruelty. But each society was aiming at the goal in a different way. There was no common meeting ground where society leaders could come together to discuss their problems with each other. There was no opportunity for one organization to observe the methods used by another. And when a problem crossed local lines, humane activity was very often completely stymied. Under these conditions, it is understandable why the new national organization immediately prepared the following statement of principles (which holds true even today): "The object of this organization is to produce such unity and conduct of action as will promote the interests common to SPCAs and humane societies wherever found." So, "United we stand, divided we fall" was one of the main reasons why AHA came into existence, and it is one of its main strengths today.

WHERE THE MONEY COMES FROM

Funds for the operation of The American Humane Association come from gifts and bequests. Gifts to AHA are tax deductible.

WHAT IT DOES

The nation's humane societies—some 1,000 strong and affiliated under the banner of The American Humane Association—have programs relating to animals, children, education, and wildlife, as well as the animal control work so vitally necessary in every community. AHA provides consultative services to motion pictures and television producers and supervises the filming of animal action. The Association provides assistance in the formation of new humane societies and municipal animal control departments. It works closely with established agencies to encourage better and more efficient programs. Among the notable programs of AHA are those which follow:

1. *Animal protection (and child protection)*—Animal protection can mean many things. Stated briefly, however, it encompasses fighting cruelty to animals wherever and whenever it exists.

2. *Emergency Animal Relief (EAR)*—This AHA department coordinates a network of humane experts who are ready to take immediate action when animals throughout the world are in distress because of some disaster: floods, blizzards, hurricanes, fire, or other natural disasters that create a need for rescue operations on a nationwide basis.

3. *Nationwide Inspection Program (NIP)*—The Nationwide Inspection Program prevents cruelty to animals in traveling shows and exhibitions. Additionally, the work of NIP includes inspection of endurance races, trail rides, and dog sled racing. The NIP was instrumental in getting The Animal Welfare Act of 1970 enacted.

4. *Information Service*—The Information Service, as the name implies, disseminates news, publicity, and information about the entire humane movement. The service carries out a wide range of activities—from fund raising from small animal shelter operations to nationwide coverage of "Be Kind to Animals Week." The information service uses newspaper and magazine articles, radio and television broadcasts, films, publications, publicity, news releases, and calendars.

Nearly 600 radio stations across the nation have joined AHA's "Pet Patrol," which is dedicated to finding and returning lost pets to their owners. In the year of 1971, over 186,000 lost animals were returned to their frantic owners.

5. *Be Kind to Animals Week (BKA)*—This is one of the oldest of the special American weeks. It was started in 1915. Its stated purpose is that of "promoting kindness on an all-out national scale." Each May, during this special week, some 500 television stations and nearly 1,000 radio stations carry broadcasts of this special event.

6. *The Patsy Awards*—This is the big, annual Hollywood event that focuses international attention on the value of kindness towards animals. These are the awards to the "Performing Animal Television Star of the Year" and to the "Picture Animal Top Star of the Year."

7. *Many other things*—In addition to the many fine programs listed above, AHA does many other things and sponsors many other programs for the prevention of cruelty and promotion of kindness to animals, among them:

   a. An annual, international "Animals in Art" poster contest; each year, the calendars, prepared painstakingly by young people in schools around the world, number nearly a quarter of a million

   b. A $10,000 humane trap contest

   c. Pet calendars

   d. A "Seal of Approval" for humane handling and dispatching of food animals

Fig. 490. The overcrowded condition of one dog dealer. (Courtesy The Humane Society of the United States, Washington, D.C.)

e. Supervision of motion picture and television animal action

f. Participation in seminars and conducting of workshops to further the humane efforts of other organizations with related interest, such as the American Veterinary Medical Association and Livestock Conservation, Inc.

HUMANE SOCIETY OF THE UNITED STATES (HSUS)

The address:
The Humane Society of the United States
1604 K Street N.W.
Washington, D.C. 20006

The Humane Society of the United States is the largest national society for the prevention of cruelty to animals. It is nationwide in coverage, with regional organizations. It does not encourage formal ties with local humane societies and SPCAs (remember, there is no national organization called the SPCA), however, it provides information and counsel to any state or local organization or government unit requesting it. Also, it works closely with humanitarians interested in establishing a humane society or shelter in their community.

The Humane Society of the United States is a voluntary, nonprofit organization working to prevent cruelty to all animals, from household pets to exotic wildlife. But its scope of concern is largely in kindness to animals—it encompasses respect for all life.

The Humane Society believes that once man has learned to respect the essence called life, he will refrain from cruelty to both animals and his fellow man. There would, therefore, be no need for animal shelters, no need for laws to protect endangered species, no need to take the federal government to court to stop inhuman practices.

Nevertheless, HSUS is realistic about the whole matter. It recognizes that a society that treats pets as toys, that considers the killing of wildlife a sign of masculinity, that sees little relationship between kindness to people and kindness to animals, needs humane societies and legal restrictions to govern its action.

WHERE THE MONEY COMES FROM

HSUS is totally dependent on private contributions; and it is not heavily endowed.

WHAT IT DOES

Point by point, the program of HSUS is:

1. *Education*—The focus of the Society's educational programs is its National Humane Education Center in Waterford, Virginia, from which a variety of programs for elementary and secondary level children are disseminated under the umbrella of KIND (Kindness in Nature's Defense). The Center's meeting facilities and animal shelter are used to train volunteer leaders and staff of state and local humane societies and government units in the conduct of humane programs and animal shelter operations. In addition, HSUS staff members conduct regional seminars throughout the United States to communicate the latest techniques in organizational leadership and management.

Thousands of school children visit the Center annually to get acquainted with animals and to learn the importance of respecting them.

The Humane Society distributes literature, films, public service announcements for radio and television, and technical reports to humane groups, civic organizations, schools, and churches to inform Americans of the problems of animals and how they can alleviate them.

2. *Legislative action*—HSUS is especially active in working with Members of Congress to draft humane legislation. With headquarters in Washington, D.C., it is often called upon by Members of Congress and the Administration to provide information and guidance in the development of legislation that will effectively protect animal life. HSUS also provides assistance to state and regional humane organizations for drafting and analyzing proposals for state legislatures and city councils.

3. *Legal action*—The Humane Society acts as a watchdog on federal agencies to insure that laws and policies concerning animals are followed. When HSUS determines that they are being thwarted, it takes legal action through the courts and regulatory

Fig. 491. *A young visitor to the National Humane Education Center, Waterford, Virginia. (Courtesy The Humane Society of the United States, Washington, D.C.)*

agencies to obtain adherence. It also works with state and local humane societies to prosecute persons guilty of cruelty to animals.

4. *Visits local humane societies*—Members of HSUS staff visit state and local humane societies throughout the United States to assist them in dealing with problems when improving the animals of their community.

SECTION VI—DOG BOOKS

Without claiming that either all or the best dog books are listed, the books in Table A-VI are recommended as the kind that will provide valuable reference material for the dog owner and caretaker and enhance the home library.

SECTION VII—DOG MAGAZINES

The dog magazines publish news items and informative articles of special interest to dog owners and caretakers. Without claiming that either all or the best dog magazines are listed, the magazines in Table A-VII will provide good reading.

SECTION VIII—COLLEGES OF VETERINARY MEDICINE

Colleges of Veterinary Medicine conduct research with animals, including dogs. Also, each of them maintains a small animal clinic. A list of the Colleges of Veterinary Medicine in the United States and Canada follows:

State	Address
Alabama	School of Veterinary Medicine, Auburn University, Auburn, 36830
Alabama	College of Veterinary Medicne, Tuskegee Institute, Tuskegee, 36088
California	College of Veterinary Medicine, University of California, Davis 95616
Colorado	College of Veterinary Medicine and Biochemical Sciences, Colorado State University, Ft. Collins, 80521
Georgia	College of Veterinary Medicine, University of Georgia, Athens, 30601
Illinois	College of Veterinary Medicine, University of Illinois, Urbana, 61801
Indiana	School of Veterinary Science and Medicine, Purdue University, Lafayette, 47907
Iowa	College of Veterinary Medicine, Iowa State University, Ames, 50010
Kansas	College of Veterinary Medicine, Kansas State University, Manhattan, 66502
Michigan	College of Veterinary Medicine, Michigan State University, East Lansing, 48823
Minnesota	College of Veterinary Medicine, University of Minnesota, St. Paul 55101
Missouri	School of Veterinary Medicine, University of Missouri, Columbia, 65201
New York	New York State Veterinary College, Cornell University, Ithaca, 14850
Ohio	College of Veterinary Medicine, Ohio State University, Columbus, 43210
Oklahoma	College of Veterinary Medicine, Oklahoma State University, Stillwater, 74074
Texas	College of Veterinary Medicine, Texas A & M University, College Station, 77843
Washington	College of Veterinary Medicine, Washington State University, Pullman 99163

IN CANADA

Province	Address
Ontario	College of Veterinary Medicine, University of Toronto, Guelph
Quebec	L'Ecole de Medicine Veterinaire, St. Hyacenthe

SECTION IX—METRIC SYSTEM

From time to time, dog owners have need to convert the U.S. Customary weights and measures into the metric system, and vice versa. Table A-IX may be used for this purpose.

TABLE A-VI
DOG BOOKS

Title of Book	Author	Publisher
American Beagling	G. G. Black	G. P. Putnam's Sons, New York, N.Y.
Animals and Men; Pub. 1965	Hermann Dembeck	Natural History Press, Garden City, N.Y.
Basic Guide to Canine Nutrition; Pub. 1970	Gaines Dog Research Center	General Foods Corporation, New York
Beagle Handbook, The	Ike Carrell	Hounds & Hunting, Bradford, Pa.
Book of the Dog, The; Pub. 1971		Hamlyn Publishing Group Limited, London, New York, Sydney, Toronto
Book of the Poodle, The	T. H. Tracy	Bonanza Books, New York, N.Y.
Breeding and Rearing of Dogs, The; Pub. 1969	R. H. Smythe	Arco Publishing Co., Inc., N.Y.
Breeding Better Livestock	Victor Rice, Frederick Andrews, Everett Warwick	McGraw-Hill Book Co., Inc., New York, Toronto, London
Canine and Feline Nutritional Requirements; Pub. 1965	Proceedings of a Symposium organized by The British Small Animals Vet. Assn., ed. by Oliver Graham-Jones	Pergamon Press, Ltd., London
Cats and Dogs; Pub. 1969	Compiled by Claire Necker	A. S. Barnes and Company, New York, N.Y.
Common Sense Book of Puppy and Dog Care (2nd ed., revised); Pub. 1968	Harry Miller	Bantam Books, Inc., New York, N.Y.
Companion Dog Training	Hans Tossutti	Howell Book House, Inc., New York, N.Y.
Complete Book of Dog Care, The; Pub. 1953	Leon F. Whitney, D.V.M.	Doubleday & Company, Garden City, N.Y.
Complete Book of Dog Obedience, The	Blanche Saunders	Howell Book House, Inc., New York, N.Y.
Complete Book of Dog Training and Care, The; Pub. 1970	J. J. McCoy	Coward-McCann, Inc., New York, N.Y.
Complete Book of Puppy Training and Care	Maxwell Riddle	Coward-McCann, Inc., New York, N.Y.
Complete Dog Book, The (revised ed.); Pub. 1968	American Kennel Club	Garden City Publishing Company, Garden City, N.Y.
Complete Novice Obedience Course, The	Blanche Saunders	Howell Book House, Inc., New York, N.Y.
Complete Puppy & Dog Book, The; Pub. 1968	Norman H. Johnson, D.V.M., with Saul Galin	Atheneum Press; Howell Book House, Inc., New York, N.Y.
Coonhunter's Handbook, The	Leon F. Whitney, D.V.M.	Holt, Rinehart & Winston, New York, N.Y.
Dog, The: A historical, psychological, and personality study; Pub. 1968	Joseph Perlson	Vantage Press, New York, N.Y.
Dog Digest	Bob Becker	American Publishers, Chicago, Ill.

(Continued)

TABLE A-VI (CONTINUED)
DOG BOOKS

Title of Book	Author	Publisher
Dog Obedience Training	Milo Pearsall and Charles Leedham	Charles Scribner's Sons, New York, N.Y.
Dog Owners Guide; Pub. 1950	Kasco Mills, Inc.	Waverly Press, New York
Dog Training: For Boys and Girls	Blanche Saunders	Howell Book House, Inc., New York, N.Y.
Dog Training Made Easy; Pub. 1960	Wm. Cary Duncan	Bell Publishing Co., Inc., New York
Dog You Care For, The; Pub. 1968	Felicia Ames	Signet Books, under the auspices of Friskies Pet Foods, a Div. of Carnation Co.
Dogs of the World; Pub. 1969	Ivan Swedrup	Arco Publishing Co., Inc., N.Y.
Dogs of the World; Pub. 1970	Dr. Erich Schneider-Leyer and Dr. E. Fitch Daglish	Arco Publishing Co., Inc., N.Y.
Elementary Spaniel Field Training	Ralph Craig	American Spaniel Club, 154 Maple Ave., Uniondale, N.Y.
Expert Obedience Training for Dogs	Winifred Strickland	The MacMillan Company, Riverside, N.J.
Family Dog, The	Richard A. Wolters	E. P. Dutton & Company, Inc., New York, N.Y.
Farm Animals	John Hammond	Edward Arnold & Co., London
Genetics and Social Behavior of the Dog; Pub. 1965	J. P. Scott and J. L. Fuller	University of Chicago Press, Chicago, Ill.
Genetics Is Easy; Pub. 1967	Philip Goldstein	Lantern Press, Inc., New York, N.Y.
Genetics of Livestock Improvement	John F. Lasley	Prentice-Hall, Inc., Englewood Cliffs, New Jersey
Groom Your Dog	Leon F. Whitney, D.V.M.	t.f.h. Publications, Jersey City, N.J.
History of Domesticated Animals, A; Pub. 1963	F. E. Zeuner	Harper & Row, New York & Evanston
How Life Begins; Pub. 1965	Jules Power	Simon & Schuster, New York
How to Breed Dogs; Pub. 1971	Leon F. Whitney, D.V.M.	Howell Book House, Inc., New York, N.Y.
How to Raise a Dog	James R. Kinney, D.V.M., and Ann Honeycutt	Simon & Schuster, Inc., New York, N.Y.
How to Raise a Dog in the City (revised); Pub. 1969	James R. Kinney, D.V.M.	Simon & Schuster, Inc., New York, N.Y.
How to Train Hunting Dogs; Pub. 1942	William F. Brown	A. S. Barnes & Co., Cranbury, N.J.
How to Train Your Bird Dog; Pub. 1956	Horace Lytle	A. F. Hochwalt Company, Dayton, Ohio
How to Trim, Groom, and Show Your Dog; Pub. 1971	Blanche Saunders	Howell Book House, Inc., New York, N.Y.
Howell Book of Dog Care and Training; Pub. 1963	E. S. Howell, M. Denlinger, and A. C. Merrick	Howell Book House, Inc., New York, N.Y.
Kennel Club Year Book, The; Pub. 1971		The Kennell Club, London

(Continued)

TABLE A-VI (CONTINUED)
DOG BOOKS

Title of Book	Author	Publisher
Koehler Method of Dog Training, The; Pub. 1972	W. R. Koehler	Howell Book House, Inc., New York, N.Y.
Koehler Method of Guard Dog Training, The	William Koehler	Howell Book House, Inc., New York, N.Y.
Lassie Method, The; Pub. 1971	Rudd Weatherwax	Western Pub. Co., Inc.
Mating and Whelping of Dogs, The; Pub. 1970	R. Portman Graham	Arco Publishing Co., Inc., N.Y.
Modern Dog Encyclopedia, The	Henry P. Davis	Stackpole and Heck, Inc., Harrisburg, Pa.
Natural Method of Dog Training, The	Leon F. Whitney, D.V.M.	M. Evans & Company, Inc., New York, N.Y.
New Art of Breeding Better Dogs, The; Pub. 1971	Kyle Onstott; revised by Philip Onstott	Howell Book House, Inc., New York, N.Y.
New Complete Beagle, The	Noted Beaglers	Howell Book House, Inc., New York, N.Y.
New Dog Encyclopedia, The; Pub. 1970	Revised and expanded updating of Henry P. Davis classic, Modern Dog Encyclopedia	Stackpole Books, Harrisburg, Pa.
New Knowledge of Dog Behavior, The; Pub. 1972	Clarence Pfaffenberger	Howell Book House, Inc., New York, N.Y.
New Standard Book on Dog Care & Training, The; Pub. 1962	Jeanette Cross and Blanche Saunders	Hawthorn Books, Inc., New York, N.Y.
Nutrient Requirements of Dogs (revised); Pub. 1962 (No. 8 of "Nutrient Requirements of Domestic Animals")	Committee on Animal Nutrition	National Academy of Sciences—National Research Council, Washington, D.C.
Nutrition of the Dog; Pub. 1943	Clive M. McCay	Comstock Publishing Co.
Our Friendly Animals and Whence They Came; Pub. 1938	Karl Patterson Schmidt	M. A. Donohue & Co., Chicago, Ill.
Personality of the Dog, The; Pub. 1964	Edited by Brandt Aymar and Edward Sagarin	Bonanza Books, New York, N.Y.
Practical Dog Breeding and Genetics; Pub. 1971	Eleanor Frankling	Arco Pub. Co., Inc., New York, N.Y.
Practical Education of the Bird Dog; Pub. 1965	J. A. Sanchez Antunano	American Field Publishing Company, Chicago, Ill.
Puppy Training & Care (revised); Pub. 1971	Maxwell Riddle	Coward-McCann, Inc., New York, N.Y.
Retriever Gun Dogs	William F. Brown	A. S. Barnes, Cranbury, N.J.
This Is the Beagle	George D. Whitney, D.V.M.	t.f.h. Publications, Jersey City, N.J.
Training Gun Dogs to Retrieve	David D. Elliott	Holt, Rinehart & Winston, New York, N.Y.
Training the Family Dog	Edna Kaehele	Lantern Press, New York, N.Y.

(Continued)

TABLE A-VI (CONTINUED)
DOG BOOKS

Title of Book	Author	Publisher
Training You to Train Your Dog	Blanche Saunders	Doubleday and Company, Inc., New York, N.Y.
Training Your Own Bird Dog (rev. ed.); Pub. 1969	Henry P. Davis	G. P. Putnam's Sons, New York, N.Y.
Training Your Retriever	James Lamb Free	Coward-McCann Pub. Co., New York, N.Y.
Training Your Spaniel	Clarence J. Pfaffenberger	Howell Book House, Inc., New York, N.Y.
Wing & Shot	Robert J. Wehle	The Country Press, Scottsville, N.Y.
World of Dogs, The; Pub. 1971	Wendy Boorer	The Hamlyn Publishing Group Limited, London
Your Dog and You	Project of 4-H Dog Care and Training Development Committee	Assisted by Ralston Purina Co.
Your Dog from Puppyhood to Old Age	Josephine Z. Rine	Sentinel Books, Inc., New York, N.Y.
Your Field Trial Beagle		Hounds & Hunting, Bradford, Pa.
Your Puppy and How to Train Him; Pub. 1968	H. V. Beamish	Funk & Wagnalls, New York, N.Y.

TABLE A-VII
DOG MAGAZINES

Publication	Address
American Brittany, The	Route 3, Box 14, Sherwood, Oregon 97140
American Cooner, The	116 E. Franklin, Sesser, Illinois 62884
American Field	222 West Adams Street, Chicago, Illinois 60606
Bloodlines Journal	321 West Cedar Street, Kalamazoo, Michigan 49007
Boxer Review, The	8760 Appian Way, Los Angeles, California 90046
Chase, The	P.O. Box 5090, 1140 Industrial Rd., Lexington, Kentucky 40505
Collie and Shetland Sheep Dog Review	8760 Appian Way, Los Angeles, California 90046
Dogs	222 Park Avenue South, New York, N.Y. 10003
Dogs in Canada	2323 Yonge Street, Toronto 12, Ontario, Canada
Dog World	10060 West Roosevelt Road, Westchester, Illinois 60153
Full Cry	Box 190, Sedalia, Missouri 65301
German Shepherd Dog Review, The	Box 1221, Lancaster, Pennsylvania 17604
German Shorthaired Pointer News	Box 395, Saint Paris, Ohio 43072
Hounds and Hunting	142 West Washington Street, Bradford, Pennsylvania 16701
Hunting Dog	Box 330, Greenfield, Ohio 45123
National Stock Dog Magazine	Route 1, Butler, Indiana 46721
Pekingese Parade	218 East 48th Street, Savannah, Georgia 31405
Popular Dogs	2009 Ranstead Street, Philadelphia, Pennsylvania 19103
Pure-Bred Dogs	51 Madison Avenue, New York, N.Y. 10010

TABLE A-IX
U.S. CUSTOMARY WEIGHTS AND MEASURES AND METRIC EQUIVALENTS

U.S. Customary	Metric
Length	
1 inch	= 2.54 centimeters
1 foot	= 30.48 centimeters
	= 0.3048 meter
1 yard	= 0.9144 meter
1 mile	= 1609.34 meters
	= 1.609 kilometers
Area	
1 square inch	= 6.452 square centimeters
1 square foot	= 0.0929 square meter
1 square yard	= 0.8361 square meter
1 acre	= 0.4047 hectare
1 square mile	= 259.0 hectares
Capacity or volume	
1 cubic inch	= 16.387 cubic centimeters
1 cubic foot	= 0.0283 cubic meter
1 cubic yard	= 0.7646 cubic meter
1 fluid ounce (U.S.)	= 29.573 milliliters
1 liquid pint (U.S.)	= 0.4732 liter
1 liquid quart (U.S.)	= 0.9463 liter
1 gallon (U.S.)	= 3.7853 liters
Weight	
1 ounce (avdp.)	= 28.50 grams
1 pound (avdp.)	= 453.592 grams
	= 0.4536 kilogram
1 ton (short)	= 0.907 ton (metric)
1 ton (long)	= 1.016 ton (metric)
	= 1016.05 kilograms
Volume per unit area	
1 gallon (U.S.)/acre	= 9.354 liters/hectare
Weight per unit area	
1 pound (avdp.)/square inch	= 0.0703 kilogram/square centimeter
1 pound (avdp.)/acre	= 1.121 kilograms/hectare
Area per unit weight	
1 square inch/pound (avdp.)	= 14.22 square centimeters/kilogram

(Continued)

TABLE A-IX
U.S. CUSTOMARY WEIGHTS AND MEASURES AND METRIC EQUIVALENTS

U.S. Customary	Metric
Length	
1 millimeter	= 0.03937 inch
1 centimeter	= 0.3937 inch
1 meter	= 39.37 inches
	= 3.281 feet
	= 1.094 yards
1 kilometer	= 0.6214 mile
Area	
1 square centimeter	= 0.155 square inch
1 square meter	= 1.196 square yards
	= 10.764 square feet
1 hectare (10,000 m^2.)	= 2.471 acres
1 square kilometer	= 0.386 square mile
	= 247.1 acres
Capacity or Volume	
1 cubic centimeter	= 0.061 cubic inch
1 cubic meter	= 35.315 cubic feet
	= 1.308 cubic yards
1 milliliter	= 0.0338 fluid ounce (U.S.)
1 liter	= 33.81 fluid ounces (U.S.)
	= 2.1134 pints (U.S.)
	= 1.057 quarts (U.S.)
	= 0.2642 gallon (U.S.)
1 kiloliter	= 264.18 gallons (U.S.)
Weight	
1 gram	= 0.03527 ounce (avdp.)
1 kilogram	= 35.274 ounces (avdp.)
	= 2.205 pounds (avdp.)
1 metric ton (1,000 kg.)	= 0.984 ton (long)
	= 1.102 tons (short)
	= 2204.6 pounds (avdp.)
Volume per unit area	
1 liter/hectare	= 0.107 gallon (U.S.)/acre
Weight per unit area	
1 kilogram/square centimeter	= 14.22 pounds (avdp.)/square inch
1 kilogram/hectare	= 0.892 pound (avdp.)/acre
Area per unit weight	
1 square centimeter/kilogram	= 0.0703 square inch/pound (avdp.)
Temperature conversion formulas	
Centigrade (Celsius)	= 5/9 (Fahrenheit − 32)
Fahrenheit	= 9/5 centigrade (Celsius) + 32
Illumination	
1 foot candle	= 10.764 lux
1 lux	= 0.0929 foot-candle

Index

Abilene, Kansas, 506
Abnormalities of development, 153
Accident, auto, 387
Accountability, 540
Accounts, enterprise, 399
Accrual basis tax reporting, 410
Advertising, dogs in, 446
Affenpinscher, 36
Afghan Hound, 36
African hunting dog, 16
Afterbirth, 178
Age: as behavior factor, 295; to breed, 167; of the stud, 170
Ailments: nutritional, 234; of older dogs, 376
Airedale Terrier, 36
Airplane, 420
Alaskan Malamute, 38
American Black-and-Tan Coonhound, 46, 122
American Field, The, 498
American Foxhound, 38
American Humane Association, 581
American Indian dogs, 23
American Kennel Club, 114
American Staffordshire Terrier, 38
American Water Spaniel, 40
Amino acid: composition chart, 254; essential, 197, 198
Anatomy of dog, 31, 32
Anemia, nutritional, 236
Appetite, 372
Aroma of food, 224
Artificial hare, 507
Artificial Insemination, 171, 174
ASPCA, 579
ASPCA Animalport, 422, 423
Attention, 295
Australian Terrier, 40
Auto accident, 387

Bacteria, 329
Bacterins, 331
Bad habits, 308
Balanced ration, 189

Barking excessively, 310
Basenji, 40
Basset Hound, 42
Bathing, 321
Beagle, 42, 482; hound trials, 492
Bear dog, 16
Bedlington, 42
Bedding, 291
Beds, 268
Bee sting, 387
Begging, 308
Behavior, 294, 536
Belgian Malinois, 44
Belgian Sheepdog, 44
Belgian Tervuren, 44
Benched shows, 463
Benching stalls, 463
Bermuda Kennel Club, Inc., 129
Bermuda shows, 472
Bernese Mountain Dog, 46
Biologics, 331
Biotin, 218
Bird dog(s), 479; field trials, 495; pointers, 479; retrievers, 482; spaniels, 482; training, 485
Bitch, conditioning for breeding, 168
Bites, dog, 387
Biting, 310
Black-and-Tan Coonhound, 46
Black tongue, 234, 236
Bleeding, 387
Bloodhound, 46
Bluetick Coonhound, 122
Bonuses for help, 405, 409
Bookkeeping, 402
Books, 586, 589
Border Collie, 551
Border Terrier, 48
Borzoi (Russian Wolfhound), 48
Boston Terrier, 48
Bouvier des Flanders, 50
Boxer, 50
Breath, bad, 372
Breed(s), 25, 35, 113; Affenpinscher, 36; Afghan Hound, 36; Airedale Terrier, 36; Alaskan Malamute, 38; American Black-and-Tan Coonhound, 46, 122; American Foxhound, 38; American Staffordshire, 38; American Water Spaniel, 40; Australian Terrier, 40; Basenji, 40; Basset Hound, 42; Beagle, 42; Bedlington, 42; Belgian Malinois, 44; Belgian Sheepdog, 44; Belgian Tervuren, 44; Bernese Mountain Dog, 46; Bloodhound, 46; Bluetick Coonhound, 122; Border Terrier, 48; Borzoi (Russian Wolfhound), 48; Boston Terrier, 48; Bouvier des Flanders, 50; Boxer, 50; Briard, 50; Brittany Spaniel, 52; Brussels Griffon, 52; Bulldog, 52; Bullmastiff, 54; Bull Terrier, 54; Cairn Terrier, 54; Chesapeake Bay Retriever, 56; Chihuahua, 56; Chow Chow, 58; Clumber Spaniel, 58; Cocker Spaniel, 58; Collie, 60; Curly-Coated Retriever, 60; Dachshund, 62; Dalmatian, 62; Dandie Dinmont Terrier, 62; Doberman Pinscher, 64; English Cocker Spaniel, 64; English Coonhound, 124; English Foxhound, 64; English Setter, 66; English Springer Spaniel, 66; English Toy Spaniel, 68; Field Spaniel, 70; Flat Coated Retriever, 70; Fox Terrier, 70; French Bulldog, 70; German Shepherd Dog, 72; German Shorthaired Pointer, 72; German Wirehaired Pointer, 72; Giant Schnauzer, 72; Golden Retriever, 74; Golden Setter, 74; Great Dane, 74; Great Pyrenees, 76; Greyhound, 76, 508, 509; Harrier, 76; Irish Setter, 78; Irish Terrier, 78; Irish Water Spaniel, 78; Irish Wolfhound, 80; Italian Greyhound, 80; Japanese Spaniel, 80; Keeshond, 82; Kerry Blue Terrier, 82; Komondor, 82; Kuvasz, 84; Labrador Retriever, 84; Lakeland Terrier, 84; Lhasa Apso, 84; Maltese, 86; Manchester Terrier, 86; Mastiff, 86; Miniature Pinscher, 86; Miniature Schnauzer, 88; Newfoundland, 88; Nonsporting, 27;

593

Norwegian Elkhound, 88; Norwich Terrier, 90; Old English Sheepdog, 90; Otter Hound, 90; Papillon, 92; Pekingese, 92; Plott Hound, 124; Pointer, 94; Police dogs, 528; Pomeranian, 94; Poodle, 94; Popularity, 28, 29; Pug, 96; Puli, 96; Redbone Coonhound, 126; Rhodesian Ridgeback, 96; Rottweiler, 96; St. Bernard, 98; Saluki, 98; Samoyed, 98; Schipperke, 100; Scottish Deerhound, 100; Scottish Terrier, 100; Sealyham Terrier, 102; Shetland Sheepdog (Sheltie), 102; Shih Tzu, 102; Siberian Husky (Siberian Chuchi), 104; Silky Terrier, 104; Skye Terrier, 104; Standard Schnauzer, 106; Sussex Spaniel, 106; Terriers, 27; Toy, 27; Vizsla, 106; Walker Coonhound, 126; Weimaraner, 108; Welsh Corgi (Cardigan), 108; Welsh Corgi, (Pembroke), 108; Welsh Springer Spaniel, 110; Welsh Terrier, 110; West Highland White Terrier, 110; Whippet, 112, 509; Wirehaired Pointing Griffon, 112; Working, 26; Working Border Collie, 551; Yorkshire Terrier, 112
Breeding, 133, 575; chart, 577; habits of, 166; selection, 160; stock, feeding, 230; systems, 157
Briard, 50
Brittany Spaniel, 52
Bruises, 387
Brushing, 318
Brussels Griffon, 52
Budgets in kennel business, 399
Bulldog, 52
Bullmastiff, 54
Bull Terrier, 54
Burns, 387, 388
Business aspects, 393
Buying, 129

Cages, 287
Cairn Terrier, 54
Calcium, 204, 206
Calorie system, 203
Calorimeter, 203
Canadian Kennel Club, 128
Canadian shows, 472
Canned: dog food, 221; meat, 222
Capital, 395
Carbohydrates, 201
Caring for new puppy, 296
Carotene conversion, 240
Car(s) chasing, 311; sickness, 388
Cart dogs, 543
Car travel, 418
Cash basis, 410
Cataracts, 154
Cat chasing, 311
Championship points, 460, 463
Characteristics, 35
Character selection, 163
Charcoal, 223
Chasing: cars, 311; cats, 311
Chewing things, 309

Chihuahua, 56
Child development, 442
Choline, 216
Chow Chow, 58
Chromosomes, 137, 142
Civilizing influence of dogs, 440
Classification, 25
Cleaning after whelping, 178
Cleaning kennel, 282
Cleft palate, 154
Closebreeding, 158
Clumber Spaniel, 58
Coat: care, 318; color, 148, 151
Coccidiosis, 340
Cocker Spaniel, 58
Colleges of Veterinary Medicine, 585
Collie, 60
Colostrum, 179
Combing, 318
Commands, 297, 300
Commercial dog food, 221; chart, 242, 254, 260; composition of, 235
Companion, 442
Companionship, 22
Composition of foods, 242, 261
Computers in kennel business, 403, 404
Conditioning: bitch, 168; show, 465
Confidence, 294
Constipation, 372, 376
Convulsions, 373
Coon Hounds, 121-27, 483; American Black-and-Tan, 122; Bluetick, 122; English, 124; Plott, 124; Redbone, 126; Walker Coonhound, 126
Copper, 210
Copulation, 171
Cough, 372
Countries, travel regulations, 424
Coursing, National Assn., 506
Crates, 287, 417
Credit, 396
Crossbreeding, 160
Cryptorchidism, 154
Curly-Coated Retriever, 60
Cuts, 388
Cynodictis, 16, 17, 18

Dachshund, 62
Daily double, 511
Dalmatian, 62
Dalmatian urine, 154
Dam, 155
Dandie Dinmont Terrier, 62
Deafness, 154, 376
Deliveryman phobia, 311
Derby events, 496
Development, abnormalities, 153
Dewclaws, 322
Diagnostic agents, 332
Diarrhea, 372
Diet formulating, 224
Digging, 311
Dingo, 22
Disease(s), 326; causes of, 329; distemper, 334, 379; hepatitis, 334, 383; infectious, 333; leptospirosis, 336, 383; nutritional,
234, 239; prevention, 330, 377; rabies, 336, 383, 416; ringworm, 336, 384; transmissible, 379, 383
Disinfectant(s), 290, 378, 382
Dislocations, bone, 388
Distemper, 334, 379
DNA structure, 143
Doberman Pinscher, 64
Dog(s): burns, 387; classification, 25-28; domestic, 16; evolution of, 16-18; family, 21; family tree, 16; famous, 447; food for, 21; genus, 21; guide organizations. Eye Dog Foundation, 518; Guide Dog Foundation for the Blind, 519; Guide Dogs for the Blind, Inc., 520; Guiding Eyes for the Blind, Inc., 522; Leader Dogs for the Blind, 522; Master Eye Foundation, 524; Pilot Dogs, Inc., 525; Seeing Eye, Inc., 515; guides for blind, 422, 513, 514; history of, 16, 17; houses, 264; location, 267; materials, 269; plans, 269; requisites of, 268; style, 267; hunters, 474; numbers, 9; parts of, 31, 32; racing, 505; semen, frozen, 173; show classes, 457-59; show(s), 454; species, 21; thumbs, 322; zoological classification, 21
Domestication of dog, 17
Dominant factors, 145, 147
Double nose, 54
Draft, 21
Dragging rear, 372
Drowning, 388
Drugs, 332
Dry dog food, 222

Ear(s), 34, 322, 390; trouble, 373
Egg fertilization, 135, 142
Eggs, 223
Egyptian Greyhound, 20
Electric shock, 389
Enclampsia, 236
Energy, 195, 201, 203; measuring, 203
England Kennel Club, 128
English Cocker Spaniel, 64
English Coonhound, 124
English Foxhound, 64
English Setter, 66
English Springer Spaniel, 66
English Toy Spaniel, 68
Enterprise accounts, 399
Entry blanks, 465
Environmental control, 276
Environment and heredity, 156
Equipment, 262, 270, 289, 297; grooming, 317, 319
Esophageal, 340
Estate planning, 411
Estrus period, 167
Eustis, Dorothy Harrison, 514
Evolution, 16, 18
Exercise, 376
Exercising machines, 289
External parasites, 361
Eye Dog Foundation, 518
Eyes, 323, 389

Fads, foibles, 224
False pregnancy, 175
Family names, 156
Famous: dogs, 447; people, 447
Farm dogs, 549; breeds, 550; housing, 552; training, 552; uses, 550; Working Border Collie, 551
Fats, 202, 260; rancidity, 203
Fear, 294
Feeding, 183; amount, 232; breeding stock, 230; lactating female, 226; obese dogs, 231; old dogs, 230; orphaned or rejected puppies, 228; pregnant female, 226; puppies, 227, 297; rules of, 232; self-feeding, 233; sick dogs, 231; special, 226; when, 233; working dogs, 230
Feed room, 280
Fee, Stud, 170
Female reproductive organs, 165
Fence, 285
Fertilization, 168
Field Spaniel, 70
Field trials, 486, 490, 497; Beagle hound, 492; Foxhound, 500; important, 497; judging methods, 497; Stakes, 496
Fighting, 389
Fire prevention, 289
First aid, 326, 384; chart, 387–92; kit, 384
Fits, 373
Flat-Coated Retriever, 70
Flatulence, 373
Fleas, 362, 379, 383
Flooring, 283
Flushing, 482
Folic acid, 214
Food, 21, 220; commercial, 221; composition, 242, 261; dry, 222; function of, 187; home formula, 220; semimoist, 222; supplements, 222; types of, 221
Foot trouble, 389
Foreign objects, 389
Formulation of diet, 226
Foxes, 16
Foxhound, 483, 500
Fox Terrier, 70
Fractured bones, 390
French Bulldog, 70
Frostbite, 390
Frothing, 373
Frozen dog semen, 173
Fungi, 330

Gaiting for show, 466
Galapagos Island, 23
Game preserves, 477
Gas, 373
Gene, 138; multiple inheritance, 147; simple inheritance, 144
Genetics of coat color, 148
German Shepherd Dog, 72; recessive white, 145, 146
German Shorthaired Pointer, 72
German Wirehaired Pointer, 72
Gestation period, 168
Giant Schnauzer, 72

Gid, 379
Gifts, tax-free, 412
Glossary, 556
Goiter, 236
Golden Retriever, 74
Golden Setter, 74
Grading up, 160
Gramaphone, 446
Great Britain shows, 472
Great Dane, 74
Great Pyrenees, 76
Greyhound, 20, 76; racing in U.S., 508; speed, 508; training, 508
Greyhound Hall of Fame, 512
Grooming, 315, 324, 418; equipment, 317, 319; room, 280; show, for, 324, 468
Growling, 310
Growth, 187
Guarding, 22
Guide Dog Foundation for the Blind, 519
Guide dog organizations, 515
Guide Dogs for the Blind, 422, 513
Guiding Eyes for the Blind, Inc., 522
Gun dog training, 486

Habits, bad, 308
Hair, matted, 320
Hairlessness, 154
Halitosis, 372
Handlers, professional, 465
Handling newborn, 178
Hare, artificial, 507
Harelip, 154
Harness dogs, 542
Harrier, 76
Head shapes, 33
Health: certificate, 415, 416; chart, 577; program, 377; signs of good, 328, 377; signs of ill, 329; problems, 371
Hearing, 528
Heartworm, 342
Heating kennel, 282
Heat, signs of, 167
Heat stroke, 390
Height measurement, 35
Help, incentive basis for, 405
Helpmate, 21
Hemophilia, 154
Hepatitis, 334, 383
Herding, 22
Heredity and environment, 138, 156
Heredity, fundamentals of, 138
Hernia, 154
Historical, 440–42, 475, 478
History, 19, 457
Hobby, 410
Hookworm, 344, 383
Hounds, 26, 482; Beagles, 482; Coonhounds, 483; Foxhounds, 483
Housebreaking, 297, 299
Houses, 262
Housing on the farm, 552
Humane organizations, 579; Humane Society of U.S., 583
Hunters, dogs, 474
Hunting, 21; breeds, 478; hounds, origin, 476; training of, 484; winners as, 498
Hydatid cyst, 383
Hydrocephalus, 154
Hyena dog, 16

Identical twins, 151
Identifying your dog, 575, 576
Illness, signs of, 329
Immunity, 330
Inbreeding, 157
Incentives, 405–9
Income taxes, 409, 410
Incomplete dominance, 147
Indian dogs, 23
Individuality, selection by, 160, 161
Infectious diseases, 333
Infertility, 174
Inheritance, 139–41, 411; multiple gene, 147; simple gene, 144
Inspirational purposes, 440
Instincts, 536
Insurance, 411
Intelligence, 295
Interest rates, 398
Intestinal threadworms, 344
Iodine, 210; deficiency, 236
Irish Setter, 78
Irish Terrier, 78
Irish Water Spaniel, 78
Irish Wolfhound, 80
Iron, 208
Italian Greyhound, 80

Jackal, 9, 10, 17
Japanese Spaniel, 80
Jaundice, 373
Judge, show, 464
Judging, 470; field trials, 493, 497
Jumping: on furniture, 309; up, 308

Keeshond, 82
Kennel Clubs, 114; American, 114; Bermuda, 129; Canadian, 128; England, 128; United, Inc., 116; licensed hunts, 501; licensed water races, 502
Kennel(s), 262, 270, 417; bookkeeping, 402; budgets, 399; business, 395; cages, 287; cleaning, 282; computers, 403; environmental control, 276; feed room, 280; fence, 285; flooring, 283; floor plan, 278; grooming room, 280; heating, 282; insulation, 283; kitchen, 279; layout, 277; location, 276, 277; materials, 281; multiunit, 270; office, 280; pens, 286; plumbing, 282; record room, 280; requisites, 273; runs, 269, 284; space requirements, 264, 279; Specifications, 281; storage area, 280; style, 281; trophy room, 280; ventilation, 283; zoning, 277
Kerry Blue Terrier, 82
Kidney damage, 377
Kitchen middens, 17
Komondor, 82
Kuvasz, 84

Labrador Retriever, 84

595

Lactating female, feeding, 226
Lactation, 188
"Laika," 446
Lakeland Terrier, 84
Lameness, 374
"Lassie," 450
Laws, dog, 578
Leader Dogs for the Blind, 522
Leash for show, 466
Leptospirosis, 336, 383
Lethals, 153; definition, 153
Lhasa Apso, 84
Liability, 411
Lice, 364
licenses, 578
Linebreeding, 159
Litter size, 151
Lost dogs, 418, 575

Magazines, 585, 590
Magnesium, 208
Magnitude of industry, 9
Mailman phobia, 311
Maintenance, body, 187
Male reproductive organs, 163, 164
Maltese, 86
Management, 404
Manager traits, 404
Manchester Terrier, 86
Manganese, 210
Manufactured dog food, 213
Marijuana dogs, 527, 539
Master Eye Foundation, 524
Mastiff, 86
Match shows, 462
Mating, 171
Maturation, 143
Measuring, 35; energy, 203
Meat, canned, 222
Medical research, 446
Medicine, giving, 385
Memory, 294
Mendelism, 138
Mendel's contribution, 137
Metric system, 585, 591
Miacis, 16, 17, 18
Military dogs, 539; cited, 540
Mineral(s), 196, 204; chart, 206; supplements, 222
Miniature Pinscher, 86
Miniature Schnauzer, 88
Mites, 366
Movie star dogs, 450–52
Multiple gene inheritance, 147
Mushers, 545
Mutations, 144

Nails, toe, 322, 390
National Coursing Assn., 506
Neighbor, good, 313
"Nemo," 541
Nephritis, 377
Nervousness, 390
Net income, 399
Newborn puppies, 178
Newfoundland, 88

Niacin, 216
Nicking, 156
Nightblindness, 236
"Nikki," 548
Nipping, 310
Nitehunts, 501
Nome run, 546
North American Sheep Dog Soc., 555
Norwegian Elkhound, 88
Norwich Terrier, 90
NRC nomenclature, 235
Nursing period, 180
Nutrients, 188
Nutritional diseases and ailments, 234–39
Nutritive: needs, 189; requirements, 190–96

Obedience: commands, 300; training, 297, 299; trials, 461
Obese dogs, 231
Office, 280
"Old Drum," 452–53
Old English Sheepdog, 90
Organs, male and female, 163, 165
Orphan puppies, 181, 228
Osteomalacia, 238
Otter Hound, 90
Outcrossing, 159
Overshot jaw, 154
Ovulation, 167

Pack dogs, 543
Palatability, 224
Pantothenic acid, 216
Papillon, 92
Parasites, 326, 330, 339, 377; control, 399; external, 361; fleas, 362, 379; lice, 364; mites, 366; ticks, 368; internal, 339; coccidiosis, 340; esophageal, 340; heartworm, 342; hookworm, 344; intestinal threadworm, 344; roundworms, 346; salmon poisoning, 346; tapeworms, 348; whipworms, 350; prevention, 339
Pariah dogs, 22
Pari-mutuel, 510
Partial dominance, 147
Partnerships, 411
Parts of, 31
Parturition, 176
Patrol, 538, 539
Pedigree, selection, 161
Pekingese, 92
Pens, 286
People, famous, 447
Perfecta, 511
Performance testing, selection, 162
Personnel, for shows, 463
Pets, 439
Pets International, Ltd., 423
Phosphorus, 204, 206
Pilot Dogs, Inc., 525
Plott Hound, 124
Poachers, 477
Pointer, 94, 479, 498; breeds, 489; number of, 488; vs Setters, 498
Poisoning, 389, 390

Poisons, 290
Police: dogs, 526, 528; breeds, 528; training, 528; officers handling dogs, 529
Pomeranian, 94
Poodle, 94; haircuts and hairdos, 469
Popularity, 28, 457
Porcupine quills, 390
Pose for show, 467
Potassium, 206
Pregnancy determination, 174; false, 175
Pregnant female: care of, 175; feeding, 226
Prehistoric records, 19
Premium lists, 465
Prepotency, 155
Prolapse of vagina, 168
Protein, 189; needs, 195; quantity of, 198, 199; sources, 200; toxicity, 201
Protozoa, 330
Psychology, 294
Psychotherapy, 443
Puberty, 166
Pug, 96
Puli, 96
Punishment, 296
Puppies: events, 496; feeding, 227, 229, 297; grooming, 316; newborn, 178; orphan, 181, 228; rejected, 228; weaning, 181
Purebred definition, 115
Purebreeding, 157
Pyridoxine, 216

Qualitative traits, 144
Quantitative traits, 147
Quiniela, 511

Rabies, 336, 383, 416
Racing: attendance, 510; daily double, 511; Greyhound in U.S., 508; history, 505; magnitude, 510; pari-mutuel, 510; perfecta, 511; place, 511; Quiniela, 511; revenue, 510; show, 511; sled dog, 547; speed, 508; standard tracks, 510; training, 508; Whippet, 511; win, 511; worldwide, 505
Ration, balanced, 189, 226
Reasoning by dogs, 295
Recessive factors, 145, 147
Record room, 280
Records, 402
Redbone Coonhound, 126
Registration, 29, 115, 117, 182; certificate, 120
Rejected puppies, 228
"Remus," 445
Renting kennels, 422
Reproduction, 188
Reproductive organs, 163, 165, 188
Retrievers, 482, 487
Rewards, 295
Rheumatism, 377
Rhodesian Ridgeback, 96
Riboflavin, 214
Rickets, 235, 238
Ringworm, 336, 384

"Rin Tin Tin," 447
Roading machine, 289
Romulus, 445
Rottweiler, 96
Roundworms, 346
Run: fence, 285; outdoor, 284; size, 285; surface, 285; wire, 269
Running away, 312

Salmon poisoning, 346
Salt, 208
Saluki, 98
Samoyed, 98
Sapling, 509
Schipperke, 100
Scottish Deerhound, 100
Scottish Terrier, 100
Scrotum examination, 468
Scurvy, 235, 238
Sealyham Terrier, 102
Seeing Eye, Inc., The, 515
Selection, 129, 160
Selenium, 210
Self-feeding, 233
Selling, 406
Semen: frozen, 172; volume, 173
Senses, 527–28
Sentry dogs, 538
Serums, 332
Serving, 443
Setters, 488, 498; vs. pointers, 498
Sex determination, 152
Shedding, 320
Sheepdog, 549; trials, 550, 553
Sheep-killing dogs, 578
Sheep measles, 383
Shetland Sheepdog (Sheltie), 102
Shih Tzu, 102
Shock, 391
Shooting dog events, 496
Show(s), 187, 465; abroad, 471; art of, 468; benched, 463; benching stalls, 463; Bermuda, 472; Canadian, 472; championship points, 460; classes, 457–61; committee, 464; conditioning, 465; entry blanks, 465; facilities, 463; gaiting, 466; Great Britain, 472; grooming, 324, 468; history, 457; judge, 464; kinds of, 462; leash, 466; match shows, 462; obedience trials, 461; personnel, 463; popularity, 457; pose, 467; premium list, 465; preparing dog, 465; purpose of, 457; ring, 463; scrotum examination, 468; specialty, 463; stance, 467; steward, 464; superintendent, 463; teeth examination, 468; veterinarian, 465
Showing dogs, 454
Show-Ring winnings, selection, 161
Siberian Husky (Siberian Chuchi), 104
Sick dogs, 231
Sight, 377, 527
Silky Terrier, 104
Simple gene inheritance, 144
Sire, 155
Skin trouble, 374
Skunk odor, 391

Skye Terrier, 104
Sled dogs, 542, 546; races, 547
Sleds, 546
Smell, 527
Snake bite, 392
Sodium chloride, 208
Soldier dogs, 533, 536; marijuana, 539; patrol, 538; procurement of, 539; sentry, 538; training, 536
Space requirements, 264
Space research, 446
Spaniels, 482, 486
Specialty shows, 463
Sperm, 142
Spiritual purposes of dogs, 440
Sporting: breeds, 25; instinct, 441
Sports, dogs in, 441
Sprains, 391
Standard Schnauzer, 106
Starch utilization, 224
Steinbeck, John, 384
Sterility, 174
Steward, show, 464
Stock dog, 549
Stomach upset, 391
"Stubby," 540
Stud, 169; age, 170; care, 169; fee, 170; management, 169; selecting, 170; service, 170
Sunstroke, 390
Supplemental feeding, 179, 222
Sussex Spaniel, 106
Systems of breeding, 157

Tail: injury, 392; shapes, 34
Tapeworms, 348
Taste, 224
Tax-free gifts, 412
Teeth, 323, 377; examination of, 468; missing, 154
Terriers, 27
Thiamin, 214
Thorn in foot, 392
Thunder, 392
Ticks, 368
Toenails, 322, 390
Tomarctus, 16, 17, 18
Tooth trouble, 375
Toxoids, 332
Toy breeds, 27
Tracks, standard race, 510
Trade secrets, 224
Training, 292; equipment, 297; guides, 297; gun dog, 486; obedience, 297, 300; police dogs, 528; retriever, 487; soldier dogs, 536; spaniel, 486; stock dogs, 552
Traits, 144, 147
Travel, 413–14; air, 420; car, 418; country requirements, 424–38; kennels, 422; state requirements, 425–27
Travels with Charlie, 384
Trembling, 376
Trials: Beagle Hound, 492; bird dog, 495; field, 490, 492, 497; Foxhound, 500; judging, 493, 497; sheep dog, 553
Tricks, 304

Trimming, 320
Trophy room, 280
Twins, identical, 151
Type, selection, 160, 161

Unbenched shows, 463
Undershot jaw, 154
Unidentified factors of vitamins, 219
United Kennel Club, Inc., 116
United Kennel hunts, 501
United Kennel water races, 502
Uses on farm, 550

Vaccination, 331
Vaccines, 331
Ventilation, kennel, 283
Veterinarian, 465
Veterinary colleges, 585
Vices, 308, 313
Viruses, 330
Visceral larva migrans, 384
Vitamin(s), 196, 205, 212; A, 212; Biotin, 218; B_{12}, 214; C, 218; Choline, 216; D, 212; E, 212; Folic acid, 214; K, 218; Niacin, 216; Pantothenic acid, 216; Pyridoxine, 216; Riboflavin, 214; supplements, 222; Thiamin, 214
Vomiting, 376

Wagering, 511
Walker (Treeing) Coonhound, 126
Watchdogs, 21
Water, 220, 282; races, 502
Waterers, automatic, 288
Weaning, 181, 228
Weight loss, 376
Weimaraner, 108
Welsh Corgi (Cardigan), 108
Welsh Corgi (Pembroke), 108
Welsh Springer Spaniel, 110
Welsh Terrier, 110
West Highland White Terrier, 110

Whelping, 176; abnormal conditions of, 178; box, 176, 288; cleaning after, 178; preparation, 176; time, 176–78
Whippet, 112; racing, 511; speed of, 509
Whipworms, 350
Wild dogs, 22
Willingness, 295
Wirehaired Pointing Griffon, 112
Wire run, 269
Wolf, 16, 17
Work, 188
Working, 26; dogs, feeding, 230
World War I dogs, 535
World War II dogs, 535
Wounds, 388

"York," 541
Yorkshire Terrier, 112

Zinc, 210
Zoning kennels, 277
Zoological scheme, 21

597